BLACK LETTER

Professional
Responsibility

Ronald D. Rotunda

George Mason University Foundation Professor of Law
George Mason University School of Law

SEVENTH EDITION

THOMSON
*
WEST

Mat #40268497

COPYRIGHT © 1984, 1988, 1992, 1995 WEST PUBLISHING CO.
COPYRIGHT © 2001, 2002 WEST GROUP
© 2004 West, a Thomson business
   610 Opperman Drive
   P.O. Box 64526
   St. Paul, MN 55164–05261
   800–328–9352

ISBN 0–314–15445–0

 PRINTED ON 10% POST CONSUMER RECYCLED PAPER

To Valerie,
My lawyer if I ever need one

*

Preface

It is said that the future will bring us not only more change but also an increase in the rate of change. That has certainly been true in the area of legal ethics. Since the American Bar Association first proposed its Model Rules of Professional Conduct, in August of 1983, there have been many important additions to this model law, dealing with issues such as the sale of a law practice, government subpoenas of attorneys, and direct mail lawyer advertising, and so forth. The work of ABA Commission 2000 resulted in substantial changes to the Model Rules in 2002, and more changes in 2003. In addition, new court decisions, proposals for multi-disciplinary practice, and the American Law Institute's entrance into the world of legal ethics, with its Restatement, Third, of the Law Governing Lawyers (2000), have all conspired to make a new edition a necessity. The law of judicial ethics also has not stood still. In August of 1990 the ABA proposed a new Model Code of Judicial Conduct, which has already been amended to take into account developments in the case law. And, of course, the case law and literature dealing with that topic has similarly increased. This edition is thus necessary, in order to keep pace with these new developments.

I am grateful that the previous six editions have appealed to a diverse group of readers: law students studying for law courses in legal ethics and the bar examination in that same subject; practitioners who represent lawyers in malpractice cases and discipline proceedings, or who want to evaluate ethics issues that confront them in their daily practice; academics teaching in the area; and judges. I am particularly pleased that various judges have told me that they have found this book to be valuable, and some have even cited it. E.g., *Pearson v. Parsons*, 541 So.2d 447, 452 (Miss. 1989); *Attorney Grievance Commission v. Ficker*,

319 Md. 305, 312, 572 A.2d 501, 504 (Ct.App. 1990); *Freeman v. Crown Mining, Inc.,* 90 Ohio App. 3d 546, 554, 555, 630 N.E.2d 19, 24, 25 (Ct. App. 1993). I hope that this new edition will be even more useful than the previous ones.

More than a few people have aided me in writing this new edition. I thank Jane Barton, my secretary. I thank Judge Noël Anketell Kramer, Superior Court of the District of Columbia, who earlier read the chapter on Judicial Ethics, and Professor W. William Hodes for his helpful suggestions. I also am grateful for the generous support of the Law & Economics Center of George Mason University School of Law.

I any work such as this, it is almost inevitable that a few errors might creep in, notwithstanding my efforts, the efforts of my computer spelling check, and the efforts of West Group's editorial staff. If any gentle reader finds any such errors, I am hopeful that one or more of the people I mentioned in the previous paragraph will assume responsibility. And, in mitigation, I plead the words of Judge Henry de Bracton over 700 years ago:

"I ask the reader, if he finds in this work anything superfluous or erroneous, to correct and amend it, pass it over with eyes half closed, for to keep all in mind and err in nothing is divine rather than human."

2 H. de Bracton, *Bracton on the Laws and Customs of England* 20 (S. Thorne trans. 1968) (circa 1250).

RONALD D. ROTUNDA

Arlington, VA
June, 2004

Summary of Contents

■ PART I: DEFINING DISCIPLINABLE CONDUCT

■ PART II: THE LAWYER'S OBLIGATION TO SUPPORT BAR ADMISSIONS AND THE DISCIPLINARY SYSTEM

■ PART III: THE LAWYER'S OBLIGATION TO THE CLIENT

■ PART IX: THE LAWYER'S OBLIGATIONS REGARDING PRO BONO ACTIVITIES

■ PART X: THE LAWYER'S OBLIGATIONS AS A JUDGE

APPENDICES

App.

*

Table of Contents

■ PART I: DEFINING DISCIPLINABLE CONDUCT

■ PART II: THE LAWYER'S OBLIGATION TO SUPPORT BAR ADMISSIONS AND THE DISCIPLINARY SYSTEM

■ PART III: THE LAWYER'S OBLIGATION TO THE CLIENT

■ PART IV: THE LAWYER'S OBLIGATION AS A MEMBER OF A FIRM

■ PART V: THE LAWYER'S OBLIGATIONS REGARDING ADVERTISING AND SOLICITATION

■ PART VI: THE LAWYER'S OBLIGATION NOT TO MISUSE THE OFFICE OF GOVERNMENT

■ PART VII: THE LAWYER'S OBLIGATION AS AN ADVOCATE

■ PART X: THE LAWYER'S OBLIGATIONS AS A JUDGE

APPENDICES

App.

Capsule Summary

■ **PART ONE: DEFINING DISCIPLINABLE CONDUCT**

I. THE DISTINCTION BETWEEN DISCIPLINABLE AND ASPIRATIONAL CONDUCT

The ethics rules distinguish between conduct to which a lawyer should aspire and conduct below which a lawyer may not go. Only failure to meet the latter subjects the lawyer to possible discipline.

The ABA House of Delegates originally approved its Model Code of Professional Responsibility on August 12, 1969, and approved later amendments until 1983, at which point it shifted to the ABA Model Rules. By now, most states have adopted some version of the Model Rules. The old Model Code created "Disciplinary Rules," or DRs, which were intended to be "mandatory in character." For violation of a DR, a lawyer may be disciplined. "Ethical Considerations," in contrast, were intended to provide guidance and assist in interpreting the policies underlying the Disciplinary Rules. The Model Rules do not use this format, but they still provide that a lawyer *must* do certain things, *should* do other things, and *may* do other things.

In 1983, the ABA turned to a new format found in the present ABA Model Rules of Professional Conduct. It subsequently amended them from time to time, with a large number of amendments in 2002. That same year, the ABA House of Delegates rejected proposals to increase the power or duty of lawyers to report on clients' financial misdeeds but, only a year later, in 2003, the ABA accepted major revisions to Rules 1.6 & 1.13 to response to the Enron Corporation bankruptcy and scandal. Most state and federal courts have adopted a version of the Model Rules as positive law to govern the lawyers within their jurisdictions. In addition, courts often cite them as evidence of the law. It is also often useful, as a pedagogical tool, to compare the present Model Rules to the former Model Code. And, a few jurisdictions still use the old Model Code format.

Disciplinary actions may include formal reprimand or disbarrment by the state or local bar association in which the lawyer is a member. A lawyer may also be liable in tort for legal malpractice or breach of fiduciary duty.

II.   THE "APPEARANCE OF IMPROPRIETY"

Language found in the Model Code and some court decisions refer to the lawyer's duty to avoid conduct that has the appearance of impropriety. But the Model Code never intended this vague standard to be used as a test and the term "impropriety" is not defined in the Code. The Model Rules nowhere adopt this standard, which the ABA has criticized as "question-begging." Before the 2002 revisions, a Comment specifically rejected the "appearance of impropriety" test; the 2002 revisions deleted this Comment as unnecessary, but the Reporter's Notes state that "No change in substance is intended." (Notes to former Comment 5 of Rule 1.9).

III.   DEFINING DISCIPLINABLE CONDUCT

A lawyer may be subject to discipline for violating any of the mandatory requirements of the ethics rules. It is also disciplinable conduct to assist or induce another to violate a Disciplinary Rule or to "attempt to violate the Rules."

In addition the lawyer may be subject to discipline for violation of certain other law, including crimes that reflect adversely on the lawyer's dishonesty, fraud, deceit, or misrepresentation.

Some of these violations—those that have a functional relationship to the practice of law—are also disciplinable even if the lawyer does not engage in them while acting in a legal capacity. For example, a lawyer who is selling a used car and defrauds a purchaser is subject to discipline for engaging in conduct involving dishonesty, fraud, and deceit.

IV. JURISDICTION

In general, a state disciplinary authority has the power to discipline a person admitted to the bar of that jurisdiction even though the acts in question occurred outside the jurisdiction. However, the general rule is that if a lawyer practices before a court in Jurisdiction A, she must obey the ethics rules of that court; still, Jurisdiction B can discipline her for violating what happened in another jurisdiction, i.e., the ethics rules of the tribunal in Jurisdiction A.

■ PART TWO: THE LAWYER'S OBLIGATIONS TO SUPPORT BAR ADMISSIONS AND THE DISCIPLINARY SYSTEMS

I. APPLICANTS TO THE BAR

The ethics rules of a given jurisdiction govern only lawyers admitted to that bar. The rules do not apply to *applicants* to the bar, but if these applicants knowingly submit any materially false information they can be disciplined if they are later admitted.

Applicants to the bar must also disclose facts necessary to correct a known misapprehension and must respond to lawful demands for information from admissions or disciplinary authorities, unless doing so violates client confidentiality rules.

In addition, an applicant to the bar in State One, who is already a member of the bar in State Two, and who knowingly submits a materially false application to State One, is subject to discipline in State Two.

Lawyers are often asked to supply character references for bar applicants. The lawyer must respond truthfully and correct any prior misstatements or clarify any misunderstandings arising from statements by the lawyer about the applicant. However, lawyers must not disclose information protected as a client secret under Rule 1.6.

II. THE LAWYER'S ROLE REGARDING REPORTING DISCIPLINABLE VIOLATIONS OF LAWYERS

Because present Model Rules strongly rely (like the predecessor Model Code) on self-regulation, they impose upon lawyers an affirmative duty of "whistle-blowing," an obligation to report other lawyers who violate the ethics rules, at least when the violations are serious. This obligation, however, is subject to the reporting lawyer's duty of client confidentiality. The Model Code appeared to impose a duty to report to oneself. The Model Rules, in contrast, require reporting "another lawyer." The Rules do not require lawyers to waive the Fifth Amendment privilege against self-incrimination.

III. THE LAWYER'S ROLE REGARDING JUDGES AND CANDIDATES FOR THE JUDICIARY

The lawyer may not, with scienter, falsely accuse a judge. Lawyers who are candidates for judicial office are under the same restrictions that are applied to incumbent judges. (See Part Ten: The Lawyer's Obligations as a Judge.)

■ PART THREE: THE LAWYER'S OBLIGATION TO THE CLIENT

I. THE DUTY OF CONFIDENTIALITY

Lawyers must *not disclose* information gained in the professional relationship (1) that is protected as an evidentiary privilege, (2) that would otherwise be embarrassing or likely detrimental to the client, or (3) that the client has requested be kept secret.

The lawyer's duty of confidentiality arises from multiple sources: the law of evidence; the work product privilege (or work product immunity), which protects the lawyer from turning over information otherwise subject to discovery or other compelled disclosure; and the law of agency, which places restrictions on the agent, who is a fiduciary of the principal.

Both the Model Code and the Model Rules prohibit the lawyer from using client information to the client's detriment, unless the client consents. The Code, unlike the Rules, also prohibited the lawyer, unless the client consents, from using client information to the lawyer's own (or a third party's) advantage, even if this information is not disclosed to anyone and is not detrimental to the client.

Notwithstanding this general requirement of nondisclosure, the Model Rules, after changes that the ABA accepted in August, 2003, decided that a lawyer may reveal information if:

(A) the client consents to disclosure, either expressly or impliedly;

(B) or, if the lawyer reasonably believes that disclosure is necessary

    (1) to prevent the client from committing a crime or fraud that is reasonably certain to result in substantial injury to financial interests or property of another and in furtherance of which the client has used or is using the lawyer's services;

    (3) to prevent, mitigate or rectify substantial injury to the financial interests or property of another that is reasonably certain to result or has resulted from the client's commission of a crime or fraud in furtherance of which the client has used the lawyer's services;

(4) to establish a claim or defense on behalf of the lawyer in a controversy between the lawyer and the client, to establish a defense to a criminal charge or civil claim against the lawyer based upon conduct in which the client was involved, or to respond to allegations in any proceeding concerning the lawyer's representation of the client; or

(6) to comply with other law or a court order.

A client may lose the privilege of confidentiality by inadvertently disclosing otherwise privileged communications to non-privileged recipients.

If the client will use a lawyer's services to further the client's criminal or fraudulent conduct, a lawyer must withdraw from representation.

The protection of confidentiality, intended to encourage clients to speak freely to their lawyers, is extended beyond current clients to encompass *prospective* clients who do not retain the services of the lawyer, as well as to *former* clients. Information which has become "generally known," however, is no longer within the protection of the confidentiality rules.

Attorneys are also required to exercise reasonable care to protect confidential information communicated by the lawyer to nonlawyer employees and to other lawyers in the same firm.

II. CONFLICTS OF INTEREST

Unless the client knowingly consents, a lawyer may not accept, or continue, employment by a client if the lawyer's exercise of professional judgment will be materially affected by the lawyer's own financial or personal interests, the interests of a current or former client, or if the representation is directly adverse to the first client. The lawyer owes to each client a duty of zealous (but not over-zealous) representation, loyalty, and preservation of confidences. If fulfilling any of these duties to one client violates a duty to another client, there is a prohibited conflict.

The Model Rules now provide that a client may waive a conflict of interest, by giving informed consent *confirmed in writing*. In some cases, however, public policy demands that even client consent cannot waive the conflict. Such cases include instances when the conflict would prevent the lawyer from providing competent and diligent representation, when the waiver is prohibited by other law, or when institutional interests would be compromised (such as when the clients are in litigation suing each other.) If a conflict arises after representation has begun, the lawyer should withdraw if the parties do not waive the conflict.

An attorney involved in a conflict of interest may be subject to discipline, tort liability, and disqualification.

If the lawyer is disqualified because of a conflict, typically this disqualification is *imputed* to every other lawyer in the same firm. If a lawyer leaves that firm and joins another, the lawyer's imputed knowledge (unlike a lawyer's actual knowledge) is not thereafter imputed to others in the new firm. A client may also waive the imputed conflict or consent to waive the conflict on the condition that the law firm screens the affected lawyer (*i.e.,* isolate the lawyer from participation through adequate procedures in the firm) from the matter.

Also, the Model Rules specifically provide that certain types of disqualifications are not imputed. For example, if two lawyers in different firms are married to each other, they may not be on opposite sides of the same case (unless the clients give informed consent), but this disqualification is not imputed to other members in the same law firm.

III. THE DUTY OF COMPETENCE AND THE SCOPE OF REPRESENTATION

The lawyer must perform services competently. A lawyer is competent if he has the "legal knowledge, skill, thoroughness and preparation reasonably necessary for the representation." Competence is not equated with experience and a lawyer may gain the necessary knowledge and skill through study and preparation or by associating in the matter with another attorney who is already competent.

In general, the client has control both as to scope of the representation and the extent to which the lawyer may waive the client's substantive rights. The lawyer and client may change the division of lawyer/client responsibility through agreements. For example, a lawyer may limit the scope of representation if reasonable under the circumstances if the client consents; or a client may authorize the lawyer to take specific action on the client's behalf without further consultation. These agreements are, however, subject to restrictions. For example, the client cannot agree to so severely limit the representation that it results in incompetent representation, because the client cannot waive his or her right to competent representation.

IV.   FEES

The lawyer may not make an agreement for, charge, or collect an unreasonable fee or an unreasonable amount for expenses. The Rules list eight factors that should be considered when determining whether a fee is reasonable:

(1)   the time and labor required, the novelty and difficulty of the questions involved, and the skill requisite to perform the legal service properly;

(2)   the likelihood, if apparent to the client, that the acceptance of the particular employment will preclude other employment by the lawyer;

(3)   the fee customarily charged in the locality for similar legal services;

(4)   the amount involved and the results obtained;

(5)   the time limitations imposed by the client or by the circumstances;

(6)   the nature and length of the professional relationship with the client;

(7)   the experience, reputation, and ability of the lawyer or lawyers performing the services; and

(8)   whether the fee is fixed or contingent.

It is the *better practice* to put agreements regarding fees, expenses, and the scope of representation in writing. The Rules *require* that contingent fees be in writing and signed by the client.

The lawyer may not charge a contingent fee in criminal cases. The Rules also prohibit contingent fees in divorce cases (while the former Code only discouraged such fee arrangements).

V.   ACCEPTING, DECLINING, AND TERMINATING REPRESENTATION

Unless the court has appointed a lawyer to represent a client, a lawyer has no obligation to accept all clients in the order in which they walk in the door. The lawyer is not normally like a taxi cab driver who must accept the next person in line. However, once the lawyer accepts a case, she is subject to various restrictions so that she has no general, absolute right of withdrawal.

If a matter is before a tribunal, the lawyer must follow that tribunal's rules, which typically require the lawyer to secure the tribunal's permission before withdrawing.

The client always has a right to discharge a lawyer at any time, with or without cause. If the client fires the lawyer, the lawyer must withdraw. (But if the matter is before a tribunal, the lawyer must still comply with the tribunal's rules, which typically require the lawyer to first secure the tribunal's permission to withdraw.) The client remains liable for any fees earned or other contractual or quasi-contractual damages. Similarly, the lawyer must return any fees not yet earned.

The lawyer must make reasonable efforts to protect the client's interests, such as giving reasonable notice to the client, surrendering papers and property to which the client is entitled, and refunding any prepayment of fees that have not yet been earned.

VI. TRUST FUND ACCOUNTS

Client funds must be placed in trust fund accounts, and any interest earned on the accounts belongs to the client unless state bar rules provide otherwise.

The lawyer must be careful not to commingle a client's funds with the lawyer's or firm's own funds. However, the lawyer may deposit his or her funds in the client trust fund account in order to pay bank service charges on that account.

The lawyer must also deposit into a client trust account any pre-paid legal fees or expenses, withdrawing them only when the fees are earned or expenses incurred.

When trust funds are in dispute between two or more persons, one of whom may be the lawyer, that property must be kept separate until the dispute is resolved. The lawyer must distribute the undisputed amount promptly.

■ PART FOUR: THE LAWYER'S OBLIGATIONS AS A MEMBER OF A FIRM

I. SUPERVISORY RESPONSIBILITY

The ethics rules do not govern the lay employees of a lawyer, but they do make it the lawyer's responsibility to assure that his employees act to protect client interests, such as the client's interests in confidentiality.

Lawyers also must exercise reasonable supervision over subordinate lawyers. The Rules make clear that a subordinate lawyer may defer to the *reasonable* judgment of the supervisory lawyer in ethical matters, but that otherwise there is no defense based on simply following orders.

A lawyer may not knowingly assist another to violate the ethics rules or violate those rules through the acts of another. The supervisory lawyer must also take reasonable remedial action to avoid or mitigate misconduct by a subordinate lawyer.

II. SHARING FEES AND RESPONSIBILITY WITH LAY PEOPLE

Lawyers have broad authority to include nonlawyer employees in profit sharing or retirement plans, but lawyers may not share *managerial* responsibilities with lay people in matters relating to the lawyer's professional legal judgment.

In general, the lawyer may not share legal fees with a nonlawyer. However, the lawyer may share court-awarded legal fees with a nonprofit organization that employed, retained, or recommended employment of the lawyer in that matter.

III. UNAUTHORIZED PRACTICE OF LAW

What is the unauthorized practice of law is a legal question, the answer to which varies from one jurisdiction to another. In general, it may be said that the essence of the practice of law is to apply the general principles of law to specific factual circumstances.

Lawyers may not practice law in a jurisdiction unless they are admitted there. In addition, lawyers must not aid nonlawyers in unauthorized practice. The Rules do not prohibit a lawyer from providing advice and instruction to nonlawyers whose employment requires knowledge of the law, such as claims adjusters, because those people are not practicing law.

Lawyers are not prohibited from employing secretaries, law clerks, or paralegals and delegating tasks to them, as long as the lawyer supervises the work and retains responsibility for the work.

A lawyer may assist a lay person who wishes to proceed *pro se*, because although that person is practicing law, they are not engaging in the *unauthorized* practice of law because a layperson can always represent himself.

Even if a lawyer is admitted to practice in State One, it is a violation of the ethics rules for a lawyer to practice law in State Two if doing so violated the rules of State Two. Because lawyers, in modern times, routinely engage in the practice of law that affects multiple jurisdictions—e.g., the lawyer in State One advises the Client, incorporated in State Two, about tort liabilities of a product of Client, when that product is used in various jurisdictions—there is often a question of *where* the lawyer is practicing and whether that practice violates the unauthorized practice rules. In 2003, the ABA substantially revised Model Rule 5.5 to deal with the problem of the multijurisdictional practice of law.

In general, a lawyer not admitted to practice in State One must not establish an office or other systematic and continuous presence in State Two (where she is not admitted to the practice of law), or hold herself out as admitted to practice in State Two. However, she may provide legal services on a temporary basis in State Two if (1) she associates with a lawyer who is admitted to practice in this jurisdiction and who actively participates in the matter; or (2) her work is reasonably related to a pending or potential proceeding before a tribunal and that tribunal authorizes her to appear (e.g. pro hac vice) or she reasonably expects to be so authorized; or (3) her work is reasonably related to a pending or potential arbitration, or other similar proceeding and are not for services for which the forum requires pro hac vice admission; or (4) her work is reasonably related to the lawyer's practice in a jurisdiction in which she is admitted to practice; or (5) she provides legal services to her employer or its organizational affiliates and the forum does not require pro hac vice admission for these services; or (6) federal law or other law authorizes her legal practice.

IV. AGREEMENTS TO RESTRICT THE RIGHT TO PRACTICE LAW

A lawyer may not be a party to an agreement that restricts his right to practice law, unless the restriction is part of a retirement benefits agreement, or is part of a valid agreement, authorized by the Model Rules, for the sale of a law practice. Lawyers may not restrict their right to practice as part of the settlement of a client controversy.

■ PART FIVE: THE LAWYER'S OBLIGATIONS REGARDING ADVERTISING AND SOLICITATION

I. ADVERTISING

Until the U.S. Supreme Court extended certain first amendment rights to lawyer's advertising their professional services, one could almost summarize the law of ethics in the sentence: Lawyers may not lie, cheat, steal, or advertise. Now, the Rules basically forbid advertising only if it is *false or misleading*. The Rules govern advertising through written, recorded, or electronic media, including "public media."

The Code had the same goal—no misleading advertising—but it reached it by imposing fairly detailed descriptions of the types of advertising that it allowed. Constitutional case law from the U.S. Supreme Court has forced the ABA, over the years, to liberalize its rules governing advertising.

The Rules provide that a lawyer may not pay others for recommending the lawyer's services, *except* that a lawyer may pay reasonable costs of advertisements or communications and pay employees engaged in marketing or development services. Lawyers may also pay the usual charges of a legal service plan, a not-for-profit referral service, or an approved lawyer referral service.

II. SOLICITATION

Lawyers may not, in general, "solicit" clients for pecuniary gain in circumstances where the prospective client might be subjected to overreaching or, because of the emotional situation, have an impaired capacity for reasoned judgment. Beyond these extreme cases, efforts to prohibit solicitation often run afoul of the constitutional protections of free speech.

The Rules, amended to conform to Supreme Court decisional law, now do not treat direct mail advertising as improper solicitation, and only have a blanket prohibition of "in-person" (*i.e.,* face-to-face), or "live telephone," or "real-time electronic" (*i.e.,* internet chat room) solicitation of prospective clients when a significant motive for the lawyer's actions is his pecuniary gain. The solicitation restriction does not apply if the person contacted is a former client, a lawyer, or has "a family, close personal, or prior professional relationship with the lawyer."

■ PART SIX: THE LAWYER'S OBLIGATIONS NOT TO MISUSE THE OFFICE OF GOVERNMENT

I. THE PUBLIC OFFICIAL WHO IS ALSO A LAWYER

Lawyers may not abuse their public positions by, for example, accepting bribes, using their names in private law firms when they no longer practice law in that firm, or implying that they have the power to influence action corruptly.

The Model Rules, like the Model Code, make clear that a lawyer may not state or imply to anyone that he has the power to influence a public official or agency on improper or irrelevant grounds.

The Model Rules also prohibit lawyers from making political contributions for the specific purpose of obtaining legal engagements. Rule 7.6.

II. THE REVOLVING DOOR

There are certain public benefits as well as possible disadvantages involved when lawyers for the government leave to enter private practice and vice versa. In an effort to draw a proper balance, the ethics rules forbid a lawyer in private practice from representing a client in a matter if that lawyer, while in the government, had personally and substantially participated in that matter, unless the appropriate government agency consents.

The former government lawyer's individual disqualification is not imputed to the entire firm if that lawyer is *screened* from the particular matter in question, is apportioned no part of the fee, and the law firm promptly gives written notice to the relevant government agency so that it can verify that the firm has complied with the provisions of this rule.

A lawyer in government service also must not negotiate for private employment with a party who is involved in a matter in which the government lawyer is then participating, personally and substantially. A lawyer for the government may not take a case in which she had personal and substantial participation while in private practice, unless substantive law imposes on that lawyer a nondelegable duty to act.

A former government attorney may not use "confidential government information" gained during his employment with the government to the "material disadvantage of that person." A former judge, arbitrator, mediator, or other third-party neutral may not accept private employment in a matter if she acted in a judicial capacity, on the merits of that case. The parties may waive this protection by informed consent.

III. SPECIAL RESPONSIBILITIES OF A PUBLIC PROSECUTOR

The public prosecutor represents not only a governmental entity but also the public interest. Because the government is a particularly powerful client, the lawyer's duty of zealousness is tempered by the obligation to avoid harassing techniques and to refrain from instituting proceedings unsupported by probable cause.

For example, the prosecutor must inform the accused of the existence of evidence that tends to negate the guilt of the accused or mitigate the punishment. The prosecutor must also inform the sentencing tribunal of all mitigating information not covered by a protective order or otherwise privileged. When proceeding *ex parte*, the prosecutor should offer the tribunal "all material facts" whether or not adverse. The prosecutor should give the accused a reasonable opportunity to obtain counsel, and should not urge an unrepresented accused to waive important pretrial rights. The prosecutor should also refrain from making unnecessary extrajudicial comments that are likely to increase public condemnation of the accused and exercise reasonable care to prevent others associated with the prosecution from doing so.

■ PART SEVEN: THE LAWYER'S OBLIGATION AS AN ADVOCATE

Although the lawyer acts as an advocate, he or she must avoid taking frivolous positions or making frivolous claims, defenses, or motions. A lawyer must be reasonably expeditious in litigation "consistent with the interests of the client." Rule 3.2.

The Model Rules clear up prior ambiguities in the law and now provide that, when appearing before a tribunal the lawyer must not mislead the tribunal, as to law or facts, or fail to correct a previously made false or misleading statement.

A lawyer must not knowingly offer false evidence and the lawyer must make reasonable remedial measures, *including disclosure to the tribunal*, if she knows that her client plans to engage in, is engaged in, or previously engaged in criminal or fraudulent conduct related to the proceeding. Additionally, a lawyer must disclose to the tribunal any legal authority in the controlling jurisdiction known to be directly adverse to his client's position.

Lawyers must avoid improper publicity that might reasonably prejudice the proceedings in both criminal and civil trials. Lawyers shall avoid improper ex parte communications with jurors or prospective jurors and they must act with decorum to avoid disruption of the tribunal.

The lawyer must also treat third parties and opposing counsel with respect. Lawyers may not mislead opposing counsel or third parties by making a false statement of material fact or law, or by failing to disclose a material fact when necessary to avoid assisting in a criminal or fraudulent act by a client.

A lawyer representing a client may not communicate with another person whom the lawyer knows to be represented by counsel unless that person's lawyer consents or the communications are authorized by other law or court order. When communicating with a person not represented by counsel, the lawyer may not state or imply he is disinterested and may offer no legal advice to the other party other than the advice to secure counsel. The lawyer must clarify any misunderstanding an unrepresented person may have as to the lawyer's role.

■ PART EIGHT: THE LAWYER'S OBLIGATIONS AS ADVISER

The lawyer must give his client candid advice, including the lawyer's opinion of what the court is likely to do and the practical effects of such a ruling. The lawyer may also advise a client on economic, political, social, and moral considerations.

The Model Rules, prior to 2002, had a Rule 2.2, that governed the lawyer as "Intermediary." It provided that the lawyer may act as an intermediary between clients with potentially conflicting interests *if* all consent and the lawyer reasonably believes that she can perform this role impartially. The 2002 revisions eliminated this Rule. The lawyer can still represent multiple clients if the lawyer complies with Rule 1.7, which is the general rule dealing with conflicts of interest of concurrent clients.

The 2002 revisions to the Model Rules added a new Rule 2.4, called "Lawyer Serving as Third–Party Neutral." In this case the lawyer serves or assists two or more persons, but these persons are not his clients. He is really acting as a mediator, or arbitrator. The lawyer must explain his role to the persons so that they understand what is going on.

The lawyer may evaluate a matter affecting a client for the benefit of a third party if the lawyer knows or reasonably should know that the client's interests will not be materially or adversely affected and the client gives informed consent to what the lawyer is doing. For example, the client may ask the lawyer to write an opinion that the client has valid title to a piece of real estate so that the client can give this letter to a third person, the prospective buyer. The seller-client is paying his lawyer to provide legal advice to a third party.

■ PART NINE: THE LAWYER'S OBLIGATIONS REGARDING PRO BONO ACTIVITIES

The ethics rules encourage, but do not require, the lawyer to volunteer to undertake pro bono activities. Recipients of pro bono legal services may include indigent persons; charitable, religious, civic, community, governmental, and educational organizations designed to meet the needs of indigent people; legal services at no fee or a substantially reduced fee; and activities for improving the law, the legal system, or the legal profession.

In addition, courts sometimes appoint lawyers to represent indigents, particularly in criminal cases. A lawyer should not refuse a court appointment to handle a pro bono case, unless the representation will result in violation of the ethical rules, or cause an "unreasonable financial burden" on the lawyer. For example, if the client or cause is "so repugnant" to the lawyer that the lawyer will not be able to adequately represent the client, then the lawyer must refuse the appointment because accepting it will violate the lawyer's duty to give competent representation.

The lawyer's obligations to his private clients do not prevent the lawyer from advocating his own personal views as to how the law should be reformed, even if the lawyer's personal views do not agree with or support the client's position.

■ PART TEN: THE LAWYER'S OBLIGATIONS AS A JUDGE

I. INTRODUCTION

In 1990 the American Bar Association approved a comprehensive revision of judicial ethics, called the Model Code of Judicial Conduct. This Code replaced the Code of Judicial Conduct, adopted in 1972. Over the years, the ABA has added various amendments to this Model Code, which governs the behavior of judges and candidates for judicial office.

II. PERSONAL BEHAVIOR

The judge shall demonstrate judicial integrity and impartiality. Judicial integrity is comprised of "probity, fairness, honesty, uprightness, and soundness of character." An independent judiciary is free of "inappropriate outside influences." The Model Judicial Code explicitly adopts and defines the "appearance of impropriety" language to test whether a violation of the integrity and independence rules has been made.

A judge shall not use the prestige of judicial office to advance private interests (her own or those of another) or convey the impression that others are in a special position to influence her.

A judge may testify as a factual witness (an eyewitness), but is prohibited from *voluntarily* testifying as a character witness. The judge will still testify—the judicial ethics rules do not grant any immunity from testifying—but the party seeking the judge will be not testifying "voluntarily" because he will be testifying pursuant to a subpoena.

The judge shall not hold membership in any organization that practices invidious discrimination on the basis of race, sex, religion, or national origin.

III. CONDUCT IN THE COURTROOM

The judge shall maintain courtroom decorum and exercise appropriate patience and temperance. She must also avoid improper ex parte communications, abstain from public comment about pending cases, refrain from criticism of jurors, and should not exercise the judicial power of appointment based on favoritism or nepotism.

Judicial duties take precedence over all the judge's other activities. Judges should not hear a case if the Code requires disqualification. A judge must be faithful to the law, maintain professional competence, and remain unswayed by fear of criticism.

The judge shall perform judicial duties without improper bias or prejudice, and shall require judicial staff and lawyers in the proceedings to do likewise.

Judicial duties include courtroom proceedings as well as administrative duties, such as filing records and the making of appointments.

Judges should not appoint a lawyer to a position, such as special master or guardian, if the judge has contributed more than a certain amount to the judge's election campaign, unless the position is substantially uncompensated, or the lawyer is selected in rotation from a list that has no regard to the lawyer's political campaign contributions, or no other lawyer is able or willing to accept the position.

The Judicial Code requires judges to report other judges and lawyers who engage in ethical violations that raise a substantial question as to the lawyer's or judge's honesty and fitness either to practice law or to judge. A judge who reports another lawyer or judge is "absolutely privileged" from any civil action based on his or her reporting.

IV. JUDICIAL DISQUALIFICATION

The judge shall hear and decide matters unless the Judicial Code requires her disqualification. Unless the parties consent, the judge should disqualify herself where her impartiality might reasonably be questioned. Such a situation may include cases where the judge sympathized with someone who physically attacked the defense lawyer.

A judge must also disqualify himself where she has actual bias or prejudice, where she is a material witness or had been a lawyer in that matter, where she knows she has more than a *de minimis* economic interest in the subject matter in controversy or party to the proceeding, or any other more than *de minimis* interest that could be substantially affected by the proceeding. A judge may also be disqualified if she knows a close family relative has such a financial interest.

Courts have created a "rule of necessity" exception to the disqualification provisions: no judge is required to disqualify herself if the basis of disqualification would require all judges to disqualify themselves. There always must be some judge to hear the case.

Under the Model Judicial Code, the parties may waive a judge's disqualification if they do so outside the presence of the judge, after there is disclosure *on the record* of the basis for disqualification. If all parties and lawyers agree, *without participation by the judge*, to waive the disqualification, the judge will then be allowed to participate. The agreement to waive disqualification must be incorporated into the record of the proceeding.

V. EXTRA–JUDICIAL ACTIVITIES

A judge may engage in extra-judicial activities if doing so does not cast doubt on her capacity to decide impartially as a judge, does not demean the judicial office, and does not interfere with the proper performance of judicial duties.

A judge may speak, write, lecture, teach, and participate in extra-judicial activities concerning the law, the legal system, and administration of justice, as well as non-legal subjects, unless such activities violate other sections of the Judicial Code.

Judges may testify at public hearings or consult with executive or legislative bodies and officials on any legal matters. Judges may also testify or consult in matters affecting the judge's own interests or when acting pro se. Judges may not, however, accept appointments to governmental positions concerned with issues of fact or policy on matters other than the improvement of the law, the legal system, or the administration of justice. The Code allows service as an officer, director, trustee, or nonlegal advisor of an organization or government agency that does not violate other sections of the Code, subject to certain restrictions.

A judge may not engage in financial or business dealings that may appear to exploit the judicial office or involve the judge in frequent transactions or continuing business relationships with lawyers or other people likely to come before that judge's court. Judges are generally prohibited from accepting gifts, bequests, favors, or loans, with certain exceptions. The Code imposes another general prohibition (with a few exceptions) against judges acting in a fiduciary capacity. The Judicial Code also forbids judges from acting as arbitrators, mediators, or law practitioners.

VI. POLITICAL ACTIVITIES

A judge, including a candidate for election or selection to the bench, is subject to some limits in political activities so as to prevent what the Judicial Code regards as inappropriate political activity. Canon 5A provides that a judge may not act as a leader of or hold office in a political organization, make speeches at, or attend, political gatherings, and may not solicit funds or make contributions to political organizations.

On the other hand, Canon 5C limits the applicability of Canon 5A. Canon 5C provides that the judge or candidate who is subject to public election may, *at any time*, attend and buy tickets for political gatherings, identify herself or himself as a member of political party, and contribute to a political organization. A judge who is a candidate may speak to gatherings on her own behalf, publicly endorse or oppose other candidates for the same judicial office in which the judge is running. The Judicial Code also regulates campaign conduct by judicial candidates for elective or appointive positions.

VII. DEFINING WHO IS A JUDGE

All of the restrictions of the Code of Judicial Conduct apply only to full-time judges. Those restrictions that are functionally appropriate also apply to part-time judges, judges pro tempore, and retired judges.

Perspective

■ I. AN HISTORICAL INTRODUCTION

The present Model Rules of Professional Conduct have a long lineage. In 1836, when the legal profession was subject to virtually no regulation, David Hoffman, a professor of law at the University of Maryland, published for his students fifty *"Resolutions In Regard to Professional Deportment."* Hoffman recommended that a lawyer's conscience be his "sole guide" (Resolution 33), and that a lawyer "espouse no man's cause out of envy, hatred or malice, toward his antagonist" (Resolution 2).

In 1854, Professor, and Judge, George Sharswood, turned to the issues raised by Hoffman and published *"A Compend of Lectures on the Aims and Duties of the Profession of Law."* Sharswood's lectures greatly influenced the Alabama Bar Association, which published a "Code of Ethics" in 1887. Lawyers in other states followed Alabama's lead, and, on August 27, 1908, a nationwide voluntary bar association, the American Bar Association, approved 32 Canons, also based on the Alabama model. See Altman, Considering the A.B.A.'s 1908 Canons of Ethics, 71 Ford.L.Rev. 2395 (2003).

Over the years various states adopted these Canons as positive law: The courts enforced these Canons, which were amended over time. In addition, the ABA purported to treat the Canons as private law governing those lawyers who chose to join that association. In 1940 it announced: "The Canons of this Association govern all its members, irrespective of the nature of their practice, and the application of the Canons is not affected by statutes or regulations governing certain activities of lawyers which may prescribe less stringent standards." ABA Formal Opinion 203 (Nov. 23, 1940) (patent lawyer may not advertise even though the U.S. Patent Office allows certain types of advertising).

In spite of the various amendments to the Canons, they were soon criticized as "generalizations designed for an earlier era." Stone, *The Public Influence of the Bar,* 48 Harv.L.Rev. 1, 10 (1934). But it was not until 1969 that the ABA adopted a completely revised set of rules, the Code of Professional Responsibility. In keeping with the view that the Code was "law" that governed ABA members regardless of state law, this Code (approved by the ABA House of Delegates on August 12, 1969) had an "effective date" of January 1, 1970. Until 1976, the membership form for the ABA also included a statement that the member promised to abide by the ABA Canons of Ethics and, later, by the ABA Code of Professional Responsibility.

The Antitrust Division of the Department of Justice, as well as other groups, noted serious antitrust problems when lawyers agree with each other to abide by certain purportedly "ethical" restrictions on, for example, advertising or fees. In 1978, in response to this criticism, the ABA formally acknowledged that its Code was really only a *Model* Code.

"The Canons of Professional Ethics and the succeeding Code of Professional Responsibility have been drafted, promulgated, and amended by agencies of the American Bar Association within the context of understanding that such codes might serve only as exemplars for the proper conduct of legal practitioners but that the power of disciplinary enforcement rests with the judiciary." ABA Informal Opinion 1420 (June 5, 1978).

To emphasize this change, the ABA eventually changed the title of its Code of Professional Responsibility so it is now called the *Model* Code of Professional Responsibility.

The ABA was quite successful in persuading state and federal courts to adopt its Model Code as positive law. State courts also cited the Model Code as evidence of the law. Similarly, though the ABA Formal and Informal Opinions interpreting the Model Code are not law, courts have cited and relied on them as influential evidence of the law.

In 1977 the ABA took the first steps toward completely revamping the Model Code. It created a Commission on Evaluation of Professional Standards (initially chaired by the late Robert J. Kutak, and thus popularly referred to as the Kutak Commission). This Commission drafted the *Model Rules of Professional Conduct*, which the ABA House of Delegates approved in August 1983. This time, the ABA House of Delegates specifically defeated a motion to set an effective date.

By the middle of 1995 nearly three-quarters of the states adopted the Model Rules, subject to various nonuniform amendments. In addition, the Model Rules are evidence of the law and have been cited as such in various court decisions, even when the states have not formally adopted a version of the Model Rules. The Model Rules are also a useful teaching tool to compare with its predecessor, the Model Code.

Note: For the sake of brevity, the Model Rules and the Model Code will often be referred to as the Rules or the Code. The Disciplinary Rules of the Code will be cited as "DR," as in DR 4B101. The Ethical Considerations of the Code will be cited as "EC," as in EC 2B21. The Model Rules will be cited as "Rule," as in Rule 1.6. The Comments will be cited by Rule number and paragraph number. The drafters of the Model Rules did not originally number the paragraphs of the Comments (or the Code Comparison, or the other divisions of the Rules), but, for ease of reference, we shall refer to them by number. The Model Rules, as amended in 2002, eliminated the "Code Comparison," and added numbers to the Comments. Thus, a citation to Rule 1.6, Comment 15, refers to the fifteenth paragraph of the Comment to Rule 1.6; a citation to Rule 1.2, Code Comparison 5 refers to the fifth paragraph of the Code Comparison to Rule 1.2. Note that this "Code Comparison" only exists in the 1983 version of the Model Rules, but it is still a useful interpretative tool. The ABA has not amended the Model Code since it first approved the Model Rules in 1983. The latest version of the Model Rules appears in an Appendix at the end of this book.

ABA Ethics 2000 Commission. In 1997, the ABA established the Commission on Evaluation of the Rules of Professional Conduct (the "Ethics 2000 Commission") to undertake a comprehensive review and evaluation of the Model Rules in light of all the changes since the ABA approved the Model Rules in 1983. On February 5, 2002, the ABA House of Delegates approved substantial changes along with many other stylistic revisions. In 2003, the ABA approved other changes to Rules 1.6 and 1.13, in response to the Enron bankruptcy scandal. This book reflects those changes.

The A.L.I. In 1986 the American Law Institute, a prestigious group of practicing lawyers, judges, and academics, began drafting a *Restatement of the Law Governing*

Lawyers. Although the ALI had never before tackled the law of lawyering, it titled this project, "Restatement of the Law Third." However, there is no Restatement Second, or Restatement First. The ALI has chosen this title not out of a perverse desire to confuse law students and practicing lawyers (though that has been a common result) but to signify that the American Law Institute was then working on a third major series of Restatements, such as the Restatement, Third, of the Law of Unfair Competition, etc. Occasionally this book will refer to the *Restatement Third of the Law Governing Lawyers* (2000), which is now in final form.

■ II. RELATIONSHIP WITH OTHER COURSES

The history of law, Maitland said, is a "seamless web." Maitland, *Prologue to a History of English Law,* 14 L.Q.R. 13 (1898). This observation is equally true of legal ethics. To write the first sentence is to make a tear in this unity. The lawyer's ethical duty to keep the client's confidences incorporates the law of evidence and the attorney-client privilege as well as the law of agency. The lawyer's duty of competence is related to the law of tort (particularly the tort of malpractice). The lawyer's agreement with the client also involves the law of contract, and takes into account that the lawyer is a fiduciary of the client.

The Model Rules represent a *proposed* law that the ABA advocates each jurisdiction adopt. Each state's version of the Model Rules is "law," (just as much as the Rules of Evidence or Rules are Civil Procedure are law), and this law must be tested against constitutional principles, particularly those related to freedom of speech. The ethics rules related to lawyer advertising, in particular, often raise free speech concerns.

In addition to the relationship with other areas of substantive law, legal ethics is a branch of history and philosophy. "There is much more to it than rules of ethics. There is a whole atmosphere of life's behavior." Wigmore, *Introduction* xxiv, in, O. Carter, Ethics of the Legal Profession (1915). And this atmosphere exists whether or not the constable is watching. Legal ethics is also related to the interdisciplinary study of law and economics, because some of the present or past ethical violations are best understood as guild rules created by a cartel of lawyers. That is why George Bernard Shaw once said that professions are "conspiracies against the laity." G.B. Shaw, Doctor's Dilemma (preface) (1911).

■ III. PREPARING FOR A PROFESSIONAL RESPONSIBILITY EXAMINATION

The "most fundamental legal skill consists of determining what kind of legal problems a situation may involve, a skill that necessarily transcends any particular specialized knowledge." Model Rules, Rule 1.1, Comment 2.

However, in an examination of legal ethics, a little specialized knowledge would not hurt. The Rules are a source of this specialized knowledge. Students should apply their traditional legal skills to the fact situation and evaluate how the Rules (or other body of law) might deal with the problem. Sometimes these Rules are too vague to be of much help; at other times they are quite specific, but one may think that they represent bad policy. A conclusion that a Rule represents bad policy is important, because the law is not static: what the law ought to be is very relevant, because the "ought" influences the "is." The fact that law is not static is what has required this new edition.

It is important to realize that the law of ethics advises the lawyer not only what one must or must not do, but also what one "should" do, or what one "may" do even if the client objects. Finally, whether or not conduct is consistent with the Rules, that conduct may subject the lawyer to malpractice liability. The Multistate Professional Responsibility Examination recognizes these important distinctions in its specific definitions of several key phrases:

1. *Subject to discipline* asks whether the conduct referred to or described in the question subjects the attorney to discipline under the provisions of the ABA Model Rules of Professional Conduct or ABA Model Code of Judicial Conduct. You are not asked if the disciplinary authorities will in fact impose discipline; the only issue is whether the lawyer or judge is subject to discipline.

2. *May* or *proper* asks whether the conduct referred to or described in the question is professionally appropriate in that it:

   a. would not subject the attorney or judge to discipline.

   b. is not inconsistent with Preamble, Comments, or text of the ABA Model Rules of Professional Conduct and ABA Model Code of Judicial Conduct.

   c. is not inconsistent with "generally accepted principles of the law of lawyering."

3. *Subject to litigation sanction* asks if the conduct in question would subject the lawyer or the lawyer's law firm to sanction by a tribunal to contempt, fine,

fee forfeiture, disqualification or other sanction.

4. *Subject to disqualification* asked if the conduct in question would subject the lawyer or his or her law firm to disqualification in a civil or criminal matter.

5. *Subject to civil liability* asks whether the conduct referred to or described in the question subjects the attorney to civil liability, such as claims for malpractice, misrepresentation, or breach of fiduciary duty. In connection with this issue, one should be aware of the relationship, if any, between being liable for malpractice and being subject to discipline.

6. *Subject to criminal liability* asks if the conduct in question would subject the lawyer for criminal liability, for participation in, or aiding and abetting, criminal acts such as insurance or tax fraud, destruction of evidence, and obstruction of justice.

■ IV. CAVEAT

A text limited in size necessarily restricts any full discussion of all the nuances of the ethics governing the practice of law. The black letter language found throughout, and the capsule summary in particular, are intended to be (and in the nature of things can only be) summaries of the basic principles of legal ethics. For a more elaborate discussion, analysis, and research tool, see, e.g., ABA/BNA, *Lawyers' Manual on Professional Conduct* (multivolume loose leaf service); R. Underwood & W. Fortune, *Trial Ethics* (1988); Ronald D. Rotunda, *Legal Ethics: The Lawyer's Deskbook on Professional Responsibility* (ABA/West Group, 2d ed. 2002); Ronald D. Rotunda & Michael I. Krauss, *Legal Ethics in a Nutshell* (West Group, St. Paul, Minnesota, 1st ed. 2003, Nutshell Series); G. Hazard & W. Hodes, *The Law of Lawyering: A Handbook on the Model Rules of Professional Conduct* (3d ed. 2001)(2 volumes); R. Hillman, *Law Firm Breakups: The Law and Ethics of Grabbing and Leaving* (1990). On the ABA Model Judicial Code, see, J. Shaman, S. Lubet, & J. Alfini, *Judicial Conduct and Ethics* (1990). On legal malpractice, see, Ronald E. Mallen & Jeffrey E. Smith, *Legal Malpractice* (4th ed. 1996) (4 volumes).

PART I

Defining Disciplinable Conduct

■ **ANALYSIS**

IV. Jurisdiction
    A.   Acts Done Outside of the Jurisdiction
        1.   In General
        2.   Rationale
        3.   Choice of Law Problems
    B.   Statutes of Limitations

I. The Distinction Between Disciplinable and Aspirational Conduct

Lawyers may only be disciplined for violating mandatory rules, but they should strive to meet the aspirational goals.

A. Ethical Considerations

The Model Code distinguished between Ethical Considerations ("EC") and Disciplinary Rules ("DR"). The Ethical Considerations are "aspirational" only. See Model Code, Preliminary Statement. Therefore, if conduct violates only an EC, it is not disciplinable. The EC's also aid in interpreting and explaining the policies underlying a DR. "They constitute a body of principles upon which the lawyer can rely for guidance in specific situations." Model Code, Preliminary Statement.

Notwithstanding the fact that a violation of an EC is not disciplinable under the Code, in some cases courts have disciplined an attorney for violating an EC. See, *Committee on Professional Ethics and Conduct of State Bar Association v. Behnke*, 276 N.W.2d 838, 840 (Iowa 1979) (violation of an EC, "standing alone," will support disciplinary action; in this case the violation was of EC 5–5). However, in most such instances, the fact that the conduct is prohibited can be derived from a DR, even though it might be expressed more clearly in the EC. Courts purporting to rely only on EC's may have failed to carefully and precisely interpret the Model Code. In short, one should not assume that if conduct expressly violates an EC, it does not also violate a more generally phrased DR.

B. Disciplinary Rules

The Disciplinary Rules, unlike the Ethical Considerations, "are mandatory in character." They state "the minimum level of conduct below which no lawyer can fall without being subject to disciplinary action." See Model Code, Preliminary Statement; DR 1–102(A)(1) (misconduct to violate a disciplinary rule).

Some of the EC's and DR's are cast in terms of what the lawyer "may" do. E.g., DR 4–101(C) (when lawyer "may" reveal a client secret or confidence). In that case the Code gives lawyers a power to be exercised in their sound discretion.

C. The Model Rules

The Model Rules do not adopt the DR–EC format. However, they draw similar distinctions between what *must* be done, what *should* be done, and what *may* be done. And, they also make clear that if a Model Rules says "shall," as opposed to "preferably," the lawyer is subject to discipline. Scope ¶ 19; Rule 8.4(a).

The format of the Model Rules distinguish between the Rule itself (which the commentators often call the "black letter Rule") and the Comments, which serve to explain the reason for a Rule, or give examples, or make distinctions, or offer advice on what a lawyer may or should not do.

There is no discipline for not complying with black letter Rules that use permissive language. For example, Rule 1.5(b) says that a fee agreement is "preferable in writing." Rule 1.6(b) discusses when lawyer "may" reveal client information. Rule 6.1 advises: "A lawyer *should* aspire to render at least (50) hours of *pro bono publico* services per year."

In contrast to the black letter Rules, many of the Comments use the term "should." These "Comments do not add obligations to the Rules but provide guidance for practicing in compliance with the Rules." Model Rules, Scope, 14.

The Comments also explain the Rules and provide interpretative guidance, though, of course, "the text of each Rule is authoritative." Rules, Scope 21. Therefore, while the black letter Rules control, one should not conclude that, because conduct violates an explicit aspirational Comment, it does not also violate a more broadly drafted Rule.

II. The "Appearance of Impropriety"

Although the former Code stated that lawyers should avoid the "appearance of impropriety," this "appearance" provision is not part of the Model Rules, is not a disciplinable standard, and is not definable unless one first defines what an "impropriety" is.

The title of Canon 9 states: "A Lawyer Should Avoid Even the Appearance of Impropriety." The titles of the Canons are not disciplinable rules themselves, but only titles of sections. They represent "axiomatic norms" (see Model Code, "Preliminary Statement"), not tests to determine when lawyers should be disciplined or disqualified. This "appearance of impropriety" standard may represent a reason behind a rule (see EC 9–3)—why, for example, some ethics rules are mechanical and absolute—but it is not a rule itself. It is significant that no Disciplinary Rule requires the lawyer to avoid the "appearance of impropriety."

Nonetheless, some courts have used this loose language as a standard of conduct. See, e.g., *Kramer v. Scientific Control Corp.*, 534 F.2d 1085 (3d Cir.1976), cert. denied,

429 U.S. 830, 97 S.Ct. 90, 50 L.Ed.2d 94 (1976). Other courts, in contrast, have warned that use of such a broad test should not substitute for analysis to demonstrate why conduct does, or does not, fit within specific disciplinary rules. *International Electronics Corp. v. Flanzer*, 527 F.2d 1288, 1295 (2d Cir.1975). As the court carefully noted in *Fund of Funds, Ltd. v. Arthur Andersen & Co.*, 567 F.2d 225, 227 (2d Cir.1977): "When dealing with ethical principles . . . we cannot paint with broad strokes. The lines are fine and must be so marked. [T]he conclusion in a particular case can be reached only after painstaking analysis of the facts and precise application of precedent." In ABA Formal Opinion 342 (1975), the American Bar Association warned that if the "appearance of impropriety" language had been made a disciplinary rule, "it is likely that the determination of whether particular conduct violated the rule would have degenerated . . . into a determination on an instinctive or even *ad hominem* basis. . . . "

The Rules reject the "appearance of impropriety" test. The drafters thought that it is too loose and vague, gives no fair warning, and allows, or even encourages, instinctive judgments by disgruntled clients. Also, one can not begin to define "appearance of impropriety" unless one first defines "impropriety," and the purported "test" does neither. The Rules, at times, impose a bright line prohibition in order to avoid an "appearance of impropriety," but that phrase, by itself, is not a test. Because "impropriety" is not defined, the term "appearance of impropriety" is question-begging, and it is not a test found in the present version of the Model Rules.

III. Defining Disciplinable Conduct

A lawyer may be disciplined for violating a mandatory requirement of the Code or Rules, or for engaging in conduct forbidden by other laws if such conduct demonstrates that the lawyer should not be entrusted with the confidence that clients normally place in a lawyer.

A. Acts Not Done in a Legal Capacity

A lawyer may be disciplined for wrongful conduct even though she was not acting in her capacity as a lawyer when engaging in the wrong, *if* the conduct functionally relates to her capacity to practice law. ABA Formal Opinion 336 (June 3, 1974) concluded that (1) any "illegal conduct involving moral turpitude," and (2) any conduct "involving dishonesty, fraud, deceit, or misrepresentation" adversely affect the lawyer's capacity to practice law. See Rule 8.4(b), (c); DR 1–102(A)(3), (4).

Example: A lawyer knowingly makes a false statement of fact about a judicial candidate. DR 8–102(A); Rule 8.2(a). He has evidenced lack of trustworthiness and is subject to discipline.

In contrast to these rules, DR 7–107 and Rule 3.6, governing trial publicity, or DR 2–101, and Rule 7.2, governing advertising, relate to a lawyer only in her *professional* capacity.

B. Categories of Disciplinable Conduct

1. Violating a Disciplinary Rule

It is, of course, disciplinable to violate a Disciplinary Rule. Rule 8.4(a); DR 1–102(A)(1). It is also disciplinable to assist or induce another to violate a Disciplinary Rule. Rule 8.4(a); DR 1–102(A)(2). The Rules add that it is disciplinable to "attempt to violate the Rules." Rule 8.4(a).

Example: Clients can talk to each other directly even if one or both of the clients are represented by counsel. Lawyers, however, may not contact the other party if the lawyer knows that the other party is represented by counsel. Rule 4.2. May a lawyer advise a client that the client can talk to the other side directly? Yes. Lawyers may advise clients what the law is, that is, lawyers may advise clients that they communicate with the opposing party directly. Rule 4.2, Comment 4. Rule 8.4 makes it clear that the lawyer does not violate Rule 8.4(a) (violating a Rule through "acts of another") by advising a client of actions that the client is lawfully entitled to make.

2. Criminal Acts

Not all illegal conduct is disciplinable. The former Model Code forbade crimes involving "moral turpitude." DR 1–102(A)(3).

The problem with the test of "moral turpitude" is that it is too vague and allows, or even invites, a court to discipline attorneys for acts that may be crimes in some states, although the crime is not connected or even relevant to the attorney-client relationship. See *Grievance Committee of Hartford County Bar v. Broder*, 112 Conn. 263, 152 A. 292 (1930) (extramarital relations with consenting person not a client; held, disciplinable).

It is not at all evident that the drafters of the Model Code intended to make disciplinable those crimes that are not functionally related to fitness to practice law, particularly because other provisions in the Code imply that such a functional relationship is necessary. See DR 1–102(A)(6), forbidding a lawyer from engaging in "any *other* conduct that adversely reflects on his fitness to practice law." (emphasis added).

In any event, the Rules adopt more precise language because "a lawyer should be professionally answerable only for offenses that indicate lack of those characteristics relevant to law practice." Rule 8.4, Comment 1. Rule 8.4(b) limits disciplinable crimes to only those that reflect "adversely on the lawyer's honesty, trustworthiness or fitness as a lawyer in other respects." Discipline is inappropriate for violations of "personal morality" such as adultery. Rule 8.4, Comment 1.

Example: Examples of disciplinable conduct include crimes of fraud or breach of trust; willful (rather than negligent) failure to file an income tax return; or "serious interferences with the administration of justice." Rule 8.4, Comment 1.

Rule 8.4, Comment 2, includes "violence" in the category of disciplinable crimes, even though violence does not necessarily indicate lack of trustworthiness or dishonesty: a drunken barroom brawl may only indicate a lawyer's bad temper, not his willingness to steal his client's money. Nonetheless, crimes of violence, particularly when the violence is quite serious, have been held disciplinable. E.g., *Matter of Webb*, 602 P.2d 408 (Alaska 1979) (first degree murder, accessory after the fact).

The Rules suggest that even a pattern of repeated minor offenses could be disciplinable if it indicates "indifference to legal obligation." Rule 8.4, Comment 2. The drafters give no examples, but repeated violations involving minor offenses may just as likely indicate an indifference only to a *particular* violation, e.g., a lawyer owns a grocery store that repeatedly is open on Sunday, in criminal violation of a local, generally unenforced, "blue law."

3. Conduct Involving Dishonesty, Fraud, Deceit, or Misrepresentation

Conduct, whether or not a crime, that involves dishonesty, fraud, deceit, or misrepresentation, is disciplinable. Rule 8.4(c); DR 1–102(A)(4). Noncriminal fraud (for those states that have such an offense) would fall under this rubric. Similarly, violations of fiduciary obligations (whether or not undertaken in one's capacity as a lawyer) would be disciplinable if they indicate dishonesty. If the action does not involve dishonesty, etc., then the lawyer is not subject to discipline. For example, a lawyer's racist and sexist remarks made outside of the representation of a client are not disciplinable, although they are despicable (although some state ethics rules have language making such speech disciplinable). See, Rotunda, *Racist Speech and Attorney Discipline*, 6 The Professional Lawyer 1 (A.B.A., No. 6, 1995).

ABA Formal Opinion 337 (Aug. 10, 1974) relied on DR 1–102(A)(4) to hold that a lawyer's surreptitious tape recording (except in the case of law enforcement that is in compliance with statutory and constitutional guidelines) without the consent or prior knowledge of all parties involved is disciplinable. The secret nature of the recording, the Opinion argued, was a form of fraud, *even if* not a crime under the local jurisdiction.

In ABA Formal Opinion 01–422 (June 24, 2001), the ABA formally withdrew (i.e., *overruled*) Formal Opinion 337, and announced that it is not inherently "misleading" for a lawyer to tape record a conversation. However, a lawyer may not record conversations in violation of the law if a jurisdiction forbids such conduct without the consent of all parties. Nor may a lawyer falsely represent that she is not recording a conversation when she, in fact, is doing so. The Committee could not agree whether a lawyer may record a client-lawyer conversation without the knowledge of the client, but the members agreed that it is inadvisable for a lawyer to do so. While many people find surreptitious tape recording to be offensive as a general matter, there are specific circumstances where the practice seems reasonable. For example, lawyers might tape record (or advise the client to tape record) in order to document obscene phone calls or threats.

4. Other Conduct

Prejudicial to the Administration of Justice. The final version of the Rules (but *not* the Proposed Final Draft of May 30, 1981) makes it disciplinable to "engage in conduct that is prejudicial to the administration of justice." Rule 8.4(d). This vague and loose standard was also found in the Model Code. DR 1–102(A)(5). The Code offered another equally vague and loose catch-all standard: "any other conduct that adversely reflects on his fitness to practice law." DR 1–102(A)(5)(b). The Model Rules, however, do not continue that vague provision.

Implying Ability to Influence Judge or Improperly Assisting Judge. The Model Rules, for unknown reasons, place in Rule 8.4 two further prohibitions that, more logically, could have been placed with the other substantive provisions in the Model Rules. One prohibition provides that a lawyer should not state or imply an ability to improperly influence a government agency or official. Rule 8.4(e). This topic is discussed further in Part 6(I)(D), below. A lawyer also may not "achieve results by means that violate" the Model Rules or other law.

The second prohibition forbids a lawyer from knowingly assisting a judge to violate the Code of Judicial Conduct. Rule 8.4(f).

The Code had similar prohibitions, but they are placed in the body of the Code. See DR 9–101(c), which is almost identical to Rule 8.4(e), and DR 7–110(A), which is somewhat related to Rule 8.4(f).

Manifesting Bias or Prejudice. Rule 8.4, Comment 4, is a new provision (added in 1999), not found in the former Model Code. It provides that a lawyer, *in the course of representing a client*, who manifests, "by words or conduct," his or her bias or prejudice on the basis of "race, sex, religion, national origin, disability, age, sexual orientation or socioeconomic status," thereby violates Rule 8.4(d) ("conduct prejudicial to the administration of justice"). This Comment does not say when the words or conduct are prejudicial to the administration of justice, although it does provide that "[l]egitimate advocacy"—a term not defined—does not violate Rule 8.4(d).

Whether this Rule is so overbroad that it violates the First Amendment is a nice question. This Comment is similar to college "speech codes" that punish offensive speech based on race, sex, sexual orientation, etc. Lower courts have typically invalidated such codes. See, e.g., Robert Sedler, *The Unconstitutionality of Campus Bans on "Racist Speech": The view from Without and Within*, 53 U. Pittsburgh L. Rev. 631 (1992); Ronald D. Rotunda, *A Brief Comment on Politically Incorrect Speech in the Wake of R.A.V.*, 47 So. Methodist U. L. Rev. 9 (1993). Consequently, this Comment, depending on how it is enforced, may raise free speech problems.

Note also that the Comment speaks of "words *or* conduct" and refers back to Rule 8.4(d), but that Rule only speaks of "conduct." In addition, the phrase "socioeconomic status" raises more questions. For example, if a lawyer tells a client, "we should lobby against the proposed reduction in the capital gains tax rate because I hate the idle rich," is that lawyer now subject to discipline, and if, he is, would discipline violate the First Amendment. See, e.g., Rotunda, *What Next? Outlawing Lawyer Jokes?*, Wall Street Journal, Aug. 8, 1995, at A12, col. 3–5. This Comment, depending on how it is enforced, may raise free speech problems.

Example: Assume that a lawyer, in the course of a trial, seeks to use a preemptory challenge to dismiss a black juror. Assume further that the judge rejects the preemptory challenge on the grounds that the lawyer exercised the challenge on racist grounds. Is the lawyer therefore subject to discipline? Comment 3, Rule 8.4 says no: "A trial judge's finding that preemptory challenges were exercised on a discriminatory basis does not alone establish a violation of this Rule." Remember however, this improper use of a preemptory challenge violates the U.S. Constitution even if the lawyer who exercises the peremptory challenge is representing a private party in a civil case, *Edmonson v. Leesville Concrete Co., Inc.*, 500 U.S. 614, 111 S.Ct. 2077, 114 L.Ed.2d 660 (1991).

Perhaps the drafters of this Comment thought that too much should not be read into a single instance in which a judge called on the lawyer to give a neutral reason for a peremptory challenge, followed by the judge not finding the neutral reason sufficient, given that the judge's finding is not typically appealable. Also, by the nature of things, many lawyers (particularly prosecutors) who have participated in a large number of trials may have lost peremptory challenge motions.

IV.   Jurisdiction

A.   Acts Done Outside of the Jurisdiction

A state disciplinary authority has, in general, the power to discipline a person admitted to the bar in that jurisdiction even though the acts complained of occurred outside the jurisdiction.

1.   In General

Consider three cases: (1) Lawyer **1** is admitted in State *A*, yet practices in State *Y* after being admitted there *pro hac vice*, i.e., for purposes of this case only. (2) Lawyer **2** is admitted in State *A* and State *Y*, but practices only in State *Y*, outside the jurisdiction of State *A*. (3) Lawyer **3**, admitted in State *A*, does not practice law at all, yet he engages in misconduct, e.g., fraud, (in State *Y*) reflecting on his ability to practice law. In all of these cases, State *A* has jurisdiction to discipline the lawyer, although the improper conduct occurred outside of State *A*'s jurisdiction. In addition, State *Y* also has jurisdiction to discipline Lawyer **1** for misconduct growing out of Lawyer **1**'s special appearance in State *Y*. E.g., *Kentucky Bar Ass'n v. Shane*, 553 S.W.2d 467 (Ky. 1977). Of course, because Lawyer **1** is not generally admitted in State *Y*, State *Y* cannot disbar him. However, State *Y* can revoke its permission for him to appear *pro hac vice* for that case and for future cases.

2.   Rationale

The rationale for the extraterritorial application of ethics rules is easy to understand. The purpose of lawyer discipline is not to punish but rather to "seek to determine the fitness of an officer of the court to continue in that capacity and to protect the courts and the public from the official ministration of persons unfit to practice." *In re Echeles,* 430 F.2d 347, 349 (7th Cir.1970). If the lawyer engages in improper conduct outside the jurisdiction of State *A*, that conduct still reflects on the ability of the lawyer to practice in State *A*. It is the lawyer's admission to practice in State *A* (not the site or physical location of his improper act) that gives State *A* the jurisdiction to discipline. E.g., *State v. Pounds,* 525 S.W.2d 547 (Tex.Civ.App.1975) (discipline of nonresident lawyer). See also, e.g., *Selling v. Radford,* 243 U.S. 46, 37 S.Ct. 377, 61 L.Ed. 585 (1917).

The Code had no specific provision governing this jurisdictional question, though it is implicit in the definition of misconduct, DR 1–102, which, by its own terms, provides no jurisdictional limitations.

The Rules explicitly codify the present law: "A lawyer admitted to practice in this jurisdiction is subject to the disciplinary authority of this jurisdiction, regardless of where the lawyer's conduct occurs." Rule 8.5(a).

3. Choice of Law Problems

If a lawyer is admitted in State *A*, then that state can discipline the lawyer for improper conduct, regardless of where the conduct occurred. Rule 8.5(a). A lawyer may be admitted in two different jurisdictions, State *A*, and State *B*. If this lawyer engages in an act (either in State *A*, or *B*, or elsewhere) that is disciplinable, State *A* may discipline a lawyer for engaging in this bad conduct in State *B*, even though State *B* punishes this same conduct less severely (e.g., a private admonition, versus suspension for one year, versus disbarment). State *A* will no doubt contend that it has higher standards than State *B*. The situation is analogous to the case where two States adopt the multistate bar examination but one State sets a lower passing rate than the other.

Now consider the case where State *A* seeks to punish the conduct that occurred in State *B*, but, that conduct did not violate the rules of State *B*. Choice of law problems are inevitable. If a lawyer practices in two jurisdictions, it is quite conceivable that conduct *forbidden* in one jurisdiction is ethically *compelled* in another. For example, State *A* may demand disclosure of client confidences in a situation where State *B* may forbid it.

The Model Code had no provisions that deal specifically with the choice of law problems. The Model Rules deal with this the issue in Rule 8.5(b).

The goal of this Rule is to insure that (1) any particular conduct of a lawyer should be subject to only one set of rules; (2) those rules should be reasonable ascertainable; and (3) there is a safe harbor for lawyers who act reasonably when there is inevitable uncertainty. Rule 8.5, Comment 3. Both jurisdictions may impose discipline, but they should both be using the same set of rules against which they measure the conduct. Disciplinary authorities should avoid proceeding against a lawyer on the basis of two inconsistent rules. Comment 6. Thus, the question is, which jurisdictional rules ought to apply.

In general, if the conduct at issue took place before a court, the disciplinary authority should apply only the rules of the jurisdiction where that court sits (unless the rules of that court provide otherwise). Assume that a lawyer is admitted generally in State *A*, and is admitted *pro hac vice* (only for purposes of a particular proceeding) in a case heard in State *B*. If that lawyer then violates the ethics rules of State *B* while appearing in the court of State *B*, State *A* should apply the ethics rules of State *B*. Rule 8.5(b)(1).

For all other conduct, if the ethics law that should apply is the law of the jurisdiction in which the conduct occurred. However, if the "predominant effect" of the conduct occurs in a different jurisdiction, then the law of that jurisdiction should apply. Rule 8.5(b)(2) & Comment 4.

Now, what happens if the lawyer has significant contacts with more than one jurisdiction and it is not clear where the "predominant effect" occurs? That is where the Rules create a safe harbor: if the lawyer conforms to the rules of a jurisdiction where the "lawyer reasonably believes the predominant effect will occur," the lawyer is safe. Rule 8.5(b)(2) & Comment 5.

If a lawyer practices both in this country and in another country, the American ethics rules still apply unless a treaty or other agreement between the affected jurisdictions says otherwise. Rule 8.5, Comment 7.

As states have adopted the Model Rules, there has been a great tendency to adopt nonuniform amendments. Thus, we may expect choice of law problems to increase.

B. Statutes of Limitations

Neither the Code nor the Rules incorporate any statute of limitations for disciplinary actions.

Because the purpose of discipline is to protect the public rather than punish the attorney, *In re Echeles*, 430 F.2d 347, 349 (7th Cir.1970), the time when the misconduct occurred is relevant only to the extent that it bears on the lawyer's present fitness to practice law. If the lawyer is accused of conduct that is also a civil tort or criminal wrong, the mere fact that the statute of limitations has run in either the civil or criminal case does not preclude disciplinary action. "Lawyer discipline and disability proceedings should not be subject to any statute of limitations." ABA Standards for Lawyer Discipline and Disability Proceedings § 4.6 (1979). "Staleness in a charge against an attorney might prevent its being considered, because an unreasonable delay in the presentation of a charge might make it impossible for an attorney to procure witnesses . . . ; but the statute of limitations itself is no defense to such a proceeding." *In re Smith*, 73 Kan. 743, 745, 85 P. 584, 586 (1906). See also, *Anne Arundel County Bar Association, Inc. v. Collins*, 272 Md. 578, 325 A.2d 724 (1974).

REVIEW QUESTIONS

1. While the Model Code distinguishes between mandatory and aspirational conduct, the Model Rules abandon this distinction and only focus on mandatory conduct.

_____ True _____ False

2. The "appearance of impropriety" test is:

    a.   a useful litmus test found in both the Model Rules and the Model Code.

    b.   a useful litmus test found only in the Model Rules.

    c.   a generalized statement found only in the Model Code and abandoned in the Model Rules as too vague to be of assistance.

    d.   a generalized statement created by the drafters of the Model Rules to guide the courts.

3. Lawyer, while driving home from a golf outing, was given a traffic ticket for speeding. In Lawyer's state, a traffic ticket is a criminal misdemeanor.

Is Lawyer *subject to discipline*?

    a.   No, because Lawyer was not acting in a professional capacity.

b.   No, because the crime does not reflect adversely on Lawyer's honesty.

c.   Yes, because the ticket shows a lack of respect for law.

4.   Lawyer is admitted in both State A and State B and primarily practices in State B. The ethics rules of State A requires the lawyer, in an ex parte proceeding, to volunteer all material facts, even if the facts are adverse to his client, and even if they are protected as secret client information. The ethics rules of State B do not permit a lawyer in this situation to offer such evidence unless his client voluntarily consents. Lawyer, who is seeking a temporary restraining order in an ex parte proceeding filed in State A, volunteers some adverse client information without securing his client's consent. The disciplinary authorities of State B seek to discipline the Lawyer for this action. Under the Model Rules, is lawyer subject to discipline in State B?

a.   Yes, because Lawyer is admitted in State B.

b.   Yes, because Lawyer primarily practices in State B.

c.   No, because Lawyer was practicing before the courts of State A.

d.   No, because Lawyer's actions took place in a different jurisdiction.

5.   Williams, an insurance adjuster, is a lawyer who has not practiced for years. He is still a member of the bar. When Friend, a good friend of his, suffered a house fire, Williams examined the premises, and greatly inflated his estimates of Friend's actual losses. Williams hoped to receive a kickback or rebate from Friend because of his actions, but Friend refused.

Is Williams *subject to discipline?*

a.   No, because Williams did not engage in such conduct in his capacity as a lawyer.

b.   No, because he received no kickback.

c.   Yes, because he submitted a fraudulent insurance claim.

d.   Yes, because he acted in a prohibited conflict of interest situation when he adjusted his friend's claim.

PART II

The Lawyer's Obligation to Support Bar Admissions and the Disciplinary System

■ **ANALYSIS**

I. Application to the Bar
  A. Applicability to Applicants and Lawyers
  B. The Requirements of No Material Falsity, Correction of Misapprehensions, and Response to Requested Information
    1. No Material Falsity
    2. Correction of Misapprehensions
    3. Requested Information
  C. Furthering the Application of Candidates for the Bar and Whistle–Blowing

II. **The Lawyer's Role Regarding Reporting Disciplinable Violations of Lawyers**
  A. The General Rule
  B. The Applicability of the Rule to the Lawyer's Own Conduct
    1. Blowing the Whistle on Oneself
    2. The Duty to Cooperate With Discipline Authorities
  C. Applicability of Privilege
    1. Self–Incrimination
    2. Client Confidences

III. **The Lawyer's Role Regarding Judges and Candidates for the Judiciary**
  A. Lawyers Criticizing and Defending Judges and Judicial Candidates
    1. Whistle–Blowing
    2. False Statements
    3. Duty to Defend
  B. Candidates for Judicial Office

I. Application to the Bar

Both the applicant for admission and the lawyer who supplies an affidavit on behalf of an applicant or who responds to inquiries in a discipline matter may not make any false statements and must affirmatively correct any known misunderstandings. The lawyer and applicant retain any evidentiary or constitutional privileges.

A. Applicability to Applicants and Lawyers

The Model Rules (like its predecessor, the Model Code) do not govern nonlawyers. However, if a nonlawyer in her bar application makes a materially false statement, the bar authorities can discipline the applicant for that misstatement when the person is admitted, even if she was not a lawyer at the time. Rule 8.1(a) & Comment 1; DR 1B102(A)(4). See Part I, section III, A, supra.

The Rules are more specific than the old Model Code on this point. The applicant may not make a false statement in connection with the bar application. Rule 8.1(a). Though the applicant is not, at the time of the application, governed by the Rules of that jurisdiction, a violation of Rule 8.1(a) may form the basis of discipline if the applicant is already a member of the bar in one jurisdiction and seeking admission elsewhere, or is subsequently admitted and thus becomes subject to the jurisdiction of the Rules. Rule 8.1, Comment 1. The applicant must also correct any prior misstatements and affirmatively clarify any misunderstanding. Id. The touchstone is candor.

B. The Requirements of No Material Falsity, Correction of Misapprehensions, and Response to Requested Information

1. No Material Falsity

The lawyer (or applicant, see supra, section I, A) may not knowingly make a *material* misstatement. Rule 8.1(a); DR 1–101(A). A statement is material if it has "the effect of inhibiting efforts of the bar to determine an applicant's fitness to practice law." *Matter of Howe*, 257 N.W.2d 420 (N.D.1977). Moreover, the misstatement must be *knowingly* false when made. There is no violation if the misrepresentation was not deliberate. *Siegel v. Committee of Bar Examiners, State Bar of California*, 10 Cal.3d 156, 110 Cal.Rptr. 15, 514 P.2d 967 (1973).

2. Correction of Misapprehensions

The Code did not specifically compel the lawyer or applicant to correct a misapprehension that may have arisen on the part of the bar authorities. However, it might be considered, in some circumstances, to be a "fraud," DR 1–102(A)(4), not to correct misunderstandings of the bar authorities.

In contrast, the Model Rules are quite clear on this point. The lawyer or applicant may not *"fail to disclose* a fact necessary to correct a misapprehension known by the person to have arisen in the matter . . . " Rule 8.1(b) (emphasis added). What is less clear is whether the duty exists even if the misapprehension was not caused by something the lawyer or applicant said. The Comment supports a broad interpretation of the duty to correct misunderstandings. It says that the Rule "also requires affirmative clarification of *any misunderstanding* on the part of the admissions or disciplinary authority of which the person involved becomes aware." Rule 8.1, Comment 1 (emphasis added).

3. Requested Information

In the case of either an application for admission or a bar disciplinary matter, the bar authorities may request information. DR 1–103(B) specifically required that the lawyer must reveal any "unprivileged knowledge" regarding another lawyer "upon proper request." This rule did not expressly apply to either the bar admission process or to a disciplinary investigation involving the lawyer's *own* conduct (although refusal to obey a lawful subpoena might be held to violate DR 1–102(A)(5)—conduct "prejudicial to the administration of justice"). The Rules specifically require a lawyer to cooperate with any "lawful demand for information" in any admissions or disciplinary investigation, including an investigation into the lawyer's own conduct. Rule 8.1(b).

The Rules (like the Code) only mandate obedience to a "lawful demand." The lawyer or applicant, of course, has the right to claim any evidentiary or constitutional privilege, but "should do so openly and not use the right of nondisclosure as a justification for failure to comply . . . " Rule 8.1, Comment 2. See also, Rule 3.4(c) (requiring lawyer to obey rules of a tribunal "except for an open refusal").

The bar can discipline a lawyer or refuse to admit an applicant because the person unlawfully obstructs the investigation. *Konigsberg v. State Bar of California,* 366 U.S. 36, 81 S.Ct. 997, 6 L.Ed.2d 105 (1961) (Konigsberg II). However, because of free speech concerns, the bar cannot punish persons simply because they are or have been members of the Communist Party. *Schware v. Board of Bar Examiners of State of N.M.,* 353 U.S. 232,

77 S.Ct. 752, 1 L.Ed.2d 796 (1957). Nor may the bar violate a person's associational and privacy rights by charging perjury if one incorrectly answers *vague* inquiries about past associations. *Baird v. State Bar of Ariz.,* 401 U.S. 1, 91 S.Ct. 702, 27 L.Ed.2d 639 (1971) (bar threatens to punish applicant for perjury if she answers incorrectly—without a requirement of scienter—whether any of her past memberships, already disclosed, were in organizations that advocated the unlawful overthrow of the Government).

Nevertheless, the bar may refuse to admit a person who is a *knowing* member (*i.e.,* a member with scienter) of an organization advocating the unlawful overthrow of the Government, with the *specific intent* to further these *unlawful* goals of the organization. *Law Students Civil Rights Research Council, Inc. v. Wadmond,* 401 U.S. 154, 164–66, 91 S.Ct. 720, 727–28, 27 L.Ed.2d 749, 759–60 (1971). See generally, 4 Ronald D. Rotunda & John E. Nowak, *Treatise on Constitutional Law: Substance and Procedure* § 20.44 (West Group Co. 3d 1999).

C. Furthering the Application of Candidates For the Bar and Whistle–Blowing

Lawyers are often asked to supply character references for bar applicants. The Code required that lawyers "shall not further," the admission of candidates to the bar whom the lawyer knows lack the required "character," "education," or "other relevant attribute." DR 1–101(B). The most natural reading of this section is that the lawyer should not file such references as to persons "known by him to be unqualified." DR 1–101(B). This interpretation is also supported by EC 1–3, which provided that, before recommending an applicant, the lawyer "should satisfy himself that the applicant is of good moral character." In other words, the lawyer need not become "a self-appointed investigator," EC 1–3, but he should not recommend an applicant if he has no basis for a recommendation (i.e., "should satisfy himself"), and definitely should not "further" the application of one known to be lacking the requisite characteristics.

Note: The last sentence of EC 1–6 affirmatively encouraged lawyers to "assist" unqualified applicants to be licensed when the disqualification (e.g., mental or emotional stability) has terminated. Similarly, lawyers should assist suspended or disbarred lawyers to restore their right to practice law when their disqualifications have terminated.

Notwithstanding this interpretation, some have argued that the rule was phrased too broadly: "An attorney could 'further' the application of a person for admission to the bar by acting as his counsel in a bar admission proceeding." Weckstein, *Maintaining the Integrity and Competence of the Legal Profession*, 48 Tex.L.Rev. 267, 271 (1970).

Consequently, the Rules do not contain any requirement similar to DR 1–101(B). A lawyer representing an applicant for admission is governed not by Rule 8.1 ("Bar Admission and Disciplinary Matters") but by the rules normally governing the attorney-client relationship. Rule 8.1, Comment 3 so provides and specifically refers to Rule 1.6, governing the need to protect the confidentiality of client information. Rule 8.1(a) prohibits the attorney or applicant from submitting any knowingly false affidavits.

No provisions of the Rules require (or even urge) a lawyer to *volunteer* unfavorable information about an applicant. However, a portion of EC 1–3 might be interpreted to encourage whistle-blowing. In context, however, EC 1–3 should not be so interpreted. EC 1–3 provided:

> "Before recommending an applicant for admission, a lawyer should *satisfy himself* that the applicant is of good moral character. Although a lawyer should not become a self-appointed investigator or judge of applicants for admission, *he should report to proper officials all unfavorable information he possesses* relating to the character or other qualifications of an applicant" (emphasis added).

A more natural reading of EC 1–3 is to regard the second sentence as modifying the first. In other words, if an applicant asks a lawyer for a recommendation, before the lawyer files the affidavit, he or she should be satisfied that the applicant is of good moral character. It is not necessary for the lawyer, in order to be satisfied, to become a self-appointed investigator, but if the lawyer (who has been asked to recommend an applicant) happens to know or come across unfavorable information, then the lawyer should report it to the bar authorities.

If the lawyer believes that the applicant is of good moral character notwith-standing the unfavorable information, the lawyer still must report the unfavorable information, and may argue that it should not be disqualifying, but should let the bar authorities evaluate it. That is the position of Model Rule 8.1(b), which prohibits the lawyer or applicant from failing to disclose a fact necessary to correct a misapprehension. known to have arisen in the matter.

Examples: Lawyer hired a summer Law Clerk in her law office. From that experience Lawyer, based on several incidents, believes that

Law Clerk is mentally unstable. Law Clerk is now applying for admission to the bar, but does not ask Lawyer for a reference. Lawyer, after learning of Law Clerk's application, does nothing; however, if the bar asks for a reference she intends to reply truthfully.

Lawyer has violated no provision of the Model Rules. Some may argue that Lawyer has failed to meet the aspirational level of EC 1–3. Lawyer has violated no DR of the old Model Code.

II. The Lawyer's Role Regarding Reporting Disciplinable Violations of Lawyers

Lawyers have an obligation to volunteer information of another lawyer's disciplinable violations unless the information is privileged under the ethics rules.

A. The General Rule

The Code required, under threat of discipline, a lawyer to voluntarily report any disciplinable violation by another lawyer to the appropriate authority. DR 1–103(A); EC 1–4. This affirmative duty of whistle-blowing applied not only against a lawyer in another firm but also against a partner or associate in the reporting lawyer's own firm. ABA Informal Opinion 1203 (Feb. 9, 1972).

This DR conferred standing on a lawyer to report an alleged conflict of interest by an opposing counsel in litigation. The charge of conflict, if successful, could then lead to that opposing counsel's disqualification. See, e.g., *Estates Theatres, Inc. v. Columbia Pictures Industries, Inc.*, 345 F.Supp. 93, 98 (S.D.N.Y.1972).

Rule 8.3(a), in general, *requires* a lawyer to report *another* lawyer's substantial violation of the Rules *if* the lawyer "knows" of the violation. "Knows" means "actual knowledge. Rule 1.0(f). The reference to "another lawyer" means that there is no duty to self-report. In addition, this violation must raise a "substantial" question about the lawyer's honesty, trustworthiness or fitness as a lawyer in other respects." Hence, the lawyer need not report a violation of many of the ethics rules that do not relate to things like honesty. For example, illegal solicitation of clients (if it is not misleading), many conflicts of interest, aiding unauthorized practice of law, etc.—all of these matters do not trigger the reporting obligation if they do not relate to things like honesty.

Note on the Impaired Lawyer: There are matters that do not relate to honesty but do clearly relate to a lawyer's "fitness as a lawyer in other respects." A lawyer who believes that another lawyer's known violations of an ethics rule raises substantial questions about her fitness to practice must report those violations to the appropriate professional authority. A lawyer who believes that another lawyer's *mental condition* materially impairs her ability to represent clients, and who knows that that lawyer continues to do so, *must report* that lawyer's consequent violation of Rule 1.16(a)(2), which requires that she withdraw from the representation of clients. ABA Formal Opinion 03–431 (Aug. 8, 2003).

Rule 8.3(b) has similar requirements as to lawyers reporting judges, if the lawyer's "knowledge" of the judge's violation of the Code of Judicial Conduct raises a "substantial" question about the judge's fitness for office.

On its face, DR 1–103(A) applied to *all* disciplinable violations, whether they were, in the reporting lawyer's view, flagrant and substantial, or minor and technical. However, an element of judgment remains, because the lawyer need not (but may) report suspected violations that are not clear violations of the discipline rules. ABA Informal Opinion 1379 (Dec. 7, 1976). See also EC 1–4 (reporting conduct believed "*clearly* to be in violation of the Disciplinary Rules") (emphasis added).

DR 1–103(A) was largely unenforced, and lawyers rarely reported other lawyers. See Note, *The Lawyer's Duty to Report Professional Misconduct*, 20 Ariz.L.Rev. 509 (1978); Marks & Cathcart, *Discipline Within the Legal Profession: Is it Self Regulation?*, 1974 U. of Ill.L.Forum 193. Until recently, in those rare cases where a court actually reprimanded a lawyer for failing to report another lawyer's wrongdoing, the lawyer was also being disciplined for other wrongs. E.g., *Matter of Bonafield*, 75 N.J. 490, 383 A.2d 1143 (1978) (per curiam)(attorney disciplined for failing to report another and for aiding another lawyer's misconduct); *Attorney Grievance Commission of Maryland v. Kahn*, 290 Md. 654, 431 A.2d 1336 (1981)(attorney disciplined for failing to report another and for aiding unethical conduct of his law firm).

The Illinois Supreme Court, in 1988, became the first court that disciplined a lawyer (who was suspended for a year) who was charged with nothing *except* failing to report another lawyer's misconduct, under circumstances where the client specifically told him not to report the other lawyer's conduct. *In re Himmel*, 125 Ill.2d 531, 127 Ill.Dec. 708, 533 N.E.2d 790 (1988). See, Rotunda, *The Lawyer's Duty to Report Another Lawyer's Unethical Violations in the Wake of Himmel*, 1988 U.Ill.L.Rev. 977. The Illinois court interpreted "unprivileged knowledge" in its version of DR 1–103(A) to mean only "confidence," the evidentiary privilege, and not "secret," the ethical privilege of DR 4–101(A). The ABA, in contrast, uses the term "privileged" in the Model Code to mean both "confidence" and "secret." ABA Formal Opinion 341 (1975). Rule 8.3 "does not require disclosure of information otherwise protected by Rule 1.6. . . . " Rule 8.3(c). Cf. EC 4–4. Thus far, other states have not followed Illinois' lead.

The Rules also impose a duty to report, but limit it so that the duty only covers conduct that raises a "substantial question" regarding the other lawyer's "honesty, trustworthiness or fitness as a lawyer." Rule 8.3(a). The drafters of the Rules hoped that, by limiting the obligation to report only the more serious violations, the duty would be more realistic and therefore might be more enforceable. Rule 8.3, Comment 3.

The Rules define "substantial" to mean "a material matter of clear and weighty importance." Rule 1.0(l). Thus, "substantial" refers not to the amount of evidence of which the lawyer is aware, but to the "seriousness of the possible offense." Rule 8.3, Comment 3.

Note: The Rules call for an exercise of judgment in reporting violations. The Rules require the judgment to be exercised with regard to the *seriousness* of the violation. The former Code required the judgment to be exercised with respect to the quantum of evidence of a violation.

Rule 8.3(c) specifically do *not* require disclose of information otherwise protected by Rule 1.6. Hence, it does not approve of *Himmel* refusal to recognize the limitation of DR 4–101 (which roughly corresponds to Rule 1.6).

Rule 8.3(c) also specifically does not require disclosure of information that the lawyer learns from participating in LAP ("Lawyer's Assistance Program"), which seeks to help lawyers and judges suffering from alcohol and drug abuse.

B. The Applicability of the Rule to the Lawyer's Own Conduct

1. Blowing the Whistle on Oneself

Must a lawyer report her own disciplinary violation? Is that not asking too much of anyone? DR 1–103(A) required a lawyer to report knowledge of unprivileged information of disciplinable conduct. Given the way in which it is drafted, DR 1–103(A) may be interpreted to require a lawyer to report his or her own misconduct. Failure to report would then be a separate disciplinable violation. This interpretation is supported by the contrasting language in DR 1–103(B), which specifically referred to "another lawyer." Of course, this interpretation would not require a lawyer to waive the fifth amendment privilege against self-incrimination because DR 1–103(A) only refers to "unprivileged knowledge or information." Thus, ABA Informal Opinion 1279 (Aug. 29, 1973) concluded:

> "Does [DR 1–103(A)]require a lawyer to 'report' his knowledge that he has, himself, violated DR 1–102, in the situation where his unethical conduct is not privileged because, for example, he clearly cannot be exposed to criminal sanctions for having engaged in such unethical conduct? We construe DR 1–103(A) as requiring the lawyer to report himself in that situation."

Some commentators have argued, without discussion, that the "reporting provision of . . . DR 1–103(A) does not appear to apply to the lawyer's own conduct." 2 R. Mallen & J. Smith, Legal Malpractice § 19.6 at 162, note 20 (3d ed. 1989). On the other hand, at least one court has ruled that a lawyer must promptly notify a client of possible malpractice claims that a client may have against him. *Tallon v. Committee on Professional Standards, Third Judicial Dept.*, 86 A.D.2d 897, 447 N.Y.S.2d 50, 51 (3d Dept. 1982) (respondent suspended for six months for this and other violations).

The Rules solve this question of interpretation by drafting with greater clarity. The relevant provision explicitly refers to knowledge regarding "another lawyer." Rule 8.3(a). The Model Rules recognize that, as a matter of realism, one does not expect a lawyer to report himself. The Rules do not impose requirements that experience has shown to be "unenforceable." Rule 8.3, Comment 3. Instead, the Rules limit the reporting obligation but expect that lawyers will comply with the more limited obligations.

2. The Duty to Cooperate With Discipline Authorities

The Rules encourage a lawyer to cooperate with discipline authorities. The Model Code, which was the immediate predecessor to the Model Rules, encouraged cooperation. E.g., EC 1–4 said that, if requested, lawyers should serve and assist disciplinary committees. DR 1–103(A) and (B) mandated cooperation. The lawyer not only must whistle-blow, DR 1–103(A), but must comply with the investigatory authority's "proper request" for information. DR 1–103(B).

The Model Rules follow that tradition. Thus Rule 8.1(b) provides that a lawyer may not "fail to respond to a lawful demand for information from an admissions or disciplinary authority . . . " Compare *State v. Weber,* 55 Wis.2d 548, 550, 200 N.W.2d 577, 580 (1972) (lawyer's deliberate refusal to cooperate is a grounds for sanction), with, *Committee on Legal Ethics of West Virginia State Bar v. Mullins,* 159 W.Va. 647, 226 S.E.2d 427, 431 (1976) (no separate violation because of refusal to cooperate).

If lawyer *#1*'s client tells lawyer *#1* that lawyer *#2* has violated a disciplinary rule, that information may be privileged under Rule 1.6. Comment 2 of Rule 8.3 states that if lawyer *#1*'s knowledge of lawyer *#2*'s discipline violation is privileged client information, then lawyer *#1* should encourage his client to waive the privilege if doing so will not "substantially prejudice the client's interests."

Lawyer Assistance Programs. Many jurisdictions have developed Lawyer Assistance Programs (LAP), where lawyers and judges help other lawyers and judges who have problems with alcohol or drugs. A promise of confidentially encourages these lawyers and judges to seek help. Rule 8.3(c) and Comment 5 recognize this fact and treat this information as if it were protected by the attorney-client privilege, so that those participating in approved LAP programs are not also required to report those who seek help.

C. Applicability of Privilege

1. Self–Incrimination

DR 1–103 restricted its application to "unprivileged knowledge" but did not define the term. Clearly the rule should not apply to knowledge protected by a constitutional privilege, such as the privilege against self-incrimination; otherwise the rule would be unconstitutional. See ABA Informal Opinion 1279 (Aug. 29, 1973) (DR 1–103 does not require lawyer to engage in self-incrimination).

The Rules are clearer on this point. The relevant sections refer to information "otherwise protected by Rule 1.6" (the confidentiality section); Rule 1.6, in turn, does not refer to self-incrimination. However, Rule 8.2, Comment 2 explicitly provides that this Rule "is subject to the provisions of the fifth amendment." See Rule 8.1(b), 8.3(c). To preserve the constitutionality of these Rules, the self-incrimination protection must be read into them. Though the Comments to Rule 8.3 are silent on this issue, its interpretation should be similar.

As a constitutional matter, bar authorities cannot sanction a lawyer simply because he or she has asserted the privilege against self-incrimination. *Spevack v. Klein,* 385 U.S. 511, 87 S.Ct. 625, 17 L.Ed.2d 574 (1967). However, the attorney may be disciplined for refusing to testify if that testimony would not expose him to criminal prosecution. *Zuckerman v. Greason,* 20 N.Y.2d 430, 285 N.Y.S.2d 1, 231 N.E.2d 718 (1967).

Consequently, the state can grant a lawyer "use immunity"—i.e., a guarantee that the compelled testimony will not be used against the person in a criminal prosecution—and then use this testimony to disbar or otherwise discipline the lawyer. The justification for allowing the use of compelled testimony for bar discipline is that bar discipline is not a criminal matter. E.g., *Matter of Ungar,* 27 A.D.2d 925, 282 N.Y.S.2d 158 (1967); *Anonymous Attorneys v. Bar Ass'n of Erie County,* 41 N.Y.2d 506, 393 N.Y.S.2d 961, 362 N.E.2d 592 (1977); *In re Schwarz,* 51 Ill.2d 334, 282 N.E.2d 689 (1972); *In re Daley,* 549 F.2d 469 (7th Cir.1977), cert. denied, 434 U.S. 829, 98 S.Ct. 110, 54 L.Ed.2d 89 (1977).

2. Client Confidences

DR 1–103 referred to "unprivileged knowledge" but did not explain if "privilege" included only the attorney-client evidentiary privilege, or the much broader privilege protected by Canon 4. (On Canon 4 "confidences" and "secrets," see Part III, section I, A, 1). DR 7–102(B)(1), governing a different issue, also speaks of "a privileged communication." ABA Formal Opinion 341 (Sept. 30, 1975) interpreted "privileged communication" in DR 7–102(B)(1) as referring to "those confidences and secrets that are required to be preserved by DR 4–101." This Formal Opinion found it undesirable to interpret "privileged" to mean only information protected as an evidentiary privilege because the lawyer's ethical duty would then vary from jurisdiction to jurisdiction, depending on the local rules of evidence. Also, the Formal Opinion argued, in some cases it might be difficult to determine which jurisdiction's evidence law should govern.

Because this interpretation of "privileged" under DR 7–102(B)(1) is equally applicable to DR 1–103, the same definition should also apply;

that is, "unprivileged knowledge" or "evidence" under DR 1–103 means any information not protected by Canon 4.

The Rules opt for this same definition, and reach this point more directly. They explicitly provide that the relevant Rules do not apply to information protected by Rule 1.6. See Rule 8.1(b), 8.3(c). Rule 1.6, of course, protects more than the attorney-client evidentiary privilege.

III. The Lawyer's Role Regarding Judges and Candidates for the Judiciary

A. Lawyers Criticizing and Defending Judges and Judicial Candidates

1. Whistle–Blowing

While DR 1–103(A) mandated a whistle-blowing role for lawyers, see section II, supra, there was no analogous disciplinary rule mandating the lawyer to make an unsolicited report of misconduct by a judge. However, DR 1–103(A) would apply to judges who are also lawyers in the relevant jurisdiction.

Note: Not all judges fall in that category. As late as 1983 there were approximately 14,000 nonlawyer judges in 44 states. Time Magazine, Sept. 26, 1983, at 62, col. 1.

If a lawyer reported a judge's misconduct to the judicial discipline authority, which many states have created, that authority could impose sanctions on the judge.

As an ethical aspiration (rather than a mandatory obligation) the former Model Code provided that a lawyer should report to "appropriate authorities" (presumably including a judicial discipline commission) any fraudulent, deceptive, or otherwise illegal conduct of any "participant in a proceeding before a tribunal" if the information is not protected as a client confidence. EC 8–5. This language would apply to judges as well as lawyers and laypeople. The Code did explicitly provide that, "upon proper request," the lawyer must reveal unprivileged knowledge or evidence regarding a judge. DR 1–103(B).

In contrast, the Rules *require* a lawyer to whistle-blow, that is, to volunteer to the appropriate authorities any nonconfidential information showing that the judge (whether or not a lawyer) violated the judicial rules if the conduct raises "a substantial question as to the judge's fitness for office . . . " Rule 8.3(b).

> *Note:* On the Code of Judicial Conduct, see Part X. On the definition of "substantial" see Rule 1.0(l), defining "substantial" as meaning "a material matter of clear and weighty importance."

2. False Statements

If a lawyer makes any charges against a judge or judicial candidate the lawyer must not knowingly speak falsely or with "reckless disregard as to its truth or falsity." Rule 8.2(a); DR 8–102. Cf. *New York Times Co. v. Sullivan,* 376 U.S. 254, 279–80, 84 S.Ct. 710, 725–26, 11 L.Ed.2d 686, 706–07 (1964).

The Code prohibited knowingly making "false statements of fact," DR 8–102(A) and "false accusations," DR 8–102(B). The Rules do not follow this terminology and simply prohibit any knowingly false "statements" (or false statements made with reckless disregard as to their truth), when the statements relate to the judge's, or judicial candidate's qualifications or integrity. Rule 8.2(a). However, Comment 1 makes clear that it is important for lawyers to be able to improve the administration of justice by being able to express "honest and candid opinions." Thus, Rule 8.2 would approve of such cases as *State Bar v. Semaan,* 508 S.W.2d 429, 432 (Tex.Civ.App.1974), which found no disciplinable offense when an attorney expressed his opinion attacking a judge; because the criticism involved opinion, there was no statement of fact that could be tested as true or false. In contrast, the Rules would *not* approve of *In re Raggio,* 87 Nev. 369, 487 P.2d 499 (1971) (per curiam), which reprimanded an attorney for charging that a judicial opinion was "shocking."

3. Duty to Defend

The Code was confused about the lawyer's duty to defend judges. It urged lawyers to defend judges and other adjudicatory officials against "unjust criticism" because these officials are not "wholly free to defend themselves." EC 8–6. See also *Rinaldi v. Holt, Rinehart & Winston, Inc.,* 42 N.Y.2d 369, 397 N.Y.S.2d 943, 366 N.E.2d 1299 (1977) (concurring opinion of Fuchsberg, J.), cert. denied, 434 U.S. 969, 98 S.Ct. 514, 54 L.Ed.2d 456 (1977) (arguing that lawyers have an affirmative duty to defend judges). Lawyers also should "be certain" of their criticisms of judges, "use appropriate language" and avoid "petty" and "unrestrained" criticism. EC 8–6. On the other hand, the same ethical consideration urged lawyers to "protest earnestly against the appointment or election of those who are unsuited for the bench." EC 8–6. And lawyers "should avoid undue solicitude for the comfort or convenience of judge[s]." EC 7–36.

The Code thus pointed in two directions regarding the lawyer's duty to defend judges.

The original draft of the Rules, in contrast, was much less protective of judges; it contained no express language that corresponded to that found in EC 8–6 regarding the lawyer's duty to defend judges. See, Rule 8.2 (Proposed Final Draft, May 30, 1981). The final version, as approved by the House of Delegates, added a paragraph to the Comment that encourages lawyers "to continue traditional efforts to defend judges and courts unjustly criticized." Rule 8.2, Comment 3. However, there is no language (like the language found in EC 8–6) urging lawyers to be "certain" of the merits of their criticism. Rather, the Rules simply urge lawyers to express "honest and candid opinions." Rule 8.2, Comment 1.

B. Candidates for Judicial Office

Judges running for retention or reelection are governed in their campaign activities by the ABA Model Code of Judicial Conduct (1990) as amended, see Part X, section VI, infra, as enacted by the individual states.

The Rules (like the former Model Code), in order to prevent lawyers campaigning for judicial office from having an unfair competitive advantage, require that the lawyer-candidate comply with the applicable provisions of the Code of Judicial Conduct. Rule 8.2(b); DR 8–102(B).

The Model Code of Judicial Conduct places various restrictions on the judge's receipt of campaign contributions and other moneys or loans. See Part X, sections V & VI, infra. Lawyers are also prohibited from giving to judges that which the judges are not allowed to accept under the Model Code of Judicial Conduct. See Rule 8.4(f) (the lawyer should not "knowingly assist a judge" in "violation of applicable rules of judicial conduct or other law"). See also DR 7–110(A).

REVIEW QUESTIONS

1. Attorney is a member of the bar and a practicing lawyer. One of his clients, Mary Smith, in the course of seeking legal advice, has just told Attorney that Smith has had financial reverses because her former lawyer (Former) has stolen

money from her. Mary Smith told Attorney that she does not want Attorney to reveal this information because of her concern for her Former's sick wife, who is Smith's sister and who would be devastated if she knew of Former's financial dealings. Attorney told her: "Unless you are willing to let me reveal this information, there is little I can do. But I assure you, I will keep your secret."

Is Attorney *subject to discipline* if he does NOT reveal this information to the disciplinary authorities?

   a. Yes, because he must report such unfavorable information to the appropriate tribunal empowered to investigate it.

   b. No, unless the amount stolen is large.

   c. Yes, if Smith's concerns for Former's wife is groundless.

   d. No, because the information is privileged.

2. Lawyer is admitted to the practice of law in State First. She is presently arguing a case in the trial court of State Second, where she was admitted *pro hac vice*. The judge in State Second told her, in open court: "The other lawyer has accused you of destroying evidence. If that is true, and if you were a member of the bar in this jurisdiction, I would seek to have you disbarred for violating the rules of this court."

Assuming that the accusation is true, is Lawyer *subject to discipline* in State First?

   a. No, because her conduct did not occur in State First.

   b. No, unless State Second first disciplines her.

   c. Yes, because she should not practice law in State Second without a license.

   d. Yes, because the discipline authorities in State First have jurisdiction over conduct engaged in elsewhere.

3. Lawyer is a real estate broker in State One and a member of the bar of State Two. In applying for a renewal for his real estate license in State One, Lawyer failed to disclose that he had just been charged with criminal fraud. This false answer to a specific question ("Have your ever been charged with a crime?") made his application materially false.

Is Lawyer, regarding this application, *subject to discipline* in State Two?

a.   No, because he was not acting as a lawyer.

b.   No, because he filed his application in State One.

c.   Yes, because he acted dishonestly.

d.   Yes, because as a lawyer he may not also be a real estate broker.

4.   Lawyer reasonably believes that Judge is a drunk, both on the bench and off, and that therefore Judge lacks any proper judicial temperament. Judge is now running for reelection, and Lawyer, in response to a reporter's questions, states: "I will not support Judge's efforts for reelection because Judge is a drunk, and his drinking interferes with his work."

Is Lawyer *subject to discipline*?

a.   Yes, because Lawyer has cast the judicial system into disrepute.

b.   No, unless Lawyer supports Judge's opponent.

c.   Yes, because the statement was made during a reelection campaign.

d.   No, because Lawyer's beliefs were reasonable and his statements were not knowingly false.

*

PART III

The Lawyer's Obligation to the Client

■ ANALYSIS

I. **The Duty of Confidentiality**
   A. The General Rule
       1. The Distinction Between the Evidentiary and the Ethical Privilege
       2. Rationale and Applicability to Information Generally Known
       3. Extension of the Protection to Prospective and Former Clients
       4. Intrafirm Communications
       5. Controlling Subordinates
       6. Applicability to Government Lawyers and Other Lawyers for an Entity
   B. Specific Prohibitions on Using or Revealing Confidential or Secret Information
       1. Revealing Client Information
       2. Using Client Information to the Disadvantage of a Client

B. Competence
    1. Defining Competence
    2. Waiving Malpractice Liability
    3. Neglect
C. Crimes or Frauds
D. The Incompetent Client

IV. **Fees**
  A. Basic Principles
    1. Reasonableness Requirement
    2. Writing Requirement
    3. Price Discrimination
    4. Suing to Collect Fees
  B. Contingent Fees
    1. Writing Requirement
    2. Offering Alternatives
    3. When Forbidden
  C. Fee Referrals

V. **Accepting, Declining, and Terminating Representation**
  A. Accepting and Declining Representation
  B. Terminating Representation
    1. Overriding Principles
    2. Mandatory and Permissive Withdrawal

VI. **Trust Fund Accounts**
  A. Establishing Trust Fund Accounts
    1. What Must Be Kept in Trust
    2. Disputes Regarding Trust Fund Property
    3. Audits of Trust Fund Accounts
    4. Interest Earned on Client Funds
  B. Client Security Funds

I. The Duty of Confidentiality

A. The General Rule

The Attorney's obligation to protect a client's confidential information extends beyond the evidentiary privilege.

Rule 1.6 imposes on the lawyer the duty to take *reasonable steps* to protect client information from unauthorized use or disclosure. ALI, Restatement, Third, of the Law Governing Lawyers, § 60(1)(b) (Official Draft 1998). For example, the lawyer does not violate Rule 1.6 by using unencrypted email because that mode of transmission offers a reasonable expectation of privacy, and unauthorized interception of email violates the law. ABA Formal Opinion 99–413 (March 10, 1999). However, if a lawyer reasonably believes that confidential client information is so sensitive that extraordinary measures are warranted, she should consult with her client as to whether another mode of transmission (such as a special messenger service) is justified.

1. The Distinction Between the Evidentiary and the Ethical Privilege

An attorney is subject to discipline for violating the attorney-client evidentiary privilege. Rule 1.6(a); DR 4–101(A), (B). In addition, the work product privilege (or work product immunity) protects the lawyer from turning over information otherwise subject to discovery or other compelled disclosure. Work product is material (other than underlying facts) prepared by a lawyer for litigation or in reasonable anticipation of litigation. A.L.I., Restatement (Third) of the Law Governing Lawyers, § 87 (Final Draft, 2000).

However, the attorney's duty goes beyond protection of the evidentiary privilege and work product immunity because the attorney is the agent of his client, who is the principal. It is a general rule of agency law that the agent must neither use nor disclose "information confidentially given to him by the principal or acquired by him during the course of or on account of his agency. . . . " A.L.I., Restatement (Second) of Agency § 395.

Thus, both the Model Rules and the Model Code require lawyers to "shun indiscreet conversations" concerning their clients. EC 4–2. Model Rule 1.6, Comment 3 goes on to explain that the principle of confidentiality is based on the attorney-client evidentiary privilege (including the work product privilege), and the rule of confidentiality established in professional ethics.

It is not necessary for the lawyer to charge a fee in order for the ethical or evidentiary privilege to attach.

The Code divides client information into two types: "confidence" and "secret." DR 4–101(A). A "confidence" is any information protected under the attorney-client evidentiary privilege. A "secret" is any other information if: (1) the client has requested that it be held "inviolate;" or (2) disclosure would embarrass the client; or (3) disclosure would likely "be detrimental to the client." The Rules are drafted to be as broad or even broader, for they protect *all* information "relating to the representation," unless the disclosures are impliedly authorized, or fall within certain named exceptions, or the client waives her rights. Rule 1.6(a).

Examples: Client asks Lawyer to represent Client in a transaction. In the course of this representation, Lawyer uncovers secret information. Pursuant to an investigation by the grand jury, Court later orders Lawyer to reveal this information to the grand jury on the grounds that it is not protected by the evidentiary privilege. Lawyer reveals this information in the grand jury room. Later reporters ask him: "Did you comply with the court order?" He answers: "Yes." Then they ask him: "What did you say to the grand jury?"

If Lawyer responds, Lawyer will commit a disciplinary violation by revealing a client's secret. In other words, virtually all information is initially within Rule 1.6, because the Rules do not demand that the client's request to treat the information as secret be express. It may be implied. Also, it is not necessary that the source of the information be the client; it is only necessary that the information be "related to the representation." Rule 1.6(a), & Comment ("all information relating to the representation, whatever its source").

Note: The former Model Code, DR 4–101(A) did not make clear whether its language, "gained in" means "because of" the professional relationship, or the more broad, "during the course of" the professional relationship (e.g., in the course of seeking business advice, the client confides to the lawyer that the client is cheating on her husband). In any event, it is quite clear that it is unnecessary, under Canon 4, that the client be the source of the information. The Model Rules agree.

Rule 1.6's basic definition of confidential information offers protection to *any* information "relating to representation of a client." All information of consequence is, at least initially, offered protection.

2. Rationale and Applicability to Information Generally Known

The purpose of this broad protection is to encourage the client to speak freely with the lawyer and to encourage the lawyer to obtain information from sources other than the client. Rule 1.6, Comments 2, 3, 4; EC 4–1.

Needless to say, this purpose would not be furthered if a lawyer would be forced to keep information confidential after it has become a matter of general knowledge. The general law of agency recognizes this exception (A.L.I., Restatement (Second) of Agency § 395), and the Rules adopt it in Rule 1.9(c)(1), which allows a lawyer to use, to the *disadvantage* of a *former* client, information otherwise protected by Rule 1.6, *if* the information is "generally known."

Note: A lawyer should not act to the detriment of a *present* client because of the duty of loyalty. This duty of loyalty extends beyond the need to protect client secrets. Rule 1.7(a), (b); DR 5–101(A).

The Code does not explicitly adopt the exception of Rule 1.9(c)(1) relating to client information that "has become generally known." In fact EC 4–4 states that the ethical duty to protect secrets exists "without regard" to "the fact that others share the knowledge." However, in context, EC 4–4 refers to *present* clients, and assumes that the secret nature of the conversation is not lost merely because the client has shared his secret with a *few* others besides the lawyer. Such sharing, beyond a strict "need to know basis," will mean the loss of the evidentiary privilege—see Proposed Federal Rule of Evidence 530(a)(4)—but not the loss of the ethical privilege. However, once the information is *generally known* (even though it once was a secret) its protection would not serve the purpose of the rule.

Inadvertent Disclosure and the Misdirected Fax. The client may inadvertently lose the attorney-client evidentiary privilege. For example, if the client voluntarily reveals a portion of his privileged communications, courts typically find that he may not withhold the remainder. Some courts even find a permanent loss of the evidentiary privilege if the lawyer or client inadvertently discloses part of the privileged communication. One wishing to preserve the privilege "must treat the confidentiality of attorney-client communications like jewels—if not crown jewels." *In re Sealed Case*, 877 F.2d 976, 980 (D.C.Cir.1989).

ABA Formal Opinion 92–368 (Nov. 10, 1992) deals with the situation where a law firm *inadvertently* receives information from the opposing party that, on its face, appears to be covered by the attorney-client privilege or is otherwise confidential. In the typical case, a clerk in a law firm mistakenly faxes a document to opposing counsel instead of faxing it to co-counsel. The Opinion concludes that the lawyer should refrain from reviewing the materials, notify the sending lawyer, and abide by that lawyer's instructions. However, if an unauthorized source, e.g., a whistle-blower, *intentionally* sends the information to counsel, then the receiving lawyer should either inform the adversary's lawyer and follow her instructions, or refrain from using the unsolicited material until a court makes a definitive resolution of the proper disposition of the materials. ABA Formal Opinion 94–382 (July 5, 1994).

The solution that these ABA Formal Opinions propose raises questions. For example, in some cases the receiving lawyer will not know if the sender is a whistle-blower or a negligent employee. (Not all whistle-blowers announce their intention in the cover memorandum attached to the fax.) Also, if the problem of the fax mistakenly sent to the lawyer occurs in a state that would regard the evidentiary privilege as lost in those circumstances, why should the ethics rules prohibit the lawyer from using the faxed information? In any event, some state bar opinions and court cases reject the proposed ABA solution. E.g., *Aerojet–General Corp. v. Transport Indemnity Insurance*, 18 Cal.App.4th 996, 22 Cal.Rptr.2d 862 (1st Dist.1993), holding that even if the documents were sent inadvertently, the lawyer who received them through no wrongdoing on his part may keep them and need not inform opposing counsel.

The Model Rules, after the 2002 revisions, added a special provision to Rule 4.4, which provides that lawyer who receives a document relating to the representation of the lawyer's client and knows or reasonably should know that the document was *inadvertently sent* must promptly notify the sender. Rule 4.4(b). Then, the sender and the receiver can argue in court whether the privilege has been lost. See Rule 4.4, Comment 2 (notifying the sender will "permit that person to take protective measures").

ALI, Restatement, Third, of the Law Governing Lawyers, § 79, Comment *h* (Official Draft, 1998) argues that an inadvertent disclosure should not constitute waiver of the evidentiary privilege if the client or other disclosing person (e.g., the lawyer) took *reasonable precautions* to guard against disclosure. Once the client knows, or should know, of the inadvertent disclosure, the client "must take prompt and reasonable steps to recover the communication, to reestablish its confidential nature, and to reassert the privilege."

3. Extension of the Protection to Prospective and Former Clients

Prospective Clients. To fulfill the purpose of protecting client information, the ethical rules encompass not only information that the lawyer learned from her clients but also secret information that she learned because a *prospective* client sought to (but did not) retain her. EC 4–1. ABA Formal Opinion 90–358 (Sept. 13, 1990) concluded that information from a would-be client seeking representation is protected by Model Rule 1.6 even though the lawyer does not undertake representation of, or perform legal work for, the would-be client.

The 2002 revisions to the Model Rules added a new section, Rule 1.18: "Duties to Prospective Clients." It explicitly provides that, even if no client-lawyer relationship ever develops, the lawyer who had discussions with a prospective client must keep that information confidential and may neither use nor reveal it in the same way that the lawyer must keep the confidences of a former client. Thus, the former and prospective client are treated the same with respect to confidences. Rule 1.18(b).

Protecting the confidences of the prospective client who does not retain the lawyer imposes an opportunity cost on the lawyer, who may be disqualified from later representing the opponent of the would-be client because the lawyer received confidences while interviewing the would-be client. ABA Formal Opinion 90–358 (Sept. 13, 1990) suggests several ways that the law firm may be able to limit these costs. It may institute procedures to identify as early as possible conflicts of prospective clients; it may limit information learned from the would-be client; it may seek waivers of confidentiality from the would-be client. This Opinion also suggests that some courts might accept the law firm's screening of the lawyer who learned the confidential information "where the information disclosed by the would-be client is not extensive or sensitive. . . . "

At the time, no Rule authorized what this ABA Opinion recommended. Now, Rule 1.18(c) & (d) deals with this problem. If a particular lawyer is disqualified because she received information from the prospective client that could be "significantly harmful," then that lawyer cannot represent a client with interests "materially adverse" to that prospective client in the same or substantially related matter. The Rule imputes this disqualification to all the members of the firm unless (2) the client and the prospective client give their informed consent and it is "confirmed in writing." Or, (2) the law firm *screens* the lawyer with the secret information and "is apportioned no part of the fee" from the matter in question, then the lawyer's disqualification is not imputed to other members of the firm. Rule 1.18(d)(2). The firm has to notify the prospective client [i.e., the prospective client who is not hiring the firm but considered it earlier] so that it can determine that the screen is truly opaque. The provision against being apportioned a fee only means that the lawyer cannot receive compensation that is "directly related" to the matter on which she is disqualified. She can receive her normal partnership share or salary that was established by prior agreement. Comment 7.

Former Clients. The fact that the *former* client no longer employs a lawyer does not terminate the lawyer's obligation to preserve the former client's confidences and secrets. Rule 1.6, Comment 18; Rule 1.9; EC 4–6.

The lawyer may not *reveal* information about a former client except if she could reveal the same information of a present client. Rule 1.9(c)(2).

The lawyer also may not *use* information about the former client except if she could use the same information of a present client, *or*, if the "information has become generally known." Rule 1.9(c)(1).

The Restatement, Third, of the Law Governing Lawyers (Official Draft 2000), § 124(2) also proposes a narrow role for screening involving *former* clients. Section 124 is entitled: "Removing Imputation." Subsection (2) allows a lawyer's personal disqualification not to be imputed *if* "there is no substantial risk that confidential information of the *former client* will be used with material adverse effect on the former client" because: (a) the information is "unlikely to be significant" in the later case; (b) adequate screening measures "eliminate participation" by the personally-prohibited lawyer in the representation; *and* (c) "timely and adequate notice of the screening has been provided to all affected clients."

4. Intrafirm Communications

Though a client may only deal with a few lawyers in a firm, the client really hires the firm. Partners and associates regularly discuss with each other the affairs of their clients and seek from each other advice regarding client affairs. Rule 1.6, Comment 5; EC 4–2. Such intrafirm communication is one of the reasons for the rule regarding imputation of attorney disqualifications. See Rule 1.10, Comment 1. See Part III, Section II, F.

Consequently, unless the client otherwise directs, a lawyer may disclose to other lawyers in the firm information protected by Rule 1.6 or Canon 4. See EC 4–2, Rule 1.6, Comment 8.

5. Controlling Subordinates

It is reasonable for lawyers to disclose client confidences to nonlawyer employees, such as secretaries, investigators, and paralegals. The ethics rules have no jurisdiction over these nonlawyer employees. See Rule 5.3, Comment 1. However, they do require that the lawyer must give "appropriate instruction and supervision" to prevent his employees or associates from violating the obligation regarding client confidences and secrets. Rule 5.3, Comment 1; DR 4–101(D); EC 4–5.

A lawyer who fails in her duty of supervision violates these disciplinary rules even though no secrets are in fact disclosed, because the disciplinable violation is the failure to supervise. Similarly, a lawyer who adequately supervises has fulfilled her obligation, even though the employee nonetheless improperly discloses a client secret or confidence.

The lawyer may give limited information from his files to an outside agency for accounting or other legitimate purposes if the lawyer exercises due care in selecting the agency. EC 4–3; Rule 5.3, Comment 1 (referring to "independent contractors"). However, the lawyer may not transfer this information if the client chooses to forbid it. EC 4–3. Cf. Rule 1.6, Comments 5, 16.

6. Applicability to Government Lawyers and Other Lawyers for an Entity

Rule 1.6 applies not only to lawyers in private practice, but also to attorneys for the government and lawyers for any other entity, such as a corporation or association. Rule 1.13, Comment 6.

B. Specific Prohibitions on Using or Revealing Confidential or Secret Information

In general the lawyer must not reveal or use a client confidence or secret unless certain exceptions are applicable.

1. Revealing Client Information

The lawyer must not reveal client confidences except under certain circumstances. These situations, found in the Rules or other law, are discussed more fully below.

2. Using Client Information to the Disadvantage of a Client

The Rules, like the former Code, forbid using client secrets or confidences to the disadvantage of the client. Rule 1.8(b); DR 4–101(B)(2). This prohibition applies equally to protect a former client, *if* the information has not become generally known. Rule 1.9(c)(1). See EC 4–6. See also, Part III, section I, A, 2, supra.

Note that a lawyer violates this rule of confidentiality even if the lawyer does not disclose the information to anyone. What is relevant is that she *uses* the information to the client's detriment. If the agent is allowed to use confidential information for purposes that cause injury to the principal, that would tend to harm the freedom of communication that should exist between principal and agent.

Example: Lawyer learned, confidentially, that Client is planning to renew the lease on the building that Client now uses. Lawyer then secretly visits Lessor and obtains the lease on Lawyer's own account but does not tell Lessor any Client information. Lawyer plans to raise the rent because she learned, in confidence, that this location is more important to Client than Lessor suspects. Lawyer has committed a disciplinable violation. Rule 1.8, Comment 5. See also, A.L.I., Restatement (Second) of Agency § 395 & Illustration 1, which states that the agent "may be required to hold this lease as constructive trustee" for the principal.

3. Using Client Information for the Advantage of the Lawyer or Third Person

Unless the client consents, the lawyer may not use a client confidence or secret for the lawyer's own advantage (or a third person's advantage). Under the Model Code, this rule is applicable whether or not the client suffers detriment. DR 4–101(B)(3).

This prohibition on the use of client information is an old one. See ABA Canons of Professional Ethics, Canon 11 (1908), and Canon 37 (1908), as amended. E.g. *Healy v. Gray*, 184 Iowa 111, 119, 168 N.W. 222, 225 (1918):

"[A]n attorney will not be permitted to make use of knowledge, or information, acquired by him through his professional relations with his client, or in the conduct of his client's business to his own advantage or profit."

It also reflects basic principles of agency law. No agent, whether or not a lawyer, may use the principal's secret information to the agent's advantage even if there is no detriment to the principal and even if using the information does not require revealing it. A.L.I., Restatement (Second) of Agency, § 388, and Comment c. The remedy in the law of agency for this breach of trust is that the agent must turn over any profits to the principal.

Example: Where "a corporation has decided to operate an enterprise at a place where land values will be increased because of such operation, a corporate officer who takes advantage of his special knowledge to buy land in the vicinity is accountable for the profits he makes, *even though such purchases have no adverse effect upon the enterprise.*" Restatement (Second) of Agency, at Comment c; id. at § 395, Comment *e* (emphasis added). This rule is not applicable if the "information is a matter of general knowledge." Id. at § 395.

The theory behind the old Model Code—and the law of agency that the Model Code reflected—is that this confidential or secret information is a form of intellectual property that belongs to the client. The lawyer may not sell it or use it to the lawyer's own advantage unless the client consents. In other words, the old Code provided that lawyer may not *use* the secret information [DR 4–101(B)(3)] to his own advantage even if the lawyer does not *reveal* the secret information [DR 4–101(B)(1)].

The Rules, surprisingly, have *no* section corresponding to DR 4–101(B)(3). Rule 1.8(b) only forbids a lawyer from using the client's secret information "to the disadvantage of the client" unless the client gives informed consent. Prior to 2002, Rule 1.8, Comment 1, seemed to negate the possibility that the Rules could be interpreted to incorporate the principle of DR 4–101(B)(3). That Comment included an illustration that said: "For example, a lawyer who has learned that the client is investing in specific real estate may not, without the client's consent, seek to acquire nearby property *where doing so would adversely affect the client's plan for investment.*" (emphasis added.) The negative implication was that there is no ethical problem if the lawyer's purchase of the land and use of the client's "insider" information does not harm the client.

The Model Rules deleted that example in the 2002 revisions. However, the Reporter's Notes negate any interpretation that the deletion was significant; the Notes only state: "This Comment was revised to state the rationale for the Rule and to clarify which transactions are covered."

Under the general Law of Agency a lawyer who used client information for the lawyer's advantage must account to the client for any profits made. The lawyer who turns to this section of the Model Rules for a safe harbor will find (when a court, pursuant to the law of agency, orders him to account to the client for any profits made) that this harbor is heavily mined. The lawyer may not use "on his own account" confidential information acquired from a former client. A.L.I., Restatement (Second) of Agency, § 395, 396(b), (c). However, it may be the case that this lawyer would not be subject to discipline under the Model Rules. Rotunda, *Proposed Restatement of the Law Governing Lawyers* (Sept. 7, 1990), reprinted in, 136 Federal Rules Decisions 236, 266–71 (1991).

The Model Rules specifically allow use of information that does not disadvantage the client. For example, "a lawyer who learns a government agency's interpretation of trade legislation during the representation of one client may properly use that information to benefit other clients." Rule 1.8, Comment 5. Of course, the lawyer simply learned the law and the information is hardly unknowable to other lawyers.

C. Exceptions

1. Client Consent

Clients may always waive their confidentiality rights. If the lawyer wants the client to consent to waive rights to confidentiality, this consent is effective only if the lawyer makes a full disclosure to the client. Rule 1.6(a), 1.8(b); DR 4–101(B)(3), (C)(1). In order for the consent to be effective, the lawyer must communicate to the client enough information to permit the client to appreciate the significance of the waiver. See Rule 1.0(e).

The Code did not explicitly provide for implied consent, but its definition of "secret" is consistent with, and perhaps assumes, this possibility. DR 4–101(A) The Rules explicitly recognize an *implied consent*, narrowly defined as "disclosures impliedly authorized in order to carry out the representation," Rule 1.6(a). For example, the lawyer may disclose information in order to satisfactorily conclude a negotiation, or the lawyer in litigation may admit a fact that "cannot properly be disputed." Rule 1.6, Comment 5.

2. When Other Provisions in the Ethics Rules Permit Disclosure

Other provisions of the ethics rules may permit or require disclosure in certain situations. The lawyer should follow these other, more specific sections when they are applicable. For example, Rule 1.13(c) authorizes disclosure "whether or not Rule 1.6 permits such disclosure. . . . " Rule 3.3(c) similarly overrides Rule 1.6. On the other hand, Rule 4.1(b) requires a lawyer to disclose in certain situations "unless disclosure is prohibited by Rule 1.6." (But note that Rule 4.1, Comment 3, authorizes the lawyer to withdraw in order to avoid assisting a client fraud and crime, and then give notice of the fact of withdrawal to anyone while disaffirming any of his opinions, documents, etc.)

Other law, for example a statute or regulation, may require a lawyer to make certain disclosures. If this other law supersedes Rule 1.6 is an issue that is beyond the scope of these Rules. However, Rule 1.6(b)(6) permits the lawyer to make those disclosures. See Comment 12 of Rule 1.6.

Similarly, the Code explicitly provides that other provisions of the Code may override the requirements of Canon 4, either by permitting, or requiring, disclosure. See, e.g., DR 7–102(A)(3); *Matter of Kerr,* 86 Wash.2d 655, 662 n.2, 548 P.2d 297, 301 n.2 (1976). See also DR 7–102(B)(2).

3. Challenging Court Orders Requiring Disclosure

The Code had an explicit provision allowing lawyers to reveal Canon 4 information when "required by law or court order." DR 4–101(C)(2). The Proposed Final Draft of the Rules had a similar provision. In 1981, the ABA House of Delegates explicitly deleted this provision from Rule 1.6 but left language in a Comment, which is now Comment 13. In addition, Rule 1.6(b)(6) now makes the same point.

The lawyer may challenge any court order requiring his testimony. However, there is no ethical requirement that the lawyer first suffer contempt before revealing client information in response to a court order. The lawyer may simply comply with the order and reveal the client secret rather than violate the order and challenge the contempt. Rule 1.6(b)(6) & Comment 13. See also DR 4–101(C)(2). Cf., e.g., *Dike v.*

Dike, 75 Wash.2d 1, 14–15, 448 P.2d 490, 498–499 (1968) (because it was proper for the lawyer to challenge the lower court order, the contempt order against the lawyer is vacated).

The lawyer should consult with the client about challenging the order, and may raise all nonfrivolous objections. If the court rejects these objections, the lawyer must consult with the client about an appeal. If the client does not seek a review of the order, the lawyer may comply with the order mandating disclosure. There is no obligation of the lawyer to be in contempt of the judge's order. Rule 1.6(b)(6) permits the court to comply with the order. Comment 13.

4. To Collect a Fee

The lawyer may reveal client confidences or secrets if necessary to establish or collect the lawyer's fee. Rule 1.6(b)(4); DR 4–101(C)(4). The purpose of this exception is to prevent the client, who is the beneficiary of a fiduciary relationship, from exploiting that relationship to the detriment of the lawyer-fiduciary. Rule 1.6, Comment 11. For example, the client ought not to be excused from a contractual obligation to pay a fee solely because the lawyer could not prove (unless he revealed a client confidence or secret) that services were in fact performed. See *Cannon v. United States Acoustics Corp.,* 532 F.2d 1118, 1120 (7th Cir.1976) (per curiam). See also, Rule 1.6, Comment 10. Similarly, the lawyer may use client confidences if necessary to collect the fee. *Nakasian v. Incontrade, Inc.,* 409 F.Supp. 1220, 1224 (S.D.N.Y.1976) (lawyer, in effort to collect fee, may use client confidences to procure attachment order against client property). Accord, ABA Formal Opinion 250 (June 26, 1943).

This right to use confidences or secrets does not mean a right to blackmail the client. The lawyer may not state to the client: "Pay the fee or I will reveal to your employer your income tax problems." The lawyer may only exercise the right to reveal client information to the extent that it is reasonably *necessary* to establish or collect the fee. There should be no extortion or unnecessary disclosure. See Rule 1.6, Comment 14.

The lawyer may also sue her former client or former employer for retaliatory discharge. However, the lawyer should only disclose client information that she believes is reasonably necessary to prove her claim. ABA Formal Opinion 01–424 (Sept. 22, 2001).

5. To Respond to a Charge of Wrongful Conduct

It has long been the rule that a lawyer is justified in disclosing client information if necessary to respond to a client's accusation of wrongful conduct. See ABA Formal Opinion 202 (May 25, 1940), relying on Canons of Professional Ethics, Canon 37 (1908, as amended). The original Canon 37 limited this exception to the case where the "lawyer is accused *by his client* . . . " (emphasis added). The Code had no such limitation. The lawyer may reveal client information "if necessary" to respond to anyone's "accusation of wrongful conduct," though the lawyer should disclose only that which is "necessary" to establish a defense to the charge. DR 4–101(C)(4). Nor is it necessary that the accuser bring any formal proceedings or actually file any lawsuit against the lawyer. E.g., *Meyerhofer v. Empire Fire & Marine Ins. Co.*, 497 F.2d 1190, 1194–95 (2d Cir.1974), cert. denied, 419 U.S. 998, 95 S.Ct. 314, 42 L.Ed.2d 272 (1974).

Originally the Rules proposed to limit this right of disclosure to cases where the client and the lawyer were involved in a lawsuit or where the lawyer had to use the client information to establish a defense to a civil or criminal claim based on conduct in which the client was involved. Draft Rule 1.7(C)(3), (Discussion Draft, Jan. 30, 1980), reprinted in T. Morgan & R. Rotunda, 1980 Selected National Standards Supplement 83 (1980). However, the Rules now are identical with the Code in this regard, though the wording is different. See Rule 1.6(b)(5).

Although Rule 1.6(b)(5) uses words such as "criminal charge," "civil claim," or "allegations in any proceeding," it is not necessary that the accuser initiate any formal proceedings before the lawyer may reveal client information. Moreover, the accuser may be someone other than the client. The Comment is quite clear on this point: "The lawyer's right to respond [to allegations of wrongful conduct] arises when an assertion of such complicity has been made. Paragraph (b)(5) *does not require the lawyer to await the commencement of an action* or a proceeding so that the defense may be established by responding *directly to a third party* who had made such an assertion." Rule 1.6, Comment 10 (emphasis added).

If it does not prejudice the lawyer's ability to establish a defense and if it is practicable to do so, the lawyer should advise the client of the third party's assertion and request that the client respond appropriately. Id. at Comment 14. However, the client cannot prevent the lawyer from establishing the lawyer's innocence.

Example: A newspaper editorial accuses Lawyer of having won an acquittal in an important criminal case many years earlier by suborning her client's perjury. Lawyer responds by writing, to the newspaper, a letter that reveals that the

Client had intentionally kept Lawyer in the dark about the perjury and that Lawyer never learned of it until years after the acquittal, when Client confessed to Lawyer on his death bed. Client, at that time, also told Lawyer never to reveal the perjury; then Client died. Lawyer also states that her version is confirmed by an associate in her office who was present during the conversation in question.

Under the Rules and the Code, Lawyer's disclosures are permissible.

Note that while the Rules give attorneys liberal authority to violate client confidences or secrets in order to defend themselves, Rule 1.6, until the 2003 revisions, did not allow attorneys to reveal such information when necessary to prevent a substantial financial fraud by the client or to rectify the consequences of a client's criminal or fraudulent act in which the lawyer's services had been used. An earlier draft of the Rules would have allowed the lawyer to reveal such information—see Draft Rule 1.6(b)(2), (3) (Proposed Final Draft, May 30, 1981)—but the ABA House of Delegates, in 1983, deleted those sections. (In August of 1991 the ABA House of Delegates again refused to accept a similar proposal.)

In 2003, the ABA—after the Enron Corporation bankruptcy and scandal—added a new Rule 1.6(b)(2) & (3), discussed immediately below.

6.   **When the Client Intends to Commit or Has Committed a Crime or Fraud**

The lawyer is the agent of the client, who is the principal. A basic principle of agency law is that:

> "An agent is privileged to reveal information confidentially acquired by him in the course of his agency in the protection of a superior interest of himself or a third person. Thus, *if the confidential information is to the effect that the principal is committing or about to commit a crime, the agent is under no duty not to reveal it.* However, an attorney employed to represent a client in a criminal proceeding has no duty to reveal that the client has confessed his guilt." A.L.I., Restatement (Second) of Agency, § 395, Comment f (emphasis added).

The old Model Code codified this common law rule (and the distinction it draws between confessions of *past* crimes and intentions to commit *future* ones). Thus the Code provided that the lawyer "may reveal" the client's intention "to commit a crime" as well as the information necessary to prevent it. DR 4–101(C)(3).

The Code did not distinguish between types of crimes—violation of a trivial offense versus premeditated murder—nor did the rule offer any guidelines to cabin the lawyer's exercise of discretion. We are only told that the attorney "may" reveal this information. However, a pre-Code ABA Formal Opinion, in considering the Canons of Professional Ethics, stated that if "the facts in the attorney's possession indicate beyond reasonable doubt that a crime will be committed," then the lawyer must disclose the client's confidences. ABA Formal Opinion 314 (April 27, 1965). The Code quoted this portion of the Formal Opinion in the footnotes (DR 4–101(C)(3) at note 16), and this Disciplinary Rule may be interpreted to adopt the test of the Formal Opinion. Thus, DR 4–103(C)(3) appeared to permit a lawyer to reveal the client's intention to commit a crime and probably required such disclosure if the lawyer knew, beyond a reasonable doubt, that the client will commit the crime.

An early draft of the Rules made some effort to draw some useful distinctions not present in the Code. First, this early draft *required* the lawyer to reveal client information if "necessary to prevent the client from committing an act that would result in death or serious bodily harm to another person. . . . " Draft Rule 1.7(b) (Discussion Draft, Jan. 30, 1980). This mandatory disclosure proposal appears to reflect already existing tort law. See, e.g., *Tarasoff v. Regents of the University of California,* 17 Cal.3d 425, 131 Cal.Rptr. 14, 551 P.2d 334 (1976), which held that when a psychotherapist knew of his patient's planned murder, the psychotherapist was liable in tort when he did not take steps to reasonably necessary under the circumstances, such as notifying the police, or the victim. 17 Cal.3d 425, 431, 551 P.2d 334, 340, 131 Cal.Rptr. 14, 20.

The next draft of the proposed Rules eliminated this mandatory disclosure proposal, but *allowed* disclosure in order "to prevent the client from committing a criminal or fraudulent act that the lawyer believes is likely to result in death or substantial bodily harm, or substantial injury to the financial interests or property of another;" or "to rectify the consequences of a client's criminal or fraudulent act in the commission of which the lawyer's services had been used." Proposed Final Draft of Model Rules, Rule 1.6(b)(2), (3) (May 30, 1981), reprinted in T. Morgan & R. Rotunda, 1980 Selected Standards Supplement 113 (1980). This draft drew some interesting distinctions involving crimes or frauds causing serious harm and circumstances where the lawyer's services had unwittingly been used (actually, misused) by the client.

The 1983 version of the Rules was much more protective of client information than either its earlier drafts or the old Model Code. The 1983 version of Rule 1.6 had no mandatory rule involving disclosure and, with respect to the fraud or crime issue, only permitted disclosure to prevent the client "from committing a criminal act that the lawyer believes is likely to result in *imminent death or substantial bodily* harm." former Rule 1.6(b)(1) (emphasis added).

All this changed in 2003, when the ABA—under pressure from the fallout of the Enron Corporation bankruptcy and scandal—changed Rule 1.6.

Rule 1.6(b)(1) now provides that the lawyer may reveal confidential client information in order to prevent "reasonably certain death or substantially bodily harm." It is no longer necessary that the future death be "imminent." For example, assume that the lawyer learns that the client accidentally discharged toxic wastes into a water supply. We can also assume that this discharge is not a crime. If neither the client nor the lawyer report this discharge, and there is a "present and substantial threat a person will suffer such harm at a later date," then the lawyer may disclose to "eliminate the threat or reduce the number of victims" who will contract a life-threatening or debilitating disease. Comment 6.

Rule 1.6(b)(2) now allows the lawyer to reveal client confidences to prevent the client from engaging in a crime or fraud "that is reasonably certain to result in substantial injury to the financial interests or property of another and in furtherance of which the client has used or is using the lawyer's services." For example, Client asks Lawyer to prepare a stock offering used to sell stock in the Client's corporation. Lawyer later learns that the documents she prepared are based on fraudulent facts and that her services were, unwittingly, used in this fraud. If the stock is sold based on these false statements, many people will eventually suffer substantial financial loss. Lawyer confronts Client who says to Lawyer, "You are done preparing the documents; I don't need you any more. Just go away." Lawyer may reveal the information to the prospective investors or to the appropriate authorities in order to prevent Client from committing the crime or fraud. Comment 7.

Rule 1.6(b)(3) now allows the lawyer to reveal client confidences to prevent, mitigate, *or rectify* the substantial injury to another person's property or financial interests of another that is reasonably certain to result from the client's crime or fraud (or has resulted from the client's crime or fraud) *if* the client has used the lawyer's services in the commission of the crime or fraud. Notice that this subsection allows the lawyer (let us call her Lawyer #1) to reveal *past* acts of the client in the special circumstances indicated. If the government charges a person with a crime, or others sue that person for a financial fraud, and that person then hires a lawyer (Lawyer #2) to represent him, Lawyer #2 must keep the client's secrets. But, if that person had used Lawyer #1's services to commit the crime or fraud, Lawyer #1 may reveal the information necessary to rectify the harm. Comment 8.

Lawyer's Discretion. Model Rule 1.6(b)(1), (2), & (3) make clear that when it gives the lawyer discretion to reveal client information, it intends that this discretion be absolute and unreviewable. See Rule 1.6, Comment 15: "A lawyer's decision not to disclose as permitted by paragraph (b) does not violate this Rule." See, Rules, "Scope," ¶ 14: "No disciplinary action should be taken when the lawyer chooses not to act or acts within the bounds of such discretion [, *i.e.,* when the Rule says 'may']." See also, Rules, "Scope," ¶ 20: "Violation of a Rule should not itself give rise to a cause of action against a lawyer nor should it create any presumption if such a case that a legal duty has been breached."

Given decisions like *Tarasoff,* supra, the efforts of the ABA House of Delegates to grant lawyers unreviewable discretion may well be unsuccessful, at least in a tort case. The Rules admit that other law may mandate disclosure [although they counsel that there should be a presumption that other law does not supersede Rule 1.6]. Rule 1.6, Comment 12

May a lawyer reveal that her client has confessed to a crime for which an innocent person is about to be punished? This question is a "much mooted" one. Charles Wolfram, *Modern Legal Ethics* 673 (1986). The lawyer's silence in such a case may permit a grave injustice to be done. *State v. Macumber,* 112 Ariz. 569, 544 P.2d 1084 (1976) held that the trial judge in a murder case had properly excluded testimony by two attorneys that a third person, now deceased, had confessed to them that he had killed the people whom the state is charging the defendant with murdering. This third person confessed to the two attorneys who had represented him when he was tried in federal court for an unrelated murder. The state court ruled that the attorney-client privilege prevented this disclosure.

The dissent argued that when this third person died and there was no chance of his prosecution for other crimes, then any privilege was merely a matter of property interest, which should not prevail over the constitutional right of the accused to introduce reliable hearsay declarations evidencing his innocence.

At one point, a proposed version of the Restatement of the Law, Third, of the Law Governing Lawyers § 132, Illustration 4 (Tentative Draft No. 2, April 7, 1989) offered an illustration based on *Macumber.* At the May, 1989 annual meeting, various American Law Institute members objected to this illustration as "grotesque," "revolting," and "disgusting." It is not right, members said, that a lawyer may reveal privileged information in a fee dispute but may not reveal information to prevent an innocent person from going to jail. By a vote of 164 to 65, the ALI members voted to strike the illustration.

The United Kingdom does not follow *Macumber.* E.g., M. Howard, P. Crance & D. Hochberg, Phipson on Evidence 500 (14th ed. 1990), noting that the evidentiary privilege "does not apply where the privilege, if granted, would prevent an accused person from calling evidence which might lead to his acquittal on a criminal charge."

Rule 1.6(b)(1) now allows the lawyer to reveal otherwise secret client information "to prevent reasonably certain death or substantial bodily harm." This subsection does *not* require that the client be involved in the death, or that the client have committed a crime, or that the client have used the lawyer's services. Rule 1.6(b)(1), after the 2002 & 2003 revisions, certainly appears to allow the lawyer to reveal this information to prevent the conviction and execution of an innocent person.

7. To Secure Legal Advice from Another Lawyer

Rule 1.6(b)(4) recognizes that lawyers sometimes need lawyers too. A lawyer (Lawyer #1), in the course of representing a client, may need legal advice to determine if a course of action is consistent with the Rules of Professional Conduct. If Lawyer #1 is a member of a large firm, he may just consult with other lawyers in the firm, or members of the Conflicts Committee, or the General Counsel of the firm. (Large law firms are tending to hire General Counsel for the firm; that way, firm lawyers can consult with the General Counsel without fear of losing the attorney-client evidentiary privilege.) A solo practitioner, or a lawyer practicing in a firm without the necessary expertise may need to consult with a lawyer not in the firm (Lawyer #2) about an ethical quandary. Rule 1.6(b)(4) explicitly permits this consultation. Even without the subsection, lawyers typically concluded that the limited disclosure to Lawyer #2 was "impliedly authorized" under Rule 1.6(a). Now, Rule 1.6(b)(4) makes that legal argument unnecessary. Comment 9. Lawyer #1's disclosure to Lawyer #2 is also covered under the attorney-client privilege.

8. Filing a Notice of Withdrawal

Both the Rules and Code agree that if the client will use a lawyer's services to further the client's "criminal or fraudulent conduct," then the lawyer must withdraw. Rule 1.16(a)(1); DR 2–110(B)(2); DR 7–102(A)(7). In some circumstances the fact of a lawyer's withdrawal from representation may amount to a disclosure of client confidences or secrets. For example, if a lawyer withdraws in such a manner as to suggest that the client intends to commit fraud, then the lawyer will have disclosed information detrimental to the client. ABA Formal Opinion 314 (Apr. 27, 1965) recognized that in some instances "the very act of disassociation would have the effect of violating Canon 37." (Canon 37 of the ABA Canons of Professional Ethics (1908, as amended) is the predecessor to DR 4–101 of the Model Code.) Nonetheless the lawyer must withdraw. (*Different considerations apply if the perjured testimony or false evidence has been offered before a tribunal.* See Model Rule 3.3, and Part VII, Section II, A, 3 "Disclosure of Facts," infra.)

If a lawyer withdraws from representation of a client, the Model Code did not specifically deal with the question whether the lawyer may formally inform third parties that the lawyer is no longer in the case. None of the early drafts of the Rules talked of filing a *Notice of Withdrawal.* However, the final version of the 1983 version contains several Comments on this new concept, created for the first time by the Rules. See discussion in, Rotunda, *The Notice of Withdrawal and the New Model Rules of Professional Conduct: Blowing the Whistle and Waiving the Red Flag,* 63 Oregon L.Rev. 455 (1984).

The Comments dealing with the "Notice of Withdrawal" are no longer in Rule 1.6 because they are no longer necessary, given the explicit authorization of the lawyer to blow the whistle on the client in cases where the client has used the lawyer's services and will commit (or has committed) a future crime or fraud that will result in substantial harm. See Rule 1.6(b)(1), (2), (3).

However, there are still two important references to the concept of a "Notice of Withdrawal." First, Rule 1.2, Comment 10 states:

"The lawyer is required to avoid assisting the client, for example, by drafting or delivering documents that the lawyer knows are fraudulent or by suggesting how the wrongdoing might be concealed. A lawyer may not continue assisting a client in conduct that the lawyer originally supposed was legally proper but then discovers is criminal or fraudulent. The lawyer *must*, therefore, withdraw from the representation of the client in the matter. See Rule 1.16(a). In some cases, withdrawal alone might be insufficient. It may be necessary for the lawyer to give notice of the fact of withdrawal and to disaffirm any opinion, document, affirmation or the like. See Rule 4.1."

Rule 4.1, Comment 3 repeats the essential words of this Comment.

The lawyer, in short, may file this Notice of Withdrawal even though its issuance may be a red flag that the client is up to no good.

Note also that this Comment does not limit to whom the Notice of Withdrawal may be sent. The Notice may apparently be sent to third parties, not merely the opposing side.

Example: Lawyer learns, on the eve of closing, that the limited partnership agreement that Lawyer has prepared for her Client is a criminal fraud under the federal securities laws. Lawyer confronts Client, who states that he will go through with the deal and if Lawyer does not like it, Lawyer can resign. The lawyer must resign. Rule 1.16(a)(1); DR 2–110(B)(2). Under the Model Rules Lawyer may also send a Notice of Withdrawal to the other side and also to the Securities & Exchange Commission. Under the Model Rules and Model Code, the lawyer may reveal this information; Rule 1.6(b)(3); DR 4–101(C)(3).

The client cannot preclude the lawyer from filing a noisy withdrawal by firing the lawyer first. "Whenever circumstances exist that would otherwise require a lawyer to withdraw, disaffirmance [of the lawyer's work product] may be in order even if the client fires her before she has a chance to do so." ABA Formal Opinion 92–366 (Aug. 8, 1992).

II. Conflicts of Interest

A. The Basic Rationale

The rules governing conflicts of interest derive, for the most part, from the need to protect client confidences and secrets, and the duty of client loyalty and zealous representation.

The rules dealing with conflicts of interest are found, primarily in Rules 1.7 through 1.13 & Rule 1.18, of the Rules; many of these provisions were derived from Canon 5 of the old Model Code. All of these specific rules derive from several basic premises.

The first is the lawyer's duty to protect secret or confidential client information, discussed in section I, supra.

Example: A conflict may develop if Lawyer simultaneously represents Client *A* and Client *B*, or now represents Client *B* and used to represent Client *A*. Lawyer may know secret information about Client *A* (the present, or former, client) and this information would be useful to Client *B*. If Lawyer does not reveal the information to *B*, Lawyer violates his or her duty of zealous representation of *B*. If Lawyer does reveal the information to *B*, Lawyer violates his or her duty to *A* to keep *A*'s secrets.

Another basic premise is the lawyer's duty of loyalty to the client. This duty exists even if there is no breach of client secrets.

Example: Lawyer for Client *D* is paid by Insurer, who insures Client *D*. Insurer instructs Lawyer (who is defending *D* in a tort suit) not to dispute Plaintiff's charge that *D*'s tortious conduct was really intentional. If the jury believes that *D* acted intentionally, Insurer will not be liable. If Lawyer follows Insurer's instructions, Lawyer is violating the duty of loyalty to *D*.

Given these policies, there are various types of conflicts. There might be a conflict between the client and the lawyer's business or personal interests; between the client and another present or former client; or between the client and a person or group who may be paying for the client's legal assistance. This section will discuss all of these categories of conflicts.

Bear in mind that the client may be able to *waive* the conflict in some instances. When a conflicts rule is designed to protect only the client, little reason exists to prohibit a lawyer from engaging in the representation when a competent and informed client desires to waive that protection. In contrast, if the conflicts rule is designed to protect a systemic interest—an interest of the system of justice—client waiver should be ineffective. With respect to the different types of conflicts, we will consider when the client may desire to waive, and under what circumstances that waiver will be effective.

Finally, the Rules (like its predecessor, the Model Code) sometime *impute* one lawyer's disqualifying conflict to all of the other lawyers in the same firm.

Because imputation applies even when the firm is very large, with branch offices in many states, the firm must adopt "reasonable procedures, appropriate for the size and type of firm and practice," to determine whether there are actual or potential conflicts, in both litigation and nonlitigative matters. Rule 1.7, Comment 3.

B. Simultaneous Representation

1. Multiple Clients in the Same Matter

(a) In General

Very often the lawyer represents two or more clients in the same matter. For example, the lawyer may be asked to represent several clients in setting up a small corporation, or a husband and wife in a house closing, or the driver and owner-passenger of a car when both have been sued for injuries arising out of an automobile accident.

It is often in the best interest of clients to share the same lawyer. Such an arrangement reduces legal fees and saves time. On the other hand such an arrangement creates the potential for conflict, so the lawyer must "weigh carefully the possibility that his judgment may be impaired or his loyalty divided if he accepts or continues the employment." EC 5–15. The mere possibility of conflict does not itself preclude the representation. Rule 1.7, Comment 8.

(b) In Litigation

The potential of conflict when representing multiple clients exists whether the representation involves litigation or counseling. However, disqualification is more likely in litigation because the lawyer acts primarily as an advocate. Rules 2.1, 3.1. Cf. EC 7–4, 7–5.

"A lawyer should never represent *in litigation* multiple clients with differing interests; and there are few situations in which he would be justified in representing *in litigation* multiple clients with potentially differing interests." EC 5–15 (emphasis added); Compare Rule 1.7, Comments 23 to 24 ("Conflicts in Litigation") with Comments 26 to 28 ("Nonlitigation Conflicts").

The lawyer may not represent both Client *A* and *B* in the case of *A v. B.* See Rule 1.7(a). E.g., *Jedwabny v. Philadelphia Transportation Co.,* 390 Pa. 231, 135 A.2d 252 (1957), cert. denied, 355 U.S. 966, 78 S.Ct. 557, 2 L.Ed.2d 541 (1958).

Rule 1.7(a) speaks to the situation where the representation of a client is *"directly adverse"* to another client. Unfortunately, the Rule does not clearly define what is "direct" or "indirect." We are told that it is the intent of Rule 1.7(b)(3) to prohibit representation of "opposing parties in litigation." Rule 1.7, Comment 23. If a lawyer represents multiple clients in litigation who are all on the same side as co-plaintiffs (or all co-defendants), Rule 1.7(a)(2) is applicable. See Rule 1.7, Comment 23. The lawyer may represent these co-plaintiffs or co-defendants if the lawyer reasonably believes he can represent all of them competently, each client gives informed consent, *confirmed in writing*, the co-clients are not taking positions against each other, and no other law prohibits the joint representation. Rule 1.7(b).

Waiver. The conflict illustrated by the case of *A v. B* where A is suing B and the lawyer wants to represent both A and B cannot be cured by consent; that is, such a conflict may not be waived, because of the systemic interest—the interest in the system of justice—recognized in both DR 5–105(C) and Rule 1.7(b)(3) & Comment 23. Consent is ineffective to cure a conflict if a disinterested lawyer would conclude that the client should not agree to the representation under the circumstances.

In the case of *A v. B,* a lawyer could not determine that he or she could adequately represent both *A* and *B.* Therefore, *A*'s and *B*'s consent, even though made after full disclosure, would not waive the conflict. The systemic interest in the fair administration of justice would prevail.

Simultaneously Representing Adverse Clients in Unrelated Matters. Not only may the lawyer not represent Clients *A* and *B* in the case of *A v. B,* but the lawyer may not sue *A* on behalf of *B,* while simultaneously representing *A* in another, *completely unrelated* matter.

Example: Lawyer represents Wife in a divorce suit against Husband while simultaneously representing Husband who is seeking to collect on his workman's compensation claim. *Memphis & Shelby County Bar Ass'n v. Sanderson,* 52 Tenn.App. 684, 378 S.W.2d 173 (1963) (lawyer disbarred).

Although the two cases—the divorce and the workman's compensation claim—are completely unrelated and create no danger of any use of confidences in one case that would or could be useful or relevant in the other case, there is a breach of loyalty. Rule 1.7, Comment 6. When an attorney represents one client in a suit against another, some adverse effect on the lawyer's exercise of independent judgment on behalf of a client may arise because of the lawyer's adversary posture towards that client in another matter. See, *I.B.M. Corp. v. Levin*, 579 F.2d 271 (3d Cir.1978). For example, in the attorney's effort to please Client *A* (who is his long-standing client) there may be a "diminution in the rigor of his representation of the client in the other matter." 579 F.2d at 280. The lawyer might not—or it might appear that he might not—fight as vigorously for one of his clients as he otherwise would.

Waiver. It is unclear whether client consent is ever effective to allow such dual representation. Although the lawyer is not representing opposing parties in the same case, there is much authority that the duty of loyalty *always* prevents effective consent. The possible ineffectiveness of client consent is illustrated by *Matter of Kelly v. Greason*, 23 N.Y.2d 368, 374–79, 296 N.Y.S.2d 937, 942–46, 244 N.E.2d 456, 459–62 (1968). Two lawyers, Kelly and Whalen, were in a law partnership. Whalen was then employed as an insurance adjuster for the Nationwide Insurance Co. Whalen had no access to any Nationwide files other than those of claims assigned to him. Nonetheless the firm handled some claims against Nationwide. There was no proof that any of the Nationwide settlements were unreasonable or unfair to either the insurance carrier or the claimants. Nor was there any prejudice to any of Nationwide's claimants by the partnership's failure to bring a negligence liability claim against the carrier. However, potentially, a claimant against an insurance company is adverse in interest to the carrier, which would most often seek to minimize any liability. Hence, "it was, prima facie, evidence of professional misconduct for the partnership to represent claimants, whether assured of Nationwide or not, in their claims against the carrier, while at the same time Whalen was also the carrier's employee." 23 N.Y.2d at 376, 296 N.Y.S.2d at 944, 244 N.E.2d at 461. The court found that discipline was appropriate unless, and *perhaps even if,* consent had been obtained from *both* clients after full disclosure.

A.B.A. Formal Opinion 112 (May 10, 1934) held that an attorney who represents an insurance company in workmen's compensation cases may not accept employment from a former general agent who is suing the insurance company. The Opinion expressly stated: "We assume that the insurance company has expressed no objection" to the lawyer's representation against the insurance company, "but that does not relieve lawyer *A* from his obligation to accept no employment from a new client in a case where fidelity to the new client may require examination of the motives and the good faith of the insurance company by which he has been and is employed in numerous other cases *and whose patronage he desires to continue.*" (emphasis added). See also, H. Drinker, Legal Ethics 111 (1953).

The purpose of this simultaneous adverse representation rule is to protect the systemic interest in the fair administration of justice as well as to protect the clients' interest in loyalty. Thus there is a substantial question whether, even "with consent in such circumstances the attorney may profit from breach of the duty of loyalty." Fordham, *There are Substantial Limitations on Representation of Clients in Litigation Which are Not Obvious in the Code of Professional Responsibility,* 33 The Bus. Lawyer 1193, 1204 (Mar.1978). "Thus, absent consent, a lawyer may not act as advocate in one matter against a person the lawyer represents in some other matter, even when the matters are wholly unrelated." Rule 1.7, Comment 6.

On the other hand, if a lawyer represents a large corporation, he or she may ordinarily represent another economic enterprise in a matter that is unrelated, even though one enterprise is competing with the other. For example, the lawyer is representing both *A* and *B* on two separate matters that are unrelated. Assume, for example, that the lawyer represents a major auto company on a securities matter. The lawyer is also representing another major auto company on a different, unrelated securities matter. Although *A* and *B* generally compete with each other, the lawyer is not suing either *A* or *B*. Nor is the lawyer giving legal advice to *A* that is to be used against *B* (or vice versa). Nor is there any violation of client confidences or secrets. In the words of the Model Rules, *A* and *B* are not "directly adverse" because they are merely "competing economic enterprises." Rule 1.7, Comment 6. Indeed, representing competing economic enterprises in unrelated litigation "does not ordinarily constitute a conflict of interest and thus *may not require consent of the respective clients.*" Comment 6 (emphasis added).

In contrast, if the lawyer were suing Client *A* on behalf of Client *B* in one matter, the lawyer should not simultaneously represent Client *A*, on a different matter, even if the two matters are completely unrelated. See, e.g., *IBM Corp. v. Levin*, discussed, supra. *As part of the duty of loyalty, a lawyer may not sue a present client.*

(c) In Negotiation

A lawyer, while acting as an advocate, cannot represent the opposite side in negotiation. A lawyer "may not represent multiple parties to a negotiation whose interests are fundamentally antagonistic to each other, but common representation is permissible where clients are generally aligned in interest even though there is some difference of interest among them." Rule 1.7, Comment 28. See also DR 5–105(A), EC 5–15. Thus a lawyer may represent several parties on the *same side* of a negotiation even though there is some difference among them. See Rule 1.7(b) (discussed below).

If a lawyer does seek to be a part of a situation involving fundamentally antagonistic multiple parties in negotiation, he should do so as a *third-party neutral,* not as an advocate. See Rule 2.4. "Lawyer Serving as Third–Party Neutral."

2. Representing Clients Notwithstanding the Existence of a Current Conflict of Interest

Rule 1.7(a) deals with the basic factual situation where a lawyer may have a conflict with a concurrent client because (1) the representation of one client is "directly adverse" to another client whom the lawyer is representing simultaneously, or (2) or the lawyer's representation of a client "will be materially limited" because of the lawyer's responsibilities to another client, a former client, a third person, or the lawyer's "personal interest."

Rule 1.7(a) sets out the general rule for dealing with conflicts of interest of current clients. Rule 1.7(b) is the subsection that provides for waiver of a conflict described by Rule 1.7(a).

In order for there to be a valid waiver, four factors must all exist.

First, the lawyer must "reasonably" believe that she will be able to provide competent and diligent representation to the affected clients notwithstanding the conflict. If she does not believe this, then the conflict is not waiverable. Rule 1.7(b)(1). "Belief" is subjective, Rule 1.0(a), but "reasonably believes" means that the lawyer has this subjective belief and that this believe is objectively reasonable. Rule 1.0(i).

Second, no other law will prohibit the representation. Rule 1.7(b)(2). For example, some states provide that one lawyer cannot represent co-defendants in a capital murder cases even if all co-defendants agree.

Third, the lawyer cannot represent one client asserting a claim against another client whom the lawyer also represents in the same litigation. Rule 1.7(b)(3). For example, Lawyer cannot represent both Plaintiff and Defendant in the case of Plaintiff versus Defendant, even if both parties agree.

Finally, the lawyer must secure from each client "informed consent," and this consent must be "confirmed in writing." Rule 1.7(b)(4). An oral consent is not worth the paper it is printed on. "Informed consent" means that the lawyer has told the client all the relevant information. Rule 1.0(e). And "confirmed in writing" means that silence does not imply consent. Instead, it means that the lawyer must transmit to the client something in writing confirming the client's earlier oral informed consent. The writing may be any tangible or electronic record, such as an email, or audio recording, or fax. It is not necessary that the client *sign* this writing. Rule 1.0(b),(n). Rule 1.7, Comment 20. The purpose of the writing is to impress upon the client the significance of the client's waiver.

"Informed consent" means that the lawyer has communicated enough information so that the client can appreciate the material risks and reasonable alternatives to the proposed course of conduct. Rule 1.0(e); Rule 1.7, Comment 18. For example, the lawyer should normally explain that if two clients engage the same attorney to represent them in a matter, and each communicates separately with the attorney, then, as between the two clients, there are no confidences: "the communicating client, knowing that the attorney represents the other party also, would not ordinarily intend that the facts communicated should be kept secret from him." *McCormick's Handbook on the Law of Evidence* § 91 at 190 (E. Cleary, ed., 2d ed. 1972). If one of the co-clients wants relevant information kept from the other co-client, then each should obtain their own separate counsel to begin with.

3.   Special Problem Areas

(a) Securing Consent

(i)   Full Disclosure

Before a lawyer may represent clients who are—or are reasonably likely to be—in conflict with each other, the lawyer must secure each client's consent. In order for there to be "informed consent," the lawyer must give each client full disclosure. Rule 1.0(e); Rule 1.7(b)(4);DR 5–105(C). In some cases, however, such full disclosure may include secrets about another client that the lawyer may not reveal under Rule 1.6. See G. Hazard, *Ethics in the Practice of Law* 24, 76 (1978). In such situations the lawyer cannot secure the adequate consent from Client *A* without violating his or her duty to keep confidential the secrets of Client *B*. Thus the lawyer cannot secure adequate consent and may not take on such representation. See Rule 1.7, Comment 19.

Full disclosure requires the lawyer to reveal "all the facts, legal implications, possible effects, and other circumstances relating to the proposed representation. A client's mere knowledge of the existence of his attorney's other representation does not alone constitute full disclosure." *Financial General Bankshares, Inc. v. Metzger*, 523 F.Supp. 744, 771 (D.D.C.1981).

(ii) Prospective Waivers

If a client may waive a conflict, it may chose to waive its objections prospectively, if the prospective waiver meets all the requirements of a present conflict of interest. The lawyer relying on this prospective waiver must show that it "reasonably contemplated" the future conflict so that the client's consent is reasonably viewed as fully informed when it was given.

However, even a prospective waiver (a present waiver of a future conflict) does not extend to disclosure or use of client confidences against the client, unless the client explicitly agreed to such disclosure or use. ABA Formal Opinion 93–372 (Apr. 16, 1993). In other words, a client may waive, prospectively, a conflict based on loyalty, but it may not normally waive, prospectively, a conflict based on breach of confidences, because a client could not know *now* what those confidences might be or their significance *in the future*. Rule 1.7(b)(4) now requires that prospective waivers be confirmed in a writing. See Rule 1.7, Comment 22.

> *Example:* Corporation located in Los Angeles hires the local office of a national law firm to negotiate and draft a lease on a Los Angeles building. The law firm asks Corporation to waive any objections to the Chicago office of the law firm representing a Chicago bank in negotiating mortgages on Chicago property, even if the mortgagor happens to be another division of Corporation. The Corporation may waive, prospectively, its objections to conflicts.

In short, the lawyer engaging in a representation that would be in violation of Rule 1.7 (unless the client, with informed consent, prospectively waived that conflict), must show that the "subsequent representation was reasonably contemplated by the waiver document, and that the subsequent representation will not result in disclosure or use of information imparted by the client in the representation existing at the time of the waiver, or any subsequent representation of that client." ABA Formal Opinion 93–372 (Apr. 16, 1993). The fact that the client is independently represented (e.g., the corporation's in-house counsel approves of the prospective waiver) makes it more likely that a court will later find the prospective waiver to be effective. Rule 1.7, Comment 22.

(iii) The "Hot Potato" Doctrine

In general, if a law firm finds itself simultaneously representing two adverse clients in two different law suits, it may not avoid the problem simply by dropping the disfavored client like a "hot potato." Absent special circumstances, if the parties do not consent to the conflict, the law firm must withdraw from representing *both* parties in the two cases. *Picker International, Inc. v. Varian Associates, Inc.,* 670 F.Supp. 1363 (N.D.Ohio 1987), *affirmed,* 869 F.2d 578 (Fed.Cir.1989). Rule 1.7, Comment 29: "Ordinarily, the lawyer will be forced to withdraw from representing all of the clients if the common representation fails."

However, sometimes it is not the law firm's fault when it finds itself in the position of representing a client in one case and being adverse to the interests of a client in another case where that client is independently represented. Consider Pennwalt Corp. v. Plough, Inc., 85 F.R.D. 264 (D.Del. 1980). A law firm represented Pennwalt for decades. In 1978, the firm began to defend Scholl against antitrust charges. In April 1979, Schering–Plough acquired Scholl as a wholly owned subsidiary. Because Plough was already a wholly-owned subsidiary of Schering–Plough, Scholl and Plough then became sister corporations. In May, 1979, the law firm filed suit against Plough on behalf of its longtime client Pennwalt. When the law firm learned a week or two later that it represented Scholl in one case while simultaneously represented Pennwalt against Scholl's parent, it sought to withdraw from representing Scholl. After the court granted that motion, Plough moved to disqualify the firm from the second case. The court agreed that counsel may not eliminate a conflict "merely by choosing to represent the more favored client and withdrawing its representation of the other." However, in this case the firm's conflict was inadvertent: the merger activities of the client created the problem. "Scholl is a corporate entity distinct from Plough and Schering–Plough," and it was highly unlikely that as of the date of the law firm's representation there was any misuse of confidential information or adverse effect on its exercise of independent judgment. Thus, the court did not mandate disqualification. See Comment 5 to Model Rule 1.7, Comment 5, approves of this case where unforeseen changes in corporate or other organizational affiliations occur.

(b) The Organization as a Client

(i) Representing the Entity
Occasionally the lawyer represents an entity, such as a corporation, union, or a governmental unit. In such cases the lawyer owes his allegiance to the incorporeal entity and not to a "stockholder, director, officer, employee, representative, or other person connected with the entity." EC 5–18. Thus Rule 1.13(a) provides that the lawyer "employed or retained by an organization *represents the organization* acting through its duly authorized constituents." (emphasis added). Cf. DR 5–107(B).

Note: One of the consultants to the ABA Commission that drafted the Model Rules noted that the Commission often rejected the language of the Model Code not because of any intent to change the meaning but only because of a preference for different phraseology. Sutton, *Professional Code Becoming Controversial Rules,* 35 Virginia L. Weekly 1, 4 col. 1 (Nov. 12, 1982).

The lawyer represents the "entity," but this legal entity can only act through its officers and other duly authorized agents. See Rule 1.13(a) and Comment 1.

The "entity" theory offers no Rosetta Stone to solve all corporate conflicts problems, but it does provide some solutions. "[I]f a competitor sues a corporate client alleging an antitrust violation, it is easy to conclude that the corporate lawyer does not represent a shareholder of defendant who is also a shareholder of plaintiff; rather, the lawyer represents the corporation as an entity." Rotunda, *Law, Lawyers, and Managers,* in The Ethics of Corporate Conduct, 127, 129 (C. Walton, ed. 1977). But what of other, more difficult cases—where the shareholders of the corporation sue derivatively, alleging that the directors have not performed their legal obligations; or the lawyer for a corporation is asked to defend it from a hostile takeover, which may be in the best economic interests of the shareholders; or the corporate lawyer discovers that one of the officers is violating a law (e.g., engaging in price-fixing), which violation would be imputed to the entity but it "benefits" the corporation *if* the corporation is not caught? Model Rule 1.13(b) & (c) provide a more useful analytical tool than the bare bones of EC 5–18. See also Comments 13 & 14 ("Derivative Actions").

Note that Rule 1.13 applies to any "organization." Often we think of corporations but the Rule is not so limited. For example, a *partnership* is an "organization" for ethics purposes even if it is considered an "aggregate" under state partnership law. Similarly, a *class action* is an organization for purposes of Rule 1.13. The lawyer represents the class as an entity, rather than each individual unnamed member of the class.

(ii) The Approach of the Model Code
The former Model Code offers some assistance in the general principles of EC 5–18. The most specific guidance is found in

EC 5–24, which stated that the lawyer should make legal judgments but defer to the business judgment of the agents of the entity: directors and officers "necessarily have the right to make decisions of business policy [but] a lawyer must decline to accept direction of his professional judgment from any layman."

(iii) The Approach of the Model Rules

The ABA substantially revised Rule 1.13 in 2003, in response to the Enron Corporation bankruptcy and scandal. For the first time, the ABA requires the lawyer to the organization not only to report up the organization chain of command in order to find out what the organization really wants, but also it now authorizes the lawyer to report outside the organization in order to prevent "substantial injury to the organization." Rule 1.13(c). This point is discussed below.

Rule 1.13(b) & (c) set up what basically is a requirement that the lawyer exhaust any internal remedies to find out what the organization really wants. These subsections provide guidance as to when a lawyer must climb up the corporate ladder (or the chain of command of any other legal entity) and exhaust these internal organizational remedies in order to determine what the entity really "wants." Once that determination is made, the lawyer then is governed, first by Rule 1.13(c) and also by the other Rules; that is, *Rule 1.13 is in addition to and does not replace other Rules,* such as Rule 1.6 (Confidentiality); Rule 1.8 (Conflicts); Rule 1.16 (Withdrawal); Rule 3.3 (Candor Towards the Tribunal); or Rule 4.1 (Truthfulness to Others). See Rule 1.13, Comment 6.

Rule 1.13(b) in part provides that if the lawyer for the entity learns that an agent of the entity is acting (or refuses to act) in a matter that is "related to the representation," *and:*

> "[(1)] is a violation of a legal obligation to the organiza-tion, *or* [(2)] a violation of law which reasonably might be imputed to the organization, *and* [(3)] is likely to re-sult in substantial injury to the organization, [*then*] the lawyer shall proceed as is reasonably necessary in the best interest of the organization." (emphasis added)

Before determining what is in the "best interest" of the entity, it is well to point out several significant ambiguities.

First, it is unclear whether clause (3)—"is likely to result in substantial injury to the organization"—modifies *both* clauses 1 and 2 or whether it only modifies clause 2. That is, must the agent's violation of a legal obligation to the entity result in substantial injury, or is the amount of injury relevant only if the agent's legal violation might be imputed to the entity? The language of Rule 1.13(b) does not number the clauses and grammatically allows either interpretation. For example, if the CEO of the corporation is engaging in massive corporate theft, that will result to injury to the corporation whether or not it is discovered. Now consider the situation where the corporation engages in price fixing. That is a crime and will result in substantial injury to the corporation *if discovered*. It is unclear whether the requirement of "substantial injury to the organization" means substantial "if discovered," or substantial "assuming that it is discovered."

It is unclear how Rule 1.13(b) is intended to apply in this situation. It makes more sense to interpret this Rule to mean substantial "assuming that it is discovered." The alternative is to encourage constituents of the entity to cover-up wrongful activity and to give a premium to the attorney who, ostrich-like, sticks his head in the sand. Rule 1.13 obligates the attorney to find out what the entity wants so that he or she can act in its best interests. The attorney cannot make that determination unless he or she first discovers what is going on: if, e.g., the entity really "wants" to commit a crime (e.g., price-fixing) then the attorney may resign or disclose pursuant to Rule 1.13(c), or take other action pursuant to other applicable rules. Rule 1.13, Comment 6 ("Relation to Other Rules").

Second, what is "substantial"? If the violation of law imputed to the organization is a crime, but the criminal penalties for the misdemeanor are relatively minor, is the violation "substantial"? 1 Geoffrey C. Hazard, Jr. & W. William Hodes, *The Law of Lawyering: A Handbook on the Model Rules of Professional Conduct* at p. 17–38 (3d ed. 2001) argues yes. "Criminal matters must normally be considered *per se* 'substantial' [so that the lawyer] would have no choice but to demand reconsideration or to put the matter to a higher authority within the organization." That conclusion is a reasonable one, although it is unfortunate that neither the Comments nor the Black Letter Rule explicitly define "substantial" to mean any crime, though it would have been easy enough to do so.

> *Example:* Agent of Corporation, in charge of one its retail subsidiaries, keeps the store open on Sunday, in violation of the city's blue laws (forbidding retail stores from being open on Sunday before noon). The penalty for violating this criminal law is only a $100 fine per Sunday, but the store makes an extra $3000 in profit by opening its doors at 11 a.m. instead of noon. Is this criminal violation (which is open and notorious) something that triggers Rule 1.13(b)?

In any event, if the requirements of Rule 1.13(b) are met, the lawyer should proceed in the "best interest" of the entity. The lawyer must weigh the seriousness and consequences of the violation, the scope and nature of the lawyer's representation, the entity's responsibility, the apparent motivation of the person involved, the organization's policies concerning such matters, and anything else deemed relevant.

Depending on how the lawyer weighs such considerations, the lawyer may decide to (1) ask that the matter be reconsidered; (2) advise that a separate legal opinion be sought to present to the organization's appropriate authority; or (3) refer the matter to higher authority. Rule 1.13(b) & Comment 4. If the matter in question is sufficiently serious and important, "referral to higher authority in the organization may be necessary. . . . " Rule 1.13, Comment 4.

Revealing Information and Whistle–Blowing. If the highest authority of the organization (e.g., the Board of Directors) engages in action (or inaction) that is "clearly a violation of law *and* is likely to result in substantial injury to the organization" then the lawyer "*may* reveal information relating to the representation whether or not Rule 1.6 permits such disclosure, *but only if* and to the extent the lawyer reasonably believes necessary to prevent substantial injury to the organization." Rule 1.13(c) (emphasis added). This subsection authorizes the lawyer to reveal information that otherwise he must keep confidential under Rule 1.6.

Withdrawal. Notice that Rule 1.13(c) does not require whistle-blowing. It says "may," not "must." If the lawyer does not whistle-blow, he may have to resign if his continued representation will result in violation of the ethics rules. See Rule 1.16(a)(1); Rule 1.13, Comment 6. If the lawyer resigns, he may still issue a noisy notice of withdrawal and "disaffirm any opinion, document, affirmation or the like." Rule 1.2, Comment 10. Comment 6 of Rule 1.13 reminds us that if the organization's lawyer learns that his services are being used to further a crime or fraud, the "Rules 1.6(b)(2) and 1.6(b)(3) may permit the lawyer to disclose confidential information. In such circumstances Rule 1.2(d) may also be applicable, in which event, withdrawal from the representation under Rule 1.16(a)(1) *may be required*." (emphasis added).

"Related to the Representation." Before Rule 1.13(c) comes into play, first the lawyer has to fill the requirements of Rule 1.13(b), which applies only when a lawyer knows that the organization is intending to act or refuses to act in a way that is a violation of law to the organization, etc. "in a matter related to the representation." See also, Rule 1.13, Comment 6: "It is not necessary that the lawyer's services be used in furtherance of the violation, *but it is required that the matter be related to the lawyer's representation of the organization.*" Rule 1.13, Comment 6.

Example: Lawyer, who represents Corporation in filing patent claims, overhears a conversation of the vice president of a division of Corporation saying that he sold a property of the Corporation after falsely telling the new owners that, as far as he knew, there were no termite problems. Lawyer, who has no responsibilities for selling that property, learned information that is "not related to the representation." Hence, the requirements of Rule 1.13 are not triggered.

The lawyer's authorization to disclose corporate wrong-doing pursuant to Rule 1.13(d) does not apply when the organization has hired the lawyer to represent it to defend against a charge of illegal conduct or to investigate an alleged violation of law. Rule 1.13(d).

Wrongful Discharge. If a lawyer makes disclosures authorized under Rule 1.13(b),(c) and "reasonably believes" that she has been discharged because of those disclosures, or she withdraws from further representation she "shall proceed" as she "reasonably believes necessary to assure that the organization's highest authority is informed of the lawyer's discharge or withdrawal." Rule 1.13(e). The highest authority of a corporation is normally the Board of Directors; sometimes it may be the independent directors. Rule 1.13, Comment 5.

(iv) **Actual or Apparent Representation of the Organization and One or More of Its Constituents**

Occasionally the lawyer representing the organization will also have a relationship with the entity's employees, who may believe that the lawyer also represents their interests. The lawyer should then clarify her role and must explain the identity of the client if it is apparent that the organization's interests are adverse to those people with whom the lawyer is dealing. Rule 1.13(g). See DR 7–104(A).

The lawyer may represent both the organization and one or more of its constituents if the normal requirements of knowing consent are met, and the potential conflict can be waived. See Rules 1.13(g); 1.7; DR 5–105(C). The organization's consent should be given by an appropriate person "other than the individual who is to be represented, or [it may be given] by the shareholders." Rule 1.13(g).

(v) **Representing Partnerships**

The partnership laws of some states treat partnerships as "aggregates" while others may treat partnerships as "entities." The ethical rules do not rely on this distinction. Rule 1.13, Comment 1, makes clear that Rule 1.13 applies equally to unincorporated associations, which is what a partnership is. A partnership has distinct legal rights and duties. It can enter into contracts, and sue in its own name. It may have objectives that are different than some of its members. The lawyer is the agent of the partnership, and may even represent the partnership in a dispute with one or more of the individual partners. In general, the lawyer representing a partnership "represents the entity rather than the individual partners *unless the specific circum-*

stances show otherwise." ABA Formal Opinion 91–361 (July 12, 1991)(emphasis added). In determining whether there is an attorney-client relationship between the partnership lawyer and one or more of its partners, one would look at factors such as whether the lawyer led the individual partner into believing that the lawyer assumed a duty of representing the individual partner; whether the individual partner was individually represented when the partnership was created; and whether there was evidence that the individual partner relied on the lawyer as his or her separate counsel.

(vi) Derivative Suits

In a derivative suit the shareholders sue on behalf of the corporation, which is unwilling to sue. In such cases the corporation may be aligned as a defendant and the other defendants may include corporate officers or directors. May the corporate counsel also defend these other corporate constituents against the claims of the corporate shareholders, or does such dual representation constitute an improper conflict of interest with the corporation? If the shareholder-plaintiffs are successful, the individual defendants may have to pay a money judgment to the corporation. The corporate-defendant then is like a reluctant plaintiff; it benefits from the lawsuit brought against it and the other defendants. A typical case opposing joint representation is *Cannon v. United States Acoustics Corp.,* 398 F.Supp. 209, 219–20 (N.D.Ill.1975), affirmed on this point, 532 F.2d 1118 (7th Cir.1976) (per curiam), which held that "these two ethical considerations [EC 5–15, 5–18] convincingly establish that in a derivative suit the better course is for the corporation to be represented by *independent* counsel from the outset; even though [existing] counsel believes in good faith that no conflict exists." (emphasis added). This new counsel should then advise as to "the role the corporation will play in the litigation." Id. See also Note, *Independent Representation for Corporate Defendants in Derivative Suits,* 74 Yale L.J. 524 (1965).

The Rules reject any *per se* rule regarding this question. Comment 14 provide that if the claim "involves serious charges of wrongdoing by those in control of the organization," then a conflict "may arise" and so the general standards of Rule 1.7 will govern "who should represent the directors and the organization." Rule 1.13, Comment 14.

A leading case is, *In re Oracle Securities Litigation*, 829 F.Supp. 1176 (N.D.Cal. 1993), which involved both a class action and a derivative suit. Because of the class action, the parties needed the court's approval to settle. The parties agreed that settlement of both the class action and derivative claims were contingent on approval of the other. The court found the class settlement fair to those who bought or sold the stock, but the settlement of the derivative action produced few benefits to the company. Further, the company's directors lacked the requisite independence to settle the derivative action and did not consult independent counsel. Legal advice about the settlement had come from the in–house general counsel. In-house lawyers have to live with management, and "are inevitably subservient to the interests of the defendant directors and officers whom they serve." Id. at 1188.

Thus, the *Oracle* court directed the corporation to hire outside counsel to advise the independent directors on the issue. The corporation, before proceeding further with the derivative action, must "retain independent counsel having no prior relationship with the corporation or the individual defendants. Although some courts have gone so far as to appoint corporate counsel in derivative actions, it seems more appropriate here to defer to the independent directors on the selection of corporate counsel. [The] 'new counsel will recognize their duty to represent solely the interests of the corporate entit[y]. And should difficulties arise, the parties or counsel may apply to the court for additional relief.' " In re Oracle Securities Litigation, 829 F.Supp. 1176, 1190 (N.D.Cal.,1993) (internal citations omitted).

(vii) The Lawyer as Director of the Corporate Client

If a law firm does a substantial amount of work for a particular corporate client, it is not uncommon for one of the partners of the firm also to be a member of the corporation's board of directors. This dual membership has potential conflicts. For example, the lawyer on the board may also be a witness to certain events and later may be asked to be both an advocate in litigation and a prospective witness. The client may be confused as to when the lawyer is giving business advice (in her capacity as a director) or legal advice (in her capacity as counsel). If the corporation is sued, the lawyer who is also a director is more likely to find herself a named defendant. At least one major legal malpractice insurer discourages lawyers from serving on boards of public companies, and excludes from its malpractice coverage those lawyers who hold top board positions, such as chairman or vice chairman. Wall Street Journal, Dec. 31, 1993, at 12, col. 1–2.

The Rules acknowledge the problem (the Model Code did not even do that), but otherwise they offer little concrete guidance except to advise that the lawyer should not wear these two hats if "there is a material risk that the dual role will compromise the lawyer's independence of professional judgment . . . " Rule 1.7, Comment 35. ABA Formal Opinion 98–410 (Feb. 27, 1998) recommends that the lawyer-director should be reasonably assured that management and other board members understand the different roles and responsibilities that the corporation's lawyer and a corporate director have. For example, sometimes matters discussed at board meetings will not receive the attorney-client privilege because the lawyer will not be acting in her capacity as lawyer. Conflicts of interest could also arise that require the lawyer to recuse herself as a director, and the lawyer may have to decline representation of the corporation in a particular matter.

(viii) **Private Attorneys on the Board of Legal Services Organizations**
An attorney in a private law firm may also be a member, officer, or director of a legal services organization engaged in pro bono activities, including lawsuits against private parties represented by the attorney's private firm. Such a situation may raise a conflict. Rule 6.3. See Part IX, Section V, B, infra for a discussion of this issue.

(ix) **Examining Client as Adverse Witness**
ABA Formal Opinion 92–367 (Oct. 16, 1992), states that a lawyer, representing Client A, who examines Client B (another client of the same firm) as an adverse witness (or conducts discovery of Client B as an adverse witness), will "ordinarily face a conflict of interest that is disqualifying" unless there is appropriate client consent, even if the law firm's representation of Client A is unrelated to the law firm's representation of

Client *B*. The law firm should decline the new representation if it does not secure appropriate consent. If the conflict arises or becomes foreseeable only *after* both representations are underway, withdrawal from one of the cases may be possible. The lawyer should consider the priority in time of the commencement of the representation as well as the balance of equities in terms of the prejudice arising from the withdrawal. Alternatively, a satisfactory solution may be to retain another lawyer solely for the purpose of examining the client of the principal lawyer.

Rule 1.7, Comment 6 acknowledges this issue: "a directly adverse conflict may arise when a lawyer is required to cross-examine a client who appears as a witness in a lawsuit involving another client, as when the testimony will be damaging to the client who is represented in the lawsuit."

The problem, however, is broader than that, for the lawyer, in cross-examining the witness, may rely on confidential information that is not generally known but that the lawyer knows because of his representation of witness (as a client) in a different matter. Then lawyer's cross-examination of his client should violate Rule 1.7(a)(2), because there is a serious risk that representing the current client in the cross-examination will compromise his duties to keep secret his knowledge of the person he is cross-examining.

Example: Shortly before trial, Plaintiff's trial attorney died. Plaintiff therefore asks Lawyer to represent him in a malpractice case, where Doctor will be an expert witness on behalf of Defendant. However, Lawyer already represents Doctor as client on various unrelated matters (such as drafting a will and drafting a lease on some property that the doctor owns). Cross examining Doctor as an adversary's expert witness "will almost inescapably be a direct adverseness under Rule 1.7(a)," precluding representation, unless (1) both clients consent, and (2) Lawyer reasonably believes that her cross examination of Doctor and her relationship with both clients will not be affected. If her belief is not reasonable, even consent will not cure the conflict. Normally, Lawyer cannot competently cross examine Doctor without challenging Doctor's qualifications and credibility. ABA Formal Opinion 92–367 (Oct. 16, 1992).

(x) Corporate Family Issues

Should separate corporations that are affiliated with each other (parent/subsidiary, or sister corporations) be treated the same for conflict purposes?

In the typical fact situation, Corporation *X*, a client of Law Firm, asks Law Firm to file suit against Corporation *A*. Corporation *A* *is not a client of Law Firm*, but Corporation *B* is, and Corporation *A* is a subsidiary of Corporation *B*. May Law Firm sue Corporation *A* while simultaneously representing its parent, Corporation *B*, on an unrelated matter? A Law Firm, of course, may not represent a client in one matter while suing it in another, even though the two matters are unrelated. Rule 1.7(a), (b)(3) and Comment 17. Should the parent and subsidiary (Corporations *A* and *B*) be treated as one client, or does the Law Firm only represent "the entity," that is, Corporation *B*?

Some cases have assumed that representing a corporation in one matter while undertaking a representation directly adverse to an affiliate of that corporation, such as a parent corporation, subsidiary, or sister corporation, is normally an improper conflict of interest. *Pennwalt Corp. v. Plough, Inc.*, 85 F.R.D. 264 (D.Del.1980).

Some ethics opinions conclude that a lawyer who represents a parent corporation may also represent a party with interests adverse to a subsidiary of the parent corporation in an unrelated matter *if*: the lawyer does not have access to confidential information adverse to the subsidiary, there is no attorney-client relationship between the attorney and subsidiary, and the parent corporation's interests are not materially affected by action against the subsidiary. New York County Lawyers' Association, Committee on Professional Ethics, Opinion 684 (July 8, 1991). California State Bar Standing Committee on Professional Responsibility and Conduct, Formal Opinion 1989–

113 (July 6, 1990), concludes that a lawyer may undertake representation adverse to a wholly owned subsidiary of the existing corporate client so long as the parent corporation is not the alter ego of the subsidiary and the subsidiary has not revealed confidential information to the lawyer with the expectation that it would not be used adversely to the subsidiary. This Opinion advises: "The percentage of ownership of stock, while a factor to consider, is by no means itself determinative."

ABA Formal Opinion 95–390 (Jan. 25, 1995), issued over several dissents, concluded that the Model Rules do not prohibit a law firm from representing a party adverse to a corporation (without consent) merely because the law firm represents, in an unrelated matter, another corporation that is affiliated (e.g., parent, subsidiary, sister corporation) with the adverse corporation. However, there may be circumstances in a particular case where it is reasonable to treat the affiliate as a client, either generally, or for purposes of client conflicts. The ABA Formal Opinion, however, explained that a "lawyer who has no reason to know that his potential adversary is an affiliate of his client will not necessarily violate Rule 1.7 by accepting the new representation without his client's consent."

For example, Formal Opinion 95–39 explained that the nature of the lawyer's dealings with the affiliates of the corporate client are such that they all become clients where the lawyer works for the corporate parent on a stock issue intended to benefit all subsidiaries and collects confidential information from all of them. Or, the lawyer's relationship with the corporate affiliate may lead that affiliate to reasonably believe that it is a client of the lawyer, as when the lawyer for a subsidiary was hired by, and reports directly to, an officer or general counsel of the parent. The relationship between the corporate client and the affiliate may be such that the lawyer must regard the affiliate as its client, such as "where the corporation is the alter ego of the other." The various dissenting opinions, in general, opposed allowing the representation, arguing that a lawyer may not take a position directly adverse to a corporate affiliate of a client.

In short, the lawyer should evaluate how separate the corporate entities really are. Are corporate formalities really observed? To what extent are the two entities really run separately? What is the nature of the charges filed against Corporation *A*? For example, does Corporation *X*'s lawsuit allege fraud or criminal conduct by Corporation *A*? Are the personnel with whom the lawyer must deal the same people? It would be difficult for the lawyer, on Day One, to call the general counsel of Parent Corporation, loyally advise her about the latest strategies on behalf of Subsidiary, and then, on Day Two, call the same general counsel and engage in tough negotiations on behalf of another client suing Parent Corporation in a RICO action.

Rule 1.7, Comment 34 basically codifies this Opinion. The ethics rules do not bar the lawyer unless "the circumstances are such that the affiliate should also be considered a client of the lawyer," or the lawyer and the organizational client have an understanding that the lawyer will avoid representation adverse to the client's affiliates, or "the lawyer's obligations to either the organizational client or the new client are likely to limit materially the lawyer's representation of the other client."

Note: Careful law firms will include parent-subsidiary information in their conflict of interest databases, so that they will be aware of possible conflict issues. They can also avoid problems by clarifying, in the initial retention agreement, the extent to which the client consents to adverse representation against an affiliate of the corporate client. See, Rotunda, *Conflict Problems When Representing Members of Corporate Families*, 72 Notre Dame Law Review 655 (1997).

(xi) Identifying the Client When Representing a Government Entity

The lawyer who represents a government entity (either full time or part time) may not simultaneously represent a private party suing that particular government entity. Rule 1.7(a). However, this lawyer may represent a private client on an unrelated matter against *another* government entity in the same jurisdiction [as long as the more general requirements of Rule 1.7(b) (representation not "materially limited") are also met]. The important point is that the two government entities are not the same client.

That leads to the question of how one determines the identity of the government client when two different government entities are involved. There can be "uncertainty" as to the identity of the client. Rule 1.0, Comment 4. For example, a lawyer may represent a local school district in an employment discrimination suit while also representing private citizens opposing the widening of a county road before the County Planning Commission.

As an initial matter, the lawyer and the government officials will decide the identity of the government client for purposes of the conflict rules. However, the lawyer may not agree to a definition so narrow that it is unreasonable. If there is no express agreement, one looks to the reasonable expectations of the lawyer and the responsible government officials, taking into account such functional considerations as how the government client is legally defined and funded, whether it has independent legal authority for the matter in which the lawyer has been retained (e.g., contracting, litigating, settling), and the extent to which the proposed representation has importance for other government components in the jurisdiction. The lawyer should resolve uncertainty in identifying the government client in favor of disclosure: disclosure of the government representation to private clients the lawyer may be representing against the government, and disclosure to the government client of any arguably conflicting representation. ABA Formal Opinion 97–405 (April, 19, 1997).

Rule 1.13, Comment 9, states that although, "in some circumstances the client may be a specific agency, it is generally the government as a whole." ABA Formal Opinion 97–405, at n. 5, retorts that this statement is not "dispositive." Comment 9 does acknowledge that when a lawyer represents a bureau, the client may be "the department of which the bureau is a part" or it may be "the government as a whole." See also, Scope, ¶ 18. Defining the actual client "is beyond the scope of these Rules." Rule 1.13, Comment 9. The government regulations may make the matter clear.

(c) Attorney for the Insured and Insurer

The insurer, in a typical liability insurance policy, normally agrees to pay any liability within the policy limits, and to provide a lawyer to defend the insured. The insured, in turn, agrees to cooperate. Rule 1.8(f) is relevant in this situation. In particular, see Rule 1.8(f)(2), which stipulates that if the lawyer accepts compensation from someone other than his client (e.g., the insurance company, which earlier agreed to pay for the cost of a lawyer in the event of a lawsuit), then that third party, the insurer, must not interfere with the professional judgment of the lawyer.

Normally the insured and the insurer have a "community of interest," ABA Formal Opinion 282 (May 27, 1950), because both wish to defend vigorously against the claim brought by plaintiff. However, conflicts may arise when the suit is for more than the policy limits and the insured is more anxious than the insurer to settle for an amount less than (or not much more than) the policy limits.

Example: Plaintiff offered to settle for $12,500 and the policy limit was $10,000. Insured was willing to add the additional $2500. Insurer initially authorized settlement of $9500. Lawyer for insured did not relay to the insured this relevant settlement information; nor did Lawyer inform insured that the settlement offer was rejected. After trial, the verdict was $225,000. Attorney believed his sole duty as to settlement was to the insurer, but never so advised insured. Therefore, Attorney could be personally liable for the judgment in excess of policy limits. *Lysick v. Walcom,* 258 Cal.App.2d 136, 65 Cal.Rptr. 406 (1968).

The lawyer's obligation to the insured requires that he respect the insured's confidences. Thus a "lawyer may not defend the insured and at the same time investigate the failure of the insured to give timely notice of the accident involved as required by the insurance policy. Nor may counsel reveal to the insurer the insured's confidential disclosure indicating that his earlier version of the accident is untrue, or that the case is not covered by the insurance policy." Aronson, *Conflict of Interest Problems of the Private Practitioner,* in Professional Responsibility: A Guide for Attorneys 91, 104 (ABA 1978).

The old Model Code merely noted the issue, but gave little concrete guidance, simply stating that "[t]ypically recurring situations involving potentially differing interests" include cases where the lawyer represents "an insured and his insurer." EC 5–17.

The case law is not entirely consistent, but the trend is to consider the lawyer in such cases to owe the duty of loyalty solely to the insured. Rather than treating such a lawyer as representing dual clients (the insured and insurer), much of the case law is best understood as treating the insured as the only client, while the insurer merely pays for the lawyer. Rule 1.8(f)(2) and DR 5–107(B) provide support for this view, because they make clear that, if one person (the "other person") pays the lawyer to render legal services for another, the lawyer may not permit that other person to interfere with the lawyer's professional judgment. See also Rule 1.8, Comment 11; Rule 5.4(c).

If the lawyer represents the insured, the Rules of Professional Conduct (and not the insurance contract) govern the lawyer's obligations to the insured. If the insurance policy authorizes the insurer to control the defense and settle within policy limits in its sole discretion, the lawyer must communicate to the insured these imitations on her representation, preferably early in the representation. After that, the lawyer may settle at the direction of the insured. If the insured tells the lawyer that he objects to a settlement, the lawyer may not settle the claim at the direction of the insurer without giving the insured an opportunity to reject the settlement and assume responsibility for his own defense, at his own expense. ABA Formal Opinion 96–403 (Aug. 2, 1996).

Later, ABA Formal Opinion 01–421 (Feb. 16, 2001), while acknowledging that insurance companies "have a legitimate interest in lawyer billing practices and in controlling expenses," advised that the lawyer may comply with insurance company litigation guidelines only where they do not "materially" impair the lawyer's own independent professional judgment on behalf of the client, or "result in his inability to provide competent representation to the insured." If the insurer insists on imposing these limits, and the insured refuses to consent to the limited representation, then the lawyer must either withdraw from the case or continue to represent the insured without compensation from the insurer.

This Opinion *explicitly* did not purport to decide whether the lawyer represents the insured, the insurer, or both. Instead, it relied on Rule

5.4(c), which provides in part that a lawyer "shall not permit a person who recommends, employs or pays a lawyer to render legal services *for another* to direct or regulate the lawyer's professional judgment in rendering . . . legal services." (emphasis added). However, that Rule assumes that the other person is a client, so the Opinion had to be rejecting the view that the lawyer *only* represents the insurance company. Indeed, the Opinion itself later refers to the insured as the "client-insured." So, at a minimum, the insured is a client. Later still, ABA Formal Opinion 03–430 (July 9, 2003) simply asserted: "Absent a conflict, the lawyer commonly represents the insurance company as well." A footnote at that point only says that "many" jurisdictions have adopted this view. Later, the same ethics opinion acknowledges that whether or not we treat the insurer as a co-client of the insured, "the lawyer's ethical obligations largely are unaffected." Id.

See also, In the Matter of the Rules of Professional Conduct and Insurer Imposed Billing Rules and Procedures, 299 Mont. 321, 2 P.3d 806 (2000). In this case defense counsel (whom the insurers appointed to represent their insureds) brought an original proceeding for declaratory relief. The issue was whether insurer-imposed billing and practice rules violated the Rules of Professional Conduct. The Montana Supreme Court held that (1) the insured is the *sole* client of defense counsel appointed by the insurer, and thus, the insurer is not a co-client of defense counsel; (2) the insurers' prior-approval requirements violated the Rules of Professional Conduct by fundamentally interfering with defense counsels' exercise of their independent judgment and their duty to give undivided loyalty to insureds; and (3) the disclosures, to insurers' third-party auditors, of detailed descriptions of professional services rendered by defense counsel required the contemporaneous, fully informed consent of insureds.

Once "the client-lawyer relationship attaches, the rules of professional responsibility, not the insurance contract or the lawyer's employer, govern the lawyer's ethical obligations to clients." ABA Formal Opinion 03–430 (July 9, 2003)(footnote omitted).

The insurance company's staff counsel (lawyers who are full-time employees of the insurance company) may ethically represent the insured as long as they tell the insured and exercise their professional judgment. In addition, the insurance staff counsel may practice under a trade name, such as a traditional law firm name ("Jane Doe & Associates"). But, they must inform their insureds-clients that they are employees of the insurance company. ABA Formal Opinion 03–430 (July 9, 2003).

While Rule 1.8(f) is often considered in the context of insurer-insured conflicts, it is not limited to that area of the law. For example, if a father hires a lawyer to represent his daughter whom the police arrested on a drunken driving charge, Rule 1.8(f) applies: the lawyer represents the daughter, not the father who is merely paying the bills. Hence, if the daughter decided to plead guilty, that is her decision, because she is the client. If the daughter does not want the father to be told of certain things related to the incident, the lawyer must respect her rights under Rule 1.6 to keep that matter confidential.

Consider another example: Client #1, a current client of Lawyer, recommends to Testator that Lawyer draft a will for Testator. Testator is not yet a client of Lawyer, and Client #1 is a potential beneficiary of Testator's will. Client #1 offers to pay for the cost of drafting the will. If Testator asks Lawyer to draft the will, Lawyer may do so as long as, FIRST, Lawyer complied with Rule 5.4(c) (if a person recommends the lawyer to another or agrees to pay the lawyer to render legal services for another, that person cannot direct or regulate the lawyer's professional judgment); SECOND, if Client #1 pays the lawyer for drafting the will, the lawyer must secure informed consent from Testator under Rule 1.8(f); THIRD, the lawyer should obtain clear guidance from Client #1 and Testator as to the lawyer's use or revelation of protected information of each in representing the other. (The lawyer also must follow Rule 1.7, which is the general conflicts rule governing conflicts among current clients). ABA 02–428 (Aug. 9, 2002).

(d) **Positional Conflicts**

A lawyer may represent Client *A*—in the case of *A vs. X*—seeking a particular legal result on one lawsuit (e.g., that the statute of limitations for tort should be tolled until the malpractice could reasonably have been discovered) and, at the same time, represent Client *B* in a completely different matter—the case of *Z vs. B*—raising very different factual issues. However, may the lawyer, on behalf of *B*, defend the contrary legal position?

The Model Code had no specific rule prohibiting a lawyer from taking different positions in different cases. Client *A* (or Client *B*) may object, but whether the lawyer responds to these objections would be a business question, not an ethical one. The Code only spoke of such positional conflicts in the pro bono context, and in that context specifically *allowed* positional conflicts. See EC 7–17 (lawyer may advocate law reform contrary to interest or desires of client); cf. EC 8–1. See also Fed.R.Civ.P., Rule 8(e)(2) (inconsistent pleadings in same case allowed).

The Rules, in contrast, raise a question about this practice but provide little guidance in answering it. Rule 1.7 Comment 24 acknowledges that "ordinarily" a lawyer "may take inconsistent legal positions in different tribunals at different times on behalf of different clients." But, a conflict of interest exists "if there is a significant risk that a lawyer's action on behalf of one client will materially limit the lawyer's effectiveness in representing another client in a different case; for example, when a decision favoring one client will create a precedent likely to seriously weaken the position taken on behalf of the other client."

So, how do we find out when that happens? Comment 24 simply lists many factors: "where the cases are pending, whether the issue is substantive or procedural, the temporal relationship between the matters, the significance of the issue to the immediate and long-term interests of the clients involved and the clients' reasonable expectations in retaining the lawyer." If there is a "significant risk of material limitation" on the lawyer's representation, then he must secure consent from both parties or "or withdraw from one or both matters." How does the lawyer decide which matter to drop? The Comment does not say.

The ALI, Restatement (Third) of the Law Governing Lawyers, § 128, Illustrations 5 and 6 (Final Draft, 2000) accept the notion of positional conflicts, but the two illustrations read like an ipse dixit rather than a rationale. Illustration 5 allows an attorney to represent Client *A* and Client *B* in damage actions brought in two different federal district courts, where the lawyer will seek to introduce certain evidence in one trial and argue against its admissibility in the other trial. Even though there is "some possibility" that the court's ruling in one case will be published and cited as persuasive authority in the other proceeding, the lawyer "may proceed with both representations without obtaining the consent of the clients involved."

In contrast, consider Illustration 6. The facts are the same, except both cases are now before the U.S. Supreme Court, which will decide the common evidentiary question. This Illustration concludes that now there is a conflict and it is so great that, "[e]ven the informed consent of both Client *A* and Client *B* would be insufficient to cure [it]." Perhaps Clients *A* and *B* (when told of the conflict in Illustration 6) might be surprised to know that their common lawyer had no obligation to tell them when he first planted the seed of the conflict in Illustration 5.

Nowadays, when it is not unusual for firms to have hundreds of members scattered among various cities, there may well be positional conflicts, like those in Illustration 5, going on all the time. Thus, California State Bar Formal Opinion 1989–108 concluded that a lawyer may ethically represent two clients who are not directly adverse to one another even if the lawyer would be arguing opposite sides of the same legal question before the same judge: positional conflicts are "common and prolific in our adversarial system of justice, [and] every time an attorney argues a point of law, it is probable that other clients will then or later be adversely affected." It would be difficult for a conflicts check even to uncover these positional conflicts because legal arguments change all the time, even within the same case. The California Opinion concluded that even if "there is a substantial likelihood that one or both clients will be prejudiced by the representation, the attorney is not acting unethically by continuing the representation," and "if the attorney chooses not to disclose the two representations the attorney does not violate his or her duty of loyalty to the client."

ABA Formal Opinion 93–377 (Oct. 16, 1993) (published long before the 2002 revisions of the Model Rules added Rule 1.7, Comment 24) argued that procedural, discovery and evidentiary issues "almost invariably turn on their particular facts, and it is therefore rare that such issues will give rise to the type of conflict problem that is the subject of this Opinion." Whether that factual assertion is correct is a matter of some dispute. Recall that the American Law Institute's example of a positional conflict involved an evidentiary question.

Note also that the 2002 revisions of the Model Rules only lists "substantive or procedural" as one factor among many.

ABA Formal Opinion 93–377 concluded that, if a lawyer is asked to advocate a position on a *substantive* legal issue that is directly contrary to the position that the lawyer (or any lawyer in the same firm) is urging in a different and unrelated matter in the *same jurisdiction*, then the lawyer should refuse to accept the second representation (or withdraw from the first representation "if otherwise permissible") if there is a "substantial risk" that the lawyer's advocacy on behalf of one client will create a legal precedent that, "even if not binding," is "likely materially to undercut the legal position being urged on behalf of the other client." However, the law firm can continue with both representations if both clients consent after full disclosure.

On the other hand, if the two matters are being litigated in different jurisdictions, *and* there is no substantial risk that either representation will be adversely affected by the other, the lawyer may proceed with both representations. In determining whether there is this substantial risk, this ABA Formal Opinion advised that the lawyer should consider, for example, whether the issue is one of federal law, where one federal judge will respectfully consider the decision of another federal judge, even if they are not in the same district or state; whether the issue is so important that its determination is likely to affect the ultimate outcome of the case; and whether the firm might "soft-pedal" or deemphasize certain arguments in order to avoid affecting the other case. See also, John Dzienkowski, *Positional Conflicts of Interest*, 71 Tex. L. Rev. 457 (1993).

(e) Moving to Disqualify Opposing Counsel

If conflicts develop during litigation, counsel may move to disqualify opposing counsel. If the conflict is such that it "taints" the fact finding process or fairness of the trial, the courts should grant the motion. *Board of Education of City of New York v. Nyquist*, 590 F.2d 1241 (2d Cir.1979). However, if the alleged ethical violation does not affect the fact finding process or the fairness of the trial (a claim by defendant that plaintiff's lawyer improperly solicited plaintiff will not taint the fact finding process), then the court should leave any enforcement of the alleged violation to the disciplinary process. See, *Lefrak v. Arabian American Oil Co.*, 527 F.2d 1136 (2d Cir.1975). Prior to 2002, a Comment to Rule 1.7 of the Model Rules advised that counsel should not use this disqualification device as a "technique of harassment." The 2002 revisions dropped this caveat because, the Reporter's Notes tell us, "it addresses questions outside the disciplinary context."

(f) Aggregate Settlements

The lawyer, on behalf of her multiple clients, may negotiate an aggregate settlement of the civil claims, or an agreement of guilty or nolo contendere pleas covering multiple clients in a criminal case. In such cases each client gives informed consent, which must include "disclosure of the existence and nature of all the claims or pleas involved and of the participation of each person in the settlement." Rule 1.8(g). Accord, DR 5–106(A).

Example: Attorney represents 18 individual plaintiffs who entered into a prior agreement that majority rule would govern acceptance of a settlement. Defendant offered $155,000 for distribution to the group, which voted 13–5 to accept it. Notwithstanding the prior agreement, each plaintiff has a right to agree or refuse to agree once the settlement was made known to them. *Hayes v. Eagle–Picher Industries, Inc.,* 513 F.2d 892 (10th Cir.1975).

A Writing: The 2002 revisions to Rule 1.8(g) added a new requirement: the informed consent must be reflected "in a writing signed by the client." It is not enough for the lawyer to send each of the clients a letter describing the terms of the settlement; the client must *sign* the letter or other writing. Rule 1.8(g) & Comment 13. The signature can be an electronic symbol. Rule 1.0(n).

Class Actions: If the lawyer represents a class, she cannot secure such a writing from every member of the class, but she should comply with the procedural rules of the court regulating notice to class members. Rule 1.8, Comment 13.

(g) Job Negotiations with Adverse Firm or Party

Many years ago, when a lawyer joined a law firm, it was, like marriage, typically for life. In modern times, when a lawyer joins a law firm, it is, like modern marriage, typically not for life. ABA Formal Opinion 96–400 (Jan. 24, 1996) discusses the situation where a lawyer is considering employment with a firm or party that she is opposing in a matter on behalf of a client. Her employment pursuits may materially limit her representation within the meaning of Rule 1.7. Therefore, the ABA Opinion advises that the lawyer "must consult with his client and obtain the client's consent before that point in the discussions when such discussions are reasonably likely to materially interfere with the lawyer's professional judgment." If the lawyer has a limited role in the matter, he ordinarily will consult with his supervisor rather than with the client directly. The time to consult and secure consent will be when the lawyer agrees "to engage in substantive discussions of his experience, clients, or business potential, or the terms of a possible association, with the opposing firm or party."

If the client does not give consent, the lawyer may not pursue the discussions until he is permitted to withdraw from the matter pursuant to Rule 1.16. ABA Formal Opinion 96–400 advises that the negotiating lawyer's conflict of interest is *not imputed* to the other lawyers in his firm, but those other lawyers must evaluate whether they have a conflict because of their own interest in their colleague's negotiations. For example, a colleague may also have an interest in leaving the law firm along with the negotiating lawyer.

Imputation. Rule 1.7, Comment 10, which the 2002 revisions added to the Model Rules, warns that, if a lawyer is discussing employment with the opponent of his client or with the law firm representing that opponent, that situation "could" materially limit his representation of his client. If so, the lawyer has a conflict, but that conflict is "personal," under Rule 1.7(a)(2) and therefore *not imputed* to the other members of his law firm under Rule 1.10(a).

(h) When Lawyer Represents Another Lawyer When the Two Lawyers Represent Clients Whose Interests are Adverse

Sometimes a lawyer proposes to form an attorney-client relationship with another lawyer, while the two lawyers are representing clients whose interests are adverse. For example, Lawyer #1 may represent Lawyer #2 (who is securing a divorce) while Lawyer #1 also represents client #1 who is suing client #2 (represented by Lawyer #2) on a real estate transaction. ABA Formal Opinion 97–406 (April 19, 1997) advises there is no per se prohibition. Instead, the issue is whether the effect of Lawyer #1's representation of Lawyer #2 is "materially limited," within the meaning of Rule 1.7(a)(2). That depends on factors such as the relative size of the fee expected, the relative importance of each case to each lawyer and their clients, the sensitivity of the matter, the similarity of the subject matter or issues involved, and the nature of the relationship of each lawyer to the other and to their third-party clients. For example, a material limitation may exist if a representing lawyer is unwilling to seek sanctions against his opponent, because that opponent is also his client in an unrelated matter.

If the representation of the other lawyer will "materially limit" the representation of the third-party client, but the lawyer reasonably believes that his personal representation of the opposing lawyer will not adversely affect his representation of his other client (the third-party client), then, Opinion 97–406 advises the lawyer to consult with the third-party client and secure her consent before accepting the representation.

If the lawyer concludes that the representation is not "materially limited," then ABA Formal Opinion 97–406 announced, without discussion, that: "neither lawyer nor his or her third-party client may compel the opposing lawyer to decline, or to withdraw from a representation of a third-party client that the opposing lawyer has concluded is permissible under the analysis above."

In some cases, the conflict is so great that the lawyer cannot reasonably ask his client to consent. Rule 1.7(b)(1). For example, Lawyer #1 is representing Lawyer #2 in disciplinary charges arising out of Lawyer #2's handling of a case before Judge Alpha. A third-party client now asks Lawyer #1 to defend him in a suit that Lawyer #2 has filed against him, also pending before Judge Alpha. Lawyer #1's duties of loyalty and confidentiality may create "an unconsentable conflict." Opinion 97–406.

Opinion 97–406 also declared that any conflict that a represented lawyer may have because of his *personal* interest in the separate matter is not necessarily imputed to the other lawyers in the firm. Imputation would depend "on the nature of the separate matter and the knowledge of the other lawyers in the firm." Later, with the 2002 revisions, the ABA Model Rules accept the conclusion that this type of *personal* conflict need *not* be imputed to other members of the firm. Rule 1.10(a).

(i) **The Lawyer as Third–Party Neutral, Such As Arbitrator or Mediator**
Rule 2.4 governs the situation where the lawyer represents no clients but serves as a third-party neutral such as an arbitrator or mediator or facilitator. Rule 2.4 is a completely new Rule that the ABA added in the 2002 revisions to the Model Rules.

One normally does not have to be a lawyer to be a third-party neutral, but if one is a lawyer, she should inform the unrepresented parties that she is not representing them and explain to them what this means in terms that they can understand. Rule 2.4(b) & Comment 3. For example, there is no attorney-client privilege between the third-party neutral and the parties to the arbitration, mediation, etc.

If a lawyer was a third-party neutral in a matter, she can later represent one of the parties under the same circumstances that a former judge can later represent one of the parties. These situations are all governed by Rule 1.12, dealing with "Former Judge, Arbitrator, Mediator or Other Third–Party Neutral."

Under Rule 1.12, if Lawyer Alpha was a third-party neutral, she cannot later represent one of the parties on that matter unless all parties consent *and* this consent is confirmed in writing. Rule 1.12(a). However, there is no imputation; in other words, Alpha's law firm can represent one of the parties if the firm screens Alpha, gives written notice to the other parties and the relevant tribunal, and is "apportioned no part of the fee." Rule 1.12(c).

Remember, being "apportioned no part of the fee" only means that Alpha cannot receive money "directly related" to this particular case. She can continue to receive her regular salary or partnership share established by prior independent agreement, even though that partnership share (3% of the partnership profits that year) will include the income from all cases including the case where she earlier was the third-party neutral. Rule 1.12, Comment 4.

(j) **Comparing the Lawyer as a Third–Party Neutral to the Lawyer As Representing Multiple Parties**
Prior to the 2002 revisions, the Model Rules had a Rule 2.2, "Intermediary." ABA Commission 2000 (the group of lawyers and others charged with revising the Model Rules) recommended delet-

ing Rule 2.2 and moving any discussion of common representation to Rule 1.7. The ABA followed these recommendations. You will find that the essence of Rule 2.2 is now found in Comments 29–33 of Rule 1.7, "Special Considerations in Common Representations."

The lawyer may act as a lawyer with multiple clients (i.e., represent all clients), and the conflicts issues relating to that are found mainly in Rule 1.7. Or the lawyer may act as an arbitrator or mediator (and represent no clients), and that is governed by Rule 2.4.

The original idea behind Rule 2.2 (now deleted) was to permit common representation when the circumstances were such that the potential benefits for the various clients outweighed the potential risks. Rule 2.2, however, contained several limitations that were not present in Rule 1.7; for example, former Rule 2.2 imposed a flat prohibition on a lawyer continuing to represent one client and not the other if intermediation failed, even though neither client objects. Consequently, if lawyers did not want to be bound by such limitations, they would choose to consider the representation as falling under Rule 1.7 rather than Rule 2.2; nothing in former Rule 2.2 or any other Rules dictated a contrary result.

Hence, in 2002, the ABA deleted old Rule 2.2 and dealt with the issues in Comments 29–33 of Rule 1.7. These Comments explain that the lawyer cannot represent multiple clients if contentious litigation or negotiations between them are imminent or contemplated. Nor can the lawyer accept multiple representation if the lawyer is unlikely to be impartial in dealing with his multiple clients; for example, if he has represented Client X for many years, it may well be the case that he cannot represent both Client X and new Client Y in a particular matter, particularly if the lawyer does not tell new Client Y of the lawyer's long-term relationship (both in the past and expected in the future).

If Lawyer represents both Clients X and Client Y, the normal rule is that there is no attorney-client privilege as between them—that is, Client X cannot expect Lawyer to keep secrets from Client Y when Lawyer represents both Client X & Client Y. Therefore Lawyer must advise both Clients X & Y of this fact and obtain their informed consent prior to undertaking the joint representation. However, there can be situations where Client X & Y freely consent to telling their common lawyer some matter that they both expect their lawyer not to reveal to the other client, such as a trade secret. Rule 1.7, Comment 31.

C. Successive Representation

A lawyer cannot represent a new client in a matter adverse to a former client if to do so results in a breach of loyalty or confidence to the former client.

The rule developed to determine conflicts in subsequent representation cases was, initially, a judicial rule, incorporated into the old Model Code only by inference in Canons 4, 5, and 9. Judge Weinfeld developed the basic test in the leading case of *T.C. Theatre Corp. v. Warner Brothers Pictures, Inc.,* 113 F.Supp. 265, 268–69 (S.D.N.Y.1953):

> "[T]he former client need show no more than that the matters embraced within the pending suit wherein his former attorney appears on behalf of his adversary are *substantially related* to the matters or cause of action wherein the attorney previously represented him, the former client. The Court will assume that during the course of the former representation confidences were disclosed to the attorney bearing on the subject matter of the representation. It will not inquire into their nature and extent. Only in this manner can the lawyer's duty of absolute fidelity be enforced and the spirit of the rule relating to privileged communications be maintained." [emphasis added].

Judge Weinfeld's "substantial relationship" test for subsequent representation cases has been quoted, relied on, cited, and followed by a host of other court decisions. E.g., *Emle Industries, Inc. v. Patentex, Inc.,* 478 F.2d 562, 570–71 (2d Cir.1973); *Schloetter v. Railoc of Indiana, Inc.,* 546 F.2d 706, 710–11 (7th Cir.1976).

The Rules, unlike the former Code, have an explicit section dealing with this problem. Rule 1.9 recognizes two interests that must be protected: loyalty and client confidences.

As a matter of client loyalty, whether or not the lawyer, in the case of *A vs. B*, learned from Client *A* secret or confidential information, that particular lawyer cannot now "switch sides" in the *same* matter and represent Client *B*. Rule 1.9(a), & Comments 1, 2, 8. "Thus, a lawyer could not properly seek to rescind on behalf of a new client a contract [that this lawyer had] drafted on behalf of the former client." Rule 1.9, Comment 1.

If the matter is not exactly the same, the lawyer still may not "switch sides" if the matters are "substantially related." *T.C. Theatre Corp.,* supra; Rule 1.9(a);

H. Drinker, Legal Ethics 115 (1953). To determine whether the matters are so related, is a question of degree. If the lawyer is involved in a "specific transaction" as opposed to a "recurrently handled type of problem," then the switching of sides is a direct breach of loyalty, and a conflict exists in the subsequent representation. In contrast, if the matter was a "recurrently handled type of problem," the lawyer may represent a new client "in a wholly distinct problem of that [general] type even though the subsequent representation involves a position adverse to the prior client." Rule 1.9, Comment 2.

Because the basic concern of Rule 1.9 is to protect the confidences of the former client (and to protect the loyalty to the extent that the lawyer is actually switching sides in the same case), a matter is "substantially related," if it involves "the same transaction or legal dispute or if there otherwise is a substantial risk that confidential factual information as would normally have been obtained in the prior representation would materially advance the client's position in the subsequent matter." Rule 1.9, Comment 3. The touchstone, in other words, is whether there are relevant confidences.

Example: Lawyer "L" has represented several banks over the years. However, a year ago he resigned from representing any of these banks when he changed law firms. He still practices in the same locality. He now plans to defend a debtor in a collection matter. Because L no longer has any banker clients, and the new collection suit is a matter unrelated to his previous employment, his former clients may not prevent him from undertaking the new representation. L need not obtain the consent of his former clients nor even inform them of his plan. Geoffrey C. Hazard, Jr. & W. William Hodes, *The Law of Lawyering: A Handbook on the Model Rules of Professional Conduct* § 13.7, Illustration 13–4, at p. 13–19 to 13–20 (3d ed. 2001).

Example: Lawyer formerly represented a client in securing environmental permits to build a shopping center. She is precluded from representing neighbors seeking to oppose rezoning of the property on the basis of environmental considerations; however, she is not precluded, on the grounds of substantial relationship, from defending a tenant of the completed shopping center in resisting eviction for nonpayment of rent. Rule 1.9, Comment 3.

Both the Rules and Code also prohibit the lawyer from using confidential or secret information acquired from the former client on behalf of a new client.

The case law, interpreting the Code, reached this result by having the definition of "substantial relationship" turn on "the possibility, or appearance thereof, that confidential information might have been given to the attorney in relation to the subsequent matter in which disqualification is sought." *Westinghouse Electric Corp. v. Gulf Oil Corp.*, 588 F.2d 221, 224 (7th Cir.1978). See also, *Westinghouse Electric Corp. v. Kerr–McGee Corp.*, 580 F.2d 1311, 1321 & n.28 (7th Cir. 1978)(holding that there was a conflict even though the law firm erected what it called a "Chinese Wall" to keep client confidences given to lawyers in the law firm's Chicago office secret from lawyers in the Washington, DC office of the same law firm). Rules 1.9(c)(1) reaches this same result by providing that the lawyer may not "use information relating to the representation to the disadvantage of the former client. . . . " See also, Rule 1.9(b)(2).

This protection of client confidences has some limits, or else a lawyer could never sue a former client. Thus it is not disqualifying if a lawyer had access to *"general information concerning the personality of a client,* which is always helpful in later suits against that client. . . ." *Unified Sewerage Agency of Washington County, Oregon v. Jelco Inc.,* 646 F.2d 1339, 1351 (9th Cir.1981). "Information that has been disclosed to the public or to other parties adverse to the former client ordinarily will not be disqualifying." Comment 3.

Similarly, there is no need to protect the former client's secret information if that information has become "generally known," Rule 1.9(c)(1), or if the former client consents to the subsequent representation. However, in order for this consent to be valid, the former client must give informed consent "confirmed in writing." Rule 1.9(a). This "confirmed in writing" requirement does *not* mandate that the former client *sign* anything; instead, it is sufficient if there is "writing that a lawyer promptly transmits to the person confirming an oral informed consent." Rule 1.0(b). If the lawyer cannot feasibly obtain or transmit the writing at the time the person gives informed consent, "then the lawyer must obtain or transmit it within a reasonable time thereafter." Id.

There is also no need to protect the former client's confidences if the other exceptions to the normal rule protecting client confidences are applicable. Rule 1.6; DR 4–101(C).

Let us assume that Lawyer was with *Firm X* (which represents *Client #1*) and then leaves *Law Firm X* to join *Law Firm Y*. While Lawyer was with the first firm, he was disqualified because someone else in the firm had the knowledge of the client's secrets and that knowledge is imputed to all other members of the law firm. When Lawyer leaves *Firm X* and joins *Law Firm Y*, does Lawyer infect *Law Firm Y* with his *imputed* knowledge?

The answer is NO. Rule 1.9(b) provides there is no need to limit the practice of a lawyer because of client secrets, when the lawyer has no actual (but only imputed) knowledge of those secrets. Thus, if Lawyer leaves *Firm X* (which represents *Client #1*) and then joins *Firm Y*, Lawyer A is not precluded from representing *Client #2*, even though Client #2's interests are materially adverse to *Client #1*, *if* Lawyer A never acquired any confidential or secret information about *Client #1* while Lawyer A was a member of *Firm X*. Cf. also, Rule 1.10(b). Otherwise, Lawyer A would be a Typhoid Mary, infecting any firm he joined with knowledge that he never actually had, but only knowledge that was imputed to him while he was with his original firm.

As to questions involving a *former government* attorney's representation against the government, see Part VI, section II, infra. The general principle to remember is that it is Rule 1.11, not Rule 1.9(a), or (b), that governs the conflict of interest obligations of a former government lawyer. However, a former government lawyer is still subject to Rule 1.9(c), which prohibits the lawyer from using information relating to her representation of the government (her former client) to the government's disadvantage except where the information has become generally known. ABA Formal Opinion 97–409 (Aug. 2, 1997); Rule 1.10(a)(1).

D. The Attorney's Personal and Financial Interests

1. Nonfinancial Interests
Lack of Belief in the Client's Cause

The mere fact that the lawyer does not believe in the justness of the client's cause is not disqualifying. Cf. EC 2–29; Rule 1.2(b) (lawyer's representation is not an endorsement of client's views). However, if the intensity of the lawyer's personal feelings is so great that she could not provide competent representation, then she should not accept the case. EC 2–30; EC 5–1; DR 5–101(A); Rule 1.16(a).

Sexual Relations with the Client

Lawyers who take unfair advantage of their clients violate their fiduciary obligations. There would be a violation of the lawyer's fiduciary obligations if the lawyer unfairly exploited the fiduciary relationship, or, during the course of the representation, entered into a sexual relationship with the client that impaired the lawyer's ability to act competently. The client's consent may not avoid the ethical problem because the lawyer's potential undue influence and the client's "emotional vulnerability" vitiate and impair "meaningful consent," ABA Formal Opinion 92–356 (July 6, 1992). Though the Model Code did not have special rules that deal precisely with the issue of a lawyer's sexual relations with a client, several states adopted specific disciplinary rules and statutes restricting sex between attorneys and their clients. See, Calif. Bus. & Prof. Code, §§ 6106.7–6106.8; Calif. Rules of Prof. Conduct, Rule 3–120. In 2002, the ABA Model Rules finally added Rule 1.8(j), providing that a lawyer "shall not have sexual relations with a client unless a consensual sexual relationship exited between them when the client-lawyer relationship commenced." See also Comments 17–19.

> **Imputation.** Rule 1.10 does *not* automatically impute this disqualification, so that if a lawyer has sexual relations with a person, someone else in that lawyer's firm can represent that person. See also, Rule 1.8(k).

> **Corporations.** Comment 19 of Rule 1.8 advises that if lawyer represents an organization such as a corporation, the lawyer should not have a sexual relationship with a constituent of that organization who supervises or regularly consults with that lawyer.

Lawyers also can be subject to malpractice. For example, a Rhode Island jury awarded a client $25,000 compensatory and $250,000 punitive damages for malpractice because of her sexual relationship with her lawyer. She testified that the lawyer handling her divorce forced her to have sex by threatening to work actively to lose custody of her child. The court did not require the client to prove that there was any adverse result in the underlying legal work done for her. (She was awarded custody, alimony, child support, and 60% of the marital assets.) *Lawyer Liable for Coerced Sex*, ABA Journal, Feb. 1993, at 24. See, Howard Brill, *Sex with the Client: Ten Reasons to Say "No!,"* 33 Santa Clara L. Rev. 651 (1993).

2. Financial Interests

(a) Business Dealings With Others

The lawyer may be involved with business dealings with others that may affect the lawyer's ability to represent the client. There is a conflict if these interests are significant and material enough to affect the lawyer's judgment. The lawyer in such cases should not accept the case unless he or she reasonably believes that the representation will not be adversely affected and the client consents. Rule 1.7(a)(2); DR 5–101(A).

(b) Business Dealings With the Client

If the lawyer deals with the client in a business transaction, the lawyer may overreach the client, who may be relying on the lawyer's independent legal judgment. The old Model Code and the Rules attempt to deal with this problem in slightly different ways.

The Code flatly forbad business relations with the client if two conditions exist: (1) the lawyer and client have differing interests, and (2) the client expects the lawyer to exercise his or her legal judgment for the protection of the client. DR 5–104(A). The client could nonetheless consent to the lawyer's involvement.

The Code also recommended that lawyers should not "seek to persuade" their clients to permit them to invest in the client's business or undertaking. EC 5–3. Even if the lawyer's efforts at persuasion are unsuccessful, he has violated this ethical aspiration by attempting to persuade the client.

The Rules do not focus on the client's expectation that the lawyer will exercise professional judgment on behalf of the client. Rather, they allow client business dealings with the lawyer if: (1) the transaction is fair and reasonable to the client; (2) the lawyer transmit the terms of the transaction to the client *in writing* so that the client can understand them; (3) the lawyer gives the client a reasonable opportunity to consult another lawyer (whether or not the client actually exercises that opportunity); and (4) the client consents *in a writing* that the *client signs.* This writing must disclose whether the client thinks that the lawyer is representing the client in the transaction. Rule 1.8(a). Rule 1.8 does not specifically forbid the lawyer from seeking to invest in the client's enterprise. (Note, however, that Rule 1.8(c) forbids the lawyer from soliciting any substantial gift from the client.)

Rule 1.8(a) applies even if the business transaction is not closely related to the lawyer's representation of the client. For example, Lawyer, who drafted a will for Client, learns that Client needs money for a business deal. Lawyer offers to lend the money to Client. The requirements of Rule 1.8(a) apply. Comment 1.

The Model Rules have no per se prohibition from a lawyer acquiring an ownership interest in a client, either as payment of a fee or as an investment opportunity (e.g., stock in the client), as long as the lawyer complies with all the requirements of Rule 1.8(a). In addition, the fee must be reasonable. The lawyer must make sure that he avoids conflicts between the client's interest and the lawyer's personal economic interests, as required by Rule 1.7(b). The lawyer must also make sure that, pursuant to Rule 2.1, he is exercising independent judgment in advising the client concerning legal matters. ABA Formal Opinion 00–418 (July 7, 2000).

See also, ABA Formal Opinion 02–427 (May 31, 2002), advising that a lawyer who acquires a contractual security interest in a client's property to secure payment of fees earned or to be earned must comply with Rule 1.8(a)[business dealings with client]. And, a lawyer who acquires a security interest in the subject matter of litigation in which the lawyer represents the client must comply with Rule 1.8(i)[governing propriety interests in litigation].

The ethics rules impose duties on lawyers, not clients. Hence, it is not the duty of the client, even if sophisticated, to recognize the conflict. Rather it is the duty of the lawyer to bring the matter to the client's attention. If the lawyer represents a client in a transaction, and also receives a personal benefit in addition to the client's fee, then the lawyer's ethical obligation is "not always fulfilled by merely disclosing" the lawyer's personal stake, explaining the potential consequences, and obtaining consent. The lawyer "must always ensure that his or her personal interest does not interfere with the unfettered exercise of professional judgment the client is entitled to expect under the circumstances. The best way to achieve this, of course, is to see that the client has independent advice." *Matter of Breen,* 171 Ariz. 250, 254, 830 P.2d 462, 466 (1992).

(c) Gifts From the Client

(i) That Do Not Require Instruments
Because of the danger that the lawyer may overreach the client and abuse the fiduciary relationship, there are certain restrictions that a lawyer should observe when accepting client gifts.

Some gifts do not involve the drafting of any instruments. In contrast, a gift given by a will demands a legal instrument that needs to be drafted. A typical case involving no legal instrument occurs when the client, happy with the lawyer's work, decides to give a gift, which may be nominal (a basket of fruit) or substantial (e.g., a large amount of cash in addition to the agreed fee, or an expensive gold watch). The Code had no disciplinary rule dealing with such cases, but an Ethical Consideration advised the lawyer to tell the client to get "disinterested advice from an independent competent person who is cognizant of all the circumstances." EC 5–5.

Because the Code draws no distinction between substantial versus nominal gifts, it went too far in regulating client gifts.

In contrast, the Rules try to deal with these problems. After the 2002 revisions, the Rules, first, prohibit the lawyer from soliciting any "substantial" gift from his client, Rule 1.8(c), whether or not the transfer of the gift calls for the drafting of a legal instrument.

In addition, the lawyer may not draft a legal instrument for the client that gives a substantial gift to the lawyer or anyone related to the lawyer, unless the lawyer or other recipient is related to the client. Rule 1.8(c). For example, if the lawyer and client are related, the lawyer can prepare an instrument that transfers ownership of the client's car and gives it to the lawyer or another relative of the client.

What does it mean to be "related"? We are all brothers under the skin, so the Rules define "related" to mean spouse, child, parent, grandchild or grandparent or anyone whom the client or lawyer maintain a close, familiar relationship. Rule 1.8(a).

The Comment goes beyond the Rule and advises that the lawyer may accept any gift that meets "general standards of fairness." Nominal gifts may simply be accepted. Rule 1.8, Comment 6.

Rule 1.8 does not prohibit lawyers from accepting substantial gifts not solicited by the lawyer, but the client can later void these gifts under the common law doctrine of undue influence, which treats client gifts as "presumptively fraudulent." Comment 6.

If the client is not a relative of the donee, and if the gift is substantial, *and* if its effectuation requires that a legal instrument be drafted, then another lawyer should offer "detached advice." Rule 1.8 Comment 7. If the gift is substantial but does not require an instrument, then Rule 1.8(c) is inapplicable and Comment 6 offers no guidance except the "general standards of fairness" test.

(ii) Lawyer Seeking to Be Named as Executor

Lawyers that do estate work often ask the client to name the lawyer or a member of the lawyer's firm executor of the client's estate, or a be named to a similar lucrative fiduciary position. A Comment to Rule 1.8 simply announces that Rule 1.8 does not forbid lawyers from seeking such appointments. Comment 8. The general conflicts of interest provision of Rule 1.7 applies if there is a "significant risk" that the lawyer's interest in being appointed will "materially limit" the lawyer's judgment in advising the client whom to choose. In other words, the lawyer should not be recommending himself when other executors are better and cost less. That is why the lawyer must advise the client of the relevant facts concerning the nature and extent of the lawyer's financial interest in the appointment and also "the availability of alternative candidates for the position."

In general, the Model Rules do not prohibit a lawyer who is serving as fiduciary of an estate or trust from appointing himself or other lawyers in his firm to represent him in that capacity. However, the compensation for the legal services must be reasonable under Rule 1.5(a), taking into account the compensation for fiduciary services. A lawyer serving as fiduciary of an estate or trust and the lawyer's firm must also satisfy the requirements of Rule 1.7 before representing a beneficiary or creditor of the estate or trust. The lawyer serving as executor of the estate and his law firm ordinarily would be prohibited from representing the beneficiary or creditor in claims against the trust or estate regardless of the client's consent. ABA Formal Opinion 02–426 (May 31, 2002).

(iii) That Require Instruments

If the effectuation of the gift requires an instrument, such as a will, the Rules require that the lawyer must not solicit such a gift for himself or his relative. In addition, he may not prepare the instrument unless the lawyer or other recipient is related to the donor. The Rules do not regulate cases where the client/donor is related to the donee. Rule 1.8(c), Comments 6–7.

If the prohibition of Rule 1.8(c) applies, its prohibition is imputed to all members of the lawyer's firm. Rule 1.8(k).

Example: Client asks Lawyer *A* to draft a will giving Lawyer *A*'s son a large sum of money. Lawyer *A* says: "I cannot draft this instrument, but my partner *B* can do it."

Lawyers *A* and *B* have violated Rule 1.8(c), (k)

Lawyer *A* now leaves the firm and joins another one. When Client makes the same request Lawyer *A* says: "I cannot draft the will but my good friend and *former* law partner, Lawyer *B* can."

Lawyers *A* and *B* have not violated 1.8(c), (k).

(d) Publication Rights

Consider the situation where the lawyer negotiates with the client for publication rights to a particular matter *before* that matter has ended and while the lawyer is still in the employ of the client. There is a danger that the lawyer, in bargaining with the client, may be able to overreach. For example, the client, needing the lawyer's services, may feel pressured to waive the attorney-client privilege, which the attorney wants, so that he can later write a more interesting book. Also, the lawyer, in his representation of the client, may be consciously or unconsciously influenced to "enhance the value of his publication rights to the prejudice of his client." EC 5–4. Accord, Rule 1.8, Comment 9.

The old Model Code prohibited the lawyer from acquiring from the client an interest in publication rights relating to the subject matter "[p]rior to the conclusion of all aspects of the matter giving rise to his employment . . . " DR 5–104(B). Out of an overabundance of caution, Code prohibited acquiring such rights if the matter giving rise to the employment still continues, even though another lawyer now represents the client and the first lawyer's employment regarding that matter has ended. EC 5–4. The Rules, in contrast, only prohibit acquiring such rights "[p]rior to the conclusion of representation of a client . . . " Rule 1.8(d).

The Code refers to "publication rights," but the Rules use a term that the drafters thought more expansive—"literary or media rights."

Rule 1.8(d) exists not only to protect the client but to protect the interest of the judicial system in competent representation. Therefore the Rules do not allow client waiver of these restrictions. California, ignoring these systemic interests and basing its decision on the California Rules—which in this respect are not modeled on the Rules—does allow client waiver. *Maxwell v. Superior Court of Los Angeles County*, 30 Cal.3d 606, 180 Cal.Rptr. 177, 639 P.2d 248 (1982).

If the lawyer represents the client in a dispute or other transaction concerning literary property, e.g., a copyright claim, the lawyer may contract for a reasonable contingent fee, that is, a reasonable share of the ownership of the literary property, assuming no other rules are violated. The prohibition on publication rights is not meant to cover this situation. Rule 1.8, Comment 9.

This restriction is imputed to all members of the firm. Rule 1.8(k).

(e) **Financial Advances to the Client**
When representing a client in a matter involving litigation the lawyer may not provide general financial assistance to the client (e.g., living expenses), but may advance or guarantee the expenses of litigation (e.g., the expenses of a medical examination, the cost of an expert witness).

The Code had a specific requirement that the client must remain "ultimately liable," DR 5–103(B), but also advised (inconsistently) that (1) lawyers should not normally sue the client to collect their fees except to prevent fraud or gross imposition, EC 2–23, and that (2) lawyers should charge the less fortunate clients no fee or a smaller fee. EC 2–16.

The Rules are more straightforward on this point. They eliminate the requirement of client reimbursement and also allow the lawyer to pay directly an indigent's litigation expenses and court costs without the client remaining ultimately liable. Rule 1.8(e)(1), (2).

This restriction is imputed to all members of the firm. Rule 1.8(k).

ABA Formal Opinion 04–432 applied Rule 1.8(k) and Rule 1.7 to the situation where the client asks the lawyer to post bail for her client. It concluded that "neither Model Rule 1.7 nor Model Rule 1.8(e) creates a *per se* prohibition against a lawyer advancing funds for, or subjecting assets to the risk of loss with respect to, a defendant client's bail bond." However, the lawyer "must reasonably believe that her resulting personal interest does not create a significant risk that her representation of the client will be materially limited." Thus, other "than in relatively unusual circumstances, the lawyer should conclude that taking such action would be improper."

(f) Limiting Malpractice Liability

The lawyer may not require the client to enter into an agreement *prospectively* limiting the lawyer's liability to that client for malpractice. Rule 1.8(h); DR 6–102(A). The old Model Code did not explicitly use the word "prospectively," but it must have been its intent. Otherwise if the former client sued the lawyer for malpractice, the former client (who now is separately represented by new counsel) could not settle with, and release, the lawyer regarding that claim.

ABA Formal Opinion 96–401 (Aug. 2, 1996), interpreting Rule 1.8(h), concluded that a lawyer may practice in a limited liability partnership if the jurisdiction's applicable law provides that the particular lawyer rendering legal services remains personally liable to the client, even though the individual lawyers have no vicarious liability for the professional actions of other lawyers in the firm. The lawyer must accurately describe the form of the business organization. Using the abbreviated designation (e.g., LLP or LLLP) is sufficient disclosure.

The Rules, unlike the Code, specifically allow the lawyer to limit her liability prospectively if the client is "independently represented in making the agreement . . . " Rule 1.8(h)(1). The rationale is that the purpose of the rule regarding malpractice liability is to prevent the attorney from overreaching the client, a fear that is unfounded if the client has separate counsel on this issue.

At first, it may be difficult to imagine situations where a lawyer would send a client down the hall to another attorney in a different law firm for the purposes of securing advice so that the client can waive malpractice liability. (One might worry that the client, once he was sent to a different law firm, might not return.) However, the typical case would probably not involve individual clients. A corporation's inside counsel, when hiring outside counsel, might find it reasonable to waive malpractice liability in some instances. Rule 1.8(h) would allow that prospective waiver because the client (the corporation) is separately represented by inside counsel.

If a client or former client has a malpractice claim or potential claim, Rule 1.8(h)(2) requires the lawyer to advise that person that independent legal representation is appropriate before settlement. See Section III, B, 2, infra. As a further protection for the client or former client thinking of settling a malpractice claim, the lawyer's advice regarding the appropriateness of independent representation must be "in writing." The ABA Section on General Practice recommended this requirement and the ABA Commission accepted it without opposition. See The Legislative History of the Model Rules of Professional Conduct 60–64 (ABA, Center for Professional Responsibility 1987).

(g) Suing Parties Represented by the Lawyer's Relatives

Assume that Lawyer *A* represents *P* who is suing *D*. Lawyer *B* represents *D*. Is there any conflict if Lawyers *A* and *B*—both in different firms—are married to each other, or related as parent, child, or sibling?

The Code had no explicit provision dealing with this issue. ABA Formal Opinion 340 (Sept. 23, 1975), dealing with the husband/wife relationship, found no per se disqualification but otherwise offered little concrete guidance. It did state, however, that if one spouse is disqualified under DR 5–105(A), the entire firm is disqualified under DR 5–105(D).

The Rules have an explicit provision regarding such relationships. It used to be a specific subsection of Rule 1.8. The 2002 revisions moved it to Rule 1.7, Comment 11. Lawyer *A* may not represent Client *P* if Lawyer *B* is the spouse, parent, child, or sibling representing Client *D*, unless the client consents. However, this prohibition is *not imputed* to the other members of either *A*'s or *B*'s firm. See Rule 1.7, Comment 11, which considers this conflict to be a "personal conflict" and not imputed to other members of the firm.

Rule 1.10(a) makes clear that "personal conflicts" are not imputed to other members of the firm. Thus, husband may not represent plaintiff while wife represents defendant (unless the clients knowingly consent), but husband's law firm may represent plaintiff while wife or wife's law firm represents defendant and there is no need to secure any client consent.

E. The Advocate as Witness

The Rules (like the predecessor Code) regulate when an advocate may simultaneously act as a witness. The primary difference is that the Rules do not impute the disqualification to other members of the disqualified lawyer's firm.

Both the Rules and the Code treat a situation where the advocate is asked to be a witness as a conflict of interests. The Code placed the relevant rules in Canon 5, the conflicts Canon—DR 5–101(B). Both DR 5–102—and the Rules specifically refer to the problem as a "conflict of interest." Rule 3.7, Comment 1.

The Code offered inconsistent rationales for the restrictions on the testifying advocate—e.g., such an advocate may be "more easily impeachable for interest" and simultaneously "the opposing counsel may be handicapped in challenging the credibility of the lawyer. . . . " EC 5–9.

The Rules offer as a primary rationale that the fact-finder may be confused if the person actually acting as an advocate before the fact-finder also offers testimony with his or her argument: "It may not be clear whether a statement by an advocate-witness should be taken as proof or as an analysis of the proof." Rule 3.7, Comment 2. The introductory sentence of Comment 2 explains that the "tribunal has proper objection when the trier of fact may be confused or misled by a lawyer serving as both advocate and witness." Comments 3 & 5 repeat that concern. The jury may be confused if the advocate gets up from counsel's chair and then sits in the witness box, and later addresses the jury in closing argument. On the other hand, that is what happens when a lawyer or anyone else represents himself pro se.

There are several important issues to remember. First, the Advocate–Witness rule (unlike the Attorney–Client privilege) does not give a lawyer any immunity from testifying; it is a limitation on advocacy. It basically provides that the advocate should withdraw if she is "likely to be a necessary witness" unless (a) the testimony relates to an uncontested issue, or (b) it relates to the nature and value of legal services in that case, or (c) disqualification would work a "substantial hardship on the client." Rule 3.7(a)(1), (2), (3); DR 5–102(A).

The Code explicitly imputed this disqualification to all lawyers in the firm, DR 5–101(B); DR 5–102(A), (B). However, given the rationale of the Rules, discussed supra, the Rules *do not automatically impute* the advocate-witness prohibition. Rule 3.7(b). Where the witness is a partner of another lawyer who is the advocate, there is no automatic imputation because there is no danger of confusing the fact–finder. Note that Rule 1.10, the general imputation rule, does not provide for imputation of Rule 3.7. Moreover, to make this conclusion perfectly clear, the 2002 revisions added Comment 5 to Rule 3.7 that explicitly states that one lawyer may act as an advocate in a trial while another one testifies as a necessary witness.

While Rule 3.7 does not impute, Rule 1.7 or Rule 1.9 may require imputation. For example, if the lawyer's testimony is likely to conflict substantially with the client's testimony, there is "a conflict of interest that requires compliance with Rule 1.7." See Rule 3.7, Comment 6. The client can waive that conflict if the lawyer complies with the waiver requirements of Rule 1.7.

Note that Rule 3.7(a)(3) states that, even if the lawyer-advocate rule applies, the lawyer can still testify if the lawyer's disqualification "would work substantial hardship on the client." The particular except—"would work substantial hardship on the client"—does not apply if there is a disqualification under Rule 1.7. In other words, if the lawyer's testimony is likely to conflict substantially with the client's testimony, then Rule 1.7 applies and the conflict is imputed to all members of the law firm even if this imputation is likely to work a substantial hardship on the client. Because Rule 1.7 takes over, the client can waive the conflict *if* the special waiver requirements of that rule are met.

If only Rule 3.7 governs the situation and prevents the lawyer from simultaneously being a witness and an advocate—if, in other words, there is no issue under Rule 1.7 or Rule 1.9—then there is no provision for client waiver. Given this rationale of confusion of the fact-finder—an interest of the judicial system rather than an interest of the client—nothing in either the Code or the Rules provides for client waiver of the advocate-witness rule. The California Rules of Professional Conduct, surprisingly, do provide for client waiver, though the case law makes no real attempt to justify why. California Rule 5–210(C). There should be no waiver of the advocate witness rule, because that rule exists to protect systemic interests—the interests in the system of justice—and not merely to protect one of the parties. E.g., *Supreme Beef Processors, Inc. v. American Consumer Industries, Inc.*, 441 F.Supp. 1064, 1068 (N.D.Tex.1977); *Draganescu v. First National Bank of Hollywood*, 502 F.2d

550, 552 (5th Cir.1974). The party represented by the advocate-witness might seek to "waive" the disqualification because of bad advice from the advocate-witness who desires to remain on the case as a litigant. And the attorney for the other side "may avoid pressing for disqualification out of a desire to avoid clashing with opposing counsel or to obtain tactical advantages." Thus, the court should act *sua sponte* if neither party moves for disqualification. *MacArthur v. Bank of New York*, 524 F.Supp. 1205, 1209 (S.D.N.Y.1981).

If the advocate-witness rule is the only reason why a lawyer is disqualified, then the disqualified lawyer may consult with the party's substitute counsel and assist in preparing for trial. *MacArthur v. Bank of New York*, 524 F.Supp. 1205, 1211 n.3 (S.D.N.Y.1981); *Jones v. Chicago*, 610 F.Supp. 350, 363 (N.D.Ill.1984). None of the reasons offered for the advocate-witness rule (confusion of fact-finder, difficulty of challenging credibility of advocate-witness, etc.) justify prohibiting the disqualified advocate-witness from consulting with the new lawyer: for example, the disqualified lawyer will not divulge any forbidden confidences or other improper information to the new lawyer, because the lawyer-witness was not disqualified for that reason; nor will the lawyer-witness, who is no longer a lawyer-advocate, be able to confuse the fact-finder.

Courts enforce the advocate-witness rule in the course of litigation. See, e.g., *Weil v. Weil*, 283 App.Div. 33, 35, 125 N.Y.S.2d 368, 370 (1953) (new trial granted because of violation of advocate-witness rule); *Supreme Beef Processors, Inc. v. American Consumer Industries, Inc.*, 441 F.Supp. 1064, 1069 (N.D.Tex.1977) (judgment vacated because of violation of advocate-witness rule); *MacArthur v. Bank of New York*, 524 F.Supp. 1205 (S.D.N.Y.1981) (mistrial because of violation of advocate-witness rule). This enforcement is proper, because a violation of the advocate-witness rule infects the truth-finding process by confusing the fact-finder, whether judge or jury.

F. Vicarious Disqualification

1. Introduction

It has long been a general rule in disqualification cases that if "a lawyer is required to decline employment or to withdraw from employment under a Disciplinary Rule, no partner or associate, or any other lawyer affiliated with him or his firm may accept or continue such employment." DR 5–105(D). One attorney's disqualification is imputed to all. E.g., *Consolidated Theatres v. Warner Brothers, Circuit Management Corp.*, 216 F.2d 920 (2d Cir.1954). And if the lawyer actually disqualified as to a particular case moves to a new firm, his disqualification is normally imputed to all the lawyers of the new firm. Id.

The Code itself provided no explicit exceptions to this general rule, but in practice it was interpreted to allow various exceptions. See, e.g., ABA Formal Opinion 342 (Nov. 24, 1975), dealing with the former government attorney, discussed in Part VI, section II, infra.

Model Rule 1.10 lays out the general rule for imputed disqualification. It is more narrowly drafted than DR 5–105(D). For the most part, it reflects the rule as it has actually been interpreted by the case law. Model Rule 1.10 is a good restatement of the law.

2. Application to Government and Former Government Lawyers

The disqualification principles of Rule 1.10 are more extensive than those provided by Rule 1.11 ("Special Conflicts Of Interest for Former and Current Government Officers and Employees "); *Rule 1.10 does not apply to the problems involving the movement between private practice and government service.* See Rule 1.10(d) ("The disqualification of lawyers associated in a firm with former or current government lawyers is governed by Rule 1.11."). See also Comment 7. These problems are considered elsewhere. See Part VI, section II, infra. The government is subject to different protections because of what is seen as the public policy benefits for the government to recruit lawyers who will not be unduly burdened in seeking later private employment because of their former affiliation with the government. Similarly, because of the government's unusually broad legal relationships, it should not be unduly hampered when it recruits a lawyer from the private sector. Rule 1.11, Comment 4.

3. Waiver and Screening

Any affected client protected by the principles of Rule 1.10 may waive its protections *if* the waiver provisions of Rule 1.7 are followed. Rule 1.10(c). In other words, each client gives informed consent, confirmed in writing; the lawyer reasonably believes that his or her representation will not be adversely affected; no other law prevents the representation; and the representation does not involve the lawyer being on both sides of the case.

If a lawyer is disqualified, and this disqualification is imputed to other members of the firm, Rule 1.10 does not provide for screening as a method of curing the disqualification. Rule 1.10 (unlike Rule 1.11) does *not* provide for a screen for *lawyers*. As Comment 2 explains, a basic premise is that "a firm of lawyers is essentially one lawyer for purposed of the rules governing loyalty to the client."

While Rule 1.10 does not itself provide for any screening mechanism—or what is sometimes called a "Chinese Wall"—around the affected attorney, the client may, if he so chooses, withhold consent, or agree to consent on the condition that a screen be placed around the affected attorney so he has no contact with the matter. Rule 1.10 does not preclude a client from knowingly waiving rights and allowing a screen.

While Rule 1.10 does not provide for a screen for a disqualified lawyer, a few cases have suggested that a screen may be sufficient to remove the imputation of the disqualification. Sometimes this suggestion is dictum, or the court is faced with a peculiar set of facts. E.g., *Nemours Foundation v. Gilbane, Aetna, Federal Ins. Co.*, 632 F.Supp. 418 (D.Del.1986) (referring to a "cone of silence" and to Rule 1.11(a), which allows screening for the former *government* attorney). See also, ABA Formal Opinion 90–358 (Sept. 13, 1990) at n. 12 (noting that some cases have referred to screening in cases not involving the former government attorney).

Screens Erected Around Non–Lawyers. Sometimes the person subject to the disqualification is a non-lawyer, such as a paralegal or legal secretary. Or the person is a lawyer but she learned of the disqualifying information while she was a non-lawyer, for example she was a law clerk in another firm the prior summer. Comment 4 allows a screen in that circumstance, because the dangers of breaching the screen are less and the burdens on the mobility of non-lawyers are greater.

4. Defining the "Firm"

Rule 1.10 applies to lawyers associated together in a law "firm," a term intended to encompass not only private law firms but also corporate legal departments and legal service organizations. See, Rule 1.0(c). Because the purpose of this rule is to protect client confidences and client loyalty (Rule 1.10, Comment 1) the definition of "firm" may vary. For example, while "firm" includes a legal aid office, it does not necessarily include lawyers employed in separate units of the same legal aid organization. Rule 1.0 Comment 4. When such lawyers are in different offices, the need to protect confidences of clients represented by different offices is lessened. The definition of "firm" for this purpose may also include co-counsel who are not members of the same firm but who are representing the same party *if* co-counsel have exchanged confidential information. In determining whether two or more lawyers should be treated as a "firm," it is relevant to know if the lawyers have mutual access to information concerning the clients that they serve. Rule 1.0, Comment 2.

Similarly the term "firm," may include lawyers who only share office space but who imply to the public that they are a partnership. Rule 1.0 Comment 2. Because these lawyers act as if they are partners, application of Rule 1.10 is necessary to protect client expectations of loyalty.

5. Lawyers Currently Associated in a Firm

Rule 1.10(a) provides the basic imputation rule for lawyers *while* they are currently associated in the same firm. This Rule states that *only the disqualification principles of certain Rules*—Rule 1.7 ("Conflict of Interest: Current Clients") and Rule 1.9 ("Duties to Former Client")—*are imputed to all the other lawyers, and this imputation exists only while these other lawyers are currently associated in the same firm as the disqualified lawyer.*

The imputation rules for Rule 1.8 are found in Rule 1.8(k), *not* in Rule 1.10. Rule 1.8(k) imputes all of its disqualification to all other lawyers in the same firm, *except* it does not impute Rule 1.8(j), dealing with a lawyer's sexual relations with a client.

It is important to remember that Rule 1.10(a) is not at all applicable to situations where one lawyer—either the one with the actual disqualification, or another lawyer with the imputed disqualification—leaves the first firm and joins another. Rule 1.10(b) and Rule 1.9 govern those situations.

Also, Rule 1.10(a) does not impute a lawyer's disqualifications based on his or her "personal interest" if that personal interest does not present a significant risk that it will materially limit the client's representation by other lawyers in the firm.

Examples: Lawyer in Firm refuses to work on tobacco cases because of his strong opposition to smoking and because he believes he cannot represent the client competently. Lawyer, however, has no interest or power to materially limit the zealousness of other lawyers in the firm that work on tobacco cases. Lawyer's disqualification is not imputed to other lawyers in the firm. Rule 1.10, Comment 3.

6. When a Lawyer Moves From One Firm to Another

(a) Introduction

Imputed knowledge is not thereafter imputed to another lawyer.

Assume that Lawyer #1 represents Client P in a matter—P v. D. Lawyer #1 cannot also represent D. Such a representation would breach Lawyer #1's duty to P. Rule 1.7(a), (b)(3). Similarly, Lawyer #2, a partner or associate in Lawyer #1's firm could not represent D because of the firm's duty of loyalty to P. **Rule 1.10(a)** & Comment 2. In addition, Lawyer #1's confidential information about Client P is imputed to all members of law Firm #1. Hence, Lawyer #1's disqualification is imputed to all members of Lawyer #1's firm.

Now assume that Lawyer #2 leaves Firm #1 and joins Firm #2. Lawyer #2's representation of D against P does *not* breach P's expectation of loyalty from Lawyer #1 or #1's firm. If the duty of loyalty prevented #2 from litigating against P, then no lawyer could ever sue a former client, yet we know that Rule 1.9 says otherwise. Lawyer #2 has no confidences to transmit to the other lawyers in Firm #2. The only client information that Lawyer #2 had is information that was *imputed* to him, *only while* he remained in Firm #2. In other words, if the knowledge that Lawyer #2 has is imputed, it is not thereafter imputed to other lawyers in his new firm. Rule 1.10(a).

On the other hand, if Lawyer #2 had acquired actual confidential knowledge about P that would be helpful to D, then Lawyer #2's representation of D would be improper because it would violate Lawyer #2's duty under Rule 1.6 to safeguard client information. **Rule 1.9(b)**.

If Lawyer #2 did not *personally* represent Client P *and* did not acquire any material secrets or confidences from Client P, neither Lawyer #2 nor #2's new firm should be disqualified from representing Client D. **Rule 1.9(b)** & Comment 5. Otherwise, mobility of the legal profession would be severely restricted, a burden not justified by any need to protect client loyalty or client information, neither one of which, by hypothesis, exists.

Moreover, if the law imputed Lawyer #2's imputed knowledge to #2's new firm, then the imputed disqualification could exist *ad infinitum* when, for example, Lawyer #3 (#2's new partner) leaves that firm and joins yet another: if Lawyer #2's imputed disqualification were imputed to Lawyer #3, is Lawyer #3's doubly-imputed knowledge also imputed to the lawyers in Lawyer #3's new firm? The general rule is no. The Rules do not treat the lawyer like a Typhoid Mary infecting all with whom me comes in contact. "[N]ew partners of a vicariously disqualified partner, to whom knowledge has been imputed during a former partnership, are not necessarily disqualified: they need only show that the vicariously disqualified partner's knowledge was imputed, not actual." *American Can Co. v. Citrus Feed Co.*, 436 F.2d 1125, 1129 (5th Cir.1971).

(b) When a Lawyer Joins a Firm

Rule 1.9(a) & (b) governs the extent to which a lawyer who joins a new firm carries with him any disqualifications from the old firm.

Assume that lawyer Alpha is a member of Firm *#1*. Firm *#1* represents *P* in a suit against *D*. Alpha herself was not involved in any representation of *P*, and Alpha has not acquired any secret or confidential information from *P* that is relevant to *D*. Alpha now leaves Firm #1 and joins Firm #2, which represents *D*.

Note that *P*'s and *D*'s interests are materially adverse to each other *and* Firm #2 (Alpha's new firm) is representing *D* in a matter that is the same as (or substantially related to) the matter in which Firm #1 (Alpha's old firm) is representing *P*. Nonetheless, both Firm #2 and Alpha may properly represent *D* against *P* because Alpha acquired from Client *P* no material information protected by Rules 1.6 or 1.9(b). This same result would be reached either under Rule 1.9(b) or under the prior case law. E.g., *Silver Chrysler Plymouth, Inc. v. Chrysler Motors Corp.*, 518 F.2d 751, 757 (2d Cir.1975) (a client cannot "reasonably expect to foreclose either all lawyers formerly at the firm or even those who have represented it on unrelated matters from subsequently representing an opposing party."). **Rule 1.10(a)** does not impute any disqualification to anyone in Firm #2.

Example: Lawyer Gamma is a member of the firm of Alpha & Beta. Alpha represents *P* in the case of *P vs. D*. Gamma, while with the law firm of Alpha & Beta, did not work on the case of *P vs. D* and acquired no knowledge relating to client *P*. Gamma then leaves the firm and joins another firm, the "second firm." "[N]either the lawyer [Gamma] individually nor the second firm is disqualified from representing another client in the same or a related manner even though the interests of the two clients conflict." Rule 1.9, Comment 5.

Now assume the same facts in the previous hypothetical except that Alpha *personally* worked for *P* in the case of *P v. D* while Alpha was with Firm #1. Alpha did not acquire any material client secrets or confidences, but she did work on that particular case. For example, she filed an appearance in court and asked for a continuance. By hypothesis, there is no need to protect the former client's secrets or confidences, but is there a need to protect any duty of loyalty owed to a former client?

Unless the former client consents, Alpha is *personally* disqualified. **Rule 1.9(a)** provides that if Alpha formerly represented a client in a matter, she may not thereafter represent another person in the same or a substantially related matter, if that other person's interest is materially adverse to the interest of the former client (unless, or course, the former client consents). See also, Rule 1.9, Comment 2 ("When a lawyer has been directly involved in a specific transaction, subsequent representation of other clients with materially adverse interests clearly is prohibited.").

Now, is Alpha's disqualification imputed to the other lawyers in Firm #2? Yes. Rule 1.10(a) explicitly imputes *all* of Rule 1.9.

(c) **When a Lawyer Leaves a Firm**

Rule 1.10(b) governs the extent to which Firm #1 is still disqualified from handling a matter when Lawyer Alpha (the cause of the initial disqualification) has left Firm #1. Basically Rule 1.10(b) states that, once Lawyer Alpha leaves Firm *#1*, Firm *#1* may then represent clients materially adverse to Firm *#1*'s former clients who had been represented by Alpha when she was with Firm *#1*, unless: the matter involved is the same as (or substantially related to) the matter in which Alpha (the formerly associated lawyer) had represented the client *and* any of the lawyers still with Firm *#1* have knowledge of the former client's material secrets or confidences (i.e., client information protected by Rules 1.6 or 1.9(c)).

In other words, if Lawyer Alpha is the sole lawyer who handled all of a client's affairs, and when she left Firm #1 she took with her the client, and all confidential information about the client, then there is no need to preclude Firm #1 from taking matters adverse to that firm's former client.

Examples: Lawyer Alpha, a member of Firm #1, represents Client *D* on various matters. Client *D* gives Alpha confidential information relating to a patent. Alpha did not relate any of the confidential information regarding the patent to any member of Firm #1. Then Alpha leaves Firm #1, takes Client *D* with him, and moves to Firm #2.

Then Client *P* asks Firm #1 to represent it in a patent infringement action against *D*. Alpha and Firm #2 represent *D* in this patent suit. Firm #1 may properly represent Client *P*. *Novo Terapeutisk Laboratorium A/S v. Baxter Travenol Laboratories, Inc.*, 607 F.2d 186 (7th Cir.1979) (*en banc*). Accord, Rule 1.10, Comment 7.

(d) Burden of Proof

The application of Rule 1.9(b) and similar rules often turns on the question of whether a lawyer had acquired material client information protected as client confidences or secrets. In that situation, the burden of proof should rest upon the firm whose disqualification is sought. Rule 1.9, Comment 6.

However, the fact that the firm must demonstrate that it is *not* the depository of material protected client information does not mean that the burden can never be met. "[I]t will not do . . . to make the standard for proof . . . unattainably high . . . particularly where . . . the attorney must prove a negative." *Laskey Bros. of W.Va., Inc. v. Warner Bros. Pictures, Inc.*, 224 F.2d 824, 827 (2d Cir.1955). See *Gas–A–Tron of Arizona v. Union Oil Co. of California*, 534 F.2d 1322, 1325 (9th Cir.1976) (per curiam), cert. denied, 429 U.S. 861, 97 S.Ct. 164, 50 L.Ed.2d 139 (1976): "[W]e are convinced that any initial inference of impropriety that arose from [Lawyer *B's*] potential physical access to the files of Exxon and Shell and from his association with lawyers who did know confidential information about them was dispelled by evidence that he saw none of the files other than those relating to the cases assigned to him heretofore described and that he heard no confidences about Exxon and Shell from the lawyers with whom he was earlier associated." The court will also allow rebuttal by attorney affidavit. *Silver Chrysler Plymouth, Inc. v. Chrysler Motors Corp.*, 518 F.2d 751, 756 (2d Cir.1975).

G. Sanctions

If an attorney is involved in a conflict of interest, he may be subject to discipline, tort liability, and disqualification.

An attorney who violates one of the ethics rules relating to conflicts of interest is subject to discipline.

If the violation causes damage to the client, the lawyer may also be liable for damages for the tort of malpractice. E.g., *Arlinghaus v. Ritenour*, 622 F.2d 629 (2d Cir.1980).

If the conflict occurs in the course of litigation, the court may also disqualify the attorney from further representation in that litigation, *if* the conflict is such that it may "taint" the fact-finding process. Compare *Board of Education of City of New York v. Nyquist*, 590 F.2d 1241 (2d Cir.1979) (no disqualification when only claim is possible "appearance of impropriety" and "no claim that the trial will be tainted . . . "), with *Ceramco, Inc. v. Lee Pharmaceuticals*, 510 F.2d 268, 271 (2d Cir.1975) ("the courts have not only the supervisory power but the duty and responsibility to disqualify counsel for unethical conduct prejudicial to his adversaries"). Thus, improper attorney solicitation of clients (see Part V, section II, infra) may merit discipline, but the court will not disqualify those lawyers because improper solicitation does not taint or prejudice the fact-finding process. *Fisher Studio, Inc. v. Loew's Inc.*, 232 F.2d 199, 204 (2d Cir.1956), cert. denied, 352 U.S. 836, 77 S.Ct. 56, 1 L.Ed.2d 55 (1956).

Sometimes, attorneys involved in conflicts may lose their fees. Judge Learned Hand noted in *Silbiger v. Prudence Bonds Corp.*, 180 F.2d 917, 920 (2d Cir.1950): "[B]y the beginning of the Seventeenth Century it had become a commonplace that an attorney must not represent opposed interests; and the usual consequence has been that he is disbarred from receiving any fee from either, no matter how successful his labors." (footnotes omitted).

Appealability. When parties litigate attorney disqualification in the course of litigation, the question arises as to when adverse trial rulings (either granting or denying disqualification) are appealable prior to the conclusion of the main case. In the federal system, the Supreme Court has ruled that in a civil case a trial court decision denying or granting disqualification is not appealable as a final decision under 28 U.S.C.A. § 1291. *Firestone Tire & Rubber Co. v. Risjord,* 449 U.S. 368, 101 S.Ct. 669, 66 L.Ed.2d 571 (1981) (order denying disqualification motion not immediately appealable); *Richardson–Merrell, Inc. v. Koller,* 472 U.S. 424, 105 S.Ct. 2757, 86 L.Ed.2d 340 (1985) (order granting disqualification motion not immediately appealable).

The Court has also held that the granting of a disqualification motion in a *criminal* case is not immediately appealable. *Flanagan v. United States,* 465 U.S. 259, 104 S.Ct. 1051, 79 L.Ed.2d 288 (1984). We should expect it to reach a similar conclusion with respect to the denial of a disqualification motion in a criminal case. See *United States v. White,* 743 F.2d 488 (7th Cir.1984) (criminal case; denial of disqualification motion not final order).

The courts do not preclude disqualification motions by applying overly strict notions of standing and laches; similarly, they do not easily find or imply client waiver of attorney conflicts. See generally, Hacker & Rotunda, *Standing, Waiver, Laches and Appealability in Attorney Disqualification Cases,* 3 Corp.L.Rev. 82 (1980).

III. The Duty of Competence and the Scope of Representation

A. Client Control
The client has the authority to make major decisions—those affecting the merits of the case, or substantially prejudicing the client's rights.

The lawyer is the agent (not the guardian) of the client, who is the principal (not the ward). See *State v. Barley,* 240 N.C. 253, 81 S.E.2d 772 (1954); *Prate v. Freedman,* 583 F.2d 42, 48 (2d Cir.1978). The lawyer must abide by his "client's decisions concerning the objectives of representation . . . " Rule 1.2(a). The Rules (like the former Code) therefore attempt to lay out basic guidelines to distinguish between those matters where the lawyer must secure client waiver and those where prior consent is unnecessary.

The lawyer is entitled to make her own decisions in matters "not affecting the merits of the cause or substantially prejudicing the rights of the client;" in other cases "the authority to make decisions is exclusively that of the client . . . " EC 7–7. See also Rule 1.2(a) (the client decides the "objectives of representation" and the lawyer must consult with the client "as to the means by which they are to be pursued."). However, sometimes a clear distinction cannot be drawn.

The ethics rules use examples in an effort to make the text more concrete. Thus, the client decides whether or not to accept a settlement offer or to plead guilty. Rule 1.2(a). In criminal cases the client has the final say as to whether or not he will testify on his own behalf. Rule 1.2(a); ABA Standards of the Defense Function, Standard 4–5.2(a)(iv).

Consider, *Linsk v. Linsk,* 70 Cal.2d 272, 278–79, 74 Cal.Rptr. 544, 547–48, 449 P.2d 760, 763–64 (1969) (internal citations and paragraphing omitted):

> "An attorney may refuse to call a witness even though his client desires that the witness testify; may abandon a defense he deems to be unmeritorious; may stipulate that the trial judge could view the premises; that a witness, if called, would give substantially the same testimony as a prior witness; and that the testimony of a witness in a prior trial be used in a later action; and he may waive the late filing of a complaint. On the other hand, an attorney may not, by virtue of his general authority over the conduct of the action, stipulate that his client's premises constituted an unsafe place to work where such a stipulation would dispose of the client's sole interest in the premises, nor may he stipulate to a matter that would eliminate an essential defense. He may not agree to the entry of a default judgment against his client, may not compromise his client's claim, or stipulate that only nominal damages may be awarded, and he cannot agree to an increase in the amount of the judgment against his client. Likewise an attorney is without authority to waive findings so that no appeal can be prosecuted, or agree that a judgment may be made payable in gold coin rather than in legal tender. An attorney is also forbidden without authorization to stipulate that the opposing party's failure to comply with a statute would not be pleaded as a defense. . . . "

While the Rules offer examples of which conduct falls on which side of a not very bright line, these examples should not be regarded as negating all other instances. Thus, the Rules state that in a criminal case it is for the client to decide whether to waive a jury trial. Rule 1.2(a). Yet in a civil case as well the attorney may not waive the client's jury trial right without client consent. E.g., *Graves v. P.J. Taggares Co.,* 94 Wash.2d 298, 616 P.2d 1223 (1980).

Similarly, the ABA Defense Functions state that the decisions on "what witnesses to call, whether and how to conduct cross-examination, what jurors to accept or strike, *what trial motions should be made,* and what evidence should be introduced" are strategic and tactical decisions "that *should be made by defense counsel* after consultation with the client." Standard 4–5.2(b) (emphasis added). However, if the trial motion relates to exclusion of evidence allegedly obtained in violation of the Constitution, the client should have the final say on that issue. Cf. *Henry v. Mississippi,* 379 U.S. 443, 85 S.Ct. 564, 13 L.Ed.2d 408 (1965).

Lawyers have a right to agree to reasonable requests of opposing counsel that do not prejudice the rights of his client, such as reasonable requests regarding court procedures, settings, continuances, waiver of procedural formalities, and similar matters that do not prejudice the rights of his client. EC 7–38. Thus, Rule 1.3, Comment 1 advises that a lawyer "is not bound, however, to press for every advantage that might be realized for a client." Later, Comment 3 adds that "A lawyer's duty to act with reasonable promptness, however, does not preclude the lawyer from agreeing to a reasonable request for a postponement that will not prejudice the lawyer's client."

Example: Defendant's Attorney asks Plaintiff's Attorney for a one week extension in the time allowed to file an Answer to the Complaint. The extension would not affect the merits of the case or prejudice Plaintiff. The ethics rules grant Plaintiff no right to forbid Plaintiff's Attorney from granting this request. Rule 1.3, Comments 1, 3; EC 7–38.

Because the attorney is an agent of the client, the attorney and client have a great deal of power, within the law of contract, to change the division of lawyer/client responsibility. For example, client may properly tell lawyer: "Use your judgment as to whether or not to accept any settlement for at least $25,000." Though the Client has the sole power to accept or reject settlements, the client may give actual authority to the attorney to act on the client's behalf. The Client may also hire the lawyer only for a specifically defined purpose. Rule 1.2, Comment 6.

Similarly, the lawyer may ask the client's permission to forego action that the lawyer believes is unjust, even though it is otherwise in the best interest of his client. EC 7–9. See also, Rule 1.2(c) (client may limit the scope of representation if the limitation is reasonable and the client gives informed consent); Rule 1.2 Comment 4 (limitations on representation may exclude actions "that the lawyer regards as repugnant or imprudent.").

The lawyer or client may also affect the extent of client control by terminating the relationship. That is, *the client can always fire the lawyer, who then must withdraw, even if the client seeks to terminate the lawyer for a less than noble reason.* Rule 1.16(a)(3); DR 2–110(B)(4). For example, if the client decides to fire the lawyer because the lawyer has hired a minority law associate, the lawyer still has no right to prevent the client from terminating the representation. The lawyer, in turn, *may* withdraw if the client insists on pursuing an objective that "the lawyer considers repugnant or with which the lawyer has fundamental disagreement," even though it is not illegal. Rule 1.16(b)(4). Cf. DR 2–110(C)(1)(a); cf. DR 7–101(B)(2). On withdrawal, see generally section V, B, infra.

The client's and lawyer's rights to control the scope of representation have some limits; that is, the power to contract may not be used to violate the ethical codes or other law. Thus, the client may not be asked to agree to representation so limited in scope as to violate Rule 1.1 requiring competence, or to surrender the right to terminate the lawyer's services or the right to settle litigation that the lawyer might wish to continue. Rule 1.2, Comment 8. Cf. DR 6–102(A). On the question of competence, see section III, B, infra.

Note: The ethics rules allow the attorney and client to agree that the attorney will present all nonfrivolous issues. And, as a matter of constitutional law, the indigent can compel appointed counsel to press a nonfrivolous appeal. *Anders v. California*, 386 U.S. 738, 87 S.Ct. 1396, 18 L.Ed.2d 493 (1967). However, as a matter of constitutional law, the indigent has no right to compel appointed counsel to present all nonfrivolous *issues* on appeal if the appointed lawyer's professional judgment is to forego certain issues. *Jones v. Barnes*, 463 U.S. 745, 103 S.Ct. 3308, 77 L.Ed.2d 987 (1983).

B. Competence

1. Defining Competence

Not only the law of malpractice but the law of ethics requires lawyers to be competent. Rule 1.1; DR 6–101(A). A lawyer is competent if he has "the legal knowledge, skill, thoroughness and preparation reasonably necessary for the representation." Rule 1.1. The framers of the Model Rules placed the requirement of competence first, because they thought that the first rule of ethics is competence.

The lawyer need not necessarily be experienced in a particular matter to be considered competent in that matter. After all, before you get experience, you have to start somewhere. Moreover, even a novice lawyer has training in the common denominator of all legal problems: legal method, the analysis of precedent and evidence, and legal drafting.

Rule 1.1, Comment 2. Cf. EC 6–1. On the other hand to develop other skills (e.g., trial practice, negotiation), training and close supervision are important. Partners in law firms have the responsibility to make reasonable efforts to insure that all of the lawyers in the firm conform to the rules of professional conduct. Rule 5.1.

The lawyer need not have the necessary degree of competence *prior to* accepting the employment. There is a first time for everything. The lawyer may properly accept the matter and then acquire the necessary competence, through study and preparation, in a novel area of law. Rule 1.1, Comment 2; DR 6–101(A)(2), EC 6–4. The Code adds a specific caveat that this preparation should not result in "unreasonable delay or expense to his client." EC 6–3. This limitation is implicit in the requirement in the Rules that the preparation be "reasonable." Rule 1.1, Comment 4. Cf. Rule 1.1, Comment 5.

The lawyer has an ethical duty to engage in continuing legal education and study in order to maintain his or her competence. Rule 1.1, Comment 6; EC 6–2.

The lawyer may also establish the necessary competence by associating in the matter with another attorney who is already competent. Rule 1.1, Comment 2; DR 6–101(A)(1). Before any association is proper, the client must consent to it. Rule 1.5(e)(2); EC 2–22, 6–3.

Because what is "competent" is a function of reasonableness, a different standard of competence applies in an emergency. A lawyer in such cases may give advice reasonably necessary in the circumstances "where referral to or consultation with another lawyer would be impractical." Rule 1.1, Comment 3.

2. Waiving Malpractice Liability

The client has a right to expect competent representation. The Code nowhere permits the client to waive the lawyer's duty of competence. In fact the Disciplinary Rules explicitly forbid the lawyer from attempting "to exonerate himself from or limit his liability to his client for his personal malpractice." DR 6–102(A). Though the language of this Rule is not explicitly limited to prospective attempts, i.e., attempts before the malpractice actually occurs, such a limitation must be read into DR 6–102(A). Otherwise it would forbid the lawyer from agreeing to a settlement offer in which the client suing for malpractice released his claim.

The Rules also forbid the lawyer from asking the client to agree to incompetent representation. (See Rule 1.2, Comment 8, referring to Rule 1.1, which requires competence.) However, later the Rules make clear that the lawyer may make an agreement "prospectively limiting the lawyer's liability to a client for malpractice" *if* the client "is independently represented in making the agreement. . . . " Rule 1.8(h)(1). The rationale is that if a second lawyer independently represents the client in making the decision to waive malpractice liability prospectively there is no danger that the first lawyer is overreaching.

This provision is logical, but as a practical matter it will be the unusual case where an individual will hire a lawyer to represent him in negotiating a retention agreement with another lawyer where the client agrees to waive malpractice liability. This section is most likely to apply in cases involving corporations, where inside counsel, in the course of hiring outside counsel, might find it reasonable to waive malpractice liability in some instances. Rule 1.8(h) would allow that prospective waiver because the client (the corporation) is separately represented by its inside counsel.

The Rules explicitly recognize that the lawyer may settle a malpractice claim or a potential claim that her client has against her. Rule 1.8(h)(2). If the client (or former client) is not separately represented in the settlement, the lawyer must advise the client *in writing* that "independent representation is appropriate. . . . "Rule 1.8(h). The purpose of this provision is to give unrepresented people the right to settle malpractice claims, while guarding against overreaching by the lawyer.

3. Neglect

Reasonable Communication. The "lawyer should fully and promptly inform his client of material developments in the matters being handled for the client," EC 9–2, and should keep his client informed of relevant considerations before the client makes decisions, EC 7–8. The Rules make clear that these requirements are not merely hortatory; to violate them is to violate a disciplinary rule. Rule 1.4(a), (b). However, these Rules are subject to a rule of reason. See Rule 1.4, Comment 2. In fact, the lawyer may even be justified in delaying the transfer of information to the client if the lawyer believes the client might react imprudently. Rule 1.4, Comment 7. Cf. Rule 1.14.

In addition to this duty of reasonable communication, the lawyer may not neglect a legal matter entrusted to him. DR 6–101(A)(3). The Rules use much more affirmative language than the old Model Code: "A lawyer shall act with reasonable diligence and promptness in representing a client." Rule 1.3.

A Pattern of Behavior. Under the former Code, a showing of neglect usually requires proof of *a pattern of behavior*. If a lawyer on one occasion forgot to file an answer to a complaint in time because of inadvertence, he could be guilty of civil malpractice if the client were damaged, but he would not be guilty of neglect. "Neglect involves indifference and a *consistent* failure to carry out the obligations which the lawyer has assumed to the client or a *conscious disregard* for the responsibility owed to the client." ABA Informal Opinion 1273 (Nov. 20, 1973). The Model Rules appear to apply the same test. The Rules warn that "no professional shortcoming is more widely resented than procrastination," and unreasonable delay can cause "needless anxiety" to a client. Rule 1.3, Comment 3.

Agreeing to Reasonable Postponements. Rule 1.3, Comment 3, makes clear that an obstreperous client has no ethical power to make the lawyer act uncivilly towards the opponent. It advises. "A lawyer's duty to act with reasonable promptness, however, does not preclude the lawyer from agreeing to a reasonable request for a postponement that will not prejudice the lawyer's client."

Example: Client tells lawyer, "I hate plaintiff; therefore do not give her a short delay to answer the interrogatories. I know she said that she wanted to attend her mother's funeral, but I don't care." Lawyer may grant the reasonable delay. Note that if Lawyer refuses to grant the delay, the other lawyer will make a motion for a short delay, the trial judge will grant it under these circumstances, and then chastise the lawyer for refusing to grant the short delay.

Waiver. Nothing in the ethics rules permits the client to waive his right that his attorney act with reasonable promptness or diligence. Even the client's refusal to pay the lawyer's fee does not justify neglect. If the client deliberately disregards his obligation to pay his attorney, the attorney may withdraw, *but only after* taking reasonable steps to protect the client's interests. Rule 1.16(b)(5) & (d); DR 2–110(A)(2) & (C)(1)(f). If the matter is before a tribunal, then the lawyer may not even withdraw unless the tribunal permits. Rule 1.16(c); DR 2–110(A)(1). In any event, until the lawyer is able to withdraw in accordance with the requirements in the ethics rules, the lawyer may not neglect the client's case. E.g., *In re Pines*, 26 A.D.2d 424, 275 N.Y.S.2d 122, 123 (1st Dept. 1966) (per curiam) (client refusal to reimburse lawyer for expenses does not justify lawyer "in refraining from proceeding in the action for over three years . . . "). Similarly, an attorney's heavy workload does not excuse his continued neglect of probate matters. *Matter of Loomos*, 90 Wash.2d 98, 579 P.2d 350 (1978).

C. Crimes or Frauds

The client's "ultimate authority to determine the purposes to be served by legal representation" (Rule 1.2, Comment 1) is limited by other law as well as by the ethics rules. Thus, the lawyer may not "counsel a client to engage, or assist a client, in conduct that the lawyer knows is criminal or fraudulent. . . ." Rule 1.2(d); See DR 7–102(A)(7); DR 7–102(A)(6).

Note: While Rule 1.2(d) uses the term "criminal or fraudulent" the Code used the broader term "illegal or fraudulent." DR 7–102(A)(7). The Code language is more open-ended and may even include violation of civil law, such as tortious conduct.

The Rules (like the Model Code) is not as clear as we would like in defining "counsel" or "assist," though they make some effort to explain by example. In general, the lawyer may present an analysis of the legal aspects of questionable conduct but may not recommend "the means by which a crime or fraud might be committed with impunity." Rule 1.2, Comment 9. See EC 7–5. The lawyer must give his "honest opinion" about the "actual consequences" of the client's acts. Id. Accord, Rule 2.1, Comment 1. It is irrelevant that the defrauded party is not a party to the transaction. For example, the lawyer may not help the client effectuate a "sham transaction" to escape tax liability. Comment 12.

The lawyer may give an "honest opinion about the actual consequences that appear likely to result from a client's conduct." The fact that the client then uses that advice to aid his crime or fraud does not, of itself, "make a lawyer a party to the course of action." Rule 1.2, Comment 9. That is because there is a "critical distinction between presenting an analysis of legal aspects of questionable conduct and recommending the means by which a crime or fraud might be committed with impunity." Comment 9.

However, even when the lawyer may not reveal such client information (see Part III, section I, supra, on confidences), the lawyer must avoid assisting the client's criminal or fraudulent purposes, for example, by drafting documents he knows are fraudulent, or by advising how the purpose might be concealed. Rule 1.2, Comment 10.

Notice of Withdrawal. If the lawyer discovers that he has been unwittingly assisting the client in conduct that the lawyer then discovers is criminal or fraudulent, then the lawyer must withdraw. Rule 1.2, Comment 10; Rule 4.1, Comment 3.

From 1983, when the ABA House of Delegates approved the Model Rules, until the 2003 revisions, the Model Rules had an important concept found in Comments to Rule 1.6. This concept was a "notice of withdrawal," which was found in the Model Rules at Rule 1.6, Comment 14. This Comment, titled, "Withdrawal," said, among other things: "after withdrawal the lawyer is required to refrain from making disclosure of the client's confidences, except as otherwise provided in Rule 1.6. Neither this rule nor Rule 1.8(b) nor Rule 1.16(d) prevents the lawyer from *giving notice of the fact of withdrawal, and the lawyer may also withdraw or disaffirm any opinion, document, affirmation, or the like.*" Rule 1.6 *no longer provides for a notice of withdrawal as the remedy for client fraud.* Instead, Rule 1.6(b)(2) & (3) provide that, if the lawyer learns that the client has used or is using the lawyer's services in order to commit a crime or fraud that is "reasonably certain" to result in "substantial injury" to another person's financial interests, the lawyer *may reveal* the information to either prevent, mitigate, or rectify the problem.

Nonetheless, the ABA did not change Rule 1.2, Comment 10 and Rule 4.1, Comment 3, both of which refer to a "Notice of Withdrawal." Both of these Comments also advise that if withdrawal is insufficient for the lawyer to stop assisting a client in criminal or fraudulent conduct, then it "may be necessary for the lawyer to give notice of the fact of withdrawal and to disaffirm any opinion, document, affirmation or the like." Rule 1.2, Comment 10. Accord, and Rule 4.1, Comment 3. So, there still is a notice of withdrawal, but its importance is substantially less significant in light of the important changes in Rule 1.6.

Prior to 2003, the ABA Model Rules did not allow the lawyer to blow the whistle on a client's financial frauds but it did allow the lawyer to waive a red flag by giving a very noisy notice of withdrawal. The withdrawal was "noisy" because it could be given to anyone (like the SEC), not just the client. Now, Rule 1.6 allows the lawyer to blow the whistle. Hence, the noisy notice of withdrawal is most likely only likely to be important in the case of frauds or crimes that are not within Rule 1.6, such as a crime or fraud that is not "reasonably certain to result in substantial injury" to the financial interests of another, under Rule 1.6(b)(2).

Note: Different considerations apply if perjured testimony or false evidence has been offered before a tribunal. See Model Rule 3.3. These issues are considered in Part VII, Section II, A, 3 ("Disclosure of Facts"), infra.

Rule 4.1(b) announces that, in representing the client, a lawyer "shall not knowingly fail to disclose a material fact to a third person when disclosure is necessary to avoid assisting a criminal or fraudulent act by a client, *unless* disclosure is prohibited by Rule 1.6 [the confidentiality section]." (emphasis added). Rule 4.1(b) cannot mean that a lawyer may assist the client in a criminal or fraudulent act if failure to so assist would amount to a disclosure prohibited by Rule 1.6. If Rule 4.1(b) means that, it conflicts with Rule 1.2(d). In such a situation, in order to avoid violating either Rule 1.2(d) or 4.1(b), the lawyer would have to withdraw under Rule 1.16(a)(1). When withdrawing, the lawyer *may waive a red flag* by filing a "notice of withdrawal." See Rule 1.4, Comment 3. The lawyer should also inform the client of the lawyer's obligations under the Model Rules. Rule 1.2(e). See generally Part III, Section I, C, 7, supra ("Filing a Notice of Withdrawal"). In addition, Rule 1.6 may itself allow disclosure.

The lawyer may counsel or assist his client "to make a good faith effort to determine the validity, scope, meaning or application of the law." Rule 1.2(d). See also, DR 2–109(A)(2); DR 7–102(A)(2); EC 7–4; DR 7–106(A).

The lawyer may not agree to be general counsel for a criminal syndicate, but may agree to undertake "a criminal defense incident to a general retainer for legal services to a lawful enterprise." Rule 1.2, Comment 9; ABA Formal Opinion 281 (Mar. 11, 1952); ABA Defense Function Standards, Standard 4–3.7(c); *In re Abrams,* 56 N.J. 271, 266 A.2d 275 (1970). In other words, the lawyer may not become general counsel to a drug cartel, but may be general counsel to a large legitimate corporation, even though one expects the government may someday charge the corporation with a criminal violation of an environmental regulation, or an antitrust violation, or another law.

D. The Incompetent Client

The client may have diminished capacity, or be under a mental disability, or the client's youth may impair his ability to render a considered judgment. In such cases the lawyer should endeavor, insofar as possible, to maintain a normal lawyer-client relationship. Rule 1.14; EC 7–12. Even if the client is under a legal disability, he or she might still be capable of understanding the matter. In that case, the lawyer should obtain all possible aid from the client. Rule 1.14, Comment 1; EC 7–12.

When the client has diminished capacity, the lawyer may take "reasonably necessary protective action," such as consulting with entities or individuals (including family members) who have the ability to protect the client. Rule 1.14(b) & Comment 3. If it is appropriate, the lawyer may seek to have the court appoint a guardian for the client. Rule 1.14(b).

The client still has the protection of Rule 1.6, but Rule 1.14(c) advises that the lawyer is "impliedly authorized" to reveal otherwise confidential information about the client, "but only to the extent reasonably necessary to protect the client's interests." For example, the lawyer may need to consult and disclose information to a medical doctor. To protect the client, the lawyer may even withhold from the client the doctor's psychiatric diagnosis of the client *if* the "examining psychiatrist indicates that disclosure would harm the client" Rule 1.4, Comment 7.

ABA Formal Opinion 96–404 (Aug. 2, 1996) attempts to deal with the problems of *clients* who have become legally incompetent to handle their own affairs. If the client is in fact incompetent, Rule 1.14(a)'s admonition to try to "maintain a normal lawyer-client relationship" with the client is not realistic. Moreover, in some states the agency relationship between lawyer and client may be dissolved automatically because of the client-principal's incompetence. Oddly enough, Rule 1.16, Comment 6, comes to an opposite conclusion. It states: "If the client has severely diminished capacity, *the client may lack the legal capacity to discharge the lawyer*, and in any event the discharge may be seriously adverse to the client's interests." (emphasis added).

Formal Opinion 96–404 counsels the lawyer to take the "least restrictive action under the circumstances." The lawyer should not seek appointment of a guardian "if other, less drastic, solutions are available." Even if a guardian is needed for some purposes, something less than a general guardianship should be sought if possible. The lawyer should petition for guardianship if the lawyer concludes it is necessary, not because someone else (such as a family member) requests it. Finally, if the lawyer is asked to recommend a guardian, any expectation the lawyer may have of future employment by the guardian must be disclosed to the appointing court, as must any different preference for a guardian that the client might have expressed.

In 1997, the ABA House of Delegates built on this Opinion by adding what are now Comments 9 and 10, dealing with "Emergency Legal Assistance." The core idea is that sometimes the health, safety or a financial interest of a person under a disability is threatened with imminent and irreparable harm. In those circumstances, "a lawyer may take legal action on behalf of such a person even though the person is unable to establish a client-lawyer relationship or make or express considered judgments about the matter, when that person" or someone acting in good faith on the client's behalf has consulted with the lawyer. Comment 9. The Comment goes on to say that the lawyer should keep the confidences of the disabled person, should not act in this capacity if the person has another lawyer, and normally should not charge a fee for the services rendered. Comment 10.

Not all authority agrees with this ABA ethics opinion. For example, California State Bar Opinion 1989–112 (1989) concluded that the lawyer may not reveal client confidences to the court and family members even when the lawyer believes that the client is incompetent.

Consider, *Matter of M.R.*, 135 N.J. 155, 638 A.2d 1274 (N.J.1994). M.R., a 21–year old woman with Down's Syndrome, was incapable of managing her day-to-day affairs. Her father and mother each wanted to be her guardian. M.R. wanted to live with her father. The court appointed a lawyer for M.R. The court determined that the lawyer should not decide for himself what is best for M.R.; that would be the function of a guardian. The lawyer should advocate what M.R. wants, short of things "patently absurd or that pose an undue risk of harm to the client."

IV. Fees

A. Basic Principles

1. Reasonableness Requirement

Fees Must Be Reasonable.

Because the lawyer is a fiduciary of the client, the lawyer is subject to discipline if the fees are not "reasonable." Rule 1.5(a). The Code used the term "clearly excessive," DR 2–106(A), but it really means "unreasonable." The former Code did not mean that a fee could be excessive, as long as they were not clearly so. Indeed, the Code itself went on to define "clearly excessive" in terms of reasonableness: "a lawyer of ordinary prudence would be left with the definite and firm conviction that the fee is in excess of a reasonable fee." DR 2–106(B). See also, EC 2–17 ("A lawyer should not charge more than a reasonable fee;" "adequate compensation is necessary").

Both the Rules and the old Code Rules list the same eight factors that are relevant in determining reasonableness. The ethics rules do not limit the determination of reasonableness to these eight factors; these are simply factors to be considered. Comment 1.

Reasonableness is determined by considering how much time and labor are required, the novelty of the legal service, and how much skill is needed to perform it. Rule 1.5(a)(1); DR 2–106(B)(1). For many lawyers the hourly rate is the most important (or possibly even the sole) factor used to determine fees. Of course, a lawyer basing the fee on the hours expended may not engage in goldbricking, that is, employing wasteful procedures in an effort to increase the number of billable hours. Rule 1.5, Comment 5.

Taking one matter may well preclude lawyers from taking other legal work. The lawyer may consider this opportunity cost; if the client is not aware of this opportunity cost, the lawyer should tell him. Rule 1.5(a)(2); DR 2–106(B)(2).

The lawyer may also consider the fees customarily charged in the locality for similar legal services. Rule 1.5(a)(3); DR 2–106(B)(3). It would be a violation of the antitrust laws for the bar association to discipline a lawyer because he has charged less than a minimum (or more than a maximum) fee. *Goldfarb v. Virginia State Bar,* 421 U.S. 773, 95 S.Ct. 2004, 44 L.Ed.2d 572 (1975). However, the mere fact that all lawyers of similar quality charge the same, or approximately the same, fee for similar services is not evidence of price-fixing, because, in a perfectly competitive economy, the prices for similar services (discounted for quality) are also the same.

If a lawyer purports to charge by the hour, it is unreasonable for a lawyer to bill more time than she has actually spends on a matter (although she can round up minimum time periods such as quarter-hours, or tenths of an hour). To bill several clients for the same time (e.g., scheduling court appearances for two clients on the same day, spending two hours at the courthouse, and billing each client the full two hours), or for the same work product (e.g., spending 15 hours preparing a research memorandum for one client, which happens to be relevant to a second client, and then billing each client the full 15 hours) violates Rule 1.5. ABA Formal Opinion 93–379 (Dec. 6, 1993).

While ABA Formal Opinion 93–379 says it is interpreting Rule 1.5, it's conclusion is really grounded on a notion of misrepresentation: if the lawyer purports to bill by the hour, then billing two different clients twice for the same hour is a misrepresentation. If the lawyer, instead, tells the client that he will prepare an opinion letter for a flat fee, and the client agrees, then it does not matter how many hours (or how few hours) the lawyer took because he was not billing by the hour.

Note: While lawyers may not conspire to fix prices, the federal antitrust laws do not forbid the state from setting prices. Price-fixing by state action is exempt from the Sherman Act. See, e.g., *Gair v. Peck*, 6 N.Y.2d 97, 188 N.Y.S.2d 491, 160 N.E.2d 43 (1959), cert. denied, 361 U.S. 374, 80 S.Ct. 401, 4 L.Ed.2d 380 (1960) (maximum prices set by the court in contingent fee causes).

ABA Formal Opinion 00–420 (Nov. 29, 2000), considers the situation where a lawyer hires a contract lawyer (an outside lawyer hired for a particular service, such as a temporary legal worker) for the client. If the lawyer bills the client for the use of the contract lawyer as a *disbursement* (an expense or a cost), then, unless the client has an understanding to the contrary, the lawyer may only charge the client the cost directly associated with the service. The lawyer cannot add a surcharge. But if the lawyer bills the client for the contract lawyer as *fees for legal services*, then the lawyer may add a surcharge (a profit) for those services, as long as the total fee is reasonable. This Formal Opinion adds that this surcharge is permissible, "whether the use and role of the contract lawyer are or are not disclosed to the client." In short, when the lawyer bills a client for "legal services," that fee may include charges for overhead and profit.

The lawyer may also take into account how much money is involved and how successful the attorney is in the particular matter. Rule 1.5(a)(4); DR 2–106(B)(4). It is not uncommon for a law firm to raise or lower a base hourly rate by a varying amount depending on the success of the negotiations, the size of the deal, and so forth. However, if the firm represented to the client that the fee would be based only on the numbers of hours worked, it should be unreasonable for the firm to retroactively change the basis of the fee.

The lawyer may adjust the bill if the circumstances or the client impose special time limitations. Rule 1.5(a)(5); DR 2–106(B)(5). The nature and length of the relationship with the client is also relevant. Rule 1.5(a)(6); DR 2–106(B)(6). That is, special circumstances might make a lawyer more likely to reduce a bill for an old client, or to cut a bill as a "loss leader," in an effort to encourage a new client to continue to retain the lawyer in other matters. If the client needs to have a matter done with unusual speed, the lawyer may be justified in raising the fee.

The lawyer may also consider his own experience, reputation, and ability. Rule 1.5(a)(7); DR 2–106(B)(7). Lawyers who are twice as good are justified in charging twice as much. If the prospective client, after hearing that boast, does not think the lawyer is worth that much, the prospective client can hire another lawyer.

The fee may be fixed or contingent. Rule 1.5(a)(8); DR 2–106(B)(8). Thus, a fee that looks large in retrospect, may not appear as large if one considers that the fee was contingent and that the lawyer risked receiving nothing.

If a client alleges that a lawyer's fee is excessive, these various factors are used in determining what is an attorney's reasonable fee, what is the fair market value of his services. It is also certainly relevant if, for example, the attorney overreached the client, abused the relationship, or was not completely candid in discussing the elements of a fee.

Some commentators have claimed that the nature of the lawyer's product make rational valuation of the individual attorney's services practically impossible. That is too pessimistic a view of the ability of the market place to value services. Courts have not found it impossible to value attorney's fees, and have found some to be excessive. E.g., *The Florida Bar v. Moriber,* 314 So.2d 145 (Fla.1975) (per curiam) (even though client may have been informed of fee of nearly $8,000 for collecting, on behalf of client, approximately $23,000 in an investor's variable payment fund, which had passed to client by operation of law, the fee was excessive). Cf. *United States v. Vague,* 697 F.2d 805, 806 (7th Cir.1983) (Posner, J.)(even a fixed fee freely bargained by competent adults who do not complain about it may be excessive). See also, Brickman & Cunningham, *Nonrefundable Retainers: Impermissible Under Fiduciary, Statutory and Contract Law,* 57 Fordham L.Rev. 149 (1988).

Note: If the lawyer is paid in property, the fee may be subject to the requirements of Rule 1.8(a), which govern business dealings between the lawyer and client, because the lawyer may have special knowledge of the value of the property. Rule 1.5, Comment 4.

Fee Shifting Statutes. To be distinguished from cases where the attorney and client bargain for a fee (later challenged as excessive) are cases involving fee shifting statutes. In those cases, such as civil rights cases, the court is authorized to require the losing party to pay the attorney's fees of the prevailing party. Under the Civil Rights Attorney's Fees Awards Act of 1976, 42 U.S.C.A. § 1988, the prevailing plaintiff ordinarily should receive an attorney's fee; in contrast, the prevailing defendant may recover an attorney's fee only if the lawsuit was vexatious, frivolous, or brought to harass or embarrass the defendant. To determine what a reasonable fee is, the "critical inquiry" is generally the appropriate hourly rate multiplied by the number of hours reasonably expended on the litigation. 4 Ronald D. Rotunda & John E. Nowak, *Treatise on Constitutional Law: Substance and Procedure* § 19.36 (West Group, 3d ed.1999).

2. Writing Requirement

A frequent cause of clients' disputes with their attorneys regarding fees is misunderstanding. Consequently, the Code advised that it "is usually beneficial to reduce [the fee arrangement] to writing. . . . " EC 2–19. The Rules raise this recommendation to the disciplinary level, but still make the language precatory. Rule 1.5(b) ("preferably in writing"). The lawyer should give this writing to the client before or a reasonable time after beginning the representation. Malpractice experts recommend that the lawyer "confirm in writing the basis of the fee." 1 R. Mallen & J. Smith, *Legal Malpractice* § 2.9 (3d ed. 1989).

As to *contingent fees*, the Code merely urged a writing, EC 2–19, but the Rules *require* it. Rule 1.5(c). This writing must state how the fee is determined and whether expenses are deducted before or after the contingent fee is calculated. If the lawyer insists on holding the client liable for certain expense even if the client loses, the lawyer must "clearly notify" the client of this unpleasant fact. These facts must be incorporated in a writing that the *client must sign*. After the matter is concluded, the lawyer must also provide a detailed statement to the client. Rule 1.5(c).

3. Price Discrimination

The Rules, like the Code, allow price discrimination. That is, the lawyer may lower a fee depending on who the client is. Because lawyers may charge less to the less wealthy, they, by necessary implication, may charge more for the same services offered to the more wealthy. See, e.g., Rule 1.5, Comment 5 ("it is proper to define the extent of services in light of the client's ability to pay"); EC 2–24, 2–25.

4. Suing to Collect Fees

On an aspirational level, the Model Code advised that lawyers should not sue the client to collect a fee "unless necessary to prevent fraud or gross imposition by the client." EC 2–23.

The Rules have no such prohibition. However, if the bar has established a mediation or arbitration system, the Rules encourage lawyers to use them if they are voluntary and to comply with them if they are mandatory. Rule 1.5, Comment 9. Cf. EC 2–23. It is ethical for lawyers to provide in their clients' retainer agreements a provision that requires binding arbitration of disputes involving lawyers' fees or malpractice claims. However, the lawyer must explain to the client the advantages and disadvantages, and the client must give informed consent. ABA Formal Opinion 02–425 (2002).

B. Contingent Fees

1. Writing Requirement

The Rules *require* (the Model Code merely encourages) all contingent fee arrangements to be in writing. See section A, 2, supra.

2. Offering Alternatives

The last sentence of what had been Comment 3 to Rule 1.5 used to say that the lawyer has no right to impose a contingent fee on a client who desires another arrangement, and the lawyer should volunteer alternative arrangements to clients if that is in the clients' best interest. The ABA deleted that sentence in 2002. The Reporter's Notes state the reason for the deletion: "If the contingent fee is reasonable, then lawyers need not offer an alternative fee nor need they inform clients that other lawyers might offer an alternative."

One would think that the lawyer, as fiduciary, should advise the client, e.g., "I only work on a contingency basis; but for this type of matter you would be better off if you retained a lawyer who worked by the hour instead of by contingency." However, no provision of the Model Rules imposes that requirement.

3. When Forbidden

Criminal Cases. Both the Code and the Rules forbid contingent fees in criminal cases because, it is said, of the lack of a *res* out of which the fee is to be paid. Rule 1.5(d)(2); DR 2–106(C); EC 2–20. However, in other areas of the law, litigation may produce no *res* and yet the attorney may be paid only if successful. E.g., *Mills v. Electric Auto–Lite Co.*, 396 U.S. 375, 90 S.Ct. 616, 24 L.Ed.2d 593 (1970)(in corporate derivative suit, corporation must pay plaintiff's attorney on a "benefits conferred" theory, although victory produced no *res*). Perhaps the reason for the rule prohibiting contingent fees in criminal cases rests on "historical accident, arising in earlier cases during a time when all contingent fee contracts were generally regarded with great suspicion. . . . " Charles Wolfram, Modern Legal Ethics 536 (1986). Its continuation may result from the desire of criminal defense counsel to be paid by their clients in advance; the ethical prohibition thus gives lawyers a good excuse to reject the efforts of those clients who might insist on a contingent fee if that alternative were possible.

It would be contrary to public policy for the state to hire a *prosecutor* on a contingency fee basis, *i.e.,* the prosecutor gets paid only if he secures a criminal conviction. *Baca v. Padilla*, 26 N.M. 223, 190 P. 730 (1920) (contract is void and there can be no recovery on it). The rationale behind this prohibition is not difficult to find: the duty of a prosecutor is to do justice, not merely to convict. The state's interest "in a criminal prosecution is not that it shall win a case, but that justice shall be done." *Berger v. United States*, 295 U.S. 78, 88, 55 S.Ct. 629, 633, 79 L.Ed. 1314 (1935).

Domestic Relations Cases. The Code finds that contingent fees in domestic relations matters are "rarely justified," EC 2–20, but it does not raise this note of discouragement to the level of discipline. In contrast, the Rules flatly forbid fees in divorce matters contingent upon "the securing of a divorce or upon the amount of alimony or support or property settlement" achieved. Rule 1.5(d)(1). The Rules do not explain the purpose of its prohibition, but the reason behind it is easy to understand. Because public policy does not encourage divorce, the lawyer's fee arrangements should not place the lawyer in a position where the lawyer might be encouraged to prevent any possible reconciliation of the parties. The lawyer who charged a contingent fee would place himself in a conflict situation, for he would lose his fee if he encouraged reconciliation.

A number of state ethics committee opinions construed Rule 1.5(d) to permit contingent fees in post-decree family law matters, i.e., collecting arrearages that have been reduced to judgment, because such fee arrangements do not implicate the same policy matters that are implicated when fees are contingent upon securing a divorce or on the amount of alimony, support or property order. In 2002, the ABA added Comment 6 to adopt that interpretation.

Other Cases. The Rules (like its predecessor, the Code) do not forbid, as a matter of attorney discipline, contingent fees in other classes of cases. Typically contingent fees exist in personal injury litigation, but they are not limited to those cases. For example, contingent fees are proper in administrative agency proceedings. EC 2–20. A common justification of contingent fees is that they allow poorer litigants to hire competent lawyers and pay them out of the judgment won. They also allow litigants to set up a fee system that gives a special incentive to their lawyers. Hence, even clients able to pay an hourly fee may prefer a contingent fee arrangement.

Neither the Rules nor the Code forbid a lawyer from accepting a contingent fee from a client who can afford a reasonable fixed fee. Also, the mere fact that liability may be clear does not, by itself, render a contingent fee inappropriate or unethical. There may be a substantial dispute as to the extent of the damages. An ABA Formal Ethics Opinion also advises that the fact that a lawyer is paid a contingent fee imposes no ethical obligation on the lawyer to solicit an early settlement offer on behalf of the client (who may not even wish to settle). The lawyer may not have enough information about the defendant's conduct and the claim to evaluate an early settlement offer. Lawyer and client may also agree that the lawyer will charge a different contingent fee rate at different stages of a matter and may increase (or decrease) the percentage taken as a fee as the amount of the recovery to the client increases. After all, it is the last dollars of recovery, not the first, that normally require the greater effort. ABA Formal Opinion 94–389 (Dec. 5, 1994).

Reverse Contingent Fees. The Model Rules do not have any *per se* prohibition of defense counsel charging contingent fees in civil cases, where the contingency is based on the amount of money (if any) that the defense counsel saves for the client, if the amount saved is reasonably determinable. Such contingent fees must also meet the other requirements of Rule 1.5. The fee must be reasonable and the client's agreement to the fee arrangement must be fully informed. Often, the amount that plaintiff claims in a case is not readily determinable, e.g., an unliquidated tort damages complaint may claim a vague amount ("damages in excess of $1 million"). If the "dollar amount of plaintiff's claim is unspecified, it is up to negotiation between the lawyer and the client defendant to establish a fair dollar figure to attribute to plaintiff's claim." Formal Opinion 93–373 (Apr. 16, 1993).

The reasonableness of the reverse contingent fee depends on the degree to which the savings from liability is reasonably ascertainable. To use the plaintiff's prayer for relief in an unliquidated tort damages claim as the *sole* basis to calculate a reverse contingent fee is unreasonable because the claim is purely speculative in amount. *Wunschel Law Firm, P.C. v. Clabaugh,* 291 N.W.2d 331 (Iowa 1980). If the plaintiff sues your client for $10 billion, and you settle the case for $100 million, you may not have really "saved" your client $9.9 billion, for the risk of a $10 billion verdict may be infinitesimal.

Conflicts of Interest. Contingent fees raise a potential conflict of interest between the attorney and client. See EC 5–7. For example, the client may wish to settle litigation while the attorney would want to press on, or vice-versa. The ethics rules attempt to reduce such conflicts, and have specific provisions—in the conflicts of interest section—dealing with contingent fees. See Rule 1.8(i); DR 5–103(A). These provisions forbid a lawyer from acquiring a proprietary interest in the client's cause of action or subject matter *except* that: (1) he may acquire a lien to secure his fees or expenses as authorized by other law (see *Lien,* in the Glossary, Appendix I) and (2) he may "contract with a client for a reasonable contingent fee in a civil case." Rule 1.8(i)(2); DR 5–103(a). *Exception 2 validates contingent fees.* However, the client may not assign to the attorney his cause of action because clients cannot waive their right to decide when to settle litigation. Rule 1.2(a); EC 7–7.

Example: Client agrees to compensate Lawyer by giving him a one-fourth interest in certain real property and mining claims. Ownership of these properties is disputed and Lawyer defends Client (and himself as well, to the extent that the Lawyer's one-fourth interest is involved). Client becomes dissatisfied with Lawyer's services and tries to discharge Lawyer, who refuses to leave. Lawyer has violated the ethics rules because he has refused to accept the client's discharge. ABA Informal Opinion 1397 (Aug. 31, 1977).

C. Fee Referrals

A division of a fee "is a single billing to a client covering the fee of two or more lawyers who are not in the same firm." Rule 1.5, Comment 7. Such divisions are commonly called "referral fees" or "forwarding fees." *The Rules (like the Code) do not regulate how lawyers divide legal fees within the same firm.* If lawyers are partners, they can divide fees anyway they wish. It is not unusual for some lawyers to be the rainmakers, who bring in a lot of the business, while other lawyers focus on more mundane matters.

The Rules allows referral fees only if several conditions exist.

FIRST, the fee division is in proportion to the services that each lawyer performs *or*, each lawyer assumes "joint responsibility" for the matter. "Joint responsibility," the Reporters Notes to the 2002 revisions tell us, means that the lawyers assume legal responsibility, including financial and ethical responsibility, "as if the lawyers were associated in a partnership." This is the interpretation that has been given to the term by a number of state ethics opinions, and Rule 1.5, Comment 7 adopts that view.

The Rules aid clients by allowing referrals and thus encouraging lawyers to refer matters to other lawyers who will be more competent to help the client. When the Rules first allowed such referrals in 1983, many lawyers have objected to this change. See, e.g., National Law Journal., (2/5/1979), at p. 18 (editorial). Oddly enough, the Rules on this point merely reinstate the rule existing under the old ABA Canons of Professional Ethics, Canon 37 (1908, as amended 1937), which allowed a division of fees with another lawyer "based upon a division of service *or* responsibility." (emphasis added). The Model Code did not allow referrals based on merely assuming responsibility, but the Model Rules clearly allow that.

SECOND, for the referral fee to be proper, the client must consent to the employment of the other lawyer after a full disclosure that a division of fees will be made. This disclosure must include the share each lawyer will receive. This agreement must be confirmed in writing. Rule 1.5(e)(2).

Prior to 2003, the Rules made clear that the client did not have to be told the share each lawyer will receive. The client had to be told of the fact of a division but need not be told of the percentage of the fee each lawyer will receive. Now, "the client must agree to the arrangement, *including the share that each lawyer is to receive.*" Rule 1.5, Comment 7.

THIRD, the total fee (including the referral fee) must be reasonable.

Thus, a referral fee is proper under the Rules if Lawyer #1 assumes joint responsibility (i.e., malpractice liability and the supervisory responsibility imposed by Rule 5.1) with Lawyer #2 for the particular matter, the total fee is reasonable, and the Client is advised and does not object.

Comment 8, added in 2002, seeks to clear up a confusion as to whether Rule 1.5(e)(1) must be satisfied when a lawyer leaves a law firm, and the departing lawyer agree to share some part of a fee to be received in the future. The Reporter's Notes advise: "Technically, the future division would be between lawyers who were no longer members of the same law firm. None of the usual reasons for requiring the client's agreement to the arrangement apply to such fee divisions, however, and this Comment is intended to make that clear."

V. Accepting, Declining, and Terminating Representation

A. Accepting and Declining Representation

The American lawyer, unlike the English barrister—or cab driver, who is bound to respond to the first hail—is not obligated to accept every client who walks through the door. But the lawyer may not reject a client because the client or the cause is unpopular. Rule 6.2; see also, EC 2–27, 2–28, 2–29, 2–30. See generally Part IX, section III, infra. On the English "Taxicab Rule" for barristers, see W.W. Boulton, *A Guide to Conduct and Etiquette at the Bar of England and Wales* 17–33 (4th ed. 1965). This English "Taxicab Rule" does not apply to solicitors.

A lawyer also may not accept a case if doing so will violate a disciplinary rule or other law, or if the lawyer cannot perform prompt and competent service. Rule 1.16(a)(1), (2), & Comment 1; EC 2–30.

B. Terminating Representation

1. Overriding Principles

The rules regarding withdrawal are more complex. One must first keep in mind several overriding principles.

FIRST, if a matter is before a tribunal, the lawyer must follow that tribunal's rules, which typically require securing the tribunal's permission before withdrawing. If the tribunal does not grant permission, the lawyer must continue in the case even though the lawyer would otherwise have a right, or duty, to withdraw. Rule 1.16(c); DR 2–110(A)(1). If the tribunal asks the lawyer why he is seeking withdrawal, the lawyer's duty to keep client confidences may prevent the lawyer from responding. Rule 1.16, Comment 3. This Comment advises the lawyer to be "mindful" of her obligations under Rule 1.6 and Rule 3.3. However, the Comment does not remind the lawyer that, in cases involving a client's crimes or fraud, the confidentiality rules do not prevent the attorney from filing a "notice of the fact of withdrawal" and withdrawing or disaffirming any opinion, document, affirmation, or the like. Rule 1.2, Comment 10, Rule 4.1, Comment 3. And, Rule 1.6 now allows the lawyer to disclose client information to prevent, mitigate, or rectify a client's serious fraud or crime if the client involved the lawyer's services.

If the client discharges the lawyer and the tribunal does not permit the lawyer to withdraw, the lawyer must comply with the orders of the tribunal. Compare Rule 1.16(a) with Rule 1.16(c).

If the matter is before a tribunal, that tribunal may simply refuse to allow the lawyer to withdraw. *E.g., Haines v. Liggett Group, Inc.,* 814 F.Supp. 414 (D.N.J.1993), where plaintiff's lawyer moved to withdraw in tobacco litigation on the grounds that the firm could no longer absorb the cost of financing the litigation. The judge, relying on Rule 1.16(c), denied the request, noting that unprofitability is an inherent risk of contingent fee litigation; the law firm cannot walk away from its contract because the case may not generate the return initially predicted.

Second (assuming that the matter is not before a tribunal or that, if it is, the tribunal agrees), the client always "has a right to discharge a lawyer at any time, with or without cause, subject to liability for payment of the lawyer's services." Rule 1.16, Comment 4. In such a case, if the client fires the lawyer, the lawyer must withdraw. Rule 1.16(a)(3); DR 2–110(B)(4).

Agency law recognizes the concept of a "power coupled with an interest," such as the lender's power to sell the house when the mortgagor defaults. See, e.g., Sell on Agency § 229 (1975). But lawyers are not agents with a power coupled with an interest. No "lawyer can continue to represent a client who does not wish to be represented." ABA Informal Opinion 1397 (August 31, 1977). See also, Rule 1.16, Comment 4. Even a lawyer's contingent fee arrangement cannot be used to prevent the client from discharging the lawyer. Id. Rule 1.8(i) (lawyer may not acquire a proprietary interest in client's cause of action). See *Richette v. Solomon,* 410 Pa. 6, 18–19, 187 A.2d 910, 917 (1963) (clause in retainer agreement prohibiting lawyer discharge is void).

Note: The power to discharge an attorney does not apply to cases controlled by other law, such as when a statute grants a term of office to a government attorney who cannot be fired except for cause. *Pillsbury v. Board of Chosen Freeholders of Monmouth*

County, 140 N.J.Super. 410, 356 A.2d 424 (1976) (per curiam), affirming, 133 N.J.Super. 526, 337 A.2d 632 (1975).

The client who discharges the lawyer is still liable for any fees earned, or for other contract or quasi-contract damages. See Rule 1.16(a)(3) and Comment 4. E.g., *Carlson v. Nopal Lines,* 460 F.2d 1209 (5th Cir.1972). And the lawyer must return any fee advances not yet earned. Rule 1.16(d).

THIRD, the lawyer must make reasonable efforts to protect the client's interests, such as giving reasonable notice to the client, surrendering papers and property to which the client is entitled, and refunding any prepayment of fees that have not yet been earned. Rule 1.16(d). Accord DR 2–110(A)(2). This duty exists not only when the attorney resigns but also when the client discharges the lawyer. E.g., *Dayton Bar Association v. Weiner,* 40 Ohio St.2d 7, 317 N.E.2d 783 (1974), cert. denied, 420 U.S. 976, 95 S.Ct. 1400, 43 L.Ed.2d 656 (1975).

2. Mandatory and Permissive Withdrawal

Given these general principles, the Rules divide withdrawal into two basic types—mandatory and permissive withdrawal. Both permissive and mandatory withdrawal are subject to the three overriding principles discussed above.

The lawyer *must* withdraw from a case if (1) continued employment would result in her violating the ethical rules or other law; if (2) the lawyer's physical or mental condition would materially impair her ability to represent her client; or (3) if the client discharges the lawyer. Rule 1.16(a).

The Rules also provide that the lawyer *may* withdraw without any reason if doing so has no material adverse effect on the client. Rule 1.16(b)(1). The Code had no such provision, but prior case law has recognized this right of an attorney, like any other agent. E.g., *Sterling v. Jones,* 255 La. 842, 846, 233 So.2d 537, 539 (1970).

The Rules, subject also to the three overriding principles discussed above, permit withdrawal (even if it causes material adverse impact to the client) if the client: persists in using the lawyer's services in an action that the lawyer "reasonably believes" is a crime of fraud; has used the lawyer to perpetrate a crime or fraud; insists on conduct the lawyer believes is repugnant or with which the lawyer has fundamental disagreement; fails substantially to fulfill an obligation to the lawyer and the client has been warned; or has made representation unreasonably difficult; or there is an unreasonable financial burden on the lawyer. Rule 1.16(b)(2)–(6).

The Rules add a catch-all—-when "other good cause for withdrawal." exists. Rule 1.16(b)(7). This catch-all is not limited to cases where the *tribunal* finds good cause.

All of these Rules of permissive withdrawal are subject to the overriding principles discussed above. For example, once the lawyer has filed an appearance, he may not withdraw from the litigation without the judge's permission to withdraw.

VI. Trust Fund Accounts

A. Establishing Trust Fund Accounts

Lawyers must be careful not to commingle a client's funds with the lawyer's own funds. The lawyer must hold client property as a fiduciary.

1. What Must Be Kept in Trust

The Rules (like the Code) require the lawyer to keep separate, identifiable accounts of client funds. The law firm may not commingle the firm's (or lawyer's) own funds with these client funds. Rule 1.15(a). For example, a law firm must not pay its debts by drawing a check on a client's trust fund account. The firm first should withdraw from that account any amount to which it is entitled. The firm then should place that amount in the firm's own account and draw a check on its own account. See, *Matter of Rabb,* 73 N.J. 272, 374 A.2d 461 (1977). The lawyer may not even temporarily borrow client funds. Such borrowing is really conversion. The lawyer can deposit his own funds in a client trust account "for the sole purpose" of paying bank service fees, and the deposit must be "only in an amount necessary for that purpose." Rule 1.15(b).

Note: The trust fund rule prohibits commingling client funds with the lawyer's funds. The client's funds must be segregated from the lawyer's funds. There is no prohibition against the lawyer keeping one client's funds with one or more other clients' funds in one trust account so long as careful records of each client's interests are kept. However, "[s]eparate trust accounts may be warranted when administering estate monies or acting in similar fiduciary capacities." Rule 1.15, Comment 1. See also, *Attorney Grievance Commission v. Boehm*, 293 Md. 476, 446 A.2d 52, 53 n. 2 (1982).

The bank account should be maintained in the state where the law office is, unless the client consents to a different place. Also, the law firm must identify other client property as such, and safeguard it appropriately. Rule 1.15(a).

Example: Client gives Lawyer bearer bonds for safe-keeping while Client is in Europe on an extended vacation. Lawyer places these bonds in the office safe, but does not identify them as belonging to Client. Lawyer has committed a disciplinable violation.

The Rules apply these trust fund rules not only to property of clients but also to property of third persons, when the property is in the lawyer's possession in connection with the representation of a client. Rule 1.15(a). This provision follows present practice. E.g., *Matter of Lurie*, 113 Ariz. 95, 546 P.2d 1126 (1976).

The lawyer must deposit into a trust fund account any prepaid legal fees and prepaid expenses, and they should be withdrawn as the fees are earned or the expenses paid. Rule 1.15(c). When the lawyer completes his services, he must return all prepaid fees that have not been earned, see Rule 1.16(d).

The lawyer must maintain complete records of all client property and render appropriate accounts to his client regarding them. Rule 1.15(a), (d). The Rules add a requirement that these records be kept for a given number of years (the Rules recommend five years) after the legal representation has ended. Rule 1.15(a).

Note: When the lawyer receives funds belonging in a trust fund account, the lawyer must promptly notify the client, or third party. Rule 1.15(d). The lawyer must then promptly pay or deliver to the client any trust funds or property that the client requests and to which the client is entitled.

2. Disputes Regarding Trust Fund Property

Occasionally the client and lawyer may have a dispute regarding trust fund property. For example, the settlement check for $90,000 may be deposited in the client account, and the lawyer would like to withdraw the agreed upon fee of one-third plus the amount to cover disbursements. But the client may claim that less than a third is due the lawyer, perhaps because of a dispute regarding whether one-third was reasonable under the circumstances, or because of a disagreement over disbursements.

The Rules lawyer may not withdraw the *disputed portion* until the dispute is resolved. Rule 1.15(e). The undisputed portion should be distributed; the lawyer may withdraw the undisputed portion of the funds from the trust fund account when due. Rule 1.15(d) & Comment 3: "The undisputed portion of the funds shall be promptly distributed." The lawyer may not, in an effort to coerce the client to give up his claim, refuse to deliver to the client the money that is undisputedly the client's.

3. Audits of Trust Fund Accounts

The Rules do not require any spot or systematic auditing by the bar authorities of client trust funds.

Note: The ABA, in its Model Standards for Lawyer Discipline and Disability Proceedings recommended that bar discipline counsel should have "ready access" to records of the location and number of client trust fund accounts held by all of the lawyers in the state. Standard 3.11(i). However, bar counsel should be able to verify the accuracy of these accounts only if there is "probable cause" that the funds have not been maintained properly or have been mishandled. Standard 13.3.

Notwithstanding the ABA's reluctance to require auditing, some states require spot checks. Some Canadian provinces require accounting certificates of trust fund accounts. Some commentators have proposed that all attorneys be bonded.

4. Interest Earned on Client Funds

Any interest earned on client trust fund accounts does not belong to the lawyer.

The Rules do not specifically deal with the question of the investment of client trust fund accounts. Usually, the funds are held for such a short time that the funds are kept in non-interest-bearing bank accounts. The administrative difficulty of apportioning to each of the clients their share of interest in a multi-client account with other clients' funds encourages non-interest bearing accounts. However, with modern computers, the assumed burden imposed by administrative difficulty should be (or soon will be) a thing of the past.

Normally a lawyer would be under no duty to invest client funds because he is usually keeping these funds in his capacity as a safeguarder, not an investor. However, in some cases the large amount of money and length of time involved may require the lawyer to secure from the client instructions regarding investments. ABA Formal Opinion 348 (July 23, 1982).

If funds are invested, the interest earned (whether small or large in amount) on the client's property belongs to the client, not to the lawyer. ABA Formal Opinion 348 (July 23, 1982). The original 1908 Canons of Professional Ethics made this point quite clearly. See Canon 11: Client funds should not "be commingled with [the lawyer's] own *or be used by* him" (emphasis added). Nor may the lawyer use interest earned to defray the expense of handling the agency account. ABA Informal Opinion 991 (July 3, 1967). The attorney may always bill the client separately for disbursements.

In recent years, the organized bar has created an exception to these basic rules. It has tried to collect the interest from the pool of trust fund accounts and use this otherwise untapped resource to fund law-related public service projects, such as indigent legal services. The nominal interest from many small accounts can quickly add up. The Law Foundation of British Columbia receives interest on Lawyer's trust fund accounts, and by 1976, interest income totaled over $2 million a year. See *In re Interest on Trust Accounts,* 356 So.2d 799, 804 (Fla.1978).

In ABA Formal Opinion 348 (July 23, 1982), the ABA ruled that the ethics rules do not stand in the way of such programs. Even without prior client consent or notice, the "interest earned on bank accounts in which are deposited client's funds, nominal in amount or to be held for short periods of time, under state-authorized programs providing for the interest to be paid to tax-exempt organizations" is not treated as funds of the client within the meaning of the ethics rules.

The Supreme Court has held that the state could require that client funds that cannot earn net interest for the client be deposited in "Interest on Lawyer's Trust Accounts" (IOLTA) and that the clients are not entitled to any compensation from the state for interest taken from these IOLTA accounts because they suffered no net loss in the context of the program at issue. *Brown v. Legal Foundation of Washington,* 538 U.S. __, 123 S.Ct. 1406, 155 L.Ed.2d 376 (2003). See Rotunda, *Found Money: IOLTA, Brown v.*

Legal Foundation of Washington, and the Taking of Property without the Payment of Compensation, 2002–2003 Cato Supreme Court Rev. 245 (2003).

B. Client Security Funds

Some states have established client security trust funds in order to offer some protection to clients whose attorneys had misappropriated their money. These funds are typically funded by periodic assessments on the members of the bar.

The Rules do not require the establishment of client protection funds, but lawyers must participate in them if other law makes that participation mandatory. If participation is voluntary, the lawyer "should" participate. Rule 1.15, Comment 6.

REVIEW QUESTIONS

1. Lawyer represented Client in a lawsuit completed over a decade ago. Lawyer has not represented Client since. Plaintiff, who was not involved in the prior litigation with Client, seeks to retain Lawyer to sue Client in another matter that is distinct from the prior litigation, but ancillary to it, and involves in part the same facts and circumstances, some of which are confidential.

It is *proper* for Lawyer to:

a.   Decline to represent Plaintiff.

b.   Refer the matter to his law partner, who was not involved in the prior litigation and who became associated with Lawyer only a year ago.

c.   Accept the representation after notifying Plaintiff and notifying Client.

d.   Refer the matter to Zeta, a lawyer in another firm, in exchange for a secret kickback of 10% of the fee that Zeta will charge Plaintiff.

2. Lawyer represents Plaintiff in a personal injury action. After successful negotiations, the case is settled. Defendant sends Lawyer a check for $30,000 payable to the order of Lawyer. One third of this amount represents Lawyer's undisputed fee. Consistent with Lawyer's ethical obligations, what may Lawyer do?

I.   Deposit the check in Plaintiff's trust fund account, inform Plaintiff, and forward a $20,000 check drawn on that account to Plaintiff.

II. Deposit the check in Lawyer's personal bank account and send to Plaintiff Lawyer's personal check for $20,000.

III. Send the check directly to Plaintiff after having endorsed it, and then ask Client to pay the fee.

    a. I & II only.

    b. I & III only.

    c. I, II, & III.

    d. III only.

    e. I only.

3. The same facts as Question 2. As between the lawyer and client, who may keep any interest earned on the funds in the client's trust fund account?

    a. The lawyer.

    b. The client.

4. Plaintiff has hired Lawyer to represent him in a lawsuit against Defendant, who in turn has filed a counterclaim against Plaintiff. A great deal of personal hatred has developed over the years between Plaintiff and Defendant, so Plaintiff orders Lawyer to pursue a hard line in the suit against Defendant. "I shall not settle," he says. "And I shall show him no mercy. I want to teach him a lesson."

Assuming that the lawsuit is not frivolous, Lawyer plans:

I. to reject Defendant's reasonable request for a continuance because Client refuses to accept Defendant's request.

II. to refuse to waive Client's affirmative defense to Defendant's counterclaim because Client refuses to consent to the waiver.

    a. Neither I nor II are *proper.*

    b. Only II is *proper.*

    c. Only I is *proper.*

    d. Both I and II are *proper.*

5. Williams is one of over 200 victims of an airline disaster case. The carrier has admitted liability and the only question remaining is the amount of damages. A few similar cases have already gone to trial with jury verdicts returned between $225,000 and $250,000 per victim. Williams asked Attorney to represent her in settlement negotiations with the carrier, which has announced that it will settle cases similar to Williams' for $235,000, a figure that is satisfactory to Williams. Therefore Williams asks Attorney to work for a reasonable hourly fee. She believes that Attorney's role will be primarily formal. Attorney, however, wants his standard one-third contingent fee.

> If Williams eventually agrees to Attorney's condition, was it *proper* for Attorney to insist upon a one-third contingent fee as a condition to taking the case?

>> a. Yes, unless no other attorney was available to work on a non-contingent basis.

>> b. No, unless a one-third contingent fee is customary in accident cases in the area where Attorney practices.

>> c. No, if under the circumstances, the contingent fee would be excessive.

>> d. Yes, because a successful prosecution of the claim produces a *res* out of which the fee can be paid.

6. John Doe requested that Attorney defend him in a murder charge. Attorney told Doe that he primarily handles civil matters, and was too busy to take the case anyway, so he gave Doe the names of three good criminal lawyers. As Doe was leaving, Attorney said, "Perhaps your case is unusually interesting. If so, I may make room to take it." Doe, in an effort to persuade Attorney to reconsider his decision, told Attorney the facts leading to his arrest, including an admission that he shot the deceased. Doe then asked Attorney what his reactions were. Attorney briefly discussed temporary insanity as a defense. However, Attorney said that the case was not interesting enough so he still refused to take the case. Doe subsequently hired another lawyer. Attorney did not charge Doe any fee.

> The prosecutor learned of Doe's conversation with Attorney and has subpoenaed Attorney to appear as a witness in Doe's trial.

Is it *proper* for Attorney to testify that Doe admitted shooting the deceased?

>> a. Yes, because the Attorney–Client relationship was never formed between Doe and Attorney.

b. Yes, because an Attorney did not charge Doe any fee.

c. No, because a lawyer may not disclose the confidence or secrets of a prospective client.

d. Yes, because Attorney told Doe that Attorney did not usually handle criminal matters.

e. No, because Attorney's testimony would be hearsay.

7. Attorney was an assistant state's attorney at the time the case of *State v. Criminal* was awaiting trial. The state Public Defender represented Criminal. Attorney could have obtained access to the file in that case but did not. Attorney, in fact, did not participate at all in this matter.

Attorney subsequently left that employment and now practices in a private law firm. Criminal has asked Attorney to represent him on the appeal from his criminal conviction in the case of *State v. Criminal*. Is it *proper* for Attorney to represent Criminal on the appeal?

a. No, because Attorney was a member of the prosecutor's office while the criminal matter was pending.

b. No, because Attorney is now, in effect, suing his former employer.

c. Yes, unless Attorney acquired confidential information concerning the case while in the prosecutor's office.

d. Yes, because Attorney had no substantial responsibility in the matter while in the prosecutor's office.

e. Both *c* and *d*.

8. Adam Advocate represents 22 plaintiffs who were victims of the same bus accident. He has negotiated with the bus company and the engine manufacturer a settlement that he reasonably believes is beneficial to all of the plaintiffs. Each plaintiff will receive between $35,000 and $250,000 in damages, the amount received being a function of the damages sustained. The defendants have stated quite clearly that they will not settle any of the 22 claims unless all 22 are settled. Adam is worried that if he reveals all of the details of the settlement to each of the 22 plaintiffs, there is a danger that the entire settlement will be upset.

If Adam reveals the entire settlement details to each of the 22 participants, is he *subject to discipline*?

a. No, but he would be engaged in a violation of his ethical aspirations.

b. Yes, because to do so might upset the entire settlement.

c. Yes, because he would violate client secrets.

d. No, because, unless he advises each of the individuals of the participation of each person in the settlement, they cannot provide informed consent.

9. Larry Lawyer engages extensively in counseling and advising clients with respect to tax matters and transactions that are largely tax-motivated. If the client-taxpayer's treatment of the transaction is not challenged by the Internal Revenue Service or if any challenge by the IRS is rejected by the courts, the transaction may result in a substantial reduction in taxes to the client. If, on the other hand, the transaction is not sustained, the taxpayer will at least be required to pay the tax he had hoped to avoid plus an interest and possibly a negligence penalty.

In advising a client on such a transaction with doubtful consequences, consider the following fee arrangements, none of which involve a criminal case:

I. Larry Lawyer and Client agree that the client will be charged a fixed fee, which includes not only the planning of the transaction but also covers representation of the client in the event the client's return is selected for audit, both before the Internal Revenue Service and in possible litigation before the Tax Court. If either the audit or the Tax Court litigation did not ensue, the lawyer would still keep the fee.

II. Larry Lawyer and Client agree on a contingent fee where Larry Lawyer is only to be paid if he accomplishes a tax saving for the client.

III. Larry Lawyer and Client agree on a fixed fee coupled with a contingency on the outcome of the case providing it is also understood that the fixed fee applies irrespective of the outcome and that the contingency applies only to the tax saving effected.

IV. Larry Lawyer and Client agree that Client will be charged for the legal services on an hourly basis.

Is Larry Lawyer *subject to discipline* for any of these fee arrangements, assuming that the fee is not "clearly excessive?"

a.   Yes, as to I, II, & IV.

b.   I only.

c.   II only.

d.   III only.

e.   IV only.

f.   I, II, III, & IV are all permitted.

10.   In a city of 200,000 Attorney Alpha represents Client Adams in the purchase of a residence. The representation was commenced in August and will continue until December, producing a fee of $300. In October, Client Brewer visits Alpha and explains that he wishes to bring a $200,000 personal injury case against Client Adams on a contingent fee basis. (The statute of limitations for this claim runs in November). Under the ethics rules what *must* Alpha do:

a.   Alpha should have another lawyer in his office handle the personal injury claim.

b.   Alpha should refer Brewer to another law firm but may claim a referral fee of ⅓ of the net fee, even if Brewer does not know of the referral fee.

c.   Alpha may accept Brewer's case, if he makes a full disclosure to Brewer of his current representation of Adams and Brewer consents.

d.   Alpha may ethically represent Brewer, but for practical reasons should not do so.

e.   Alpha cannot represent Brewer.

11.   Which of the following "fee schedules" are permitted after *Goldfarb v. Virginia State Bar*?

I.   The state legislature sets a fee of 5% of the gross estate in probate cases.

II.   The state Supreme Court sets a fee ranging from 10% to 20% in personal injury cases.

III. The local, voluntary bar mandates a minimum fee of $150 for an uncontested divorce.

IV. The state voluntary bar surveys every member of its association, and reports that in one downstate county, lawyers charge from $175 to $295 for an uncontested adoption.

    a.   Neither I, II, III, nor IV.

    b.   Only I & II.

    c.   Only I, II & IV.

    d.   All are permitted.

*

PART IV

The Lawyer's Obligation as a Member of a Firm

■ **ANALYSIS**

I. Introduction

Part 5 of the Rules has a specific section dealing with "Law Firms and Associations." Many of these provisions had no explicit counterpart in the Code. For the most part, however, Part 5 of the Rules does not change the law. Rather, it codifies and amplifies provisions found in scattered sections of the Code; it also elaborates on topics already implicit in the law of agency and tort.

II. Supervisory Responsibility Over Other Lawyers or Nonlawyer Employees

A. Lawyers

The partners or other supervisors in a law firm have the duty to make reasonable efforts to assure that all of the lawyers in the firm comply with the ethics rules. Rule 5.1(a). Cf. DR 4–101(D); EC 4–5. This duty similarly applies to other lawyers with general supervisory powers, such as the head of a corporate law department, the head of a government agency, or the shareholders of a professional legal corporation. Rule 5.1, Comment 1. The Rules do not specify what the appropriate procedural safeguards are. Whether the measures are reasonable depends on all the facts and the measures may vary depending on the size of the firm. Rule 5.1, Comment 3.

Even if a lawyer is not a partner or other general supervisor with managerial authority, he or she may have direct supervisory authority over another lawyer. Rule 5.1(b). For example, a senior associate may have some authority over a junior associate. Such a supervisor has the same responsibility as a partner or manager to assure compliance with the ethical rules by those lawyers under her direct supervisory authority. Rule 5.1(b). These managers must make sure that the firm has policies and procedures to detect conflicts of interest, keep client trust funds safe, train lawyers, etc. Comment 2. If the lawyer is ignorant of a conflict because of the law firm's failure to institute appropriate procedures, such ignorance will not excuse a lawyer's violation of this Rule. Rule 1.7, Comment 3. While the partner's or general manager's responsibilities relate to *all* lawyers in the firm, the supervisory lawyer's responsibilities relate only to those lawyers under her direct supervisory authority. Rule 5.1(b).

As a general principle, a lawyer may not knowingly assist another to violate the ethics rules or to violate those rules through the acts of another. Rule 8.4(a); DR 1–102(A)(2). Consequently, a lawyer is responsible for another lawyer's ethics violation if the first lawyer orders the second to engage in misconduct, or knowingly ratifies the second lawyer's misconduct. Rule 5.1(c)(1). The managing lawyer is also responsible for the other lawyer's ethical misconduct if the supervisory lawyer fails to take reasonable remedial action to avoid or mitigate the misconduct. Rule 5.1(c)(2). Cf. DR 1–103(A). For example, if a supervisory lawyer knows that a subordinate lawyer misrepresented a matter to an opposing party in negotiation, not only the subordinate but also the supervisor has a duty to correct the resulting misapprehension. Rule 5.1, Comment 4.

Wrongful Discharge. In recent years attorneys who have been fired by their clients or their law firm for refusal to engage in unethical activity have brought wrongful discharge suits, even though they are at-will employees. The courts have split on this issue, but the trend favors this cause of action. See, *Wieder v. Skala*, 593 N.Y.S.2d 752, 80 N.Y.2d 628, 609 N.E.2d 105 (1992) (lawyer who alleges that he was discharged from law firm because he insisted that his firm comply with its ethical obligation to report a fellow associate to the state bar disciplinary authorities has a cause of action for breach of contract; the duty to comply with the state bar's ethical rules is an implied-in-law condition of the employment contract). The fact that a client (or a law firm) has the right to fire an attorney for no reason does not imply a right to fire for the wrong reason. Of course, because clients can always fire their counsel at any time, with or without cause (Rule 1.16, Comment 4) the remedy for wrongful discharge would not be reinstatement but damages. The Model Rules do not prohibit a lawyer from suing her former client and employer for wrongful discharge, but the lawyer must take care not to disclose client information beyond that information the lawyer reasonably believes is necessary to establish her claim. ABA Formal Opinion 01–424 (September 22, 2001).

Comparing Tort and Ethical Liability. One should keep in mind the distinction between Rule 5.1 and tort liability, as well as the distinction, within Rule 5.1, between the failure to supervise and ordering or ratifying of unethical conduct.

Example 1:   Lawyer *A* is the supervisor of Lawyer *B*. Neither the firm nor Lawyer *A* exercises any care to assure that Lawyer *B* will protect client confidences. Nonetheless, Lawyer *B* in fact has not violated any confidences. Lawyer *A* has violated Rule 5.1(b), but not Rule 5.1(c). Lawyer *A* is also not liable to the client in tort, because there are no damages.

Example 2: Assume, in the above example, that Lawyer *A* does exercise reasonable supervisory care over Lawyer *B*, but Lawyer *B* nonetheless violates a client's confidences, causing the client monetary damage. Lawyer *A* has not violated Rule 5.1(b) or 5.1(c), but is liable in tort under a theory of vicarious liability.

Example 3: Assume, in Example 2, that Lawyer *A* discovers Lawyer *B*'s breach of confidence in time that he could prevent it, but Lawyer *A* acts unreasonably and fails to take any remedial action. Lawyer *A* has not violated Rule 5.1(b) but he has violated Rule 5.1(c)(2), and is also liable in tort, under a theory of vicarious liability.

B. Nonlawyer Employees

A lawyer's responsibility over nonlawyer employees parallels that over subordinate lawyers. See Rule 5.3. Cf. DR 4–101(D); EC 4–5; DR 7–107(J).

III. Responsibility of a Lawyer Subject to Supervision by Another Lawyer

A lawyer cannot escape responsibility for ethical misconduct merely by claiming that he followed orders. Rule 5.2(a); *In re Knight,* 129 Vt. 428, 430, 281 A.2d 46, 48 (1971) (per curiam) ("inexperienced attorney" under "domination" of experienced practitioner suspended for ethical violation; he could not "assign to another his duty to his oath").

On the other hand, if the ethical violation is not clear, the subordinate lawyer may defer to the judgment of the supervisory attorney. The subordinate does not violate his ethical duties if she follows the supervisor's "reasonable resolution of an arguable question of professional duty." Rule 5.2(b). Cf. Rule 1.13(b)(2) (in resolving ethical problem, lawyer for organization may advise that outside counsel supply separate legal opinion).

IV. Sharing Fees and Responsibility with Laypeople

A. Sharing Fees

In general, a lawyer or law firm cannot "share legal fees with a nonlawyer. . . . " Rule 5.4(a); DR 3–102(A). Similarly, a corporation such as Wal–Mart, or any nonlawyer, such as Donald Trump cannot own a law firm, or form a partnership with a law firm. Rule 5.4(b); DR 3–103(A). A corporation may certainly choose to have in-house counsel to represent it, but the corporation may not make a profit by using its in-house counsel to provide services to third parties for a fee, because that would constitute prohibited fee-sharing.

For example, ABA Formal Opinion 95–392 (April 24, 1995) concludes that there is improper fee-sharing if the corporation "rents out" its in-house counsel to perform legal work for other clients and collects a fee for the services at an hourly rate higher than the cost to the corporation of employing the lawyers. Also, if in-house corporate counsel successfully litigates a case for the corporation and seeks an award of attorney's fees under a fee-shifting statute, the lawyer may *not* share with her corporate employer a "reasonable attorney's fee" based on an hourly rate that exceeds the cost that the corporation incurred in employing the lawyer. To do so would also constitute improper fee-sharing with a nonlawyer. The ABA Opinion explained that involvement of nonlawyers, such as corporate employers, in the legal process may impair the lawyer's independent professional judgment because laypeople are not subject to the ethics rules governing lawyers, and fee-splitting between the lawyer and layperson poses the possibility of control by the layperson, interested in his profit more than the client's fate.

However, there are several significant limitations to the fee-sharing prohibition. One important exception allows lawyers to include nonlawyer employees in a compensation or retirement plan "even though the plan is based in whole or in part on a profit-sharing arrangement." Rule 5.4(a)(3). This exception is long-standing. See DR 3–102(A)(3).

Example: At the end of the year Law Firm gives each secretary a bonus because the firm just settled a significant case on very favorable terms. The firm's actions do not constitute a prohibited sharing of fees.

In addition, a law firm may agree to pay money to the estate of a deceased lawyer (or to other specified persons) for a reasonable period of time after the lawyer's death. Rule 5.4(a)(1); DR 3–102(A)(2). The estate is not a "lawyer," but there is no risk that the estate will interfere with the professional judgment of any lawyers remaining in the firm. The estate is merely the passive recipient of funds.

The Model Rules (since 1990) allow a lawyer to sell her law practice to another lawyer. Rule 1.17. To conform to that principle, the ABA added Rule 5.4(a)(2), which provides that if a lawyer (e.g., Lawyer *A*) purchases the law practice of "a deceased, disabled, or disappeared lawyer," (e.g., Lawyer *B*), then Lawyer *A* may agree to pay the purchase price to the estate or other representative of Lawyer *B*. The sale of a law practice is discussed at the end of this chapter, at section VI, B, below.

Note: Rule 5.4(a)(1),(2) and DR 3–102(A)(1),(2) do not apply to a lawyer who *retires* from a law firm. A deceased lawyer obviously cannot exercise any continuing oversight or be available for consultation regarding legal matters. A retired lawyer, however, can. In addition, when lawyers leave the law firm and retire from practice, a restriction on their right to compete with their former law firm does not interfere with the client's right to choose her lawyer because the lawyer, by hypotheses, is retired and the client cannot choose him. Thus, different rules apply to sharing fees with retired lawyers, Rule 5.6(a); DR 2–108(A), or to sharing fees with lawyers in other firms. Rule 1.5(e); DR 2–107(A). See Part III, Section IV, C, supra, regarding sharing fees with lawyers.

Sharing Fees in Pro Bono Cases. May a lawyer share court-awarded legal fees with a nonlawyer entity such as the ACLU, NAACP, etc.? For many years the language of Rule 5.4 appeared to prohibit that result and some cases enforced the literal language. ABA Formal Opinion 93–374 (June 7, 1993) reached the opposite result and concluded that the lawyer may share court-awarded legal fees with a not-for-profit, bona fide pro bono organization because there is no realistic risk of compromising the lawyer's independent judgment. Rule 5.4(a)(4), which the ABA added in the 2002 revisions, codifies that conclusion so that a lawyer may now share court-awarded legal fees with a non-profit organization that employed, retained, or recommended the lawyer to handle the case.

Partnerships with Lawyers in Sister States and Foreign Lawyers. If a law partnership has offices in several states, but not all the lawyers in the partnership are admitted in all jurisdictions, then the listings of the law firm (*e.g.*, the letterhead, bar listing, professional card) should list the pertinent jurisdictional limitations on the lawyer's ability to practice. ABA Formal Opinion 90–357 (May 10, 1990).

The situation is a little different if the law firm in the United States seeks to form a partnership with lawyers in a foreign country, as opposed to a sister state. ABA Formal Opinion 01–423 (September 22, 2001) concludes that the Model Rules allow U.S. lawyers to form law partnerships (or other entities) with foreign lawyers, for the purpose of practicing law, as long as the foreign lawyers are members of a recognized legal profession in a foreign jurisdiction and the arrangement is otherwise in compliance with the law of jurisdictions where the firm practices. However, members of a profession that is not recognized as a legal profession by the foreign jurisdiction would be considered "nonlawyers" so that admitting them to partnership would violate Rule 5.4. Before accepting a foreign lawyer as a partner, the responsible lawyers in American law firm must take reasonable steps to ensure that the foreign lawyer qualifies under this ethical standard.

B. Sharing Responsibility

Although lawyers may include lay employees in a profit-sharing arrangement, the lawyer may not give these people managerial control. Thus, lay people cannot be partners in law firms. See, e.g., Rule 5.4(b): "A lawyer shall not form a partnership with a nonlawyer if any of the activities of the partnership consist of the practice of law." Accord, DR 3–103(A). Perhaps some day the Model Rules will change, and Wal–Mart or Sears will be allowed to own a law firm. It is interesting to note that on January 1, 1991, Washington, D.C. became the first jurisdiction to amend its version of Rule 5.4(b) and allow nonlawyers to become partners in law firms, subject to various conditions (the effect of which is to prohibit Wal–Mart or Sears from owning a law firm).

Similarly, if the lawyer is practicing law in the form of a professional legal corporation, no lay person may be a director or officer (or have similar responsibility regardless of the title), or control the lawyer's legal judgment, or own any financial interest (except that a deceased lawyer's fiduciary representative may hold the lawyer's interest for a reasonable period of time during the administration of the estate). Rule 5.4(d); DR 5–107(C).

If someone other than the client pays for the client's legal services, the lawyer's obligations are still to the client. The lawyer may not allow the third party (who is paying for the services or who recommended the lawyer) to interfere with the lawyer's professional judgment. Rule 5.4(c); DR 5–107(B). Cf. Rule 1.8(f).

C. Law–Related Services

Someday, Sears or Wal–Mart may be able to own a law firm. In the meantime, may a law firm own and operate a department store? May it own an ancillary business, such as a patent consulting firm? In August of 1991, the ABA House of Delegates narrowly approved (197–186) a new rule to deal with this question, Model Rule 5.7, "Provision of Ancillary Services." At its August, 1992 annual meeting, the ABA repealed this Rule, by a vote of 190–183. It was the first time that the ABA House of Delegates simply repealed, outright, a Rule. At its February, 1994 midyear meeting the ABA approved a new Rule 5.7, entitled "Responsibilities Regarding Law–Related Services."

"Law-related services" are services that are reasonably performed in conjunction with, and are related to, legal services, and that, if performed by a nonlawyer, would not be the unauthorized practice of law. Rule 5.7(b). Examples include "title insurance, financial planning, accounting, trust services, real estate counseling, legislative lobbying, economic analysis, social work, psychological counseling, tax return preparation, and patent, medical or environmental consulting." Rule 5.7, Comment 9.

Various law firms, particularly in the Washington, D.C. area, have created subsidiaries to perform these services. Customers may include clients and nonclients. The existence of these subsidiaries raises various ethical issues mainly relating to conflicts of interest and attorney-client privilege. Rule 5.7(a) provides that a lawyer is subject to all of the Model Rules when providing these services if (1), he provides them in circumstances that are indistinct from his provision of legal services to clients, *or* (2), the lawyer (individually or with others) controls a separate entity that provides these law-related services *and* he does not take reasonable measures to make sure that the recipient of the law-related services knows that they are not legal services and that therefore the protections of the lawyer-client relationship (e.g., attorney-client privilege, conflict of interest rules) do not apply.

Note: If a lawyer provides law-related services that are distinct from his provision of legal services to clients, and he makes clear that the protections of the lawyer-client relationship do not apply, then, with respect to those law-related services, the lawyer is not subject to those provisions of the Model Rules that apply to lawyers when acting as lawyers (e.g., advertising, conflicts of interest, disclosure of confidential information). *However*, the lawyer is still subject to those portions of the Model Rules that apply to lawyers even if they are not acting in their capacity as lawyers. See, e.g., Rule 8.4(c) (lawyer may not engage in conduct "involving dishonesty, fraud. . . . "). Rule 5.7, Comments 1, 2, 3, 8, 10.

If a jurisdiction does not adopt this proposed rule, the lawyer is still governed by existing Rule 1.8(a), which already regulates business transactions with a client.

V. Unauthorized Practice of Law and Multijurisdictional Practice of Law

What constitutes the unauthorized practice of law is a matter of state law. The Model Rules and Model Code merely incorporate by reference these local rules, and provide that if a lawyer violates state law regarding unauthorized practice, that violation is also disciplinable. Rule 5.5 & Comment 1. See also DR 3–101(A); EC 3–5.

Typically, state laws provide that it is a defense to a lawsuit for the payment of fees that the party seeking fees engaged in the unauthorized practice of law. The unauthorized practice of law may also be a criminal violation. For example, a court sentenced a paralegal in Green Bay, Wisconsin, to nine months in jail for helping people file petitions in federal bankruptcy court in Madison. (He was released on probation after 30 days.) Wall St. Journal, Aug. 28, 1991, at B4, col. 6 (Midwest Ed.).

The court might also enjoin the unauthorized practice or use its contempt powers to enforce unauthorized practice rules. In 1985, the Arizona state legislature repealed the statute prohibiting the unauthorized practice of law. Nonetheless, the state supreme court continued to enforce the prohibition by using of its contempt powers against disbarred lawyers. *In re Creasy*, 198 Ariz. 539, 12 P.3d 214 (2000).

The loss of the attorney client privilege is *not* a remedy for unauthorized practice because of the general rule that a client or prospective client secures the protection of the attorney client privilege even if he or she communicates with someone who is a fraud or charlatan, so long as the confiding client "reasonably believes that the imposter is a lawyer." Restatement of the Law Governing Lawyers, § 72(1), comment *e* (Official Draft 2000). The client or prospective client does not lose the protection merely because the lawyer failed to pay his bar dues, or is practicing outside the jurisdiction in which he is admitted. *E.g., Georgia–Pacific Plywood Co. v. United States Plywood Corp.*, 18 F.R.D. 463, 465 (S.D.N.Y.1956).

The purported purpose of the privilege is to safeguard the client or prospective client. That purpose is hardly furthered when the client acts reasonably in dealing with a pretender or a member of the bar who has not yet received *pro hac vice* admission and the court punished the reasonable client by denying the protection of the privilege. When a client hires a lawyer, he does not usually ask the lawyer to supply a receipt for his most recent bar dues.

The state law definitions of unauthorized practice are varied and often confused. See Rhode, *Policing the Professional Monopoly: A Constitutional and Empirical Analysis of Unauthorized Practice Prohibitions*, 34 Stan.L.Rev. 1 (1981). When the lawyer is practicing within the jurisdiction of a state is not always clear, in the modern world of cellular phones, email, and so forth. *El Gemayel v. Seaman*, 72 N.Y.2d 701, 536 N.Y.S.2d 406, 533 N.E.2d 245 (1988) held that a foreign lawyer did not practice law in New York when he telephoned the client and her daughter in New York and discussed the progress of legal proceedings in Lebanon. The lawyer, in this case, was not physically present in New York and did not have an office in that state. The court allowed him to collect his fees. The court distinguished *Spivak v. Sachs*, 16 N.Y.2d 163, 263 N.Y.S.2d 953, 211 N.E.2d 329

(1965), which held that a California lawyer engaged in unauthorized practice when he assisted an acquaintance in securing a New York divorce. The lawyer spent about 14 days in New York, attending meetings and reviewing documents, recommending a change in New York counsel, and rendering his opinion as to the proper jurisdiction for the divorce action.

A particularly controversial decision is *Birbrower, Montalbano, Condon & Frank, P.C. v. Superior Court (ESQ Business Services, Inc.)*, 17 Cal.4th 119, 70 Cal. Rptr.2d 304, 949 P.2d 1 (Cal. 1998). A New York law firm represented a California company in claims it had against another company. California law governed the contract. The New York firm partners traveled to California for a few brief trips on several occasions. Ultimately, the dispute was settled, the California client refused to pay, and the court upheld this refusal, because it said that the law firm was engaged in the unauthorized practice of law in California. Many commentators have attacked this decision as ignoring the fact that many law firms give advice to clients in different jurisdictions.

In contrast to *Birbrower*, the Restatement of the Law Governing Lawyers, § 3 (Official Draft, 2000) provides that a lawyer admitted to practice in one jurisdiction may provide legal services (1) at any place within that jurisdiction, (2) before a tribunal in another jurisdiction if the lawyer complies with the requirement for temporary or regular admission before that tribunal, and (3), "at a place within a jurisdiction to the extent that the lawyer's activities *arise out of or are otherwise reasonably related* to the lawyer's practice under Subsection (1) or (2)." (emphasis added). Rule 5.5(c)(3) adopts the Restatement's position on this issue.

To some extent unauthorized practice rules can represent guild rules, efforts to protect a cartel and prevent reform that might lead to competition from nonlawyers. The late Professor Arthur Sutherland once remarked that one can hardly imagine a medical doctor speaking at a meeting of a county medical society and discussing the possible elimination of some disease by public health measures, and then qualifying his remarks by the statement that many practitioners make a living out of treating this disease; and that "unless the physicians are vigilant to prevent the adoption of such measures, this source of business will be taken from them. Yet speakers at bar association meetings are frequently heard to make similar observations about the effects of proposed reforms." Quoted in, Martin Mayer, *The Lawyers* 28 (1967).

"The definition of the practice of law is established by law and varies from one jurisdiction to another." Rule 5.5, Comment 2. In general it may be said that a person practices law when he *applies the law to the facts of a particular case.* "Functionally, the practice of law relates to the rendition of service for others that call for the professional judgment of a lawyer. The essence of the professional judgment of the lawyer is his educated ability to relate the general body of and philosophy of law to a specified legal problem of a client. . . . " EC 3–5. See, e.g., *State v. Winder*, 42 A.D.2d 1039, 348 N.Y.S.2d 270 (1973) (no unauthorized practice in distribution of do-it-yourself divorce kits with forms and instructions because the kit did not contain personalized advice applied to a particular person).

If a police officer tells you that the speed limit is 55 m.p.h., or the court clerk tells you that reply briefs should be printed on blue-backed paper, these people use the law, but they are not practicing the law; they are not applying the law to a specific fact situation and using legal judgment. EC 3–5. If a lawyer instructs these people (or similar people, such as a claims adjuster) about the law, the lawyer is not normally engaging in the unauthorized practice of law because these people, the recipients of the lawyer's aid, do not practice law.

The lawyer may delegate various tasks to secretaries, law clerks, or paralegals, and, so long as the lawyer supervises the delegated work and is responsible for it, there is no unauthorized practice. EC 3–6; Rule 5.5, Comments 1, 3.

The rule against unauthorized practice only applies to a person seeking to represent another. A lay person may represent himself, even if doing so requires that the lay person appear in court and otherwise practice law. EC 3–7. In fact, in criminal cases defendants have a constitutional right to defend themselves. *Faretta v. California*, 422 U.S. 806, 95 S.Ct. 2525, 45 L.Ed.2d 562 (1975).

If a lay person wishes to proceed *pro se*, a lawyer may assist him. This assistance does not violate the rule against aiding a lay person in the unauthorized practice of law because the lay person, while practicing law, is not engaged in the *unauthorized* practice of law. A nonlawyer may represent himself. Rule 5.5, Comment 3.

Example: Lay Person enters a law library and asks the librarian (who is also a lawyer), "Where may I find the books and forms on writing a will. I want to write a will for myself and save the costs of a lawyer." The librarian says, "Books and forms dealing with wills and trusts are in aisle 4." The librarian has not aided the lay person in the "unauthorized" practice of law.

The unauthorized practice rules treat individuals differently than corporations. While an individual may represent himself, the typical rule is that corporations may *not* appear *pro se*. Because a corporation is a separate legal entity, this incorporeal entity can only appear through others, who must be lawyers if the representation involves the practice of law. E.g., *Simbraw, Inc. v. United States*, 367 F.2d 373 (3d Cir.1966) (per curiam).

The fact that a person is a graduate of a law school does not make him authorized to practice law unless he is admitted to the bar of the relevant jurisdiction. "Authority to engage in the practice of law conferred in any jurisdiction is not per se a grant of the right to practice elsewhere, and it is improper for a lawyer to engage in practice where he is not permitted by law or by court order to do so." EC 3–9. See DR 3–101(B); Rule 5.5(a).

The Code encourages members of the bar, as well as the organized bar itself, to remove unnecessary restrictions on interstate practice. See EC 3–9; EC 8–3. The Rules, interestingly, do not have any corresponding exhortation in favor of removing needless barriers to entry.

Model Rule 5.5, after the 2002 revisions, allows a lawyer who is admitted in one state (State *A*) to provide *temporary* legal services in a state in which she is not admitted (State *B*), even though she does not associate with a lawyer in State *B* if the services are "reasonably related" to the lawyer's practice in State *A*. See Rule 5.5(c)(2), (3). For example, a client's activities may involve multiple jurisdictions, such as when a multinational corporation surveys potential business sites and seeks its lawyer's services in assessing the relative merits of each. Comment 14.

In general, Rule 5.5, after its extensive revisions, now provides that:

A lawyer not admitted to practice law in State *A*, may not practice law in State *A* in violation of State *A*'s rules, or help another to do so. Rule 5.5(a).

A lawyer admitted in State *A* may practice in State *B* on a "temporary basis" if she associates with a lawyer admitted in State *B* who "actively participates" in the matter. Rule 5.5(c)(1).

A lawyer admitted in State *A* may provide temporary services "reasonably related" to a proceeding before a tribunal or potentially before a tribunal in State *B* if the lawyer "reasonably expects" to be admitted *pro hac vice* (that is, "admission for the purposes of the particular case"). Rule 5.5(c)(2). She could meet with clients, interview witnesses, and review documents. Comments 9 & 10.

A lawyer admitted in State *A* but not in State *B* may provide temporary legal services related to a pending or potential mediation, arbitration, or other alternative dispute resolution if her services are "reasonably related" or arise out of her practice in State *A* if the forum does not require *pro hac vice* admission for those services. Rule 5.5(c)(3).

A lawyer admitted in State *A* but not in State *B* may provide legal services in State *B* if those services are "reasonably related" to her practice in State *A*.

Rule 5.5(c)(4). For example, she works for a multinational corporation that has business interests in various jurisdictions and the corporation seeks her legal advice on transactions in these various jurisdictions she may give this advice without being admitted in every jurisdiction. Comment 14. Lawyers who give advice, and aid in putting together various transactions have no procedure to become admitted *pro hac vice* for purposes of a particular transaction, so the Rule does not require it.

The above provisions all relate to lawyers who are admitted in one jurisdiction but practice law temporarily in another jurisdiction. The situation is different when a lawyer is admitted in State *A*, but has a physical presence in, and gives legal advice in, State *B*:

Rule 5.5(d) provides for two instances when such a lawyer may properly provide legal services in a jurisdiction in which the lawyer is not admitted but has an office or other type of continuous presence in the jurisdiction.

First, a lawyer admitted in State *A* but not in State *B* may provide legal services in State *B* if those services are provided to her employer (or its affiliates) and State *B* does not require *pro hac vice* admission for those services. Rule 5.5(d)(1). For example, a lawyer may be in-house counsel or a government lawyer. This lawyer is physically located in State *B*, but only admitted in State *A*; the Rules conclude that this lawyer's ability to represent her employer does not create any unreasonable risks to her client, because the client is sophisticated enough to evaluate the lawyer's qualifications. Comment 16. A more restrictive rule could make life very difficult for the government or large corporations who shift lawyers and other personnel from office to office in different states throughout the country.

Second, Rule 5.5(d)(2) allows a lawyer admitted in one jurisdiction to provide legal services in a different jurisdiction if federal law or other law so provides.

She may provide legal services to her employer (i.e., as in-house counsel or government lawyer) inside a jurisdiction in which she is not admitted, as long as she is not before a tribunal. Rule 5.5(d) and Comment 16. If she is before a tribunal, she must secure *pro hac vice* admission.

Example: assume that Lawyer is admitted in Illinois and drafts a will and estate plan for Client *A*, in Illinois. Later, Client *A* moves to Florida, and requests Lawyer to draft a codicil to *A*'s will. Lawyer does so and visits Client A in Florida to obtain the necessary signatures, but she never opens an office in Florida. Rule 5.5(c)(4) authorizes this activity.

VI. Agreements to Restrict the Right to Practice Law

A. Restrictive Covenants

The Rules, like its predecessor, the Code, prohibit a lawyer from requiring or agreeing to accept an employment contract restricting a lawyer's right to practice law after termination of the relationship created by the agreement. However, such a requirement may be imposed as a condition to the payment of retirement benefits. Rule 5.6(a); DR 2–108(A).

Such restrictive covenants violate the discipline rules even if they are limited to a stated period and geographic area. ABA Formal Opinion 300 (Aug. 7, 1961). Moreover, most courts do not enforce such agreements. *Cohen v. Lord, Day & Lord*, 75 N.Y.2d 95, 551 N.Y.S.2d 157, 550 N.E.2d 410 (1989)(law firm partnership agreement that conditions payment of earned but uncollected partnership revenues upon a withdrawing partner's obligation to refrain from the practice of law in competition with the former law firm restricts the practice of law in violation of New York's DR 2–108(A) "and is unenforceable in these circumstances as against public policy."). Contra, *Howard v. Babcock*, 6 Cal.4th 409, 25 Cal. Rptr.2d 80, 863 P.2d 150 (1993), arguing that law firms should be treated no differently from other business partnerships, such as accountants' and doctors' practices, which California permits to enter into agreements restricting competition: "A revolution in the practice of law has occurred requiring economic interests of the law firm to be protected as they are in other business enterprises." Justice Kennard wrote a vigorous and thoughtful dissent. Note, in this case, the court enforced a contract that violated the ethics rules that the same court had promulgated.

Similarly, lawyers may not restrict their right to practice as part of the settlement of a client's controversy. Rule 5.6(b); DR 2–108(B).

In general, the lawyer also may not participate or comply with a settlement agreement that prevents her from *using* information gained during the representation in later representations against the opposing party or a related party. An agreement not to use information learned during the representation would effectively restrict the lawyer's right to practice and thus would violate Rule 5.6(b). ABA Formal Opinion 00–417 (April 7, 2000). Yet, Rule 5.6(b) does not prevent lawyers "from agreeing *not to reveal* information about the facts of the particular matter to the terms of its settlement." ABA Formal Opinion 00–417 (emphasis in original). The restriction on "using" client information applies only to the use of the information to *the disadvantage* of the former client. Rule 1.9(c)(1), dealing with duties to *former* clients, makes that quite clear. The "subsequent use of information relating to the representation of a former client is treated quite liberally as compared to restrictions regarding disclosure of client information." ABA Formal Opinion 00–417.

Rule 5.6(b) is not implicated when lawyers accept restrictions on the use of information where this agreement is entered into as a condition of receiving the information. Nor does this Rule apply to protective orders that courts impose during litigation.

Rule 5.6(b) prohibits lawyers from participating in an agreement restricting their right to practice law as part of the settlement of a controversy between clients. Thus, Rule 5.6(b) would *not* apply to disciplinary proceedings brought by the bar or by an administrative agency with jurisdiction over some part of the lawyer's practice where the lawyer himself is a party. In such proceedings, a settlement may "involve the lawyer agreeing to suspension or disbarment from practice before the agency itself; and this is plainly not forbidden by Rule 5.6(b)." ABA Formal Opinion 95–394 (July 24, 1995). For example, the Federal Office of Thrift Supervision may settle a case with a law firm on the condition that two partners are barred from representing any savings association and banks that carry federal deposit insurance.

Rule 5.6(b) otherwise applies not only where the controversy is between private parties, but also where a party is a governmental entity.

Clients always have a right to discharge their lawyers at any time and hire new counsel. (See Part III, Section V.) If lawyers were forced to (or forced others to) agree to restrictive covenants, then there would be restraints, not only on the lawyer's professional autonomy, but also on the client's freedom to choose a lawyer. Rule 5.6, Comment 1. Rule 5.6 thus limits Rule 1.2(a), which generally provides that the lawyer must abide by the client's decisions concerning settlement. ABA Formal Opinion 93–371 (Aug. 16, 1993).

Rule 5.6 is virtually identical to DR 2–108, which in turn reflects pre-Code authority. ABA Formal Opinion 300 (Aug. 7, 1961). Some lawyers have vigorously attacked Rule 5.6 without appreciating its very traditional origins. See Jackson & Atlas, *The Ethics of Stealing Clients*, 69 A.B.A.J. 706, 707 (1983) ("Firms are being bled and even destroyed [but Rule 5.6 does] nothing to protect the attorney who has built a law practice.").

The introductory clause to Rule 5.6 makes clear that both Rule 5.6(a) & (b) prohibit lawyers from "participat[ing] in offering or making" the prohibited agreement. Thus a lawyer may not unethically agree to the restriction and opposing lawyer may not propose or require the restriction. For example, a lawyer may not accept or propose a restriction in an employment agreement prohibiting counsel for a corporation from representing anyone in any future action against the corporation. While the former lawyer for the corporation could not ethically engage in subsequent adverse representation that is *substantially related* to the prior representation, a prohibition of *all* future adverse representation, including matters that are *unrelated,* violates Rule 5.6(a). ABA Formal Opinion 94–381 (May 9, 1994).

B. Sale of Law Practice

The Model Code prohibited a lawyer from "selling" the law practice (EC 4–6) because, it is announced, "clients are not merchandise." ABA Formal Opinion 266 (June 2, 1945). However, the Code did not concern itself with division of fees among lawyers within the same firm. DR 2–107. Thus, a firm could always add another lawyer as a partner in the firm, and have that new partner purchase equity in the firm. This equity typically includes not only the cost of physical assets like law books and desks, but also "good will," that is, the expectation of continued business. Thus, under the Model Code there was a disparity of treatment between the sole practitioners, who were forbidden from selling "good will." Cf. *O'Hara v. Ahlgren, Blumenfeld & Kempster,* 127 Ill.2d 333, 130 Ill.Dec. 401, 537 N.E.2d 730 (1989), holding that a sole practitioner may not sell good will.

California responded to such concerns by adopting a new rule allowing for the sale of a law practice by a living or deceased lawyer. Rule 2–300, California Rules of Professional Conduct. The California State Bar urged the ABA to adopt a similar rule, and it did so in February, 1990, when it added Rule 1.17, "Sale of Law Practice."

Comment 1 to Rule 1.17 reaffirms that "[c]lients are not commodities that can be purchased and sold at will." However, the remainder of that Comment, and the ones that follow, explain the proper way to sell the law practice as an on-going concern. Rule 1.17 imposes various restrictions when one "sells the business," that is, sells the law practice or an "area of the law practice," such as estate law, or trademark law.

First, the seller must cease to engage in the practice of law entirely (or cease to practice in an area of law practice) in the jurisdiction (or a particular geographic area) [the state court adopting Rule 1.17 should choose one of these alternatives]. However the seller may returns to private practice due to unanticipated circumstances. Rule 1.17 & Comment 1, 2. A seller who becomes in-house counsel, or works for the Government, or a legal services entity, is not considered to be returning to private practice. Comment 3. That is because the lawyer, in that case, will not be competing for private clients of the lawyer to whom he just sold his practice.

Second, the seller must sell the entire practice (or an area of law practice) to a single purchaser (subject to client consent, and assuming that there is no disqualifying conflict). The reason this rule prohibits piecemeal sale of less than an entire area of practice (or an area of law practice) is to protect clients "whose matters are less lucrative and who might find it difficult to secure other counsel if the sale could be limited to substantial fee-generating matters." Comment 6. It is incongruous that the ABA, which has objected to "too much litigation" [see, Rotunda, *Lawyers and Professionalism: A Commentary on the Report of the American Bar Association Commission on Professionalism,* 18 Loyola U. of Chicago L.Rev. 1149, 1159 (1987)] drafted Rule 1.17 so that it forces the purchaser to subsidize those clients with the less lucrative cases, including clients with lawsuits that the purchaser candidly evaluates should not have been brought to begin with. The purchaser cannot avoid accepting the clients with the less lucrative cases by trying to raise their fees, because Rule 1.17(d) prohibits raising any fees because of the sale. The purchaser must honor the existing free agreements between the seller and the client. Rule 1.17(d) & Comment 10. These restrictions, we are told, are intended to prevent the seller from financing the sale by increasing the new clients' fees.

Third, the sale of a law practice raises questions regarding client confidentiality, because the purchaser is not the lawyer whom the clients hired. Consequently, each of the seller's clients must receive written notice of: the proposed sale, the right to retain other counsel, and the right to take possession of his file. Rule 1.17(c)(1),(2). (Even after the sale, a client may always transfer the representation to another lawyer. Comment 8.) Of course, not all clients may respond to this notice. Thus, Rule 1.17(c)(3) provides that the client should also be notified that the client's consent to the sale is *presumed, if* the client does not respond within 90 days. If the client cannot be given notice, the purchaser must secure a court order authorizing the transfer. The court can determine if there have been reasonable efforts to find the clients and whether it serves the legitimate interests of those absent clients to have the purchaser continue the representation of them. To protect the client's confidentiality, the seller may disclose to the court *in camera* information about the proposed representation only to the extent necessary to obtain this order. Rule 1.17, Comment 8.

Recall that if a lawyer divides fees with another lawyer in a different law firm, each lawyer must assume joint responsibility for the representation. Rule 1.5(e)(1). Rule 1.17 does not refer to that section; in fact, Comment 15 to Rule 1.17 specifically provides that this Rule does not apply to the transfer of legal representation unrelated to the sale of a practice (or area of practice). One would think, as a logical matter, that the responsibilities assumed under Rule 1.17 should be no less than those assumed pursuant to Rule 1.5(e)(1).

Rule 1.17, Comment 11, notes that the seller has the obligation to exercise competence in identifying a qualified purchaser. While the seller cannot exercise continuing supervision (he has, after all, left the practice), it does not appear unreasonable to make him share joint malpractice liability (as if they were partners) with the person whom he had handpicked to buy his practice. Such a rule would assure that the seller picks carefully, and it is no more onerous than the burden placed by Rule 1.5(e)(1). However, except for Comment 11, Rule 1.17 does not provide for any seller's liability.

Disposition of Client Files and Property when a Sole Practitioner Dies. If a law firm has more than one attorney, the death of one of the lawyers does not end the law practice, because there is a least one other attorney to carry on the work. However, in the case of sole practitioners who do not first sell their practice, there arises the question of what happens to the files of the various clients. Rule 1.1 and DR 6–101(A)(1), requiring competence, and Rule 1.3 and DR 6–101(A)(3), prohibiting neglect, support the obligation of a sole practitioner to make plans to assure that client matters (e.g., document filings, statute of limitations) are not neglected in the event of her death. ABA Formal Opinion 92–369 (Dec. 7, 1992) recommends that the sole practitioner have a plan to provide for the protection of her clients' interests in the event of her death. The plan should designate another lawyer who would make reasonable efforts to notify the clients of the sole practitioner's death, review the files, and determine which need immediate attention. Because the designated lawyer does not represent these clients, she should only review as much of the files as needed to identify the clients and determine which files need immediate attention.

REVIEW QUESTIONS

1. Thomas is an attorney who specializes in plaintiff tort cases. All of his cases are contingent fee cases. His law firm employed James, an investigator who is not a lawyer. They have the following financial arrangement: James will receive, yearly, 5% of the law firm's net income. Thus, if Thomas loses all of his cases in a given year, James will receive nothing. James is not involved in making any professional judgments; only Thomas does that.

Is Thomas *subject to discipline* for this fee arrangement?

a.   Yes, unless each client consents after full disclosure.

b.   No, because lawyers may include nonlawyer employees in a compensation plan based on a profit sharing arrangement; investigators have to get paid and their pay in fact comes out of clients' fees. Thomas' arrangement simply recognizes that economic fact.

c.   Yes, because it involves James in the unauthorized practice of law.

d.   This arrangement does not violate any disciplinary rule but it is discouraged by the ethical aspirations.

e.   Yes, because an attorney may not divide his legal fees with any non-attorney.

2.   Lawyer Able entered into a partnership with Accountant Baker and Insurance Agent Clark. They decided to name the partnership Able, Baker and Clark. The partnership maintains its offices in a building owned by Lawyer Able and carries on its business in a suite of offices composed of a waiting room, law and tax book library, and offices. Each member of the partnership has a private office for himself and his secretary that is adjacent to the waiting room and library. They have a small, dignified sign on the door that says "Able, Baker, and Clark; Legal, Accounting and Insurance Services." All of the monies received by any partner go into the common bank account, from which they pay all expenses with the remaining profits divided equally: one-third (⅓) to each of the partners.

Is Lawyer Able *subject to discipline?*

I.   Yes, because Able has shared his legal fees with non-lawyer who are not employees but partners of the firm.

II.   Yes, because a lawyer shall not form a partnership with a nonlawyer if any of the activities of the partnership consist in the practice of law.

The best answer is:

a.   Both I and II.

b. Neither I nor II.

c. I only.

d. II only.

3. Attorney Jones is the majority shareholder of Collection Agency, Inc. If Collection Agency's collection efforts have not been successful, Jones authorizes Collection Agency's Manager, who has graduated from law school but is not admitted to the bar, to use his (Manager's) best judgment to write an appropriate collection letter. The letter is typed on Jones' legal letterhead. If Manager decides, the letter may contain a statement that the matter has been referred to Attorney Jones and that suit will be filed in five days if payment is not received. Jones authorizes Manager to sign Attorney Jones' name to the letter. Jones does not personally review each letter before it is sent.

Is Attorney Jones *subject to discipline?*

a. Yes, because Attorney may not threaten suit to gain advantage in a civil case.

b. Yes, because the letter is a threat.

c. Yes, because Collection Agency, through Manager, is engaging in the unauthorized practice of law.

d. No, because Manager is authorized to act as Jones' agent.

e. No, because Attorney is the majority shareholder of Collection Agency, Inc.

4. Attorney asks Secretary to file a copy of Client's confidential papers. Attorney then leaves the office early. Attorney's instructions are quite clear, and Secretary in the past has followed them. But that night, Secretary is rushed and leaves the confidential papers on the top of the conference table. Later that night, some clients in a different matter meet at the firm with another attorney in the firm. These other clients use the conference table, see the confidential documents, express surprise, and tell the firm's attorney, who locks up the papers.

Is Attorney *subject to discipline?*

a. No, because she reasonably supervised Secretary.

b. No, because Attorney is not responsible for Secretary.

c. Yes, under a theory of vicarious liability.

d. Yes, because the other clients saw the confidential documents.

*

PART V

The Lawyer's Obligations Regarding Advertising and Solicitation

■ ANALYSIS

I.   **Lawyer Advertising and Solicitation**
   A.   Introduction
      1.   Historical and Constitutional Background
      2.   The Bar's Response to *Bates*
   B.   Use of the Media
      1.   The Model Code
         (a)   Scope
         (b)   Content

I. Lawyer Advertising and Solicitation

A. Introduction

1. Historical and Constitutional Background

The Canons of Ethics of 1908 originally allowed lawyers to advertise. Publication of business cards in newspapers and directories as well as advertisements of a lawyer's specialty were quite common, but some of them created problems. For example, one 1911 lawyer's ad in the Los Angeles Daily Times included the following (in all capital letters): "WE GET THE COIN." See, Oliver, *Lawyer Advertising,* Calif. Lawyer, July, 1987, at 29. By 1937 a complete redraft of Canon 27 severely restricted lawyer advertising. See ABA Formal Opinion 276 (Sept. 20, 1947). The organized bar maintained this virtual prohibition until the 1970's when consumer groups, attorneys, and others began actively opposing the bar's position.

The Supreme Court opened the door to legal advertising in *Bates v. State Bar of Arizona,* 433 U.S. 350, 97 S.Ct. 2691, 53 L.Ed.2d 810 (1977), which held that the First Amendment protects truthful newspaper advertising of availability and fees for routine legal services. However, the Court allowed the states to subject legal advertising to reasonable restrictions on time, place and manner, and to prohibit false or misleading advertising.

Ohralik v. Ohio State Bar Association, 436 U.S. 447, 98 S.Ct. 1912, 56 L.Ed.2d 444 (1978) turned to the question of solicitation and held that a state may constitutionally discipline a lawyer who solicits clients in-person under circumstances likely to create undue pressure on the client. *Ohralik* responded to a question left open in *Bates* regarding the greater potential for overreaching when the attorney solicits business face to face rather than through the media.

In a companion case, *In re Primus,* 436 U.S. 412, 98 S.Ct. 1893, 56 L.Ed.2d 417 (1978), the Court recognized that certain types of solicitation are entitled to special protection. *Primus* involved an American Civil Liberties Union (ACLU) lawyer who spoke to a group of women and later, through a letter, offered free legal services to a woman allegedly deprived of her civil rights. The Court extended the First Amendment's protection for free speech and association to the lawyer's activities and struck the state's efforts to reprimand the ACLU lawyer for solicitation.

In re R.M.J., 455 U.S. 191, 102 S.Ct. 929, 71 L.Ed.2d 64 (1982) invalidated additional restrictions on lawyer advertising. Missouri reprimanded R.M.J. because he had deviated from the precise listing of certain areas of practice included in the state's Rule 4. For example, R.M.J.'s advertisement listed "real estate" but Rule 4 used the term "property;" R.M.J. listed "contracts" but Rule 4 did not list that term at all. Because the state could neither demonstrate that R.M.J.'s listing was deceptive nor show that its restrictions promoted any substantial interests, a unanimous U.S. Supreme Court found the state limitations unconstitutional. The Court also invalidated a part of Rule 4 that prohibited a lawyer from identifying the jurisdictions in which he is licensed to practice.

R.M.J. had also emphasized in large, boldface type that he was a member of the U.S. Supreme Court bar. Justice Powell, for the Court, conceded that this fact was "relatively uninformative," but, nonetheless, held that R.M.J. could not constitutionally be disciplined for advertising it: the record did not show that it was misleading, and Rule 4 did not specifically identify it as misleading, nor place a limitation on its type size, nor require any explanatory disclaimer explaining the significance (or lack thereof) of U.S. Supreme Court bar admission.

Zauderer v. Office of Disciplinary Counsel of Supreme Court of Ohio, 471 U.S. 626, 105 S.Ct. 2265, 85 L.Ed.2d 652 (1985) held that a state may not discipline an attorney who ran newspaper advertisements containing nondeceptive illustrations (in this case, a drawing of a Dalkon Shield Intrauterine Device) and legal advice (in this case, the advice that product liability tort claims may not yet be barred by the statute of limitations). However, the Court explained, the state could discipline a lawyer for failure to include in his advertisements information reasonably necessary to make his advertisement not misleading. In this case the lawyer advertised that he would represent clients on a contingent fee basis and "if there is no recovery, no legal fees are owed by our clients." The lawyer did not disclose that the client might still be liable for litigation costs. The state has broader power to mandate disclosure than it has to prohibit advertising. The lawyer's "constitutionally protected interest in *not* providing any particular factual information in his advertising is minimal." (emphasis in original). However, the Court added that disclosure requirements do implicate free speech, and "unjustified or unduly burdensome disclosure requirements might offend the First Amendment by chilling protected commercial speech."

Shapero v. Kentucky Bar Association, 486 U.S. 466, 108 S.Ct. 1916, 100 L.Ed.2d 475 (1988) held that free speech guarantees preclude the states from imposing blanket bans on direct mail advertising. Directed mail is simply a more efficient form of advertising than blanket mailings.

In *Peel v. Attorney Registration and Disciplinary Commission of Illinois,* 496 U.S. 91, 110 S.Ct. 2281, 110 L.Ed.2d 83 (1990), the Court (with no majority opinion) ruled that the First Amendment prohibited Illinois from censuring a lawyer for truthfully stating that he was "certified as a civil trial specialist by the National Board of Trial Advocacy," a bona fide private organization.

Ibanez v. Florida Department of Business and Professional Regulation, 512 U.S. 136, 114 S.Ct. 2084, 129 L.Ed.2d 118 (1994) held that the Florida Board of Accountancy violated free speech when it reprimanded Silvia Ibanez, an attorney (who argued her own case), because she truthfully advertised that she was a Certified Public Accountant and a Certified Financial Planner. The state Board of Accountancy licensed her as a CPA and a bona fide private organization certified her as a CFP.

2. The Bar's Response to *Bates*

The American Bar Association immediately responded to *Bates* by amending DR 2–101, by creating a complex list of items that an attorney may include in an advertisement, and prohibiting anything that it did not expressly permit. The Model Rules, in contrast, take the opposite approach: anything not expressly prohibited is allowed. Rule 7.1 broadly prohibits "false or misleading statements." Subject to this requirement, Rule 7.2 permits a lawyer to advertise through a broad spectrum of media. Over the years, the ABA amended Part 7 of the Model Rules, *Information About Legal Services,* to tear down the barriers to advertising so that now the general rule of Rule 7.1 is that a communication is "false or misleading" only if it "contains a material misrepresentation of fact or law, or omits a fact necessary to make the statement considered as a whole not materially misleading."

The constitutionality of any specific law restricting truthful lawyer advertising is not completely uncertain after *Bates* and its offspring. Consequently, any ethics rules that impose specific restrictions, either on their face or as applied, may, in the future, fall to constitutional challenges. The ABA Model Rules, particularly after the 2002 revisions, seek to avoid this problem by focusing on a general prohibition of what is truly false and misleading in a material way. For example, prior to the

2002 revisions, Rule 7.1(c) simply announced that the lawyer could not compare her services with other lawyers' services unless the comparison can be factually substantiated. The 2002 revisions simply deleted Rule 7.1(c), but added Comment 3, which explains an appropriate disclaimer may be helpful in precluding a finding that the statement is misleading.

B. Use of the Media

1. The Model Code

The Code regulations on use of the media began with a general prohibition of "false, fraudulent, misleading, deceptive, self-laudatory or unfair" statements or claims. DR 2–101(A). The Code then listed 25 categories of information that may be advertised, subject to the requirement of DR 2–101(B) that any communication be presented "in a dignified manner." DR 2–101(B) (1–25).

(a) Scope

The Code permitted advertising through both print and broadcast media. DR 2–101(B). *Bates* had reserved the question as to the extent of constitutional protection in light of the possible "special problems of advertising on the electronic broadcast media."

The Code also provided that the advertising may cover only the geographic area in which the lawyer resides, or maintains offices, or where a "significant" number of her clients reside. DR 2–101(B).

(b) Content

A lawyer could present biographical information such as her name, DR 2–101(B)(1), schools attended, DR 2–101(B)(5), and foreign language ability, DR 2–101(B)(14). Advertisements could also include office information such as hours, DR 2–101(B)(19) and fee information, DR 2–101(B)(20–25). If contingent fees are advertised, the publicity had to include a statement that the percentage is computed before or after deduction of costs. DR 2–101(B)(22).

As a general rule, the Code prohibited lawyers from identifying themselves in their advertisements as specialists in a particular field of law. DR 2–102(A); DR 2–105; EC 2–14. This rule allowed several exceptions. First, the Code recognizes the traditional exception for patent lawyers. DR 2–105(A)(1).

Note: EC 2–14 also included the fields of admiralty and trademark. This EC is contrary to DR 2–105(A)(1). The ABA

House of Delegates amended DR 2–105(A)(1) in 1977 (eliminating admiralty and trademark) and *forgot* to amend the corresponding EC.

Second, the Code permitted lawyers to advertise their specialty *if* certified by the appropriate state agency, DR 2–105(A)(3). Furthermore, lawyers could indicate that their practice is limited to certain areas only by using state-designated terms. DR 2–105(A)(2).

These restrictions regarding advertising of truthful information obviously raised constitutional problems. If a lawyer only handles real estate matters, should he not be able to advertise that, whether he uses state designated terms or not? *In re R.M.J.*, discussed in section I, A, 1, supra, so held.

The Code provided that any person wishing to advertise information not on the "approved list" could apply to the appropriate state agency for an expansion of the Code. DR 2–101(C).

(c) Other Regulations

The Code also imposed detailed regulations of other aspects of lawyer advertising besides mode, range, and content. If a lawyer used the broadcast media, the lawyer must pre-record the advertisement and retain a copy. DR 2–101(D). If a lawyer advertised a specific service for a set fee, the lawyer must render the service for that fee for a reasonable time after the advertisement appears. DR 2–101(E),(F), & (G).

(d) Conclusion

It is not necessary to remember these old, complex restrictions. But it is necessary to appreciate the background that led to the current Rules. The organized bar, in brief, did not welcome advertising with open arms. See, Ronald D. Rotunda, *Lawyer Advertising and the Philosophical Origins of the Commercial Speech Doctrine, Lawyer Advertising and the Philosophical Origins of the Commercial Speech Doctrine,* 36 U. Richmond L. Rev. 91 (2002)(Allen Chair Symposium of 2001).

2. The Model Rules

(a) Scope

The Model Rules, like the Model Code, recognize the public's need to know about the availability and quality of legal services. *See, e.g.,*

Rule 7.2, Comment 1; EC 2–10. The Rules, however, approach regulation of lawyer advertising more liberally and less technically than the Code. The Rules recognize that the "interest in expanding public information about legal services ought to prevail over considerations of tradition." Rule 7.2, Comment 1. Thus, the Rules permit truthful advertising through any medium except with "direct contact with prospective clients," "in-person solicitation," which is narrowly defined and governed by Rule 7.3. See section II, infra. Furthermore, unlike the Code, the Rules do not restrict the advertisement's geographic reach.

(b) Content

The Rules ban false or misleading communications about a lawyer's services. After the 2002 revisions, there is no blanket prohibition of an advertisement of a lawyer's *past* jury awards. However, because each case is fact-bound, an advertisement could be misleading if it led a reasonable person to form an unjustified expectation. For example, an advertisement that said, "I have averaged over $1 million for each tort award for plaintiffs, and I can do that same for you," should be misleading. Rule 7.1, Comment 3. Just because a lawyer secured a million dollar fee in one personal injury case does not mean that such a victory will be repeated. The new plaintiff may well have a different set of facts or be subject to different law. However, the lawyer can include an "appropriate disclaimer" to preclude a finding that the report of past achievements is misleading. Comment 3.

The Rule also forbids factually unsubstantiated statements that compare one lawyer's services with another's, *if* the claims would lead a reasonable person to think that the comparison can be substantiated. Here again, an appropriate disclaimer or qualifying language can prevent a finding of materially false or misleading communication. Rule 7.1 Comment 3.

Rule 7.1 also forbids any material misrepresentation of law or fact, or any *omission* of "a fact necessary to make the statement considered as a whole not materially misleading." Cf. Securities & Exchange Commission Rule 10b–5. *Zauderer v. Office of Disciplinary Counsel of Supreme Court of Ohio,* 471 U.S. 626, 653 n.15, 105 S.Ct. 2265, 2283 n.15, 85 L.Ed.2d 652 (1985) upholds the constitutionality of such a disclosure rule as long as it is not "unduly burdensome" and not too vague.

The Rules also place some regulations on a lawyer's communication of fields of practice. A lawyer may communicate through advertising that the lawyer's practice does or does not include particular fields of law. Rule 7.4(a). The Rules, unlike the Code, do *not* require that the lawyer use certain designations (specifically approved by the state regulatory authority) in order to describe these fields. See DR 2–105(A)(2).

Prior to February, 1989, a Comment to Rule 7.4 had provided that the lawyer may not state that his practice "is limited to" or is "concentrated in" a particular area. Now, there is no such restriction. In light of the modern lawyer advertising cases, the pre–1989 version would probably be unconstitutional, unless the state could meet the difficult burden of demonstrating that the use of language such as "is limited to" is misleading (while "is not limited to" is not misleading).

In 1992 the ABA amended Rule 7.4 in response to *Peel v. Attorney Registration and Disciplinary Commission,* 496 U.S. 91, 110 S.Ct. 2281, 110 L.Ed.2d 83 (1990). The ABA amended it again in 2002 and made it even more accommodating. The new Rule generally allows a lawyer to call herself "certified as a specialist," if the ABA or an appropriate state authority approves the organization and the advertisement "clearly" identifies the name of the certifying organization. In short, if a bona fide organization certifies the lawyer, she can communicate that she is certified as a specialist in a particular field of law.

In *Peel,* a divided Court ruled that free speech guarantees prohibited Illinois from disciplining an attorney who had accurately stated on his letterhead that the National Board of Trial Advocacy had certified him as a "Certified Civil Trial Specialist." The plurality concluded that Peel's statement was neither potentially nor actually misleading (the National Board of Trial Advocacy was a bona fide organization that had made a reasonable inquiry into Peel's fitness), and the state did not have a sufficient interest to justify a categorical ban on the use of such statements. The plurality noted that terms like "air conditioning specialist" or "foreign car specialist" are common, and the public does not think that they imply a claim of formal recognition by the state.

Rule 7.4(b), (c), continue to accept the historical specialties allowed in admiralty and patent law.

The present version of Rule 7.4, amended after *Peel*, provides that a lawyer may not state or imply that he is certified as a specialist unless the ABA or the appropriate state authority has approved the organization that is doing the certifying. Rule 7.4(d). The Reporter's Notes to this section explain that "it is both necessary and constitutionally permissible for the states to protect prospective clients against potentially misleading claims of certification by requiring the organizations conferring the certification to be approved by an appropriate state authority or accredited by the ABA."

Rule 7.4(d)(2) now requires that the name of the certifying organization be clearly identified. The purpose of this rule is to enable prospective clients to make further inquiry about the certification program.

The Rules (unlike the Code) require that any advertising contain the name of at least one lawyer responsible for its content. Rule 7.2(c).

(c) Other Regulations

The ABA, in 2002, followed the recommendations of Commission 2000 and eliminated the requirement that a lawyer who uses broadcast media retain a copy of the advertisement. In contrast, the Code required records be kept, apparently with no time limit. DR 2–101(D) (" . . . shall be retained . . . ").

C. Firm Names, Letterheads, and Other Personal Publicity

1. Trade Names and Firm Names

(a) Trade Names & Web Addresses

The Code prohibited lawyers in private practice from practicing under a trade name, such as "The 47th Street Law Office," whether or not it was misleading. DR 2–102(B). The Rules are more logical and prohibit the use of trade names in private practice only if the name is misleading or falsely implies a connection with a government agency or public legal services organization. Rule 7.5(a).

Rule 7.5, Comment 1 now allows a lawyer or law firm to use a "distinctive website address." A law firm's website address is a professional designation governed by Rule 7.5. Thus, a law firm may not use a website address that violates Rule 7.1. For example, a website that was "we_ always_ win.com" would be misleading.

Note: It is constitutional for the state to have a blanket prohibition of trade names. *Friedman v. Rogers*, 440 U.S. 1, 99 S.Ct. 887, 59 L.Ed.2d 100 (1979). However, there may be constitutional problems when the state bans one type of trade name ("the 44th Street Clinic") but not another ("Jones & Smith"—when Jones is no longer with the firm because he is dead); then, the asserted justification is undercut by the state's own actions.

A firm name that uses the name of a deceased partner is really a form of trade name. Rule 7.5, Comment 1, recognizes this fact. The Code pretends that such names are not trade names and consequently the Code does not bother to distinguish them from other trade names. See section (b), infra. The Rules avoid these problems by allowing trade names, such as the "ABC Legal Clinic."

(b) Firm Names

DR 2–102(B) prohibited lawyers from practicing under a firm name that contains names other than those of the lawyers in the firm, on the grounds that such a name is misleading; however, it permitted (where otherwise lawful) firm names to contain the names of deceased or retired members of the firm, in a continuing line of succession. The Code apparently recognized that a well known firm name develops value and good will, over the years. Also, the Code specifically allowed professional corporations to use certain initials ("P.C." or "P.A.") to indicate the nature of the organization. DR 2–102(B).

The Rules take a more liberal position on firm names, prohibiting only names that are, in fact, misleading. Thus it allows trade names (unless they falsely imply a connection with a governmental or charitable agency), and the use of the name of a deceased or retired member in a continuing line of succession. Rule 7.5(a) and Comment 1.

Leaving aside the question of deceased or retired partners, only a member of a law firm actively and regularly practicing with that firm may be named in a firm name. Consequently the names of lawyers acting in judicial, executive, or administrative capacities may not appear in firm names or on professional notices during the period in which the lawyer is serving in that capacity, unless that lawyer is still actively and regularly practicing law with the firm. Rule 7.5(c) (prohibiting the use of the name of a lawyer serving in public office during any substantial period in which the lawyer is not regularly practicing with the firm). Accord, DR 2–102(B).

Both the Rules and the Code permit a lawyer to state or imply that a lawyer is a member of a partnership or organization, such as a professional legal corporation, only where such is in fact the case. Rule 7.5(d); DR 2–102(D).

2. Professional Cards, Signs, Letterheads

The Code, unlike the Rules, had quite specific and detailed regulations governing professional cards, signs, and letterheads. The Code began with a general prohibition against the use of professional cards, office signs, letterheads, and other similar types of personal publicity. DR 2–102(A). However, it permitted several types of personal publicity that serve to assist clients in locating and identifying an attorney, if it is in "dignified form." DR 2–102(A).

The Code's detailed regulation extended to business cards. It permitted only professional cards that carry the lawyer's name, profession, telephone number, and the name of the lawyer's law firm, the names of the firm's members or associates, and limitations on practice to the extent that DR 2–105 approves of those limits. DR 2–102(A)(1). A lawyer could use these cards for identification. DR 2–102(A)(1). DR 2–102 also created a limited exception for the use of "brief" professional announcement cards, DR 2–102(A)(2), office signs, DR 2–102(A)(3), and letterheads, DR 2–102(A)(4).

The Code did not permit partnerships among lawyers licensed in different jurisdictions unless each lawyer's jurisdictional limitations were indicated on the letterhead and on other permissible publicity. DR 2–102(D). Rule 7.5(b) governs this situation and is substantially similar to the Code.

The Rules, unlike the Code, do not engage in such regulatory detail. Rule 7.5(a) simply prohibits the use of a "firm name, letter or other professional designation that violates Rule 7.1," which bans misleading or false statements.

3. Lawyer Identification

(a) The Model Code

The Code had a special provision allowing the "limited and dignified" identification of a lawyer's name and profession in certain circumstances. DR 2–101(H). These circumstances included political advertisements (if germane), public notices (only if germane), announcements of business, civic, professional or political organizations (if the lawyer is an officer or director), legal documents, legal textbooks prepared by the identified lawyer, or in public notices whenever the identification is reasonably pertinent to some purpose "other than the attraction of clients." The Code said that if it is proper to identify a lawyer as a lawyer and the author of a book, it is also proper to identify the author as a lawyer in dignified advertisements for the book. DR 2–101(H)(5).

(b) The Model Rules

The Rules, in contrast, make no special exception for such lawyer identification because it does not need to do so. Its less restrictive regulatory scheme does not prohibit truthful identification of a lawyer as a lawyer.

II. Solicitation

A. Introduction

One may think of solicitation as a form of advertising on a retail, rather than a wholesale, level. The Code imposed strict rules against most solicitation, and made a distinction between general media advertising and improper "in-person" solicitation, which involves contact with specific prospective clients motivated by pecuniary gain. EC 2–2, 2–3 & 2–4.

In contrast, the Rules, as they have been amended in response to various Supreme Court decisions that invalidated earlier Rules on First Amendment grounds, now make a distinction that forbids "in-person [*i.e.*, face to face] or live [*i.e.*, non-prerecorded] telephone contact," or "real-time electronic contact" [*i.e.* internet chat rooms] where the lawyer engages in such actions because his "pecuniary gain" is a "*significant* motive". Rule 7.3(a).

Rule 7.3(a)(2) permits in-person or live telephone contact or electronic contact *if* the recipient is another lawyer or has a family or prior professional relationship with the lawyer. In addition, a Comment simply announces that Rule 7.3(a) is "not intended to prohibit a lawyer from participating in constitutionally protected activities of public or charitable legal-service organizations or bona fide political, social, civic, fraternal, employee or trade organizations whose purposes include providing or recommending legal services to its members or beneficiaries."

The purpose of this comment is to recognize that there are constitutional limitations on regulators attempting to prohibit lawyers from cooperating with nonprofit organizations that assist their members or beneficiaries to secure legal counsel necessary for redress of grievances. See *United Transportation Union v. State Bar*, 401 U.S. 576, 91 S.Ct. 1076, 28 L.Ed.2d 339 (1971), which held that a state court injunction that enjoined a union from giving legal aid to its members or their families violated the First Amendment right of the union and its members to engage in collective activity to obtain meaningful access to the courts. The union recommended selected attorneys to its members and their families, and secured a commitment from those attorneys that the maximum fee charged would not exceed 25% of the recovery.

Rule 7.3 specifically allows "direct contact with prospective clients," even if the lawyer's significant motive is her self-interested pecuniary gain, in a limited class of cases—the person contacted is a lawyer or family member or close personal friend, or the person had a prior professional relationship with the lawyer (*i.e.*, a former client). However, even then, the lawyer may not engage in such solicitation if the prospective client told the lawyer that he did not want to be solicited. No, means no. Rule 7.3(b)(1).

In addition, the Rules forbid any solicitation that involved coercion, duress, or harassment. Rule 7.3(b)(2). For example, the lawyer in *Ohralik v. Ohio State Bar Association*, 436 U.S. 447, 98 S.Ct. 1912, 56 L.Ed.2d 444 (1978), visited the prospective client in her hospital room where she was lying in traction. He sought to represent her and on the second visit she signed a contingent free agreement. He sought to represent another client, also an accident victim, on the very day she came home from the hospital, and used a concealed tape recorder, to have evidence of her oral assent to the representation. The Rules forbid that.

B. Direct Contact With Client

The Rules restrict two types of solicitation. The first type involves direct contact between a lawyer and a prospective client. The second involves a lawyer's effort to obtain a recommendation or client referral from a third party.

Under the former Code, lawyers could not recommend their services or those of their partners to a prospective client unless that person initiated the consultation. DR 2–103(A). Similarly, lawyers who rendered unsolicited advice to prospective clients could not usually accept employment arising from such advice. DR 2–104(A). A lawyer could, however, accept employment resulting from unsolicited advice to a close friend or relative. Unsolicited advice to a former client in order to secure business was also permitted if the advice was germane to a matter the lawyer formerly handled for such client. DR 2–104(A)(1). Similarly, a lawyer could accept employment resulting from participation in educational activities sponsored by a qualified legal services organization. DR 2 104(A)(2). The Code generally permitted a lawyer to accept employment resulting from a lawyer's spoken or written legal scholarship, so long as he does not tout his own professional qualifications. DR 2–104(A)(4).

Under the Code a lawyer could not accept employment from a client who sought that lawyer's services as a result of prohibited solicitation. DR 2–103(E). Consequently, a lawyer could not accept employment if the lawyer knew that the client has been solicited by the lawyer's employee, partner, or other lawyer affiliated with such lawyer. Cf. DR 1–102(A)(2).

The Rules' restrictions are expressed in much less detail, and have been amended over the years as the ABA has reluctantly responded to Supreme Court decisions that have protected various forms of advertising as free speech. The Rules now prohibit solicitation by "in-person or live telephone or real-time electronic contact" of a prospective client with whom the lawyer has no prior professional or family relationship when "a significant motive" is the lawyer's pecuniary gain. Rule 7.3(a).

Florida Bar v. Went for It, Inc., 515 U.S. 618, 115 S.Ct. 2371, 132 L.Ed.2d 541 (1995) held (5 to 4) that it was constitutional for the state to prohibit plaintiff-attorneys (but not defense-attorneys) from sending direct mail solicitations to victims and their relatives for 30 days following an accident or disaster. The state argued that the 30–day ban protected the privacy of victims and their loved ones against invasive, unsolicited contact by lawyers and prevented the erosion of confidence in the legal profession that such invasions engendered. The narrow majority thought it important that, even with the ban: "Florida permits lawyers to advertise on prime-time television and radio as well as in newspapers and other media. They may rent space on billboards. They may send untargeted letters to the general population, or to discrete segments thereof." See, Rotunda, *Professionalism, Legal Advertising, and Free Speech In the Wake of Florida Bar v. Went For It, Inc.*, 49 Arkansas Law Review 703 (1997); Rotunda, *Lawyer Advertising and the Philosophical Origins of the Commercial Speech Doctrine, Lawyer Advertising and the Philosophical Origins of the Commercial Speech Doctrine*, 36 U. Richmond L. Rev. 91 (2002)

The Rules used to distinguish mass mailings (which were allowed) from direct, targeted mailings (which were not), claiming that "[d]irect mail solicitation cannot be effectively regulated by means less drastic than outright prohibition." See, former Comment 5 to Rule 7.3 (1988 version). However, targeted mailing does not involve face-to-face contact, and the recipient can simply throw the mail away. Targeted mailing is really only a more efficient form of advertising than a mass mailing. Indeed, in *Bates v. State Bar of Arizona,* 433 U.S. 350, 402 n.12, 97 S.Ct. 2691, 2718 n.12, 53 L.Ed.2d 810 (1977), Powell, J., concurring in part and dissenting in part, joined by Stewart, J., admitted that there was no "principled basis" to distinguish advertisements in newspapers from "handbills, and mail circulations." If you can give a handbill to someone, you ought to be able to mail him the handbill.

In February of 1987 two ABA entities initially proposed that Rule 7.3 be amended to allow targeted mailing, but they withdrew this proposal after the ABA Board of Governors opposed it. Then *Shapero v. Kentucky Bar Association,* 486 U.S. 466, 108 S.Ct. 1916, 100 L.Ed.2d 475 (1988) ruled that, pursuant to the First Amendment, states may not categorically prohibit lawyers from seeking business by sending truthful, nondeceptive letters to potential clients known to face particular legal problems.

In February, 1989, the ABA responded to *Shapero* by amending Rule 7.3, which now allows direct mail or prerecorded telephone contact unless the recipient has indicated that he or she does not wish to be solicited by the lawyer, or the solicitation involves coercion, duress, or harassment. Any written solicitation must include the words "Advertising Material" on the outside envelope and at the beginning and ending of any recorded message, unless the recipient is a family member or a lawyer or is someone with whom the lawyer had a close personal or prior professional relationship. The touchstone of the new Rule is to protect the prospective client from direct, personal encounters or live telephone persuasion or real-time electronic contact from a lawyer because those situations are fraught with the possibility of "undue influence, intimidation, and over-reaching." Rule 7.3, Comment 1. In addition, in light of the possibility of direct mail or prerecorded telephone advertising, there is no pressing need for such personal encounters because the direct mailing can always invite the prospective client to call the lawyer's office if the recipient wishes more information.

Chat Rooms. The ABA added a new restriction in 2002, by treating "real-time electronic contact" as in-person solicitation. The Rules acknowledge that "electronic media, such as the Internet, can be an important source of information about legal services, and lawful communication by electronic mail is permitted by this Rule." Rule 7.2, Comment 3. But Rule 7.3(a) prohibits the solicitation of a prospective client through a real-time electronic exchange that is not initiated by the prospective client.

One could treat these electronic communications as a writing. One has to type the message. The recipient does not have to respond. We all receive junk email from people, e.g., seeking help to transport $50 million from Nigeria or offering to sell us a pill that will make the opposite sex adore us. But we do not have to respond to that email. The ABA, however, treats chat rooms like face-to-face contact.

Comment 1 of Rule 7.3 simply announces that "real-time electronic contact" from the lawyer to the prospective client will "subject the layperson to the private importuning of the trained advocate in a direct interpersonal encounter." Later, Comment 3 adds: "real-time electronic persuasion," like a live telephone contact, "may overwhelm the client's judgment." There is no effort to explain or support these statements.

Comment 2 offers a different rationale: "The contents of direct in person or, live telephone or real-time electronic conversations between a lawyer to and a prospective client can be disputed and are may not be subject to third party scrutiny. Consequently, they are much more likely to approach (and occasionally cross) the dividing line between accurate representations and those that are false and misleading." It is true that oral statements can be disputed, but what goes on in a chat room is not oral communication. The recipient can print out and save whatever the lawyer sent him or her. The Internet Service that supports the chat room may keep all records of all the email sent to the chat room for many years.

For purposes of keeping track of what is said, it is easier to do that for chat rooms than for email (which is not "real-time" contact unless the sender and recipient are both using an instant-messenger service or both have broad band service). Yet, the Reporter's Notes make clear that "real-time" refers to chat rooms and not to all email. The ABA Commission recommended "that lawyer solicitation by real-time electronic communication (e.g., an Internet chat room) be prohibited." That is because: "Differentiating between e-mail and real-time electronic communication, the Commission has concluded that the interactivity and immediacy of response in real-time electronic communication presents the same dangers as those involved in live telephone contact."

C. Obtaining Recommendations or Client Referrals

The Model Code prohibited a lawyer from paying a person or organization for a recommendation or giving a reward for such a recommendation, but she could pay reasonable and customary fees or dues to a legal service organization that recommends her services. DR 2–103(B). The Code even prohibited a lawyer from requesting a person or organization to recommend the lawyer's services. DR 2–103(C). The Code did permit a lawyer to pay media advertisers for their services [if lawyers publish advertisements, they have to pay for them], but lawyers may not pay for professional publicity in a news item. DR 2–101(I). The lawyer could also request referrals from bar association-sponsored lawyer referral services, and legal service organizations, and pay them usual and reasonable dues and fees. DR 2–103(C)(1),(2).

Rule 7.2(b) is much less restrictive. It forbids a lawyer from giving anything of value in exchange for a recommendation, except that she (1) may pay for media advertising; (2) may purchase a law practice pursuant to Rule 1.17; (3) she may be part of a reciprocal referral agreement (discussed below); and (4), she may pay the "usual charges" of legal service plan or of a not-for-profit or qualified lawyer referral service. A "qualified lawyer referral service" is one that has been approved by the appropriate regulatory authority. Other than that, a lawyer may not pay someone for channeling professional work. Rule 7.2, Comment 6.

Reciprocal referral agreements. The reference in Rule 7.2 to a reciprocal referral agreement was part of the 2002 revisions. Lawyers may now agree to refer clients to other lawyers, or even a nonlawyer professional, on the condition or understanding that the beneficiaries of that referral will refer back business to them. Lawyers for very many years have been able legally to refer a case (typically a tort case) to another lawyer in exchange for a referral fee. Rule 1.5(e) (division of fees of lawyers not in the same firm). But Rule 7.2(b)(4) is quite different: it allows a lawyer to refer business to another lawyer or to a *non*lawyer in exchange for getting business referrals in the future.

These reciprocal referrals are fraught with risks, because the lawyer may be referring the client to lawyer #1 (or accountant #1) instead of a person who would be better for the client (e.g., lawyer #2 (or accountant #2)). The new Rule concludes that there is no need for a blanket prohibition if the lawyer follows certain caveats. The reciprocal referral agreement must not be exclusive and the lawyer must inform the client of the referral agreement. Rule 7.2(b)(4) & Comment 8. Then, the client will be able evaluate the referral in light of the fact that his lawyer is getting paid to give it. If the reciprocal referral agreement creates any conflicts of interest, that will be governed by Rule 1.7. The Comment adds that reciprocal referral agreements should not be of indefinite duration and should be reviewed periodically to determine whether they comply with these Rules. Comment 8. This Comment also makes clear that this Rule does not concern itself referrals or divisions of revenues or net income "among lawyers within firms comprised of multiple entities." So, rainmakers need not be worried.

Qualified Lawyer Referral Services. Rule 7.2(b)(2) allows a lawyer to pay the usual charges of a legal service plan *or* a not-for-profit *or* a qualified lawyer referral service. These revisions also came with the 2002 revisions.

A "legal service plan" is a prepaid or group legal service plan or any similar delivery system that assists prospective clients to secure legal representation. Rule 7.2 Comment 6. A "lawyer referral service" is any organization that holds itself out to the public as a lawyer referral service. The Comment tells us that laypersons understand these referral services to be "consumer-oriented organizations that provide unbiased referrals to lawyers with appropriate experience in the subject matter of the representation and afford other client protections, such as complaint procedures or malpractice insurance requirements." Comment 6.

One should bear in mind that a "legal service plan" is not a "legal services organization;" the "legal services organization" provides direct legal services to clients and is included in the definition of a "law firm," [see Rule 1.0(c)] and prepaid and group legal service plans.

The new Rule allows lawyers to pay the usual charges of a *for-profit* lawyer referral service, but only if it has been approved by an appropriate regulatory authority as affording adequate protections for prospective clients. Comment 6. In addition, the lawyer must be reasonably assured that the activities of the plan or service are compatible with the lawyer's obligations. For example, the plan's advertising must not be false or misleading. Comment 7.

D. Departing Lawyers Soliciting Clients of Their Former Law Firm

One does not normally think of soliciting present clients, because they have already hired the law firm. A firm sending them unsolicited information about their possible legal needs, is only being pro-active, taking the initiative. However, there are situations where lawyers within a firm depart and want to take some of the clients with them. The partnership agreement may explain how the firm should handle these break-ups, but any agreement must comply with the ethical rule that provides that a partnership or employment agreement may not restrict the right of a lawyer to practice after leaving except an agreement concerning benefits upon retirement. Rule

5.6(a). Thus, lawyers retain the right to practice law in competition with their former firm. But, to what extent may they seek to take with them ("solicit") the clients of that firm (or, in the view of the departing lawyers, "their clients")?

In a sense, the clients are clients of the "law firm," but in another sense the clients only deal with individual flesh and blood human beings, some of whom will be leaving to start a new firm and compete with the old one. The clients may wish to follow the individual lawyers with whom they have dealt with in the past. Clients are not merchandise; they have the right to follow the lawyer when she changes law firms.

There are also some free speech interests at stake. A lawyer should be able to tell the truth, e.g., that she is leaving one firm and starting a new firm and the clients are free to follow her. Yet, the ethics opinions do not favor departing lawyers making statements disparaging of their former law firm. ABA Formal Opinion 99–414 (Sept. 8, 1999), at n. 11. Nevertheless, one should distinguish disparaging remarks that are factually verifiable from other types of disparaging remarks. For example, if a lawyer left the firm because it had discriminated against her on account of race or sex, the free speech interests dictate that she should be able to tell that to her clients at Law Firm #1.

The right of free speech does not include the right to lie. The departing lawyer may not lie or mislead others as to why she is leaving. *In re Smith*, 843 P.2d 449 (Ore.1992) suspended a lawyer for four months for misrepresentations in connection with his leaving his old firm. The lawyer had each new law firm client sign letters retaining him individually. When he opened his new firm, he then sent these clients letters that falsely implied that nothing material had changed.

The general principle one can derive from the cases is that, unless the firm agreement is more permissive, when a lawyer leaves a law firm, she may solicit clients on whose matters she had previously worked "actively and substantially," only *after* she adequately and timely informs the firm of her intent to contact clients for that purpose. ALI, Restatement, Third, of the Law Governing Lawyers, Third, § 9(3) (Official Draft 2000). "Informing the client of the lawyer's departure in a timely manner is critical to allowing the client to decide who will represent him." ABA Formal Opinion 99–414 (Sept. 8, 1999).

A lawyer leaving a law firm "does not have a prior professional relationship with a client sufficient to permit in-person or live telephone solicitation solely by having worked on a matter for the client along with other lawyers in a way that afforded little or no direct contact with the client." The lawyer may contact these firm clients by letter or recorded communication after she has departed the law firm. ABA Formal Opinion 99–414 (Sept. 8, 1999).

When a lawyer decides to leave a law firm, she might not leave alone. She ethically may consult with other partners and associates and employees who decide to leave together subject to three caveats: First, the lawyers and other personnel should do nothing otherwise prohibited (such as impermissibly soliciting clients); second, they must not misuse firm resources (such as copying files or client lists without permission); and third, they should take no other action detrimental to the interests of the firm or of clients, other than whatever detriment may befall the firm due to their departure. Restatement, Third, § 9, Comment *i*.

If the clients of law firm #1 decide to retain the lawyers of law firm #2 (made up of lawyers who departed from law firm #1), then law firm #1 must turn its files over to the law firm designated by the clients. ABA Formal Opinion 99–414 (Sept. 8, 1999).

In short, there is no impermissible solicitation when the departing lawyer notifies her current clients that she is departing because the lawyer has a present professional relationship with them. She may similarly inform clients with whom she has a family relationship.

E. Legal Services Organizations

With great specificity and detail, the old Model Code defined the types of legal service organizations from which a lawyer could accept a recommendation or client referral. DR 2–103(D) authorized referrals from, public defender, military legal assistance, and bar association referral services. A brief look at some of these restrictions tells us how much as changed in the last few decades. Under the Code, the recommending or referring organization could exert no influence and could not interfere with the lawyer's exercise of independent professional judgment on behalf of a client. DR 2–103(D). The Code extensively regulated other legal services organizations such as employee or union legal benefits plans. DR 2–103(D)(4)(a–g). This set of complicated rules drew various distinctions involving for-profit and not-for-profit plans; open and closed plans; plans where the organization "bears ultimate liability of its members" (i.e., a typical insurance plan where the insurer bears liability and chooses the attorney to defend the insured); and plans that the lawyer initiated. DR 2–103(D)(4).

The Rules, in contrast, do not have such a Byzantine set of rules, though they do have a general rule requiring a lawyer to guarantee his professional independence (Rule 5.4), and there are the general restrictions regarding solicitation, Rule 7.3. Comment 8 to Rule 7.3 makes clear that Rule 7.3(d) allows an attorney to participate in (but not own or direct) a prepaid legal service plan even though the plan uses personal contact to solicit potential members generally (but does not target particular persons who are known to need legal services in a particular matter).

ABA Formal Opinion 87–355 (Dec. 14, 1987) reaffirms the Model Rules approval of a lawyer participating in a for-profit prepaid legal service plan if the plan allows the lawyer to exercise independent judgment on behalf of the clients, to keep client confidences, and to practice competently. The participating lawyer must ensure that the plan involves neither improper advertising, nor improper solicitation, nor improper fee sharing, and must be in compliance with other applicable law. Rule 7.2(b)(2) codifies these relaxed restrictions.

Rule 7.2(b)(2) allows a lawyer to pay the usual charges of a legal service plan *or* a not-for-profit *or* a qualified lawyer referral service. These changes also came with the 2002 revisions. A "legal service plan" is a prepaid or group legal service plan or any similar delivery system that helps prospective clients to secure legal representation. Rule 7.2 Comment 6. A "lawyer referral service" is any organization that holds itself out to the public as a lawyer referral service. The Comment tells us that laypersons understand these referral services to be "consumer-oriented organizations that provide unbiased referrals to lawyers with appropriate experience in the subject matter of the representation and afford other client protections, such as complaint procedures or malpractice insurance requirements." Comment 6.

The new Rule allows lawyers to pay the usual charges of a *for-profit* lawyer referral service, but only if it has been approved by an appropriate regulatory authority as affording adequate protections for prospective clients. Comment 6. In addition, the lawyer must be reasonably assured that the activities of the plan or service are compatible with the lawyer's obligations. For example, the plan's advertising must not be false or misleading. Comment 7.

III. Political Contributions to Obtain Government Legal Work or Legal Engagements or Appointments by Judges

DR 2–103(B) provided that a lawyer "shall not compensate or give anything of value to a person or organization to recommend or secure his employment by a client or as a reward. . . . " This section roughly corresponds to Model Rule 7.2(b), discussed above.

In 2000, the ABA added an entirely new section that has no counterpart in the Model Code. Rule 7.6 provides: "A lawyer *or law firm* shall not accept a government legal engagement or an appointment by a judge if the lawyer or law firm makes a political contribution or solicits political contributions for the purpose of obtaining or being considered for that type of legal engagement or appointment." This provision forbids lawyers from accepting judicial engagements in circumstances where judges may not offer such engagements. See, ABA Model Code of Judicial Conduct, Canon 3C(5). Cf. Canon 3E(1)(e), Canon 5C(3). This Rule represents the first time that the Model Rules have regulated a "law firm" instead of individual lawyers within a firm.

State and federal law already forbid bribery, *if* there is proof of a *quid pro quo*. And the Model Rules emphasize the obvious by stating that a lawyer who commits bribery is subject to discipline. Rule 8.4(b), cited by Rule 7.6, Comment 6.

To prevent "laundering" of political contributions, Rule 7.6 is intended to cover a political action committee or other entity owned "or controlled" by a lawyer or law firm. Comment 3.

This new Rule may be difficult to enforce because it makes crucial a very subjective element: did the lawyer or law firm make the political contribution "for the purpose of obtaining or being considered" for a legal engagement? For example, assume several lawyers in a law firm contribute to a Democratic candidate for mayor. Comment 1 acknowledges that lawyers "have a right to participate in the political process." That person becomes mayor and later hires the law firm to represent the city in various matters, all allowed under state law. Is the law firm violating Rule 7.6 if one of the lawyers hoped (but could not be certain) that the new mayor would favor a law firm that included his supporters? In addition, unlike ordinary campaign finance laws (which regulate the candidate who *receives* the contribution as well as donors who give it), Model Rule 7.6 only regulates the lawyer who gives the money, not the politician who receives the funds. And neither the donor nor recipient will be violating any state or federal laws.

When Rule 7.6 was being debated, the National Organization of Bar Counsel (representing lawyers who prosecute discipline cases) warned the ABA that it would be difficult to enforce, short of bribery. Supporters of the Rule argued that it would be "largely self-enforcing" except in "extreme circumstances." See, Rotunda, Legal Ethics: The Lawyer's Deskbook on Professional Responsibility § 51A–2 (ABA, West Group, 2000).

REVIEW QUESTIONS

1. George Uncle, the uncle of Attorney Beta, asked her to lecture to a retired persons' association on the topic, "Estate Planning and Lawyers." Attorney Beta agrees. In her talk, she does not tout her professional reputation and engages in no direct, private communications. Consistent with Beta's responsibilities under the Model Rules, select the most accurate statement:

   a. Her speech *is improper* because a lawyer should not give advice to laypeople that they need a lawyer.

   b. Her speech *is improper* unless Beta refuses to accept employment from the advice, except she may accept employment from Uncle because he is a relative.

   c. It *is proper* for Beta to accept employment at the meeting from those attending because she does not tout her own professional reputation, and she may address social or fraternal organizations whose members seek legal advice.

   d. Her speech *is proper only if* Beta refuses to accept employment from the advice, including employment from Uncle.

2. *A & B*, both attorneys, assumed duties as officers and directors of the First National Bank. Before and after banking hours they maintained a partnership engaged in the private practice of law. The law partnership was in a separate office in a section of the bank building rented to various offices, including other law offices. They did not solicit any law business stemming from the banking activities and the bank did not engage in any advertising that directly or indirectly benefited *A* and *B* in the practice of law. They occasionally referred clients to an accountant who worked down the hall from them. In return, the accountant would sometimes refer her clients to *A & B* for legal work. *A & B* informed their clients of this agreement. If, in the judgment of *A & B*, it was best for the client to be referred to another accountant, *A & B* would refer to their client to that accountant with whom they had no reciprocal referral agreement.

   I. *A* and *B* are aiding in the unauthorized practice of law.

   II. *A* and *B* are involved in an inherent conflict of interest between their banking interests and their legal interests and their clients' accounting interests.

III. *A* and *B* have violated no disciplinary rules.

The best answer is:

a. I only

b. II only

c. I and II

d. III only

3.   *A, B, & J* are attorneys whose sole professional relationship is that they are full-time salaried employees of *C* Corporation and constitute its Legal Department. The President of *C* Corporation has requested *A, B, & J*, in corresponding with third parties, to use letterheads that do not disclose that *A, B, & J* are members of the Legal Department of the corporation. Much of the correspondence warns the addressees of possible violations by the addressees of contracts with *C* Corporation. The President of the corporation feels that a letterhead that does not identify the signatory as a member of the Legal Department of the corporation would tend to sound more impressive to the recipients. The letterhead would read:

A, B, & J, a Partnership of Attorneys at Law [Street address] [telephone number]

I.   The letterhead is a *violation of the rules* unless the Board of Directors authorized it, because the corporate attorneys owe their obligations to the corporate entity and not any member thereof.

II. The letterhead *is proper* because it represents customary advertising.

III. The letterhead *is proper* under the rules *if* A, B, & J shared the same offices.

IV. The letterhead *is improper* because A, B, & J are not in fact partners.

The best answer is:

a. I and IV

b. II only

c. I only

d. III only

e. IV only

4. The Supreme Court in *Bates v. State Bar of Arizona*, 433 U.S. 350, 97 S.Ct. 2691, 53 L.Ed.2d 810 (1977) held, inter alia, that:

I. The state may regulate legal advertising in order to assure its truthfulness.

II. Legal advertising on radio and television are subject to the same restraints as those on the print media.

III. In-person solicitation is constitutionally protected.

IV. Advertising the quality of legal services is constitutionally protected.

The best answer is:

a. Neither I, II, III, nor IV

b. I, II, & IV, only

c. I only

d. I and IV only

5. Attorney practices largely in the areas of tax, wills and estates, and trusts. Attorney learned of a new Internal Revenue Service regulation that may affect provisions in a will she prepared for Former Client two years ago. Attorney has not heard from Former Client since she drew the will.

Is Attorney *subject to discipline* if she telephones Former Client to tell him of the new IRS ruling?

a. No, unless Attorney's significant motive is to secure employment by Former Client.

b. No, because Former Client is a former client.

c. Yes, because Attorney is engaged in direct contact using a live telephone.

d. Yes, because Attorney would be soliciting legal business from someone no longer her client.

6. Attorney, the only adjunct (i.e., part-time) faculty member at Law School, asked that the following statement be included in the law school catalog.

"The state-approved certifying agency has certified that Attorney, an adjunct member of our faculty, is a certified practicing specialist in the subject that she teaches."

Is Attorney *subject to discipline* if the statement is included in Law School's catalog?

a. Yes, unless Attorney limits her practice to the subjects she teaches.

b. No, if Attorney is in fact experienced in the subjects she teaches.

c. Yes, because the designation of Attorney as a specialist appears in a publication intended for persons other than members of the bar.

d. Yes, if the statement is false.

*

PART VI

The Lawyer's Obligation Not to Misuse the Office of Government

■ **ANALYSIS**

I. The Public Official Who Is Also a Lawyer

Lawyers holding public office may not use their public positions in order to obtain improper advantage for their clients.

A. Firm Names

In many instances a lawyer may hold a public position and be allowed to practice law or another occupation. For example, a part-time mayor, state legislator, or city council member typically is allowed to continue the practice of law.

In such cases the lawyer's law firm may continue to use the lawyer's name in the firm name as long as that lawyer engages in active and regular practice with the firm. Rule 7.5(c); DR 2–102(B). If the lawyer is not so engaged, it is misleading to allow the firm to continue to use his name in firm communications because it may imply a connection that no longer exists. See ABA Informal Opinion 1205 (Feb. 9, 1972).

B. Using a Public Position to Obtain Special Advantage

The lawyer-legislator may be in an advantageous position to offer legislation, in her capacity as a legislator, in order to benefit her private client. Canon 8 of the former Model Code specifically considered this problem. Oddly enough, the Rules do not directly address it, though some of its general provisions are applicable.

The Code provided that a lawyer-legislator may accept private clients but is prohibited from using his public position to obtain a "special advantage in legislative matters for himself or for a client" only in those cases "where he knows or *it is obvious* that such action is not in the public interest." DR 8–101(A)(1) (emphasis added). This section is not so much a meaningful prohibition as it is a license, because of the difficulty of meeting any test using the phrase: "it is obvious." Thus, there is no *per se* prohibition against a lawyer accepting a retainer from a private client who is likely to be affected by proposed legislation. ABA Informal Opinion 1182 (Dec. 5, 1971). The requirement of "special advantage" means "a direct and peculiar advantage." The "not in the public interest" standard means legislation "clearly inimical to the best interests of the public as a whole." Id.

However, this license does not mean that a lawyer-legislator may ethically receive anything of value from a private client *in exchange for* introducing or voting for legislation. That transaction amounts to a bribe and is directly prohibited by DR 8–101(A)(3). Cf. Rules 3.5(a); 8.4(b). The old Model Code also explicitly prohibited the lawyer-legislator (or similar person) from accepting anything of value from anyone if the lawyer "knows or it is *obvious* that the offer is for the purpose of influencing his action as a public official." DR 8–101(A)(3) (emphasis added).

This prohibition applied whether or not the lawyer fulfills his part of the bargain, i.e., whether the lawyer in fact uses, or attempts to use, his influence corruptly, in violation of DR 8–101(A)(3). It also applies if the bargain is only implicit.

Example: In re D'Auria, 67 N.J. 22, 24, 334 A.2d 332, 333 (1975) held that it is improper for a judge handling worker's compensation matters to accept numerous "free" lunches from lawyers or insurance companies who had cases then pending before the judge. Though there was no explicit evidence proving the corrupt intent of those who offered the "free" lunch, the facts and setting probably convinced the court that the purpose of the offer was "obvious." As economists would say, "There is no such thing as a free lunch."

Where the factual background is less compelling, the result is different. Cf. ABA Informal Opinion 1182 (Dec. 5, 1971) (no per se violation of DR 8–101(A)(3) when facts only show that a lawyer-legislator represented in legal matters a person also affected by contemplated legislation).

Though the Rules have no direct counterpart to DR 8–101(A)(3), a fact situation that meets the stiff requirements of that DR probably also meets the general prohibitions of Rule 8.4(c) or (d), prohibiting dishonesty and conduct prejudicial to the administration of justice.

Just as the lawyer-official may not accept anything of value offered to influence her own actions as a public official, neither may a lawyer seek to influence a public official (or juror) improperly. Rule 3.5(a); Cf. EC 7–35; DR 9–101(C).

Rule 7.6 prohibits any lawyer or law firm from accepting a government legal engagement (such as being hired as municipal bond counsel) or appointment by a judge (e.g., being appointed as special referee) if the lawyer or law firm made a political contribution or solicited a political contribution "*for the purpose of obtaining or being considered* for the legal engagement or appointment." The test is very strict: the lawyer would not have made the political contribution "but for" the desire to be considered for the legal engagement or appointment. Rule 7.6, Comment 5.

Oddly enough, "political contributions" do not include uncompensated services such as being chairman of the judge's reelection campaign. Rule 7.6, Comment 2. Why? Because the Comment says so.

C. Attempts to Influence a Tribunal

A lawyer may not use his public position in order to gain a corrupt advantage for himself or his client. DR 8–101(A)(2); Rule 3.5(a). The basic question is whether the effort to influence the tribunal was corrupt.

Example: A lawyer-legislator appears before the state commerce commission to urge a rate increase on behalf of a private client. This lawyer-legislator is also on the state house committee that oversees the state commerce commission and sets the administrators' salaries. Such circumstantial facts alone do not show anything improper. The lawyer-legislator must also have actually engaged in an overt attempt to exert *improper* influence over the state commerce commission. ABA Informal Opinion 1182 (Dec. 5, 1971). See also *State ex rel. Nebraska State Bar Ass'n v. Holscher*, 193 Neb. 729, 738, 230 N.W.2d 75, 80 (1975).

D. Implying the Power to Influence Improperly

A lawyer, whether or not a public official, may not state "or imply" to anyone that she has the power to influence a public official or agency on improper or irrelevant grounds or to achieve results by any means that violate the Rules or other law. Rule 8.4(e); DR 9–101(C).

This prohibition applies whether or not the lawyer actually exercises the influence. This prohibition also applies whether or not the lawyer could, in fact, exercise such influence.

Example: Lawyer tells Client: "You are lucky you hired me. The judge hearing your case is my old college roommate and good friend. He'll do what he can to help me." Lawyer has violated Rule 8.4(e) and DR 9–101(C) whether or not the judge even knows of Lawyer.

The rationale for this rule is that such suggestions by lawyers serve no valid purpose and undermine public confidence in the legal system, even if the implication is false. EC 9–4. See, Rotunda, *Ethical Problems in Federal Agency Hiring of Private Attorneys*, 1 Georgetown J. Legal Ethics 85, 121–22 (1987).

In *Matter of Sears*, 71 N.J. 175, 364 A.2d 777 (1976), the attorney wrote an official of his company-client implying that the attorney would or could improperly influence a federal judge in connection with an S.E.C investigation of that company. Though there was no evidence that the attorney communicated *ex parte* with the judge, the attorney wrote an official of the corporate client as follows:

> "When you talk to Bob [Vesco], will you please tell him that I have made contact re the above and have done all that I can properly be done [sic] under the circumstances."

The Ethics Committee found that this letter was referring to Vesco's earlier request that the lawyer approach the federal judge. The lawyer characterized the letter "as merely 'rain-making'—that is, an effort to mollify a client who had been pressuring him to undertake a specific action." The state supreme court found a violation of DR 9–101(C):

> "In the instant case, the Vesco request was aimed at influencing the S.E.C. suit and was highly improper. By fostering the impression that he had satisfied or could satisfy that request, respondent's conduct fell directly within the ambit of DR 9–101(C)."

71 N.J. at 191, 364 A.2d at 785.

II. The Revolving Door

A. The Former Government Lawyer

When a lawyer who works for the Government leaves that position and accepts private employment, the commentators talk about the "revolving door" between governmental service and private employment. The goal of the rules in this area is to limit potential abuses—e.g., the risk of improper use of confidential government information or the risk that the government lawyer might use that position to benefit a future private employer—without unduly restricting the ability of the government to attract lawyers. See Rule 1.11, Comment 4. There are public advantages, within limits, to leaving open the door between government service and private practice. The revolving door between government service and private practice may be a good thing.

The basic Code provision is DR 9–101(B):

> "A lawyer shall not accept *private* employment in a *matter* in which he had *substantial responsibility* while he was a *public employee*." (Emphasis added).

The italicized words emphasize the breadth and limitations of this rule, which must be read in connection with DR 5–105(D). DR 5–105(D) imputed the disqualification of DR 9–101(B) to every other lawyer in the firm. The Model Rules *reject* this automatic imputation and allow the disqualified lawyer to be timely screened from the matter in question, as discussed below. Rule 1.11(b)(1); Rule 1.11(c).

ABA Formal Opinion 342 (Nov. 24, 1975) is quite old in terms of years, but it is still influential, and much of it is reflected in the present version of Model Rule 1.11. ABA Formal Opinion 342 addressed the following issues:

1. Private Employment

"Private employment" means work "as a private practitioner." If a lawyer in private practice has accepted, as one of his clients, a government agency, that lawyer is accepting *private* employment from the government agency. E.g., *General Motors Corp. v. City of New York*, 501 F.2d 639 (2d Cir.1974) (private lawyer accepts contingent fee case from New York City). This term, however, does not cover the situation where one government agency recruits a lawyer presently employed by another agency because there is no realistic danger that a lawyer will abuse his government office for private gain merely because he moves from one salaried government position to another salaried government position.

2. Matter

This term refers to "a discrete and isolatable transaction or set of transactions between identifiable parties."

Example 1: Lawyer represents Government in suing Widget, Inc. for a strip-mining violation. The Lawyer leaves the Government and represents Widget, Inc. in defending against this suit. Or, Lawyer represents a class action plaintiff suing Widget for pollution damage growing out of the same facts. The various suits involve the same "matter."

Example 2: Lawyer for a congressional committee helps draft a new law governing the coal industry and establishing requirements for returning the land back to its natural form after strip mining. Lawyer then leaves the congressional committee and begins work for Coal Co., Inc. involving the same point of *law*. The two situations are not the same "matter" because there is no discrete transaction between identifiable parties in a particular situation. Drafting a law for the government does not disqualify a lawyer from later private employment involving the same point of law.

3. Substantial Responsibility

A government lawyer does not have "substantial responsibility" over a matter if she only gives perfunctory approval or disapproval. The lawyer should have "had such a heavy responsibility for the matter in question that it is unlikely he did not become personally and substantially involved in the investigative or deliberative processes regarding that matter."

4. Public Employee

This term encompasses every capacity in which the lawyer is employed by the government. It is not necessary that the employment be in one's capacity as a lawyer. One might be the administrative head of an agency.

5. Imputation

ABA Formal Opinion 342 concluded that there was no pressing public need, under DR 5–105(D), to apply an inflexible imputation of the DR 9–101(B) disqualification. Such inflexibility is costly because it restricts government recruitment and limits a client's choice of lawyers. Thus, in spite of the broad language of DR 5–105(D), the Formal Opinion concluded that the former government lawyer's disqualification is not imputed to the other lawyers in his new firm *if* the former government lawyer is "screened, to the satisfaction of the government agency concerned, from participation in the work and compensation of the firm on any matter over which as a public employee he had substantial responsibility."

6. The Approach of the Model Rules

Rule 1.11 is in many respects substantially similar to DR 9–101(B), as court decisions actually interpreted that rule. However, Model Rule 1.11 is much more specific and clear. First, it expressly incorporates the requirements of other law, such as government conflict of interest law.

The Rule also requires that a firm screening a disqualified lawyer notify "promptly" the governmental agency *in writing*, so that the agency may assure itself that the firm has complied with the requirements of this rule. Rule 1.11(a)(2). "Promptly" means "as soon as practicable" after the need for screening becomes apparent. Rule 1.11, Comment 7. While the lawyer must notify the government agency, there is *no* requirement that any notice be given to any *other* adverse *party* to enable it to ascertain that there has been compliance with this Rule. Compare Rule 1.11(c) with Rule 1.11(a)(2).

Rule 1.0(k) defines "screened" to mean that the law firm isolates the lawyer from any participation in the matter by imposing "reasonably adequate" procedures so that the screened lawyer protects the information that the ethics rules or other law obligate the isolated lawyer is protect.

Note: Because part of Formal Opinion 342 speaks of the need to permit "the one protected by DR 9–101(B) to waive" its protection, the question may arise as to whether a government agency may unreasonably refuse to "waive," e.g., to withhold its waiver only for tactical reasons. See *Kesselhaut v. United States*, 555 F.2d 791, 794 (Ct.Cl. 1977) (per curiam) (government's unjustified withholding of consent to a screening not binding on the court). The Model Rules avoid this issue and reach the result in *Kesselhaut* because they do not require any government consent as to screening. The government must receive notice so that it can ascertain that the screening is timely and effective, but it has no power to withhold consent to a proper screening. However, the former government lawyer does need consent from the government if that former government lawyer wants to be able *personally* to represent another client in a matter in which he had participated earlier personally and substantially as a government official. Rule 1.11(a).

Rule 1.11(b)(1) also provides that the screened lawyer must be "apportioned no part of the fee" from the disqualifying matter. This rule is less restrictive than Formal Opinion 342 because the Rule explicitly allows the screened lawyer to receive "a salary or partnership share established by prior independent agreement." The Rule only prohibits "*directly* relating the attorney's compensation to the fee" in the disqualifying matter. Rule 1.11, Comment 6 (emphasis added).

Rule 1.11(c) has a special provision regarding confidential government information. "Confidential government information" is defined as information obtained pursuant to government authority and not available to the public. The former government attorney cannot use such confidential information about a person to the "material disadvantage of that person." Rule 1.11(c). The Rules do not impute this special restriction on the former government lawyer to other members of his firm *if* the firm *screens* the former government lawyer from the matter in question and apportions to him no part of the fee from that matter.

The lawyer in government service also must not negotiate for private employment with a party who is involved in a matter in which the government lawyer is then participating, personally and substantially. Rule 1.11(d)(2)(ii).

Note: Law clerks seeking private employment are treated differently. See Rule 1.12(b) and the next section, C(1), infra.

B. The Private Lawyer Moving Into Government Practice

A lawyer for the government may not take a case in which she had personal and substantial participation while in private practice, unless the appropriate government agency gives informed consent, confirmed in writing. Rule 1.11(d)(2)(i).

The disqualification imposed on the former private practitioner now in government service is not imputed to any other lawyers within the government. See Rule 1.10. To impute would place a tremendous cost on the government—a cost not justified by public policy. The lawyer cannot ethically reveal her former client's secrets to her new colleagues. See Rule 1.6; Canon 4. And, there is little financial incentive to breach this screen or Chinese Wall because a salaried government lawyer has no "financial interest in the success of departmental representation that is inherent in private practice." The duty of a government lawyer is "to seek just results rather than the results desired by a client." ABA Formal Opinion 342 (Nov. 25, 1975). This government official should, however, be screened from participation in the particular matter. Id. Rule 1.10 (the general rule governing imputation) does *not* govern imputations related to the former *government* lawyer now in private practice. See Rule 1.10, Comment 7.

In 2002, the ABA approved changes to Rule 1.11 specifically applying Rules 1.7 and 1.9 to the conflicts of interest of former and current government officers and employees. See Rule 1.11 (a)(1) and 1.11(d)(1).

C. The Former Judge

1. The General Rule

A *former judge* may not accept private employment in a matter if she acted in a judicial capacity, on the merits of that case. DR 9–101(A); Rule

1.12(a) ("participated personally and substantially"). This disqualification rule applies not only to judges but to other persons who have acted in a "judicial capacity," such as a hearing officer, special master, or referee. Rule 1.12(a), Comment 1. *Powers v. State Dept. of Social Welfare,* 208 Kan. 605, 493 P.2d 590 (1972) (DR 9–101(A) applies to referee in social welfare department). See also EC 5–20 (impartial mediator or arbitrator).

If the judge's *law clerk* "personally and substantially" participated with the judge on the case, then the law clerk is also disqualified from later representing anyone in the same matter. Rule 1.12(a). The judge's law clerk may, however, negotiate for employment with a party or attorney who is involved in a matter—even though the clerk is participating personally and substantially on that matter—so long as the clerk notifies the judge. Rule 1.12(b).

In 2002, the ABA changed the Rule to expand it to apply to lawyers who served as arbitrators, mediators, and other third-party neutrals. Rule 1.12(a). These lawyers are prohibited from representing clients in a matter in which the lawyer participated personally and substantially, unless all parties to the proceedings give their informed consent, confirmed in writing. Rule 1.12(1) and Comment 2. Imputation and screening procedure for disqualified former third-party neutrals is the same as for former judges, adjudicators, and law clerks. See Rule 1.12(c); See also (2) and (3) infra.

The Rules do not disqualify a *partisan arbitrator—i.e.,* the partisan member of a multimember arbitration panel—from later representing a party to the arbitration because that type of arbitrator did not serve, in that matter, as an impartial decision-maker. Rule 1.12(d).

2. Waiver

The general rule requiring disqualification of the former judge, adjudicator, or third-party neutral is for the protection of the parties. Consequently, they may waive this protection by giving informed consent, confirmed in writing. Rule 1.12(a). Cf. Model Code of Judicial Conduct, Canon 3F (1990), which provides for waiver of certain disqualifications by a sitting judge.

3. Imputation and Screening

The disqualification of the former judge, adjudicator, or third-party neutral is *not* imputed to any other lawyer in the disqualified lawyer's new law firm if two conditions exist: first, the disqualified lawyer should be timely screened from the disqualifying matter and be apportioned no part of the fee from it; second, the law firm should promptly give written notice to the parties and the appropriate tribunal so that they can determine that the screening is adequate. Rule 1.12(c). This screening and notice provision parallels the rule regarding the former government lawyer, but adds a requirement of notification to the parties in addition to notification to the tribunal. See Rule 1.11(b).

III. Special Responsibilities of a Public Prosecutor

The duty of the public prosecutor is to seek justice, not merely to convict. Rule 3.8, Comment 1; EC 7–13. From this principle, there have developed certain limitations that modify the duty of zealous behavior.

A. Criminal Cases

A prosecutor may not institute charges if he knows that they are not supported by probable cause. DR 7–103(A); Rule 3.8(a). Ordinarily a lawyer may bring any nonfrivolous action. See DR 2–109(A); 7–102(A)(1); Rule 3.1.

The prosecutor must inform the accused of the existence of evidence of which the prosecutor is aware, if that evidence tends to negate the guilt of the accused or mitigate the punishment. DR 7–103(B); Rule 3.8(d). The prosecutor should not intentionally fail to follow certain leads because he believes the information secured might damage his case. EC 7–13.

The prosecutor must also inform the sentencing tribunal of all mitigating information not covered by a protective order or otherwise privileged. Rule 3.8(d). Whenever the prosecutor is proceeding *ex parte,* as in a grand jury hearing, he should offer the tribunal "all material facts" whether or not adverse. Rule 3.3(d); Rule 3.8(d).

The prosecutor should give the accused a reasonable opportunity to obtain counsel, and should not urge an unrepresented accused to waive important pretrial rights, such as the right to a preliminary hearing. Rule 3.8(b), (c). Cf. DR 7–104(A)(2). However, if the accused has decided to appear *pro se,* the government attorney must negotiate directly with the accused. Rule 3.8, Comment 2. Cf. EC 3–7.

The Model Rules place ethical limits on a prosecutor who seeks to subpoena an attorney.

Over the last several decades, the Government has appeared to increase its subpoenas of criminal defense lawyers to testify before the grand jury. In the

District of Massachusetts, for example, the Federal Government, during most of the 1980's, subpoenaed attorneys in approximately 10% to 32% of the criminal cases. *United States v. Klubock*, 832 F.2d 649, 658 (1st Cir.1987) (amended panel opinion), affirmed by equally divided en banc court, 832 F.2d 664 (1st Cir. 1987). The Government often seeks information on the amount of the fee paid to the attorney, whether it was paid in cash, and whether the client or a third party paid it. The answers to these questions are relevant in light of various federal laws such as the Racketeer Influenced and Corrupt Organizations Act, 18 U.S.C.A. §§ 1961—1968 and the Continuing Criminal Enterprise Statute, 21 U.S.C.A. §§ 848—853. The fee information may be useful in determining whether any fee is subject to forfeiture because it was acquired through certain criminal activity, or is evidence of a criminal enterprise.

An attorney, just like any other witness who is called to testify before the grand jury, can always raise any applicable privilege, such as the attorney-client evidentiary privilege. However, attorneys have typically argued that they should not even be subpoenaed unless there is first an adversary hearing before a judge, who is to determine that the information is not privileged, the evidence is "essential," and that there is "no other feasible alternative" to secure this evidence. After most courts rejected this position, *e.g.*, *United States v. Perry*, 857 F.2d 1346 (9th Cir.1988), the ABA (in February, 1990) addressed the issue and imposed strict requirements on prosecutors who subpoena defense counsel. In 1995 the ABA *deleted* that rule. The ABA then adopted the diluted, rule is now found in Rule 3.8(e) and Comment 4.

Rule 3.8(e) imposes some requirements on the prosecutor, but they are not too overly restrictive. It only provides that the prosecutor should not subpoena a lawyer in a criminal proceeding to provide evidence about a past or present client unless the prosecutor "reasonably believes" that the evidence is not privileged, is essential, and there is no other feasible way to get the information. This Rule does *not* require the prosecutor to seek the judicial permission or make any special showing to a court.

In *United States v. Klubock*, 832 F.2d 649 (1st Cir.1987) (*en banc*)(per curiam), an equally divided court approved a federal rule that was much more restrictive than the present version of Rule 3.8(e). The ethics rule in *Klubock* made it "unprofessional conduct for a prosecutor to subpoena an attorney to a grand jury *without prior judicial approval* in circumstances where the prosecutor seeks to compel the attorney/witness to provide evidence concerning a person who is represented by the attorney/witness." Note that this ethics rule was much stricter than the present version of Rule 3.8(e). Some federal courts have invalidated, on supremacy clause grounds, similar state rules to the extent that the state seeks to apply that Rule to federal prosecutors. E.g., *Baylson v. Disciplinary Board of Supreme Court of Pennsylvania*, 764 F.Supp. 328 (E.D.Pa.1991), holding that a state rule patterned after Rule 3.8(e) cannot be enforced against federal prosecutors. The rule "distorts evidentiary privileges, disrupts existing subpoena practice, and compromises the authority and function of the modern grand jury."

In 1999, Congress took the matter into its own hands and expressly made federal lawyers subject to state ethics rules. This law, called the McDade Amendment, is found at 28 U.S.C.A. § 530B.

Rule 3.8(f) prohibits prosecutors from making extra judicial comments that are substantially likely to heighten public disapproval of the accused, except when statements serve a legitimate law enforcement function and serve to inform the public regarding the nature and extent of the prosecutor's action. The rule reminds prosecutors to exercise reasonable care to prevent others assisting the prosecutor in the criminal case (such as investigators and law enforcement personnel) from making a statement that the prosecutor would be prohibited from making under Rule 3.6 or Rule 3.8. Rule 3.8(f) and Comment 6. For example, the prosecutor can announce the indictment, but she should avoid unnecessary comments, such as "he's obviously guilty."

B. Civil Cases

The old Model Code said that the government lawyer's special duty to seek justice extends to civil or administrative proceedings. The lawyer should not use her position or the government's economic power to "harass parties," or to cause "unjust settlements or results." EC 7–14. If the government lawyer believes that litigation is unfair, she should use her discretionary power not to proceed, or offer such a recommendation to her superiors. EC 7–14.

ABA Formal Opinion 94–387 (Sept. 26, 1994) concluded that the Model Rules do *not* require a lawyer to inform the opposing party in negotiations that the statute of limitations has run on her client's claims (though the lawyer must not make affirmative misrepresentations). Indeed, it would violate Rules 1.3 and 1.6 to reveal this information without client consent. The lawyer may also file a suit to enforce a time-barred claim (unless the rules of the jurisdiction prohibit that). Finally, there is no basis in the Model Rules to hold a lawyer representing the government in a *civil* case to any different ethical standard: "the government lawyer operating within the adversarial system has no greater or lesser right or duty than the private lawyer to sit in presumptive judgment of the client's cause." (Footnote omitted).

Formal Opinion 94–387 drew a dissent that rejected all of its conclusions. It also argued, citing EC 7–14, that the "worst part of this opinion is its theory that government lawyers do not owe a greater duty to the public than other lawyers, particularly the pettifogger described in this opinion." Cf. *Freeport–McMoRan Oil & Gas Co. v. Federal Energy Regulatory Commission*, 962 F.2d 45 (D.C.Cir.1992). FERC counsel did not bother to disclose in its brief that FERC had no objection to vacating challenged orders, which were superseded by a subsequent FERC order, and while the challenged orders were in effect the plaintiffs suffered no injury. The court vacated the orders and, at oral argument, FERC counsel rejected the idea that counsel for a public agency has any special obligations. Mikva, J., for the court, cited EC 7–14 and responded: "We find it astonishing that an attorney for a federal administrative agency could so unblushingly deny that a government lawyer has obligations that might sometimes trump the desire to pound an opponent into submission." 962 F.2d at 48. However, in the context of this case, a private lawyer, just like a government lawyer, would be obliged to inform the court that the law had changed. Rule 3.3(a)(2). In other words, this opinion does not show that government lawyers have higher duties than private lawyers in civil cases. Rule 3.8 imposes special duties on government lawyers but only in the context of criminal prosecutions.

REVIEW QUESTIONS

1. While working for the Department of Justice, Attorney had the major responsibility for initiating a suit against Cosmetic Co. for an antitrust violation. Attorney then left the Department of Justice and went into private practice in the capital city of her home state. The State Attorney General now is seeking to hire Attorney (for a contingent fee) as a special prosecutor to help in a case against Cosmetic Co. based on the same facts in the Department of Justice suit. Attorney will also continue her private practice.

Is it *proper* for Attorney to accept the employment?

a. Yes, unless attorney will be required to take a position on behalf of the State that is adverse to the Department of Justice interests.

b.   Yes, if Cosmetic Co. consents after full disclosure.

c.   No, because Attorney had substantial responsibility for this matter while she was a public employee.

d.   No, because it gives the appearances of impropriety for Attorney to accept various clients when all of them seek to sue the same defendant.

e.   Yes, because her new employer, for this case, is also a governmental unit.

2.   Attorney Doe has tried many contested cases before Judge. Doe believes that Judge lacks judicial temperament and is not too bright. Doe also believes that Attorney Roe would make an excellent judge. Doe wishes to defeat Judge and assist Roe in getting elected.

Doe tells the local reporter, "I support candidate Roe because I believe Judge is not too bright."

Is Doe *subject to discipline*?

a.   Yes, because Doe practices before Judge.

b.   Yes, because Doe is criticizing a sitting judge.

c.   No, because Doe believes that she is telling the truth.

d.   No, unless the reporter publishes the comment.

3.   State's Attorney seeks an indictment against Deft for extortion. State's Attorney knows that there is no probable cause to support the indictment, but believes that he can use the indictment (and subsequent plea bargaining) as a bargaining chip with Deft in order to secure Deft's testimony against others.

Is State's Attorney *subject to discipline?*

a.   No, because State's Attorney has a duty to prosecute zealously.

b.   No, if State's Attorney has acted in good faith with no personal vindictiveness against Deft.

c.   Yes, unless the Grand Jury in fact indicts.

d.   Yes, because there is no probable cause.

4.   Lawyer is a practicing attorney and also a member of a Special Commission appointed by the Governor to recommend law reform. Client, a divorced husband, has asked Lawyer to handle a legal problem regarding child custody. Lawyer researches the law and finds that it is, in her view, unjust toward husbands. Her view is shared by many, but not all, experts. Lawyer asks the Commission to recommend a change in the law to correct the problem. Lawyer, with Client's consent, discloses to the Commission her relationship with Client, but she does not disclose the name of the client. The new bill, if enacted, would greatly strengthen Client's case.

Is Lawyer *subject to discipline?*

a. Yes, because she misused her public office to help a private client.

b. Yes, because the bill is not necessarily for the public good, given the objections of some experts.

c. No, because Lawyer disclosed to the Special Commission that the interests of a client may be materially benefited by the position the Special Commission takes.

d. No, because her duty of zealous representation of client required Lawyer to act the way she did even if the bill is contrary to the public interest.

e. Yes, because Lawyer did not disclose the name of the client.

*

PART VII

The Lawyer's Obligation as an Advocate

■ ANALYSIS

I. Frivolous and Dilatory Positions

Lawyers may not assert frivolous positions.

Lawyers may not assert frivolous positions, claims, defenses, or motions. Rule 3.1; DR 7–102(A); DR 2–109(A); *In re Sarelas*, 360 F.Supp. 794 (N.D.Ill.1973) (attorney suspended and fined for filing frivolous immigration appeals); *In re Bithoney*, 486 F.2d 319 (1st Cir.1973) ("baseless defenses").

Rule 3.4(a) & (d) prohibit frivolous discovery requests or the failure to make a reasonably diligent effort to comply with discovery requests. See, e.g., Wall Street Journal, Feb. 29, 1995, at B8, col. 6, reporting that a law firm representing Apple Computer paid to settle a tort claim against Apple. The law firm itself footed the bill for the settlement because it discovered that, due to an oversight, it had failed to turn over to plaintiff documents subject to discovery, and the trial judge had threatened to declare a mistrial or impose sanctions. The document omissions came to light when the law firm was about to turn over the same documents to another plaintiff in a different case.

The mere fact that a legal position is "creative" or contrary to existing law does not make that position frivolous. The existing law often has ambiguities and always has potential for change. Rule 3.1, Comment 1. Therefore a lawyer may make a "good faith argument for an extension, modification or reversal of existing law." Rule 3.1; DR 2–109(A)(2); DR 7–102(A)(2). See also Rule 3.4(c) (lawyer should not knowingly disobey tribunal unless there is "open refusal based on an assertion that no valid obligation exists.") Cf. DR 7–106(A).

The duty to refrain from asserting frivolous claims includes pursuing dilatory tactics, which are not permissible even in criminal cases. *State v. Darnell*, 14 Wash.App. 432, 542 P.2d 117, 120 (1975). See also, Rule 3.2; DR 7–102(A)(1). However, the duty to avoid frivolous claims does not preclude the attorney from putting the state to its burden of proof in a criminal case. Rule 3.1. The government, in every criminal case, has the constitutional duty to prove every element of the charge if defendant pleads not guilty. The government cannot constitutionally shift that burden to the defendant. *Mullaney v. Wilbur*, 421 U.S. 684, 95 S.Ct. 1881, 44 L.Ed.2d 508 (1975).

Note: The language of the Rules regarding dilatory motions is phrased more affirmatively than that of the Code. Rule 3.2 requires the lawyer to make "reasonable efforts to expedite litigation consistent with the interests of the client," while DR 7–102(A)(1) and DR 2–109(A)(1) forbid a lawyer from delaying when the lawyer "*knows* or it is *obvious* that such action would serve *merely to harass* or maliciously injure another." (emphasis added).

Whether the case is civil or criminal, the lawyer need not first fully substantiate the facts before making a claim. Nor does the claim become frivolous merely because the lawyer believes that the client will not prevail. The lawyer may expect to develop vital evidence by discovery. Rule 3.1, Comment 2. Discovery, after all, comes after the complaint is filed, not before. But, "if the pleading or oral representation when made is without any reasonable basis and is designed merely to embarrass or [for] . . . some other ill-conceived or improper motives, such a pleading or oral representation would clearly be subject to disciplinary action." *State v. Anonymous (1974–5)*, 31 Conn. Sup. 179, 326 A.2d 837, 838 (1974).

Note: The drafters of the Model Rules claimed that, unlike DR 7–102(A)(1), the test of Rule 3.1 is "an objective test." See Rule 3.1, Code Comparison 1. Note, however, that this "objective" test defines "not frivolous" in terms of a "good faith argument" for a change or modification in the law. Rule 3.1. When a test [very similar to that found in DR 7–102(A) and DR 2–109(A)], is defined in part in terms of motivation, it is hardly objective.

Rule 11, Federal Rules of Civil Procedure. In 1983, Rule 11 of the Federal Rules of Civil Procedure was amended to provide that every pleading, motion, or other paper must be signed by an individual lawyer; this signature certifies that she has read the paper, that to the best of her knowledge, "formed after reasonable inquiry," it is well grounded in fact and is warranted by existing law or good faith argument to extend, modify, or reverse existing law, and that it is not filed for any improper purpose. For violation of this rule the court may sanction the party *or the attorney.*

Rule 11 spawned a great deal of controversy over its scope, meaning, procedures, and application. Opponents claim that it has chilled lawyers' enthusiasm over pursuing novel legal theories; that it is biased against plaintiffs, particularly against plaintiffs in civil rights suits; that it has not reduced but has increased the expenses of litigation by imposing satellite litigation. Since adoption of Rule 11 in 1983 there have been thousands of decisions dealing with Rule 11 sanctions; in one case alone the lawyers (to vindicate their reputation) spent $100,000 to reverse a $3,000 sanction. In some circuits, a very few judges are responsible for a disproportionate number of Rule 11 sanctions. E.g., 3 ABA/BNA Lawyers' Manual on Professional Conduct 266–67 (Aug. 19, 1987); Rotunda, *Learning the Law of Lawyering,* 136 U.Pa.L.Rev. 1761, 1773–75 (1988); Kramer, *Viewing Rule 11 as a Tool to Improve Professional Responsibility,* 75 Minn.L.Rev. 793 (1991).

The Advisory Committee on the Federal Rules of Civil Procedure responded to these criticisms, and a new Rule 11 went into effect in late 1993. The Advisory Committee Notes to the 1993 amendments explained that the new Rule 11 "places greater constraints on the imposition of sanctions and should reduce the number of motions for sanctions presented to the court." The new Rule 11 provides protection against sanctions if the challenged paper, claim, defense, etc. is withdrawn or appropriately corrected. Federal Rule 11(c)(1)(A). The judge's sanctions "shall be limited to what is sufficient to deter repetition" of the conduct and sanctions may include "directives of a nonmonetary nature" or an order to pay a penalty to the court, or an order to pay the movant "some or all of the reasonable attorneys' fees and other expenses incurred as a direct result of the violation." Federal Rule 11(c)(2).

II. Responsibilities Toward the Tribunal

A. Candor

1. Disclosure of Representative Capacity

A lawyer appearing before a tribunal may not mislead the tribunal regarding the fact that the lawyer appears in a representative capacity.

The identity of the lawyer's client is rarely privileged. See, e.g., *Colton v. United States*, 306 F.2d 633, 637 (2d Cir.1962). Even when it is, the lawyer may not mislead the tribunal—whether it be judicial, administrative, or legislative—regarding the fact that the lawyer appears in a representative capacity. It is not misleading for a lawyer to disclose that she appears on behalf of another, whose name is privileged; it is misleading for the lawyer to pretend that she appears pro se when in fact she does not. DR 7–106(B)(2); DR 1–102(A)(4); Rule 8.4(c); cf. Rule 3.9.

As a general rule, the attorney-client evidentiary privilege does not protect the identity of the client. In judicial as well as nonadjudicative proceedings (such as those involving lobbying), the government has a legitimate need to know "who is being hired, and who is putting up the money, and how much." *United States v. Harriss*, 347 U.S. 612, 625, 74 S.Ct. 808, 816, 98 L.Ed. 989, 1000 (1954) (upholding disclosure provisions of Federal Lobbying Act, 2 U.S.C.A. § 261 et seq.). Accord, Rule 3.9; DR 7–106(B)(2); ABA Canons of Professional Ethics (1908, as amended), Canon 26: "[I]t is unprofessional for a lawyer [appearing before legislative or other bodies] to conceal his attorneyship. . . . "

2. Disclosure of Adverse Legal Authority

A lawyer is subject to discipline if she knowingly makes a false statement of law or fact to a tribunal or if she fails to correct a false statement of law or fact that she made previously to the tribunal. Rule 3.3(a)(1).

A lawyer must also disclose to a tribunal any legal authority in the controlling jurisdiction that he knows is directly adverse to his client's position and that opposing counsel has not disclosed. Rule 3.3(a)(2). See also, DR 7–106(B)(1).

Rule 3.3 does not require the lawyer to make "a disinterested exposition of the law. . . . " Rule 3.3, Comment 4. The lawyer is engaged in advocacy, not a seminar discussion. But he must disclose pertinent, adverse legal authority in the controlling jurisdiction. Of course, after disclosing these decisions he may seek to distinguish them, or challenge their soundness, or present reasons that he believes would warrant the court in not following them in the pending case. ABA Formal Opinion 146 (July 17, 1935).

Note that Rule 3.3(a)(2) does not speak of "controlling authorities." It is broader and refers to "legal authority in the controlling jurisdiction." This Rule follows the principle of ABA Formal Opinion 280 (June 18, 1949), which rejects the narrow view that the lawyer must only cite decisions that are decisive of the pending case. Rather, the disclosure rule applies to "a decision directly adverse to any proposition of law on which the lawyer expressly relies, which would reasonably be considered important by the judge sitting on the case." The test the lawyer should use: Is the decision that opposing counsel has overlooked one that the court should clearly consider in deciding the case? Would a reasonable judge properly feel that a lawyer who advanced a proposition adverse to the undisclosed decision was lacking in candor and fairness to him? Would the judge consider himself misled by an implied representation that the lawyer knew of no adverse authority?

Case law has adopted a similar test. See *In re Greenberg*, 15 N.J. 132, 137, 104 A.2d 46, 49 (1954) ("limiting it, however, to decisions of the courts of this State and, with respect to federal questions, to decisions of the courts of the United States").

The Rules extend the duty to disclose adverse legal authority until the proceedings are concluded "even if compliance requires disclosure of information otherwise protected by Rule 1.6." Rule 3.3(c). In other words, if a lawyer, in the course of representing a client, discovers adverse legal authority within the meaning of Rule 3.3(a)(2), the lawyer must disclose that authority to the tribunal, even if it is information that would otherwise be protected by Rule 1.6.

Comparison of Rule 3.9 with Rule 3.3. Rule 3.9 applies only when the lawyer is representing a client in a *non*adjudicative proceeding of a legislative body or administrative agency. Rule 3.9. For example, the lawyer may be acting as a lobbyist or testifying in support of a proposed law or rule.

Rule 3.9 applies if the lawyer or the lawyer's client is presenting *evidence or argument* at a legislative or administrative proceeding. Rule 3.9 does *not* apply in situations where the agency is a formal adversary, such as when the lawyer is representing a client in negotiations or other bilateral transaction with the government, or is applying for a government license. It also does *not* apply when the matter is related to the client's compliance with generally applicable reporting requirement such as the filing of income tax returns, or in connection with a government investigation or examination of the client. Those representations are governed by Rules 4.1 through 4.4, dealing with adversaries. Rule 3.9, Comment 3.

Comment 3 of Rule 3.9 is consistent with the holding of ABA Formal Opinion 93–375 (August 6, 1993) that Rule 3.9 is inapplicable in connection with a bank examination. This Opinion said that in representing a client in a bank examination, a lawyer "may not under any circumstances lie to or mislead agency officials," but the lawyer is under "no duty to disclose weaknesses in her client's case or otherwise reveal confidential information protected under Rule 1.6."

Rule 3.9 does not incorporate Rule 3.3(d), which governs *ex parte* proceedings, because those proceedings involve applications for a type of relief—a temporary restraining order, a default judgment—that are simply inapplicable to the *non*adjudicative proceedings governed by Rule 3.9. Similarly, Rule 3.9 explicitly does not incorporate the portions of Rule 3.4 governing, for example, a lawyer's obligations regarding discovery, or the limitations on a lawyer asserting personal knowledge, because they are often inapplicable before municipal councils, legislatures, and agencies acting in a rule-making capacity. Of course, if the agency before which the lawyer appears has particular rules of procedure that impose duties beyond those of Rule 3.9, the lawyer must follow them.

3. Disclosure of Facts

(a) Affirmative Misrepresentation

The general principle is that a lawyer may not make any misrepresentation or engage in any dishonest, fraudulent, or deceitful conduct. Rule 8.4(c); DR 1–102(A)(4). A specific corollary of this principle is that a lawyer may not make a false statement of fact to a tribunal. Rule 3.3(a)(1); DR 7–102(A)(5). Nor may the lawyer offer evidence that he knows to be false. Rule 3.3(a)(3); DR 7–102(A)(4). In addition, the lawyer has discretion to refuse to offer evidence ("other than the testimony of a defendant in a criminal matter") that he or she "reasonably believes is false." Rule 3.3(a)(3). Similarly the lawyer may not falsify evidence or aid in its creation or preservation if he knows, or it is obvious that the evidence is false. Rule 3.4(b); DR 7–102(A)(6).

Compensating Witnesses. DR 7–109(C) provided that a lawyer "shall not pay, offer to pay, or acquiesce in the payment of compensation to a witness contingent on the content of his testimony or the outcome of a case." However, this DR allowed the lawyer to pay a witness expenses reasonably incurred in attending the trial and testifying, and reasonable compensation for her loss of time in attending the trial. The witness, for example, might have to miss a day of work and be docked one day's pay. In addition, the lawyer could pay a reasonable fee for the professional services of an expert witness. The lawyer could pay the expert (an accountant, a medical examiner, etc.) for his time, but not for his opinion.

Rule 3.4(b) does not adopt this language. Instead, it incorporates, by reference, the laws of the local jurisdiction, so a lawyer may not "offer an inducement to a witness that is prohibited by law." If other law prohibits bribes, then a lawyer who offers to bribe a witness is subject to discipline (in addition to being subject to imprisonment for violating the criminal law).

Under Rule 3.4(b), may a lawyer offer compensation to a witness contingent on the content of the outcome of the case? Assume the lawyer says: "I will pay you, a fact witness or an expert witness, $500 per hour for your testimony, but only if my client wins the case." Comment 3 to Rule 3.4 says: "The common law in most jurisdictions is that it is improper to pay an occurrence witness [i.e., an eye witness, or a fact witness] any fee for testifying and that it is improper to pay an expert witness a contingent fee." So, one must look to other law to see if the lawyer may offer to pay a witness contingent on the outcome of the case.

ABA Formal Opinion 96–401(Aug. 2, 1996) interpreted Rule 3.4(b) and concluded that a lawyer may compensate a non-expert witness for the time spent in attending a deposition or trial, or the time spent in meeting with a lawyer to prepare for testimony (as long as other law does not forbid the arrangement, and as long as the payments are not conditioned on the content of the testimony).

ABA Formal Opinion 96–401 also allows a lawyer to pay the witness for time preparing and discussing the testimony even if the payments do not represent lost wages for the witness. If the lawyer pays the witness for time discussing the testimony and then does not use the witness, an outsider may conclude that the lawyer really was paying for the content of the testimony, the lawyer learned that content was not satisfactory, and so the lawyer did not use the prospective witness. Or, the prospective witness may figure out that the only way to keep getting paid for this lucrative second job is to keep telling the lawyer that which the lawyer wants to hear.

(b) Misrepresentations by Omission

It is not always necessary to volunteer adverse facts when appearing before a tribunal. However, in some circumstances, the "failure to make a disclosure is the equivalent of an affirmative misrepresentation." Rule 3.3, Comment 3. Because lawyers may not affirmatively misrepresent—Rule 8.4(c)—they must make the necessary affirmative disclosures in such circumstances. Hence, Rule 3.3(d) requires a lawyer to inform the tribunal of material facts, even if the facts are adverse, when the lawyer is involved in an *ex parte* proceeding. The lawyer cannot rely on the adversarial system to disclose these facts because, by hypothesis, the proceeding is *ex parte* and the other parties are not there.

(c) Remedial Measures

Commentators have long debated the degree of disclosure appropriate when the lawyer discovers that he or she has submitted material, false evidence, e.g., that the client or a witness has lied. Some have argued, particularly in criminal cases, that keeping client confidences must prevail. See, e.g., Monroe Freedman, *Ethics in an Adversary System* (1975); Monroe Freedman, *Understanding Lawyers' Ethics* 109–41 (1990). Others have rejected that conclusion. E.g., Rotunda, *Book Review of Lawyers' Ethics in an Adversary System*, 89 Harv.L.Rev. 622 (1976). See generally, Rule 3.3, Comments 5 to 14. The Rules clearly come down on the side of disclosure.

If the lawyer has offered material evidence and later learns of its falsity, under the Rules the lawyer "must take reasonable remedial measures." Rule 3.3(a)(3). This duty applies "even if compliance requires disclosure of information otherwise protected" by the confidentiality requirements of Rule 1.6. See Rule 3.3(c). Similarly, the lawyer's duty continues "to the conclusion of the proceeding" even though "compliance requires disclosure of information otherwise protected by Rule 1.6." Rule 3.3(c).

Rule 3.3(b) requires a lawyer who knows that a client plans to commit, is committing, or has committed criminal or fraudulent conduct related to the proceeding to take "reasonable remedial measures" to prevent this conduct. *Disclosure to the tribunal is considered reasonable, if necessary.* Rule 1.6, which imposes a duty of confidentiality on the lawyer, does *not* prevent the lawyer from disclosing the necessary information to the tribunal.

The duties that Rule 3.3(a) and (b) impose continue until the proceedings have concluded. Rule 3.3(c). In a criminal case, a verdict of acquittal should conclude the proceedings, given that the double jeopardy clause prevents the state from retrying the defendant. In a criminal case, if the defendant was convicted, the defendant may wish to appeal to secure a new trial or an outright reversal; the defendant should not be able to benefit from his earlier perjury, and so the proceeding should probably not be treated as "concluded" until at least the time for direct appeal (as opposed to collateral attack via a writ of habeas corpus) has passed. In a civil case, the proceedings should probably be treated as concluded when the time for appeal has passed. See Rule 3.3, Comment 13.

The lawyer, in order to comply with the candor requirements of Rule 3.3, may even have to reveal to the court the unfortunate fact that his client committed perjury. First, of course, the lawyer should seek to persuade the client to correct the falsehood. Rule 3.3, Comment 6. The lawyer should "remonstrate with the client confidentially" (Rule 3.3, Comment 10) and, if the client is still adamant, the lawyer "must take further remedial action," which may include withdrawal from the representation, if permitted and if such withdrawal will undo the effect of the false evidence.

It is not enough for the lawyer, like Pontius Pilate, to wash his hands of the situation. If withdrawal will not remedy the situation, the lawyer must disclose the relevant information to the court. The lawyer's obligation is to take reasonable remedial measures. The court then decides what to do next: (1) make a statement to the trier of fact; (2) order a mistrial; (3) "or perhaps nothing." Id. See Rotunda, *Client Fraud: Blowing the Whistle, Other Options,* 24 TRIAL Magazine 92 (Nov. 1988). See also Rule 3.3, Comment 15.

Note: It is unclear what happens if the judge orders a hearing when the lawyer discloses the perjury of the client, who disputes the charge. It is unlikely that lawyer can represent the client at the hearing (the lawyer will be a witness), so the judge may call a mistrial. An unscrupulous client with street smarts may seek to produce a series of mistrials to escape prosecution. The court, presumably, will not allow that abuse of the system. There is constitutional support for the proposition that the client may lose his right to appear at trial. Cf. *Illinois v. Allen,* 397 U.S. 337, 90 S.Ct. 1057, 25 L.Ed.2d 353 (1970) (defendant's courtroom disruption justifies conducting trial without defendant's presence). If the defendant seeks to produce a series of mistrials, the court may find a forfeiture of any right to a new hearing on the question of his perjury. See Westen, *Away from Waiver: A Rationale for the Forfeiture of Constitutional Rights in Criminal Procedure,* 75 Mich.L.Rev. 1214 (1977).

The Code was not clear regarding the lawyer's duty to remedy the lack of candor towards a tribunal. It drew a distinction between client fraud and fraud by those who are not clients, such as witnesses. DR 7–102(B)(2) provided that if the lawyer "clearly" learns that someone "other than the client has perpetrated a fraud upon a tribunal," then the lawyer "shall promptly reveal the fraud to the tribunal." However, if the client "in the course of representation" has "perpetrated a fraud upon a person or tribunal," then the lawyer must "promptly call upon his client to rectify" it. If his client refuses or is unable to do so, the lawyer must "reveal the fraud to the affected person or tribunal, *except when the information is protected as a privileged communication.*" DR 7–102(B)(1) (emphasis added). The ABA added the italicized language in 1974. Many states *refused* to adopt this 1974 amendment.

Matters became even more confusing when ABA Formal Opinion 341 (Sept. 30, 1975) interpreted "privileged" to include both "confidences" and "secrets" within the meaning of Canon 4. The drafters of ABA Formal Opinion 341 may have thought that this interpretation made DR 7–102(B)(1) a bar to disclosure. However, by incorporating Canon 4, Formal Opinion 341 also incorporated all of Canon 4's exceptions, including the exception for disclosure necessary to prevent "crimes" such as fraud. Those exceptions were "broad enough to engulf the new rule promulgated by Opinion 341." Rotunda, *When the Client Lies: Unhelpful Guides from the ABA*, 1 Corp.L.Rev. 34, 39 (1978). Under this interpretation of DR 7–102(B)(1), the lawyer has a duty to disclose the perjury. Rule 3.3, Code Comparison 4.

The Model Rules clear up the confusion. Rule 3.3(b), which the ABA added in 2002, makes clear that a lawyer "who represents a client in an adjudicative proceeding and who knows that a person intends to engage, is engaging or has engaged in criminal or fraudulent conduct related to the proceeding shall take reasonable remedial measures, including, if necessary, disclosure to the tribunal." The lawyer may refuse to offer evidence that lawyer "reasonably believes is false," but the lawyer must allow a criminal defendant to testify if the lawyer only reasonably believes the testimony will be false. Rule 3.3(a)(3).

Moreover, the commentary also provides that, if a court insists that a criminal defendant be permitted to testify in the defendant's defense (or to give a narrative statement), the lawyer commits no ethical violation in allowing the client to do so even if the lawyer knows the client intends to lie. Comments 7 and 9. However, the lawyer must still take "reasonable remedial measures," including disclosure to the tribunal if that is what is necessary to "undo the effect of the false evidence." Comment 10.

If a jurisdiction requires, as a constitutional matter, that the lawyer present the accused as a witness, then if the accused wishes to testify and "the lawyer reasonably believes but does not know that the testimony will be false," or "even if counsel knows the testimony will be false," the lawyer must follow the constitutional requirement. Rule 3.3, Comments 7 and 9.

The U.S. Constitution does *not* give the defendant any right to present perjured testimony. The leading case is *Nix v. Whiteside*, 475 U.S. 157, 106 S.Ct. 988, 89 L.Ed.2d 123 (1986). The Supreme Court, with no dissent, held that there is no violation of the Sixth Amendment right to effective assistance of counsel when the lawyer refuses to cooperate with the criminal defendant in presenting perjured testimony at the trial. In that case the lawyer told the defendant Whiteside that if he (Whiteside) insisted on committing perjury, then "it would be my duty to advise the Court of what he [Whiteside] was doing and that I felt he was committing perjury; also, that I probably would be allowed to impeach that particular testimony." The lawyer also said that he would seek to withdraw from further representation. Whiteside, to buttress his self-defense claim in a murder charge, wanted to testify that he had seen something "metallic" in the victim's hand. In fact, until a week before trial, Whiteside had consistently stated that he had not actually seen the victim with a gun. When asked about the change in testimony, Whiteside said: "If I don't say I saw a gun I'm dead."

At trial Whiteside testified and admitted that he had not actually seen a gun in the defendant's hand. Whiteside was convicted and claimed ineffective assistance of counsel because his counsel's admonition had prevented him from giving false testimony. The Eighth Circuit actually granted habeas relief to Whiteside but the Supreme Court reversed, relying in part on Model Rule 3.3.

ABA Formal Opinion 87–353 (April 20, 1987) advised that the disclosure obligation of Rule 3.3 is "strictly limited" to the case where "the lawyer *knows* that the" evidence is false. The lawyer's suspicions are not enough." (emphasis in original). If the lawyer cannot dissuade the client from testifying perjuriously, and if the lawyer cannot withdraw from representation, the lawyer either should not call the client as a witness (when the lawyer knows "that the only testimony the client would offer is false"), or call the client and question him only on those matters that would not produce perjury. If the client does testify falsely, the lawyer must disclose the false testimony under Rule 3.3(a)(3) and (b).

In short, if the lawyer offers evidence that the lawyer "knows to be false," or comes to know of its falsity, the lawyer must take "reasonable remedial measures," including, if necessary, disclosure to the tribunal. Rule 3.3(a), (b), (c).

The Client as Narrator. The lawyer cannot avoid her responsibility by having the client testify in a narrative form, without his lawyer questioning him. Some jurisdictions still allow the criminal defendant to testify using a "narrative approach"—i.e., the witness simply testifies and his or her lawyer asks no questions, but the ABA Model Rules reject that approach. ABA Formal Opinion 87–353 concluded that the Model Rules reject the narrative approach that was outlined in Proposed ABA Defense Function Standard 4–77 (1979). A lawyer "can no longer rely on the narrative approach to insulate him from a charge of assisting a client's perjury." Later editions of the Defense Function Standards now refer to ABA Model Rule 3.3. See Defense Function Standard 4–7.5 & Commentary (ABA, 1991). If the lawyer is in a jurisdiction that allows the narrative approach, and she puts her client on the stand and says, "Tell your story," what happens if the opposing lawyer objects because the vague question would allow the client's answer to include hearsay and other inadmissible testimony?

(d) Ex Parte Proceedings

The Model Rules place upon the lawyer a special affirmative duty in ex parte proceedings to disclose all material facts (whether or not thought to be adverse) so that the tribunal can make an informed decision. Rule 3.3(d). In an ex parte proceeding, one cannot rely on the adversary system to uncover the truth. Because the lawyer cannot rely on the other side to balance her presentation, she has this broader affirmative duty. Rule 3.3, Comment 14.

The principle of Rule 3.3(d) finds support in the case law going back many years. Cf. *Precision Instrument Mfg. Co. v. Automotive Maintenance Machinery Co.*, 324 U.S. 806, 818, 65 S.Ct. 993, 999, 89 L.Ed. 1381, 1388 (1945) (patent applicant must report to the Patent Office all facts concerning possible fraud or inequities underlying patent application).

(e) Pretrial Discovery

If a lawyer in a civil case discovers that her client has lied in a deposition, the lawyer must take all reasonable methods to remedy the fraud. The lawyer may have acted completely innocently. For example, the other party's attorney asked a question during deposition, to which her client responded with an answer that the lawyer thought was correct at the time. However, the client later admits privately to his lawyer that he lied in the deposition. Even though the lawyer does not rely on that deposition to file a motion for summary judgment, and no misrepresentations took place in open court, Rules 3.3(a)(3) and (b) apply to pretrial discovery situations because neither Rule requires that the tribunal must have been aware of the false evidence. Rule 3.3, Comments 1 & 10 (added in 2002) make that clear. Rule 3.3 requires the lawyer to take reasonable remedial measures to rectify the perjury. For example, the lawyer should first remonstrate with the client. If that fails, the lawyer must take other measures.

A "noisy withdrawal" [see Rule 4.1, Comment 3] may not be entirely effective to undo the fraud's impact on the case. For example, the opposing party might drop the case or settle it, in reliance on the false deposition, in spite of the noisy withdrawal by opposing counsel. Then the lawyer must disclose: "Direct disclosure under Rule 3.3, to the opposing party or if need be to the court, may prove to be the only reasonable remedial measure in the client fraud situations most likely to be encountered in pretrial proceedings." ABA Formal Opinion 93–376 (Aug. 6, 1993).

B. Trial Publicity

Rule 3.6 attempts to balance the right of free speech with the right to a fair trial. Rule 3.6, after it was amended in response to *Gentile v. State Bar of Nevada,* 501 U.S. 1030, 111 S.Ct. 2720, 115 L.Ed.2d 888 (1991), discussed immediately below, is more sympathetic to the first amendment concerns than was the former Model Code provision: DR 7–107. Rotunda, *Media Accountability In Light of the First Amendment,* 21 Social Philosophy & Policy 269 (Cambridge University Press, No. 2, 2004).

Note: Any limits on a lawyer's right to comment raise questions regarding possible unconstitutional restrictions on the lawyer's First Amendment rights. Several courts have found various first amendment problems with DR 7–107. See *Chicago Council of Lawyers v. Bauer,* 522 F.2d 242 (7th Cir.1975), cert. denied sub nom., *Cunningham v. Chicago Council of Lawyers,* 427 U.S. 912, 96 S.Ct. 3201, 49 L.Ed.2d 1204 (1976); *Markfield v. Association of the Bar of City of New York,* 49 A.D.2d 516,

370 N.Y.S.2d 82 (1975), appeal dismissed, 37 N.Y.2d 794, 375 N.Y.S.2d 106, 337 N.E.2d 612 (1975); *Hirschkop v. Snead*, 594 F.2d 356 (4th Cir.1979) (per curiam). In *Gentile v. State Bar of Nevada*, 501 U.S. 1030, 111 S.Ct. 2720, 115 L.Ed.2d 888 (1991), a very divided Supreme Court held that a Nevada Supreme Court Rule governing a lawyer's pretrial statements about a case (a Rule almost identical to the original version of Model Rule 3.6) incorporated a standard that was consistent with the First Amendment, but was void for vagueness as interpreted. Different majorities of the Court supported each holding. Justice Kennedy, for the Court, concluded that the "notwithstanding" language [now found in Model Rule 3.6(b)] purported to create a safe harbor, listing statements that can be made (e.g., the general nature of the claim or defense, information contained in a public record) without fear of discipline. Nevada's decision to discipline Gentile in spite of this purported safe harbor provision raised concerns of vagueness and selective enforcement. The Rule misled Gentile to believe that he could make statements on those issues at a press conference, even if he knows or reasonably should know that these statements will have a substantial likelihood of prejudicing an adjudicative proceeding. See Rotunda, *Can You Say That?*, 30 Trial Magazine 18 (December, 1994). The new Rule 3.6(b) does create a safe harbor and should avoid the problem that existed in *Gentile*. Rule 3.6, Comment 4.

DR 7–107 distinguished between criminal and civil cases by imposing a few more restrictions of speech in criminal cases. DR 7–107(F) also applied the restrictions of criminal cases to professional discipline proceedings and juvenile proceedings. However, the Code provided that none of the restrictions on trial publicity—whether in a civil or criminal case—applied if the lawyer is (1) replying to charges of misconduct publicly made against the lawyer or (2) participating in any proceeding of any legislative, administrative, or other investigative body. DR 7–107(I).

In contrast, Rule 3.6(a) adopts a general test restricting speech if the extrajudicial statement "will have a substantial likelihood of materially prejudicing an adjudicative proceeding in the matter." The Code used a test less protective of the free speech interests: "reasonably likely to interfere with a fair trial" or similar proceeding. See DR 7–107(D), (F), (G)(5), & (H)(5).

DR 7–107(C)(7) allowed the attorney to describe, at the time of seizure, physical evidence seized except for a confession, admission, or statement.

Rule 3.6 does not allow such announcements, viewing them as "substantially prejudicial. . . . " Rule 3.6, Code Comparison 1.

DR 7–107 stated specifically what attorneys may or may not publicly disclose. Rule 3.6, in contrast, treats these specifics as illustrations of conduct that will usually meet the "substantial likelihood" test of Rule 3.6(a).

Whether the case is civil or criminal, with or without a jury, it is important to remember that there are matters as to which extrajudicial statements are allowed, including, e.g., information contained in a public record, a request for assistance in obtaining evidence, a warning of the danger concerning an individual if there is reason to believe that there exits the likelihood of substantial harm, the scheduling or results of any steps in litigation, the general nature of the claim, the general scope of an investigation, the identity of the accused, and the identity of the arresting and investigating officers. Rule 3.6(b); DR 7–107(B),(G).

Rule 3.6(c) adds a right not found in the Code: a lawyer may make an extrajudicial statement that would otherwise be improper, if it is in response to statements by others, when a reasonable lawyer believes that the response is necessary to avoid prejudicing his client. The statement should be limited to information necessary to mitigate any undue prejudice created by the statements made by others. In a sense, the lawyer can fight fire with fire, by using his free speech rights to counteract negative publicity about his client.

Rule 3.8(f) is also not found in the old Model Code. It warns *prosecutors* to refrain from making any extrajudicial comments that serve no legitimate law enforcement purpose and have a substantial likelihood of heightening public opprobrium of the accused. It further requires prosecutors to exercise reasonable care to prevent those working with them in the criminal case from making the prohibited comments.

C. Decorum and *Ex Parte* Communications

1. Disruption of the Tribunal
Both the Rule and the Code forbid the lawyer from disrupting the tribunal. Rule 3.5(d); DR 7–106(C)(6). *In the Matter of McAlevy*, 69 N.J. 349, 354 A.2d 289 (1976), the court severely reprimanded an attorney who, at a side bar conference, threatened (in vulgar terms) physical violence to the Deputy Attorney General, and who later attacked the Deputy Attorney General during a conference in the judge's chambers. When the judge and his law clerk tried to separate the two men now locked in combat, they were

drawn into the fight and at one point all four men were rolling on the floor. The judge suffered minor injuries. See Rotunda, *The Litigator's Professional Responsibility*, 25 TRIAL Magazine 98 (Mar. 1989).

The lawyer, however, may disobey a tribunal's order if there is an "*open refusal based on an assertion that no valid obligation exists. . . .*" Rule 3.4(c) (emphasis added). See also DR 7–102(A).

2. Ex Parte Communications

Lawyers may not engage in improper ex parte communications during the proceeding with jurors or prospective jurors [Rule 3.5(b), (c); *DR 7–108*] *or with judges.* Rule 3.5(b); DR 7–110(B). Similarly, lawyers may not engage in improper efforts to influence judges, jurors, prospective jurors, or other officials during the proceeding. Rule 3.5(a); DR 7–108(A); DR 7–110(A). The old Model Code was much more specific that the Model Rules in describing the forbidden conduct. The Rules simply incorporate the requirements of other law. Rule 3.5(a)("by means prohibited by law"),(b), and (c).

Lawyers may communicate with a juror or prospective juror following the discharge of the jury, unless other law or a court order prohibits the communication, or the juror made it known to the lawyer that she did not wish to communicate with the lawyer, or the communication involves misrepresentation, coercion, duress, or harassment. Rule 3.5(c).

3. Arguments During Trial

During the trial the lawyer may not "allude" to any matter not reasonably believed to be relevant, or supported by admissible evidence. Nor may the lawyer, in closing argument or otherwise, assert his personal opinion or knowledge regarding facts at issue, unless he is actually testifying as a witness. Rule 3.4(e); DR 7–106(C)(1), (3), and (4). However, he may argue for any nonfrivolous position or conclusion based on his analysis of the evidence. DR 7–106(C)(4); Rule 3.1.

Example 1:   In closing argument Lawyer states: "How can you believe Witness? I've seen many people testify over the years, and in my experience, Witness is lying. I don't believe him, can you?" Lawyer's action is *improper*, even if Lawyer really believes that Witness is lying.

Example 2:   In closing argument Lawyer states: "How can you believe Witness? His testimony contradicts the sworn testimony of three other people who, unlike Witness, have no financial interest in this case." Lawyer's action is *proper*.

III. Responsibilities Toward Opposing Counsel and Other Persons

A. Candor

Lawyers have certain affirmative obligations of *candor* to a tribunal, e.g., to disclose material adverse legal authority, see Section II(A), supra. However, with respect to opposing parties or third parties, the lawyer's duty is more limited. The fundamental principle is that lawyers may not *knowingly misrepresent* either a material fact or law to opposing parties or other persons. Rule 4.1(a); Rule 8.4(c); DR 7–102(A)(5); DR 7–102(A)(4). This principle applies whether the lawyer is involved in litigation or negotiation.

A partially true, but misleading statement or omission is equivalent to an affirmative false statement. Rule 4.1, Comment 1. In other words, a half-truth is a whole lie.

Example: Plaintiff's Lawyer plans to file a claim against Defendant. Lawyer and Plaintiff know that the statute of limitations has run, but they hope that Defendant and her counsel will not plead the statute. During the course of negotiations, Plaintiff's Lawyer discovers that Defendant and her counsel are unaware of the limitations defense. Plaintiff's Lawyer is careful not to make any affirmative misrepresentation about the facts showing that the claim is time-barred. Plaintiff's Lawyer is acting properly. "Indeed, the lawyer may not, consistent with her responsibilities to her client, refuse to negotiate or break off negotiations merely because the claim is or becomes time-barred." ABA Formal Opinion 94–387 (Sept. 26, 1994).

Note: The Model Rules simply announce in the Comments: "Under generally accepted conventions in negotiation, certain types of statements ordinarily are not taken as statements of material fact. Estimates of price or value placed on the subject of a transaction and a party's intentions as to an acceptable settlement of a claim are ordinarily in this category, and so is the existence of an undisclosed principal except where nondisclosure of the principal would constitute fraud." Rule 4.1, Comment 2. See also, ABA Informal Opinion 1283 (Nov. 20, 1973)(unethical in settlement negotiations to represent that class action will be brought if this intention is false). While the Model Code would probably exclude "puffing" or immaterial misstatements, nothing in the Model Code specifically approved of the exceptions found in Rule 4.1, Comment 2.

ABA Formal Opinion 93–370 (Feb. 5, 1993) explains that Rule 4.1, Comment 2 really only allows a "certain amount of posturing or puffery in settlement negotiations" as an "acceptable convention *between opposing counsel.*" But a party's actual "bottom line" is a material fact. This Formal Opinion concedes that: "A deliberate misrepresentation or lie *to a judge* in pretrial negotiations would be improper under Rule 4.1." (emphasis added.) The lawyer, however, may "ordinarily" misstate, to another lawyer, his "party's intentions as to an acceptable settlement of a claim," according to Rule 4.1, Comment 2.

Example: Assume that Lawyer's Client dies in the midst of settlement negotiations of a pending lawsuit in which Client was the plaintiff. *Lawyer has duty to volunteer* this information to opposing counsel and the court that her Client has died. ABA Formal Opinion 95–397 (Sept. 18, 1995). This Opinion states that a lawyer's failure to voluntarily disclose this fact is the equivalent of an affirmative misrepresentation. While the Opinion is not very good in explaining why the lawyer must volunteer this fact but not others, the law of agency supplies a rationale. Under the law of agency, the death of the principal (the client) automatically terminates the agency. If Lawyer continues her representation, it will be on behalf of a *different* client, and that is a material fact that she must disclose. The case law agrees. *Virzi v. Grand Trunk Warehouse & Cold Storage Co.*, 571 F. Supp. 507 (E.D.Mich. 1983).

A corollary to this prohibition against material misrepresentation is that a lawyer may not unlawfully obstruct access to, alter, or conceal evidence, or witnesses, or encourage a witness to testify falsely. Rule 3.4(a),(b); DR 7–109(A), (B), (C); DR 7–106(C)(7).

Note: The Code specifically prohibits a lawyer from paying a witness any money contingent on the outcome of the case. DR 7–109(C). The lawyer may advance, guarantee, or acquiesce in the payment of (1) a witness's expenses in attending or testifying; (2) compensation for the witness' loss of time because of attending or testifying, and (3) a reasonable fee for an expert witness' professional services. DR 7–109(C). The Rules have no such explicit provision, but a Comment assumes that the "common law rule in most jurisdictions is that it is improper to pay an occurrence witness any fee for testifying and that it is improper to pay an expert witness a contingent fee." Rule 3.4, Comment 3.

Rule 4.1(b) provides that a lawyer shall not knowingly "fail to disclose a material fact" when disclosure is necessary to avoid assisting a criminal or fraudulent act by a client, *unless* disclosure is prohibited by Rule 1.6." (emphasis added). Rule 1.6 governs client confidences. As explained elsewhere (see Part III, Section III, C, supra) Rule 4.1(b) does not require a lawyer to assist a client in a crime or fraud even if failure to assist would amount to a disclosure prohibited by Rule 1.6. Rather, the lawyer must not assist, must withdraw, and may also file a notice of withdrawal. If the failure to disclose a material fact involves a tribunal, Rule 3.3—not Rule 4.1(b)—is applicable; the lawyer's remedy in such a case is provided by Rule 3.3(b). This remedy may require disclosure of the perjury to the tribunal because of the lawyer's duty of candor to the tribunal. See Part VII, Section II, A, supra.

B. Communications

1. Persons Represented by Counsel

If a lawyer for a client (Lawyer #1) knows that another person is represented by his own attorney (Lawyer #2), then Lawyer #1 may not communicate with the person represented by Lawyer #2 in that matter unless Lawyer #2 consents. Rule 4.2. The obvious reason for this requirement is to prevent lawyers from overreaching the persons they contact. Rule 4.2; DR 7–104(A)(1).

A lawyer may represent a nonparty (e.g., a complaining witness in a rape prosecution). If the lawyer knows that a witness is represented by a lawyer in the matter in question, the lawyer who wants to talk to that person should either subpoena that person or should seek the consent of that person's counsel. Rule 4.2, Comment 2 makes clear that the requirement of counsel's consent "also covers any person who is represented by counsel concerning the matter to which the communication relates."

Applying this Rule to all "persons" (instead of limiting it to "parties") is quite consistent with the rationale of preventing overreaching. A new comment (added in 2002) explains the purpose of the rule: to ensure the proper functioning of the legal system by protecting a represented person "against possible *overreaching* by other lawyers who are participating in the matter, interference by those lawyers with the client-lawyer relationship and the uncounselled disclosure of information relating to the representation." Rule 4.2, Comment 1 (emphasis added).

Rule 4.2 applies even if the represented person initiates the contact with the lawyer. ABA Formal Opinion 95–396 (July 28, 1995), at 17; Rule 4.2, Comment 3. The way for the represented person to waive the rule is for the person's lawyer to give consent to the contact. People v. Green, 274 N.W.2d 448, 453 (Mich. 1979), holding that defendant's willingness to speak does not "excuse compliance" with the ethical prohibition, which is designed to protect these persons from overreaching by the other lawyer.

If the lawyer "knows" that a person (whether or not a party) is represented by a lawyer in the matter in question, the lawyer must seek the consent of that person's counsel. "Know" means "actual knowledge," but a lawyer cannot evade the consent requirement by "closing [her] eyes to the obvious." Rule 4.2, Comments 8.

However, if the lawyer does not represent anyone in the matter, she may respond to an inquiry from a person represented by his own lawyer.

Example: Lawyer #1 represents Client A in the matter of A vs. B. Lawyer #2 is a friend of Client A but is not involved in the matter at all. Client A asks Lawyer #2 some advice about the matter. Lawyer #2 may respond. Rule 4.2, Comment 4.

Other Law Authorizing Contact. Rule 4.2 does not inapplicable if *other law* (a statute, regulation, a court order) authorizes Lawyer #1 to communicate directly with a person about the subject of the representation.

- Other law may authorize a party in a controversy with a government agency to speak to government officials about the matter. Rule 4.2, Comments 5, 6.

- Prosecutors question witnesses or targets in grand jury proceedings, without their counsel's presence because the rules governing grand juries authorize such questioning. Comment 5.

- In criminal cases (or civil enforcement actions) the prosecutor may wish to secure evidence from a suspect covertly (by wiring an undercover agent or informant) without seeking permission from the suspect's counsel. Rule 4.2 allows government lawyers, either directly or through agents, to engage in investigative activities, *until* there is the commencement of a criminal or civil enforcement proceeding. Comment 5. Defense attorneys have argued that such investigative techniques violate Rule 4.2, and that courts should enforce these rules by suppressing any evidence acquired by their violation. E.g., Norton, *Ethics and the Attorney General,* 74 Judicature 203 (Dec.–Jan.1991). The U.S. Attorney General has argued that prosecutors are authorized "by law" to make such contacts directly or through agents. Thornburgh, *Ethics and the Attorney General: The Attorney General Responds,* 74 Judicature 290 (April–May 1991). Rule 4.2 now does not stand in the way of these investigations if they are done "prior to the commencement of criminal or civil enforcement proceedings."

- In a class action, defense attorneys may secure a court order allowing communication with members of the plaintiff class in appropriate circumstances. Comment 6.

- The constitutional right to "petition the government for redress of grievances" may authorize a party to contact government parties directly without violating Rule 4.2. Comment 5. The First Amendment and the general public policy of ensuring a citizen's right to access government decision-makers, both affect Rule 4.2. ABA Formal Opinion 97–408 (Aug. 2, 1997)

The requirements of Rule 4.2 are inapplicable if the communication does not concern the subject of representation but rather another, separate matter.

In addition, "parties to a matter may communicate directly with each other. . . . " Rule 4.2, Comment 2. This Rule does not prohibit lawyers from advising principals to speak directly with their counterparts. Rule 4.2, Comment 3.

Rule 8.4(a) states that a lawyer may not violate a Rule "through the acts of another," but the 2002 amendments to Rule 8.4, Comment 1 make clear that lawyers *do not* violate Rule 8.4 by "advising a client concerning action that the client is lawfully entitled to take."

If lawyer *A* (on behalf of Client *A*) makes a settlement offer to the opposing party's lawyer (lawyer *B*), but lawyer *A* believes that lawyer *B* will not communicate that offer to Client *B*, even then, lawyer *A* may *not* communicate directly with Client *B* to determine whether the offer has been communicated. But, lawyer *A* may advise Client *A* that Client *A* may communicate directly with Client *B* about the offer. ABA Formal Opinion 92–362 (July 6, 1992).

Rule 4.2 and Organizations. *If a corporation or other entity is represented by counsel, then alter egos of that organization are also treated as persons represented by that counsel for purposes of the rule restricting communications to persons represented by counsel.* ABA Informal Opinion 1410 (Feb. 14, 1978). If the officers and employees that the lawyer proposes "to interview *could commit the corporation* because of their authority as corporate officers or employees or for some other reason the law cloaks them with authority, then they, as the alter egos of the corporation, are parties for purposes of DR 7–104(A)(1)." (emphasis added). In the 2002 revisions, the ABA finally make clear that corporations or other represented organization are covered by Rule 4.2. This Rule 4.2 prohibits communications with a constituent of the organization "who supervises, directs or regularly consults with the organization's lawyer concerning the matter or has authority to obligate the organization with respect to the matter or whose act or omission in connection with the matter may be imputed to the organization" for civil or criminal liability purposes. Rule 4.2, Comment 7.

If the witness is merely a low level corporate employee who does not fit this test, then the interviewing lawyer need not secure any permission from the party's lawyer before interviewing the intended witness. If this nonparty witness has independent representation, the lawyer seeking the interview should secure the permission of the witness' personal lawyer for this matter. See, Hacker & Rotunda, *Ethical Restraints on Communications with Adverse Expert Witnesses*, 5 Corp.L.Rev. 348 (1982). See also, *In re Investigation of FMC Corporation*, 430 F.Supp. 1108 (S.D.W.Va.1977).

In addition, Rule 4.2 should be interpreted to protect the organization's attorney-client privilege when the lawyer contacts a constituent of that organization. During the original ABA debates on Rule 4.2, the Reporter for the Model Rules said that "the purpose of Rule 4.2 was to protect the lawyer-client relationship against breach by a lawyer representing another." See The Legislative History of the Model Rules of Professional Conduct 148 (ABA, 1987). The 2002 revisions made clear that when the lawyer communicates with a current or former constituent of an organization, the lawyer "may not use methods of obtaining evidence that violate the legal rights of the organization." Rule 4.2, Comment 7. For example, the lawyer should not mislead the current or former constituent in a way to secure information protected by the constituent's attorney-client privilege.

The purpose of Rule 4.2 is to prevent improvident settlements and a surrender of legal position on the part of a momentarily uncounselled, but represented, party and to enable the corporation's lawyer to maintain an effective lawyer-client relationship with members of management. "Thus, in the case of corporate and similar entities, the anticontact rule should prohibit contact with those officials, *but only those,* who have the legal power to bind the corporation in the matter or who are responsible for implementing the advice of the corporation's lawyer, or any member of the organization whose own interests are directly at stake in a representation." Charles Wolfram, *Modern Legal Ethics* 613 (1986) (emphasis added). Thus, if an employee's only relation to a case is that he or she is a witness, the employee "should be freely accessible to either lawyer." Id. See also, ABA Formal Opinion 117 (1934).

The anticontact principle of Rule 4.2 also protects someone who is not high up in the organization but whose act or omission regarding the matter in question "may be imputed to the organization for purposes of civil or criminal liability." Rule 4.2, Comment 7. For example, if plaintiff is suing a corporation for damages due to a truck accident, the lawyer for plaintiff should not contact the corporate employee who drove the truck without securing permission from the corporation's lawyer.

In 2002, the ABA deleted the broad and potentially open-ended reference to "any other person . . . whose statement may constitute an admission on the part of the organization." Some people thought that this prohibited communication with any person whose testimony would be admissible against the organization as an exception to the hearsay rule. That is not the law.

Note: If the witness whose is an employee is separately represented, then the lawyer who wants to talk to that witness need only secure permission for the employee's lawyer. Comment 7.

Encouraging Witnesses Not to Talk. On behalf of his client, the lawyer may *request* an unrepresented nonclient witness to refrain from voluntarily giving relevant information to another party *if* the witness is the client's relative, employee, or agent whose interests will not be adversely affected if this request is honored. Rule 3.4(f). The lawyer, however, cannot forbid such witnesses from being interviewed. Whether they are in fact interviewed is up to them. They can always insist on being subpoenaed and then deposed.

Former **Employees of Organizations.** The lawyer does *not* have to secure consent from the organization's lawyer in order to talk to a former employee or other constituent of the organization. Comment 7 now makes that clear. Previously courts had split on this issue. ABA Formal Opinion 91–359 (March 22, 1991) notes that prohibiting such communications would make it more expensive for the lawyer to obtain information about her case, because she would have to proceed by way of deposition of the former employee rather than by interview if the lawyer for the corporation refused consent.

2. Persons Not Represented by Counsel

Rule 4.3 and DR 7–104(A)(2) restrict the lawyer's communications with unrepresented persons. If a person is not represented by counsel, the lawyer may neither state nor imply that the lawyer is disinterested. If the unrepresented person does not understand the lawyer's role, the lawyer should try to correct the misunderstanding. A lawyer may not give legal advice, other than the advice to secure counsel, to an unrepresented person whose interests may be adverse to the lawyer's client's interests. Rule 4.3 and Comment 2.

Example: Attorney for Employer prepares settlement papers in a workman's compensation case. Employee, who signs these papers, is not represented. Attorney does not advise or mislead Employee as to the law or Lawyer's role in this matter. Attorney also advises the court, which must approve the settlement, that Employee is appearing pro se. Attorney's actions are proper. ABA Formal Opinion 102 (Dec. 15, 1933).

C. Harassing Techniques

A lawyer's duty to represent a client competently and effectively does not allow a lawyer to harass another person, to violate another's legal rights, or to use means that serve no substantial purpose but to "embarrass, delay, or burden a third person. . . ." Rule 4.4(a). See also, DR 7–102(A)(1); DR 7–106(C)(2); DR 7–108(D), (E).

Note—Threatening
Criminal Charges: The Code forbade a lawyer from threatening to present or presenting "criminal charges solely to obtain an advantage in a civil matter." DR 7–105(A). See also EC 7–21. *The Rules have no such provision.*

The Model Rules have no section corresponding to DR 7–105(A). But that does not mean that there are no restrictions: if the lawyer's threats amount to criminal extortion under state law, then Rule 8.4(b) would apply. See Model Penal Code § 223.4 (1962) (crime of theft by extortion to accuse anyone of criminal offense in order to obtain property not honestly claimed as indemnification for harm caused by conduct relating to the accusation). Assuming that there is no violation of other law (such as the state law of extortion), the Rules do *not* prohibit a lawyer, in a civil claim, from using the possibility of presenting criminal charges against the opposing party to gain relief for her client, *provided that* the criminal matter is related to the civil claim, the lawyer reasonably believes that the civil claim and the possible criminal charge are warranted, and the lawyer does not attempt to exert "improper influence" over the criminal process. The lawyer may also agree (and have her client agree) to refrain from pursuing criminal charges in return for satisfaction of the civil claim, assuming that other law does not prevent this agreement. ABA Formal Opinion 92–363 (July 6, 1992).

However, ABA Formal Opinion 94–383 (July 5, 1994) has a different view of a lawyer who threatens to file a *disciplinary complaint* against an opposing lawyer in order to gain advantage in a civil case (or agrees not to report the lawyer if a satisfactory settlement is made). The Opinion acknowledged that the Model Rules have no express prohibition, but, if the disciplinary violation is one that Rule 8.3(a) requires the lawyer to report, then the lawyer must report, rather than threaten to report in the absence of a satisfactory settlement. If Rule 8.3(a) is inapplicable, the Formal Opinion still objected, and argued that such action will "frequently" violate "one of the more general restraints on advocacy imposed by the Model Rules." It referred to Rule 4.4, prohibiting a lawyer from using means that have no substantial purpose other than to embarrass or burden a third party. It even claimed that "such a threat may prejudice the administration of justice" in violation of Rule 8.4(d).

If counsel does file a disciplinary complaint against the opposing lawyer, that fact alone normally neither requires nor permits the lawyer to withdraw from representing the client in the matter. Formal Opinion 94–384 (July 5, 1994). However, the filing of a complaint may create or expose circumstances that do justify withdrawal. For example, if the lawyer seeks to defend the accusation by exposing client confidences (Rule 1.6(b)(4)) his interests diverge from his client's.

The Misdirected Fax and Similar Mishaps. Lawyers sometimes receive documents unintentionally sent or produced by opposing parties or their lawyers. In 2002, the ABA added to Rule 4.4 a statement providing that a lawyer who receives such a document, and "knows or reasonably should know that the document was inadvertently sent," must notify the sender promptly so the sender may take protective measures. Rule 4.4(b); Rule 4.4, Comments 2 and 3. The purpose of this notice to the sending lawyer is to allow him to take whatever steps might be necessary or available to protect the interests of the sending lawyer's client. The Rules do not mandate that the receiving lawyer return the document, but that is something the sending lawyer could ask the court to require by motion. The court might simply allow the receiving lawyer to take advantage of her adversary's mistake.

REVIEW QUESTIONS

1. The State's Attorney of Blanke County has an office practice of sending to the defendant of copy of the letter that State's Attorney simultaneously sends to defendant's counsel containing an offer to plea bargain. This letter basically states that if the defendant will plead guilty to a lesser crime (e.g., attempted robbery) the government will not proceed on charges of a greater crime (e.g., robbery).

Are State's Attorney's actions *proper?*

a. State's Attorney has an ethical obligation to plea bargain and sending a copy of the letter offering a bargain helps fulfill this duty.

b. State's Attorney may not send a copy of the plea bargain letter to the defendant unless the state's attorney in good faith believes that defense counsel will not inform defendant of the plea bargain.

c. State's Attorney must not send a copy of the plea bargain letter to defendant unless defense counsel consents.

d. State's Attorney must send a copy of the plea bargain letter to fulfill his duty to assure that defendant is kept informed on all of those matters in which the decisions are exclusively for the client.

2. In closing arguments, Attorney makes the following statements.

I. "The evidence indicates that the witness is a liar."

II. "I know for a fact that the road was slick when the accident occurred."

III. "In my opinion the defendant is liable for the accident."

Is Attorney *subject to discipline?*

    a. Yes, because of II & III, only.

    b. Yes, because of II, only.

    c. Yes, because of I & II, only.

    d. No.

    e. Yes, because of I, II, & III.

3. Attorney is asked by his regular client, Millionaire, to file a suit against the United States, and "take it to the Supreme Court if necessary" in order to seek a declaratory judgment that the progressive income tax is unconstitutionally confiscatory as applied to him. Attorney advised Millionaire that the suit is baseless, but Attorney finally agreed to file the suit on receipt of a $10,000 retainer.

Is Attorney *subject to discipline?*

    a. Yes, because no portion of the fee was earned when Attorney accepted the retainer.

    b. Yes, because it is unethical to present a claim not warranted under existing law unless it can be supported by a good faith argument for reversal, or modification, or extension of existing law.

    c. No, because Attorney fully advised Millionaire that the suit was baseless and Millionaire paid the retainer with full knowledge.

    d. No, if the fee in these circumstances is reasonable.

4. Decedent's last will left her estate to a trust to be used to improve the public schools of the district in which she lived throughout her lifetime.

Niece and Nephew, Decedent's only surviving relatives, are contesting Decedent's will. The case will be heard before a judge and jury. Attorney, who represents the estate is contacted by a newspaper reporter shortly before the trial begins.

Assuming the statements are true, it is *proper* for Attorney to tell the reporter:

I.   "The response in our motion, which we just filed, summarizes the evidence showing that Niece and Nephew did not visit Decedent a single time during the last lonely year of her life in Twilight Time Nursing Home."

II. "Our answer states that just before Decedent's will was drafted, Decedent discussed with several persons the possibility of leaving her estate to her church and/or public schools. Decedent specifically stated to said persons that she did not want to leave anything to Niece and Nephew."

III. "If anyone has any evidence that relates to this case, we would like them to come forward."

IV. "I have no comment whatsoever."

    a.   IV only.

    b.   II or IV, but not I and III.

    c.   I and II, but not III.

    d.   I, II and III or IV.

5. The defendant corporation has three witnesses who will testify at trial. Assume the corporate client agrees to reimburse all monies advanced by the lawyer. *Under the disciplinary rules*, on behalf of this corporate client:

I.   The attorney may pay travel expenses for a witness who must come from a distant city.

II. The attorney may pay a witness $48 for lost wages for spending one day at trial (the witness is normally employed at $6 an hour for an 8 hour day).

III. The attorney may pay $2500 to an expert for his testimony, if that fee is a reasonable one.

IV. The attorney may guarantee an expert witness a fee of $400 to $3500, depending on the outcome of the case.

    a.   Only actions I and II are nondisciplinable.

b.   Only actions I and III are nondisciplinable.

c.   Only actions I, II and III are nondisciplinable.

d.   All four actions are permitted.

*

PART VIII

The Lawyer's Obligations as Adviser

■ ANALYSIS

I. Adviser Versus Advocate

When the client consults the attorney as advocate, the attorney may urge upon the courts any nonfrivolous interpretation of the law that favors the client; when the client consults the attorney as adviser, the attorney should give the client his or her good faith opinion on how the courts will likely rule, and the full effects of such a decision.

When the client asks the lawyer to represent him in litigation, the lawyer may urge the tribunal to adopt any permissible construction of the law. A permissible construction would include *any nonfrivolous position*, such as a good faith argument, supported by facts, for extension, modification, or reversal of existing law. Rule 3.1; EC 7–4; DR 7–102(A)(1), (2); DR 2–109(A).

When the client asks the lawyer to supply legal advice, the lawyer must render her candid opinion of what the court is *likely* to do. She should also inform her client of the practical effects of such a ruling. Rule 2.1; EC 7–5. The lawyer's efforts to comfort the client cannot limit her duty to give an honest assessment of unpleasant facts. Rule 2.1, Comment 1.

In offering legal advice, the lawyer need not limit her comments to purely technical legal considerations but may refer to economic, political, social and moral considerations. The lawyer may offer her judgment as to what effects are morally just as well as legally permissible. Rule 2.1; EC 7–8, 7–9. The lawyer who couches her advice too narrowly ill-serves her client. Rule 2.1, Comment 2. However, the client, not the lawyer, ultimately must make the final decision whether to accept the lawyer's judgment based on nonlegal considerations. EC 7–8.

The client may ask the lawyer, either expressly or impliedly, to limit her advice to only technical legal matters. The lawyer should follow this limitation, unless the client's inexperience indicates that she must say more. Rule 2.1, Comment 3. Normally the lawyer need not give advice that the client has not sought, but she "may initiate advice to a client when doing so appears to be in the client's interest." Rule 2.1, Comment 5. See EC 7–8 ("lawyer ought to initiate this decision-making process").

II. Mediation Among Multiple Clients

The lawyer may represent multiple clients with potentially conflicting interests in order to mediate these differences if the clients give informed consent, confirmed in writing.

Because clients often desire mediation to save costs and time, it is "common practice" for attorneys to act "for both partners in drawing articles of copartnership or drawing agreements for the dissolution of copartnership, in acting for both the grantor and the grantee in the sale of real property, in acting for both the seller and purchaser in the sale of personal property, in acting for both the lessor and the lessee in the leasing of property, and in acting for both the lender and borrower in handling a loan transaction . . . " *Lessing v. Gibbons,* 6 Cal.App.2d 598, 606, 45 P.2d 258, 261 (1935).

The Model Code made few references to the basic concept of the lawyer as intermediary between clients. DR 5–105(b) recognized that the lawyer may represent multiple clients with differing interests if, under DR 5–105(c), the clients consent and it is "obvious" that the lawyer can represent each adequately. See also, EC 5–20, concerning the lawyer as "impartial arbitrator or mediator."

The ABA Model Rules, when the House of Delegates first approved them in 1983, added a new Rule 2.2, titled, "Intermediary." This Rule governed lawyers acting as intermediaries between multiple clients and was supposed to fill the gap and recognize the important role that lawyers played when representing multiple clients with a similar goal–such as representing three or four people who want to start up a small business and have the lawyer draft articles of incorporation or a partnership agreement. However, this Rule 2.2 was not really influential, and one could see it as simply a specific application of what was already covered by Rule 1.7, dealing with the conflicts of interest when the lawyer represented current clients.

Consequently, in 2002, the ABA House of Delegates deleted Rule 2.2. Now, *no* Rule has the designation, "Rule 2.2." The Reporter's Explanation tells us why Rule 2.2 was stricken——because the concept of "intermediation," as distinct from "common representation" or "mediation" has not been well understood and Rule 2.2 was simply not helpful in clarifying the distinction. The relationship between Rule 2.2 and Rule 1.7, which addresses current conflicts of interest generally, caused confusion, so most of the content of Rule 2.2 was moved to the Comments to Rule 1.7. In addition, the Bar's initial resistance to the idea of common representation (which appeared awkward and difficult prior to the adoption of the Model Rules in 1983) was no longer an issue, thereby eliminating the need for a separate rule.

Comments 29 through 33 of Rule 1.7 now address situations that had been covered by Rule 2.2, but they replace the term "Intermediation" with the more easily understood term, "Common Representation" to describe cases where the lawyer is mediating between his own clients. Pursuant Rule 1.7, the lawyer should generally not represent the clients in a mediation if a conflict of interest exists. There is, initially, a conflict if representation of one client will be "directly adverse" to the other or if there is a significant risk that the representation of one or more clients will be "materially limited" by the common representation.

However, Rule 1.7 does *not* prohibit such a representation, notwithstanding the conflict described above, *if* the lawyer reasonably believes she can provide competent and diligent representation to all clients, the representation is not prohibited by law, the representation "does not involve the assertion of a claim by one client against another client represented by the lawyer in the same litigation or other proceeding before a tribunal," *and* the clients give *informed consent, confirmed in writing.* Rule 1.7.

Some conflicts of interest are, however, not consentable. See Rule 1.7 Comments 14–17 ("Prohibited Representations"). Unfortunately, the Comments do not give a laundry list of prohibited or non-consentable representations. They offer a few examples. For instance, state substantive law may provide that a lawyer may not represent multiple defendants in a capital case, even if all the defendants knowingly consent. Rule 1.7(b)(2) & Comment 16. And, the lawyer may not assert a claim on behalf of one client against another client in the same litigation. Rule 1.7(b)(3).

> *Example:* Lawyer may not represent Defendant–1 and Defendant–2 in the case of Plaintiff vs. Defendants 1 & 2 *if* Defendant–1 will be asserting a cross claim against Defendant–2.

The Comments do offer a general test to determine if clients can waive the conflict. The lawyer must inform each client of the effects of group representation on the attorney-client privilege. See Rule 1.7(b)(4). Cf. Rule 1.7, Comment 30 (generally "as between commonly represented clients the privilege does not attach"). The clients should understand that the lawyer will not act in a partisan role on behalf of one of the clients to the detriment of the others. Id. at Comment 32.

The lawyer must also believe that she will provide "competent and diligent" representation to each of her clients. Rule 1.7(b)(1).

The lawyer has an equal duty of loyalty to each client in a common representation. All clients in the representation have the right to be fully informed concerning the representation when their interests might be affected, as well as the right to expect that the lawyer will use that information to that client's benefit. Rule 1.7, Comment 31; See also Rule 1.4. When obtaining the clients' informed consent, the lawyer should advise each client that information will be shared between clients and that the lawyer must withdraw if one client decides that some material matter should be kept confidential from another commonly-represented client. Rule 1.7, Comment 31. All clients in the common representation maintain the protection of Rule 1.9 concerning the obligations to a former client and each client reserves the right to discharge the lawyer per Rule 1.16.

In such a mediation or multiple representation, the lawyer engages in a more nonadversarial approach to resolving a dispute or entering into a transaction. These comments to Rule 1.7, like the former Rule 2.2, recognize that, for both economic and noneconomic reasons, clients often need one lawyer to represent multiple interests. "Many lawyers fulfill such needs in their everyday practice without even realizing that their conduct is governed by the law as intermediary provision." Dzienkowski, *Lawyers as Intermediaries: The Representation of Multiple Clients in the Modern Legal Profession*, 1992 U.Ill.L.Rev. 741, 816–17.

III.   The Lawyer as Evaluator

Clients may sometimes hire the lawyer to evaluate a matter for the benefit of third parties.

The Rules have a provision explicitly governing a role that lawyers, particularly in recent times, have undertaken—the lawyer as evaluator for the benefit of a third party. Rule 2.3. At least one major New York law firm has found this practice so lucrative that it now has a special team to conduct these evaluations. Many courts will tend to dismiss shareholder suits against officials if a reputable law firm finds the officials to be without blame after an investigation and evaluation, and companies often believe that they can avoid more extensive government inquiries by showing that they are willing to clean their own house. Cohen, *Firms Faulted for "Independent" Inquiries*, Wall St. Journal, June 14, 1989, at B1, col. 4–6.

The lawyer is an evaluator, for example, when she issues a legal opinion concerning the title of property rendered at the seller's request to give comfort to the prospective purchaser. Or, the lawyer may issue a letter opining that the legality of securities registered for sale under the securities laws. Rule 2.3, Comment 1. See also, ABA Formal Opinion 335 (1974). Another example of the lawyer as evaluator occurs when the lawyer for a corporation responds to an auditor's request for information. Rule 2.3, Comment 6.

Note: If the client asks for confidential advice, which is not given to non-clients, the lawyer is an adviser, not an evaluator. In other words, Rule 2.1 governs, not Rule 2.3.

Evaluation for the benefit of a third party should be distinguished from investigation for the benefit of a client. A prospective purchaser may retain a lawyer to do a title search on property that the purchaser is planning to purchase. The lawyer's client is the purchaser, not the vendor, and the lawyer's duty of loyalty is only to his client. In contrast, if the vendor retains a lawyer to furnish a title opinion that the vendor plans to show to the purchaser to bolster his claim that the title is a good one, then the lawyer is retained by the client (the vendor) to *evaluate* the property for the benefit of a nonclient (the purchaser). Rule 2.3, Comment 2. The lawyer's duty of loyalty is to the client, id., but the lawyer may also have legal obligations to the third parties who rely on the evaluation. Restatement (Second) of Torts § 552.

To protect the clients, and to take into account the needs of third parties, Rule 2.3 places some restrictions on "evaluations." The lawyer must reasonably believe that conducting an evaluation is compatible with other aspects of the lawyer's relationship with the client. Rule 2.3(a). For example, if the lawyer had been an advocate defending the client on charges of fraud, it would usually not be compatible for the lawyer to conduct an evaluation of the same or related transaction. Id. at Comment 3.

When the lawyer knows or reasonably should know that an evaluation for a third party is likely to materially and adversely affect the client's interests, the lawyer should not provide the evaluation unless he first secures the client's informed consent. Rule 2.3(b). To obtain informed consent, the lawyer must adequately explain to the client the important possible effects on the client's interests. Rule 2.3(c) & Comment 5; See also Rule 1.6(a) & Rule 10(e).

The client may place limits on the scope of an evaluation, e.g., by excluding certain issues, or placing time constraints. Or, some persons may simply refuse to cooperate. Rule 2.3 Comment 4. The lawyer's evaluation should disclose in the evaluation all material limits. Under no circumstances may the lawyer knowingly make a false statement of material fact or law when providing an evaluation. Rule 2.3 Comment 4. Accord, Rule 4.1

To the extent that the client authorizes the lawyer to show the evaluation to third parties, there can be no client confidences. But otherwise, all information relating to the evaluation is confidential because of the lawyer-client relationship. Rule 2.3(c). See also, *Diversified Industries, Inc. v. Meredith*, 572 F.2d 596 (8th Cir.1977).

IV. Lawyer as Third–Party Neutral

A lawyer may also act as a neutral party in alternative dispute resolution proceedings.

In 2002, the ABA added a new Rule 2.4, "Lawyer Serving As Third–Party Neutral."

In addition to serving as an advisor or evaluator, a lawyer may serve as a third-party neutral by assisting two non-clients in dispute resolution. Rule 2.4(a). In this instance, the lawyer has no client. Instead, he is acting as an arbitrator, mediator, conciliator, or evaluator. Rule 2.4 & Comment 1. Because alternative dispute resolution has increased in popularity during recent years, the ABA House of Delegates added Rule 2.4 in 2002 to address issues particular to this type of proceeding.

First, under Rule 2.4, the lawyer must assure that the parties understand his role as third-party neutral. The lawyer must inform the unrepresented parties that he is not representing them. Cf. Rule 4.3 (lawyer dealing with unrepresented persons must inform them that he does not represent them). If the lawyer knows or reasonably should know that a party does not understand the lawyer's role, the lawyer must fully clarify the difference between his role as a third-party neutral and one who represents a client. Rule 2.4(b).

Conflicts of interest may arise if a lawyer who served as a third-party neutral is asked to represent one of the clients in the same matter. These conflicts are dealt with by Rule 1.12. See Rule 2.4 Comment 4.

When representing clients in an alternative dispute-resolution matter, a lawyer is governed by the Rules of Professional Conduct. When such a proceeding takes the form of a binding arbitration or in any other "tribunal," then Rule 3.3 controls the lawyer's duty of candor. In other alternative dispute-resolution proceedings, Rule 4.1 governs that duty. See Rule 2.4 Comment 5.

REVIEW QUESTIONS

1. Lawyer represents Bank, which asks him to examine some old mortgage papers. Lawyer discovers a very interesting and material fact—that several of these old mortgages, though carrying low interest rates, allow Bank to reset the rates every five years. Therefore Bank could now raise the mortgage rate several points. None of the Bank officers apparently had understood that the Bank could raise the mortgage rate on some of these old mortgages. Attorney also believes that if the Bank actually raises the rates suddenly and dramatically, the Bank's reputation will suffer.

  a. Attorney *may* simply refuse to tell the Bank officers about the old mortgage papers unless they ask him a specific question about them.

  b. Attorney *must* inform the Bank officers about the old mortgage papers but *may* also advise them that any sudden increase in the old mortgage loans might hurt the goodwill of Bank.

c. Attorney *must* inform the Bank officers about the old mortgage papers but *may not* also give them nonlegal, moral or business advice because he is a lawyer, not a business adviser.

d. Attorney *must not* inform the Bank officers about the old mortgage papers if he reasonably believes that they will act in a way that will hurt the Bank shareholders by damaging the goodwill of Bank.

2. Husband and Wife came to Attorney's office together. They told him they were separated and both wanted a divorce. The spouses were in agreement that Wife should have custody of the two children but were unable to agree on the amounts of spousal support and child support. They asked if Attorney would be willing to serve as impartial mediator in an attempt to help them reach a reasonable agreement. Attorney said "Yes" and informed them that he would not represent either party while trying to mediate the dispute. With his help, the spouses reached an agreement that Attorney reduced to writing and the parties signed. Shortly thereafter Husband changed his mind about custody, discharged Attorney, and hired Alpha to represent him in an attempt to get immediate custody of the two children. Attorney, at Wife's request, then filed a petition for divorce.

Without Husband's consent, Attorney represented Wife at the hearing on temporary custody.

Was Attorney's conduct proper?

a. No, because after acting as an impartial mediator, a lawyer should not represent either of the parties in the dispute unless both parties agree.

b. No, because a lawyer's proper role is that of an advocate, not a mediator.

c. Yes, because the divorce was pending.

d. Yes, because Husband voluntarily discharged Attorney and hired new counsel.

e. Attorney's conduct is not encouraged but is permissible and does not subject him to discipline.

PART IX

The Lawyer's Obligations Regarding Pro Bono Activities

■ ANALYSIS

I. Engaging in Pro Bono Activities

Both the Model Code and the Model Rules encourage, but do not require, lawyers to engage in pro bono activities.

A. Definitions

1. Representing Clients

Pro Bono Publico means, "for the public good," or for the welfare of the whole. As applied to the work of lawyers, it usually refers to work that lawyers do without fee, or with no expectation of a fee, or for a reduced fee for litigants of limited means. Pro bono work also includes representation of charitable organizations, such as the Y.M.C.A., the Boy Scouts, the A.C.L.U., and the N.A.A.C.P. on a no fee or reduced fee basis. ABA Rule 6.1, Comment 6 (e.g., "social service, medical research, cultural and religious groups" may qualify as pro bono).

If a lawyer represents a client on a pro bono basis, it does not imply that the client is necessarily right, or that the public interest is served only if the client's claim is vindicated. Rather, it means that the public interest is served because that client's views are represented. The client then has his or her day in court.

2. Representing Causes

Law reform activities (when a lawyer, without fee, represents a cause rather than a client) are also considered pro bono. Rule 6.1, Comments 2, 8. Such activities may include: (1) testifying before legislative or administrative hearings urging law reform; (2) lobbying for law reform in the selection and retention of judges; (3) participating in bar association activities.

Again, the fact that the lawyer engages in law reform activities does not imply that the lawyer's view of law reform is correct. Rather, the public is served because lawyers offer their services, judgment, and experience, to promote causes that they, in good faith, believe promote law reform.

3. Rule 6.1

When the ABA first adopted the Model Rules, Rule 6.1 was a vague call urging lawyers to engage in pro bono work for people of limited means or for public service or charitable groups. In February, 1993, the ABA House of Delegates approved a much more specific Rule, although it is still aspirational and not intended to be enforced by discipline.

In 2002, the ABA further amended the Rule to include the opening sentence "Every lawyer has a professional responsibility to provide legal services to those unable to pay." Although the rule remains aspirational (the Rules keep the language "should aspire"), the new language emphasizes that lawyers should comply with the recommendation. Comment 11 further urges law firms to "act reasonably to enable all lawyers to provide the pro bono services called for by this Rule."

The revised Rule 6.1 urges lawyers to aspire to provide at least 50 hours of pro bono services a year for persons of limited means, or for charitable, religious, etc. organizations designed primarily to meet the needs of persons of limited means. States may choose a higher or lower number, or express the number as a percentage of a lawyer's professional time. Work may include legal representation in court, legal advice, lobbying, free training, or mentoring to persons of limited means. Rule 6.1, Comment 2.

If any of these 50 hours are unfulfilled, then lawyers can fulfill the "remaining [aspirational] commitment" by engaging in pro bono work for individuals or groups seeking to protect civil rights or public rights (e.g., environmental rights), by pro bono work for charitable, religious, civil, etc. organizations (e.g., bar association activities, Law Day activities, legislative lobbying). Rule 6.1(b) & Comment 5–8.

B. Encouraged But Not Required

1. The Individual Lawyer

The Rules (like the old Model Code) do not *require* a lawyer to engage in pro bono activities. In fact, in the Code, no disciplinary rule even dealt with this issue. Only in the ethical considerations did we find the concern expressed that persons who are unable to pay "all or a portion of a reasonable fee" still should be able to obtain "necessary legal services," and that, consequently, "lawyers should support and participate in ethical activities designed to achieve that objective." EC 2–16.

The Code said that it is an "obligation" of each lawyer to render "free legal services to those unable to pay reasonable fees" (EC 2–25), but failure to meet this "obligation" is not disciplinable.

The Rules, unlike the Code, refer to pro bono services in the Black Letter (Model Rule 6.1) as well as the Comments. However, Rule 6.1 is the only Black Letter Rule that never uses the word "shall" and only uses the word "should." [Rule 1.5(b) does use the word "preferably."]

Though Rule 6.1 is not enforced through the disciplinary process (Rule 6.1, Comment 12), it does have symbolic importance. The drafters of the Model Rules believed that a reference to pro bono activities should at least be made in the Black Letter Rules, even though they were unable to secure acceptance of a mandatory pro bono requirement.

2. Law Firms

In 2002, the ABA added a new comment, Comment 11, to Rule 6.1, which encourages law firms to "act reasonably to enable and encourage all lawyers in the firm to provide the pro bono legal services" suggested by the Rule. This, too, is intended to be persuasive, and is not enforced by discipline.

3. Legal Aid Organizations

Some lawyers are more forthcoming than others in offering free (or reduced fee) legal services to those unable to pay the normal fee. In addition, in an effort to provide more representation for those unable to hire private lawyers, the state and federal governments, and some foundations, fund various legal service organizations, which hire lawyers to represent the poor. These organizations take the form of legal aid offices, state public defender offices (for the defense of criminal cases), and bar-sponsored lawyer referral services. Lawyers "should support all proper efforts" of these programs. EC 2–25; EC 2–16; EC 2–33. Accord, Rule 6.1, Comment 3.

4. Nonprofit and Court–Annexed Limited Legal Services Programs

The ABA added Rule 6.5 in 2002. It addresses lawyer participation in programs such as legal-advice hotlines and pro se clinics designed to assist people, on a short-term basis, who cannot otherwise afford legal representation. Fearing that strict application of the conflict-of-interest rules might deter lawyers from serving as volunteers in nonprofit and court-annexed limited legal services programs, the ABA added Rule 6.5 to clarify the relationship between such limited representation and the conflict rules. See Rules 1.7 and 1.9, addressed in Parts Three and Four, supra.

The purpose of Rule 6.5 is to relax the conflict requirements of Rules 1.7, 1.9, and 1.10, in order to make it easier for the lawyer to provide pro bono representation in the archetype or paradigm that Rule 6.5 had in mind: the legal-advice hotline or pro se clinic, both of which provides short-term, limited legal assistance to poor persons who otherwise would go unrepresented.

Otherwise, the lawyer must comply with the Rules of Professional Conduct when providing limited legal services. Rule 6.5, Comment 2.

Under Rule 6.5, a lawyer is subject to Rule 1.7, governing conflicts of interest related to current clients, and Rule 1.9(a), which deals with duties to former clients, **only if** the lawyer *knows* that the representation of the client involves a conflict of interest. Rule 6.5(a)(1). This provision renders it unnecessary for the lawyer to do a comprehensive conflicts check, which is not feasible under the circumstances and would deter many lawyers from serving in this capacity.

In addition, Rule 6.5(a)(2) makes clear that conflicts of interest are imputed the lawyer, pursuant to Rule 1.10, *only if* the lawyer volunteering with the non-profit or court-annexed program *knows* that another lawyer associated with the lawyer in a law firm is disqualified by Rule 1.7 or 1.9(a) with respect to the matter. This Rule protects the lawyer from an inadvertent conflict.

The short-term and limited nature of the representation provided by the nonprofit or court-annexed program distinguishes the lawyer's responsibilities from ongoing representations. The lawyer must obtain the client's informed consent as to the limited scope of the representation. If limited representation is not reasonable under the circumstances, the lawyer may provide advice to the client, but must also inform the client that further assistance of counsel is needed. Rule 6.5 Comment 2.

Rules 1.6 (Confidentiality) and 1.9(c) (Conflicts) apply to such limited representations, except as the other provisions indicate. Rule 6.5 Comment 2. In addition, the Rule does not impute a personal disqualification of a lawyer participating in the limited legal services program to other lawyers in the program. Rule 6.5 Comment 4. In addition, the lawyer's short-term representation providing limited legal services does not preclude that lawyer's law firm from representing a client with interests adverse to the client represented in relation to the program. Id. The purpose of this provision is to remove what otherwise would be an opportunity cost to the law firm by preventing it from representing paying clients when one of its lawyers, for a very short time, represents a pro bono client.

If the representation becomes ongoing, however, Rules 1.7, 1.9(a), and 1.10 become applicable. Rule 6.5 Comment 5.

II. Fees

In order to be engaged in pro bono work, it is not necessary that the lawyer work for free. The lawyer may charge a reduced fee.

A. Indigents Versus the Middle Class

If the client in a pro bono case cannot afford to pay a fee, the lawyer should charge no fee. Rule 6.1, Comment 1; EC 2–24, 2–25. However, often a person of moderate means can afford some fee but—because of the complexity of the matter—cannot afford the lawyer's customary fee. Then the lawyer should charge a reduced fee. Rule 6.1, Comment 1; EC 2–16, 2–24.

B. Price Discrimination

The Model Rules do not set a minimum fee—to do so would violate the antitrust laws, see Part III, Section IV, A, 1—but it recognizes that lawyers normally work for pay and may even require advance payment of a fee. Rule 1.5, Comment 4. The former Code recognized that "adequate compensation is necessary in order to enable the lawyer to serve his client effectively and to preserve the integrity and independence of the profession." EC 2–17.

A lawyer, therefore, may charge a "reasonable fee" of clients able to afford it. Those clients who only can afford less, should be charged a lesser fee. The Rules (and the former Code) therefore, in effect, approve of price discrimination: a lawyer may charge one client less (or more) than another client is charged, based on the clients' ability to pay. If one charges a client less because the client is less wealthy, the other side of the coin must be that one is charging another client more because that client is wealthier. Thus Rule 1.5, Comment 5 states: "it is proper to define the extent of services in light of the client's ability to pay."

Example: Attorney represents Client *A*, another lawyer, in the purchase of a home. Attorney charges $50 per hour for her services. Attorney also represents Client *B*, a wealthy manufacturer, in the purchase of his home. Attorney charges $90 per hour for her services. Client *C*, an indigent, asks Attorney to represent him in reviewing his rental contract with Landlord in a low income housing project. Attorney charges nothing. Finally, Client *D*, a person of moderate means, asks attorney to represent him in the purchase of his moderate cottage. Attorney charges $40 per hour for her services, which is all that *D* can afford. Assuming that none of these charges is unreasonably high, Attorney has done nothing improper.

C. Sharing Court–Awarded Fees with Pro Bono Organizations

Rule 5.4(a) prohibits, in general, a lawyer from sharing fees with a nonlawyer, subject to a few limited exceptions. Rule 7.2(b) prohibits payment of a referral fee, again with a few limited exceptions. Before the 2002 changes, discussed below, ABA Formal Opinion 93–374 (June 7, 1993) considered the situation where a non-profit pro bono organization asks an attorney to undertake pro bono litigation. The Opinion concluded that the lawyer (whether an employee of the organization or a member of a law firm) may agree in advance or later to turn over some or all of the court-awarded fees to the non-profit organization.

ABA Formal Opinion 93–374 (June 7, 1993) attracted a strong dissent, arguing that the majority's interpretation of the Rules was contrary to their plain meaning. Also disagreeing was an earlier court decision, *American Civil Liberties Union/Eastern Missouri Fund v. Miller,* 803 S.W.2d 592 (Mo.), cert. denied, 500 U.S. 943, 111 S.Ct. 2239, 114 L.Ed.2d 481 (1991), which held that Missouri's Rule 5.4(a) prohibited a former ACLU staff attorney from complying with his employment contract, which required him to turn over court-awarded fees. After that decision, the ACLU won a court order permanently enjoining Missouri from enforcing its ethical rules so as to invalidate the fee turn-over provision in the ACLU employment contract. *Susman v. Missouri,* No. 91–4429–CC–C–5 (W.D. Mo., June 1, 1992).

In 2002, the ABA cleared up the confusion by adding Rule 5.4(a)(4), which now makes clear that a lawyer may share court-awarded fees with a nonprofit organization that employed, retained, or recommended the lawyer's employment in the matter. This change makes sense, because it would not further the purpose of this rule to apply the normal prohibition of the turnover of fees to lay organizations in these circumstances.

III. The Decision to Accept a Pro Bono Case

A lawyer need not accept every client who walks in the office, but the lawyer should not refuse a case because the cause or client is unpopular. Nor should the lawyer lightly turn down appointed cases.

A. Proper and Improper Reasons to Reject Pro Bono Employment

The lawyer is not like the cab driver waiting at a taxi stand. The lawyer need not accept every client who walks through the door. However, it is improper for a lawyer to refuse a case for the wrong reason. To achieve the goal of making legal services fully available, a lawyer "should not lightly decline proffered employment," a principle that "requires" that a lawyer accept "his share of tendered employment which may be unattractive both to him and to the bar generally." EC 2–26.

For example, a lawyer must refuse a case because he is too busy to give it his competent attention. Rule 1.1; Rule 6.2; EC 2–30; DR 6–101(A)(1). Comment 2. A lawyer also must refuse a case if the client seeks to maintain a frivolous action or one brought only to harass another. EC 2–30; DR 2–109(A); DR 7–102(A)(1); Rule 3.1.

On the other hand, a lawyer should not decline representation merely because the client, or the client's cause, is unpopular (EC 2–27, Rule 6.2, Comment 1), or because influential members of the community oppose the lawyer's involvement. EC 2–28.

In addition, a lawyer need not refuse a case merely because he or she does not believe in the merits of a client's case, or believes, in a criminal case, that the client is guilty. EC 2–29. However, if the lawyer's personal feelings are so intense that his effective representation is impaired, then he must not take the case. Model Rule 6.2(c) & Comment 2; EC 2–30.

B. Appointed Cases

A lawyer should not refuse a court appointment to handle a pro bono case except for "compelling reasons." EC 2–29; Rule 6.2(a). In addition, the Rules allow a lawyer to refuse an appointed case if taking it would result in "an unreasonable financial burden. . . . " Rule 6.2(b).

The Code has no such specific provision, but earlier case law has allowed this excuse when the burden is truly unreasonable rather than merely minor. Compare *People ex rel. Conn v. Randolph*, 35 Ill.2d 24, 219 N.E.2d 337 (1966) (State paid fee in excess of statutory maximum allowed in appointed case in order to prevent an unconstitutional taking of property when the financial burden was staggering), with *People v. Sanders*, 58 Ill.2d 196, 317 N.E.2d 552 (1974) (only $250 statutory maximum awarded in capital punishment case because financial burden in this instance is not unreasonable), and *Brown v. Board of County Commissioners of Washoe County*, 85 Nev. 149, 451 P.2d 708 (1969) (minor loss of income should be borne by attorney).

While courts have held that there is no constitutional right to compensation for compelled jury service, *Maricopa County v. Corp.*, 44 Ariz. 506, 39 P.2d 351 (1934) (per curiam), the difference between compelled jury service and compelled legal representation is not only in the amount of time and effort typically required, but also in the nature of the limited and discrete class burdened. The burden of uncompensated criminal defense representation is borne only by trial lawyers while the burden of jury service does not single out any discrete class of individuals. A purpose of the just compensation clause is to prevent the majority from requiring discrete classes of people to bear special burdens without just compensation. Thus the Alaska Supreme Court held that, under the state Constitution, the court could not compel a private attorney to represent an indigent criminal defendant unless the state paid just compensation, defined as, "the compensation received by the average competent attorney operating in the open market." *DeLisio v. Alaska Superior Court*, 740 P.2d 437, 443 (Alaska 1987) (overruling prior cases).

While it is improper for a lawyer to refuse a case because the client is unpopular, EC 2–27, the lawyer should not take a case if his or her own personal feelings against the client or cause are so strong that the lawyer could not do a competent job. Rule 6.2(c); EC 2–30.

> *Caveat:* The Code says that "[c]ompelling reasons [not to take a case] do not include such factors as the repugnance of the subject matter . . . " EC 2–29. In contrast, Rule 6.2(c) states that a proper reason to refuse to accept an appointed case is that "the client or the cause is so repugnant . . . " to the lawyer. See also Rule 6.2, Comment 1 ("A lawyer ordinarily is not obliged to accept a client whose character or cause the lawyer regards as repugnant."). These two sections are not really in conflict. EC 2–30 explains that a lawyer should decline representation if "the intensity of his personal feelings" may "impair his effective representation . . . ," and Comment 1 to Rule 6.2 qualifies the reference to repugnancy by explaining that it is modified by the lawyer's responsibility to provide pro bono service.

IV. Mandatory Pro Bono Service

A. Proposals

The Model Rules do not presently require that lawyers engage in mandatory pro bono service, but the idea has been periodically proposed and justified under various theories.

It is settled that in individual cases the courts have the power to compel attorneys to accept appointment to cases before the court. "Attorneys are officers of the court, and are bound to render service when required by such an appointment." *Powell v. Alabama,* 287 U.S. 45, 73, 53 S.Ct. 55, 65, 77 L.Ed. 158, 172 (1932). Less certain is the extent to which counsel must assume this burden with little or no compensation. See section III, B, supra.

A related question is the extent to which a state bar association or the state disciplinary machinery can or should require mandatory pro bono representation in civil, rather than criminal cases, and mandatory pro bono counseling and advice in nonlitigative situations.

In California, for example, the state legislature considered, and defeated, a bill requiring active members of the bar to engage in a minimum of 40 hours per year of mandatory pro bono work for no fee or a "substantially reduced" fee. Assembly Bill No. 4050 (1976).

Thomas Ehrlich, the first President of the Legal Services Corporation, was also a member of the ABA Commission that drafted the Model Rules. He argued, "with enthusiasm" that the Rules should mandate (not merely encourage) pro bono activities by private attorneys to help the poor. Ehrlich, *Rationing Justice,* 34 The Record of the Association of the Bar of the City of New York 729, 743 (Dec. 1979).

The Model Rules initially proposed:

> "A lawyer *shall* render unpaid public interest legal service . . . [and] shall make an annual report concerning such service to the appropriate regulatory authority." Proposed Rule 8.1, Discussion Draft (Jan. 30, 1980), reprinted in T. Morgan & R. Rotunda, 1980 Selected National Standards Supplement 142 (1980).

There was much opposition, however, from ABA members, and the Commission withdrew its proposal.

B. Rationale

Proponents of mandatory pro bono service offer various rationales. The former President of the Legal Services Corporation argued that lawyers, but not medical doctors, are obliged to offer free service because "lawyers are an essential part of the public justice system, with monopolistic access to the workings of the system. With that monopoly comes a public obligation to help ensure the sound workings of the system—otherwise the rationing of justice becomes warped in ways that are dangerous not only to poor people, who are denied an opportunity to use the system, but also to the public generally, which is denied a legal system that works fairly." Ehrlich, *Rationing Justice,* 34 Record of the Association of the Bar of the City of New York 729, 743 (Dec. 1979).

Others reply that while lawyers have a legal monopoly to the practice of law, medical doctors have a legal monopoly over the practice of medicine. Thus, the President of the California State Bar once proposed that medical doctors, lawyers, and dentists all should be obligated to contribute one-half day per month of free services. San Jose Mercury, Nov. 29, 1976, at 26, col. 1. In 1987, the ABA Journal and the Journal of the American Medical Association each published an editorial advocating that "all doctors and all lawyers, as a matter of ethics and good faith, should contribute a significant percentage of their total professional efforts without expectation of financial remuneration." They said that 50 hours a year was "an appropriate minimum amount." 73 A.B.A.J. 55 (Dec. 1, 1987).

In reply, some have argued that the fact that there is a legal monopoly proves little: if the monopoly is bad, it should be eliminated; if the monopoly is good and needed, then its existence adds little to the pro bono debate. Some states monopolize the sale of liquor, but do not provide free alcohol to those who cannot afford it. The ABA Commission that drafted the Model Rules initially proposed a *mandatory* pro bono requirement, and did not rely on any theory of legal monopoly. The ABA Commission relied on "the lawyer's commitment to the law's idea of equal justice." Proposed Model Rule 8.1, Comment 1 (Discussion Draft, Jan. 30, 1980), reprinted in T. Morgan & R. Rotunda, 1980 Selected National Standards Supplement 142 (1980).

Others argue that to say that free legal services to the poor and less advantaged will promote justice does not lead to the conclusion that it is an individual lawyer's duty to provide such services for free. These people argue that it is society's duty to fund services and pay the lawyers who perform them. See, e.g., *State v. Green*, 470 S.W.2d 571, 573 (Mo.1971), where the court said that it "will not *compel* the attorneys . . . to discharge *alone* a 'duty which constitutionally is the burden of the State' "(emphasis in original); *State ex rel. Scott v. Roper*, 688 S.W.2d 757 (Mo.1985) (en banc)(extensive historical discussion and holding that court does not have power to appoint counsel in civil cases without compensation). See also Shapiro, *The Enigma of the Lawyer's Duty to Serve*, 55 N.Y.U.L.Rev. 735, 738–39 (1980): "Although frequently urged as rooted in the firmest of traditions, the 'duty to serve' in fact has a history shrouded in obscurity, ambiguity, and qualification. . . . " The state's imposition of this duty "raises substantial constitutional issues and is perhaps even more vulnerable on economic and other policy grounds."

C. Mandatory Pro Bono and Alternative Service

Some proposals for mandatory pro bono provide forms of alternative service. For example, if Lawyer Alpha is appointed by the court to represent an indigent, can Alpha, a partner in a large firm, fulfill this responsibility by assigning the case to one of the young associates? Lawyers in solo practice or in small firms often believe that this opt out in effect places a proportionately heavier burden on them, because it is easier for the larger firms to find a less expensive associate in their office. Moreover, when the firms are large enough and there is always a supply of young associates who do not have any client base yet, the marginal cost to the larger firm (of assigning a young associate to a pro bono activity) may be close to zero.

Alternatively, can lawyer Alpha fulfill his pro bono responsibility by paying another lawyer in a different firm to do the work? Can Alpha simply buy out of this obligation? Such a buy out is equally available to solo practitioners as well as members of the larger firms. The burden, however, is relatively greater for the poorer lawyer.

If Alpha can simply buy out, then mandatory pro bono is really a tax, and, as such, some argue that it is better for the state legislature to tax each lawyer directly and use that money to hire attorneys to staff legal aid offices. This tax could be made progressive.

Others reply that what is needed is not just the lawyer's money but the lawyer's time. "The responsibility for pro bono service should be borne *by each lawyer individually.*" Proposed Model Rule 8.1, Comment 1 (Discussion Draft, Jan. 30, 1980) (emphasis added), reprinted in T. Morgan & R. Rotunda, 1980 Selected National Standards Supplement 142 (1980). There is support for this view in some language of the Model Code and Model Rules. See EC 2–25: "[P]*ersonal involvement* in the problems of the disadvantaged can be one of the most rewarding experiences in the life of a lawyer" (emphasis added). Accord, Rule 6.1, Comment 1 (same).

Yet, some contend that if the real purpose of pro bono work is to help the poor, the poor would be better helped by a legal service lawyer specializing in their problems rather than a municipal bond lawyer who was forced to learn about the law of evictions. Contra, Ehrlich, *Rationing Justice,* 34 Record of the Association of the Bar of the City of New York 729, 744 (Dec. 1979): "But many legal aid programs have found that, with relatively modest amounts of training, even bond indenture lawyers can re-emerge from their specialist shells."

If pro bono service is not feasible for some lawyers (e.g., a state might impose legal restrictions on government lawyers or judges that restrict their ability to perform pro bono activities), then lawyers should make financial contributions to support pro bono services. Rule 6.1, Comments 5, 10.

V. Law Reform Activities Affecting Private Clients

For reasons of public policy, it is not generally considered a conflict of interest for a lawyer to engage in pro bono activities even though such activities are adverse to the interests of the lawyer's private clients.

A. The Lawyer's Personal Views

1. Law Reform Activities Adverse to a Private Client's Interests

A lawyer only represents a client in the lawyer's professional capacity. It is not necessary that the lawyer agree with, adopt, or support his or her client's views. "The obligation of loyalty to his client applies only to a lawyer in the discharge of his professional duties and implies no obligation to adopt a personal viewpoint favorable to the interests or desires of his client." EC 7–17. Accord, Rule 1.2(b). Lawyers who abhor cigarettes may represent tobacco companies without taking up the smoking habit.

In fact, the Code specifically provided that a lawyer "may take positions on public issues and espouse legal reforms he favors without regard to the individual views of any client." EC 7–17. The Rules are not as specific in this respect, though their general tenor supports the principle expressed in EC 7–17. The first sentence of Model Rule 6.4 states that a lawyer may be a director, officer, or member of a group involved in law reform activities "notwithstanding that the reform may affect the interests of a client of the lawyer." If there is no breach of loyalty when the lawyer is a member of an organization advocating law reform contrary to a client's interest, there should be little argument that there is a breach of loyalty when the lawyer speaks out on his own behalf. Cf. EC 8–4. In both cases the Code and Rules conclude that the benefits to clients because of the conflicts rules are outweighed by the social costs of using these rules to prohibit lawyers from engaging in law reform efforts, either individually or through bar associations, legal service organizations, the A.C.L.U., and similar groups.

The client may not like the fact that the lawyer is publicly advocating law reform views contrary to the client's private interests. The client may always fire the lawyer, Rule 1.16(a)(3), but the client may not properly charge that the lawyer acted unethically in taking the contrary position. In practice, of course, the client may not discharge the lawyer because lawyers are not fungible. If you are a good enough lawyer, your clients will let you get away with a lot.

Example: Attorney normally represents corporations defending against charges of job discrimination brought by the Equal Employment Opportunity Commission. Attorney is also a member of the NAACP and NOW. Attorney publicly endorses the lobbying activities of both organizations in their efforts to strengthen the power of the EEOC to fight racial and gender discrimination in employment. It might be adverse to the interests of Attorney's corporate clients if the powers of the EEOC are increased. Attorney has, nonetheless, acted properly.

2. Law Reform Activities Supportive of a Private Client

The Client's interest and the personal law reform interests of the lawyer may coincide. If the lawyer is representing a private client while, for example, appearing before a legislative committee and asking for law reform, the lawyer may not mislead the committee as to the true identity of the client. Rules 3.9 & 4.1(a); DR 7–106(B). If the attorney is representing XYZ Corp., she may not pretend to be representing her own views. If the identity of the client is privileged or secret, the lawyer should at least alert the committee that she is representing a private client whose identity cannot be revealed. Id. Cf. Rule 6.4.

If the lawyer personally believes in an item of law reform and his own belief coincides with the interest of his client, it was unclear under the Model Code whether the lawyer must nonetheless disclose that fact even if such disclosure does not identify the client. See EC 8–4, which only states that if the lawyer purports to act on behalf of the public, then the lawyer should conscientiously believe in the position advocated.

Rule 6.4 is much more specific, at least in the situation where the lawyer serves an organization involved in law reform. "When the lawyer knows that the interests of a client may be materially benefitted by a decision in which the lawyer participates, the lawyer shall disclose that fact but need not identify the client." The disclosure of the fact of representation helps to preclude the suspicion that the lawyer exercised improper influence on behalf of a client.

B. Membership on a Legal Service Board

Often attorneys are members of the Board of Directors of a Legal Services Organization. In fact, after Congress established the federal Legal Services Corporation in 1974, see 42 U.S.C.A. § 2996b, in order to offer noncriminal legal services to indigents, the relevant regulations required that at least 60% of the local governing bodies should be attorneys admitted in that state and supportive of the delivery of quality legal services to the poor. 45 C.F.R. § 1607.3(b) (1982).

If an attorney in private practice is on a legal services board, in a matter of time it may be almost inevitable that the staff members of the legal services organization, on behalf of an indigent client, will file suit against one of the private attorney's private clients, or defend the indigent against suit brought by the private client. There is, however, no conflict of interest because the private attorney who is a member of the Board does not have an attorney-client relationship with the legal service organization's clients. ABA Formal Opinion 345 (July 12, 1979); Rule 6.3, Comment 1. The individual legal service clients do not confer with the Board members; nor do they place any confidences or secrets with these Board members, ABA Formal Opinion 334 (Aug. 10, 1974). "The Board's role is restricted solely to establishment of broad policy for the Program, and not the management of or the direct participation in Program client representation." ABA Formal Opinion 345 (July 12, 1979). See also 45 C.F.R. § 1607.4(b) (1982)(same). Cf. DR 5–107(B) (lawyer should not permit person who employs him to render services for another to direct his professional judgment); Rule 5.4(c) (same); ABA Formal Opinion 334 (Aug. 10, 1974) (same). Finally, public policy favors having active practitioners involved in the activities of legal service organizations. ABA Formal Opinion 345 (July 12, 1979); Rule 6.3, Comment 1.

ABA Formal Opinion 345 (July 12, 1979), based on the Model Code, concludes, nonetheless, that there remains a problem when a Board member represents a client adverse to the client of a legal services program. Perhaps, said the Opinion, one of the lawyers might feel self-restrained in exercising zeal. Or, a client (particularly an indigent one) may acquiesce only because he believes that he has no choice in the matter.

Consequently, Formal Opinion 345 concluded that the clients on both sides must be made aware of the Board member's role. The lawyers and clients on either side should "feel comfortable," and "if, in the course of the representation, it becomes apparent that independent representation is not being afforded on both sides or one or the other of the clients perceives that it is not afforded, *no matter what the reality,* then the lawyers should assist in change of counsel for one or both clients." (Emphasis added). If the Board member's law firm is large enough, the Opinion continued, a lawyer other than the Board member should represent the firm's clients in disputes with the legal services program, so that the Board member is not directly involved. This ABA Formal Opinion "urges" the Board member's law firm to provide "screening procedures." Cf. Rule 1.11. Finally, because of the "extreme value" of having active lawyers serve as Board members, the legal services staff lawyer "should not seek unfairly to gain advantage for their clients by disqualification of the Board member or his firm." ABA Formal Opinion 345 (July 12, 1979).

The approach of the Model Rules is simply different. The Rules try to solve the problem of any perceived conflicts by selectively screening the private lawyer from the decision-making process of the legal services organization. If the private lawyer is also a member, director, or officer of the legal services organization, then the private lawyer should not "knowingly" participate in any decision or action of the legal services organization if such participation would be inconsistent with the lawyer's obligation, under Rule 1.7, to his or her private clients. (Rule 1.7 is the general rule governing conflicts of interest with regard to current clients.) Similarly, the private lawyer should not knowingly participate in a decision on behalf of the legal services organization if the decision could have a "material adverse effect" on a legal services' client whose interests are adverse to the lawyer's private client. The private lawyer, then, is not disqualified from serving on the Board; that lawyer is disqualified from participating in certain Board decisions.

The legal services organization is also encouraged to establish written policies regarding the role of the legal services decision-making process in order to enhance the credibility of the assurances that it gives to its indigent clients. Model Rule 6.3, Comment 2.

REVIEW QUESTIONS

1. Hiram Lawyer is an attorney with great prestige in the legal community. He has been asked by the court to represent an accused burglar who is indigent. Hiram:

   a. *Should* refuse to take the case if he has read about the case in newspapers and believes the defendant is probably guilty.

   b. *May* refuse to take the case if doing so would hurt his reputation, because a lawyer's reputation is his stock in trade.

    c.   *Should not* take the case if the intensity of his personal feeling may impair the effective representation of the prospective client.

    d.   *Should* take the case unless it requires him to align himself against influential members of the community.

2.   Lloyd Smith is a local attorney who is also a member of the State Bar Committee on Corporate Law. That Committee is considering whether to propose changes in the state's corporate statutes in order to allow directors to hold meetings and take binding votes by telephone. One of Smith's clients is very supportive of the new proposed law and asks Smith to vote for the proposed law in the Committee. Is it *proper* for Smith to support the proposed law?

    a.   Yes, if Smith discloses the fact that one of his clients would benefit and if he espouses only those changes in the law that he conscientiously believed to be in the public interest.

    b.   Yes, because he owes duty to his client to fight zealously for that client's interests and must do so even if he personally does not agree with the proposed changes.

    c.   No, because Smith was involved in a conflict of interest in representing this private client and also being a member of the state bar committee dealing with matters that impinged on the client's interests.

    d.   No, because Smith must disqualify himself, even if Smith would have supported the proposed law without the client's request.

3.   Delta, a lawyer and the head of the state disciplinary authority, has asked Alpha, also a lawyer, to sit on one of the state hearing boards responsible for hearing charges of disciplinary violations. The board is normally composed of two lawyers and one lay person. The state pays no compensation for such services.

Alpha *should:*

    a.   sit on the board because in doing so he can assist in the administration of the Disciplinary Rules, but he will not be disciplined if he refuses.

    b.   refuse to sit unless the state pays reasonable compensation, because in so doing he can assist in improving the enforcement of the Disciplinary Rules.

    c.   refuse to sit so long as there is a lay member of the board.

4.   Attorney Able is an associate in a large law firm, Davis, Edwards, and Finkel. He regularly serves as a volunteer on a nonprofit hotline to assist local low-income residents in disputes with landlords. Able recently received a call from Mrs. Baker, a tenant of an apartment complex owned by Mr. Carter, a client of the firm. Two weeks before, Partner Davis drafted a new lease for Carter, raising the rent at the apartment complex. Able has never met or heard of Carter and does not know that his law firm represents Carter.

Is Attorney Able *subject to discipline* for advising Mrs. Baker?

a.   Yes, if Carter is a client of the firm and Able gave advice adverse to Carter's interests.

b.   No, unless Able knows about the work done for Carter by Davis.

c.   Yes, because Able should have engaged in a comprehensive conflicts check before undertaking Baker's representation.

d.   No, because Able is an associate

*

PART X

The Lawyer's Obligations as a Judge

■ ANALYSIS

IV. Judicial Disqualification

    A.   An Introductory Note

    B.   Disqualification Where Impartiality Might Reasonably Be Questioned

        1.   Introduction

        2.   Objective Test

        3.   The Rule of Necessity

        4.   Generally Questioning the Impartiality of the Judge

        5.   Judge's Prior or Present Connection With Attorney

        6.   Judge's Intemperate Remarks

        7.   Judge's Religion

        8.   Where the Judge Knows a Party, Witness, or Attorney

        9.   When Judge's Former Law Clerk Represents a Party

        10. Where Judge Participated in Prior Related Case

    C.   Disqualification for Personal Bias or Prejudice

        1.   Introduction

        2.   Extrajudicial Bias

        3.   Actual Bias or Prejudice in General

    D.   Disqualification When the Judge Is a Former Lawyer or Material Witness

    E.   Disqualification for Financial Interests or Interests That Could Be Substantially Affected by the Outcome of the Proceeding

        1.   Introduction

        2.   Economic Interests

            (a)   Legal or Equitable Interest

            (b)   The Subject Matter in the Controversy

            (c)   A *"De Minimis"* Interest

            (d)   The Judge's Family

            (e)   Knowledge of Economic Interests

            (f)   Exceptions to Economic Interest Disqualification

                (i)   Mutual Funds

                (ii)   Civic Organizations

                (iii)   Financial Institutions and Mutual Insurance Companies

                (iv)   Government Bonds

            (g)   Other Interests

            (h)   Judicial Campaign Contributions by a Party Before the Court

    F.   Disqualification Based on Family Relationships

        1.   Introduction

        2.   Party to the Proceeding

I. An Introductory Note

A. A Short History

In 1924 the ABA House of Delegates promulgated the first judicial code of ethics, called the Canons of Judicial Ethics. An important catalyst to the 1924 Canons of Judicial Ethics was the revelation, in the early 1920's, that Kenesaw Mountain Landis, a federal judge, was engaging in private employment and supplementing his federal salary of $7,500 with a more generous yearly salary of $42,500 for being the major league baseball commissioner. The ABA adopted a resolution of censure of the judge. Armstrong, *The Code of Judicial Conduct*, 26 Southwestern L.J. 708, 709 (1972); C. Wolfram, *Modern Legal Ethics* 965 n.72 (West Pub. Co. Practitioner's ed. 1986). Even though Chief Justice Taft was chairman of the ABA Committee that drafted the 1924 Judicial Canons, many states did not adopt them, with their "curious mixture of generalized, hortatory admonitions and specific rules of standards of pro-scribed conduct." Sutton, *A Comparison of the Code of Professional Responsibility with the Code of Judicial Conduct*, 1972 Utah L.Rev. 355, 255–56. Nearly a half century later, the ABA House of Delegates replaced these Canons with the Code of Judicial Conduct (1972), written in more conventional statutory form. This Judicial Code was, at least in part, a reaction to the events that led to Justice Fortas's resignation from the Supreme Court and the financial and other disclosures that came about when the U.S. Senate rejected President Nixon's nomination of Federal Circuit Judge Haynsworth, and then Judge Circuit Judge Carswell. Many states widely adopted the 1972 Code (subject, of course, to various nonuniform amendments).

The United States Judicial Conference adopted a version as well, and its most recent version is at. 175 F.R.D. 363 (1998). In 1990, the ABA House of Delegates approved a comprehensive revision, called the Model Code of Judicial Conduct, which the ABA has continued to amend over the years.

B. Some General Comparisons Between the 1990 Judicial Code and the 1972 Judicial Code

The 1990 Model Code is in the same format as the 1972 Code, but many of the sections are renumbered and reorganized. The 1990 Code has 5 Canons, while the 1972 Code has 7.

The 1990 Code, unlike the 1972 Code, is gender neutral. The drafters of the 1990 Code also intended to offer clearer standards than those offered by the 1972 Code, but sometimes they did not succeed.

C. Terminology

The 1972 Code used the term "should" in the Canons and text and, as a consequence, some jurisdictions thought that "should" only expressed an aspirational standard. (Although the Preface to the 1972 Code indicated it intended mandatory standards, some jurisdictions omitted the Preface).

The 1990 Code eliminates this confusion by using the term *"shall"* in the text and *"must"* in the Commentary to indicate that a standard is mandatory, and violation of that standard subjects the judge to discipline. The 1990 Code uses *"may"* to indicate that the judge has permissible discretion. *"Should"* or *"should not"* is intended to be hortatory.

D. The Structure of the 1990 Judicial Code

The 1990 Code has a *Preamble,* which explains that the Code is divided into a series of *Canons,* which are broad statements. Specific rules under each Canon are called *Sections.* After this Preamble, there is a section called *Terminology,* which puts in one place all of the terms of art used in the 1990 Code. When these terms appear in the body of the 1990 Code, an asterisk (*) accompanies them, indicating to the reader to turn to the Terminology section. At the end of the 1990 Code is an *Application Section,* which discusses what types of persons are covered by the 1990 Code. The Canons, the Sections, Terminology, and Application Section are authoritative. The *Commentary* (which follows various Sections) is intended to provide guidance, but it is not intended to be a statement of additional rules.

The Judicial Code does not number the paragraphs in its Preamble or Terminology, or the Comments that follow the black letter rules. For ease of reference, they are numbered in brackets in the appendix and we refer to here by number.

E. Interpreting the 1990 Judicial Code

The Preamble explains that the 1990 Code is not intended to be a basis for civil or criminal liability. The text of the Canons and Sections is intended to be binding and to govern the conduct of judges, but not "every transgression will result in disciplinary actions." Preamble 5.

The 1990 Code is not intended to be an exhaustive guide, and the standards that it offers are to be interpreted as *rules of reason,* a point that the Preamble makes several times. Preamble 3, 5. A "minor violation of a rule need not invariably result in discipline." *ABA's Standing Committee Report on 1990 Code, Legislative Draft* 2 (1990). Lawyers are not supposed to invoke these Canons for "mere tactical advantage," Preamble 4, a principal that should prove difficult to enforce, because the adversary system, by its very nature, gives many incentives to lawyers to use laws, rules, and precedent for "mere tactical advantage."

Note: Because the ABA replaced the 1972 Code with the 1990 Code, this chapter will focus, in the main, on the 1990 Code, *not* the 1972 Code. However, much case law decided under the 1972 Code is still relevant under the 1990 Code because many of the substantive provisions are basically unchanged (although many of the sections are renumbered). The drafters of the 1990 Code did not write on a clean slate. Hence we will also refer to cases decided under the 1972 Code as well as the Reporter's Notes to the 19972 Code, when appropriate. *You should assume that any citation to a Code section is to the 1990 Code, unless the text indicates otherwise.* During the course of this chapter, we will compare differences between the two Codes when such a comparison is useful.

II. Personal Behavior

A. Canon One
A judge shall uphold the integrity and independence of the judiciary.

1. Purpose of Canon One
Canon 1 sets the tone for the rest of the Model Code of Judicial Conduct (1990). The public must not only have confidence in the reliability of judicial procedures, but also in the integrity of the judges. The basic purpose of the Code is to "assure that judges will be worthy of . . . independence and deserving of . . . confidence." See *New Standards of Judicial Conduct*, 46 Fla.B.J. 268, 269 (1972) (Quoting R. Traynor, Chairman of the ABA Special Committee on Standards of Judicial Conduct). Canon 1 introduces the parameters of that goal.

2. Judicial Independence
Canon 1 maintains that an independent judiciary is an indispensable element of justice, and that judges must strive to see that the independence of the judiciary is preserved. The comments to Canon 1 explain that an independent judiciary is one that is free of inappropriate outside influences.

The rationale of Canon 1 is to preserve an independent judiciary and thereby ensure a free society. Risks of conflicts would arise if a judge, under the *control* of the government, were called upon to decide a case in which the government is a party. Similarly, if judges remained members of the legislature, they might not be able to apply impartially the laws they passed. See E. Thode, *Reporter's Notes to [1972] Code of Judicial Conduct* 45–46 (1973) [hereinafter cited as *Reporter's Notes* (1972)].

The ABA amended the Terminology section of the Model Code in 2003 to include a definition of "impartiality" as the "absence of bias or prejudice in favor of, or against, particular parties or classes of parties, as well as maintaining an open mind in considering issues that may come before the judge." Terminology 9.

3. Judicial Integrity

The drafters explain that a judge cannot be disciplined for violating the first clause of the second sentence of Canon 1A, which provides that the judge *"should* participate in maintaining and enforcing high standards of conduct" (emphasis added). *ABA's Standing Committee Report on 1990 Code, Legislative Draft* (1990), at 8. Nonetheless, this hortatory statement is evidence of the Code's goal of assuring public confidence in the judiciary. The Canon 1A commentary defines a judiciary of integrity as "one in which judges are known for their probity, fairness, honesty, uprightness, and soundness of character."

Courts seldom rely on Canon 1 as the sole basis for disciplinary action even though the second clause of the second sentence provides that judges *"shall* personally observe" high standards of conduct. (emphasis added). Courts do, however, refer to Canon 1 in their opinions when the judge's conduct constitutes a separate violation of a more specific section of the Code. Because any violation of the Judicial Code impairs the "integrity" of the judiciary, this Canon is often cited, though never primarily relied upon. E.g., *In re Larkin*, 368 Mass. 87, 333 N.E.2d 199 (1975) (judge's repeated attempts to give illegal campaign contributions to the governor violated Canon 1, and other sections). Courts prefer to rely on the specific language of other Canons rather than the general language found in Canon 1.

Note: The Code of Judicial Conduct is a *Model* Code and is not enforceable in any jurisdiction unless officially adopted by that jurisdiction. (The title to 1972 Code does not include the word "Model," although it is a "model" or proposed code of conduct for judges. The 1990 Code incorporates "model" as part of its title.) The basis for discipline in *In re Larkin* was Massachusetts' adoption of the ABA Model Judicial Code as its own standards of judicial conduct. Any future citation of a case indicates that the jurisdiction has adopted a version of the applicable Canon as its own.

ABA Informal Opinion 1452 (March 20, 1980) offers an example of conduct that it concludes might impair the integrity of the judiciary and violate Canon 1. The issue concerned the propriety of an appellate court bargaining with a union that represented the court's secretaries where the union was also a frequent litigant before the court. The ABA concluded that the integrity of the court could be compromised because the secretaries were privy to nonpublic information related to undecided cases in which the union was a litigant, and therefore interpreted Canon 1 to prohibit the judge from bargaining with the union. With whom, then, are the secretaries to bargain? "We observe," the Informal Opinion concludes, some laws pertaining to collective bargaining "exclude from coverage confidential employees." Thus, apparently, the Judicial Code, in effect, prevents judges' secretaries from having a union! A peculiar result, some might say, and hardly compelled by the vague language of Canon 1.

4. Duty to Report Violations

Canon 1 implicitly requires a judge to report any known violations of the Code to the proper disciplinary authority, because, as the Comment to Canon 1 explains, judges "must comply with the law, including the provisions of this Code." No court or disciplinary authority, however, has needed to cite Canon 1 when disciplining judges for failure to report violations of the Judicial Code because the Code contains an explicit duty to report in Canon 3D(1), (2), discussed infra.

B. Canon Two

A judge shall avoid impropriety and the appearance of impropriety in all of the judge's activities.

1. Applies Whether Judge Is on or Off the Bench

Canon 2 compels a judge to observe high standards of conduct whether on or off the bench because public esteem for the judiciary is affected by the judge's behavior in either situation. Comment 2 to Canon 2A explicitly notes that the duty to avoid impropriety or its appearance "applies to both the professional and personal conduct of a judge." Thus, a judge was publicly reprimanded for openly engaging in sexual acts while in an automobile parked in a public parking lot. *In re Lee,* 336 So.2d 1175 (Fla.1976). Some courts, however, take a more liberal attitude toward out-of-court behavior, and hold that such conduct is not punishable unless it affects the judicial role. See, e.g., *Matter of Dalessandro,* 483 Pa. 431, 397 A.2d 743 (1979) (judge not disciplined for having open adulterous relationship; the acts of adultery, however, were not committed in the open, nor in a parking lot). The cases in this area of sexual misconduct "are nearly impossible to reconcile." Steven Lubet, *Beyond Reproach: Ethical Restrictions on the Extrajudicial Activities of State and Federal Judges* 40 (1984).

"Off-bench" conduct more likely affects the judicial role if the conduct is illegal. The court in *Dalessandro* emphasized that the judge's adulterous relationship was not contrary to Pennsylvania law. Illegal conduct was the basis for disciplining "off-bench" behavior in *Matter of Sawyer,* 286 Or. 369, 594 P.2d 805 (1979). *Sawyer* disciplined a judge for teaching part-time in a state college in violation of a state constitutional provision. The court suspended the judge from office during the period of time that he was a teacher.

Note: If otherwise allowed by law, Canon 4A and Canon 4B (discussed below) permit a judge to teach on subjects concerning the law, the legal system, and the administration of justice; Canon 4B also allows a judge to teach nonlegal subjects if teaching does not demean the judicial office or interfere with the performance of judicial duties.

2. Appearance of Impropriety and the Standard of Review

Although the Model Rules of Professional Conduct reject the "appearance of impropriety" standard as too vague to be a useful test, Model Rule 1.5, Comment 5 (discussed in Part I, § 2, supra), the Model Judicial Code adopts it in the introductory sentence to Canon 2: "A judge shall avoid impropriety and the appearance of impropriety in all of the judge's activities." Canon 2A, Comment 2, admits that this standard "is necessarily cast in general terms," and offers this test:

> "whether the conduct would create in reasonable minds a perception that the judge's ability to carry out judicial responsibilities with integrity, impartiality and competence is impaired."

Given this purported test, judicial conduct under this Canon should be scrutinized objectively. The standard is whether the conduct would appear to a reasonable person to demonstrate partiality or prejudice public esteem for the judicial office. "The guiding consideration is that the administration of justice should reasonably appear to be disinterested as well as be so in fact." *Public Utilities Commission of District of Columbia v. Pollak,* 343 U.S. 451, 467, 72 S.Ct. 813, 823, 96 L.Ed. 1068, 1079 (1952) (separate statement of Frankfurter, J.), quoted in, *School District of Kansas City, Missouri v. Missouri,* 438 F.Supp. 830, 835 (W.D.Mo.1977).

"Impropriety" is, at best, a very vague standard. After all, we cannot begin to define "appearance of impropriety" unless we know what is an "impropriety." Thus, cases disciplining a judge for engaging in impropriety typically rely on a more specific standard found elsewhere in the Code. But the court, after relying on a more specific section, will often add the violation of this more general standard, perhaps as a makeweight.

The following cases and ABA opinions are examples of conduct violative of other sections of the Judicial Code or other statutory or common law standards of conduct; in all instances the conduct was also held to violate Canon 2 and thus they help explain, by way of example, the meaning of "impropriety" or "appearance" thereof.

Spruance v. Commission on Judicial Qualifications, 13 Cal.3d 778, 119 Cal.Rptr. 841, 532 P.2d 1209 (1975). The judge conducted court in a "bizarre and unjudicial manner" by treating attorneys in a cavalier and rude manner, subjecting an attorney to an improper cross-examination when he took the stand in support of a motion to disqualify the judge, demeaning the deputy district attorney in open court and placing him under physical restraint because the deputy appealed the judge's disposition of another case, expressing disbelief in the defendant's testimony by creating a sound commonly referred to as a "raspberry," and giving the defendant "the finger" for coming in late in a traffic matter. The Court removed him from judicial office.

In *School District of Kansas City, Missouri v. Missouri,* 438 F.Supp. 830 (W.D.Mo.1977), the trial judge recused himself in a case where his former law firm represented the plaintiff, even though the firm's personnel had changed over the years during which the judge had been on the bench. The judge denied the defendant's motion for disqualification based on 28 U.S.C.A. § 455, but then disqualified himself for reasons based in part on Canon 2 principles.

The judge in *School District* believed the overriding consideration favoring recusal was the avoidance of the appearance of impropriety.

Therefore he transferred the case to a judge completely removed from any charge of partiality. It must be remembered that the judge recused himself on his own motion; under Canon 3E(1)(b), disqualification is not mandatory when the presiding judge's former law firm merely represents a party in the case. Canon 3E(1)(b) compels disqualification in such a case only when the judge had been a member of the firm *while* the firm was representing the party in the very matter now pending before the judge.

Commentary 1 to Canon 2A states that the restrictions on judges' speech imposed by Sections 3(B)(9) and (10) are essential to maintaining judicial integrity, impartiality, and independence.

3. Compliance With the Law

(a) When Acting in a Judicial Capacity

Canon 2A provides that the judge shall "comply with the law," which is defined to include not only "court rules" but also "statutes, constitutional provisions, and decisional law." Terminology 11. In *Matter of Sawyer,* 286 Or. 369, 594 P.2d 805 (1979), the judge failed to comply with a state constitutional restriction. *Matter of Cieminski,* 270 N.W.2d 321 (N.D.1978) held that a judge violated Canon 2A when he failed to follow a state rule of criminal procedure that mandated a verbatim record of the initial appearance and arraignment of the defendants. Such conduct was improper even though the judge did not have a court reporter or tape recorder readily available. *United States v. Long,* 656 F.2d 1162 (5th Cir.1981) overturned a defendant's sentence of life imprisonment because the trial judge failed to consider a presentence report before sentencing, in violation of Federal Rule of Criminal Procedure 32. Although this case did not involve a disciplinary proceeding, the appellate court relied in part on Canon 2A's "compliance with the law" requirement in ordering that the case be sent to another judge on remand. Because the trial judge had stated that no presentence report could change his mind, he in effect had stated that he would not comply with the law and therefore could not make an impartial decision with respect to the defendant's sentence.

Aside from the self-evident requirement that a judge comply with statutory and procedural law, a judge violates Canon 2 if she interferes with other judicial orders or proceedings.

Example: Matter of Conda, 72 N.J. 229, 370 A.2d 16 (1977) (per curiam) censured a surrogate for altering the designation of bank depositories set forth in orders by the county court judges. Apparently, the surrogate believed the county court had no authority to designate the banks where settlements of minors should be deposited. The New Jersey Supreme Court held that, even if the county court lacked authority to designate the bank, altering the order without the consent of the signatory judge was inexcusable. The surrogate also violated Canon 2 by using the office facilities and employees for personal political purposes in violation of a New Jersey Supreme Court rule.

(b) When Not Acting in a Judicial Capacity

A judge must respect and comply with the law even when not acting in a judicial capacity. Thus, a judge was removed from office when he unlawfully entered a neighbor's house and ransacked the house while searching for a gun in response to the neighbor's threat that she would use the gun to "blow the brains out" of members of the judge's family. This violation of law was held also to be a violation of Canon 2A, and was in itself sufficient grounds for removal. *Matter of Duncan*, 541 S.W.2d 564 (Mo.1976).

Consider *In re Conduct of Roth*, 293 Or. 179, 645 P.2d 1064 (1982) (per curiam). In *Roth*, a judge discovered his estranged wife together with Allen, a male friend, in a parked car. The judge proceeded to hit the car with his own car, thereby injuring Allen. The court in *Roth* relied on the "compliance with the law" language found in Canon 2A in censuring the judge. The judge argued that there must be a prior conviction before a judge can be disciplined for not "complying with the law." The court, however, held that no prior conviction was necessary because the court could determine for itself whether the judge had committed a crime, using the "clear and convincing evidence" standard of proof. Thus, although the judge had not been convicted of any crime, sufficient evidence existed for the court to determine that the judge did not comply with the law.

4. Independence of Judgment

Canon 2B provides that *a judge should not allow family, social, political, or other relationships to influence the judge's judicial conduct or judgment.*

See *Cuyahoga County Board of Mental Retardation v. Association of Cuyahoga County Teachers of Trainable Retarded*, 47 Ohio App.2d 28, 351 N.E.2d 777

(1975) (judge required, under Canons 2B and 3E(1)(d)(i) of the 1990 Code [that is, Canon 3C(1)(d)(i) of the 1972 Code], to disqualify himself where his brother was a member of the Board of Mental Retardation, a party to the proceedings). See also, *Matter of Del Rio*, 400 Mich. 665, 256 N.W.2d 727 (1977), appeal dismissed, 434 U.S. 1029, 98 S.Ct. 759, 54 L.Ed.2d 777 (1978) (judge demonstrates improper influence when he fixes a ticket for a friend).

The 1990 Code added the reference to "political" relationships to highlight the need for judges to be immune to influence by political relationships. *ABA's Standing Committee Report on 1990 Code, Legislative Draft* 9 (1990).

A judge should also not allow "other relationships to influence his judicial conduct or judgment." This principle prohibited a judge from giving legal advice to a person outside of the courtroom where that person later brought suit based on the judge's advice and the case came before the same judge. *Scogin v. State*, 138 Ga.App. 859, 227 S.E.2d 780 (1976).

Note: Although not discussed by the court, this conduct also may have violated Canon 4G's prohibition against a judge practicing law, discussed below.

However, a judge may provide a pro se litigant with a legal memorandum explaining procedural requirements, provided the other party also receives the memorandum. ABA Informal Opinion 1311 (March 11, 1975). This Informal Opinion implies that if both parties were represented by counsel, then offering the memorandum to one party would be unnecessary and would probably demonstrate partiality.

5.   Preserving the Prestige of Office

A judge shall not lend the prestige of judicial office to advance her private interests or the private interests of another person, nor should she convey the appearance that others are in a special position to influence her.

An ABA Informal Opinion forbids a full time judge from being an honorary director of a bank, even though he has only advisory powers and no power to vote. ABA Informal Opinion 1385 (Feb. 17, 1977). The situation conveyed the impression that others are in a position of influence and lent the prestige of the judicial office to the advancement of the private ventures. This Informal Opinion emphasizes that even the *appearance* of lending prestige is a violation of Canon 2. The propriety of a judge as an officer or director of a business is more fully discussed *infra,* in examining Canon 4D(1)(a) of the 1990 Code [which is Canon 5C of the 1972 Code, on which this Opinion also relied].

A judge conveys the impression that others are in a position to influence him when the judge fixes traffic tickets at the request of a police chief, even though the judge has good intentions and wants to alleviate a heavy court calendar. *Matter of Holder,* 74 N.J. 581, 379 A.2d 220 (1977).

A judge who leaves the bench and returns to the private practice of law may not continue to use the title, "judge" or "The Honorable." Nor should he or his staff answer the phone by saying, "Judge X's office." He should not encourage others to refer to him as "Judge X." ABA Formal Opinion 95–391 (April 24, 1995).

Examples: Judge who writes a letter on judicial stationery to the City Council complaining about a proposal to widen the street in front of Judge's house acted improperly because he used judicial letterhead for his personal business. Canon 2B, Comment 1.

Judge #1 writes a letter to Judge #2, who is sentencing a former business associate of Judge #1. Judge #1 urges Judge #2 to take into account the former business associate's ill health. Judge #1 has acted improperly because he *initiated* the communication. Canon 2B, Comment 3. Judge #1, however, may reply to a formal request from Judge #2.

A part-time judge should be held to violate this standard where—in a jurisdiction where the judge is permitted to practice law—the judge has his private law office receptionist answer his telephone with: "Judge X's office, may I help you?" ABA Informal Opinion 1473 (July 20, 1981).

6. The Judge as Witness

(a) Testifying as to Factual Matters

Some people may argue that a judge lends his prestige to advance the interests of others when he testifies as a witness on behalf of one party. The judge, of course, is not presiding, but the fact finder, knowing that the witness is also a judge, may feel the judge should know the best position in a given case because of the authority and legal knowledge associated with the judicial office. On the other hand, the judicial office should not excuse the judge from offering eyewitness or other factual information, any more than the prestige of a Bishop would immunize the holder of that office from offering relevant factual testimony.

Thus a *judge may testify as an eyewitness.* In one case, the judge who was to preside over a criminal matter was approached by an attorney regarding the timing of the trial. The attorney claimed that at this ex parte meeting he spoke only of the *timing* of the trial, and did not state any concern for the *outcome* of the trial. The judge said that he had cautioned the attorney not to talk about any of his assigned cases, but that nonetheless the attorney talked not only about the timing of the case but his interest in the outcome. The judge then wrote to the parties of his meeting and recused himself. At the trial, to establish that this attorney (whom defendants called as a witness) had an interest in the case, the new presiding judge allowed the Government to call the former presiding judge to testify as to his version of the meeting in order to attack the credibility of the other witness. *United States v. Frankenthal*, 582 F.2d 1102 (7th Cir.1978).

Frankenthal explicitly declined to adopt any rule that a judge who is *not* presiding in a case may never testify in a criminal case. There is no federal rule generally exempting a nonpresiding judge from the normal obligation to respond as a witness when he has information material to a criminal or civil proceeding. *Dennis v. Sparks*, 449 U.S. 24, 101 S.Ct. 183, 66 L.Ed.2d 185 (1980). This principle is also generally true in the state courts. See 97 C.J.S., Witnesses § 16. A nonpresiding judge does not violate any Canon of Judicial Conduct by testifying as to factual matters.

Note: Rule 605 of the Federal Rules of Evidence prohibits a *presiding* judge from testifying at the trial.

(b) Testifying as a Character Witness
Canon 2 prohibits a judge from "voluntarily" testifying as a character witness. The judge shall not exploit the dignity and prestige of judicial office by testifying voluntarily as a character witness. On the other hand, a judge does not have any privilege to refuse to testify if a party has officially subpoenaed him.

If a party wishes a judge to testify as a character witness, the party must subpoena the judge. The judge then must obey the subpoena. If the party asks the judge to appear voluntarily as a character witness, the judge must refuse.

A judge, however, may ask to be subpoenaed. *United States v. Callahan*, 588 F.2d 1078 (5th Cir.1979), cert. denied, 444 U.S. 826, 100 S.Ct. 49, 62 L.Ed.2d 33 (1979). In that case, the defendant's attorney called a judge as a character witness in a prosecution for tax evasion. The attorney subpoenaed the judge, but the district court questioned the purpose of the subpoena. The trial court claimed that if the judge/witness was really a voluntary witness, and the subpoena was a mere technical strategy to comply with the Code, then the judge might still violate the Code by being in effect a "voluntary" character witness. The district court allowed the judge to decide for himself whether he would testify, and the following day the judge/witness refused to testify.

On appeal the circuit court concluded that the district court was in error. The trial court had no power to bar the judge/witness from testifying under a legally valid subpoena, even if the judge/witness, in order to comply with the rule, had asked for the subpoena. The Fifth Circuit, however, went on to hold that the error in this case was harmless because the witness had (the court claimed) himself decided not to testify after having heard the trial judge's gratuitous and erroneous lecture on the Judicial Code.

The Fifth Circuit's conclusion in *Callahan*, that the district court erred, is sound because the Code specifically bars only voluntary, i.e., nonsubpoenaed, testimony. If a subpoena is issued, then the testimony is no longer voluntary. Any other result would open to question all character witness testimony by a judge and would erode the Code's policy of *permitting* testimony by judicial witnesses who are subject to subpoena. The Commentary to this section explicitly states that the judge may "testify when properly summoned." Canon 2B, Comment 5. This section offers no privilege against testifying. Any other rule would permit the judge to create an immunity merely by stating that the summons was "welcomed." On the other hand, Comment 5 of Canon 2B adds an ambiguous sentence that did not exist in the 1972 Code: "Except in unusual circumstances where the demands of justice require, a judge should discourage a party from requiring the judge to testify as a character witness."

7. Membership in Organizations That Practice Invidious Discrimination

Canon 2C mandates that a "judge shall not hold membership in any organization that practices invidious discrimination on the basis of race, sex, religion or national origin."

In August of 1984 the ABA added a Comment to Canon 2 prohibiting the judge from holding membership in a group that *invidiously* discriminates. In the 1990 Code the ABA moved this prohibition into the black letter standard. Notice that Canon 2C uses the term, "shall."

This issue has generated a lot of controversy over the years. Some judges have complained that they should not be second class citizens. The Model Rules of Professional Conduct, after all, place no such restriction on lawyers. On the other hand, judges (unlike lawyers) are state employees who decide cases, including civil rights issues, and, as Comment 1 to Canon 2C explains, the judge's membership in discriminatory organizations creates perceptions of impartiality. Rotunda, *Racist Speech and Attorney Discipline,* 6 The Professional Lawyer 1 (A.B.A., No. 6, 1995).

Comment 1 recognizes that it may be difficult to decide if an organization practices "invidious" discrimination, because the mere fact that no member of a minority race is a member of a club does not necessarily mean that the club discriminates on the basis of race. The issue is whether the organization "arbitrarily excludes" members based on the forbidden characteristics. The drafters specifically rejected the alternative of leaving "to each individual's judge's conscience the determination of whether an organization practices invidious discrimination." *ABA's Standing Committee Report on the 1990 Code, Legislative Draft* 5 (1990).

An organization may discriminate on a basis relating to race, sex, religion, or national origin, but that such discrimination is not necessarily "invidious." In that case, Canon 2C does not prohibit membership in such groups. For example, the judge may join a group promoting ethnic or cultural values, such as the "Sons of Italy." Canon 2C, Comment 2 also explains that it is inapplicable to groups whose membership limitations could not be constitutionally proscribed.

Example: Judge belongs to a church as well as to a church-related fraternal organization. Membership in both organizations is limited to those who are church members. Judge has not violated Canon 2C's prohibition against discrimination on the basis of religion, because the organizations are "dedicated to the preservations of religious, ethnic or cultural values of legitimate common interest to its members. . . . " Canon 2C, Comment 1.

Canon 2C limits its scope to invidious discrimination on the basis of race, sex, religion, or national origin, because these have received special protection in the constitutional case law. *ABA's Standing Committee Report on 1990 Code, Legislative Draft* 14 (1990). However, if the law of the judge's jurisdiction prohibits discrimination on another basis, for example, sexual preference, if the judge violates that law the judge "also violates Canon 2 and Section 2A and gives the appearance of impropriety." Canon 2C, Comment 2.

Example: Judge belongs to an organization that practices invidious discrimination on the basis of sexual preference. The jurisdiction has no law prohibiting such discrimination. Judge has not violated Canon 2C. If the jurisdiction banned such discrimination, Judge would be violating Canon 2 and Canon 2A.

If the judge is not a member of an invidiously discriminatory club, the judge is still subject to discipline, if he or she regularly uses such a club, or arranges for meeting there. The judge's conduct does not violate Canon 2C, but it violates Canon 2 ("appearance of impropriety") and Canon 2A ("diminishes public confidence in the integrity and impartiality of the judiciary"). Canon 2C, Comment 3.

Comment 2 to Canon 2C also states that a judge who publicly manifests a "knowing approval of invidious discrimination" violates Canon 2 and 2A.

Note: To the extent that this Comment seeks to discipline a judge for what he or she *says* as opposed to what he or she *does*, it raises free speech problems, particularly when the judge's comments are made while not on the bench. As one noted judge has remarked: a judge's off-bench comments should deserve full First Amendment protection even if the remarks are "discourteous, offensive, vile, insulting, degrading, humiliating, ill-mannered and boorish." Mosk, *Judges Have First Amendment Rights*, 2 Calif. Lawyer 30, 76 (No. 9, Oct. 1982). See also, Westin, *Out–of–Court Commentary by U.S. Supreme Court Justices, 1790–1962: Of Free Speech and Judicial Lockjaw*, 62 Colum.L.Rev. 633 (1961).

Time Limits. When a judge first learns that he or she belongs to a club that engages in invidious discrimination under Canon 2C (or if the judge's participation is prohibited by Canons 2 and 2A) the judge should either resign, or take "immediate efforts" to have the group stop discriminating. While the judge is engaged in this effort, he or she *must* suspend participation in the club. If the club has not stopped its invidious discrimination within one year after the judge first learned of its practices, the judge must then resign "immediately." Canon 2C, Comment 3.

III. Conduct in the Courtroom

Canon 3 of the Code of Judicial Conduct provides that a judge shall perform the duties of the judicial office impartially and diligently.

A. Defining "Judicial Duties"

Canon 3A declares that a judge's "judicial duties" take precedence over *all* the judge's other activities. This declaration is significant in light of the nonjudicial duties permitted by Canon 4 (governing extra-judicial duties), discussed below. The judge must always be aware that her nonjudicial duties, whether or not specifically authorized by Canon 4, are subordinate to her judicial duties.

The 1990 Code drafters based this section (with minor changes) on the 1972 Code. The task of defining "judicial duties" proved illusive to the 1972 Code's drafters. See *Reporter's Notes [1972]* at 50–51. "Judicial duties" obviously includes the traditional adjudicative duties such as presiding in court. It might also include other duties that are not adjudicative but nevertheless essential to an efficient judicial system. Such duties could include administrative duties or appointing members of local boards or agencies. The ABA decided to define "judicial duties" as "all the duties of . . . office prescribed by law." This definition includes duties provided by constitution, statute, rule, regulation, or common law. "If the activity is one that is prescribed in a judge's jurisdiction as a duty of the judicial office, it is a judicial duty for the purposes of the *Code*." Id.

B. Adjudicative Responsibilities

1. Affirmative Duty to Hear Cases

Canon 3B(1) is new in the 1990 Code. It provides that a judge has an affirmative duty to hear a case ("shall hear and decide"), *unless* the judge is required to be disqualified ("except those [matters] in which disqualification is required"). Thus it should be improper for a judge, out of an abundance of caution, always to grant a party's motion seeking the judge's disqualification, when disqualification is not really required. (If Canon 3E, "Disqualification," discussed below, requires disqualification, then, of course the judge must disqualify herself.) The drafters added Canon 3B(1) "to emphasize *the judicial duty to sit* and to minimize potential abuse of the disqualification process." *ABA's Standing Committee on 1990 Code, Legislative Draft* 15 (1990).(emphasis added) *Public policy forbids a judge to disqualify himself for frivolous reasons, because unnecessary disqualifications delay the proceedings, overburden other judges, and encourage improper judge-shopping.*

Prior to the 1974 amendment to 28 U.S.C.A. § 455, federal courts generally held that a judge had a "duty to sit" in cases where there was no technical violation of the disqualification statute, although there may have been a "question" of impartiality. The amended section 455 modifies the "duty to sit" rule by requiring disqualification if there is a *reasonable* question as to the judge's impartiality. The test is objective: would a "reasonable person" knowing all the circumstances come to the conclusion that the judge's "impartiality might reasonably be questioned." Thus, judges still should *not* disqualify themselves merely to avoid difficult or controversial cases. *See* e.g., H.R. Rep.No.1453, 93d Cong., 2d Sess. 5 (1974).

2. Faithful to the Law, Maintaining Professional Competence, and Unswayed by Fear of Criticism

Faithful to the Law. Canon 3B(2) places three main duties on judges. First, it states that a judge should be "faithful to the law." (The "law" is defined broadly in Terminology 11.) This phrase reminds judges that they are part of a system that places limits and obligations on them.

Matter of Hague, 412 Mich. 532, 315 N.W.2d 524 (1982) discussed those limits. A trial judge had discussed several complaints filed under the city's firearm control ordinance. The judge, in dismissing the complaints, held the firearm control ordinance unconstitutional on the basis of the state's preemption doctrine. These dismissals were then reversed on appeal. The trial judge thereafter dismissed similar complaints, again holding the firearm control ordinance unconstitutional; this time he claimed to base his decisions on the Second Amendment to the United States Constitution. Again, his dismissals were reversed on appeal. Undaunted by the appellate court, the judge continued to dismiss similar complaints using the same rationales that the appellate court had consistently rejected in the previous cases. For this conduct, and other alleged violations of the Judicial Code, the state's disciplinary tribunal recommended that the judge be suspended from office for 60 days without pay.

The state supreme court accepted the recommendation. As to the dismissals of the firearm control complaints, the court remarked that failure to follow stare decisis is not per se judicial misconduct. The court noted, however, that a judge must be "faithful to the law" as required by Canon 3B(2), and cannot impose his personal view of an issue simply to thwart the law clearly and repeatedly announced by an appellate court.

The conduct in this case presented an easy fact situation for the supreme court. The trial judge had publicly argued that the appellate court did not make the law in the state and that he did not have to follow any appellate decision. Judges do not necessarily violate Canon 3B(2) merely by deciding cases contrary to appellate decisions. The Michigan Supreme Court emphasized that the dismissals involved in *Hague* were not the result of reasoned judgment, but rather the product of personal prejudices. If the judge frames his decision in the context of reasoned decision making, a decision contrary to the apparent state of the law should not violate the "faithful to the law" standard of Canon 3B(2).

The Reporter's Notes to the 1972 Code offer another example of the limits and obligations placed upon judges under Canon 3B(2) of the 1990 Code [Canon 3A(1) of the 1972 Code]. The ABA Committee drafting the Judicial Code had received complaints that some judges did not uphold the attorney-client relationship between attorneys and their indigent clients, and that the judges applied different substantive legal standards to indigent litigants than those applied to nonindigent litigants. The ABA Committee decided not to define a specific standard to address this problem, believing that the phrase "faithful to the law" means that, whatever the standard involved, it should be administered the same, whether the litigant is indigent or not. *Reporter's Notes [1972]* at 51. The

ABA's conclusion gained judicial recognition in *Matter of Bennett*, 403 Mich. 178, 267 N.W.2d 914 (1978), where the Court held that a judge violated Canon 3 when he improperly sought to terminate the appointment of public defenders and appointed substitute counsel in their places. The terminations were improper because the judge interfered with the attorney-client relationship by cutting off the indigent defendants from their counsel without request or explanation. In addition, the terminations were "further evidence of a lack of judicial temperament. It gave the appearance not of a judiciously reasoned decision, but rather of an arbitrary exercise of judicial power." 267 N.W.2d at 921.

Maintain Professional Competence. Canon 3B(2) also states that a judge should maintain professional competence in the law. This aspiration encourages judges to keep abreast of recent developments and changes in the law. In full compliance with the spirit of the Judicial Code, the Board of Governors of the New Hampshire Judges Association relied on this Canon in adopting a resolution requiring judges to attend a minimum of one judicial education conference each calendar year, unless excused for good cause. *In re Proposed Rule Relating to Continuing Education for District and Municipal Court Judges*, 115 N.H. 547, 345 A.2d 394 (1975).

"Unswayed by Partisan Interests, Public Clamor, or Fear of Criticism." Canon 3B(2)'s statement that a judge should be unswayed by partisan interests, public clamor, or fear of criticism reemphasizes the requirement of judicial independence earlier articulated in Canon 1, discussed above.

3. Courtroom Decorum

Canon 3B(3) requires a judge to maintain order and decorum in the courtroom. Thus a judge violated Canon 3B(3) when he held criminal arraignments in his chambers in circumstances where the procedures created security problems, crowded the courtroom, and were therefore inconsistent with the proper conduct of the court. The judge was censured for this violation and other violations of the Code. *In re Dwyer*, 223 Kan. 72, 572 P.2d 898 (1977).

In another case, the "maintaining order and decorum" standard justified a judge ordering the defendant to be quiet when the defendant was conversing with his attorney in a loud voice that could be heard by others in the courtroom. *State v. Lovelace*, 227 Kan. 348, 607 P.2d 49 (1980).

The defendant in that case asserted on appeal that the judge's comments prejudiced the jury. The appellate court did not agree, citing Canon 3B(3) as authority justifying the judge's actions.

Canon 3B(3) also grants judges the power to preserve or restore order in the courtroom by temporarily ejecting disruptive and disorderly persons, including attorneys. *Matter of Hague,* 412 Mich. 532, 315 N.W.2d 524 (1982). A judge may not, however, have attorneys removed from the courtroom merely because of a professional or personal disagreement with the attorney.

4. Judicial Patience and Temperament

Although the Code requires judges to maintain order and decorum in court proceedings, judges must balance this duty with Canon 3B(4), which provides that a judge "shall be patient, dignified, and courteous to litigants, jurors, witnesses, lawyers, and others with whom the judge deals in his official capacity." However, the duty to hear proceedings with patience "is not inconsistent with the duty to dispose promptly of the business of the court." Canon 3B, Comment 1; Canon 3B(8). This Canon also requires the judge to require similar conduct of the lawyers and of staff and others subject to the judge's direction and control.

A proper judicial temperament is probably one of the most, if not the most, important qualities of a judge. That rare breed of lawyer, the trial litigator, often expresses admiration for those judges who by inclination or careful self-control exhibit the proper judicial character, who treat all parties with patience and with fairness, and who handle the case load with reasonable dispatch. See, Rotunda, *Remembering Judge Walter R. Mansfield,* 53 Brooklyn L.Rev. 271 (1987).

The "patience and dignity" standard of Canon 3B(4) speaks in broad and ambiguous terms not susceptible to precise definition. The following are examples of behavior that courts have found violative of Canon 3B(4).

Matter of Ross, 428 A.2d 858 (Me.1981) (per curiam) involved a judge who used abusive and vulgar language against persons appearing before him. For example, in one such case, the judge told a defendant, "[T]he Court could really be a 'dink,' "and, "Young man, you will remember that the likes of you I chew up and spit out before breakfast, and I never have breakfast until 8:00 o'clock at night." The court said that intemperate language is on occasion understandable, but vile, obscene, and abusive language is inexcusable. The judge was suspended for 90 days without pay.

In re Rome, 218 Kan. 198, 542 P.2d 676 (1975) involved a judge who granted a convicted prostitute two years probation. In granting probation, the judge wrote a humorous opinion in poetic verse. The local newspaper reprinted the opinion, and the prostitute became the primary topic of conversation around town. Although neither the prostitute nor her parents complained, the judge was censured by the disciplinary commission. The court upheld the censure, not because the opinion was written in verse, but because the prostitute was portrayed in a "ludicrous or comical situation."

Note: The judge contended that the First Amendment protected his conduct. The state supreme court held that the judge's right to free speech was limited by the Code of Judicial Conduct, and First Amendment rights do not exempt a judge from discipline for proven judicial misconduct. *See, also, Halleck v. Berliner,* 427 F.Supp. 1225, 1241 (D.D.C.1977) ("The need for public confidence in and respect for the judiciary requires some reasonable limits on the freedom of a judge to say what he pleases from the bench . . . "). On the other hand, other judges, without being subjected to discipline, have written opinions in verse that appear to make light of someone's problems. E.g., *Fisher v. Lowe,* 122 Mich.App. 418, 333 N.W.2d 67 (1983) (opinion and West headnotes in verse).

In re Jordan, 290 Or. 303, 314, 622 P.2d 297, 308 (1981). At the defendant's sentencing, the judge told the defendant, "I know why you won't tell me why you've been drinking. It's because you're chicken shit." The judge was removed from office for this remark and other violations of the Code.

Canon 3B(4) also states that a judge should require his staff, court officials, and others subject to his discretion and control to conform to the same standards of patience and dignity required of the judge.

This requirement does not mean, however, that the judge must be the "keeper" of his staff or attorneys appearing in his courtroom. A judge does not violate Canon 3A(3) if his staff is rude or undignified toward others *if* the judge does not have knowledge of such instances of rudeness; if he had knowledge, he is not liable if he acted reasonably in trying to correct the problem, even though his efforts were to no avail. *Matter of Kohn,* 568 S.W.2d 255 (Mo.1978).

Judges can help fulfill their responsibilities to require lawyers and staff under their jurisdiction to refrain from sexual harassment by being good role models themselves. Comment 2 to Canon 3B(4) explains that the judge personally "must refrain from speech, gestures or other conduct that could reasonably be perceived as sexual harassment. . . . " Judges engaged in sexist behavior have been disciplined in such circumstances.

Matter of Del Rio, 400 Mich. 665, 256 N.W.2d 727 (1977), appeal dismissed, 434 U.S. 1029, 98 S.Ct. 759, 54 L.Ed.2d 777 (1978). The judge, who was suspended for five years without pay for his behavior, constantly subjected attorneys, spectators, litigants, and witnesses appearing before him to discourtesy, harassment, unjust criticism, and abuse. In one bench trial, the judge persisted in talking on the telephone during critical testimony from the complainant and another witness. When the prosecutor requested the judge's attention, the judge ordered him into chambers where he gave the prosecutor an insulting tongue-lashing. The judge also boasted about his sex life to female attorneys, and asked them for dates. When the attorneys refused, they were often treated with disdain when later appearing professionally before the judge. The same judge had ordered an 11–year–old youngster to be locked up alone for one half hour in the "bullpen" for causing a disturbance in the courtroom during a field trip.

The Illinois Courts Commission reprimanded a judge for disparaging remarks directed to three women defense lawyers. He told one pregnant lawyer, for example, that "if your husband had kept his hands in his pockets, you would not be in the condition you are in." He told another, "Ladies should not be lawyers." *In re Circuit Judge Arthur J. Cieslik, 2 Ill. Courts Commission* 111 (1987). See, Angel, *Sexual Harassment by Judges,* 45 U.Miami L.Rev. 817 (1991).

Geiler v. Commission on Judicial Qualifications, 10 Cal.3d 270, 110 Cal.Rptr. 201, 515 P.2d 1 (1973), *cert. denied,* 417 U.S. 932, 94 S.Ct. 2643, 41 L.Ed.2d 235 (1974) removed the judge for "willful misconduct," and conduct "prejudicial to the administration of justice." The judge, among other things, approached the court commissioner from behind in a public corridor and grabbed his testicles, made lustful references to female clerks, used vulgar and profane language in conversations with clerks, and invited two female attorneys into his chambers where he discussed the salacious nature of evidence in several rape cases, using profane terms to describe bodily functions.

5. Performing Judicial Duties Without Bias or Prejudice

Canon 3B(5) requires the judge to perform judicial duties "without bias or prejudice." While performing judicial duties, the judge, by words or conduct "shall not" display "bias or prejudice based upon race, sex, religion, national origin, disability, age, sexual orientation or socioeconomic status, and shall not permit staff, court officials and others subject to the judge's direction and control to do so."

Notice that this litany of the types of bias that the judge must guard against is broader than the list in Canon 2C. However, Canon 2C governs the off-bench behavior, *i.e.,* the types of organizations that the judge must not join. Canon 3B(5) governs the judge "in the performance of judicial duties." Because the judge must perform these duties impartially and fairly, any manifestation of bias "impairs the fairness of the proceeding and brings the judiciary into disrepute." Canon 3B(5), Comment 1. The judge must also guard against facial expression and body language that might communicate an appearance of bias.

6. Requiring Lawyers Before the Judge to Refrain From Manifesting Improper Bias

Canon 3B(6) provides that the judge "shall require lawyers in proceedings before the judge to refrain from manifesting by words or conduct, bias or prejudice based upon race, sex, religion, national origin, disability, age, sexual orientation or socio-economic status, against parties, witnesses, counsel or others." However, this section does not preclude "legitimate advocacy" when those factors are at issue.

Lawyers are officers of the court, and so judges have the power—and Canon 3B(6) gives judges the duty—to prevent attorneys from manifesting improper prejudice. The judge's duty to "require" means that the judge must exercise "reasonable direction and control over the conduct of those persons subject to the judge's direction and control." Terminology 20.

7. Avoidance of Ex Parte Communications

(a) Right to Be Heard

Canon 3B(7) requires a judge to accord every person "who has a legal interest in a proceeding" (or that person's lawyer) full right to be heard according to law. Thus a judge violates Canon 3B(7) when he denies the state an opportunity to be heard in a criminal case. In

Matter of Edens, 290 N.C. 299, 226 S.E.2d 5 (1976), the defendant's guilty plea was not given in open court in the presence of the assistant district attorney or prosecuting officer; the guilty plea was accepted without prior notice to the assistant district attorney; and the judge signed the judgment in the court clerk's office, out of the presence of (and without notice to) the assistant district attorney.

Note: If Canon 3(B)(7) requires the presence of, or notice to, a party, if that party is represented by counsel, it is counsel who is to be present or to whom notice shall be given. Rule 3B(7), Comment 3.

A judge violates Canon 3B(7) if he imposes sentence without affording the defendant the hearing to which he is entitled by law. *Matter of Ross,* 428 A.2d 858 (Me.1981). See also *In re Conduct of Jordan,* 290 Or. 669, 672, 624 P.2d 1074, 1076 (1981) (per curiam) (judge disciplined because, inter alia, he began criminal trial and entered a finding of "guilty" in the absence of defendant).

Notes: This ethical requirement is supported by the due process requirement embodied in the United States Constitution.

Although ex parte communications are generally not permitted, Canon 3B(7)(e) permits ex parte communications that are "expressly authorized by law." Many states, for example, have enacted domestic abuse statutes, authorizing ex parte protective orders for the protection of the petitioners.

(b) Ex Parte Communications

(i) Introduction

Canon 3B(7) prohibits a judge from initiating or considering ex parte communications concerning a pending or impending proceeding unless the communication is about: scheduling, or for administrative purposes, or emergencies that do not deal with substantive issues, and the judge promptly notifies all the other parties, Canon 3B(7)(a) & (a)(i), (a)(ii); or, falls within the "disinterested expert on the law" exception, Canon 3B(7)(b), as discussed *infra;* or, is with court personnel, Canon 3B(7)(c), discussed *infra;* or, the parties consent to the judge conferring separately in an effort to mediate or settle the case, Canon

3B(7)(d), discussed *infra;* or is authorized by law, Canon 3B(7)(e), discussed *supra. In re Conduct of Jordan,* 290 Or. 669, 671, 624 P.2d 1074, 1075 (1981) (per curiam) (judge disciplined when—at the conclusion of a preliminary hearing—he talked privately to a potential witness about her testimony at a future trial). Cf. Canon 3B(7), Comment 6 (judge must not independently investigate facts in a case).

> *Note:* The "impending proceeding" limitation intended to discourage forum shopping by a party or lawyer who tries to assess the judge's predilections on a particular fact situation before a claim is filed. See *Reporter's Notes [1972]* at 54.

Even if the ex parte communication does not concern a pending proceeding, the judge should be aware that if a proceeding related to the communication subsequently comes before her, that earlier communication may require her disqualification under Canon 3E(1) because her "impartiality might reasonably be questioned." Thus, recusal was required when a person merely explained her legal problem to the judge, he gave advice, and that case later came before him. *Scogin v. State,* 138 Ga.App. 859, 227 S.E.2d 780 (1976).

A judge clearly violates the ex parte communication prohibition if he considers ex parte communications on substantive matters [Canon 3B(7)(a)] from a party or lawyer in a pending proceeding, or initiates such communications. *See In re Dekle,* 308 So.2d 5 (Fla.1975) (per curiam). In that case, after oral argument before the state supreme court, the attorney for one party handed Justice Dekle a legal memorandum. Dekle erroneously thought the memorandum was a duly filed amicus submission because the attorney mentioned that he had already presented the memo to another justice for use in preparing the majority opinion. When the justice originally assigned to write the majority opinion decided to join the dissent, Justice Dekle was assigned to write for the majority. In drafting his opinion, he relied on the memorandum that had not been filed. The use of the memorandum violated Canon 3B(7)(a) even though Justice Dekle thought, erroneously, that the memo had been duly filed. The court found that Dekle's conclusion was not reasonable.

Therefore, judging Dekle by objective and not subjective intent, the court held that the misconduct warranted judicial discipline. The court, in effect, concluded that Justice Dekle should have known the memo was beyond his power to consider. Even if there is no actual harm to any party, a judge who intentionally commits an act that he knew or should have known was beyond his power is guilty of misconduct. The court reprimanded the judge, adding in dicta that removal would be proper if there was a clear showing of corrupt motive or a deliberate wrong.

One court has even held that a judge violates Canon 3B(7) if he attends a public meeting when he should have known that its purpose was to raise money for criminal defendants whose cases were then pending before the superior court where the judge sat, but *not* before this particular judge, who was the chief judge. *Matter of Bonin,* 375 Mass. 680, 378 N.E.2d 669 (1978). The public meeting included a lecture by Gore Vidal on "Sex and Politics in Massachusetts." The defendants in the criminal case were indicted for alleged sexual acts between men and boys. The court argued that the judge, by attending the meeting, exposed himself to ex parte statements and arguments on matters pending before his court.

Note: Judges are human beings who cannot (and need not) divorce themselves from the real world, public discussions, newspapers, and the like. Canon 4A, Comment 1. The Massachusetts Court acknowledged that normally "any judge would be entirely free to attend a public lecture about sex and politics whether or not sponsored by a 'gay' group." Yet the Court said that Judge Bonin's actions were different because the lecture concerned cases pending in the Superior Court where he was chief justice. The Massachusetts Court showed little sensitivity to First Amendment concerns. Judge Bonin had not been assigned to hear the case and would make no ruling regarding it, so the reference to hearing "one sided argumentation" was not too relevant. When he was on the bench, he made no comment concerning the case. And when he was off the bench (when he was at the large meeting), he also made no remarks or statements about the case. Some people might infer from Bonin's attendance at the meeting that he supported the cause, but it was "at least equally likely that it would be interpreted as being motivated by curiosity or interest in the remarks of the well-known featured speaker." Steven Lubet, *Beyond Reproach: Ethical Restrictions on the Extrajudicial Activities of State and Federal Judges* 44 (1984).

Contrast an incident involving Justice Benjamin N. Cardozo. Shortly *before* he authored the leading tort decision of *Palsgraf v. Long Island R.R. Co.,* 248 N.Y. 339, 162 N.E. 99 (1928), the facts of that case were used as the focus for a debate at a meeting of the American Law Institute. Cardozo attended the meeting and listened to the discussion on unforeseeable plaintiffs, but he did not vote on the question. By a single vote, and after a "long and lively debate," the American Law Institute voted that there should be no liability. Cardozo was obviously never reprimanded for attending the ALI discussion. See John T. Noonan, Jr., *Persons and Masks of the Law: Cardozo, Holmes, Jefferson, and Wythe as Makers of the Masks* 147–49 (1976).

It is improper for judges to hear new versions of the facts of a case before them, *ex parte*, out of the presence of the lawyers. But judges often hear arguments about the governing law outside of the lawyers' presence, because they are supposed to be looking at principles larger than particular litigants in a particular case. Thus it is perfectly proper for law schools to ask judges to judge moot court cases about issues that may be before them. Judges may also read law review articles arguing about what the law should be.

In *State v. Valencia,* 124 Ariz. 139, 602 P.2d 807 (1979), the trial judge had sentenced the defendant to death but the court reversed because of an ex parte communication between the victim's brother and the trial judge prior to sentencing. The victim's brother told the judge that the family wanted the death penalty imposed. The court reversed even though the judge had not committed himself to a position after his conversation with the victim's brother; the judge merely stated that he had a difficult decision to make and would consider all the facts.

Although the appellate court did not specifically rely on Canon 3B(7) in its holding, it was cited in support of reversal.

(ii) Disinterested Expert Exception

Canon 3B(7)(b) provides: *"A judge may obtain the advice of a disinterested expert on the law applicable to a proceeding before the judge if the judge gives notice to the parties of person consulted and the substance of the advice, and affords the parties reasonable opportunity to respond."* The rule permitting ex parte communications if there is notice to the parties applies only to disinterested experts on the law; a judge cannot absolve any other ex parte communication from impropriety merely by giving notice to the parties and an opportunity for them to respond.

When the judge seeks a disinterested expert on the law, the judge does not need to secure the parties' consent in such circumstances. Nor does the requirement of "notice" mean "prior notice." The judge only need tell the parties the name of the person consulted and the substance of the advice, and give the parties a reasonable opportunity to respond. This exception recognizes both the judge's interest in seeking expert legal advice to help her decide complex questions of law and the interest of the parties in the adversary system.

This rule, by its own terms, only applies to experts *on the law,* not to all experts. See *E.I. du Pont de Nemours & Co. v. Collins,* 432 U.S. 46, 57, 97 S.Ct. 2229, 2235, 53 L.Ed.2d 100, 110 (1977), holding that it was error for the Court of Appeals to employ a Professor of Business Administration to assist the Court in understanding the record in the case. The Professor would give his economic observations and discuss a variety of data and economic observations that could not be examined and tested by the traditional methods of the adversary process. What the lower court did was wrong. The Court did not cite Canon 3B(7)(b).

Unless the rule governing ex parte communications make a specific exception, the restrictions on ex parte communications include communications by persons who are not parties to the proceedings, such as law teachers and other lawyers. Canon 3B(7), Comment 1. Law professors have no special privilege to visit with their former students who have become judges and discuss a case ex parte.

An appropriate and desirable procedure for obtaining the advice of a disinterested expert is to have the expert file an amicus curiae brief. Canon 3B(7), Comment 4. Filing such a brief, however, is not a prerequisite for compliance with the Code. In fact, the *Reporter's Notes [1972]* suggest that the ex parte advice need not even be in writing; the advice could be received in a telephone conversation. See *Reporter's Notes [1972]* at 54.

(iii) Court Personnel Exception

Canon 3B(7)(c) makes clear that this Canon does not preclude a judge from consulting with "court personnel whose function is to aid the judge in carrying out the judge's adjudicative responsibilities or with other judges." Thus, in general a judge may communicate with his law clerks, other judges, and other court personnel who aid him in carrying out his adjudicative responsibilities. It is not necessary for the judge in such cases to give the parties either notice or an opportunity to respond.

ABA Informal Opinion 1346 (Nov. 26, 1975) examines the scope of the phrase "court personnel." The judge wanted to obtain answers to specific criminal law issues through law students working in the law school's legal information center. The Opinion concluded that "court personnel" refers only to immediate employees of the court over whose activities the judge exercises supervision. Therefore, the judges could only obtain and use the answers in a pending proceeding if the judge gave notice to the parties of the person who was consulted and the substance of the advice received, and then afforded the parties a reasonable opportunity to respond.

While Canon 3B(7)(c), broadly authorizes the judge to consult "with other judges," Comment 9 to this Canon advises: "[i]f communication between the trial judge and the appellate court with respect to a proceeding is permitted, a copy of any written communication or the substance of any oral communication should be provided to all parties." This statement is new to the 1990 Code, and it will be interesting to see how this principle will be interpreted in practice, particularly in jurisdictions where appellate and trial judges are in the same building, and often eat and socialize together.

Prior case law recognizes that there must be at least some limitations to communications *on particular cases* between trial and appellate judges. In *Matter of Cunningham,* 57 N.Y.2d 270, 273, 456 N.Y.S.2d 36, 37, 442 N.E.2d 434, 435 (1982) the court censured an appellate judge who wrote two letters to a trial judge that referred to several pending cases by name; the appellate judge, among other things, assured the trial judge that there "is no way I would ever change a sentence that you had imposed. You can do whatever you want to whenever you want to and I'll agree with you . . . I take the position that you know the case and as sentencing judge you can do whatever you damn well please." He also wrote: if "I catch the appeal, I will affirm as always, on a judge's discretion."

Although a judge can converse with his law clerks regarding a pending matter, certain communications are still prohibited under Canon 3B(7), because the "judge must not independently investigate the facts in a case and must consider only the evidence presented." Canon 3B(7), Comment 6. The judge must make reasonable efforts to supervise law clerks and other personnel on the judge's staff. Id., Comment 9.

Price Brothers Co. v. Philadelphia Gear Corp., 629 F.2d 444 (6th Cir.1980), cert. denied, 454 U.S. 1099, 102 S.Ct. 674, 70 L.Ed.2d 641 (1981), illustrates a case where the judge's law clerk became a factual witness. In that case, the trial judge's law clerk visited the plaintiff's manufacturing plant to view some machines alleged to be malfunctioning in breach of the defendant's warranties. The defendant's attorney requested the judge to amend his findings of fact to reflect the visit by the law clerk. The judge refused the request without commenting on whether his clerk actually made the trip. The appellate court reversed and remanded, ordering the district court to consider whether there was any ex parte communication in violation of Canon 3B(7). The trial court was to determine (1) whether the clerk had visited the plant, (2) whether the trip had been at the direction of the judge, (3) whether the clerk had conversations with the plaintiff's employees, (4) whether any observations had been made at the plant, (5) whether the information had been reported to the judge, and (6) when the defense counsel had learned of the trip and whether the defendant had expressly or tacitly approved of the trip.

In *Kennedy v. Great Atlantic and Pacific Tea Co.,* 551 F.2d 593 (5th Cir.1977), the judge's law clerk, without the judge's knowledge, went to the defendant's store after a rainstorm to determine whether the floor was wet at the place the plaintiff alleged that he had fallen. The floor was indeed wet, and when the judge learned of his clerk's discovery, he instructed his clerk to inform the defendant's lawyer to foster a settlement. (Compare, subsection (iv), immediately below, on Settlement Conferences.) The parties did not settle, and at trial the judge informed the plaintiff's lawyer of the clerk's observation. The plaintiff's counsel subsequently called the judge's clerk as a witness, and judgment was rendered in favor of the plaintiff.

The appellate court vacated the judgment because the clerk's visit to the site of the accident was an ex parte "communication" that "infected" the jury, the members of whom must have thought that the clerk's observation had some special importance if the clerk had taken the trouble to visit the property.

(iv) Settlement Conferences

Canon 3B(7)(d) provides that a judge may, "with the consent of the parties, confer separately with the parties and their lawyers in an effort to mediate or settle matters pending before the judge." This section did not have a counterpart in the prior Judicial Code.

This exception to the normal *ex parte* rule does not give the judge *carte blanche* to receive, from one of the parties, evidence about the merits of the case, or tell one of the parties how she will rule in the case if the parties do not settle. Rather, it simply allows the judge to mediate a settlement. It has long been the rule that the judge may not cajole a settlement. *Brooks v. Great Atlantic & Pacific Tea Co.,* 92 F.2d 794, 796 (9th Cir.1937). If the judge's participation in settlement is so extensive that she becomes a witness to important fact issues, she must be disqualified. *Collins v. Dixie Transport, Inc.,* 543 So.2d 160 (Miss.1989).

Unless the client waives his right under Rule 1.6 or DR 4–101 to keep the information confidential, a lawyer may not reveal to a judge the limits of his settlement authority or the lawyer's advice to the client regarding settlement. And the judge, even when participating in pretrial settlement discussions, may not require the lawyer to reveal such information, although she may make an inquiry. If the lawyer, in response, expresses reticence to disclose this information on ethical grounds, the judge should not pursue the inquiry further, and the lawyer must decline to answer, and must not lie to the judge. ABA Formal Opinion 93–370 (Feb. 5, 1993).

8. Prompt Disposition of Business

Canon 3B(8) states that a judge "shall dispose of all judicial matters promptly, efficiently, and fairly." This Canon is the ABA's response to reports of judges who procrastinated in deciding proceedings ripe for decision, judges with heavy dockets who were very irregular in their court appearances, and judges who, by regularly arriving late to court, unreasonably delayed jurors, witnesses, parties, and lawyers. See *Reporters Notes* at 54.

"Prompt disposition" means that the judge must devote "adequate time to judicial duties," and be "punctual in attending court and expeditious in determining matters under submission." The judge must also insist on similar conduct by court officials, litigants, and their lawyers. Canon 3B(8), Comment 2. The duty of prompt disposition of judicial business is not inconsistent with the duty to be patient and deliberate. Canon 3B(4), Comment 1. Rotunda, *Remembering Judge Walter R. Mansfield*, 53 Brooklyn L.Rev. 271, 274–76 (1987).

If a judge fails to conclude matters within a statutorily prescribed time limit, he is not disposing of business promptly, within the meaning of Canon 3B(8). *Matter of Anderson*, 312 Minn. 442, 252 N.W.2d 592 (1977). This Canon is not limited, however, to statutorily prescribed limits, as made clear by the Commentary and *Reporter's Notes [1972]*. What constitutes "adequate" time and being "punctual," or "expeditious," however, are issues resolvable only in the context of a particular proceeding.

9. Public Comments

Under **Canon 3B(9),** a judge shall not, while a proceeding is pending or impending *in any court,* make any public comment that might reasonably be expected to affect its outcome or impair its fairness. In addition, the judge must not make any *nonpublic* comment "that might substantially interfere with a fair trial or hearing." The judge is also obligated to require similar abstention on the part of court personnel subject to his direction and control.

Note: .... "Court personnel" do not include attorneys who are in the proceeding before the judge. Terminology 5. Model Rule 3.6 regulates their conduct. Canon 3B(9), Comment 1.

When the public comment prohibition is applicable, it extends to comments about proceedings in any court, not just proceedings before the judge making the comments.

Canon 3B(9), of course, allows judges to make public statements "in the course of their official duties . . . " and to explain court procedures to the public. However, this provision gives a judge no *carte blanche* authority. A "judge is strictly prohibited from public comment on the merits of a pending case," even though she is "encouraged to explain a pending case in abstract terms." *Matter of Sheffield,* 465 So.2d 350, 355 (Ala.1984). The *Sheffield* court suspended a judge for two months without pay for, among other things, making some comments to a reporter (who had called him in the evening before a hearing) about the merits of a case.

Truth is stranger than fiction. In *State ex rel. Commission on Judicial Qualifications v. Rome,* 229 Kan. 195, 623 P.2d 1307 (1981) (per curiam) the court removed a judge from office for various violations, including writing a memorandum decision that stated as conclusions various factual matters that were being contested in two criminal cases, and then trying to get these statements publicized by hand-delivering a copy of the memorandum to one reporter and mailing other copies to two news stations.

Consistent with the Judicial Code, court personnel may be authorized, pursuant to established guidelines, to release certain information regarding a pending or impending proceeding. See *Reporter's Notes [1972]* at 55–56. Presumably this practice is allowed under the provision allowing judges (and therefore, court personnel) to make "public statements in the course of their official duties," or to explain "for public information the procedures of the court."

In *United States v. Microsoft Corp.,* 253 F.3d 34 (D.C. Cir. 2001), *cert denied,* 534 U.S. 952, 122 S.Ct. 350, 151 L.Ed.2d 264 (2001), the United States and individual states brought antitrust action against the manufacturer of a personal computer operating system and Internet web browser. The trial judge found various violations, but the D.C. Circuit reversed and remanded, vacated the remedies decree, and held that the district judge's ex parte comments to the press while the case was pending required his disqualification on remand. The judge's extra-judicial comments created the appearance that he was not acting impartially, within the meaning of the disqualification statute, and members of public could reasonably question whether the judge's desire for press coverage influenced his judgments.

The court allowed the motion to disqualify the district judge to be considered for the first time on appeal, even though the motion was based on press accounts of the judge's comments about case, rather than on record evidence, because the plaintiffs did not dispute the comments attributed to judge in the press, and did not request an evidentiary hearing. The question was whether the judge's disqualification should be prospective only (disqualification of the judge from participation in any further hearings on the matter), or retroactive.

The D.C. Circuit ordered "disqualification of the District Judge retroactive, but only to the date he entered the order breaking up Microsoft." While the court agreed that the trial judge's conduct "destroyed the appearance of impartiality," Microsoft had not "alleged nor demonstrated that it rose to the level of actual bias or prejudice." The trial judge's comments to the press analogized "Microsoft to Japan at the end of World War II," his other comments, and his "evident efforts to please the press," would "give a reasonable, informed observer cause to question his impartiality in ordering the company split in two." Thus the court disqualified the judge on the remand, vacated the remedies that he imposed, but accepted his findings of fact that Microsoft engaged in illegal monopolization. See, Rotunda, *Judicial Comments on Pending Cases: The Ethical Restrictions and the Sanctions—A Case Study of the Microsoft Litigation*, 2001 U. Ill. L. Rev. 611 (2001).

Judge sued in personal capacity. This section does not apply to a judge who is a litigant in a *personal* capacity. Such a judge is treated like any other litigant, and any comments the judge makes about the case are not made in his capacity as a judge. But this section does apply to judges sued in their official capacity, such as by writ of mandamus. Canon 3B(9), Comment 1.

10. Pledges, promises or commitments.

Canon 3B(10) prohibits judges from making "pledges, promises or commitments that are inconsistent with the impartial performance of the adjudicative duties of the office" with respect to matters that are likely to come before the court. The ABA added this provision in August, 2003 in response to *Republican Party v. White*, 536 U.S. 765, 122 S.Ct. 2528, 153 L.Ed.2d 694 (2002), which invalidated a Minnesota judicial canon that prohibited a "candidate for a judicial office" from "announc[ing] his or her views on disputed legal or political issues" (the "announce clause").

White held that the announce clause both prohibited speech based on its content and burdened a category of speech at the core of the First Amendment–campaign speech about the qualifications of candidates for public office. First, the clause was not narrowly tailored to serve impartiality (or its appearance) in the traditional sense of the word, *i.e.*, as a lack of bias for or against either party to the proceeding, because it does not restrict speech for or against particular parties. It was also "woefully underinclusive" in achieving "impartiality" (or its appearance) in the sense of openmindedness. For example, it did not purport to prevent judges from giving their views on disputed issues in the course writing dissents or concurrences. In addition, "judges often state their views on disputed legal issues outside the context of adjudication—in classes that they conduct, and in books and speeches. Like the ABA Codes of Judicial Conduct, the Minnesota Code not only permits but encourages this." Thus, under the Minnesota judicial ethics rule, a candidate for judicial office may not say "I think it is constitutional for the legislature to prohibit same-sex marriages." However, he may say the very same thing up until the day before he declares himself a candidate, "and may say it repeatedly (until litigation is pending) after he is elected." The judicial ethics rule (adopted by the elected judges) seemed to prohibit the speech of challengers more than it prevented the speech of incumbents. See, Rotunda, *Judicial Campaigns in the Shadow of Republican Party v. White*, 14 The Professional Lawyer 2 (ABA, No. 1, 2002).

11. Media in the Courtroom

When the ABA first published the Judicial Code in 1972, it contained a Canon 3A(7), which was an almost absolute prohibition of the broadcast media in the courtroom. The Canon first stated the general rule that a "judge should prohibit broadcasting, televising, recording, or taking photographs in the courtroom and areas immediately adjacent thereto during sessions of court or recesses between sessions . . . " The Canon then delineated several narrow exceptions. In *Chandler v. Florida,* 449 U.S. 560, 101 S.Ct. 802, 66 L.Ed.2d 740 (1981), the United States Supreme Court held that there is no per se constitutional prohibition against media coverage in the courtroom, and each case must be viewed on its own facts. See generally, 4 R. Rotunda & J. Nowak, *Treatise on Constitutional Law: Substance and Procedure* § 20.25 (West Group, 3d ed. 1999).

In reaction to *Chandler*'s rejection of a per se approach against media in the courtroom, the ABA amended Canon 3A(7) on August 11, 1982. The revised version, like its previous counterpart, begins with a general prohibition of media coverage in the courtroom. However, the revised version contains a more expansive exception to the general prohibition. Rotunda, *Dealing with the Media: Ethical, Constitutional, and Practical Parameters,* 84 Ill.BarJ. 614 (December 1996).

Finally, when the ABA adopted the 1990 Code, it eliminated any reference to the issue of media in the courtroom. The drafters of the 1990 Code explained that they deleted former Canon 3A(7) "because it addresses a matter of court administration, not judicial ethics, which is more appropriately regulated by separate court rules." *ABA's Standing Committee Report on 1990 Code, Legislative Draft* 22 (1990). Rotunda, *Reporting Sensational Trials: Free Press, a Responsible Press, and Cameras in the Courts,* 3 Communications Law and Policy 295 (No. 2, Spring, 1998).

12. Criticism of Jurors

Canon 3B(11) instructs judges not to criticize or commend jurors for their verdict other than in a court order or opinion in a proceeding, but they may express appreciation to jurors for their service to the judicial system and the community.

The purpose of this section is to "protect jurors from improper influence by judges and to preserve the appearance of fairness in judicial decision-making." *ABA's Standing Committee Report on 1990 Code, Legislative Draft* 22 (1990).

13. Judicial Use of Nonpublic Information

Canon 3B(12) provides that judges shall not disclose or use nonpublic information acquired in a judicial capacity for any purpose unrelated to judicial duties.

Nonpublic information is information that, by law, is not available to the public, such as information offered in grand jury proceedings, presentence reports, dependency cases, psychiatric reports, and information sealed by court order, impounded, or communicated *in camera*. Terminology 15.

C. Administrative Responsibilities

1. Sound Judicial Administration

Canon 3C(1) provides that a judge "shall" diligently discharge administrative responsibilities "without bias or prejudice and maintain professional competence in judicial administration. . . . "

Thus, a judge was suspended without pay for one month when he flagrantly and persistently disregarded a local rule requiring judges to compile and file accurate and complete records on pending matters. *Matter of Carstensen*, 316 N.W.2d 889 (Iowa 1982).

A judge does not have to violate administrative rules, however, to violate Canon 3C. A judge also violates Canon 3C(1) if she fails to supervise her staff, infrequently attends court, or fails to maintain court records in a manner that would maintain professional competence and facilitate the performance of administrative responsibilities. *Matter of Briggs*, 595 S.W.2d 270 (Mo.1980). A judge also violates Canon 3C if he charges traffic violators more money to be paid as a fine than the amount officially reported as paid to the county. *In re Anderson*, 412 So.2d 743 (Miss.1982) (judge removed from office). (It is amazing, is it not, what some people try to get away with?)

Canon 3C(1) also provides that a judge "should" cooperate with other judges and court officials in administrating court business. A judge violated this requirement when he refused his administrative superior's order to file weekly and monthly reports of his activities; obstinacy was the only apparent reason for his conduct. *In re McDonough*, 296 N.W.2d 648 (Minn.1979). The judge in *McDonough* also violated Canon 3C(1) by failing to get along with his administrative superior to the extent necessary to carry out judicial duties. The judge apparently accused his superior of lying, making false assumptions, and being grossly ignorant; he also cursed at and was generally disrespectful to his superior.

Canon 3C(2) mandates that judges require their staff and those court officials subject to their control to observe the standards of "fidelity and diligence" that apply to the judge and "to refrain from manifesting bias or prejudice in the performance of their official duties." Canon 3C(2). A judge violated this Canon when he refused to take action against his clerk after learning that the clerk illegally granted a limited driving privilege to her brother-in-law and reduced traffic fines without authority to do so. *Matter of Briggs*, 595 S.W.2d 270 (Mo.1980).

Canon 3C(3) governs judges with supervisory power over other judges. Supervisory judges must take "reasonable measures" to assure that other judges promptly dispose of matters before them and they properly perform their other judicial responsibilities. This section is new to the 1990 Code.

2. Making Appointments

Under Canon 3C(4), a judge shall not make unnecessary appointments to employment positions, and shall appoint impartially, only on the basis of merit, avoiding nepotism and favoritism. Appointees include assigned counsel, referees, commissioners, special masters, receivers, guardians, and personnel such as clerks, secretaries, and bailiffs. It is no defense that the parties to the case consent to the appointment of, for example, the assigned counsel. Canon 3C(4), Comment 1.

A judge violated Canon 3C(4) when he overwhelmingly appointed his friends and political supporters to represent indigent defendants in criminal cases. *Spruance v. Commission on Judicial Qualifications*, 13 Cal.3d 778, 119 Cal.Rptr. 841, 532 P.2d 1209 (1975) (44% of cases appointed to the judge's two friends; the remaining 56% of appointments were received by 22 other attorneys, no one of whom received more than 3 appointments; the judge should have known the proper procedures required in appointing counsel). The problem in *Spruance* was not that the judge appointed people he knew; it was that he did not appoint impartially and on the basis of merit. A judge may properly appoint someone (other than a close relative) whom he knows well, "if the appointment itself is necessary and the person objectively merits the appointment." *ABA's Standing Committee Report on 1990 Code, Legislative Draft* 24 (1990).

Difficult cases arise where a judge appoints someone on the basis of merit, yet there is also evidence of favoritism. A divided court refused to censure a judge who appointed his lover as chief cashier because the appointee was "well qualified for the appointment." *Matter of Dalessandro*, 483 Pa. 431, 397 A.2d 743, 759 (1979) (per curiam).

A judge cannot evade Canon 3C(4) by laundering judicial appointments. *Spector v. State Commission on Judicial Conduct*, 47 N.Y.2d 462, 418 N.Y.S.2d 565, 392 N.E.2d 552 (1979) cited Canon 3C(4) in admonishing a judge who appointed other judges' sons to represent defendants, knowing that those judges would in return appoint his son.

A judge obviously violated Canon 3C(4) where he made sexual relations a condition of employment, terminated one employee for refusing to continue having sex with him, and terminated another employee for refusing to have sex with him. *In re Hammond*, 224 Kan. 745, 585 P.2d 1066 (1978) (judge censured, although he would have been removed if ill health had not already forced his retirement).

A judge also shall not approve compensation beyond the fair value of services rendered. Canon 3B(4). If the compensation is excessive, it is no defense that the parties consent to the award of compensation. Canon 3C(4), Comment 1.

Pay to Play. In 1999, the ABA added a new Canon 3C(5) because of concern about lawyers making political contributions to judges and then judges appointing these lawyers as special masters, guardians, receivers, etc. Lawyers often referred to these contributions as "pay to play," because some lawyers felt that they had to make the contributions in order to be considered for some appointments. See Rotunda, *Competitive Bidding Would End "Pay-to-Play,"* 20 National Law Journal A23 (June 29, 1998).

Canon 3C(5) now provides that judges should not appoint someone to such a position if the judge knows (or learns) that the appointee has contributed more than a certain amount to the judge within a certain period of years. (The rule leaves it up to each jurisdiction to decide what is the time period and what is the amount that triggers the prohibition.) There are a few exceptions for situations where the appearance of impropriety is virtually nonexistent. Thus, the restrictions on the appointment of a political contributor do not apply if the position is substantially uncompensated, or the lawyer is selected by rotation from a list that is compiled without regard to political contributions, or the judge or another presiding judge determines that no other competent lawyer is willing or able to accept the position.

D. Duty to Report Unethical Conduct of Others

Canon 3D governs the judge's disciplinary responsibilities. It is divided into three parts. The first part governs judges reporting judges; the second part governs judges reporting lawyers; and the third part provides that no judges may be subject to civil liability because they have discharged their disciplinary responsibilities, an activity that is "absolutely privileged."

This Canon is intended to be somewhat analogous to the lawyer's duty to report under Rule 8.3 of the Model Rules of Professional Conduct.

Canon 3D(1). A judge who receives information that indicates "a substantial likelihood that another judge" has violated the Judicial Code "*should* take appropriate action." If the judge has "knowledge" that another judge has committed a violation of the Judicial Code and that violation "raises a substantial question" as to the other judge's fitness for office, the judge "*shall* inform the *appropriate authority.*" (emphasis added).

The "*appropriate action* "may include direct communication with the judge or lawyer in question, or other direct action, or reporting a lawyer's misconduct to the "appropriate authority." Canon 3D, Comment 1. The "*appropriate authority*" is the "authority with responsibility for initiation of disciplinary process with respect to the violation to be reported." Terminology 2. "*Knowledge*" means "actual knowledge of the fact in question." A person's knowledge "may be inferred from circumstances." Terminology 10.

Canon 3D(2). This section parallels Canon 3D(1), but it applies to judges reporting lawyers. The judge "should" take "appropriate action" if the judge has "information indicating a substantial likelihood" that the lawyer has violated the state's version of the Model Rules. If the judge has "knowledge" that the lawyer has committed a violation that "raises a substantial question as to the lawyer's honesty, trustworthiness or fitness as a lawyer in other respects," the judge "shall" inform the "appropriate authority."

Although a judge violates the Judicial Code—at least in theory—if she does not report misconduct within the requirements of Canon 3B(3), judges rarely bring violations of the lawyers' or judges' ethical codes to the attention of the proper authorities. Statistics indicate that lay persons file the greatest percentage of disciplinary complaints, not lawyers or other judges.

In light of these statistics, the drafters of the 1990 Judicial Code tried to encourage more reporting. The rule regarding reporting was changed specifically from the 1972 Judicial Code to require judges to report to a disciplinary authority "significant misconduct of lawyers and other judges, thus diminishing the number of instances in which judges take it upon themselves to impose sanctions for professional misconduct without such reporting." *ABA's Standing Committee on 1990 Code, Legislative Draft* 25 (1990). This new rule also encourages judges to take other remedial steps, such as referring, in appropriate cases, a lawyer or judge to a bar-sponsored substance abuse treatment agency. Id.

Canon 3D(3). To encourage reporting, Canon 3D(3) provides that judicial activities under Canon 3D(1) & (2) are "absolutely privileged" and there shall be "no civil action" against the judge for such reporting. Contrast Model Rule 8.3 and DR 1–103(A), neither of which provide any "absolute privilege" for lawyers who report other lawyers or judges.

If a judge refers a lawyer's unethical conduct to the proper disciplinary authority, the judge does not necessarily have to recuse himself from hearing the post-conviction motions of the attorney's client, particularly where that attorney no longer represents the client. *Honneus v. United States*, 425 F.Supp. 164 (D.Mass.1977).

IV. Judicial Disqualification

A. An Introductory Note

Canon 3E of the 1990 Judicial Code (Canon 3C of the 1972 Judicial Code) governs judicial disqualification, which is perhaps the most litigated area of the Code of Judicial Conduct. Canon 3E shares many similarities with 28 U.S.C.A. § 455. (There are, as well, a few important differences, discussed below). See, e.g., *Laird v. Tatum*, 409 U.S. 824, 825, 93 S.Ct. 7, 8, 34 L.Ed.2d 50, 51 (1972) (Memorandum of Rehnquist, J., denying recusal motion and stating that ABA Judicial Conduct Standards not "materially different" from standards in federal statute). Consequently, in an effort to analyze and illustrate Canon 3E, we will refer not only to state cases but also to relevant federal cases interpreting 28 U.S.C.A. § 455. It may be assumed that the applicable language in the Judicial Code and this federal statute are substantially identical unless otherwise indicated.

Note: Two additional federal disqualification statutes of interest include: 28 U.S.C.A. § 47, which prohibits a judge from hearing an appeal in any case over which he presided as a trial judge; and, 28 U.S.C.A. § 144, which disqualifies district court judges for actual bias or prejudice as alleged in a party's affidavit.

Waiver. Canon 3F provides a procedure where the parties may waive any disqualification imposed by Canon 3E. The federal statute only allows waiver if the judge is disqualified because his or her impartiality might reasonably be questioned. 28 U.S.C.A. § 455(e). We shall discuss the waiver issue later.

B. Disqualification Where Impartiality Might Reasonably Be Questioned

1. Introduction

Canon 3E(1)—and 28 U.S.C.A. § 455(a)—provide generally that a judge "shall disqualify himself or herself in any proceeding in which the judge's impartiality might reasonably be questioned. . . . " Subsequent subsections add specific instances where the judge must be disqualified, but those instances are *in addition* to any other case where the judge's impartiality might reasonably be questioned.

The judge should disclose on the record information that the parties or their lawyers "might consider relevant" to the disqualification issue, even if the judge believes that there is no real basis for disqualification. Canon 3E(1), Comment 2. This disclosure should be "broad" to assure that the parties are aware of the relevant facts. *ABA's Standing Committee Report on 1990 Code* 26 (1990).

2. Objective Test

Prior to the 1974 amendment to 28 U.S.C.A. § 455, federal courts generally held that a judge had a "duty to sit" in cases where there was no technical violation of the disqualification statute, although there may have been a "question" of impartiality. The amended section 455 modifies the "duty to sit" rule by requiring disqualification if there is a *reasonable* question as to the judge's impartiality. The test is objective: would a "reasonable person" knowing all the circumstances come to the conclusion that the judge's "impartiality might reasonably be questioned." Thus, judges still should not disqualify themselves merely to avoid difficult or controversial cases. *See* e.g., H.R. Rep.No.1453, 93d Cong., 2d Sess. 5 (1974).

Similarly, the test of Canon 3E(1) is also objective. It requires that the judge's partiality "might *reasonably* be questioned." (emphasis added). Canon 3B(1), a new section added to the 1990 Code, reaffirms this principle. It requires judges to decide matters "except those in which disqualification is required." The drafters added this section "to emphasize the judicial duty to sit and to minimize potential abuse of the disqualification process." *ABA's Standing Committee on 1990 Code, Legislative Draft* 15 (1990). *Public policy forbids a judge to disqualify himself for frivolous reasons, because that would delay the proceedings, overburden other judges, and encourage improper judge-shopping.*

3. The Rule of Necessity

Canon 3E(1), Comment 3, recognizes that Courts have created an exception to the disqualification provisions: no judge is required to disqualify himself if the basis for disqualification would require every judge to disqualify himself. This "rule of necessity" was created to give every person effective redress in the courts.

For example, *United States v. Will*, 449 U.S. 200, 101 S.Ct. 471, 66 L.Ed.2d 392 (1980), considered whether Congress could repeal or modify a statutorily defined formula for annual cost-of-living increases in the salary of federal judges. Every federal judge, from the district court level to the Supreme Court, had a financial interest in the outcome of the proceeding. The Court held that the "rule of necessity" precluded disqualification. "The declared purpose of § 455 is to guarantee litigants a fair forum in which they can pursue their claims. Far from promoting this purpose, failure to apply the Rule of Necessity would have a contrary effect, for without the Rule, some litigants would be denied their right to a forum." 449 U.S. at 217, 101 S.Ct. at 481, 66 L.Ed.2d at 407.

In some cases the judge who is disqualified may be the only person who is available at the moment to handle the matter (such as a temporary restraining order) on an emergency basis. That judge then must disclose the disqualifying facts on the record, and use "reasonable efforts" to transfer the matter. Canon 3E(1), Comment 3.

4. Generally Questioning the Impartiality of the Judge

The catch-all disqualification provision in Canon 3E(1)—where the judge's "impartiality might reasonably be questioned"—while measured according to an objective standard of conduct, is still subject to the particular circumstances of each case. Canon 3E(1), Comment 1 offers one example—where the judge was thinking of leaving the bench and negotiating for employment with a law firm, and that firm was appearing before the judge in a matter.

The following cases offer other examples where a judge disqualified himself or herself, or a higher court held that the judge should be disqualified on the grounds that the judge's impartiality might reasonably be questioned, or where the judge or higher court found no reasonable question of impartiality and therefore no disqualification.

5. Judge's Prior or Present Connection With Attorney

Rinden v. Marx, 116 N.H. 58, 351 A.2d 559 (1976) involved an attorney who was a defendant before the judge on drunken driving charges. Previously, the attorney *qua* attorney had served a complaint on the judge because the judge was a clerk of a corporate defendant and was the person authorized to receive service of process. The corporate defendant was covered by sufficient liability insurance, so there was no chance that the judge would be personally liable for any adverse judgment. In the absence of actual bias or prejudice, the judge did not have to disqualify himself. The disposition of the drunken driving charges against the attorney would have no effect on the civil suit.

Contrast *Smith v. State*, 239 Ga. 477, 238 S.E.2d 116 (1977), where the Supreme Court of Georgia reversed the defendant's conviction of theft and selling marijuana because of the trial judge's refusal to disqualify himself. During the trial, a deputy struck the defense counsel, who then moved for a postponement stating that, because of the beating, he was unable to represent his client on that day. The trial judge denied the motion, and even sympathized with the deputy because the deputy had earlier been subjected to defense counsel's derogatory questioning concerning sexual activities with an informer in the case. The state supreme court held that a judge has a duty to protect counsel for either party, and where the judge fails to perform this duty after knowledge of the attack and shows that his sympathies are with the attackers, his impartiality might reasonably be questioned.

ABA Informal Opinion 1477 (Aug. 12, 1981) recommended that a judge recuse himself when a party is represented by the judge's own attorney, whether that attorney is representing the judge in a personal matter or in a matter pertaining to the judge's official position or conduct. It is irrelevant whether or not the lawyer charged a fee. Furthermore, disqualification is required even if it is the lawyer's partner or associate who is the one appearing before the judge. Accord, *Texaco, Inc. v. Chandler*, 354 F.2d 655 (10th Cir.1965) (trial judge disqualified because counsel for a party had recently represented judge in unrelated case against judge for civil damages because of judge's official activity).

6. **Judge's Intemperate Remarks**

    In *Nicodemus v. Chrysler Corp.*, 596 F.2d 152 (6th Cir.1979), the plaintiff sought reinstatement in an unfair employment practices suit. The judge, who granted the plaintiff's preliminary injunction, had stated:

    > "This thing is the most transparent and the most blatant attempt to intimidate witnesses and parties that I have seen in a long time. I don't believe anything that anybody from Chrysler tells me because there is nothing in the record that is before me and in my experience in dealing with this case that gives me reason to believe that they are worthy of credence by anybody. They are a bunch of villains and they are interested only in feathering their own nests at the expense of everybody they can, including their own employees, and I don't intend to put up with it."

The trial judge also said that he was awarding $1000 in attorney fees "not necessarily because the employment laws allow it but because I believe" that the company is trying to "defy the court." Because these and similar remarks were hardly temperate and were "unsupported by the record," the appellate court reversed the preliminary injunction and disqualified the trial judge from further considering the case. The Court of Appeals noted that "this is not our first encounter with intemperate language by this particular district judge."

Contrast *In re International Business Machines Corp.*, 618 F.2d 923 (2d Cir.1980). IBM claimed that the trial judge was biased because 86% of 10,000 oral motions made and 74 out of 79 written motions were decided against IBM and in favor of the government. The appellate court held that adverse rulings alone do not create the appearance of impartiality. "A trial judge must be free to make rulings on the merits without the apprehension that if he makes a disproportionate number in favor of one litigant, he may have created the impression of bias." 618 F.2d at 929. See also, *Lazofsky v. Sommerset Bus Co.*, 389 F.Supp. 1041 (E.D.N.Y.1975) (judge does not demonstrate partiality merely because his rulings in a proceeding favor one party over the other).

7. Judge's Religion

Idaho v. Freeman, 507 F.Supp. 706 (D.Idaho 1981) involved a judge hearing a case concerning the constitutionality of Congress' extension of the ratification period for the Equal Rights Amendment. The Mormon Church generally opposed the ERA, and the judge was a Mormon and a regional representative of that Church. However, he was never required nor requested to promote the church's position, and his duties as a representative did not relate to the ERA. The judge concluded that his religious affiliation did not require him to disqualify himself. (The trial judge later held that the extension was unconstitutional, a ruling that the Supreme Court dismissed as moot.)

8. Where the Judge Knows a Party, Witness, or Attorney

As a general rule, the judge's obligation to disqualify herself where her "impartiality might reasonably be questioned" does not mean that a judge must automatically recuse herself simply because someone she might know casually is involved in litigation before her, either as a party, a witness, or as an attorney. In a small town, in particular, a judge may have a casual acquaintance with many people who become involved in some way with a trial. For example, in *Commonwealth v. Perry*, 468 Pa.

515, 364 A.2d 312 (1976), a murder trial, the judge was acquainted with the victim, a police officer, who had often appeared in court as a witness. The judge had also attended the victim's funeral. The defendant sought reversal of his conviction because the judge did not recuse himself. The divided court held that, in the absence of actual prejudice, the judge did not have to disqualify himself merely because of this personal acquaintance with the victim; judges do not live in a vacuum and a contrary rule could result in a judge being disqualified in many cases. The majority reasoned that a judge should be permitted to form social relationships and society should not reasonably expect judges to be prejudiced merely because of the fact of that relationship. Any other result would deter many qualified persons from seeking a judicial office.

See also, *Cheney v. U.S. District Court*, 541 U.S. ___, 124 S.Ct. 1391, 158 L.Ed.2d 225 (2004) (Memorandum Opinion of Scalia, J.) (Memorandum Opinion) rejecting a motion to disqualify Justice Scalia because he was in a party of approximately 30 people who went duck hunting and Vice President Cheney was also in the group, and a litigant. There were no claims of ex parte conversations.

However, there are certain circumstances where a judge's personal acquaintance requires disqualification. *In re Conduct of Jordan*, 290 Or. 669, 624 P.2d 1074 (1981) (per curiam) involved a defendant who served on a library board with the judge. The judge stated that he could not believe that the defendant had committed the alleged acts. Therefore, the judge's impartiality might reasonably be questioned, for if there is a conflict in the evidence, a reasonable person would expect the judge to be inclined to believe the testimony offered on behalf of the defendant.

Even if the case is tried to a jury, a judge's personal bias in favor of, or against, a litigant should require disqualification. Neither the ABA Model Code of Judicial Conduct nor the federal statute draws any distinction based on the possibility of a jury or bench trial, perhaps recognizing that the judge's bias regarding a party can infect the entire proceeding, may be tacitly or implicitly communicated to the jury, and might affect the judge's actions in a host of discretionary rulings (e.g., whether to grant a continuance or judgment N.O.V., whether to rule that a damage verdict in a civil case is "excessive," or whether to impose a more severe sentence in a criminal case).

9. When Judge's Former Law Clerk Represents a Party

A judge is not automatically disqualified from presiding over a case because her former law clerk represents a party in the litigation. Because many clerks continue to practice law in the jurisdiction where they served as clerks, an absolute disqualification rule would deter highly qualified people from serving as law clerks.

No specific Code provision creates a *per* se rule prohibiting a judge from hearing a case where the judge's former law clerk is participating as a lawyer. Canon 3E(1)(b) does not apply because the law clerk was not a lawyer with whom the judge had previously practiced law. Canon 3E(1)(d)(ii) is also inapplicable unless the former law clerk is also the judge's spouse or a person within the third degree of relationship to either the judge or her spouse.

Note: However, *there are ethical restrictions on the former law clerk because of that former clerk's prior association with the judge.* Model Rule of Professional Conduct 1.12(c) does not allow a lawyer to represent anyone in connection with a matter in which the lawyer "participated personally and substantially" as a law clerk to a judge, unless all parties to the proceeding "consent after consultation." If a lawyer is disqualified under this section, no other lawyer in the firm may handle the matter unless the former law clerk is effectively screened, pursuant to Model Rule 1.12(c)(i), & (2). See also, Model Rule 1.12(b)(law clerk for judge may negotiate for employment with law firm that has a case before the judge in which the judicial clerk is participating personally and substantially but only after the judicial clerk first notifies the judge). See Jones, *Some Ethical Considerations for Judicial Clerks*, 4 Georgetown J. Legal Ethics 771 (1991).

In certain circumstances, however, a judge may have to disqualify himself under the catch-all provision of Canon 3E(1) [or 28 U.S.C.A. § 455(a)] if his impartiality might reasonably be questioned because of his former law clerk's participation in the case. Consider the following cases.

In *Simonson v. General Motors Corp.*, 425 F.Supp. 574 (E.D.Pa.1976), a law student worked one day per week as a judicial intern and was also employed by a local law firm. In one case before the judge, the defendant was represented by the same law firm that employed the intern. The plaintiff moved to reassign the case to another judge alleging that the intern's dual responsibilities created the "appearance of impropriety." The judge denied the motion and instituted the following procedures to insure that the judge's impartiality could not be reasonably questioned:

(1) instructed the student not to participate in the litigation as a judicial intern, (2) instructed the law clerks not to give the student any assignments related to the litigation, or discuss the case with him, and (3) instructed the student to make arrangements with his law firm not to perform legal services on this particular case. This case, in effect, presaged Model Rule 1.12(b) & (c).

Fredonia Broadcasting Corp. v. RCA Corp., 569 F.2d 251 (5th Cir.1978), reversed the trial judge because he did not disqualify himself when his former law clerk was an associate in the law firm representing one of the parties. The law clerk was on the judge's staff *during* the first trial and belonged to the law firm when the case was again before the judge on remand. The court of appeals required disqualification because the former law clerk "had been exposed to the trial judge's innermost thoughts about the case," and therefore the party represented by the clerk's law firm had an unfair advantage in the case. The court emphasized, however, that it was not holding that a former law clerk could never practice before the judge, but in this particular case the law clerk was "actively involved as counsel for a party in a case in which the law clerk participated during his clerkship." Id. at 256. If this fact situation would occur now, the judge could avoid disqualification if his former law clerk would be screened in accordance with Model Rule 1.12(c).

10. Where Judge Participated in Prior Related Case

Parties often seek to disqualify a judge on the basis of the judge's prior participation in a case involving the same party or the same facts. Absent some showing of hostility or actual bias, however, a judge should not be disqualified merely because of earlier judicial contacts with the party. This principle is really no different than the situation where the judge knows of damaging evidence that he later excludes at trial. The judge, even in a bench trial, is presumed to be able to screen out the excluded evidence.

For example, a judge is not required to disqualify himself in a criminal action because of a decision adverse to the party in a prior criminal case involving different and unrelated criminal charges. *State v. Cabiness*, 273 S.C. 56, 254 S.E.2d 291 (1979). Similarly, a sentencing judge is not automatically disqualified from hearing a habeas corpus motion that claims that the trial was unfair. *Panico v. United States*, 412 F.2d 1151 (2d Cir.1969), cert. denied, 397 U.S. 921, 90 S.Ct. 901, 25 L.Ed.2d 102 (1970).

A judge is also not disqualified from hearing a case if an appellate court reverses the judge's ruling and remands the case back to the trial court. *Mayberry v. Maroney*, 558 F.2d 1159 (3d Cir.1977).

In *State v. Beshaw*, 134 Vt. 347, 359 A.2d 654 (1976), the defendant, convicted of burglary, asserted on appeal that the judge should have disqualified himself because, in a prior proceeding, the judge had cited the defendant for contempt for kicking a metal stand at the judge. Because the contempt proceeding was not material to the present case and had occurred 19 months earlier, the Vermont Supreme Court held that the judge did not abuse his discretion in refusing to disqualify himself. Though the court affirmed the judge, it did suggest that perhaps the judge should have disqualified himself under Canon 3C(1) because his impartiality might reasonably have been questioned.

The plaintiffs in *Meeropol v. Nizer*, 429 U.S. 1337, 97 S.Ct. 687, 50 L.Ed.2d 729 (1977), were sons of Julius and Ethel Rosenberg. The Rosenbergs were executed in 1953 following their convictions for conspiracy to commit espionage. The Meeropols sued attorney Louis Nizer for libel, invasion of privacy, and infringement of copyright. They also filed a motion before U.S. Supreme Court Justice Marshall, as Circuit Justice, to designate judges from other circuits to sit as appellate judges because the Second Circuit judges were associates, friends, or consultants of judges who had presided over the previous trial of the Meeropols' parents. Fourteen years earlier, Justice Marshall had been a member of the second circuit panel that denied post-conviction relief to Morton Sobell, the Rosenbergs' codefendant. Raising the disqualification issue *sua sponte*, Justice Marshall did not feel disqualification was necessary because he did not believe his " 'impartiality' to decide the extent of a circuit justice's powers under § 291(a) 'might reasonably be questioned' in light of this participation in a case not related to the present action." 429 U.S. at 1338 n.2, 97 S.Ct. at 689 n.2, 50 L.Ed.2d at 731 n.2. Justice Marshall then ruled that he had no authority to disqualify all of the judges on the appeals panel or to transfer the appeals to another circuit.

However, in *Rice v. McKenzie*, 581 F.2d 1114 (4th Cir.1978), a judge was required to disqualify himself under 28 U.S.C.A. § 455 where, as a federal judge reviewing a habeas corpus petition, he was required to consider a case that he had helped to decide as chief justice of the state supreme court. The court recognized that generally a judge is not precluded from presiding in a case because of an earlier decision in which he participated. In this case, however, the judge's impartiality could reasonably be questioned because, as a district judge, the judge was reviewing the constitutionality of what he previously approved as chief justice of the state supreme court.

Note: 28 U.S.C.A. § 47 prohibits a judge from sitting on an appellate panel to review a case that he had decided as a trial judge. Section 47 did not apply to this case, however, because the judge had not been the trial judge on the case.

C. Disqualification for Personal Bias or Prejudice

1. Introduction

Canon 3E(1) first provides that a judge should disqualify herself whenever her impartiality might reasonably be questioned, "including but not limited to [specified] instances . . . . " The Code then delineates specific instances where the judge's impartiality *would* be questioned. One of those instances, of course, is where a judge has actual bias or prejudices.

Canon 3E(1)(a) and 28 U.S.C.A. § 455(b)(1) thus provide that a judge must disqualify herself where she has *"a personal bias or prejudice concerning a party, or a party's lawyer, or personal knowledge of disputed evidentiary facts concerning the proceeding."*

In 2003, the ABA added another instance in which a judge should disqualify himself. Canon 3E(1)(f) requires a judge to recuse himself when he "has made a public statement that *commits*, or appears to commit, the judge with respect to" an issue or controversy in the proceeding. (emphasis added). The ABA added this instance in 2003, in response to *Republican Party v. White*, 536 U.S. 765, 122 S.Ct. 2528, 153 L.Ed.2d 694 (2002), which invalidated a Minnesota judicial canon that prohibited a "candidate for a judicial office" from "announc[ing] his or her views on disputed legal or political issues" (the "announce clause"). *White* did not decide the constitutionality of this provision, which may be referred to as the "commit clause." Rotunda, *Judicial Campaigns in the Shadow of Republican Party v. White,* 14 The Professional Lawyer 2 (ABA, No. 1, 2002).

This clause dovetails with **Canon 5A(3)(d)(i)**, which provides that a judge or judicial candidate must not make "pledges, promises or commitments" inconsistent with his duty of impartiality. This clause was also amended in response to the *White* case. **Canon 5A(3)(d)(ii)** governs elections and provides that the judge may not "knowingly misrepresent" facts concerning his election opponents.

Note: 28 U.S.C.A. § 455, unlike Canon 3E(1), does not categorize the specific instances requiring disqualification as examples where a judge's impartiality might reasonably be questioned. Section 455(b) begins, "He shall also disqualify himself in the following circumstances." The language change was not intended to alter application of the federal statute from situations where Canon 3E would require disqualification.

2. Extrajudicial Bias

Both Canon 3E(1)(a) and 28 U.S.C.A. § 455(b)(1) require disqualification only if there is bias concerning a *party*, as distinguished from bias concerning an issue in the case. This distinction reflects the Code's intent that a judge need not disqualify himself if bias arises from his beliefs as to the *law* that applies to a case. A judge may have fixed beliefs about principles of law that would not mandate disqualification. Otherwise, a judge could not write books or articles or speak on legal subjects, activities expressly permitted under Canon 4B. Indeed, after deciding cases and creating precedent for years, if would be incredible if the judge did not form some fixed ideas about the law. E.g., *Samuel v. University of Pittsburgh*, 395 F.Supp. 1275 (W.D.Pa.1975).

In *Papa v. New Haven Federation of Teachers*, 186 Conn. 725, 444 A.2d 196 (1982), the trial judge was presiding over an attempt to enjoin teachers from striking. Seeking to disqualify the judge, the defendants asserted the judge was biased because of a speech he had earlier given criticizing teachers' strikes in general. This speech was given before the case arose and did not specifically address the case. Although the judge's statements were extrajudicial in nature, the state supreme court analogized the judge's statements to judicial expressions of opinion about specific laws, the obligation to obey those laws, and the consequences of disobedience. If disqualification is not required for judicial expressions of opinion about the law, noted the court, then extrajudicial opinions on points of law should not require disqualification as long as the comments do not raise a reasonable question that the judge will prejudge a pending or impending case. The judge in this case was disqualified, however, for giving another interview to a reporter concerning the pending proceeding. That interview violated Canon 3A(6) of the 1972

Code [Canon 3B(9) of the 1990 Code]. See also, *In the Matter of Sheffield*, 465 So.2d 350 (Ala.1984), which suspended a judge for two months, without pay, because he (among other things) had a telephone interview with a reporter where the judge commented on the merits of a pending case.

The Extra–Judicial Source Rule. Even if the judge makes judgments against a party, such a "bias" is not normally considered improper and grounds for disqualification if the judgment is based on *facts* learned about a party *during the very proceeding* at which the judge sits. The judge, after all, is supposed to make judgments and decisions based on what is learned at the hearing. Similarly, courts generally hold that a judge's participation over separate jury trials of codefendants does not constitute reasonable grounds for questioning the judge's impartiality in a subsequent jury trial involving a remaining codefendant. See *United States v. Cowden*, 545 F.2d 257 (1st Cir.1976), cert. denied, 430 U.S. 909, 97 S.Ct. 1181, 51 L.Ed.2d 585 (1977).

In examining the reasons for the "extrajudicial source" rule, the court in *United Nuclear Corp. v. General Atomic Co.*, 96 N.M. 155, 249, 629 P.2d 231, 325 (1980), quoting *In re International Business Machines Corp.*, 618 F.2d 923, 930 (2d Cir.1980) explained:

> "[A] judge is not merely a passive observer. He must . . . shrewdly observe the strategies of the opposing lawyers, perceive their efforts to sway him by appeals to his predilections. He must cannily penetrate through the surface of their remarks to their real purposes and motives. He has an official obligation to become prejudiced in that sense. Impartiality is not gullibility. Disinterestedness does not mean child-like innocence. If the judge did not form judgements of the actors in those court-house dramas called trials, he could never render decisions."

However, the situation is different, if the source of this bias as to facts was an "extrajudicial source." *United States v. Grinnell Corp.*, 384 U.S. 563, 86 S.Ct. 1698, 16 L.Ed.2d 778 (1966). "The alleged bias and prejudice to be disqualifying must stem from an extrajudicial source and result in an opinion on the merits on some basis other than what the judge learned from his participation in the case." 384 U.S. at 583, 86 S.Ct. at 1710.

Although a judge generally does not have to disqualify himself if he acquires knowledge through his judicial duties, the fact that a judge's remarks or behavior take place in the judicial context does not exclude them from scrutiny and from requiring recusal if they reflect such pervasive prejudice as would constitute bias against one of the parties.

Thus, in *State v. Harry*, 311 N.W.2d 108 (Iowa 1981), the judge was required to recuse himself for prejudicial statements made in a judicial context. According to the affidavit of the defendant's attorney, the judge accused the defendant's attorney of delaying tactics and informed the attorney that if the attorney allowed an innocent man to go on trial because of the defendant's silence, the judge would make it difficult for the defendant at his own trial. The prosecution claimed the judge should not recuse himself because the statements did not arise from an extra-judicial source. The state supreme court did not rely on Canon 3E(1)(a), but rather required disqualification because of a violation of Canon 3A(3) of the 1972 Code [Canon 3B(4) of the 1990 Code], which required the judge to be patient, dignified, and courteous to litigants, lawyers, and others.

3. Actual Bias or Prejudice in General

Instances of actual bias or prejudice, like the appearance of impartiality, are often fact-bound and should therefore be examined on a case-by-case basis. The following cases explore several situations where courts have found actual bias or prejudice, or the lack thereof.

In *Commonwealth v. Leventhal*, 364 Mass. 718, 307 N.E.2d 839 (1974), the defendant moved for a new trial, asserting that the trial judge was biased for numerous reasons. The defendant alleged the judge had an "intimate relationship" with the chief prosecution witness. This "intimate relationship" only amounted to the judge's having taught the witness in a bar review course 35 years previously, and having written a letter of recommendation for admission to the bar. The court dismissed this ground as frivolous. The defendant also asserted that the judge made prejudicial remarks during the trial, displaying to the jury that the judge believed the defendant was guilty. The court held that these remarks did not demonstrate bias, for the judge normally has a great deal of discretion in commenting on the trial to the jury. Finally, the defendant claimed the judge was biased because the judge was a defendant in a civil suit that the defendant had brought against the judge. The court noted that a lawsuit between a judge and a party may require disqualification in certain circumstances, but a party cannot disqualify a judge simply by bringing a separate action against him after the principal suit has commenced. It would then be too easy for a litigant to create a "conflict" and go judge shopping.

Department of Revenue v. Golder, 322 So.2d 1 (Fla.1975). The issue in the underlying case was the constitutionality of an estate tax statute. At the time of the statute's enactment, the justice writing the opinion in the case was special tax counsel to the Florida House of Representatives and prepared a preliminary memorandum of law supporting the constitutionality of the proposed statute. The judge's prior involvement with the statute did not constitute bias because the views expressed in the memorandum were developed independently of any particular controversy or party. Also, the views as to the constitutionality of the statute were not extra-judicial.

See also *Laird v. Tatum*, Memorandum of Justice Rehnquist, 409 U.S. 824, 93 S.Ct. 7, 34 L.Ed.2d 50 (1972). Justice Rehnquist refused to disqualify himself in this case: his previous participation was limited to testifying on similar legal issues before a Senate Subcommittee; although the *Laird* case itself was then in the lower courts, and Rehnquist did briefly refer to the case in Senate testimony, he never was counsel of record, did not even consult on that case, and was not otherwise involved with it.

Note: 28 U.S.C.A. § 455(b)(3) now requires a judge to disqualify himself "[w]here he has served in government employment and in such capacity participated as counsel, adviser or material witness concerning the proceeding or expressed an opinion concerning the merits of the particular case in controversy." The Model Judicial Code, in contrast, has a less broad provision requiring disqualification when the judge served as a lawyer or was a material witness in the matter in controversy. Canon 3E(1)(b). [28 U.S.C.A. § 455(b)(2) corresponds to this less broad prohibition.] These provisions are discussed in the following section.

In *State v. Linsky*, 117 N.H. 866, 379 A.2d 813 (1977) the state sought to enjoin the defendants from demonstrating at a nuclear power plant. The defendants alleged the judge had prejudged the issues because of certain statements he made at the arraignment. The court held the judge was not biased because the judge subsequently had stated that he was not prejudging the defendants' guilt and would reach a verdict only on the evidence. The defendants also claimed the judge had personal knowledge of disputed evidentiary facts through newspapers, radio, and a meeting between the judge and defense counsel, thereby creating the possibility that the judge could be called as a witness. The court held that such knowledge did not require disqualification because the facts of which the judge had knowledge would probably not be material at trial and the evidence could be obtained from other sources. One might also add that if knowledge gathered from news media mandated disqualification, then only judges who never read newspapers or listened to the radio or television could hear cases. The court noted that information learned at the judge's meeting with defense counsel probably was not "material" to any trial. Finally, the court held that it would be inappropriate for defense counsel to object to his own meeting with the judge; if defense counsel had not wanted the meeting, he should not have had it. To hold otherwise would allow any counsel to harvest the seeds of disqualification that counsel had planted himself.

In *State v. Ahearn,* 137 Vt. 253, 403 A.2d 696 (1979) the defendant was charged with assault and robbery with a deadly weapon. The defendant appeared pro se and physically attacked the judge during the trial. The appellate court noted that "much of the defendant's conduct was intended to harass the court and generally disrupt the judicial process." The defendant sought reversal of his conviction because of an unfair trial. One of the grounds asserted was the judge's failure to disqualify himself because of the physical attack. The court held that the defendant's attack did not require disqualification because it was a "scheme" to drive the judge out of the case. The defendant also argued that his harsh sentence demonstrated the judge's bias. The court noted that the judge probably should have recused himself because his impartiality might reasonably be questioned. But the sentence itself did not demonstrate actual bias in light of the defendant's crimes and his twelve previous felony convictions. The failure to disqualify, therefore, was within the trial judge's discretion and was not reversible error.

Commonwealth v. Boyle, 498 Pa. 486, 447 A.2d 250 (1982) held that bias did not exist just because a trial judge's rulings in a former trial were similar to rulings in a pretrial proceeding. "If the rulings at the second trial constituted a fair exercise of discretion, the fact that a trial judge had previously ruled in a similar manner under similar circumstances is to be expected." 498 Pa. at 491, 447 A.2d at 252. Similarly, a judge does not demonstrate partiality merely because his rulings in a proceeding tend to favor one party over the other. *Lazofsky v. Sommerset Bus Co.,* 389 F.Supp. 1041 (E.D.N.Y.1975).

United States v. Poludniak, 657 F.2d 948 (8th Cir.1981). The judge in this case was presiding over a case where a U.S. Senator was an extortion victim. In a previous newspaper article, the judge had stated that he hoped to talk with senators to obtain additional funds to hire more marshals for courthouse security. Because the Senator involved in the case was a victim, not a party, the judge did not have to disqualify himself.

Contrast, *United States v. Brown,* 539 F.2d 467 (5th Cir.1976). In this case, it was learned that the trial judge had mentioned at a swimming pool that he was going to preside over the defendant's trial and that he was "going to get that nigger." The court reversed defendant's conviction on appeal because the judge's statement did not "comport with the appearance of justice" and demonstrated the judge's personal bias, and "it could not be said from the record alone that appellant received a fair trial."

United States v. Holland, 655 F.2d 44 (5th Cir.1981) (per curiam). In the first trial of this case, the judge, with no objection from any counsel, had an unrecorded conversation with the jury in the jury room. The defendant, on appeal, argued that the judge's conduct was error and won a new trial. At the second trial, the same trial judge stated that, because of the defendant's appeal, he was going to increase the defendant's sentence. On appeal after second trial, the appellate court held that the judge's remarks demonstrated actual bias and also the appearance of partiality. The case was remanded for a third trial, and the judge was disqualified from presiding over further proceedings in the case.

D. Disqualification When the Judge Is a Former Lawyer or Material Witness

Canon 3E(1)(b) requires disqualification where (1) a judge served as a lawyer in the matter in controversy, (2) a lawyer, with whom the judge previously practiced law, served as a lawyer during such association in the matter now pending before the judge, or (3) the judge has been a material witness concerning the matter in controversy.

Note: While the Judicial Code refers to a "lawyer in the matter", 28 U.S.C.A. § 455(b)(2) refers to judges who had served as a lawyer while in "private practice." However, the drafters of the federal statute added a new subsection, § 455(b)(3), which provides that a judge is disqualified "[w]here he has served in *governmental* employment and in such capacity participated as counsel, adviser or material witness concerning the proceeding or expressed an opinion concerning the merits of the particular case in controversy." (emphasis added). A judge should disqualify himself, for example, if he acted as an Assistant U.S. Attorney in the case before he became a judge. *Mixon v. United States,* 608 F.2d 588 (5th Cir.1979). This very broad disqualification provision, § 455(b)(3), also provides that judges who previously served in a governmental capacity (whether or not they served as lawyers) are disqualified if, in that capacity, they advised on, were a material witness concerning, or expressed any opinion about the merits of a *particular* case. *See* H.R.Rep. No. 1453, 93d Cong., 2d Sess. 6 (1974).

Canon 3E(1)(b), Comment 1 discusses the application of this disqualification provision to prior governmental employment. A "lawyer in a governmental agency does not ordinarily have an association with other lawyers employed by that agency" within the meaning of this subsection. The drafters used the word "ordinarily" to indicate that disqualification does not usually result from these relationships. *ABA's Standing Committee Report on 1990 Code, Legislative Draft* 27 (1990).

Thus, a judge who was formerly employed by the Securities and Exchange Commission would not have to disqualify himself under Canon 3E(1)(b) simply because another former or present member of the SEC brings a case before the judge. However, the judge must still disqualify himself under the catch-all provision of Canon 3E(1), *if* the fact-situation is such that his impartiality might reasonably be questioned. Furthermore, a judge would have to disqualify himself under Canon 3E(1)(b) if the SEC matter before him were one in which he had personally served as a lawyer with the SEC.

In *Matter of O'Brien,* 437 N.E.2d 972 (Ind.1982) (per curiam), a part-time judge (who was also authorized to practice law) represented the husband in a dissolution of marriage proceeding. The judge prepared the petition and served the summons on the wife. At the hearing on the matter, the regular judge was absent, and the judge who represented the husband was selected as judge *pro tempore*! The judge then entered the dissolution decree and approved the property settlement. Even though the parties consented to the judge/lawyer acting as judge *pro tempore,* the judge's conduct still violated Canon 3E(1)(b), as well as DR 9–101(A) and DR 1–102(A)(5). The judge was reprimanded and admonished.

Canon 3E(1)(b) requires disqualification only if the judge acted as a lawyer in the *matter in controversy*. Thus, a judge did not disqualify himself when he was passing on the constitutionality of an estate tax statute even though, three years earlier—when he was special tax counsel to the state legislature—he had written a preliminary memorandum concluding that the statute was constitutional. *Department of Revenue v. Golder*, 322 So.2d 1 (Fla.1975). Canon 3E(1)(b) requires disqualification only if the bias is based upon prior contacts with a *proceeding*, and not simply because of familiarity with a legal issue.

Note: If this case had involved a federal judge, 28 U.S.C.A. § 455(b)(3) would have been applicable. It requires disqualification of the judge who, when she was a government employee, had "expressed an opinion concerning the merits of the particular *case* in controversy." (emphasis added.) Because the judge had not expressed an opinion about the merits of the particular case, the federal statute also should not require disqualification.

The second clause of Canon 3E(1)(b) (as well as § 455(b)(2) of 28 U.S.C.A.) requires judicial disqualification when a judge's former law partner or associate has served as a lawyer in the matter, but only if the lawyer served as counsel *while* the judge was also practicing law with the lawyer. In other words, a judge should not participate in a case that his former law firm handled, even though the firm is no longer involved, if the judge was a member of the firm when it was acting as counsel. Thus, in *Hall v. Hall*, 242 Ga. 15, 247 S.E.2d 754 (1978), a judge did not have to disqualify himself in a divorce proceeding where the wife's counsel was the judge's former law partner in the absence of proof that the wife's representation began before the judge left his legal practice. (Of course, one must always bear in mind that, depending on the fact situation, the judge may still have to recuse himself under the catch-all provision of Canon 3E(1) where there is a reasonable question as to the judge's impartiality. The longer the judge is on the bench, the less likely the need for disqualification under the general provisions of Canon 3E(1).)

E. Disqualification for Financial Interests or Interests That Could Be Substantially Affected by the Outcome of the Proceeding

1. Introduction

Canon 3E(1)(c) mandates disqualification when a judge "knows" that he or she, "individually or as a fiduciary," has an "economic interest" (that is not "de minimis") in the subject matter in controversy or in a party to the proceeding, or has any other more than "de minimis" interest that could be substantially affected by the proceeding. Canon 3E(1)(c) also mandates disqualification if the judge "knows" that his or her spouse, parent or child (no matter where they are residing), or any other "member of the judge's family residing in the judge's household" has a similar "economic interest" (that is not "*de minimis*") or any other more than "*de minimis*" interest that could be substantially affected by the proceeding.

Introductory Definitions. This rule uses various terms of art defined in the Terminology section. In the order in which they are used in this Canon, **"knows"** means "actual knowledge of the fact in question." However, a person's knowledge "may be inferred from circumstances." Terminology 10. **"Fiduciary"** includes such relationships as "executor, administrator, trustee, and guardian." Terminology 8. (Note that Canon 4E prohibits a judge from acting as a fiduciary except for the estate, trust, or person of a member of his family, and only if such service will not interfere with the proper performance of his judicial duties.) **"Member of the judge's family residing in the judge's household"** means "any relative of the judge, by blood or marriage, or a person treated by the judge as a member of the judge's family, who resides in the judge's household." Terminology 14.

"Economic interest" is a lengthy definition, which will be discussed below. Subject to a few exceptions, it means a legal or equitable interest that is "*more than a de minimis,*" or a relationship such "as officer, director, advisor or other active participant in the affairs of a party." Terminology 7(ii). Note that any legal or equitable interest in a party is, by definition, a disqualifying "economic interest" only if it is more than de minimis. If the judge is an officer, director, etc. in a party, that is automatically disqualifying, and the issue of "*de minimis*" is not applicable. The drafters used the term "economic interest" instead of "financial interest" (which is what the 1972 Code used) in order to emphasize that an economic interest included a *relationship,* such as officer or director of a party. **"De minimis"** means "an insignificant interest that could not raise reasonable question as to a judge's impartiality." Terminology 6.

2. Economic Interests

(a) Legal or Equitable Interest

Unless the economic interest is a relationship such as an officer or director, the economic interest must be legal or equitable in nature before it is disqualifying. Terminology 7. (This "economic interest"—

unless it is a relationship—must also be, by definition, more than "de minimis," a term discussed below.)

For example, *In re Virginia Electric & Power Co.*, 539 F.2d 357 (4th Cir.1976) involved VEPCO, a public utility, attempting to recover damages caused by defective pump supports for its nuclear power plant. Because of a fuel adjustment clause, VEPCO was permitted to charge its customers directly for the amount that VEPCO claimed as damages. If VEPCO won its suit, it might be required to return to its customers that part of the award representing the surcharge. Customers could receive a $70 to $100 refund. The presiding judge was a VEPCO customer. The court upheld the judge's refusal to disqualify himself under this section because the judge merely had a contingent interest in the litigation, not a legal or equitable financial interest. VEPCO customers would only receive a refund if the Virginia State Corporation Commission authorized a return of the surcharge. The court also held that the judge did not have any other interest that would be substantially affected by the outcome of the case. *See also, Dacey v. Connecticut Bar Association*, 170 Conn. 520, 368 A.2d 125 (1976) (judge did not have legal or equitable financial interest in case where plaintiff was suing the state bar association for libel and any judgment adverse to the bar association could raise bar dues).

Similarly, a judge's interest as a ratepayer or taxpayer should not be a "legal or equitable" economic interest. Such interests, however, could require disqualification if it is "any other" interest that is "more than de minimis" and could be "substantially affected" by the outcome of the proceeding. Canon 3E(1)(c).

Although the judge's economic interest must be legal or equitable before the judge will be disqualified, this interest need not have the traditional indicia of ownership, such as a title or other physical representation of ownership. In *Taylor v. Public Convalescent Service*, 245 Ga. 805, 267 S.E.2d 242 (1980), a pauper was appealing a default judgment that had been entered in the justice of the peace court. Before the pauper could perfect his appeal, the justice of the peace had to determine the validity of the pauper's affidavit, claiming that he could not pay court costs. Under local rules, approval of the pauper's affidavit could deny (or, at least delay) the justice of the peace from receiving a portion of his income, because the justice of the peace received court costs as fees. The state supreme court required disqualification in this case because the justice of the peace had a direct economic interest in whether or not the pauper would succeed on his affidavit. This structural set-up is defective because it gives the judge a financial interest in the controversy.

(b) The Subject Matter in the Controversy

In order for Canon 3E(1)(c) to be applicable, the judge's economic interest must be "in the subject matter in controversy." *Commonwealth v. Keigney*, 3 Mass.App.Ct. 347, 329 N.E.2d 778 (1975) addressed this issue. In this case, the defendant pled guilty to armed robbery while masked, larceny of a motor vehicle, and unlawfully carrying a revolver in a motor vehicle. The presiding judge, a former stockholder and board member of the bank named in the indictment, was an accommodation maker for a friend's $1,500 note held by the bank. In the defendant's motion for a new sentencing trial, he argued that the judge should have disqualified himself because of his past pecuniary relationship with the bank. The court held that in the absence of actual bias or prejudice, the judge was not required to disqualify himself. The disposition of the indictment could not have resulted in the judge having to pay the note.

(c) A "*De Minimis*" Interest

The 1972 Code. The 1972 Judicial Code required the judge to disqualify himself if he (or spouse or minor child in his household) had a "financial interest" in the subject matter in controversy. See, Canons 3C(1)(c) & 3D (1972 Judicial Code). The 1972 Code, in general, defined "financial interest" to mean legal or equitable interest "*however small.*" Canon 3C(3)(b) (1972 Judicial Code). However, the parties and their lawyers could waive this disqualification. Thus, under the 1972 Code, a judge would be disqualified from a case where International Business Machines is a party, if she owns even one share of IBM stock, and even if the value of the stock will be unaffected by the litigation, but the parties and lawyers could always effectuate a proper waiver. J. Shaman, S. Lubet, & J. Alfini, *Judicial Conduct and Ethics* § 5.20 at 138 (1990).

The drafters of the 1972 Judicial Code thought that it would be too difficult to interpret an ambiguous concept such as "substantial" financial interest. If the substantiality test were applied to financial interests, it would not be clear whether the judge's financial interest should be compared to the total of all financial interests of others in the party, or the total of all the judge's financial interests. *See Reporter's Notes [1972]* at 65. In either case, judges would have to expose the value of their entire stock portfolio to the parties in order to determine whether the judge's economic interest was "substantial." Many judges did not want to reveal that much information about their financial affairs.

The "however small" qualification to the financial interest conflict could lead to some anomalous results. Consider, *In re Cement Antitrust Litigation (MDL No. 296)*, 688 F.2d 1297 (9th Cir.1982), affirmed, 459 U.S. 1191, 103 S.Ct. 1173, 75 L.Ed.2d 425 (1983) (per curiam), where the judge's wife owned some stock in several of the plaintiff class members. The judge recused himself at the defendants' request, but the plaintiffs sought to have the judge reappointed because of the complicated nature of the case. After concluding that unnamed class members were parties within the meaning of 28 U.S.C.A. § 455(d)(4)—which also defines "financial interest" to include "a legal or equitable interest, however small"—, the appellate court upheld the judge's decision to recuse himself. The Ninth Circuit's disdain for this result is reflected in the following statement: "[A]fter five years of litigation, a multi-million dollar lawsuit of major national importance, with over 200,000 class plaintiffs, grinds to a halt over Mrs. Muecke's $29.70." 688 F.2d at 1313. On the other hand, one might point out that whenever one draws a bright line, there will always be cases close to the line that some argue should go the other way. The alternative to a bright line is a vague one, and vagueness leads to more litigation, not less.

Note: In *Union Carbide Corp. v. United States Cutting Service, Inc.*, 782 F.2d 710 (7th Cir.1986), a divided panel held that, at least in some cases—in this case, in the midst of a large antitrust class action—a judge could "cure" the disqualification resulting from her husband's ownership of stock by selling the stock. Congress, in 1988, subsequently codified this result in § 455(f).

The 1990 Code. The drafters of the 1990 Code provide that when "economic interest" refers to ownership, it means "ownership of more than a de minimis legal or equitable interest. . . . " Terminology 7. And they, in turn, define "de minimis" to mean "an insignificant interest that could not raise reasonably question as to a judge's impartiality." Terminology 6. Judges, thus, are not required to disqualify themselves under Canon 3E(1)(c) unless they have more than a de minimis legal or equitable ownership in the subject matter in controversy or in a party to the proceeding. In addition, they must disqualify themselves if there is any other interest that is "more than de minimis" and "that could be substantially affected by the proceeding." Canon 3E(1)(c).

Note: Given the punctuation in Canon 3E(1)(c), the more natural reading is that if the judge (or relevant family member) **has a relationship such as an officer,** director, etc. in a party, or has **more than a de minimis economic interest** in the subject matter in controversy or a party to the proceeding, then the judge must be disqualified. However, if the judge (or relevant family member) has **any other interest,** then this other interest must satisfy two criteria: *first,* it must be **more than de minimis,** and *second,* this interest is such that it **could be substantially affected by the proceeding.**

The drafters of the 1990 Judicial Code are exceedingly pithy in explaining this significant new requirement that the interest be more than de minimis. They simply announce that they added this requirement "to obviate the need for disqualification where a judge's financial interest is de minimis and would not affect impartiality." *ABA's Standing Committee Report on 1990 Code, Report,* at 6 (1990). See also, *ABA's Standing Committee on 1990 Code, Legislative Draft,* at 5 (1990)("more than de minimis" was included "to preclude disqualification based on any de minimis legal or equitable interest. . . . "). Moser, *The 1990 ABA Code of Judicial Conduct,* 4 Georgetown J. of Legal Ethics 731, 752 & n. 82 (1991), discusses this issue but merely repeats the definition in the Terminology section.

Unfortunately, the drafters offer no test to determine when an interest is "de minimis." Obviously, a judge will not be disqualified under the 1990 Judicial Code if she owns one share of I.B.M. stock and I.B.M. is a party. But what if she owns 200 shares, with a tax basis of over $15,000? Is that de minimis? What if she owns 100 shares, but her entire net worth is only $75,000? Does one compare her I.B.M. shares to her total stock portfolio, or to her net worth, or to some absolute standard? What if she has a stock portfolio with a tax basis of over $3 million, and I.B.M. stock is only .5% of her portfolio. Is the amount de minimis as to her? Does the answer change if the market value (as opposed to the tax basis) of I.B.M. stock is $25,000, and the market value of her portfolio is $4 million, so that I.B.M. stock comprises .625% of her portfolio? What if her net worth is $6 million?

Many judges (like other people) like to keep their financial information private. Canon 4I, Comment 1, recognizes that a "judge has the rights of any other citizen, including the right to privacy of the judge's financial affairs, except to the extent that limitations established by law are required to safeguard the proper performance of the judge's duties." While proclaiming an interest in the privacy of a judge's financial affairs, the drafters have ironically drafted a rule that should give litigants the right to learn a lot more about a judge's financial affairs. The "de minimis" rule makes such information material, for in order to learn whether a financial interest is "de minimis," the litigants may need to have a good picture of the judge's net worth.

(d) The Judge's Family

Canon 3C(1)(b) extends the net of disqualification to cases where the judge's family owns disqualifying interests. If either the spouse, parent, or child (no matter where they are residing), or any other "member of the judge's family residing in the judge's household" (an expression defined in Terminology 14) has an economic interest or other interest that would disqualify the judge if the judge had that interest, then that interest is, in effect, imputed to the judge, who then must disqualify himself. However, this disqualification provision only applies *if* the judge knows of the interest. Thus, let us turn to the question of "knowledge."

(e) Knowledge of Economic Interests

Canon 3E(1)(c)—as well as 28 U.S.C.A. § 455(b)(4)—requires disqualification only if the judge "knows" of the disqualifying economic interest. Canon 3E(2)—and 28 U.S.C.A. § 455(c)—thus require that a judge inform himself about his own financial interests. If the judge does not keep himself so informed, he would be subject to sanctions for violating the Code. Otherwise the Judicial Code would place a premium on ignorance. But ignorance is not always bliss. This requirement of knowledge *precludes the use of a "blind trust"* to avoid disqualification. See *Reporter's Notes to 1972 Judicial Code,* at 64–65.

Although a judge *shall* keep informed of his or her own *personal and fiduciary* economic interests, the judge need only make a "reasonable effort" to learn of the personal economic interests of his or her spouse and minor children residing in the judge's household. The Canons realistically recognize that there may be limits to what a judge can do to require others to keep him or her informed of all financial dealings. Relevant factors to determine whether a reasonable effort has been made should include the following: "Did the interest of the spouse or child come from the judge or from another source? Does the spouse or child know the nature of the interest, or is he or she the beneficiary of a blind trust? Has the spouse's or child's financial interest been supervised by the judge in the past, or has the judge not been involved in the handling of the interest?" *Reporter's Notes to 1972 Judicial Code* at 68. It should also be relevant if the judge and spouse file separate tax returns.

As to other members of the judge's family who do not fall under Canon 3E(2), Canon 3E(1)(c) requires the judge to disqualify herself only if she has actual knowledge of the financial interest of such persons. The simple reality is that such persons often act independently of the judge, and so this section pragmatically does not require her to exert an effort to gain knowledge of such persons' economic interests.

(f) Exceptions to Economic Interest Disqualification
The definition of "Economic Interest" excludes several types of economic interest. Terminology 7. Cf. 28 U.S.C.A. § 455(d)(4).

(i) Mutual Funds
Λ judge must disqualify himself if he has an economic interest (i.e., more than a de minimis interest) in a mutual fund that is a party to the proceeding before him. He need not disqualify himself, however, simply because he owns shares in a mutual fund that directly owns shares in a party that appears before him, *unless* the judge participates in the management of the fund. In other words, if the judge owns more than a de minimis amount of shares in Fidelity Magellan Mutual Fund, and

Fidelity Magellan Mutual Fund is a party before the judge, he has a disqualifying interest. However, if I.B.M. is a party before him, the fact that he owns shares in Fidelity Magellan Mutual Fund (which, in turn, owns shares in I.B.M.) is not disqualifying, *unless* the judge (1) participates in the management of the fund, or (2) "a proceeding pending or impending before the judge could substantially affect the value of the interest."

Note: The drafters tell us that this second clause was added "to cover situations such as an investment club where the outcome of a proceeding involving the club might affect the value of the judge's interest." *ABA's Standing Committee Report on 1990 Code, Legislative Draft* 5 (1990). However, one would think that if the judge was a member of an investment club, that situation is already covered by the language [in Terminology 7(i)] including the judge who holds investments in, and participates in the management of, a "common investment fund."

In any event, the rule regarding mutual funds is easy to justify. The judge lacks control over the fund's investment decisions. Moreover, it is not easy to determine (at any given time) the components of a mutual fund's portfolio, for they are constantly changing. In addition, judges have a need for some nondisqualifying investments.

(ii) Civic Organizations

Terminology 7(ii) provides that if the judge or her spouse, parent or child hold an office in an educational, religious, charitable, fraternal, or civic organization, that does not create any "economic interest" in securities held by the organization. Thus, if she is an officer in her local church, and the church owns 100 shares of IBM stock, the judge need not disqualify herself simply whenever IBM is a party before her. However, if the church is a party before her, and she is an officer of her church, she must disqualify herself because "economic interest" includes the relationship of officer, director, advisor, or other active participant in the affairs of a party.

(iii) Financial Institutions and Mutual Insurance Companies

Terminology 7(iii) explains that the interest of a policy holder in a mutual insurance company, or the deposit in a mutual savings association, or credit union, or similar proprietary interest, is an "economic interest" only if the pending or impending proceeding could substantially affect the value of the interest.

(iv) **Government Bonds**

Terminology 7(iv) provides that ownership of government securities is not an "economic interest" in the issuer (e.g., the State of Illinois) unless the proceeding could substantially affect the value of the bonds. In other words, simply because a judge owns a certain number of municipal bonds of Chicago does not mean that he must disqualify himself in every case where Chicago is a party. Similarly, merely because a judge owns $5,000 (or $500,000) of U.S. Bonds does not require her to disqualify herself in every case where the U.S. Government is a party.

However, if an issue concerning the bonds themselves were the subject of the litigation before the judge (e.g., was it legal for the state to extend the time when the bonds were due), and the judge owned these bonds, then the judge has a disqualifying economic interest if the proceeding before the judge could substantially affect the value of the securities.

(g) **Other Interests**

In addition to disqualification for economic interests in the subject matter in controversy, a judge will be disqualified for "any other more than de minimis interest" *if* that interest "could be substantially affected by the outcome of the proceeding." Canon 3E(1)(c) and 28 U.S.C.A. § 455(b)(4). Similarly, the judge must disqualify herself if her spouse, parent, or child (or any member of the judge's family *if* that member is residing in the judge's household) has an interest in the proceeding that is more than de minimis.

(h) **Judicial Campaign Contributions by a Party Before the Court**

The ABA added Canon 3E(1)(c) in 1999, in response to concerns by lawyers making political contributions to judges before whom they appear. If the judge knows of the campaign contribution, or learns about it because a party files a timely motion, then Canon 3E(1)(c) comes into effect. (This Model Canon does not tell us what the time period is; each jurisdiction makes that decision.) This Canon requires the judge to disqualify herself if the campaign contribution is above a certain amount. See Rotunda, *Appearances Can Be Deceiving: Should the Law Worry About Campaign Money Looking Dirty When the Facts Show That the System's Clean?*, The Legal Times, Sept. 15, 2003, at p. 84.

Canon 3E(1)(c) does not stipulate what the amount of the contribution should be. Each jurisdiction should pick a reasonable amount. The Canon does require the judge to "aggregate" all contributions from any one source over a period. The terminology section, in the beginning of the Canons, defines "aggregate" to include not only contributions in cash but contributions in kind as well. "Aggregate" also includes contributions indirectly made but with the understanding that they will be used to support a candidate or oppose the opponent. Terminology 1.

As part of the definition of "aggregate" the Code also tells us that sometimes one does not count, in aggregating contributions, those contributions made to retention elections. The language says if one makes the contribution indirectly "with the understanding that they will be used to support the election of the candidate or to oppose the election of the candidate's opponent," that contribution does not count, if this indirect contribution is made in a "retention" election. A "retention" election is one where the judge runs to retain her judicial office but the judge does not have an opponent. She runs against her record as a judge. The Canons do not explain the rationale for the distinction it is drawing.

F. Disqualification Based on Family Relationships

1. Introduction

Canon 3E(1)(d) provides that a judge will be disqualified if the judge, the judge's spouse, a person "within the third degree of relationship" to either of them, or spouses of any of the foregoing persons, is a party, or officer, director or trustee of a party, is a lawyer in the proceeding, "is known by the judge to have more than a de minimis interest that could be substantially affected by the proceeding," or is likely to be a material witness. This disqualification provision is so expansive because the Code's drafters felt "that to maintain the appearance of impartiality the disqualification standard should encompass all persons within the third degree of relationship to a judge or his spouse even though the relationship arises only through marriage." *Reporter Notes to 1972 Judicial Code* at 67–68.

The degree of relationship, referred to in Canon 3E(1)(d) is measured according to the civil law system. The civil law system counts as one degree each person in the chain from the judge to the common ancestor and from the common ancestor to the person whose relationship raises the issue. Happily, we do not have to remember all that (although it may be useful in a bar bet), because Terminology 21 defines the third degree of relationship to include the following persons: great-grandparent, grandparent, parent, uncle, aunt, brother, sister, child, grandchild, great-grandchild, nephew, or niece. Of course, even if the judge's or his spouse's relative does not fall within the third degree of relationship, the judge still may be disqualified under the general impartiality standard of Canon 3E(1). See, e.g., *Gray v. Barlow,* 241 Ga. 347, 245 S.E.2d 299 (1978) (judge disqualified where relatives were related in the 6th degree but also held security interests in the parties' property in case where plaintiff sought removal of obstruction to his property).

2. Party to the Proceeding

Canon 3E(1)(d)(i) [and 28 U.S.C.A. § 455(b)(5)(i)] requires disqualification where any of the parties covered under this disqualification provision is a party to the proceeding or an officer, director, or trustee of a party. For example, in *Cuyahoga County Board of Mental Retardation v. Association of Cuyahoga County Teachers of Trainable Retarded,* 47 Ohio App.2d 28, 351 N.E.2d 777 (1975), a judge was obligated to recuse himself when his brother was a member of the plaintiff/board.

3. Acting as Lawyer in the Proceeding

Canon 3E(1)(d)(ii) [and 28 U.S.C.A. § 455(b)(5)(ii)] requires disqualification if a person falling within that section—the judge's spouse or any third degree relative (or spouse of such a relative) of either the judge or the judge's spouse—is a lawyer in the proceeding.

Note: Recall that Canon 3E(1)(b) [cf. 28 U.S.C.A. § 455(b)(2) & (3)] also requires a judge to disqualify himself if he had acted as a lawyer in the matter in controversy.

The Commentary to Canon 3E(1)(d)(ii) explains an important caveat to this disqualification provision. Canon 3E(1)(d)(ii) does not automatically disqualify a judge simply because a lawyer in the proceeding is a member of the law firm with which a relative of the judge is affiliated. In other words, the disqualification caused by the relative's personal appearance in the action is *not imputed* to the members of that relative's firm. The judge may still be disqualified under the catch-all provision of Canon 3E(1), however, if his impartiality might reasonably be questioned. A judge may also be disqualified under Canon 3E(1)(d)(iii) if the judge knows that the lawyer-relative has an interest in the law firm that could be substantially affected by the outcome of the proceeding.

Consider, for example, *Potashnick v. Port City Construction Co.*, 609 F.2d 1101 (5th Cir.1980). The judge's father was the senior partner in the law firm representing the plaintiffs. The judge's father, however, was not participating in the case. The court held that the judge was not disqualified under 28 U.S.C.A. § 455(b)(5)(ii) [which corresponds to Canon 3E(1)(d)(ii)], but then held that he was disqualified under § 455(b)(5)(iii) [which corresponds to Canon 3E(1)(d)(iii)]. The judge's father received a 1% share of the firm's income. Although the fee in this case could not be affected by the outcome of the decision because the fee was based on an hourly fixed rate, the court held that disqualification is required even if the lawyer-relative's interest has a mere potential to be affected by the outcome of the case. The case could have been handled on a contingent fee basis, or a favorable result may have justified a higher fee. Furthermore, the decision in the case could affect the firm's reputation, its relationship with its clients, and its ability to attract new clients. The court concluded, therefore, that the judge's father had interests that could substantially be affected by the outcome of the case.

In contrast, in *United States ex rel. Weinberger v. Equifax, Inc.*, 557 F.2d 456 (5th Cir.1977), the judge's son was an associate in the law firm representing the defendant but the son did not personally participate in the case. The judge was therefore not disqualified under 28 U.S.C.A. § 455(b)(5)(ii). The court also held the judge was not disqualified under § 455(b)(5)(iii) because as an associate the son did not have an interest that could be substantially affected by the outcome of the case. Regarding the impartiality standard under 28 U.S.C.A. § 455(a), the court held that the judge did not abuse his discretion in concluding that his impartiality could not reasonably be questioned.

In *SCA Services, Inc. v. Morgan*, 557 F.2d 110 (7th Cir.1977), the Seventh Circuit interpreted the disqualification provisions broadly to favor disqualification. The judge's brother was a partner in the law firm representing one of the parties, but he did not directly participate in the case, thereby precluding disqualification under 28 U.S.C.A. § 455(b)(5)(ii). Nonetheless, the court required disqualification under both § 455(b)(5)(iii) and § 455(a) because the brother would share in the fees generated by the case. Furthermore, the court argued that the judge's impartiality could be reasonably questioned because it is reasonable to assume that brothers enjoy a close personal and family relationship and would probably support each other's interests.

S.J. Groves & Sons Co. v. International Brotherhood of Teamsters, Chauffeurs, Warehousemen and Helpers of America, Local 627, 581 F.2d 1241 (7th Cir.1978) is another case where the judge's brother was a partner in the law firm representing one of the parties. In this case, however, the law firm withdrew from the case before the judge had made any discretionary rulings. The court held the judge did not abuse his discretion in refusing to disqualify himself where the firm had no continuing interest in the case and there was no evidence that the judge forced the firm's withdrawal through delay or other means. The court noted, however, that it probably would be better for a judge to recuse himself in such circumstances to avoid hardship on the parties.

McCuin v. Texas Power & Light Co., 714 F.2d 1255 (5th Cir.1983) added an important qualification to the situation where the judge's close relative is a lawyer in the firm representing one of the parties. In that case, six years after the plaintiffs filed a discrimination suit, defendant added as co-counsel the trial judge's brother-in-law. In a companion case another defendant added the judge's brother-in-law shortly after it filed its answer. The court was concerned that a litigant could disrupt trial preparation by disqualifying a judge whose rulings are expected to be unfavorable by "the simple expedient of finding one of the judge's relatives who is willing to act as counsel. . . . " Congress, however, has not given federal litigants the right of preemptory challenge to a judge. Thus the court interpreted § 455 to mean that "counsel may not be chosen solely or primarily for the purpose of disqualifying the judge." The district court threatened with such maneuvers "need not confine itself to grievance proceedings against errant counsel." The judge who was initially assigned to the case and who is threatened with disqualification should disqualify himself as soon as he became aware that his brother-in-law had been enrolled as counsel. The Fifth Circuit then simply announced that if the new judge thought the employment of the brother-in-law was "stratagem" or a "sham," the new judge should then disqualify counsel. The case would then be reassigned to the first judge.

4. An Interest That Could Be Substantially Affected by the Outcome

Canon 3E(1)(d)(iii) mandates disqualification where a person covered under this section "is known by the judge to have more than a de minimis interest that could be substantially affected by the outcome of the proceeding." This interest could be a non-economic as well as an economic interest. Furthermore, in order for this section to apply, the interest must be both (1) more than "de minimis" (a term vaguely defined in the Terminology (6), and (2) this more than "de minimis" interest is something that "could be substantially affected by the proceeding." [Note that 28 U.S.C.A. § 455(b)(5)(iii) is analogous to Canon 3E(1)(d)(iii) except the federal statute does not allow even de minimis interests.]

The judge has no affirmative duty to become aware of the interests of his relatives under this subsection unless the relative is a spouse or minor child residing in his household. Canon 3E(2).

5. Material Witness in the Proceeding

Canon 3E(1)(d)(iv). Canon 3E(1)(d) [and 28 U.S.C.A. § 455(b)(5)] requires the judge's disqualification whenever a person covered in this section "is to the judge's knowledge likely to be a material witness in the proceeding." Note that it is not enough that the relative will likely be a witness, but the testimony also must be "material" before the judge is required to disqualify himself. Parties cannot mandate judicial disqualification simply by calling a judicial relative as a witness for a nonmaterial matter. The Judicial Canons do not explain what is meant by "material," but the standard is probably somewhat analogous to that of Model Rule 3.7, of the Model Rules of Professional Conduct (the advocate-witness rule).

6. Judicial Campaign Contributions

Canon 3E(1)(e). This provision requires a judge to disqualify herself if she knows (or learns by a timely motion) that a party or a party's lawyer has contributed more than a certain amount [the Model Judicial Code leaves the amount to be determined by the jurisdiction that adopts the Code] or an amount that is more than a "reasonable and appropriate," if the jurisdiction does not adopt a specific amount. This provision mandates disqualification because it might "appear" improper for the judge to decide a case if she has accepted a large contribution from one of the parties. This subsection does not say what the judge should do if *both* parties have made identical campaign contributions, though the plain language says she must still disqualify herself.

In some jurisdictions, the contributions may be anonymous so the only way the judge would learn of the contribution is if the one side knew that the other side had made it and then disclosed that by timely motion. But if the judge did not know of the contribution, how could it affect her judgment?

Canon 3E(1)(e) assumes that the campaign contribution, if more than a certain amount, may affect the judge's impartiality. Intriguingly, the little empirical work that has been done is unable to show a connection between contributions and favorable decisions. In fact, there is a slight negative correlation. Rotunda, *A Preliminary Empirical Inquiry into the Connection between Judicial Decision Making and Campaign Contributions to Judicial Candidates*, 14 The Professional Lawyer 16 (ABA, No. 2, 2003).

Canon 3E(1)(f). Canon 3E(1)(f) provides that a judge or judicial candidate may not make a public statement that "commits" or "appears to commit" the judge with respect to an issue or controversy in the proceeding before the judge. Canon 5A(3)(d)(i) imposes a similar prohibition. If the judge does commit herself (or appears to do so), she must disqualify herself for that proceeding.

G. Remittal of Judicial Disqualification

Note: The waiver of disqualification provisions in the ABA Code of Judicial Conduct and the federal disqualification statute differ significantly. The two disqualification provisions will therefore be treated separately.

1. Canon 3F

If the judge is disqualified by the Canon 3E, Canon 3F permits the parties to waive disqualification unless the basis for disqualification is the judge's personal bias or prejudice concerning a party.

Canon 3F describes clearly the procedure for waiver. To secure a proper waiver, the judge discloses on the record the basis for the disqualification, and then (assuming that the basis is not personal bias or prejudice) asks the parties and lawyers, to consider, *outside of the presence of the judge,* whether to waive disqualification. If the parties and lawyers, *without participation by the judge,* all agree that the judge should not be disqualified, then the judge may participate. (Canon 3F states that the judge may participate if "the judge is then willing to participate," but one would think that the judge would not have asked the parties to waive the disqualification to begin with if he had not been willing to participate.) The agreement regarding this waiver "shall be incorporated in the record of the proceeding."

This question of waiver of disqualification, the Code emphasizes, must be made independently of the judge. Thus, if one of the parties rejects waiver, the judge is not supposed to know who it is. A judge "must not solicit, seek or hear comment on possible" waiver "unless the lawyers jointly propose remittal after consultation as provided in the rule." Canon 3F, Comment 1. It is all right if a party acts through counsel "if counsel represents on the record that the party has been consulted and consents." Id.

The 1972 Judicial Code required that the waiver be reduced to a writing, signed by all the parties and their lawyers, and be incorporated in the record of the proceeding. Canon 3D, 1972 Judicial Code. The 1990 Judicial Code inexplicably omits this important safeguard for the parties, and then, in the last sentence of the Comment to Canon 3F advises: "As a practical matter, a judge may wish to have all parties and their lawyers sign the remittal agreement."

Even under the 1972 Judicial Code, some courts were lax in requiring a written waiver. E.g., *Haire v. Cook*, 237 Ga. 639, 229 S.E.2d 436 (1976), stating that: "A waiver of disqualification of a judge may be effected expressly by agreement, or *impliedly* by proceeding without objection with the trial of the case with knowledge of the disqualification." (emphasis added.)

The wisdom of such cases is open to question. Of course we do not want the parties to plant error by not waiving in writing and then raising the writing requirement if the trial decision on the merits is not to their liking. But judges can easily foreclose this possibility by simply requiring that the waiver be put in writing. The purpose of imposing the writing requirement on both the lawyers *and* the parties "independently of the judge's participation" is to prevent the judge from cajoling the parties and their lawyers to waive important rights. It is also to make sure that lawyers consult their clients outside of the judge's presence. The writing serves to impress upon the parties the significance of the waiver. Some lawyers, after all, may be sycophants, falling over themselves in an effort to please the judge, and thus too willing to waive their clients' rights. Judges should not be able to pressure a waiver of disqualification by figuratively cloaking the judge's fist in a velvet glove. The writing procedure minimizes the chance that a party or lawyer will feel coerced into an agreement.

2. 28 U.S.C.A. § 455(e)

The federal disqualification statute permits waiver of disqualification only where the judge would be disqualified under § 455(a), when "his impartiality might reasonably be questioned." This provision of the statute was changed from the Code because the drafters believed that "confidence in the impartiality of federal judges is enhanced by a more strict treatment of waiver." H.R.Rep. No. 1453, 93d Cong., 2d Sess. 7 (1974). Thus there can be no waiver of any ground of disqualification set out in § 455(b). The only procedural requirement set out in the statute for waiver of disqualification is that the basis for disqualification be disclosed on the record.

The federal statute, § 455(e), is silent regarding the requirement of a waiver in writing by the parties and the attorneys, but the Judicial Conference of the United States, by rule, has adopted such a requirement. See 175 F.R.D. 363, 371–72 (1998). Unfortunately, in practice many federal judges do not know of the Judicial Conference Requirement, and so there are many unreported decisions where the writing requirement is often ignored.

V. Extra–Judicial Activities

Canon 4 requires the judge to conduct extra-judicial activities so as to minimize the risk of conflict with judicial obligations.

A. An Introductory Note

The 1972 Judicial Code had three separate Canons dealing with a judge's extrajudicial activities. Canon 4 of the 1972 Code stated: "A judge may engage in activities to improve the law, the legal system and the administration of justice." Canon 5 of the 1972 Code provided: "A judge should regulate his extra-judicial activities to minimize the risk of conflict with his judicial duties." And Canon 6 of the 1972 Code created a reporting section: "A judge should regularly file reports of compensation received for quasi-judicial and extra-judicial activities." All three of these Canons dealt with the same general subject: a judge's extra-curricular activities. Moreover, under the 1972 Judicial Code, whether an organization was governed by Canon 4 or Canon 5 was very important, because Canon 5 placed significantly more limitations on a judge's participation than did Canon 4 of the 1972 Code. Unfortunately, the 1972 Judicial Code was ambiguous in distinguishing between these two types of organizations.

Happily, the 1990 Code eliminated the confusion between a Canon 4 and a Canon 5 organization by lumping together these two Canons, along with Canon 6. They now are all part of Canon 4 of the 1990 Code.

Canon 3A of the 1990 Code states that a judge's judicial duties take precedence over all the judge's other activities. Yet Canon 4, Comment 1 advises that a "judge should not become isolated from the community in which the judge serves." To completely separate a judge from extra-judicial activities "is neither possible nor wise." Hence, Canon 4A permits a judge to engage in certain quasi-judicial activities so long as these activities do not cast reasonable doubt on his capacity to act impartially as a judge; do not demean the judicial office; and do not interfere with the proper performance of his judicial duties.

Note: The drafters used the phrase "demean the office" instead of "detract from the dignity of his office" to indicate injurious conduct, not merely undignified conduct, because the latter, in some cases, might not be prohibited. *ABA's Standing Committee on 1990 Code, Legislative Draft* 34 (1990).

The Commentary to Canon 4 recognizes that a judge's legal experience places him "in a unique position" to improve the law. Public policy encourages judges to engage in quasi-judicial activities either alone or through bar associations, judicial conferences, or other such organizations. That the judge publicly advocates her opinions on the law, that she has prejudged the *law*, does not imply that she will prejudge the *facts* of a case. If, as Judge Frank acknowledged, "bias" and "partiality" are defined to mean "the total absence of preconceptions in the mind of the judge, then no one has ever had a fair trial and no one ever will. The human mind, even at infancy, is no blank piece of paper. We are born with predispositions; and the process of education, formal and informal, creates attitudes in all men which affect them in judging situations, attitudes which precede reasoning in particular cases and which, therefore, by definition, are prejudices." *In re J.P. Linahan, Inc.,* 138 F.2d 650, 651 (2d Cir.1943). Moreover, as a practical matter, whether or not the judge participates in such activities, she will have definite views on the law and what it should be. "Proof that a Justice's mind at the time he joined the Court was a complete *tabula rasa* in the area of constitutional adjudication would be evidence of lack of qualification, not lack of bias." *Laird v. Tatum,* 409 U.S. 824,

835, 93 S.Ct. 7, 14, 34 L.Ed.2d 50 (1972) (memorandum of Rehnquist, J.). For this reason, a judge was not required to disqualify himself in a homicide case simply because he was a member of the Criminal Law Revision Commission that had drafted the criminal code under which the defendant was convicted. *State v. McKenzie*, 186 Mont. 481, 608 P.2d 428 (1980) (relying on Canon 4 of the 1972 Judicial Code). [Later, defendant sought habeas relief, on other grounds. *McKenzie v. Risley*, 915 F.2d 1396 (9th Cir.1990).]

On the other hand, if the judge indicates bias, even during off-bench behavior, that bias may "cast reasonable doubt" on the judge's ability to act with impartiality. Canon 4A, Comment 1. Even "jokes or other remarks demeaning individuals on the basis of race, sex, religion, national origin, disability, age, sexual orientation or socioeconomic status" fall in this category. Id.

B. Speaking, Writing, and Teaching

Canon 4B broadly provides that a judge may speak, write, lecture, teach, and participate in other extra-judicial activities concerning the law, the legal system, and administration of justice, *and non-legal subjects as well,* unless such activities violate other sections of the Judicial Code. Canon 4B, Comment 2. Thus a judge may teach a law course, write law review articles, and publish his judicial philosophy, without being required to disqualify himself. Nor does the fact that a judge has published his views prior to his confirmation affect his ability to sit on a case raising a similar legal issue. Thus Justice Jackson participated in the decision of one case that raised an issue on which he had earlier written an opinion as Attorney General. *McGrath v. Kristensen*, 340 U.S. 162, 71 S.Ct. 224, 95 L.Ed. 173 (1950). Jackson, by the way, concurred in the opinion of the Court even though it was contrary to his opinion as Attorney General. Compare 340 U.S. at 176, 71 S.Ct. at 233 with 39 Op.Atty.Gen. 504 (1940). Jackson quoted Lord Westbury who had earlier stated (when his Lordship repudiated one of his previous opinions): "I can only say that I am amazed that a man of my intelligence should have been guilty of giving such an opinion." 340 U.S. at 178, 71 S.Ct. at 233.

Judges may seek improvement in the law, both procedurally and substantively, and they "may express opposition to the persecution of lawyers and judges in other countries because of their professional activities." Canon 4B, Comment 1.

C. Governmental, Civic or Charitable Activities

1. Public Hearings and Consultations

Under **Canon 4C(1),** a judge may testify at public hearings before a legislative or administrative body, or "otherwise consult with, an executive or legislative body or official," on any legal matters, whether they are substantive or procedural, and whether or not they relate to court organization. The judge may also testify or consult in matters affecting the judge's interests or when the judge is acting pro se. The 1972 Judicial Code drew various distinctions between public hearings and private consultations. The 1990 Code draws no such distinctions.

2. Extra–Judicial Appointments

Canon 4C(2) provides that a judge shall not accept appointment to a governmental position that is concerned with issues of fact or policy on matters "other than the improvement of the law, the legal system, or the administration of justice." The Commentary suggests that the reasons for this prohibition are to conserve judicial manpower and to protect the courts from involvement in extra-judicial matters that may be controversial. Canon 4C(2), Comment 1. A judge, however, may represent units of government on ceremonial occasions or in connection with historical, educational, and cultural activities. There is nothing wrong when a judge cuts the "blue ribbon."

Canon 4C(2) disapproves of other governmental appointments of judges to nonjudicial duties, including, for example, President Johnson's appointment of Chief Justice Earl Warren to preside over the Commission investigating President John Kennedy's assassination, or President Roosevelt's appointment of Justice Robert Jackson to be the Chief American Prosecutor at the Nuremberg trials.

Canon 4C(2) only governs governmental appointments, not non-governmental appointments. Thus, for example, a judge may not accept appointment to serve on the Board of Trustees of the *State University*, because that is a governmental appointment. But he or she can accept appointment to serve on the Board of Trustees of a *State Law* School, because a law school is a governmental agency devoted to the improvement of law, the legal system, or the administration of justice. And, under Canon 4C(3), discussed immediately below, the judge may accept appointment to the Board of Trustees of a *Private University*, because Canon 4C(3) says so. Such an appointment is not a governmental appointment because the university is private. See, Canon 4C(2), Comment 2. (Remember, whenever we draw bright lines, items that are close to the line could, perhaps, be just as comfortably on the other side of the line. Remember, also, that judges had a lot of input into the drafting of the Judicial Code, and so, at least to some extent, it allows what many judges like to do, and prohibits what many judges do not want to do.)

3. Charitable and Civic Organizations

Canon 4C(3) provides that "a judge may serve as an officer, director, trustee or nonlegal advisor of an organization or governmental agency devoted to the improvement of the law, the legal system or the administration of justice or of an educational, religious, charitable, fraternal or civil organization not conducted for profit," subject to various restrictions, and assuming that the appointment does not violate some other section of the Judicial Code.

Notice that Canon 4C(3) provides that the educational, civic, etc. organization must not be conducted "for profit." The 1972 Judicial Code required that such civic organizations not be conducted "for the economic or political advantage of its members." (See, Canon 5B of the 1972 Code.) The reason the change is that the drafters wanted to make clear that judges may participate in nonprofit judicial organizations even though they support increases in judicial compensation, an activity that is intended to benefit the members. *ABA's Standing Committee Report on 1990 Code, Legislative Draft* 38 (1990).

The requirement that membership in such fraternal, civic, etc. organizations is subject to other requirements of the Judicial Code simply emphasizes the obvious: while there is no per se rule against the judge serving on the board of such an organization, in particular cases it may violate another provision of the Judicial Code. For example, the judge cannot be on the board of an organization that practices invidious discrimination against race, sex, religion, or national origin, in violation of Canon 2C. In addition, service on the board of some organizations may cast doubt on the judge's capacity to act impartially, in violation of Canon 4A(1).

Canon 4C(3)(a). Recall that Canon 3E(1)(c) requires judges to disqualify themselves if they have an economic interest in a party to a proceeding. "Economic interest" is defined to include a "relationship such as officer, director or other active participant in the affairs of a party. . . . "

Terminology 7(ii). Thus, if the judge is, for example, an officer of a fraternal organization, and that organization is involved in a lot of litigation, the judge would find that he or she must be disqualified in a lot of cases. Hence, Canon 4C(3)(a) provides that the judge "shall not serve" as an officer, director, etc. of the organization (civic, fraternal, etc.) if: (1), the organization is likely to be engaged in proceedings that would ordinarily come before the judge [Canon 4C(3)(a)(1)]; or (2), it is likely to be engaged frequently in adversary proceedings before the court of which the judge is a member, or any court subject to the appellate jurisdiction of the court of which the judge is a member [Canon 4C(3)(a)(2)]. The judge, in other words, must arrange her extra-judicial affairs so that she does not put herself in a position where she must frequently disqualify herself.

Canon 4C(3)(b). Canon 4C(3)(b) places additional restrictions on membership solicitation and fund-raising solicitation that applies not only to the judge who is an officer, director, etc. of the organization (civic, fraternal, etc.), but also to one *who is merely a member.* The basic theme behind these specific restrictions is that the judge must not use (or appear to use) the prestige of judicial office to raise funds in a coercive manner. Canon 4C(3)(b), Comment 1. The specific rules and comments are all elaborations of this theme. Thus Canon 4C(3)(b)(iv) explains, the judge "shall not use or permit the use of the prestige of judicial office for fund raising or membership solicitation."

For example, the judge "shall not personally participate" in fund-raising activities, *but may* solicit funds from other judges over whom the judge does not exercise supervisory or appellate authority. Canon 4C(3)(b)(1). The reason for this exception is to allow judges to solicit funds for judicial organizations. Moreover, the dangers of overreaching are nil because the soliciting judge cannot solicit in cases where he or she might exert improper influence. Similarly, the judge may solicit other persons for membership "if neither those persons nor persons with whom they are affiliated are likely ever to appear before the court on which the judge serves. . . . " Canon 4C(3)(b), Comment 1. The judge who is an officer of such an organization may send a general membership solicitation over the judge's signature. Id.

Even in cases where the judge shall not personally participate, he or she may assist in planning fund-raising events and may participate in management and investment of funds. Canon 4C(3)(b)(1). Similarly, the judge may attend an organization's fund-raising event, but may not be the speaker or guest of honor. Comment 3.

D. Financial Activities

1. Financial and Business Dealings

Canon 4D(1) *provides that a judge shall not engage in financial and business dealings that "may reasonably be perceived to exploit" the judicial office or involve the judge in frequent transactions or continuing business relationships with "lawyers or other persons likely to come before the court on which the judge serves."* Judges should never foster the appearance that patronizing a judge's business will benefit a litigant, or that failure to patronize will work to the litigant's disadvantage.

Thus a judge may not use confidential information learned while a judge for private gain. Canon 4D(1), Comment 2. And the judge "should discourage" family members from engaging in dealings that "would reasonably appear to exploit the judge's judicial position."

A judge exploited his judicial position and was involved in transactions with persons before him in violation of Canon 4D(1) where the judge charged parties more for legal notices required in probate matters than the expenses the judge incurred in securing the notices. *In re Douglas,* 135 Vt. 585, 382 A.2d 215 (1977). This conduct also violated Canons 1 and 2 of the Code.

Canon 4D(2) permits a judge to hold and manage investments of the judge and the judge's family, including real estate. This Canon does not limit the judge to passive investment activity, for it specifically allows the judge to engage "in other remunerative activity," unless, of course, these activities contravene some other provision of the Judicial Code.

Canon 4D(3) limits an expansive reading of Canon 4D(2), because Canon 4D(3) prohibits a judge from serving as an officer, director, manager, general partner, advisor, or employee of "any business entity," except for a family business (assuming, of course, that no other provision of the Judicial Code is violated). That is, the judge may "manage and participate in" a closely held business of the judge or members of the judge's family, or a business entity "primarily engaged in investment of the financial resources of the judge or members of the judge's family."

For example, a judge is prohibited from being even an "honorary" director of a bank, a position allowing the judge to attend meetings and express his opinion concerning bank matters, but not giving him a vote. ABA Informal Opinion No. 1385 (Feb. 17, 1977). The arrangement might appear to exploit the judicial office. Similarly, a judge "must avoid participating in a closely-held family business if the judge's participation would involve misuse of the prestige of judicial office." Canon 4D(3), Comment 2.

Canon 4D(4) requires the judge to manage his investments and other financial investments so as to minimize the number of cases in which she is disqualified. If some investment or financial investment requires the judge to be disqualified frequently, then she should divest herself of that investment as soon as she can do so "without serious financial detriment."

2. Receiving Gifts

Canon 4D(5) establishes a general prohibition on a judge accepting a gift, bequest, favor, or loan from anyone, subject to various exceptions noted below. (Note this provision does not cover campaign contributions, which Canon 5 governs.) The drafters adopted this general prohibition of noncampaign gifts to avoid the appearance of impropriety and possible actual impropriety by the judge accepting such a gifts or loans. Of course, the donor might wish to avoid this restriction by bestowing the gift on someone in the judge's family residing in the judge's household. Thus, the judge is instructed to urge such family members not to receive such bequests, though the Code recognizes that, as a practical matter, the judge cannot be expected to know or control all the financial and business dealings of family members, even those residing in the household.

Note: Terminology 14 broadly defines "member of the judge's family residing in the judge's household" as "any relative of a judge by blood or marriage, or a person treated by a judge as a member of the judge's family, who resides in the judge's household."

Canon 4D(5) then lists several important exceptions to the general prohibition on receiving gifts.

Canon 4D(5)(a). The first exception relates to a gift incident to a public testimonial; or complementary books, or tapes, or "other resource materials" supplied by publishers for official use; or an invitation to the judge and "spouse or guest" to attend a bar-related function or activity devoted to the improvement of the law, the legal system, or the administration of justice. The public testimonial gift must not come from a donor organization whose members comprise (or frequently represent) the same side in litigation (Comment 2), for then acceptance could raise an appearance of impropriety.

Also, one should keep in mind a distinction as to who pays for functions. As Comment 1 notes: subsection 4D(5)(a) governs a judge's acceptance of an invitation to a law-related function; in contrast, the judge's acceptance of an invitation that an individual lawyer or group of lawyers pay for is governed by Canon 4D(5)(h), discussed below.

Canon 4D(5)(b). This second group of exceptions covers gifts, awards, or benefits incident to the business or profession of the judge's spouse or family member residing in the judge's household. This exception reflects the fact that the judge's spouse may have an independent professional life. It is permissible that the benefit is for the use of both the spouse (or family member) and the judge. However, the purpose of this exception is not to allow the donor to launder the gift by using the spouse or other family member to accept gifts that are really meant for the judge, so this rule requires that the benefit could not reasonably be understood as intending to influence the judge in the performance of judicial duties.

Canon 4D(5)(c). The provision allows acceptance of "ordinary social hospitality." Judges may accept ordinary social hospitality "even from lawyers who practice before them." J. Shaman, S. Lubet, & J. Alfini, *Judicial Conduct and Ethics* § 7.28 at 201 n. 226 (1990). There are common sense limits to this exception, which are discussed below.

The drafters had difficulty determining what social hospitality to permit. *Reporter's Notes [1972]* at 84. The drafters adopted the "ordinary social hospitality" standard, thus permitting the standard to vary from place to place according to local customs.

Example: A month at the mountain cabin of a lawyer-friend who practices in the judge's court is *not* ordinary social hospitality and is prohibited. See *Reporter's Notes [1972]* at 84–85.

Canon 4D(5)(d) allows acceptance of a gift from a relative or friend for a special occasion, such as a wedding or birthday. However, the gift must be "commensurate with the occasion and the relationship." The gift must not be "excessive in value. . . . " Canon 4D(5)(d), Comment 1.

Note: Canon 4D(5)(d) does not simply allows the judge to accept all wedding gifts. There may be circumstances where doing so might appear to exploit the judicial office. For example, if the judge, getting married while in office, invited many lawyers practicing before the judge to the wedding (even though these lawyers were not personal friends), the lawyers might feel coerced into offering gifts. The gift must be commensurate not only with the occasion but also with the relationship. The Judicial Code implies that wedding invitations must be bona fide, and non-bona fide invitations really "exploit the judge's judicial position. . . . " Canon 4D(1)(a).

Canon 4D(5)(e) allows acceptance of a gift, loan, etc. from a relative or close friend whose "appearance or interest in a case would in any event require disqualification" under Canon 3E. The judge's acceptance of such a gift from such a person does not create any possibility that the judge might be exploiting the judicial office. The acceptance is a moot point, for the judge will have to disqualify herself anyway.

Canon 4D(5)(f) allows acceptance of a loan from a lending institution in its regular course of business on the same terms generally available to persons who are not judges.

In re McDonough, 296 N.W.2d 648 (Minn.1979), addressed the problem of a judge receiving a loan from a financial institution. In that case, the judge received preferential treatment from a bank in the form of an unsecured loan of over $20,000 and a large number of uncharged overdrafts on his wife's checking account. The loan was used to pay family and medical expenses beyond the judge's control. The court held that the judge did not violate what is now Canon 4D(5)(f) because there was no evidence that the bank's treatment of the judge was motivated by the fact he was a judge. In other words, other persons who were (like the judge) good credit risks could receive similar treatment. The court felt that it was common knowledge that financial institutions take community reputation and professional stature into consideration when extending credit or assessing fees. (The court suggested, however, that the judge should give security for the loan or perhaps refinance through another bank. The court also warned the judge that he should not sit on cases involving the bank either as a party, guardian, or trustee.)

Canon 4D(5)(g) permits acceptance of "a scholarship or fellowship awarded on the same terms applied to other applicants."

These listed exceptions are quite realistic and logical. Judges, like everyone else, may need to secure a mortgage from the bank, or the judge's child may win a scholarship. The judge may get married and the judge's friends will want to send wedding gifts. None of these loans or gifts are, or normally should be, prohibited.

Canon 4D(5)(h) offers the last exception to the general prohibition on gifts found in Canon 4D(5). This provision permits acceptance of "any *other* gift, bequest, favor, or loan *only if* the donor is not a party or other person" whose interests have come or are likely to come before the judge. (emphasis added). If such a gift, bequest, favor, or loan exceeds $150, the judge must report it in the same manner he or she reports compensation under Canon 4H, discussed below.

Example: A judge violated Canon 4D(5)(h) when he borrowed money regularly from attorneys who appeared before him, even though he always paid back the loans. *Matter of Anderson,* 312 Minn. 442, 252 N.W.2d 592 (1977) (judge suspended without pay for 3 months for this and other violations of the Judicial Code).

A judge must also be aware of the general propriety standard of Canon 2B. For example, in *Matter of Bonin,* 375 Mass. 680, 378 N.E.2d 669 (1978), the court held that a judge's activities did not violate Canon 5D(5)(h), but his activities did violate Canon 2B. When the judge was an Assistant Attorney General, he had performed legal services for an insurance agency and obtained jobs for relatives of the company's president. The company paid for the judge's reception when he was sworn in, and also paid his rental payments for a leased automobile. The judge had filed a report disclosing these gifts and thus had not violated Canon 4H. In addition, there was no indication that the insurance company or its affiliate or officers had any cases pending in the court where the judge sat. The court held, however, that receipt of the leased automobile as a gift created the appearance of impropriety because the judge had appointed relatives of the company's president to staff positions while he had been an Assistant Attorney General.

E. Fiduciary Activities

Canon 4E. The drafters, concerned about the judicial "appearance of impropriety," placed limits on a judge when acting in a fiduciary capacity. **Canon 4E(1)** generally prohibits a judge from serving as an executor, administrator or other personal representative, trustee, guardian, attorney in fact, or other fiduciary. A judge violated this prohibition when he handled personal checking accounts on behalf of persons who were having difficulty managing their own finances. *Matter of Cieminski*, 270 N.W.2d 321 (N.D.1978) (judge censured for this and other violations of the Judicial Code).

A judge may act in such capacity, however, for the estate, trust, or person of a member of his or her family, *but only if* such service will not interfere with the proper performance of judicial duties. Note that a member of the judge's family is defined as a judge's "spouse, child, grandchild, parent, grandparent, or other relative or person with whom the judge maintains a close familial relationship." Terminology 13 & 14. It is not necessary that the family member reside in the household.

Note: Under the Effective Date of Compliance section of the Judicial Code, if a new judge was serving as a fiduciary when selected as a judge, the new judge may continue to act as a fiduciary, but only for the period of time to avoid "serious adverse consequences to the beneficiary of the fiduciary relationship," and, in no event, longer than one year. See, Application of the Code of Judicial Conduct, § F, Comment 1.

Canon 4E(2) provides that a judge shall not serve as a fiduciary if it is "likely" that the judge, as fiduciary, would be engaged in proceedings that would ordinarily come before him. The judge is also disqualified if the estate, trust, or ward, in fact becomes involved in adversary proceedings in the court on which he serves or one under its appellate jurisdiction.

Canon 4E(3) provides that a judge, when acting as a fiduciary, is subject to the same restrictions on financial activities that apply to a judge acting in her personal capacity. The Commentary suggests that a judge should resign as trustee under this provision if her duties as a judge violated her duties as a fiduciary.

Example: If it would result in detriment to the trust to divest it of holdings, but retention of those holdings would place the judge in violation of Canon 4D(4), then the judge should resign as trustee.

F. Arbitration and the Practice of Law

1. Arbitration and Mediation

Canon 4F prohibits a judge from acting as an arbitrator or mediator or otherwise perform judicial functions in a private capacity, unless expressly authorized by law. The *Reporter's Notes to the 1972 Code of Judicial Conduct* at 89, suggest various reasons to justify the prohibition:

(1) the arbitration proceeding could come before the court on which the judge sits;

(2) the court could be drawn into social and political controversies in which a judge acted as an arbitrator;

(3) the judicial office might be exploited by those seeking to use its dignity and prestige in support of an arbitration award; and

(4) judicial time could be diverted in a case in which a judge's fee as arbitrator would be large.

The drafters of the 1990 Code continue these restrictions.

2. Practice of Law

Canon 4G. In order to avoid the appearance of impropriety and conflicts of interest Canon 4G prohibits a judge from practicing law. The drafters left the definition of "practice of law" to the law of each jurisdiction.

This prohibition is quite natural. One who is a full time judge in name, should also be a full time judge in fact. Thus, a probate judge cannot continue to draft deeds, wills, contracts, and other legal instruments, or act as an attorney for executors, administrators, or guardians. ABA Informal Opinion 1294 (June 17, 1974). A judge can, however, continue to practice law if his election to judicial office is being contested, so long as he has not actually assumed his office by taking the prescribed oath. *Reed v. Sloan*, 475 Pa. 570, 381 A.2d 421 (1977). But once a judge actually assumes his office he may not continue to practice law, even on matters he had started before becoming a judge. *In re Ryman*, 394 Mich. 637, 232 N.W.2d 178 (1975); *In re Piper*, 271 Or. 726, 534 P.2d 159 (1975).

The prohibition against the practice of law does not apply to the judge who is acting *pro se*. In addition, a judge may give uncompensated legal advice and even draft documents to members of the judge's family.

G. Compensation, Reimbursements, and Reporting

Introductory Note: Canon 4I provides that the Judicial Code does not require a judge to disclose his income, debts, investments, or other assets except as provided in Canons 3E [disqualification] and 3F [remittal of disqualification], this Canon [Canon 4], and other law. The Comment to this section emphasizes that judges have the same rights as other citizens to privacy of financial affairs "except to the extent that limitations established by law are required to safeguard the proper performance of judicial duties."

1. Canon 4H Generally

Canon 4H(1) provides that a judge may receive not only reimbursement of expenses, but also compensation for extra-judicial activities permitted by the Judicial Code, provided that the source of the payments does not give the appearance of impropriety or of influencing the judge in performing judicial duties. Canon 4H then adds other restrictions on a judge's receipt of compensation or reimbursement.

2. Compensation

Canon 4H(1)(a) limits the amount of compensation that judges may receive for non-judicial duties. The amount must be reasonable and should not be more than what a person who is not a judge would receive for the same activity.

3. Expense Reimbursement

Canon 4H(1)(b) limits expense reimbursement to the "actual cost" of travel, food, and lodging. Furthermore, these expenses must be "reasonably incurred" by the judge. A judge may also be reimbursed for the expenses of the judge's "spouse or guest" if that person's presence is "appropriate to the occasion." Any amount reimbursed over those expenses reasonably incurred is considered compensation. This distinction is important because compensation for non-judicial duties must be publicly reported under Canon 4H(2), while reimbursement for expenses need not be.

4. Public Reports

Canon 4H(2) sets out the manner for reporting compensation. The judge must report the date, place, and nature of any activity for which compensation was received, the name of who paid the compensation, and the amount received.

Notes: Canon 4D(5)(h) requires a similar report for gifts over $150. Reports must be made at least once a year and should be filed as a public document in the court clerk's office or other office designated by rule of court.

Compensation or income of a spouse attributed to the judge by operation of community property law is not considered the judge's income, and thus is not subject to these requirements.

VI. Political Activities

A. Introduction

Canon 5 of the ABA Model Code of Judicial Conduct, concerning political activity, requires judges and judicial candidates to refrain from inappropriate political activity. Canon 5 is divided into several sections—Section A, governing the general political conduct of all judges and candidates for judicial office; Section B, dealing with candidates seeking appointment to judicial office or a judge seeking appointment to another governmental office; Section C, governing judges and candidates subject to public election; Section D, dealing with incumbent judges; and Section E, governing applicability. Canon 5, in short, applies as a model code whether judges are selected by public election or by a merit selection (appointive) system.

B. General Political Conduct

Canon 5A places broad restrictions on the political activity of a judge or a candidate for election to judicial office, subject to various exceptions. The purpose of this section is to limit the active participation of a judge (or candidate for judicial office) in the election process of any other political candidate

Note: There may be practical problems in enforcing the Judicial Code against those who are not judges. If the candidate is successful and becomes a judge, he or she would then be subject to appropriate sanctions for any misdeeds as a candidate. In addition, if the candidate is a lawyer, DR 8–103(A) and Model Rule 8.2(b) require the lawyer to follow these provisions of the Judicial Code. Canon 5E.

Note also: A "candidate" is defined in Terminology 3. In general, it refers to anyone seeking selection or election to judicial office. The term has the same meaning when applied to elected or appointed judges.

Canon 5A(1)(a) prohibits a judge or candidate from acting as a "leader" of, or holding any office in, a political organization. **Canon 5A(1)(b)** prohibits such persons from making speeches for a political organization or candidate, or from publicly endorsing another candidate for public office. However, public endorsement requires more than mere public association. Thus, Comment 5 to Canon 5A(1) makes clear that a candidate for judicial office does not publicly endorse another candidate for public office merely by having the candidate's name on the same ticket.

Canon 5A(1)(a), (b), (c), (d), & (e) prohibit the judge or candidate from making speeches on behalf of a political organization, attending political gatherings, or soliciting funds or making contributions to a political organization or to another political candidate, attending political gatherings, or purchasing tickets for political party dinners or other functions. However, the judge or candidate may vote. [Yes indeed, Comment 1 to Canon 5A(1) explicitly states that the judge or candidate retains the right to participate as a voter.] A judge or judicial candidate also retains the right to respond to false information concerning a judicial candidate. The judge or judicial candidate may "privately" express his or her views on judicial candidates or other candidates for office. (Yes, the drafters thought it necessary for Comment 4 to make this caveat. A contrary rule would raise very serious first amendment concerns.) And, an "office in a political organization" means exactly that: a candidate who is a county prosecutor, for example, does not hold an office in a "political" organization. Comment 3.

Canon 5A(1) explicitly provides that Canons 5B(2), 5C(1), and 5C(3) are authorized exceptions to the limitations of Canon 5A. These exceptions consume much of the restrictions that Canon 5A(1) impose. Thus, **Canon 5B(2)** allows a candidate for *appointment* to judicial office, or a judge seeking appointment to another judicial office, to communicate with the appointing authority and its agents, to seek support from other appropriate organizations and individuals. **Canon 5C(1)** allows judges and candidates subject to public election to be involved in a great deal of political activity (unless otherwise prohibited by law); they may purchase tickets and attend political gatherings, identify themselves as members of a political party, and contribute to a political organization. And, **Canon 5C(3)** allows candidates for judicial election to be listed on election materials with the names of other candidates and to appear in promotions of the ticket. The ABA, in short, prefers merit selection of judges. But, not all states have merit selection, and if judges and candidates must campaign in partisan elections, then the Model Code of Judicial Conduct realistically acknowledges that it is difficult to take the politics out of politics.

Canon 5A(2) requires a judge to resign from judicial office if she is a candidate for a *non*-judicial office either in a party primary or in a general election. However, this prohibition does not apply to a judge who is serving as a delegate or running as a candidate for delegate to a state constitutional convention (if otherwise permitted by law).

C. Campaign Conduct

1. Generally

Canon 5A(3)(a) requires candidates for judicial office to maintain appropriate dignity. Although a member of the judge's family is free to do things forbidden to a judicial candidate, the judicial candidate "shall encourage" her family members to adhere to the same political activity standards of Canon 5 applicable to judicial candidates. It is difficult to see how the requirement to "encourage" will be subject to any realistic enforcement mechanism.

Canon 5A(3)(b) provides that a candidate shall prohibit public officials or employees "who serve at the pleasure of the candidate" from doing that which the judicial candidate is prohibited from doing under Canon 5. In addition, the candidate "shall discourage" other employees or officials who are "subject to the candidate's direction and control" from doing that which the candidate must not do under Canon 5. Finally, the candidate "shall not authorize or knowingly permit any other person" to do for the candidate what the candidate is prohibited from doing. **Canon 5A(3)(c).**

Canon 5A(3)(d) regulates the type of campaign that a candidate for judicial office can conduct. A candidate shall not: make pledges, promises or commitments that are inconsistent with the impartial performance of the adjudicative duties of the office or misrepresent his (or his opponent's) identity, qualifications, present position, or other fact. However, **Canon 5A(3)(e)** allows the candidate to respond to personal attacks or attacks on his record [assuming that this response does not violate Canon 5A(3)(d)].

The rules intend to protect candidates from improper questioning in opinion polls, interviews, or questionnaires. They do not prevent a candidate from promising to improve court administration. And an incumbent judge may make "private statements" to other judges or court personnel in performance of judicial duties. In any public statement, a candidate "should emphasize" the candidate's duty to uphold the law regardless of one's personal views. Canon 5A(3)(d), Comment 1.

Example: The judicial candidate (whether seeking election or appointment) may not properly state: "Elect me, and I will favor high verdicts in personal injury lawsuits."

Constitutional Note: Canon 5A(3)(d)(i) raises free speech problems. *Buckley v. Illinois Judicial Inquiry Board,* 997 F.2d 224 (7th Cir.1993), invalidated an Illinois Rule somewhat similar to Canon 5A(d)(i) (*before* it was amended in 2003), holding that a state rule prohibiting judicial candidates from making pledges or promises of conduct in office and from announcing views on disputed legal or political issues violated the

First Amendment. Although the state had a legitimate interest in preserving the impartiality of those elected to judicial office, the rule reached far beyond the speech that could reasonably be interpreted as committing the candidate in a way that would compromise impartiality if he or she succeeded in the election. The clause dealing with "disputed legal or political issues" was too broad and unconstitutionally vague. In the particular facts of this case, one of the litigants (a sitting judge) had distributed campaign literature truthfully claiming that he had never reversed a rape conviction.

Later, *Republican Party v. White*, 536 U.S. 765, 122 S.Ct. 2528, 153 L.Ed.2d 694 (2002), invalidated a Minnesota judicial canon that prohibited a "candidate for a judicial office" from "announc[ing] his or her views on disputed legal or political issues" (the "announce clause"). The Court did not decide if the "commit" clause is consistent with free speech. The ABA modified Canon 5A(d)(i) in 2003, in response to *White*, to prohibit the judicial candidate from making any "pledges, promises or commit-ments" inconsistent with her duties of impartial performance of her judicial duties. If the judge violates this obligation, she must disqualify herself in the relevant proceeding. Canon 3E(1)(f). It is the hope of the ABA, in redrafting this clause, to take into account the free speech concerns of *White*. Rotunda, *Judicial Elections, Campaign Financing, and Free Speech,* 2 Election Law Journal 79 (No.1, 2003).

2. Solicitation of Campaign Funds

Candidates for *appointive* judicial office are not permitted to engage in the fund-raising activities permitted other judicial candidates. **Canon 5B(1).**

Although a judicial candidate subject to public election may not person-ally solicit or accept campaign contributions, or "personally solicit publicly stated support," he can establish committees to conduct cam-paigns, solicit and accept "reasonable campaign contributions," manage the expenditure of funds for his campaign, as well as to obtain public statements of support and "reasonable campaign contributions" for the candidacy (even from lawyers). **Canon 5C(2).**

Note: This campaign committee provision is an explicit exception to Canon 5A(3)(c)'s prohibition on third persons performing those things that judges are prohibited from doing.

The Judicial Code also requires each jurisdiction to place time limits on the solicitation of campaign funds. Canon 5C(2). Each jurisdiction may specify its own time limits, but the Judicial Code suggests that a campaign committee should solicit funds no earlier than one year before an election [the 1972 Judicial Code proposed 90 days] and no later than 90 days after the last election in which a candidate participates during the election year. To solicit campaigns after the election may smell of tribute. On the other hand, judges who run for election have campaign expenses, and soliciting contributions after the election has proven to be a useful means of securing necessary contributions. This Judicial Canon also prohibits the use of campaign contributions for the private benefit of the candidate or others.

Note: The 1972 Code prohibited the campaign committee from revealing the names of the contributors to the candidate unless the candidate was required by law to file a list of his campaign contributors. The 1990 Code does not have such a restriction. First, most jurisdictions now require the candidates to disclose the names of the contributors, so a secrecy provision is unrealistic. Second, the judge should know the names of contributors in order to determine whether recusal is advisable. Canon 5C(2), Comment 1 notes: "Though not prohibited, campaign contributions of which a judge has knowledge, made by lawyers or others who appear before the judge, may be relevant to disqualification under Section 3E."

Solicitation of campaign funds raises a problem with no easy solution. Judges who run in elections need money. Unless the state provides the money, candidates must raise it, and the most likely source of funds are those most interested in judicial elections—the lawyers. Yet financial gifts by lawyers raise questions of partiality. In the multi-billion dollar *Pennzoil v. Texaco* case, the Texas state trial court judge received a $10,000 contribution from Pennzoil's chief trial attorney, "[w]ithin days of being assigned the Pennzoil case. . . . " The trial judge described it as a "princely sum." Petzinger & Solomon, *Texaco Case Spotlights Questions on Integrity of the Courts in Texas*, Wall Street Journal, Nov. 4, 1987, at 1, 20 column 2. See also, *More of the Same*, Forbes, Sept. 7, 1987 at 8 (in the last 3 ½ years all nine members of the Texas Supreme Court "openly accepted campaign contributions from lawyers with cases pending before them," which Texas law allowed).

VII. Application of the Judicial Code: Defining Who is a Judge

A. Introduction

The final section of the ABA Model Code of Judicial Conduct, "Application of the Code of Judicial Conduct," defines who is a judge and what sections of the Judicial Code are inapplicable to part-time judges or judges *pro tempore*.

The Judicial Code is intended to apply to all persons who perform "judicial functions," whether or not they are lawyers. Application of the Code of Judicial Conduct, § A. It is surprising but true that not all judges in the United States are lawyers. Cf. *North v. Russell*, 427 U.S. 328, 96 S.Ct. 2709, 49 L.Ed.2d 534 (1976).

To perform a "judicial function" it is not necessary that the person be a judge of a court of general jurisdiction. For example, a referee in bankruptcy, special master, court commissioner, or magistrate is a judge for the purposes of this Code.

All persons who fall in this category of "judge" should comply with the Judicial Code, subject to four exceptions: (1) Retired Judge subject to recall; (2) Continuing Part-time Judge; (3) Periodic Part-time Judge; and (4) Pro Tempore Part-time Judge. All these types of judges (except for retired judge subject to recall) are defined in the Terminology section of the Model Judicial Code.

B. Retired Judge

A retired judge who is subject to being recalled as a judge, and who is not allowed to practice law, is not ever required to comply with Canon 4E (dealing with fiduciary activities), and is only required to comply with Canon 4F (service as an arbitrator or mediator) while he is serving as a judge.

Retired judges *not* subject to recall to judicial service are not mentioned in § B of "Application," because, by implication, they are not governed by the Judicial Code.

C. Continuing Part–time Judge

A judge is classified as continuing part-time if he serves repeatedly on a part-time basis by election or under a continuing appointment. This definition includes a retired judge subject to recall who is permitted to practice law. Terminology 4.

Example: Alpha is a judge in a court of general jurisdiction who receives the same salary as other judges in that capacity. She is forbidden from engaging in any other occupation but only works every other morning because she works fast and her docket is up-to-date. She is a full-time judge required to comply with all provisions of the Judicial Code.

If one is a continuing part-time judge, then that person need not comply with Canon 3B(9) (dealing with public comments on pending or impending cases) except while serving as a judge. This person, however, is not ever required to comply with Canons 4C(2), 4D(3), 4E(1), 4F, 4G, 4H, 5A(1), 5B(2), and 5D. A part-time judge who is practicing law part-time shall not do so in the court on which he serves or in any court subject to the appellate jurisdiction of the court on which he serves. Application, § C(2). In addition, he should not act as a lawyer in any proceeding or related proceeding in which he had served as judge. Id.

D. Periodic Part–Time Judge

A "periodic part-time" judge is a judge who serves or expects to serve repeatedly on a part-time basis but under a separate appointment for each limited period of service. Terminology 16. Such a person need not comply with Canon 3B(9) except while serving as a judge. This person does not have to comply with Canons 4C(2), 4C(3)(a), 4D(1)(b), 4D(3), 4D(4), 4D(5), 4E, 4F, 4G, 4H, 5A(1), 5B(2), and 5D. Application, § D(1). In addition, a part-time judge who is practicing law part-time shall not do so in the court on which she serves or in any court subject to the appellate jurisdiction of the court on which she serves. Application, § D(2). In addition, she should not act as a lawyer in any proceeding or related proceeding in which she had served as judge. Id.

E. Pro Tempore Part–Time Judge

A pro tempore part-time judge is someone who serves or expects to serve as a judge once or only sporadically on a part-time basis under separate appointment for each period of service or case heard. While acting as a judge, he is excused from Judicial Canons 2A, 2B, 2B(9), and 4C(1), except while serving as a judge. In addition, this type of judge is not required to comply at any time with Canons 2C, 4C(2), 4C(3)(a), 4C(3)(b), 4D(1)(b), 4D(3), 4D(4), 4D(5), 4E, 4F, 4G, 4H, 5A(1), 5A(2), 5B(2), and 5D. A pro-tempore part-time judge must not act as a lawyer in any proceeding or related proceeding in which he had served as a judge, except as otherwise permitted by the adopting state's version of Model Rule 1.12(a), of the Model Rules of Professional Conduct.

REVIEW QUESTIONS

1. State Governor is on trial for federal tax fraud. He plans to call Judge, his life-long friend, as a character witness. Governor had appointed Judge to the State Supreme Court several years ago.

> When Governor asked Judge to testify on his behalf, Judge responded: "You know, under our rules, you must subpoena me. I cannot appear voluntarily, but after I receive an official summons I will be pleased to testify on your behalf."

Is Judge *subject to discipline?*

    a.   Yes, if he responds to the official summons.

    b.   No, if he responds to an official summons.

    c.   No, because Governor had appointed him to the state supreme court.

    d.   Yes, because the judge has immunity from giving character testimony.

2. Judge First is on a panel of state appellate judges who are ruling on an issue of comparative fault. In trying to interpret the application of a new statute, he asked the advice of Clerk (who is his law clerk), and Judge Second, another appellate judge who was not on his panel and Judge Third, an appellate judge who is on the same panel as Judge First. He never informed counsel of any of these conversations.

Are Judge First's actions *proper?*

    a.   No, because he initiated *ex parte* communications concerning a pending proceeding.

    b.   No, because Judge Second was not on the same appellate panel.

    c.   No, because Clerk is not another judge.

    d.   Yes, because there are no restrictions on a judge's communications with experts on the law.

    e.   Yes, because First and Second are other judges, and Clerk is a court employee.

3. In the case of *P. vs. D.*, the Chief Justice of the State Supreme Court announced at the beginning of oral argument: "I own 100 shares of the stock of

D., Inc., worth $7,100. I'll recuse myself from this case and we'll bring in another judge, unless you have no problem with my stock ownership." Counsel for P. and for D. turned to each other, briefly discussed the matter privately, and then each said on the record: "We have no problem, your Honor." The Chief Justice then declared the disqualification waived. The Chief Justice believed that her financial interest is substantial.

Did Chief Justice act *properly*?

a.   No, because the judge did not secure a proper waiver of the parties and lawyers.

b.   No, because the parties cannot waive judicial disqualifications.

c.   Yes, because any disqualification was waived.

d.   No, because the Chief Justice should not have threatened to recuse himself when her financial interest was less than $10,000.

4.   Judge, while a practicing attorney, represented class action plaintiffs in a complex consumer fraud case. Judge, in that case acquired no relevant client confidences or secrets because he was only involved in various legal questions rather than factual issues: he was then an associate, and he worked on some legal background memos regarding some venue issues. The senior partners in his firm worked substantially on the case.

Several years have passed and Judge is now a judge, and this same class action suit has now been brought before him. He has been asked to rule on several substantive issues of law having nothing to do with his earlier work on the venue matters.

Is it *proper* for Judge to so rule?

a.   Yes, if the attorneys each exercise a waiver of disqualification.

b.   Yes, because Judge acquired no relevant confidences or secrets in the prior representation.

c.   No, because Judge had served as a lawyer in the controversy now before him.

d.   No, unless his former law firm is no longer involved in representing any of the parties.

5. Judge is getting married and has invited Lawyer to his wedding. He and Lawyer are very close friends and Lawyer, an active litigator, appears before Judge. Lawyer plans to buy Judge a wedding gift costing $300. Under the circumstances, the cost of this gift is not surprising, given the occasion and the long friendship and relationship between Judge and Lawyer.

Is it *proper* for Judge to accept this gift?

a. No, because Lawyer appears in Judge's court often.

b. Yes, because the gift is a wedding gift.

c. Yes, but only if Judge reports the gift as compensation.

d. No, because the gift cost was more than $100.

6. Judge, the Chief Justice of the State Supreme Court, is planning to run for his party's nomination for Governor.

When should Judge *resign* his judgeship?

a. When he first becomes a candidate in his party's primary.

b. After the primary, if he wins it.

c. After the general election, if he wins it.

7. A judge who is disqualified from hearing a case because of a provision of the Code of Judicial Conduct—

a. may nevertheless hear the case, whatever the nature of the disqualification, if the parties and their lawyers independently agree that the judge may participate in the proceedings.

b. may not hear the case involving the disqualification, whatever its nature and without regard to any purported waivers by the clients or lawyers.

c. may nevertheless hear the case if the reason for the disqualification is based on the judge's economic interests and the parties and their lawyers (out of the presence of the judge) agree that the judge may participate in the proceedings and that the judge's interest is insubstantial.

d. may nevertheless hear the case if the reason for the disqualification is based on the fact that the judge has a personal bias or prejudice concerning a party, assuming that the parties and their lawyers independently agree that the judge may participate in the proceedings, and that his capacity as a witness will not affect his objectivity.

8. Judge is presently serving on her state's trial court. In several opinions she has refused to provide any protection to state prison inmates who are disciplined by prison authorities for violating the prison's rules of conduct. Judge is now running for election to her state's supreme court. She is vigorously opposed by several organizations concerned with the conditions under which prisoners are incarcerated in the state's prison. In an interview, the local reporter has asked her about her attitude on the subject of prisoners' rights.

Judge says:

I.   "I promise always to act impartially."

II. "In my opinion, incarceration for the commission of a crime carries with it a loss of civil liberties in prison discipline proceedings. I will not change my view, even with respect to the Jones case, which is now before the court and raises the same issue that was involved in my previous prisoner rights cases, and that's why the people should elect me to the supreme court."

III. "I am convinced I was right in those cases and I promise the people of this state that I will make the same decision in the Jones case, a case quite similar to the earlier cases you mentioned."

Were Judge's statements *proper*?

a.   Yes, as to I only.

b.   Yes, as to II only.

c.   Yes, as to I & II only.

d.   Yes, as to I, II, & III.

*

Answers to Review Questions

■ PART I

1. *False.* While the Model Rules do not use the term "ethical consideration," both the Model Code and the Model Rules guide a lawyer as to what must, may, and should be done in different circumstances.

2. *c.*

3. *b.* The answer is the same under the Model Rules and the old Model Code, though the latter does uses the "moral turpitude" language. See Model Rule 8.4(b).

4. *c.* See Model Rule 8.4(b)(1).

5. *c.* See DR 1–102(A)(4); Model Rule 8.4(c).

■ PART II

1. *d.* Model Rule 8.3(a) & (c); DR 1–103(A). *In re Himmel*, 125 Ill.2d 531, 533 N.E.2d 790 (1988) should not change this answer because the information, at this point, is still covered by the attorney/client evidentiary privilege.

2. *d.* Model Rule 8.5(a), (b)(1); DR 1–102(A)(4).

3. *c.* Model Rules 8.4(c) & 8.5; DR 1–102(A)(4). Note that Lawyer has only been *charged* with criminal fraud. He has not been convicted (at least, not yet). But Lawyer, when asked, falsely failed to disclose that he had been charged with criminal fraud. His dishonesty is his *present failure to disclose, i.e.,* his false answer to a specific question.

4. *d.* Model Rule 8.2(a); DR 8–102(A).

■ PART III

1. *a.* See Model Rules 1.5(e)(2) & 1.9(a); DR 2–107(A); DR 4–101. Note that it is not enough, in "c", to inform the parties; they must consent and waive the conflict.

2. *b.* See Model Rule 1.15; DR 9–102. N.B. It would be the unusual lawyer who would choose option III, but it is an ethically permissible option.

3. *b.* See Part II, section VII, B, supra.

4. *b.* Model Rule 1.2(a), Comment 1 & Rule 1.3, Comment 3; EC 7–7, 7–8;

5. Under the Model Rules, the answer is *c*. See Rule 1.5, Comment 3. Under the Model Code the answer is also **c**. See DR2–106(B).

6. *c.* Model Rules, Scope 17 (some duties, like confidentiality, "attach when the lawyer agrees to consider whether a client-lawyer relationship shall be established."); Rule 1.18 ("Duties to Prospective Client"). See EC 4–1; DR 4–101(A).

7. *e.* Rule 1.11(a). If Attorney had acquired confidential information, he would be disqualified under Rule 1.9(c) or Canon 4, DR 9–101(B).

8. *d.* Model Rule 1.8(g); DR 5–106.

9. *f.* Rule 1.5(d); DR 2–106(C).

10. *e.* Model Rule 1.7(a). Note, consent *only* by Brewer is not enough. Rule 1.7(c)(4) Note also that the referral fee referred to in alternative *b* is not even permitted by the Model Rules. See, Rule 1.5(e)(2); DR 5–105(C).

11.   *c.*   I & II are state action. IV is not setting a fee.

■ PART IV

1.   *b.*   Model Rule 5.4(a)(3); DR 3–102(A)(3). See, e.g., ABA Committee on Ethics, Informal Opinion 1440 (1979)(law firm's law administrator may be included in the law firm's profit-sharing plan); Arthur Garwin, *When Bonuses Boomerang*, ABA Journal, Feb. 1997, at 83.

2.   *a.*   Model Rule 5.4(a) & (b); DR 3–102(A) & (B).

3.   *c.*   Model Rule 5.5, Comments 1, 2; DR 3–101(A); EC 3–5. The manager is making an unsupervised judgment that the letter should contain a threat of suit.

4.   *a.*   Model Rule 5.3 & Comments 1, 2; DR 4–101(D).

■ PART V

1.   *c.*   Model Rule 7.3 & Comment 4, stating that 7.3(a) is not intended to prevent a lawyers from participating in constitutionally protected activities of bona fides social, civic, fraternal, etc. organizations who purposes include recommending legal services to its members. Even the old Model Rules allowed such speeches and did not regard them as solicitation. See, DR 2–104(A)(4).

2.   *d.*   Rule 1.8(f) & Comment 12; Rule 7.2(b)(4) & Comment 8. Cf. Rule 1.5(e).

3.   *e.*   Model Rule 7.5(d); DR 2–102(C). N.B. ABA Formal Opinion 03–430 (July 9, 2003) deals with two main issues: (1) the propriety of insurance staff counsel representing the insurance company and its insureds, and (2) the permissible names for an association of insurance staff counsel. This opinion concludes that insurance staff counsel may practice under a trade name or under the names of one or more of the practicing lawyers, provided the lawyers function as a law firm and disclose their affiliation with the insurance company to all insureds whom they represent. This opinion is inapplicable to the question, because the letterhead is affirmatively misleading; it says: "A, B, & J, a Partnership of Attorneys at Law" when, in fact, A, B, & J are not partners.

4.   c.   *Bates v. State Bar of Arizona* (1977) did not rule on the other issues.

5.   *b.*   Model Rule 7.3 (a)(2) allows solicitation of a person who had a "prior professional relationship with the lawyer." See also, DR 2–104(A)(1).

6.   *d.*   Model Rules 7.4(d); 7.1. See, DR 2–105(A).

■ PART VI

1. *c.* Model Rule 1.11(a)(2) & Comments 3 & 5 (which notes that it does not matter if the lawyer is acting adversely to the former government client). See Section II, A(1) of Part VI & DR 9–101(B).

2. *c.* Rule 8.2(a); DR 8–102(A).

3. *d.* Model Rule 3.8(a); DR 7–103(A).

4. *c.* Model Rule 6.4 seems to be applicable, because Lawyer is a member of an organization involved in law reform. Lawyer made the necessary disclosures and so is not violating Rule 6.4. See also, DR 8–101(A)(1).

■ PART VII

1. *c.* Model Rule 4.2; DR 7–104(A).

2. *a.* Model Rule 3.4(e) & Comment 2; DR 7–106(C)(3).

3. *b.* Model Rule 3.1; DR 7–102(A)(1), (2); DR 2–109(A).

4. *d.* See Rule 3.6(b)(2),(5). Note that the lawyer does not have to say anything; Rule 3.6 governs what the lawyer may say, not what the lawyer must say.

5. Under the Model Code the answer is *c.* See DR 7–109(C). Under the Model Rules the answer is less clear. Rule 3.4(b), Comment 3 tells that *c* remains the correct answer in a typical jurisdiction, which prohibits a person to pay an expert witness a contingent fee.

■ PART VIII

1. *b.* Model Rule 2.1, Comments 1 & 2; EC 7–8; 7–9; DR 7–101(A)(1).

2. *a.* Model Rule 1.12(a). See also, Model Rule 2.2. DR 5–105(A) & (C); EC 5–20;

■ PART IX

1. *c.* Model Rule 6.2. EC 2–27; EC 2–29; EC 2–30.

2. *a.* Model Rule 6.2. EC 8–1; EC 8–4.

3. *a.* Model Rule 6.1. EC 1–4.

4. *b.* Rule 6.5(b) & Comment 4.

■ PART X

1. *b.* Model Judicial Code, Canon 2B. The last sentence of Canon 2B states simply that "A judge shall not testify voluntarily as a character witness." Intriguingly, the last sentence of Canon 2B, Comment 5 advises (on an *aspirational* level) that "[e]xcept in unusual circumstances where the demands of justice require, a judge *should* discourage a party from requiring the judge to testify as a character witness." (emphasis added)

2. *e.* Model Judicial Code, Canon 3B(7)(c) and Comment 9.

3. *a.* We know that the judge's ownership of stock in a party is a disqualifying interest, under Model Judicial Code, Canon 3E(1)(c) if the ownership is not de minimis. Terminology 5, 6. We don't know enough to conclude that the judge is wrong in her assessment that the stock ownership is not de minimis, so we shall assume that she is correct. Model Judicial Code, Canon 3F requires that the judge ask the lawyers *and* the parties to consider a waiver *out of the presence of the judge.* That was not done here.

4. *c.* Model Judicial Canon 3E(1)(b). This disqualification can be waived, but the waiver is not proper unless the lawyers *and* the parties agree to waive it. Canon 3F.

5. *b.* Model Judicial Code, Canon 4D(5)(d).

6. *a.* Model Judicial Canon 5A(2). Judge is clearly now a candidate. Terminology 3.

7. *c.* Model Judicial Code, Canon 3E & 3F. The judge cannot waive a disqualification if its basis is the judge's personal bias or prejudice concerning a party.

8. *a.* Code of Judicial Conduct, Canon 5A(3)(d), and Comment 1.

*

A Sample Examination

INSTRUCTIONS

This examination consists of three questions. You are to answer all of them in light of the relevant ABA codes, supplemented where appropriate by other materials and considerations discussed in this course.

If any facts that you think are necessary to answer a question are missing, make appropriate assumptions and alternative assumptions of fact. Identify what assumptions you made and explain why you believe such assumptions were required. Each question is weighted in proportion to the suggested time. You have a total of 3½ hours.

QUESTION ONE *(Forty–Five Minutes)*

Plaintiff is an individual seeking to prosecute a class action involving construction of a standard life insurance policy. Plaintiff has asked Attorney to file a class action. Attorney would advance the needed funds, and Plaintiff agreed to remain liable for all costs of the litigation; that is, Plaintiff will pay for all costs out of any recovery. However, if the litigation were unsuccessful, and there is no recovery, Plaintiff would not have sufficient funds to repay Attorney. Is Attorney engaged in an improper conflict of interest if Attorney, in effect, finances the law suit?

Would it affect the conflicts issue if Plaintiff were a legal secretary employed by Attorney's law office?

For a discussion of these issues, see *Janicik v. Prudential Ins. Co.*, 451 A.2d 451, 458–60 & nn. 9–12 (Pa.Super.1982).

QUESTION TWO *(Ninety Minutes)*

Closed, Inc. was a close corporation dominated by Pres, its chief executive officer. Pres and members of his family owned the stock. Law Firm did both the corporate legal representation of Closed, Inc. and the personal legal work for Pres and his family, but all legal services were billed to Closed, Inc. regardless of whether the work performed was corporate or private.

Pres had a falling out with his family members, who were continually at odds with each other. The members of Pres' family formed a voting trust; Law Firm did not prepare this trust. However, Law Firm continued to advise Pres and the other members of the board regarding their problems. Pres thought that Law Firm's actions were a display of disloyalty to him.

Pres reconciled with Wife; then Wife sued the other family members, and the board of directors of Closed, Inc. in order to break the voting trust that Wife had earlier joined. Partner of Law Firm represented the board members in defending this suit. Wife objected, so Partner withdrew and had an associate in Law Firm handle the defense.

Finally, Pres regained control of Closed, Inc. and fired all the people whom he felt had been disloyal. These terminated employees formed a new corporation, called New Corp., to compete with Closed. Pres also fired Law Firm. New Corp. hired Law Firm to represent it. Law Firm, now in the employ of New Corp., advised it that the non-competition contracts that New Corp.'s employees had signed with Closed, Inc. (before the employees had been fired by Closed, Inc.) were, for the most part, invalid. Law Firm, when it had been working for Closed, Inc., had handled litigation for Closed, Inc. regarding these contracts. Though Law Firm had not originally drafted them, Law Firm had, from time to time, suggested changes in their format. Partner in Law Firm was also a stockholder and investor in New Corp., Inc.

Are Partner and Law Firm subject to discipline?

For a discussion of these issues, see *In re Banks*, 283 Or. 459, 584 P.2d 284 (1978)(per curiam).

QUESTION THREE *(Forty–Five Minutes)*

Utility is suing Defendant for damages in a complex case involving the manufacture of pump supports for a nuclear power station. Utility is the utility providing power in the area. Trial Judge is a customer of Utility. In fact, all judges in the state are customers of Utility. Pursuant to a fuel adjustment clause, all of Utility's customers have been directly surcharged an amount that Utility now claims as an element of damages. If Utility is successful, it may have to refund to its customers, including Trial Judge, a part of its damage award. This refund to Trial Judge would amount to between $70 and $100. Judge thought that his interest in the hypothetical $100 might require him to recuse himself. He told the parties about his problem. Four months later, after many pleadings in the case, Defendant moved to disqualify Trial Judge. Defendant did not allege any personal bias on the part of Trial Judge.

Should Trial Judge disqualify himself under ABA Model Code of Judicial Conduct 3E or under 28 U.S.C.A. § 455?

For a discussion of these issues, see *In re Virginia Electric & Power Co.*, 539 F.2d 357 (4th Cir.1976).

QUESTION FOUR *(Thirty Minutes)*

The Government is investigating XYZ Corp. for alleged violations of the criminal law. Corp. is complaining that the Government is interviewing XYZ Corp.'s agents and employees without first obtaining the permission of the general counsel of XYZ Corp. Some of the agents and employees of XYZ Corp. are hourly employees. Others are salaried. None have personal counsel. The Government has brought suit only against the corporate entity.

Is it ethical for the Government to interview the agents and employees without first securing the consent of XYZ Corp.'s general counsel? Are there any restrictions as to different types of employees or agents? If the Government is or may be acting improperly, what, if anything, can a court do? Or is the matter solely for the attorney disciplinary commission?

For a discussion of these issues, see *In re Investigation of FMC Corp.*, 430 F.Supp. 1108 (S.D.W.Va.1977). [00ff]

APPENDIX C

The American Bar Association Model Rules of Professional Conduct

AUGUST, 2003

The ABA House of Delegates adopted the Model Rules of Conduct on August 2, 1983. They were amended over the years and were subject to substantial modifications in August, 2001, and February and August, 2002, which were in response to changes proposed by the ABA Commission on Evaluation of the Rules of Professional Conduct, popularly called "Ethics, 2000." Only a year later, in August, 2003, the ABA amended Rule 1.6 and Rule 1.13 in response to the Enron corporate bankruptcy scandal. This version reflects all of these changes.

CONTENTS

COUNSELOR

ADVOCATE

TRANSACTIONS WITH PERSONS OTHER THAN CLIENTS

LAW FIRMS AND ASSOCIATIONS

PUBLIC SERVICE

PREAMBLE: A LAWYER'S RESPONSIBILITIES

[1]   A lawyer, as a member of the legal profession, is a representative of clients, an officer of the legal system and a public citizen having special responsibility for the quality of justice.

[2]   As a representative of clients, a lawyer performs various functions. As advisor, a lawyer provides a client with an informed understanding of the client's legal rights and obligations and explains their practical implications. As advocate, a lawyer zealously asserts the client's position under the rules of the adversary system. As negotiator, a lawyer seeks a result advantageous to the client but consistent with requirements of honest dealings with others. As an evaluator, a lawyer acts by examining a client's legal affairs and reporting about them to the client or to others.

[3]   In addition to these representational functions, a lawyer may serve as a third-party neutral, a nonrepresentational role helping the parties to resolve a dispute or other matter. Some of these Rules apply directly to lawyers who are or have served as third-party neutrals. See, e.g., Rules 1.12 and 2.4. In addition, there are Rules that apply to lawyers who are not active in the practice of law or to practicing lawyers even when they are acting in a nonprofessional capacity. For example, a lawyer who commits fraud in the conduct of a business is subject to discipline for engaging in conduct involving dishonesty, fraud, deceit or misrepresentation. See Rule 8.4.

[4]   In all professional functions a lawyer should be competent, prompt and diligent. A lawyer should maintain communication with a client concerning the representation. A lawyer should keep in confidence information relating to representation of a client except so far as disclosure is required or permitted by the Rules of Professional Conduct or other law.

[5]   A lawyer's conduct should conform to the requirements of the law, both in professional service to clients and in the lawyer's business and personal affairs. A lawyer should use the law's procedures only for legitimate purposes and not to harass or intimidate others. A lawyer should demonstrate respect for the legal system and for those who serve it, including judges, other

lawyers and public officials. While it is a lawyer's duty, when necessary, to challenge the rectitude of official action, it is also a lawyer's duty to uphold legal process.

[6] As a public citizen, a lawyer should seek improvement of the law, access to the legal system, the administration of justice and the quality of service rendered by the legal profession. As a member of a learned profession, a lawyer should cultivate knowledge of the law beyond its use for clients, employ that knowledge in reform of the law and work to strengthen legal education. In addition, a lawyer should further the public's understanding of and confidence in the rule of law and the justice system because legal institutions in a constitutional democracy depend on popular participation and support to maintain their authority. A lawyer should be mindful of deficiencies in the administration of justice and of the fact that the poor, and sometimes persons who are not poor, cannot afford adequate legal assistance. Therefore, all lawyers should devote professional time and resources and use civic influence to ensure equal access to our system of justice for all those who because of economic or social barriers cannot afford or secure adequate legal counsel. A lawyer should aid the legal profession in pursuing these objectives and should help the bar regulate itself in the public interest.

[7] Many of a lawyer's professional responsibilities are prescribed in the Rules of Professional Conduct, as well as substantive and procedural law. However, a lawyer is also guided by personal conscience and the approbation of professional peers. A lawyer should strive to attain the highest level of skill, to improve the law and the legal profession and to exemplify the legal profession's ideals of public service.

[8] A lawyer's responsibilities as a representative of clients, an officer of the legal system and a public citizen are usually harmonious. Thus, when an opposing party is well represented, a lawyer can be a zealous advocate on behalf of a client and at the same time assume that justice is being done. So also, a lawyer can be sure that preserving client confidences ordinarily serves the public interest because people are more likely to seek legal advice, and thereby heed their legal obligations, when they know their communications will be private.

[9] In the nature of law practice, however, conflicting responsibilities are encountered. Virtually all difficult ethical problems arise from conflict between a lawyer's responsibilities to clients, to the legal system and to the lawyer's own interest in remaining an ethical person while earning a satisfactory living. The Rules of Professional Conduct often prescribe terms for resolving such conflicts. Within the framework of these Rules, however, many difficult issues of professional discretion can arise. Such issues must be resolved through the exercise of sensitive professional and moral judgment guided by the basic principles underlying the Rules. These principles include the lawyer's obligation zealously to protect and pursue a client's legitimate interests, within the bounds of the law, while maintaining a professional, courteous and civil attitude toward all persons involved in the legal system.

[10] The legal profession is largely self-governing. Although other professions also have been granted powers of self-government, the legal profession is unique in this respect because of the close relationship between the profession and the processes of government and law enforcement. This connection is manifested in the fact that ultimate authority over the legal profession is vested largely in the courts.

[11] To the extent that lawyers meet the obligations of their professional calling, the occasion for government regulation is obviated. Self-regulation also helps maintain the legal profession's independence from government domination. An independent legal profession is an important force in preserving government under law, for abuse of legal authority is more readily challenged by a profession whose members are not dependent on government for the right to practice.

[12] The legal profession's relative autonomy carries with it special responsibilities of self-government. The profession has a responsibility to assure that its regulations are conceived

in the public interest and not in furtherance of parochial or self-interested concerns of the bar. Every lawyer is responsible for observance of the Rules of Professional Conduct. A lawyer should also aid in securing their observance by other lawyers. Neglect of these responsibilities compromises the independence of the profession and the public interest which it serves.

[13] Lawyers play a vital role in the preservation of society. The fulfillment of this role requires an understanding by lawyers of their relationship to our legal system. The Rules of Professional Conduct, when properly applied, serve to define that relationship.

SCOPE

[14] The Rules of Professional Conduct are rules of reason. They should be interpreted with reference to the purposes of legal representation and of the law itself. Some of the Rules are imperatives, cast in the terms "shall" or "shall not." These define proper conduct for purposes of professional discipline. Others, generally cast in the term "may," are permissive and define areas under the Rules in which the lawyer has discretion to exercise professional judgment. No disciplinary action should be taken when the lawyer chooses not to act or acts within the bounds of such discretion. Other Rules define the nature of relationships between the lawyer and others. The Rules are thus partly obligatory and disciplinary and partly constitutive and descriptive in that they define a lawyer's professional role. Many of the Comments use the term "should." Comments do not add obligations to the Rules but provide guidance for practicing in compliance with the Rules.

[15] The Rules presuppose a larger legal context shaping the lawyer's role. That context includes court rules and statutes relating to matters of licensure, laws defining specific obligations of lawyers and substantive and procedural law in general. The Comments are sometimes used to alert lawyers to their responsibilities under such other law.

[16] Compliance with the Rules, as with all law in an open society, depends primarily upon understanding and voluntary compliance, secondarily upon reinforcement by peer and public opinion and finally, when necessary, upon enforcement through disciplinary proceedings. The Rules do not, however, exhaust the moral and ethical considerations that should inform a lawyer, for no worthwhile human activity can be completely defined by legal rules. The Rules simply provide a framework for the ethical practice of law.

[17] Furthermore, for purposes of determining the lawyer's authority and responsibility, principles of substantive law external to these Rules determine whether a client-lawyer relationship exists. Most of the duties flowing from the client-lawyer relationship attach only after the client has requested the lawyer to render legal services and the lawyer has agreed to do so. But there are some duties, such as that of confidentiality under Rule 1.6, that attach when the lawyer agrees to consider whether a client-lawyer relationship shall be established. See Rule 1.18. Whether a client-lawyer relationship exists for any specific purpose can depend on the circumstances and may be a question of fact.

[18] Under various legal provisions, including constitutional, statutory and common law, the responsibilities of government lawyers may include authority concerning legal matters that ordinarily reposes in the client in private client-lawyer relationships. For example, a lawyer for a government agency may have authority on behalf of the government to decide upon settlement or whether to appeal from an adverse judgment. Such authority in various respects is generally vested in the attorney general and the state's attorney in state government, and their federal counterparts, and the same may be true of other government law officers. Also, lawyers under the supervision of these officers may be authorized to represent several government agencies in intragovernmental legal controversies in circumstances where a private lawyer could not represent multiple private clients. These Rules do not abrogate any such authority.

[19]   Failure to comply with an obligation or prohibition imposed by a Rule is a basis for invoking the disciplinary process. The Rules presuppose that disciplinary assessment of a lawyer's conduct will be made on the basis of the facts and circumstances as they existed at the time of the conduct in question and in recognition of the fact that a lawyer often has to act upon uncertain or incomplete evidence of the situation. Moreover, the Rules presuppose that whether or not discipline should be imposed for a violation, and the severity of a sanction, depend on all the circumstances, such as the willfulness and seriousness of the violation, extenuating factors and whether there have been previous violations.

[20]   Violation of a Rule should not itself give rise to a cause of action against a lawyer nor should it create any presumption in such a case that a legal duty has been breached. In addition, violation of a Rule does not necessarily warrant any other nondisciplinary remedy, such as disqualification of a lawyer in pending litigation. The Rules are designed to provide guidance to lawyers and to provide a structure for regulating conduct through disciplinary agencies. They are not designed to be a basis for civil liability. Furthermore, the purpose of the Rules can be subverted when they are invoked by opposing parties as procedural weapons. The fact that a Rule is a just basis for a lawyer's self-assessment, or for sanctioning a lawyer under the administration of a disciplinary authority, does not imply that an antagonist in a collateral proceeding or transaction has standing to seek enforcement of the Rule. Nevertheless, since the Rules do establish standards of conduct by lawyers, a lawyer's violation of a Rule may be evidence of breach of the applicable standard of conduct.

[21]   The Comment accompanying each Rule explains and illustrates the meaning and purpose of the Rule. The Preamble and this note on Scope provide general orientation. The Comments are intended as guides to interpretation, but the text of each Rule is authoritative.

RULE 1.0: TERMINOLOGY

(a) "Belief" or "believes" denotes that the person involved actually supposed the fact in question to be true. A person's belief may be inferred from circumstances.

(b) "Confirmed in writing," when used in reference to the informed consent of a person, denotes informed consent that is given in writing by the person or a writing that a lawyer promptly transmits to the person confirming an oral informed consent. See paragraph (e) for the definition of "informed consent." If it is not feasible to obtain or transmit the writing at the time the person gives informed consent, then the lawyer must obtain or transmit it within a reasonable time thereafter.

(c) "Firm" or "law firm" denotes a lawyer or lawyers in a law partnership, professional corporation, sole proprietorship or other association authorized to practice law; or lawyers employed in a legal services organization or the legal department of a corporation or other organization.

(d) "Fraud" or "fraudulent" denotes conduct that is fraudulent under the substantive or procedural law of the applicable jurisdiction and has a purpose to deceive.

(e) "Informed consent" denotes the agreement by a person to a proposed course of conduct after the lawyer has communicated adequate information and explanation about the material risks of and reasonably available alternatives to the proposed course of conduct.

(f) "Knowingly," "known," or "knows" denotes actual knowledge of the fact in question. A person's knowledge may be inferred from circumstances.

(g) "Partner" denotes a member of a partnership, a shareholder in a law firm organized as a professional corporation, or a member of an association authorized to practice law.

(h) "Reasonable" or "reasonably" when used in relation to conduct by a lawyer denotes the conduct of a reasonably prudent and competent lawyer.

(i) "Reasonable belief" or "reasonably believes" when used in reference to a lawyer denotes that the lawyer believes the matter in question and that the circumstances are such that the belief is reasonable.

(j) "Reasonably should know" when used in reference to a lawyer denotes that a lawyer of reasonable prudence and competence would ascertain the matter in question.

(k) "Screened" denotes the isolation of a lawyer from any participation in a matter through the timely imposition of procedures within a firm that are reasonably adequate under the circumstances to protect information that the isolated lawyer is obligated to protect under these Rules or other law.

(l) "Substantial" when used in reference to degree or extent denotes a material matter of clear and weighty importance.

(m) "Tribunal" denotes a court, an arbitrator in a binding arbitration proceeding or a legislative body, administrative agency or other body acting in an adjudicative capacity. A legislative body, administrative agency or other body acts in an adjudicative capacity when a neutral official, after the presentation of evidence or legal argument by a party or parties, will render a binding legal judgment directly affecting a party's interests in a particular matter.

(n) "Writing" or "written" denotes a tangible or electronic record of a communication or representation, including handwriting, typewriting, printing, photostating, photography, audio or videorecording and e-mail. A "signed" writing includes an electronic sound, symbol or process attached to or logically associated with a writing and executed or adopted by a person with the intent to sign the writing.

Comment

Confirmed in Writing

[1] If it is not feasible to obtain or transmit a written confirmation at the time the client gives informed consent, then the lawyer must obtain or transmit it within a reasonable time thereafter. If a lawyer has obtained a client's informed consent, the lawyer may act in reliance on that consent so long as it is confirmed in writing within a reasonable time thereafter.

Firm

[2] Whether two or more lawyers constitute a firm within paragraph (c) can depend on the specific facts. For example, two practitioners who share office space and occasionally consult or assist each other ordinarily would not be regarded as constituting a firm. However, if they present themselves to the public in a way that suggests that they are a firm or conduct themselves as a firm, they should be regarded as a firm for purposes of the Rules. The terms of any formal agreement between associated lawyers are relevant in determining whether they are a firm, as is the fact that they have mutual access to information concerning the clients they serve. Furthermore, it is relevant in doubtful cases to consider the underlying purpose of the Rule that is involved. A group of lawyers could be regarded as a firm for purposes of the Rule that the same lawyer should not represent opposing parties in litigation, while it might not be so regarded for purposes of the Rule that information acquired by one lawyer is attributed to another.

[3] With respect to the law department of an organization, including the government, there is ordinarily no question that the members of the department constitute a firm within the meaning of the Rules of Professional Conduct. There can be uncertainty, however, as to the identity of the client. For example, it may not be clear whether the law department of a corporation represents a subsidiary or an affiliated corporation, as well as the corporation by which the members of the department are directly employed. A similar question can arise concerning an unincorporated association and its local affiliates.

[4] Similar questions can also arise with respect to lawyers in legal aid and legal services organizations. Depending upon the structure of the organization, the entire organization or different components of it may constitute a firm or firms for purposes of these Rules.

Fraud

[5] When used in these Rules, the terms "fraud" or "fraudulent" refer to conduct that is characterized as such under the substantive or procedural law of the applicable jurisdiction and has a purpose to deceive. This does not include merely negligent misrepresentation or negligent failure to apprise another of relevant information. For purposes of these Rules, it is not necessary that anyone has suffered damages or relied on the misrepresentation or failure to inform.

Informed Consent

[6] Many of the Rules of Professional Conduct require the lawyer to obtain the informed consent of a client or other person (e.g., a former client or, under certain circumstances, a prospective client) before accepting or continuing representation or pursuing a course of conduct. See, e.g., Rules 1.2(c), 1.6(a) and 1.7(b). The communication necessary to obtain such consent will vary according to the Rule involved and the circumstances giving rise to the need to obtain informed consent. The lawyer must make reasonable efforts to ensure that the client or other person possesses information reasonably adequate to make an informed decision. Ordinarily, this will require communication that includes a disclosure of the facts and circumstances giving rise to the situation, any explanation reasonably necessary to inform the client or other person of the material advantages and disadvantages of the proposed course of conduct and a discussion of the client's or other person's options and alternatives. In some circumstances it may be appropriate for a lawyer to advise a client or other person to seek the advice of other counsel. A lawyer need not inform a client or other person of facts or implications already known to the client or other person; nevertheless, a lawyer who does not personally inform the client or other person assumes the risk that the client or other person is inadequately informed and the consent is invalid. In determining whether the information and explanation provided are reasonably adequate, relevant factors include whether the client or other person is experienced in legal matters generally and in making decisions of the type involved, and whether the client or other person is independently represented by other counsel in giving the consent. Normally, such persons need less information and explanation than others, and generally a client or other person who is independently represented by other counsel in giving the consent should be assumed to have given informed consent.

[7] Obtaining informed consent will usually require an affirmative response by the client or other person. In general, a lawyer may not assume consent from a client's or other person's silence. Consent may be inferred, however, from the conduct of a client or other person who has reasonably adequate information about the matter. A number of Rules require that a person's consent be confirmed in writing. See Rules 1.7(b) and 1.9(a). For a definition of "writing" and "confirmed in writing," see paragraphs (n) and (b). Other Rules require that a client's consent be obtained in a writing signed by the client. See, e.g., Rules 1.8(a) and (g). For a definition of "signed," see paragraph (n).

Screened

[8] This definition applies to situations where screening of a personally disqualified lawyer is permitted to remove imputation of a conflict of interest under Rules 1.11, 1.12 or 1.18.

[9]   The purpose of screening is to assure the affected parties that confidential information known by the personally disqualified lawyer remains protected. The personally disqualified lawyer should acknowledge the obligation not to communicate with any of the other lawyers in the firm with respect to the matter. Similarly, other lawyers in the firm who are working on the matter should be informed that the screening is in place and that they may not communicate with the personally disqualified lawyer with respect to the matter. Additional screening measures that are appropriate for the particular matter will depend on the circumstances. To implement, reinforce and remind all affected lawyers of the presence of the screening, it may be appropriate for the firm to undertake such procedures as a written undertaking by the screened lawyer to avoid any communication with other firm personnel and any contact with any firm files or other materials relating to the matter, written notice and instructions to all other firm personnel forbidding any communication with the screened lawyer relating to the matter, denial of access by the screened lawyer to firm files or other materials relating to the matter and periodic reminders of the screen to the screened lawyer and all other firm personnel.

[10]   In order to be effective, screening measures must be implemented as soon as practical after a lawyer or law firm knows or reasonably should know that there is a need for screening.

RULE 1.1: COMPETENCE

A lawyer shall provide competent representation to a client. Competent representation requires the legal knowledge, skill, thoroughness and preparation reasonably necessary for the representation.

Comment

Legal Knowledge and Skill

[1]   In determining whether a lawyer employs the requisite knowledge and skill in a particular matter, relevant factors include the relative complexity and specialized nature of the matter, the lawyer's general experience, the lawyer's training and experience in the field in question, the preparation and study the lawyer is able to give the matter and whether it is feasible to refer the matter to, or associate or consult with, a lawyer of established competence in the field in question. In many instances, the required proficiency is that of a general practitioner. Expertise in a particular field of law may be required in some circumstances.

[2]   A lawyer need not necessarily have special training or prior experience to handle legal problems of a type with which the lawyer is unfamiliar. A newly admitted lawyer can be as competent as a practitioner with long experience. Some important legal skills, such as the analysis of precedent, the evaluation of evidence and legal drafting, are required in all legal problems. Perhaps the most fundamental legal skill consists of determining what kind of legal problems a situation may involve, a skill that necessarily transcends any particular specialized knowledge. A lawyer can provide adequate representation in a wholly novel field through necessary study. Competent representation can also be provided through the association of a lawyer of established competence in the field in question.

[3]   In an emergency a lawyer may give advice or assistance in a matter in which the lawyer does not have the skill ordinarily required where referral to or consultation or association with another lawyer would be impractical. Even in an emergency, however, assistance should be limited to that reasonably necessary in the circumstances, for ill-considered action under emergency conditions can jeopardize the client's interest.

[4]   A lawyer may accept representation where the requisite level of competence can be achieved by reasonable preparation. This applies as well to a lawyer who is appointed as counsel for an unrepresented person. See also Rule 6.2.

Thoroughness and Preparation

[5]   Competent handling of a particular matter includes inquiry into and analysis of the factual and legal elements of the problem, and use of methods and procedures meeting the

standards of competent practitioners. It also includes adequate preparation. The required attention and preparation are determined in part by what is at stake; major litigation and complex transactions ordinarily require more extensive treatment than matters of lesser complexity and consequence. An agreement between the lawyer and the client regarding the scope of the representation may limit the matters for which the lawyer is responsible. See Rule 1.2(c).

Maintaining Competence

[6]   To maintain the requisite knowledge and skill, a lawyer should keep abreast of changes in the law and its practice, engage in continuing study and education and comply with all continuing legal education requirements to which the lawyer is subject.

RULE 1.2: SCOPE OF REPRESENTATION AND ALLOCATION OF AUTHORITY BE-TWEEN CLIENT AND LAWYER

(a) **Subject to paragraphs (c) and (d), a lawyer shall abide by a client's decisions concerning the objectives of representation and, as required by Rule 1.4, shall consult with the client as to the means by which they are to be pursued. A lawyer may take such action on behalf of the client as is impliedly authorized to carry out the representation. A lawyer shall abide by a client's decision whether to settle a matter. In a criminal case, the lawyer shall abide by the client's decision, after consultation with the lawyer, as to a plea to be entered, whether to waive jury trial and whether the client will testify.**

(b) **A lawyer's representation of a client, including representation by appointment, does not constitute an endorsement of the client's political, economic, social or moral views or activities.**

(c) **A lawyer may limit the scope of the representation if the limitation is reasonable under the circumstances and the client gives informed consent.**

(d) **A lawyer shall not counsel a client to engage, or assist a client, in conduct that the lawyer knows is criminal or fraudulent, but a lawyer may discuss the legal consequences of any proposed course of conduct with a client and may counsel or assist a client to make a good faith effort to determine the validity, scope, meaning or application of the law.**

Comment

Allocation of Authority between Client and Lawyer

[1]   Paragraph (a) confers upon the client the ultimate authority to determine the purposes to be served by legal representation, within the limits imposed by law and the lawyer's professional obligations. The decisions specified in paragraph (a), such as whether to settle a civil matter, must also be made by the client. See Rule 1.4(a)(1) for the lawyer's duty to communicate with the client about such decisions. With respect to the means by which the client's objectives are to be pursued, the lawyer shall consult with the client as required by Rule 1.4(a)(2) and may take such action as is impliedly authorized to carry out the representation.

[2]   On occasion, however, a lawyer and a client may disagree about the means to be used to accomplish the client's objectives. Clients normally defer to the special knowledge and skill of their lawyer with respect to the means to be used to accomplish their objectives, particularly with respect to technical, legal and tactical matters. Conversely, lawyers usually defer to the

client regarding such questions as the expense to be incurred and concern for third persons who might be adversely affected. Because of the varied nature of the matters about which a lawyer and client might disagree and because the actions in question may implicate the interests of a tribunal or other persons, this Rule does not prescribe how such disagreements are to be resolved. Other law, however, may be applicable and should be consulted by the lawyer. The lawyer should also consult with the client and seek a mutually acceptable resolution of the disagreement. If such efforts are unavailing and the lawyer has a fundamental disagreement with the client, the lawyer may withdraw from the representation. See Rule 1.16(b)(4) Conversely, the client may resolve the disagreement by discharging the lawyer. See Rule 1.16(a)(3).

[3] At the outset of a representation, the client may authorize the lawyer to take specific action on the client's behalf without further consultation. Absent a material change in circumstances and subject to Rule 1.4, a lawyer may rely on such an advance authorization. The client may, however, revoke such authority at any time.

[4] In a case in which the client appears to be suffering diminished capacity, the lawyer's duty to abide by the client's decisions is to be guided by reference to Rule 1.14.

Independence from Client's Views or Activities

[5] Legal representation should not be denied to people who are unable to afford legal services, or whose cause is controversial or the subject of popular disapproval. By the same token, representing a client does not constitute approval of the client's views or activities.

Agreements Limiting Scope of Representation

[6] The scope of services to be provided by a lawyer may be limited by agreement with the client or by the terms under which the lawyer's services are made available to the client. When a lawyer has been retained by an insurer to represent an insured, for example, the representation may be limited to matters related to the insurance coverage. A limited representation may be appropriate because the client has limited objectives for the representation. In addition, the terms upon which representation is undertaken may exclude specific means that might otherwise be used to accomplish the client's objectives. Such limitations may exclude actions that the client thinks are too costly or that the lawyer regards as repugnant or imprudent.

[7] Although this Rule affords the lawyer and client substantial latitude to limit the representation, the limitation must be reasonable under the circumstances. If, for example, a client's objective is limited to securing general information about the law the client needs in order to handle a common and typically uncomplicated legal problem, the lawyer and client may agree that the lawyer's services will be limited to a brief telephone consultation. Such a limitation, however, would not be reasonable if the time allotted was not sufficient to yield advice upon which the client could rely. Although an agreement for a limited representation does not exempt a lawyer from the duty to provide competent representation, the limitation is a factor to be considered when determining the legal knowledge, skill, thoroughness and preparation reasonably necessary for the representation. See Rule 1.1.

[8] All agreements concerning a lawyer's representation of a client must accord with the Rules of Professional Conduct and other law. See, e.g., Rules 1.1, 1.8 and 5.6.

Criminal, Fraudulent and Prohibited Transactions

[9] Paragraph (d) prohibits a lawyer from knowingly counseling or assisting a client to commit a crime or fraud. This prohibition, however, does not preclude the lawyer from giving an

honest opinion about the actual consequences that appear likely to result from a client's conduct. Nor does the fact that a client uses advice in a course of action that is criminal or fraudulent of itself make a lawyer a party to the course of action. There is a critical distinction between presenting an analysis of legal aspects of questionable conduct and recommending the means by which a crime or fraud might be committed with impunity.

[10]   When the client's course of action has already begun and is continuing, the lawyer's responsibility is especially delicate. The lawyer is required to avoid assisting the client, for example, by drafting or delivering documents that the lawyer knows are fraudulent or by suggesting how the wrongdoing might be concealed. A lawyer may not continue assisting a client in conduct that the lawyer originally supposed was legally proper but then discovers is criminal or fraudulent. The lawyer must, therefore, withdraw from the representation of the client in the matter. See Rule 1.16(a). In some cases, withdrawal alone might be insufficient. It may be necessary for the lawyer to give notice of the fact of withdrawal and to disaffirm any opinion, document, affirmation or the like. See Rule 4.1.

[11]   Where the client is a fiduciary, the lawyer may be charged with special obligations in dealings with a beneficiary.

[12]   Paragraph (d) applies whether or not the defrauded party is a party to the transaction. Hence, a lawyer must not participate in a transaction to effectuate criminal or fraudulent avoidance of tax liability. Paragraph (d) does not preclude undertaking a criminal defense incident to a general retainer for legal services to a lawful enterprise. The last clause of paragraph (d) recognizes that determining the validity or interpretation of a statute or regulation may require a course of action involving disobedience of the statute or regulation or of the interpretation placed upon it by governmental authorities.

[13]   If a lawyer comes to know or reasonably should know that a client expects assistance not permitted by the Rules of Professional Conduct or other law or if the lawyer intends to act contrary to the client's instructions, the lawyer must consult with the client regarding the limitations on the lawyer's conduct. See Rule 1.4(a)(5).

RULE 1.3: DILIGENCE

A lawyer shall act with reasonable diligence and promptness in representing a client.

Comment

[1]   A lawyer should pursue a matter on behalf of a client despite opposition, obstruction or personal inconvenience to the lawyer, and take whatever lawful and ethical measures are required to vindicate a client's cause or endeavor. A lawyer must also act with commitment and dedication to the interests of the client and with zeal in advocacy upon the client's behalf. A lawyer is not bound, however, to press for every advantage that might be realized for a client. For example, a lawyer may have authority to exercise professional discretion in determining the means by which a matter should be pursued. See Rule 1.2. The lawyer's duty to act with reasonable diligence does not require the use of offensive tactics or preclude the treating of all persons involved in the legal process with courtesy and respect.

[2]   A lawyer's work load must be controlled so that each matter can be handled competently.

[3]   Perhaps no professional shortcoming is more widely resented than procrastination. A client's interests often can be adversely affected by the passage of time or the change of

conditions; in extreme instances, as when a lawyer overlooks a statute of limitations, the client's legal position may be destroyed. Even when the client's interests are not affected in substance, however, unreasonable delay can cause a client needless anxiety and undermine confidence in the lawyer's trustworthiness. A lawyer's duty to act with reasonable promptness, however, does not preclude the lawyer from agreeing to a reasonable request for a postponement that will not prejudice the lawyer's client.

[4] Unless the relationship is terminated as provided in Rule 1.16, a lawyer should carry through to conclusion all matters undertaken for a client. If a lawyer's employment is limited to a specific matter, the relationship terminates when the matter has been resolved. If a lawyer has served a client over a substantial period in a variety of matters, the client sometimes may assume that the lawyer will continue to serve on a continuing basis unless the lawyer gives notice of withdrawal. Doubt about whether a client-lawyer relationship still exists should be clarified by the lawyer, preferably in writing, so that the client will not mistakenly suppose the lawyer is looking after the client's affairs when the lawyer has ceased to do so. For example, if a lawyer has handled a judicial or administrative proceeding that produced a result adverse to the client and the lawyer and the client have not agreed that the lawyer will handle the matter on appeal, the lawyer must consult with the client about the possibility of appeal before relinquishing responsibility for the matter. See Rule 1.4(a)(2). Whether the lawyer is obligated to prosecute the appeal for the client depends on the scope of the representation the lawyer has agreed to provide to the client. See Rule 1.2.

[5] To prevent neglect of client matters in the event of a sole practitioner's death or disability, the duty of diligence may require that each sole practitioner prepare a plan, in conformity with applicable rules, that designates another competent lawyer to review client files, notify each client of the lawyer's death or disability, and determine whether there is a need for immediate protective action. Cf. Rule 28 of the American Bar Association Model Rules for Lawyer Disciplinary Enforcement (providing for court appointment of a lawyer to inventory files and take other protective action in absence of a plan providing for another lawyer to protect the interests of the clients of a deceased or disabled lawyer).

RULE 1.4: COMMUNICATION

(a) A lawyer shall:

(1) promptly inform the client of any decision or circumstance with respect to which the client's informed consent, as defined in Rule 1.0(e), is required by these Rules;

(2) reasonably consult with the client about the means by which the client's objectives are to be accomplished;

(3) keep the client reasonably informed about the status of the matter;

(4) promptly comply with reasonable requests for information; and

(5) consult with the client about any relevant limitation on the lawyer's conduct when the lawyer knows that the client expects assistance not permitted by the Rules of Professional Conduct or other law.

(b) A lawyer shall explain a matter to the extent reasonably necessary to permit the client to make informed decisions regarding the representation.

Comment

[1] Reasonable communication between the lawyer and the client is necessary for the client effectively to participate in the representation.

Communicating with Client

[2] If these Rules require that a particular decision about the representation be made by the client, paragraph (a)(1) requires that the lawyer promptly consult with and secure the

client's consent prior to taking action unless prior discussions with the client have resolved what action the client wants the lawyer to take. For example, a lawyer who receives from opposing counsel an offer of settlement in a civil controversy or a proffered plea bargain in a criminal case must promptly inform the client of its substance unless the client has previously indicated that the proposal will be acceptable or unacceptable or has authorized the lawyer to accept or to reject the offer. See Rule 1.2(a).

[3]   Paragraph (a)(2) requires the lawyer to reasonably consult with the client about the means to be used to accomplish the client's objectives. In some situations—depending on both the importance of the action under consideration and the feasibility of consulting with the client—this duty will require consultation prior to taking action. In other circumstances, such as during a trial when an immediate decision must be made, the exigency of the situation may require the lawyer to act without prior consultation. In such cases the lawyer must nonetheless act reasonably to inform the client of actions the lawyer has taken on the client's behalf. Additionally, paragraph (a)(3) requires that the lawyer keep the client reasonably informed about the status of the matter, such as significant developments affecting the timing or the substance of the representation.

[4]   A lawyer's regular communication with clients will minimize the occasions on which a client will need to request information concerning the representation. When a client makes a reasonable request for information, however, paragraph (a)(4) requires prompt compliance with the request, or if a prompt response is not feasible, that the lawyer, or a member of the lawyer's staff, acknowledge receipt of the request and advise the client when a response may be expected. Client telephone calls should be promptly returned or acknowledged.

Explaining Matters

[5]   The client should have sufficient information to participate intelligently in decisions concerning the objectives of the representation and the means by which they are to be pursued, to the extent the client is willing and able to do so. Adequacy of communication depends in part on the kind of advice or assistance that is involved. For example, when there is time to explain a proposal made in a negotiation, the lawyer should review all important provisions with the client before proceeding to an agreement. In litigation a lawyer should explain the general strategy and prospects of success and ordinarily should consult the client on tactics that are likely to result in significant expense or to injure or coerce others. On the other hand, a lawyer ordinarily will not be expected to describe trial or negotiation strategy in detail. The guiding principle is that the lawyer should fulfill reasonable client expectations for information consistent with the duty to act in the client's best interests, and the client's overall requirements as to the character of representation. In certain circumstances, such as when a lawyer asks a client to consent to a representation affected by a conflict of interest, the client must give informed consent, as defined in Rule 1.0(e).

[6]   Ordinarily, the information to be provided is that appropriate for a client who is a comprehending and responsible adult. However, fully informing the client according to this standard may be impracticable, for example, where the client is a child or suffers from diminished capacity. See Rule 1.14. When the client is an organization or group, it is often impossible or inappropriate to inform every one of its members about its legal affairs; ordinarily, the lawyer should address communications to the appropriate officials of the organization. See Rule 1.13. Where many routine matters are involved, a system of limited or occasional reporting may be arranged with the client.

Withholding Information

[7]   In some circumstances, a lawyer may be justified in delaying transmission of information when the client would be likely to react imprudently to an immediate communication. Thus,

a lawyer might withhold a psychiatric diagnosis of a client when the examining psychiatrist indicates that disclosure would harm the client. A lawyer may not withhold information to serve the lawyer's own interest or convenience or the interests or convenience of another person. Rules or court orders governing litigation may provide that information supplied to a lawyer may not be disclosed to the client. Rule 3.4(c) directs compliance with such rules or orders.

RULE 1.5: FEES

(a) **A lawyer shall not make an agreement for, charge, or collect an unreasonable fee or an unreasonable amount for expenses. The factors to be considered in determining the reasonableness of a fee include the following:**

(1) **the time and labor required, the novelty and difficulty of the questions involved, and the skill requisite to perform the legal service properly;**

(2) **the likelihood, if apparent to the client, that the acceptance of the particular employment will preclude other employment by the lawyer;**

(3) **the fee customarily charged in the locality for similar legal services;**

(4) **the amount involved and the results obtained;**

(5) **the time limitations imposed by the client or by the circumstances;**

(6) **the nature and length of the professional relationship with the client;**

(7) **the experience, reputation, and ability of the lawyer or lawyers performing the services; and**

(8) **whether the fee is fixed or contingent.**

(b) **The scope of the representation and the basis or rate of the fee and expenses for which the client will be responsible shall be communicated to the client, preferably in writing, before or within a reasonable time after commencing the representation, except when the lawyer will charge a regularly represented client on the same basis or rate. Any changes in the basis or rate of the fee or expenses shall also be communicated to the client.**

(c) **A fee may be contingent on the outcome of the matter for which the service is rendered, except in a matter in which a contingent fee is prohibited by paragraph (d) or other law. A contingent fee agreement shall be in a writing signed by the client and shall state the method by which the fee is to be determined, including the percentage or percentages that shall accrue to the lawyer in the event of settlement, trial or appeal; litigation and other expenses to be deducted from the recovery; and whether such expenses are to be deducted before or after the contingent fee is calculated. The agreement must clearly notify the client of any expenses for which the client will be liable whether or not the client is the prevailing party. Upon conclusion of a contingent fee matter, the lawyer shall provide the client with a written statement stating the outcome of the matter and, if there is a recovery, showing the remittance to the client and the method of its determination.**

(d) **A lawyer shall not enter into an arrangement for, charge, or collect:**

(1) **any fee in a domestic relations matter, the payment or amount of which is contingent upon the securing of a divorce or upon the amount of alimony or support, or property settlement in lieu thereof; or**

(2) a contingent fee for representing a defendant in a criminal case.

(e) A division of a fee between lawyers who are not in the same firm may be made only if:

(1) the division is in proportion to the services performed by each lawyer or each lawyer assumes joint responsibility for the representation;

(2) the client agrees to the arrangement, including the share each lawyer will receive, and the agreement is confirmed in writing; and

(3) the total fee is reasonable.

Comment

Reasonableness of Fee and Expenses

[1] Paragraph (a) requires that lawyers charge fees that are reasonable under the circumstances. The factors specified in (1) through (8) are not exclusive. Nor will each factor be relevant in each instance. Paragraph (a) also requires that expenses for which the client will be charged must be reasonable. A lawyer may seek reimbursement for the cost of services performed in-house, such as copying, or for other expenses incurred in-house, such as telephone charges, either by charging a reasonable amount to which the client has agreed in advance or by charging an amount that reasonably reflects the cost incurred by the lawyer.

Basis or Rate of Fee

[2] When the lawyer has regularly represented a client, they ordinarily will have evolved an understanding concerning the basis or rate of the fee and the expenses for which the client will be responsible. In a new client-lawyer relationship, however, an understanding as to fees and expenses must be promptly established. Generally, it is desirable to furnish the client with at least a simple memorandum or copy of the lawyer's customary fee arrangements that states the general nature of the legal services to be provided, the basis, rate or total amount of the fee and whether and to what extent the client will be responsible for any costs, expenses or disbursements in the course of the representation. A written statement concerning the terms of the engagement reduces the possibility of misunderstanding.

[3] Contingent fees, like any other fees, are subject to the reasonableness standard of paragraph (a) of this Rule. In determining whether a particular contingent fee is reasonable, or whether it is reasonable to charge any form of contingent fee, a lawyer must consider the factors that are relevant under the circumstances. Applicable law may impose limitations on contingent fees, such as a ceiling on the percentage allowable, or may require a lawyer to offer clients an alternative basis for the fee. Applicable law also may apply to situations other than a contingent fee, for example, government regulations regarding fees in certain tax matters.

Terms of Payment

[4] A lawyer may require advance payment of a fee, but is obliged to return any unearned portion. See Rule 1.16(d). A lawyer may accept property in payment for services, such as an ownership interest in an enterprise, providing this does not involve acquisition of a proprietary interest in the cause of action or subject matter of the litigation contrary to Rule 1.8 (i). However, a fee paid in property instead of money may be subject to the requirements of Rule 1.8(a) because such fees often have the essential qualities of a business transaction with the client.

[5]   An agreement may not be made whose terms might induce the lawyer improperly to curtail services for the client or perform them in a way contrary to the client's interest. For example, a lawyer should not enter into an agreement whereby services are to be provided only up to a stated amount when it is foreseeable that more extensive services probably will be required, unless the situation is adequately explained to the client. Otherwise, the client might have to bargain for further assistance in the midst of a proceeding or transaction. However, it is proper to define the extent of services in light of the client's ability to pay. A lawyer should not exploit a fee arrangement based primarily on hourly charges by using wasteful procedures.

Prohibited Contingent Fees

[6]   Paragraph (d) prohibits a lawyer from charging a contingent fee in a domestic relations matter when payment is contingent upon the securing of a divorce or upon the amount of alimony or support or property settlement to be obtained. This provision does not preclude a contract for a contingent fee for legal representation in connection with the recovery of post-judgment balances due under support, alimony or other financial orders because such contracts do not implicate the same policy concerns.

Division of Fee

[7]   A division of fee is a single billing to a client covering the fee of two or more lawyers who are not in the same firm. A division of fee facilitates association of more than one lawyer in a matter in which neither alone could serve the client as well, and most often is used when the fee is contingent and the division is between a referring lawyer and a trial specialist. Paragraph (e) permits the lawyers to divide a fee either on the basis of the proportion of services they render or if each lawyer assumes responsibility for the representation as a whole. In addition, the client must agree to the arrangement, including the share that each lawyer is to receive, and the agreement must be confirmed in writing. Contingent fee agreements must be in a writing signed by the client and must otherwise comply with paragraph (c) of this Rule. Joint responsibility for the representation entails financial and ethical responsibility for the representation as if the lawyers were associated in a partnership. A lawyer should only refer a matter to a lawyer whom the referring lawyer reasonably believes is competent to handle the matter. See Rule 1.1.

[8]   Paragraph (e) does not prohibit or regulate division of fees to be received in the future for work done when lawyers were previously associated in a law firm.

Disputes over Fees

[9]   If a procedure has been established for resolution of fee disputes, such as an arbitration or mediation procedure established by the bar, the lawyer must comply with the procedure when it is mandatory, and, even when it is voluntary, the lawyer should conscientiously consider submitting to it. Law may prescribe a procedure for determining a lawyer's fee, for example, in representation of an executor or administrator, a class or a person entitled to a reasonable fee as part of the measure of damages. The lawyer entitled to such a fee and a lawyer representing another party concerned with the fee should comply with the prescribed procedure.

RULE 1.6: CONFIDENTIALITY OF INFORMATION

(a) A lawyer shall not reveal information relating to the representation of a client unless the client gives informed consent, the disclosure is impliedly authorized in order to carry out the representation or the disclosure is permitted by paragraph (b).

(b) A lawyer may reveal information relating to the representation of a client to the extent the lawyer reasonably believes necessary:

(1) **to prevent reasonably certain death or substantial bodily harm;**

(2) **to prevent the client from committing a crime or fraud that is reasonably certain to result in substantial injury to the financial interests or property of another and in furtherance of which the client has used or is using the lawyer's services;**

(3) **to prevent, mitigate or rectify substantial injury to the financial interests or property of another that is reasonably certain to result or has resulted from the client's commission of a crime or fraud in furtherance of which the client has used the lawyer's services;**

(4) **to secure legal advice about the lawyer's compliance with these Rules;**

(5) **to establish a claim or defense on behalf of the lawyer in a controversy between the lawyer and the client, to establish a defense to a criminal charge or civil claim against the lawyer based upon conduct in which the client was involved, or to respond to allegations in any proceeding concerning the lawyer's representation of the client; or**

(6) **to comply with other law or a court order.**

Comment

[1]   This Rule governs the disclosure by a lawyer of information relating to the representation of a client during the lawyer's representation of the client. See Rule 1.18 for the lawyer's duties with respect to information provided to the lawyer by a prospective client, Rule 1.9(c)(2) for the lawyer's duty not to reveal information relating to the lawyer's prior representation of a former client and Rules 1.8(b) and 1.9(c)(1) for the lawyer's duties with respect to the use of such information to the disadvantage of clients and former clients.

[2]   A fundamental principle in the client-lawyer relationship is that, in the absence of the client's informed consent, the lawyer must not reveal information relating to the representation. See Rule 1.0(e) for the definition of informed consent. This contributes to the trust that is the hallmark of the client-lawyer relationship. The client is thereby encouraged to seek legal assistance and to communicate fully and frankly with the lawyer even as to embarrassing or legally damaging subject matter. The lawyer needs this information to represent the client effectively and, if necessary, to advise the client to refrain from wrongful conduct. Almost without exception, clients come to lawyers in order to determine their rights and what is, in the complex of laws and regulations, deemed to be legal and correct. Based upon experience, lawyers know that almost all clients follow the advice given, and the law is upheld.

[3]   The principle of client-lawyer confidentiality is given effect by related bodies of law: the attorney-client privilege, the work product doctrine and the rule of confidentiality established in professional ethics. The attorney-client privilege and work product doctrine apply in judicial and other proceedings in which a lawyer may be called as a witness or otherwise required to produce evidence concerning a client. The rule of client-lawyer confidentiality applies in situations other than those where evidence is sought from the lawyer through compulsion of law. The confidentiality rule, for example, applies not only to matters communicated in confidence by the client but also to all information relating to the representation, whatever its source. A lawyer may not disclose such information except as authorized or required by the Rules of Professional Conduct or other law. See also Scope.

[4]   Paragraph (a) prohibits a lawyer from revealing information relating to the representation of a client. This prohibition also applies to disclosures by a lawyer that do not in

themselves reveal protected information but could reasonably lead to the discovery of such information by a third person. A lawyer's use of a hypothetical to discuss issues relating to the representation is permissible so long as there is no reasonable likelihood that the listener will be able to ascertain the identity of the client or the situation involved.

Authorized Disclosure

[5]   Except to the extent that the client's instructions or special circumstances limit that authority, a lawyer is impliedly authorized to make disclosures about a client when appropriate in carrying out the representation. In some situations, for example, a lawyer may be impliedly authorized to admit a fact that cannot properly be disputed or to make a disclosure that facilitates a satisfactory conclusion to a matter. Lawyers in a firm may, in the course of the firm's practice, disclose to each other information relating to a client of the firm, unless the client has instructed that particular information be confined to specified lawyers.

Disclosure Adverse to Client

[6]   Although the public interest is usually best served by a strict rule requiring lawyers to preserve the confidentiality of information relating to the representation of their clients, the confidentiality rule is subject to limited exceptions. Paragraph (b)(1) recognizes the overriding value of life and physical integrity and permits disclosure reasonably necessary to prevent reasonably certain death or substantial bodily harm. Such harm is reasonably certain to occur if it will be suffered imminently or if there is a present and substantial threat that a person will suffer such harm at a later date if the lawyer fails to take action necessary to eliminate the threat. Thus, a lawyer who knows that a client has accidentally discharged toxic waste into a town's water supply may reveal this information to the authorities if there is a present and substantial risk that a person who drinks the water will contract a life-threatening or debilitating disease and the lawyer's disclosure is necessary to eliminate the threat or reduce the number of victims.

[7]   Paragraph (b)(2) is a limited exception to the rule of confidentiality that permits the lawyer to reveal information to the extent necessary to enable affected persons or appropriate authorities to prevent the client from committing a crime or fraud, as defined in Rule 1.0(d), that is reasonably certain to result in substantial injury to the financial or property interests of another and in furtherance of which the client has used or is using the lawyer's services. Such a serious abuse of the client-lawyer relationship by the client forfeits the protection of this Rule. The client can, of course, prevent such disclosure by refraining from the wrongful conduct. Although paragraph (b)(2) does not require the lawyer to reveal the client's misconduct, the lawyer may not counsel or assist the client in conduct the lawyer knows is criminal or fraudulent. See Rule 1.2(d). See also Rule 1.16 with respect to the lawyer's obligation or right to withdraw from the representation of the client in such circumstances, and Rule 1.13(c), which permits the lawyer, where the client is an organization, to reveal information relating to the representation in limited circumstances.

[8]   Paragraph (b)(3) addresses the situation in which the lawyer does not learn of the client's crime or fraud until after it has been consummated. Although the client no longer has the option of preventing disclosure by refraining from the wrongful conduct, there will be situations in which the loss suffered by the affected person can be prevented, rectified or mitigated. In such situations, the lawyer may disclose information relating to the representation to the extent necessary to enable the affected persons to prevent or mitigate reasonably certain losses or to attempt to recoup their losses. Paragraph (b)(3) does not apply when a person who has committed a crime or fraud thereafter employs a lawyer for representation concerning that offense.

[9]   A lawyer's confidentiality obligations do not preclude a lawyer from securing confidential legal advice about the lawyer's personal responsibility to comply with these Rules. In most

situations, disclosing information to secure such advice will be impliedly authorized for the lawyer to carry out the representation. Even when the disclosure is not impliedly authorized, paragraph (b)(4) permits such disclosure because of the importance of a lawyer's compliance with the Rules of Professional Conduct.

[10]   Where a legal claim or disciplinary charge alleges complicity of the lawyer in a client's conduct or other misconduct of the lawyer involving representation of the client, the lawyer may respond to the extent the lawyer reasonably believes necessary to establish a defense. The same is true with respect to a claim involving the conduct or representation of a former client. Such a charge can arise in a civil, criminal, disciplinary or other proceeding and can be based on a wrong allegedly committed by the lawyer against the client or on a wrong alleged by a third person, for example, a person claiming to have been defrauded by the lawyer and client acting together. The lawyer's right to respond arises when an assertion of such complicity has been made. Paragraph (b)(5) does not require the lawyer to await the commencement of an action or proceeding that charges such complicity, so that the defense may be established by responding directly to a third party who has made such an assertion. The right to defend also applies, of course, where a proceeding has been commenced.

[11]   A lawyer entitled to a fee is permitted by paragraph (b)(5) to prove the services rendered in an action to collect it. This aspect of the rule expresses the principle that the beneficiary of a fiduciary relationship may not exploit it to the detriment of the fiduciary.

[12]   Other law may require that a lawyer disclose information about a client. Whether such a law supersedes Rule 1.6 is a question of law beyond the scope of these Rules. When disclosure of information relating to the representation appears to be required by other law, the lawyer must discuss the matter with the client to the extent required by Rule 1.4. If, however, the other law supersedes this Rule and requires disclosure, paragraph (b)(6) permits the lawyer to make such disclosures as are necessary to comply with the law.

[13]   A lawyer may be ordered to reveal information relating to the representation of a client by a court or by another tribunal or governmental entity claiming authority pursuant to other law to compel the disclosure. Absent informed consent of the client to do otherwise, the lawyer should assert on behalf of the client all nonfrivolous claims that the order is not authorized by other law or that the information sought is protected against disclosure by the attorney-client privilege or other applicable law. In the event of an adverse ruling, the lawyer must consult with the client about the possibility of appeal to the extent required by Rule 1.4. Unless review is sought, however, paragraph (b)(6) permits the lawyer to comply with the court's order.

[14]   Paragraph (b) permits disclosure only to the extent the lawyer reasonably believes the disclosure is necessary to accomplish one of the purposes specified. Where practicable, the lawyer should first seek to persuade the client to take suitable action to obviate the need for disclosure. In any case, a disclosure adverse to the client's interest should be no greater than the lawyer reasonably believes necessary to accomplish the purpose. If the disclosure will be made in connection with a judicial proceeding, the disclosure should be made in a manner that limits access to the information to the tribunal or other persons having a need to know it and appropriate protective orders or other arrangements should be sought by the lawyer to the fullest extent practicable.

[15]   Paragraph (b) permits but does not require the disclosure of information relating to a client's representation to accomplish the purposes specified in paragraphs (b)(1) through (b)(6). In exercising the discretion conferred by this Rule, the lawyer may consider such factors as the nature of the lawyer's relationship with the client and with those who might be injured by the client, the lawyer's own involvement in the transaction and factors that may extenuate the

conduct in question. A lawyer's decision not to disclose as permitted by paragraph (b) does not violate this Rule. Disclosure may be required, however, by other Rules. Some Rules require disclosure only if such disclosure would be permitted by paragraph (b). See Rules 1.2(d), 4.1(b), 8.1 and 8.3. Rule 3.3, on the other hand, requires disclosure in some circumstances regardless of whether such disclosure is permitted by this Rule. See Rule 3.3(c).

Acting Competently to Preserve Confidentiality

[16]   A lawyer must act competently to safeguard information relating to the representation of a client against inadvertent or unauthorized disclosure by the lawyer or other persons who are participating in the representation of the client or who are subject to the lawyer's supervision. See Rules 1.1, 5.1 and 5.3.

[17]   When transmitting a communication that includes information relating to the representation of a client, the lawyer must take reasonable precautions to prevent the information from coming into the hands of unintended recipients. This duty, however, does not require that the lawyer use special security measures if the method of communication affords a reasonable expectation of privacy. Special circumstances, however, may warrant special precautions. Factors to be considered in determining the reasonableness of the lawyer's expectation of confidentiality include the sensitivity of the information and the extent to which the privacy of the communication is protected by law or by a confidentiality agreement. A client may require the lawyer to implement special security measures not required by this Rule or may give informed consent to the use of a means of communication that would otherwise be prohibited by this Rule.

Former Client

[18]   The duty of confidentiality continues after the client-lawyer relationship has terminated. See Rule 1.9(c)(2). See Rule 1.9(c)(1) for the prohibition against using such information to the disadvantage of the former client.

RULE 1.7: CONFLICT OF INTEREST: CURRENT CLIENTS

(a) **Except as provided in paragraph (b), a lawyer shall not represent a client if the representation involves a concurrent conflict of interest. A concurrent conflict of interest exists if:**

(1) **the representation of one client will be directly adverse to another client; or**

(2) **there is a significant risk that the representation of one or more clients will be materially limited by the lawyer's responsibilities to another client, a former client or a third person or by a personal interest of the lawyer.**

(b) **Notwithstanding the existence of a concurrent conflict of interest under paragraph (a), a lawyer may represent a client if:**

(1) **the lawyer reasonably believes that the lawyer will be able to provide competent and diligent representation to each affected client;**

(2) **the representation is not prohibited by law;**

(3) **the representation does not involve the assertion of a claim by one client against another client represented by the lawyer in the same litigation or other proceeding before a tribunal; and**

(4) each affected client gives informed consent, confirmed in writing.

Comment

General Principles

[1]   Loyalty and independent judgment are essential elements in the lawyer's relationship to a client. Concurrent conflicts of interest can arise from the lawyer's responsibilities to another client, a former client or a third person or from the lawyer's own interests. For specific Rules regarding certain concurrent conflicts of interest, see Rule 1.8. For former client conflicts of interest, see Rule 1.9. For conflicts of interest involving prospective clients, see Rule 1.18. For definitions of "informed consent" and "confirmed in writing," see Rule 1.0(e) and (b).

[2]   Resolution of a conflict of interest problem under this Rule requires the lawyer to: 1) clearly identify the client or clients; 2) determine whether a conflict of interest exists; 3) decide whether the representation may be undertaken despite the existence of a conflict, i.e., whether the conflict is consentable; and 4) if so, consult with the clients affected under paragraph (a) and obtain their informed consent, confirmed in writing. The clients affected under paragraph (a) include both of the clients referred to in paragraph (a)(1) and the one or more clients whose representation might be materially limited under paragraph (a)(2).

[3]   A conflict of interest may exist before representation is undertaken, in which event the representation must be declined, unless the lawyer obtains the informed consent of each client under the conditions of paragraph (b). To determine whether a conflict of interest exists, a lawyer should adopt reasonable procedures, appropriate for the size and type of firm and practice, to determine in both litigation and non-litigation matters the persons and issues involved. See also Comment to Rule 5.1. Ignorance caused by a failure to institute such procedures will not excuse a lawyer's violation of this Rule. As to whether a client-lawyer relationship exists or, having once been established, is continuing, see Comment to Rule 1.3 and Scope.

[4]   If a conflict arises after representation has been undertaken, the lawyer ordinarily must withdraw from the representation, unless the lawyer has obtained the informed consent of the client under the conditions of paragraph (b). See Rule 1.16. Where more than one client is involved, whether the lawyer may continue to represent any of the clients is determined both by the lawyer's ability to comply with duties owed to the former client and by the lawyer's ability to represent adequately the remaining client or clients, given the lawyer's duties to the former client. See Rule 1.9. See also Comments [5] and [29].

[5]   Unforeseeable developments, such as changes in corporate and other organizational affiliations or the addition or realignment of parties in litigation, might create conflicts in the midst of a representation, as when a company sued by the lawyer on behalf of one client is bought by another client represented by the lawyer in an unrelated matter. Depending on the circumstances, the lawyer may have the option to withdraw from one of the representations in order to avoid the conflict. The lawyer must seek court approval where necessary and take steps to minimize harm to the clients. See Rule 1.16. The lawyer must continue to protect the confidences of the client from whose representation the lawyer has withdrawn. See Rule 1.9(c).

Identifying Conflicts of Interest: Directly Adverse

[6]   Loyalty to a current client prohibits undertaking representation directly adverse to that client without that client's informed consent. Thus, absent consent, a lawyer may not act as an advocate in one matter against a person the lawyer represents in some other matter, even when the matters are wholly unrelated. The client as to whom the representation is directly

adverse is likely to feel betrayed, and the resulting damage to the client-lawyer relationship is likely to impair the lawyer's ability to represent the client effectively. In addition, the client on whose behalf the adverse representation is undertaken reasonably may fear that the lawyer will pursue that client's case less effectively out of deference to the other client, i.e., that the representation may be materially limited by the lawyer's interest in retaining the current client. Similarly, a directly adverse conflict may arise when a lawyer is required to cross-examine a client who appears as a witness in a lawsuit involving another client, as when the testimony will be damaging to the client who is represented in the lawsuit. On the other hand, simultaneous representation in unrelated matters of clients whose interests are only economically adverse, such as representation of competing economic enterprises in unrelated litigation, does not ordinarily constitute a conflict of interest and thus may not require consent of the respective clients.

[7]   Directly adverse conflicts can also arise in transactional matters. For example, if a lawyer is asked to represent the seller of a business in negotiations with a buyer represented by the lawyer, not in the same transaction but in another, unrelated matter, the lawyer could not undertake the representation without the informed consent of each client.

Identifying Conflicts of Interest: Material Limitation

[8]   Even where there is no direct adverseness, a conflict of interest exists if there is a significant risk that a lawyer's ability to consider, recommend or carry out an appropriate course of action for the client will be materially limited as a result of the lawyer's other responsibilities or interests. For example, a lawyer asked to represent several individuals seeking to form a joint venture is likely to be materially limited in the lawyer's ability to recommend or advocate all possible positions that each might take because of the lawyer's duty of loyalty to the others. The conflict in effect forecloses alternatives that would otherwise be available to the client. The mere possibility of subsequent harm does not itself require disclosure and consent. The critical questions are the likelihood that a difference in interests will eventuate and, if it does, whether it will materially interfere with the lawyer's independent professional judgment in considering alternatives or foreclose courses of action that reasonably should be pursued on behalf of the client.

Lawyer's Responsibilities to Former Clients and Other Third Persons

[9]   In addition to conflicts with other current clients, a lawyer's duties of loyalty and independence may be materially limited by responsibilities to former clients under Rule 1.9 or by the lawyer's responsibilities to other persons, such as fiduciary duties arising from a lawyer's service as a trustee, executor or corporate director.

Personal Interest Conflicts

[10]   The lawyer's own interests should not be permitted to have an adverse effect on representation of a client. For example, if the probity of a lawyer's own conduct in a transaction is in serious question, it may be difficult or impossible for the lawyer to give a client detached advice. Similarly, when a lawyer has discussions concerning possible employment with an opponent of the lawyer's client, or with a law firm representing the opponent, such discussions could materially limit the lawyer's representation of the client. In addition, a lawyer may not allow related business interests to affect representation, for example, by referring clients to an enterprise in which the lawyer has an undisclosed financial interest. See Rule 1.8 for specific Rules pertaining to a number of personal interest conflicts, including business transactions with clients. See also Rule 1.10 (personal interest conflicts under Rule 1.7 ordinarily are not imputed to other lawyers in a law firm).

[11]   When lawyers representing different clients in the same matter or in substantially related matters are closely related by blood or marriage, there may be a significant risk that

client confidences will be revealed and that the lawyer's family relationship will interfere with both loyalty and independent professional judgment. As a result, each client is entitled to know of the existence and implications of the relationship between the lawyers before the lawyer agrees to undertake the representation. Thus, a lawyer related to another lawyer, e.g., as parent, child, sibling or spouse, ordinarily may not represent a client in a matter where that lawyer is representing another party, unless each client gives informed consent. The disqualification arising from a close family relationship is personal and ordinarily is not imputed to members of firms with whom the lawyers are associated. See Rule 1.10.

[12] A lawyer is prohibited from engaging in sexual relationships with a client unless the sexual relationship predates the formation of the client-lawyer relationship. See Rule 1.8(j).

Interest of Person Paying for a Lawyer's Service

[13] A lawyer may be paid from a source other than the client, including a co-client, if the client is informed of that fact and consents and the arrangement does not compromise the lawyer's duty of loyalty or independent judgment to the client. See Rule 1.8(f). If acceptance of the payment from any other source presents a significant risk that the lawyer's representation of the client will be materially limited by the lawyer's own interest in accommodating the person paying the lawyer's fee or by the lawyer's responsibilities to a payer who is also a co-client, then the lawyer must comply with the requirements of paragraph (b) before accepting the representation, including determining whether the conflict is consentable and, if so, that the client has adequate information about the material risks of the representation.

Prohibited Representations

[14] Ordinarily, clients may consent to representation notwithstanding a conflict. However, as indicated in paragraph (b), some conflicts are nonconsentable, meaning that the lawyer involved cannot properly ask for such agreement or provide representation on the basis of the client's consent. When the lawyer is representing more than one client, the question of consentability must be resolved as to each client.

[15] Consentability is typically determined by considering whether the interests of the clients will be adequately protected if the clients are permitted to give their informed consent to representation burdened by a conflict of interest. Thus, under paragraph (b)(1), representation is prohibited if in the circumstances the lawyer cannot reasonably conclude that the lawyer will be able to provide competent and diligent representation. See Rule 1.1 (competence) and Rule 1.3 (diligence).

[16] Paragraph (b)(2) describes conflicts that are nonconsentable because the representation is prohibited by applicable law. For example, in some states substantive law provides that the same lawyer may not represent more than one defendant in a capital case, even with the consent of the clients, and under federal criminal statutes certain representations by a former government lawyer are prohibited, despite the informed consent of the former client. In addition, decisional law in some states limits the ability of a governmental client, such as a municipality, to consent to a conflict of interest.

[17] Paragraph (b)(3) describes conflicts that are nonconsentable because of the institutional interest in vigorous development of each client's position when the clients are aligned directly against each other in the same litigation or other proceeding before a tribunal. Whether clients are aligned directly against each other within the meaning of this paragraph requires examination of the context of the proceeding. Although this paragraph does not preclude a lawyer's multiple representation of adverse parties to a mediation (because mediation is not a proceeding before a "tribunal" under Rule 1.0(m)), such representation may be precluded by paragraph (b)(1).

Informed Consent

[18] Informed consent requires that each affected client be aware of the relevant circumstances and of the material and reasonably foreseeable ways that the conflict could have

adverse effects on the interests of that client. See Rule 1.0(e) (informed consent). The information required depends on the nature of the conflict and the nature of the risks involved. When representation of multiple clients in a single matter is undertaken, the information must include the implications of the common representation, including possible effects on loyalty, confidentiality and the attorney-client privilege and the advantages and risks involved. See Comments [30] and [31] (effect of common representation on confidentiality).

[19] Under some circumstances it may be impossible to make the disclosure necessary to obtain consent. For example, when the lawyer represents different clients in related matters and one of the clients refuses to consent to the disclosure necessary to permit the other client to make an informed decision, the lawyer cannot properly ask the latter to consent. In some cases the alternative to common representation can be that each party may have to obtain separate representation with the possibility of incurring additional costs. These costs, along with the benefits of securing separate representation, are factors that may be considered by the affected client in determining whether common representation is in the client's interests.

Consent Confirmed in Writing

[20] Paragraph (b) requires the lawyer to obtain the informed consent of the client, confirmed in writing. Such a writing may consist of a document executed by the client or one that the lawyer promptly records and transmits to the client following an oral consent. See Rule 1.0(b). See also Rule 1.0(n) (writing includes electronic transmission). If it is not feasible to obtain or transmit the writing at the time the client gives informed consent, then the lawyer must obtain or transmit it within a reasonable time thereafter. See Rule 1.0(b). The requirement of a writing does not supplant the need in most cases for the lawyer to talk with the client, to explain the risks and advantages, if any, of representation burdened with a conflict of interest, as well as reasonably available alternatives, and to afford the client a reasonable opportunity to consider the risks and alternatives and to raise questions and concerns. Rather, the writing is required in order to impress upon clients the seriousness of the decision the client is being asked to make and to avoid disputes or ambiguities that might later occur in the absence of a writing.

Revoking Consent

[21] A client who has given consent to a conflict may revoke the consent and, like any other client, may terminate the lawyer's representation at any time. Whether revoking consent to the client's own representation precludes the lawyer from continuing to represent other clients depends on the circumstances, including the nature of the conflict, whether the client revoked consent because of a material change in circumstances, the reasonable expectations of the other clients and whether material detriment to the other clients or the lawyer would result.

Consent to Future Conflict

[22] Whether a lawyer may properly request a client to waive conflicts that might arise in the future is subject to the test of paragraph (b). The effectiveness of such waivers is generally determined by the extent to which the client reasonably understands the material risks that the waiver entails. The more comprehensive the explanation of the types of future representations that might arise and the actual and reasonably foreseeable adverse consequences of those representations, the greater the likelihood that the client will have the requisite understanding. Thus, if the client agrees to consent to a particular type of conflict with which the client is already familiar, then the consent ordinarily will be effective with regard to that type of conflict. If the consent is general and open-ended, then the consent ordinarily will be ineffective, because it is not reasonably likely that the client will have understood the material risks involved. On the other hand, if the client is an experienced user of the legal services involved and is reasonably informed regarding the risk that a conflict may arise, such consent is more likely to

be effective, particularly if, e.g., the client is independently represented by other counsel in giving consent and the consent is limited to future conflicts unrelated to the subject of the representation. In any case, advance consent cannot be effective if the circumstances that materialize in the future are such as would make the conflict nonconsentable under paragraph (b).

Conflicts in Litigation

[23]   Paragraph (b)(3) prohibits representation of opposing parties in the same litigation, regardless of the clients' consent. On the other hand, simultaneous representation of parties whose interests in litigation may conflict, such as coplaintiffs or codefendants, is governed by paragraph (a)(2). A conflict may exist by reason of substantial discrepancy in the parties' testimony, incompatibility in positions in relation to an opposing party or the fact that there are substantially different possibilities of settlement of the claims or liabilities in question. Such conflicts can arise in criminal cases as well as civil. The potential for conflict of interest in representing multiple defendants in a criminal case is so grave that ordinarily a lawyer should decline to represent more than one codefendant. On the other hand, common representation of persons having similar interests in civil litigation is proper if the requirements of paragraph (b) are met.

[24]   Ordinarily a lawyer may take inconsistent legal positions in different tribunals at different times on behalf of different clients. The mere fact that advocating a legal position on behalf of one client might create precedent adverse to the interests of a client represented by the lawyer in an unrelated matter does not create a conflict of interest. A conflict of interest exists, however, if there is a significant risk that a lawyer's action on behalf of one client will materially limit the lawyer's effectiveness in representing another client in a different case; for example, when a decision favoring one client will create a precedent likely to seriously weaken the position taken on behalf of the other client. Factors relevant in determining whether the clients need to be advised of the risk include: where the cases are pending, whether the issue is substantive or procedural, the temporal relationship between the matters, the significance of the issue to the immediate and long-term interests of the clients involved and the clients' reasonable expectations in retaining the lawyer. If there is significant risk of material limitation, then absent informed consent of the affected clients, the lawyer must refuse one of the representations or withdraw from one or both matters.

[25]   When a lawyer represents or seeks to represent a class of plaintiffs or defendants in a class-action lawsuit, unnamed members of the class are ordinarily not considered to be clients of the lawyer for purposes of applying paragraph (a)(1) of this Rule. Thus, the lawyer does not typically need to get the consent of such a person before representing a client suing the person in an unrelated matter. Similarly, a lawyer seeking to represent an opponent in a class action does not typically need the consent of an unnamed member of the class whom the lawyer represents in an unrelated matter.

Nonlitigation Conflicts

[26]   Conflicts of interest under paragraphs (a)(1) and (a)(2) arise in contexts other than litigation. For a discussion of directly adverse conflicts in transactional matters, see Comment [7]. Relevant factors in determining whether there is significant potential for material limitation include the duration and intimacy of the lawyer's relationship with the client or clients involved, the functions being performed by the lawyer, the likelihood that disagreements will arise and the likely prejudice to the client from the conflict. The question is often one of proximity and degree. See Comment [8].

[27]   For example, conflict questions may arise in estate planning and estate administration. A lawyer may be called upon to prepare wills for several family members, such as husband

and wife, and, depending upon the circumstances, a conflict of interest may be present. In estate administration the identity of the client may be unclear under the law of a particular jurisdiction. Under one view, the client is the fiduciary; under another view the client is the estate or trust, including its beneficiaries. In order to comply with conflict of interest rules, the lawyer should make clear the lawyer's relationship to the parties involved.

[28] Whether a conflict is consentable depends on the circumstances. For example, a lawyer may not represent multiple parties to a negotiation whose interests are fundamentally antagonistic to each other, but common representation is permissible where the clients are generally aligned in interest even though there is some difference in interest among them. Thus, a lawyer may seek to establish or adjust a relationship between clients on an amicable and mutually advantageous basis; for example, in helping to organize a business in which two or more clients are entrepreneurs, working out the financial reorganization of an enterprise in which two or more clients have an interest or arranging a property distribution in settlement of an estate. The lawyer seeks to resolve potentially adverse interests by developing the parties' mutual interests. Otherwise, each party might have to obtain separate representation, with the possibility of incurring additional cost, complication or even litigation. Given these and other relevant factors, the clients may prefer that the lawyer act for all of them.

Special Considerations in Common Representation

[29] In considering whether to represent multiple clients in the same matter, a lawyer should be mindful that if the common representation fails because the potentially adverse interests cannot be reconciled, the result can be additional cost, embarrassment and recrimination. Ordinarily, the lawyer will be forced to withdraw from representing all of the clients if the common representation fails. In some situations, the risk of failure is so great that multiple representation is plainly impossible. For example, a lawyer cannot undertake common representation of clients where contentious litigation or negotiations between them are imminent or contemplated. Moreover, because the lawyer is required to be impartial between commonly represented clients, representation of multiple clients is improper when it is unlikely that impartiality can be maintained. Generally, if the relationship between the parties has already assumed antagonism, the possibility that the clients' interests can be adequately served by common representation is not very good. Other relevant factors are whether the lawyer subsequently will represent both parties on a continuing basis and whether the situation involves creating or terminating a relationship between the parties.

[30] A particularly important factor in determining the appropriateness of common representation is the effect on client-lawyer confidentiality and the attorney-client privilege. With regard to the attorney-client privilege, the prevailing rule is that, as between commonly represented clients, the privilege does not attach. Hence, it must be assumed that if litigation eventuates between the clients, the privilege will not protect any such communications, and the clients should be so advised.

[31] As to the duty of confidentiality, continued common representation will almost certainly be inadequate if one client asks the lawyer not to disclose to the other client information relevant to the common representation. This is so because the lawyer has an equal duty of loyalty to each client, and each client has the right to be informed of anything bearing on the representation that might affect that client's interests and the right to expect that the lawyer will use that information to that client's benefit. See Rule 1.4. The lawyer should, at the outset of the common representation and as part of the process of obtaining each client's informed consent, advise each client that information will be shared and that the lawyer will have to withdraw if one client decides that some matter material to the representation should be kept from the other. In limited circumstances, it may be appropriate for the lawyer to proceed with the representation when the clients have agreed, after being properly informed, that the lawyer will keep certain information confidential. For example, the lawyer may reasonably

conclude that failure to disclose one client's trade secrets to another client will not adversely affect representation involving a joint venture between the clients and agree to keep that information confidential with the informed consent of both clients.

[32] When seeking to establish or adjust a relationship between clients, the lawyer should make clear that the lawyer's role is not that of partisanship normally expected in other circumstances and, thus, that the clients may be required to assume greater responsibility for decisions than when each client is separately represented. Any limitations on the scope of the representation made necessary as a result of the common representation should be fully explained to the clients at the outset of the representation. See Rule 1.2(c).

[33] Subject to the above limitations, each client in the common representation has the right to loyal and diligent representation and the protection of Rule 1.9 concerning the obligations to a former client. The client also has the right to discharge the lawyer as stated in Rule 1.16.

Organizational Clients

[34] A lawyer who represents a corporation or other organization does not, by virtue of that representation, necessarily represent any constituent or affiliated organization, such as a parent or subsidiary. See Rule 1.13(a). Thus, the lawyer for an organization is not barred from accepting representation adverse to an affiliate in an unrelated matter, unless the circumstances are such that the affiliate should also be considered a client of the lawyer, there is an understanding between the lawyer and the organizational client that the lawyer will avoid representation adverse to the client's affiliates, or the lawyer's obligations to either the organizational client or the new client are likely to limit materially the lawyer's representation of the other client.

[35] A lawyer for a corporation or other organization who is also a member of its board of directors should determine whether the responsibilities of the two roles may conflict. The lawyer may be called on to advise the corporation in matters involving actions of the directors. Consideration should be given to the frequency with which such situations may arise, the potential intensity of the conflict, the effect of the lawyer's resignation from the board and the possibility of the corporation's obtaining legal advice from another lawyer in such situations. If there is material risk that the dual role will compromise the lawyer's independence of professional judgment, the lawyer should not serve as a director or should cease to act as the corporation's lawyer when conflicts of interest arise. The lawyer should advise the other members of the board that in some circumstances matters discussed at board meetings while the lawyer is present in the capacity of director might not be protected by the attorney-client privilege and that conflict of interest considerations might require the lawyer's recusal as a director or might require the lawyer and the lawyer's firm to decline representation of the corporation in a matter.

RULE 1.8: CONFLICT OF INTEREST: CURRENT CLIENTS: SPECIFIC RULES

(a) A lawyer shall not enter into a business transaction with a client or knowingly acquire an ownership, possessory, security or other pecuniary interest adverse to a client unless:

(1) the transaction and terms on which the lawyer acquires the interest are fair and reasonable to the client and are fully disclosed and transmitted in writing in a manner that can be reasonably understood by the client;

(2) the client is advised in writing of the desirability of seeking and is given a reasonable opportunity to seek the advice of independent legal counsel on the transaction; and

(3) the client gives informed consent, in a writing signed by the client, to the essential terms of the transaction and the lawyer's role in the transaction, including whether the lawyer is representing the client in the transaction.

(b) A lawyer shall not use information relating to representation of a client to the disadvantage of the client unless the client gives informed consent, except as permitted or required by these Rules.

(c) A lawyer shall not solicit any substantial gift from a client, including a testamentary gift, or prepare on behalf of a client an instrument giving the lawyer or a person related to the lawyer any substantial gift unless the lawyer or other recipient of the gift is related to the client. For purposes of this paragraph, related persons include a spouse, child, grandchild, parent, grandparent or other relative or individual with whom the lawyer or the client maintains a close, familial relationship.

(d) Prior to the conclusion of representation of a client, a lawyer shall not make or negotiate an agreement giving the lawyer literary or media rights to a portrayal or account based in substantial part on information relating to the representation.

(e) A lawyer shall not provide financial assistance to a client in connection with pending or contemplated litigation, except that:

(1) a lawyer may advance court costs and expenses of litigation, the repayment of which may be contingent on the outcome of the matter; and

(2) a lawyer representing an indigent client may pay court costs and expenses of litigation on behalf of the client.

(f) A lawyer shall not accept compensation for representing a client from one other than the client unless:

(1) the client gives informed consent;

(2) there is no interference with the lawyer's independence of professional judgment or with the client-lawyer relationship; and

(3) information relating to representation of a client is protected as required by Rule 1.6.

(g) A lawyer who represents two or more clients shall not participate in making an aggregate settlement of the claims of or against the clients, or in a criminal case an aggregated agreement as to guilty or nolo contendere pleas, unless each client gives informed consent, in a writing signed by the client. The lawyer's disclosure shall include the existence and nature of all the claims or pleas involved and of the participation of each person in the settlement.

(h) A lawyer shall not:

(1) make an agreement prospectively limiting the lawyer's liability to a client for malpractice unless the client is independently represented in making the agreement; or

(2) settle a claim or potential claim for such liability with an unrepresented client or former client unless that person is advised in writing of the desirability

of seeking and is given a reasonable opportunity to seek the advice of independent legal counsel in connection therewith.

(i) A lawyer shall not acquire a proprietary interest in the cause of action or subject matter of litigation the lawyer is conducting for a client, except that the lawyer may:

(1) acquire a lien authorized by law to secure the lawyer's fee or expenses; and

(2) contract with a client for a reasonable contingent fee in a civil case.

(j) A lawyer shall not have sexual relations with a client unless a consensual sexual relationship existed between them when the client-lawyer relationship commenced.

(k) While lawyers are associated in a firm, a prohibition in the foregoing paragraphs (a) through (i) that applies to any one of them shall apply to all of them.

Comment

Business Transactions Between Client and Lawyer

[1]   A lawyer's legal skill and training, together with the relationship of trust and confidence between lawyer and client, create the possibility of overreaching when the lawyer participates in a business, property or financial transaction with a client, for example, a loan or sales transaction or a lawyer investment on behalf of a client. The requirements of paragraph (a) must be met even when the transaction is not closely related to the subject matter of the representation, as when a lawyer drafting a will for a client learns that the client needs money for unrelated expenses and offers to make a loan to the client. The Rule applies to lawyers engaged in the sale of goods or services related to the practice of law, for example, the sale of title insurance or investment services to existing clients of the lawyer's legal practice. See Rule 5.7. It also applies to lawyers purchasing property from estates they represent. It does not apply to ordinary fee arrangements between client and lawyer, which are governed by Rule 1.5, although its requirements must be met when the lawyer accepts an interest in the client's business or other nonmonetary property as payment of all or part of a fee. In addition, the Rule does not apply to standard commercial transactions between the lawyer and the client for products or services that the client generally markets to others, for example, banking or brokerage services, medical services, products manufactured or distributed by the client, and utilities' services. In such transactions, the lawyer has no advantage in dealing with the client, and the restrictions in paragraph (a) are unnecessary and impracticable.

[2]   Paragraph (a)(1) requires that the transaction itself be fair to the client and that its essential terms be communicated to the client, in writing, in a manner that can be reasonably understood. Paragraph (a)(2) requires that the client also be advised, in writing, of the desirability of seeking the advice of independent legal counsel. It also requires that the client be given a reasonable opportunity to obtain such advice. Paragraph (a)(3) requires that the lawyer obtain the client's informed consent, in a writing signed by the client, both to the essential terms of the transaction and to the lawyer's role. When necessary, the lawyer should discuss both the material risks of the proposed transaction, including any risk presented by the lawyer's involvement, and the existence of reasonably available alternatives and should explain why the advice of independent legal counsel is desirable. See Rule 1.0(e) (definition of informed consent).

[3]   The risk to a client is greatest when the client expects the lawyer to represent the client in the transaction itself or when the lawyer's financial interest otherwise poses a significant risk

that the lawyer's representation of the client will be materially limited by the lawyer's financial interest in the transaction. Here the lawyer's role requires that the lawyer must comply, not only with the requirements of paragraph (a), but also with the requirements of Rule 1.7. Under that Rule, the lawyer must disclose the risks associated with the lawyer's dual role as both legal adviser and participant in the transaction, such as the risk that the lawyer will structure the transaction or give legal advice in a way that favors the lawyer's interests at the expense of the client. Moreover, the lawyer must obtain the client's informed consent. In some cases, the lawyer's interest may be such that Rule 1.7 will preclude the lawyer from seeking the client's consent to the transaction.

[4]   If the client is independently represented in the transaction, paragraph (a)(2) of this Rule is inapplicable, and the paragraph (a)(1) requirement for full disclosure is satisfied either by a written disclosure by the lawyer involved in the transaction or by the client's independent counsel. The fact that the client was independently represented in the transaction is relevant in determining whether the agreement was fair and reasonable to the client as paragraph (a)(1) further requires.

Use of Information Related to Representation

[5]   Use of information relating to the representation to the disadvantage of the client violates the lawyer's duty of loyalty. Paragraph (b) applies when the information is used to benefit either the lawyer or a third person, such as another client or business associate of the lawyer. For example, if a lawyer learns that a client intends to purchase and develop several parcels of land, the lawyer may not use that information to purchase one of the parcels in competition with the client or to recommend that another client make such a purchase. The Rule does not prohibit uses that do not disadvantage the client. For example, a lawyer who learns a government agency's interpretation of trade legislation during the representation of one client may properly use that information to benefit other clients. Paragraph (b) prohibits disadvantageous use of client information unless the client gives informed consent, except as permitted or required by these Rules. See Rules 1.2(d), 1.6, 1.9(c), 3.3, 4.1(b), 8.1 and 8.3.

Gifts to Lawyers

[6]   A lawyer may accept a gift from a client, if the transaction meets general standards of fairness. For example, a simple gift such as a present given at a holiday or as a token of appreciation is permitted. If a client offers the lawyer a more substantial gift, paragraph (c) does not prohibit the lawyer from accepting it, although such a gift may be voidable by the client under the doctrine of undue influence, which treats client gifts as presumptively fraudulent. In any event, due to concerns about overreaching and imposition on clients, a lawyer may not suggest that a substantial gift be made to the lawyer or for the lawyer's benefit, except where the lawyer is related to the client as set forth in paragraph (c).

[7]   If effectuation of a substantial gift requires preparing a legal instrument such as a will or conveyance the client should have the detached advice that another lawyer can provide. The sole exception to this Rule is where the client is a relative of the donee.

[8]   This Rule does not prohibit a lawyer from seeking to have the lawyer or a partner or associate of the lawyer named as executor of the client's estate or to another potentially lucrative fiduciary position. Nevertheless, such appointments will be subject to the general conflict of interest provision in Rule 1.7 when there is a significant risk that the lawyer's interest in obtaining the appointment will materially limit the lawyer's independent professional judgment in advising the client concerning the choice of an executor or other fiduciary. In obtaining the client's informed consent to the conflict, the lawyer should advise the client concerning the

nature and extent of the lawyer's financial interest in the appointment, as well as the availability of alternative candidates for the position.

Literary Rights

[9] An agreement by which a lawyer acquires literary or media rights concerning the conduct of the representation creates a conflict between the interests of the client and the personal interests of the lawyer. Measures suitable in the representation of the client may detract from the publication value of an account of the representation. Paragraph (d) does not prohibit a lawyer representing a client in a transaction concerning literary property from agreeing that the lawyer's fee shall consist of a share in ownership in the property, if the arrangement conforms to Rule 1.5 and paragraphs (a) and (i).

Financial Assistance

[10] Lawyers may not subsidize lawsuits or administrative proceedings brought on behalf of their clients, including making or guaranteeing loans to their clients for living expenses, because to do so would encourage clients to pursue lawsuits that might not otherwise be brought and because such assistance gives lawyers too great a financial stake in the litigation. These dangers do not warrant a prohibition on a lawyer lending a client court costs and litigation expenses, including the expenses of medical examination and the costs of obtaining and presenting evidence, because these advances are virtually indistinguishable from contingent fees and help ensure access to the courts. Similarly, an exception allowing lawyers representing indigent clients to pay court costs and litigation expenses regardless of whether these funds will be repaid is warranted.

Person Paying for a Lawyer's Services

[11] Lawyers are frequently asked to represent a client under circumstances in which a third person will compensate the lawyer, in whole or in part. The third person might be a relative or friend, an indemnitor (such as a liability insurance company) or a co-client (such as a corporation sued along with one or more of its employees). Because third-party payers frequently have interests that differ from those of the client, including interests in minimizing the amount spent on the representation and in learning how the representation is progressing, lawyers are prohibited from accepting or continuing such representations unless the lawyer determines that there will be no interference with the lawyer's independent professional judgment and there is informed consent from the client. See also Rule 5.4(c) (prohibiting interference with a lawyer's professional judgment by one who recommends, employs or pays the lawyer to render legal services for another).

[12] Sometimes, it will be sufficient for the lawyer to obtain the client's informed consent regarding the fact of the payment and the identity of the third-party payer. If, however, the fee arrangement creates a conflict of interest for the lawyer, then the lawyer must comply with Rule. 1.7. The lawyer must also conform to the requirements of Rule 1.6 concerning confidentiality. Under Rule 1.7(a), a conflict of interest exists if there is significant risk that the lawyer's representation of the client will be materially limited by the lawyer's own interest in the fee arrangement or by the lawyer's responsibilities to the third-party payer (for example, when the third-party payer is a co-client). Under Rule 1.7(b), the lawyer may accept or continue the representation with the informed consent of each affected client, unless the conflict is nonconsentable under that paragraph. Under Rule 1.7(b), the informed consent must be confirmed in writing.

Aggregate Settlements

[13] Differences in willingness to make or accept an offer of settlement are among the risks of common representation of multiple clients by a single lawyer. Under Rule 1.7, this is one of

the risks that should be discussed before undertaking the representation, as part of the process of obtaining the clients' informed consent. In addition, Rule 1.2(a) protects each client's right to have the final say in deciding whether to accept or reject an offer of settlement and in deciding whether to enter a guilty or nolo contendere plea in a criminal case. The rule stated in this paragraph is a corollary of both these Rules and provides that, before any settlement offer or plea bargain is made or accepted on behalf of multiple clients, the lawyer must inform each of them about all the material terms of the settlement, including what the other clients will receive or pay if the settlement or plea offer is accepted. See also Rule 1.0(e) (definition of informed consent). Lawyers representing a class of plaintiffs or defendants, or those proceeding derivatively, may not have a full client-lawyer relationship with each member of the class; nevertheless, such lawyers must comply with applicable rules regulating notification of class members and other procedural requirements designed to ensure adequate protection of the entire class.

Limiting Liability and Settling Malpractice Claims

[14]   Agreements prospectively limiting a lawyer's liability for malpractice are prohibited unless the client is independently represented in making the agreement because they are likely to undermine competent and diligent representation. Also, many clients are unable to evaluate the desirability of making such an agreement before a dispute has arisen, particularly if they are then represented by the lawyer seeking the agreement. This paragraph does not, however, prohibit a lawyer from entering into an agreement with the client to arbitrate legal malpractice claims, provided such agreements are enforceable and the client is fully informed of the scope and effect of the agreement. Nor does this paragraph limit the ability of lawyers to practice in the form of a limited-liability entity, where permitted by law, provided that each lawyer remains personally liable to the client for his or her own conduct and the firm complies with any conditions required by law, such as provisions requiring client notification or maintenance of adequate liability insurance. Nor does it prohibit an agreement in accordance with Rule 1.2 that defines the scope of the representation, although a definition of scope that makes the obligations of representation illusory will amount to an attempt to limit liability.

[15]   Agreements settling a claim or a potential claim for malpractice are not prohibited by this Rule. Nevertheless, in view of the danger that a lawyer will take unfair advantage of an unrepresented client or former client, the lawyer must first advise such a person in writing of the appropriateness of independent representation in connection with such a settlement. In addition, the lawyer must give the client or former client a reasonable opportunity to find and consult independent counsel.

Acquiring Proprietary Interest in Litigation

[16]   Paragraph (i) states the traditional general rule that lawyers are prohibited from acquiring a proprietary interest in litigation. Like paragraph (e), the general rule has its basis in common law champerty and maintenance and is designed to avoid giving the lawyer too great an interest in the representation. In addition, when the lawyer acquires an ownership interest in the subject of the representation, it will be more difficult for a client to discharge the lawyer if the client so desires. The Rule is subject to specific exceptions developed in decisional law and continued in these Rules. The exception for certain advances of the costs of litigation is set forth in paragraph (e). In addition, paragraph (i) sets forth exceptions for liens authorized by law to secure the lawyer's fees or expenses and contracts for reasonable contingent fees. The law of each jurisdiction determines which liens are authorized by law. These may include liens granted by statute, liens originating in common law and liens acquired by contract with the client. When a lawyer acquires by contract a security interest in property other than that recovered through the lawyer's efforts in the litigation, such an acquisition is a business or financial transaction with a client and is governed by the requirements of paragraph (a). Contracts for contingent fees in civil cases are governed by Rule 1.5.

Client-Lawyer Sexual Relationships

[17]   The relationship between lawyer and client is a fiduciary one in which the lawyer occupies the highest position of trust and confidence. The relationship is almost always unequal;

thus, a sexual relationship between lawyer and client can involve unfair exploitation of the lawyer's fiduciary role, in violation of the lawyer's basic ethical obligation not to use the trust of the client to the client's disadvantage. In addition, such a relationship presents a significant danger that, because of the lawyer's emotional involvement, the lawyer will be unable to represent the client without impairment of the exercise of independent professional judgment. Moreover, a blurred line between the professional and personal relationships may make it difficult to predict to what extent client confidences will be protected by the attorney-client evidentiary privilege, since client confidences are protected by privilege only when they are imparted in the context of the client-lawyer relationship. Because of the significant danger of harm to client interests and because the client's own emotional involvement renders it unlikely that the client could give adequate informed consent, this Rule prohibits the lawyer from having sexual relations with a client regardless of whether the relationship is consensual and regardless of the absence of prejudice to the client.

[18] Sexual relationships that predate the client-lawyer relationship are not prohibited. Issues relating to the exploitation of the fiduciary relationship and client dependency are diminished when the sexual relationship existed prior to the commencement of the client-lawyer relationship. However, before proceeding with the representation in these circumstances, the lawyer should consider whether the lawyer's ability to represent the client will be materially limited by the relationship. See Rule 1.7(a)(2).

[19] When the client is an organization, paragraph (j) of this Rule prohibits a lawyer for the organization (whether inside counsel or outside counsel) from having a sexual relationship with a constituent of the organization who supervises, directs or regularly consults with that lawyer concerning the organization's legal matters.

Imputation of Prohibitions

[20] Under paragraph (k), a prohibition on conduct by an individual lawyer in paragraphs (a) through (i) also applies to all lawyers associated in a firm with the personally prohibited lawyer. For example, one lawyer in a firm may not enter into a business transaction with a client of another member of the firm without complying with paragraph (a), even if the first lawyer is not personally involved in the representation of the client. The prohibition set forth in paragraph (j) is personal and is not applied to associated lawyers.

RULE 1.9: DUTIES TO FORMER CLIENTS

(a) A lawyer who has formerly represented a client in a matter shall not thereafter represent another person in the same or a substantially related matter in which that person's interests are materially adverse to the interests of the former client unless the former client gives informed consent, confirmed in writing.

(b) A lawyer shall not knowingly represent a person in the same or a substantially related matter in which a firm with which the lawyer formerly was associated had previously represented a client

(1) whose interests are materially adverse to that person; and

(2) about whom the lawyer had acquired information protected by Rules 1.6 and 1.9(c) that is material to the matter;

unless the former client gives informed consent, confirmed in writing.

(c) A lawyer who has formerly represented a client in a matter or whose present or former firm has formerly represented a client in a matter shall not thereafter:

(1) use information relating to the representation to the disadvantage of the former client except as these Rules would permit or require with respect to a client, or when the information has become generally known; or

(2) reveal information relating to the representation except as these Rules would permit or require with respect to a client.

Comment

[1]   After termination of a client-lawyer relationship, a lawyer has certain continuing duties with respect to confidentiality and conflicts of interest and thus may not represent another client except in conformity with this Rule. Under this Rule, for example, a lawyer could not properly seek to rescind on behalf of a new client a contract drafted on behalf of the former client. So also a lawyer who has prosecuted an accused person could not properly represent the accused in a subsequent civil action against the government concerning the same transaction. Nor could a lawyer who has represented multiple clients in a matter represent one of the clients against the others in the same or a substantially related matter after a dispute arose among the clients in that matter, unless all affected clients give informed consent. See Comment [9]. Current and former government lawyers must comply with this Rule to the extent required by Rule 1.11.

[2]   The scope of a "matter" for purposes of this Rule depends on the facts of a particular situation or transaction. The lawyer's involvement in a matter can also be a question of degree. When a lawyer has been directly involved in a specific transaction, subsequent representation of other clients with materially adverse interests in that transaction clearly is prohibited. On the other hand, a lawyer who recurrently handled a type of problem for a former client is not precluded from later representing another client in a factually distinct problem of that type even though the subsequent representation involves a position adverse to the prior client. Similar considerations can apply to the reassignment of military lawyers between defense and prosecution functions within the same military jurisdictions. The underlying question is whether the lawyer was so involved in the matter that the subsequent representation can be justly regarded as a changing of sides in the matter in question.

[3]   Matters are "substantially related" for purposes of this Rule if they involve the same transaction or legal dispute or if there otherwise is a substantial risk that confidential factual information as would normally have been obtained in the prior representation would materially advance the client's position in the subsequent matter. For example, a lawyer who has represented a businessperson and learned extensive private financial information about that person may not then represent that person's spouse in seeking a divorce. Similarly, a lawyer who has previously represented a client in securing environmental permits to build a shopping center would be precluded from representing neighbors seeking to oppose rezoning of the property on the basis of environmental considerations; however, the lawyer would not be precluded, on the grounds of substantial relationship, from defending a tenant of the completed shopping center in resisting eviction for nonpayment of rent. Information that has been disclosed to the public or to other parties adverse to the former client ordinarily will not be disqualifying. Information acquired in a prior representation may have been rendered obsolete by the passage of time, a circumstance that may be relevant in determining whether two representations are substantially related. In the case of an organizational client, general knowledge of the client's policies and practices ordinarily will not preclude a subsequent representation; on the other hand, knowledge of specific facts gained in a prior representation that are relevant to the matter in question ordinarily will preclude such a representation. A former client is not required to reveal the confidential information learned by the lawyer in order to establish a substantial risk that the lawyer has confidential information to use in the subsequent matter. A conclusion about the

possession of such information may be based on the nature of the services the lawyer provided the former client and information that would in ordinary practice be learned by a lawyer providing such services.

Lawyers Moving Between Firms

[4]   When lawyers have been associated within a firm but then end their association, the question of whether a lawyer should undertake representation is more complicated. There are several competing considerations. First, the client previously represented by the former firm must be reasonably assured that the principle of loyalty to the client is not compromised. Second, the rule should not be so broadly cast as to preclude other persons from having reasonable choice of legal counsel. Third, the rule should not unreasonably hamper lawyers from forming new associations and taking on new clients after having left a previous association. In this connection, it should be recognized that today many lawyers practice in firms, that many lawyers to some degree limit their practice to one field or another, and that many move from one association to another several times in their careers. If the concept of imputation were applied with unqualified rigor, the result would be radical curtailment of the opportunity of lawyers to move from one practice setting to another and of the opportunity of clients to change counsel.

[5]   Paragraph (b) operates to disqualify the lawyer only when the lawyer involved has actual knowledge of information protected by Rules 1.6 and 1.9(c). Thus, if a lawyer while with one firm acquired no knowledge or information relating to a particular client of the firm, and that lawyer later joined another firm, neither the lawyer individually nor the second firm is disqualified from representing another client in the same or a related matter even though the interests of the two clients conflict. See Rule 1.10(b) for the restrictions on a firm once a lawyer has terminated association with the firm.

[6]   Application of paragraph (b) depends on a situation's particular facts, aided by inferences, deductions or working presumptions that reasonably may be made about the way in which lawyers work together. A lawyer may have general access to files of all clients of a law firm and may regularly participate in discussions of their affairs; it should be inferred that such a lawyer in fact is privy to all information about all the firm's clients. In contrast, another lawyer may have access to the files of only a limited number of clients and participate in discussions of the affairs of no other clients; in the absence of information to the contrary, it should be inferred that such a lawyer in fact is privy to information about the clients actually served but not those of other clients. In such an inquiry, the burden of proof should rest upon the firm whose disqualification is sought.

[7]   Independent of the question of disqualification of a firm, a lawyer changing professional association has a continuing duty to preserve confidentiality of information about a client formerly represented. See Rules 1.6 and 1.9(c).

[8]   Paragraph (c) provides that information acquired by the lawyer in the course of representing a client may not subsequently be used or revealed by the lawyer to the disadvantage of the client. However, the fact that a lawyer has once served a client does not preclude the lawyer from using generally known information about that client when later representing another client.

[9]   The provisions of this Rule are for the protection of former clients and can be waived if the client gives informed consent, which consent must be confirmed in writing under paragraphs (a) and (b). See Rule 1.0(e). With regard to the effectiveness of an advance waiver, see Comment [22] to Rule 1.7. With regard to disqualification of a firm with which a lawyer is or was formerly associated, see Rule 1.10.

RULE 1.10: IMPUTATION OF CONFLICTS OF INTEREST: GENERAL RULE

(a) While lawyers are associated in a firm, none of them shall knowingly represent a client when any one of them practicing alone would be prohibited from doing

so by Rules 1.7 or 1.9, unless the prohibition is based on a personal interest of the prohibited lawyer and does not present a significant risk of materially limiting the representation of the client by the remaining lawyers in the firm.

(b) When a lawyer has terminated an association with a firm, the firm is not prohibited from thereafter representing a person with interests materially adverse to those of a client represented by the formerly associated lawyer and not currently represented by the firm, unless:

(1) the matter is the same or substantially related to that in which the formerly associated lawyer represented the client; and

(2) any lawyer remaining in the firm has information protected by Rules 1.6 and 1.9(c) that is material to the matter.

(c) A disqualification prescribed by this rule may be waived by the affected client under the conditions stated in Rule 1.7.

(d) The disqualification of lawyers associated in a firm with former or current government lawyers is governed by Rule 1.11.

Comment

Definition of "Firm"

[1]   For purposes of the Rules of Professional Conduct, the term "firm" denotes lawyers in a law partnership, professional corporation, sole proprietorship or other association authorized to practice law; or lawyers employed in a legal services organization or the legal department of a corporation or other organization. See Rule 1.0(c). Whether two or more lawyers constitute a firm within this definition can depend on the specific facts. See Rule 1.0, Comments [2]—[4].

Principles of Imputed Disqualification

[2]   The rule of imputed disqualification stated in paragraph (a) gives effect to the principle of loyalty to the client as it applies to lawyers who practice in a law firm. Such situations can be considered from the premise that a firm of lawyers is essentially one lawyer for purposes of the rules governing loyalty to the client, or from the premise that each lawyer is vicariously bound by the obligation of loyalty owed by each lawyer with whom the lawyer is associated. Paragraph (a) operates only among the lawyers currently associated in a firm. When a lawyer moves from one firm to another, the situation is governed by Rules 1.9(b) and 1.10(b).

[3]   The rule in paragraph (a) does not prohibit representation where neither questions of client loyalty nor protection of confidential information are presented. Where one lawyer in a firm could not effectively represent a given client because of strong political beliefs, for example, but that lawyer will do no work on the case and the personal beliefs of the lawyer will not materially limit the representation by others in the firm, the firm should not be disqualified. On the other hand, if an opposing party in a case were owned by a lawyer in the law firm, and others in the firm would be materially limited in pursuing the matter because of loyalty to that lawyer, the personal disqualification of the lawyer would be imputed to all others in the firm.

[4]   The rule in paragraph (a) also does not prohibit representation by others in the law firm where the person prohibited from involvement in a matter is a nonlawyer, such as a paralegal or legal secretary. Nor does paragraph (a) prohibit representation if the lawyer is

prohibited from acting because of events before the person became a lawyer, for example, work that the person did while a law student. Such persons, however, ordinarily must be screened from any personal participation in the matter to avoid communication to others in the firm of confidential information that both the nonlawyers and the firm have a legal duty to protect. See Rules 1.0(k) and 5.3.

[5]   Rule 1.10(b) operates to permit a law firm, under certain circumstances, to represent a person with interests directly adverse to those of a client represented by a lawyer who formerly was associated with the firm. The Rule applies regardless of when the formerly associated lawyer represented the client. However, the law firm may not represent a person with interests adverse to those of a present client of the firm, which would violate Rule 1.7. Moreover, the firm may not represent the person where the matter is the same or substantially related to that in which the formerly associated lawyer represented the client and any other lawyer currently in the firm has material information protected by Rules 1.6 and 1.9(c).

[6]   Rule 1.10(c) removes imputation with the informed consent of the affected client or former client under the conditions stated in Rule 1.7. The conditions stated in Rule 1.7 require the lawyer to determine that the representation is not prohibited by Rule 1.7(b) and that each affected client or former client has given informed consent to the representation, confirmed in writing. In some cases, the risk may be so severe that the conflict may not be cured by client consent. For a discussion of the effectiveness of client waivers of conflicts that might arise in the future, see Rule 1.7, Comment [22]. For a definition of informed consent, see Rule 1.0(e).

[7]   Where a lawyer has joined a private firm after having represented the government, imputation is governed by Rule 1.11(b) and (c), not this Rule. Under Rule 1.11(d), where a lawyer represents the government after having served clients in private practice, nongovernmental employment or in another government agency, former-client conflicts are not imputed to government lawyers associated with the individually disqualified lawyer.

[8]   Where a lawyer is prohibited from engaging in certain transactions under Rule 1.8, paragraph (k) of that Rule, and not this Rule, determines whether that prohibition also applies to other lawyers associated in a firm with the personally prohibited lawyer.

RULE 1.11: SPECIAL CONFLICTS OF INTEREST FOR FORMER AND CURRENT GOVERNMENT OFFICERS AND EMPLOYEES

(a) Except as law may otherwise expressly permit, a lawyer who has formerly served as a public officer or employee of the government:

(1) is subject to Rule 1.9(c); and

(2) shall not otherwise represent a client in connection with a matter in which the lawyer participated personally and substantially as a public officer or employee, unless the appropriate government agency gives its informed consent, confirmed in writing, to the representation.

(b) When a lawyer is disqualified from representation under paragraph (a), no lawyer in a firm with which that lawyer is associated may knowingly undertake or continue representation in such a matter unless:

(1) the disqualified lawyer is timely screened from any participation in the matter and is apportioned no part of the fee therefrom; and

(2) written notice is promptly given to the appropriate government agency to enable it to ascertain compliance with the provisions of this rule.

(c) Except as law may otherwise expressly permit, a lawyer having information that the lawyer knows is confidential government information about a person acquired when the lawyer was a public officer or employee, may not represent a private client whose interests are adverse to that person in a matter in which the information could be used to the material disadvantage of that person. As used in this Rule, the term "confidential government information" means information that has been obtained under governmental authority and which, at the time this Rule is applied, the government is prohibited by law from disclosing to the public or has a legal privilege not to disclose and which is not otherwise available to the public. A firm with which that lawyer is associated may undertake or continue representation in the matter only if the disqualified lawyer is timely screened from any participation in the matter and is apportioned no part of the fee therefrom.

(d) Except as law may otherwise expressly permit, a lawyer currently serving as a public officer or employee:

(1) is subject to Rules 1.7 and 1.9; and

(2) shall not:

(i) participate in a matter in which the lawyer participated personally and substantially while in private practice or nongovernmental employment, unless the appropriate government agency gives its informed consent, confirmed in writing; or

(ii) negotiate for private employment with any person who is involved as a party or as lawyer for a party in a matter in which the lawyer is participating personally and substantially, except that a lawyer serving as a law clerk to a judge, other adjudicative officer or arbitrator may negotiate for private employment as permitted by Rule 1.12(b) and subject to the conditions stated in Rule 1.12(b).

(e) As used in this Rule, the term "matter" includes:

(1) any judicial or other proceeding, application, request for a ruling or other determination, contract, claim, controversy, investigation, charge, accusation, arrest or other particular matter involving a specific party or parties, and

(2) any other matter covered by the conflict of interest rules of the appropriate government agency.

Comment

[1]   A lawyer who has served or is currently serving as a public officer or employee is personally subject to the Rules of Professional Conduct, including the prohibition against concurrent conflicts of interest stated in Rule 1.7. In addition, such a lawyer may be subject to statutes and government regulations regarding conflict of interest. Such statutes and regulations may circumscribe the extent to which the government agency may give consent under this Rule. See Rule 1.0(e) for the definition of informed consent.

[2]   Paragraphs (a)(1), (a)(2) and (d)(1) restate the obligations of an individual lawyer who has served or is currently serving as an officer or employee of the government toward a former government or private client. Rule 1.10 is not applicable to the conflicts of interest addressed by this Rule. Rather, paragraph (b) sets forth a special imputation rule for former government

lawyers that provides for screening and notice. Because of the special problems raised by imputation within a government agency, paragraph (d) does not impute the conflicts of a lawyer currently serving as an officer or employee of the government to other associated government officers or employees, although ordinarily it will be prudent to screen such lawyers.

[3]   Paragraphs (a)(2) and (d)(2) apply regardless of whether a lawyer is adverse to a former client and are thus designed not only to protect the former client, but also to prevent a lawyer from exploiting public office for the advantage of another client. For example, a lawyer who has pursued a claim on behalf of the government may not pursue the same claim on behalf of a later private client after the lawyer has left government service, except when authorized to do so by the government agency under paragraph (a). Similarly, a lawyer who has pursued a claim on behalf of a private client may not pursue the claim on behalf of the government, except when authorized to do so by paragraph (d). As with paragraphs (a)(1) and (d)(1), Rule 1.10 is not applicable to the conflicts of interest addressed by these paragraphs.

[4]   This Rule represents a balancing of interests. On the one hand, where the successive clients are a government agency and another client, public or private, the risk exists that power or discretion vested in that agency might be used for the special benefit of the other client. A lawyer should not be in a position where benefit to the other client might affect performance of the lawyer's professional functions on behalf of the government. Also, unfair advantage could accrue to the other client by reason of access to confidential government information about the client's adversary obtainable only through the lawyer's government service. On the other hand, the rules governing lawyers presently or formerly employed by a government agency should not be so restrictive as to inhibit transfer of employment to and from the government. The government has a legitimate need to attract qualified lawyers as well as to maintain high ethical standards. Thus a former government lawyer is disqualified only from particular matters in which the lawyer participated personally and substantially. The provisions for screening and waiver in paragraph (b) are necessary to prevent the disqualification rule from imposing too severe a deterrent against entering public service. The limitation of disqualification in paragraphs (a)(2) and (d)(2) to matters involving a specific party or parties, rather than extending disqualification to all substantive issues on which the lawyer worked, serves a similar function.

[5]   When a lawyer has been employed by one government agency and then moves to a second government agency, it may be appropriate to treat that second agency as another client for purposes of this Rule, as when a lawyer is employed by a city and subsequently is employed by a federal agency. However, because the conflict of interest is governed by paragraph (d), the latter agency is not required to screen the lawyer as paragraph (b) requires a law firm to do. The question of whether two government agencies should be regarded as the same or different clients for conflict of interest purposes is beyond the scope of these Rules. See Rule 1.13 Comment [9].

[6]   Paragraphs (b) and (c) contemplate a screening arrangement. See Rule 1.0(k) (requirements for screening procedures). These paragraphs do not prohibit a lawyer from receiving a salary or partnership share established by prior independent agreement, but that lawyer may not receive compensation directly relating the lawyer's compensation to the fee in the matter in which the lawyer is disqualified.

[7]   Notice, including a description of the screened lawyer's prior representation and of the screening procedures employed, generally should be given as soon as practicable after the need for screening becomes apparent.

[8]   Paragraph (c) operates only when the lawyer in question has knowledge of the information, which means actual knowledge; it does not operate with respect to information that merely could be imputed to the lawyer.

[9]   Paragraphs (a) and (d) do not prohibit a lawyer from jointly representing a private party and a government agency when doing so is permitted by Rule 1.7 and is not otherwise prohibited by law.

[10]   For purposes of paragraph (e) of this Rule, a "matter" may continue in another form. In determining whether two particular matters are the same, the lawyer should consider the extent to which the matters involve the same basic facts, the same or related parties, and the time elapsed.

RULE 1.12: FORMER JUDGE, ARBITRATOR, MEDIATOR OR OTHER THIRD–PARTY NEUTRAL

(a) Except as stated in paragraph (d), a lawyer shall not represent anyone in connection with a matter in which the lawyer participated personally and substantially as a judge or other adjudicative officer or law clerk to such a person or as an arbitrator, mediator or other third-party neutral, unless all parties to the proceeding give informed consent, confirmed in writing.

(b) A lawyer shall not negotiate for employment with any person who is involved as a party or as lawyer for a party in a matter in which the lawyer is participating personally and substantially as a judge or other adjudicative officer or as an arbitrator, mediator or other third-party neutral. A lawyer serving as a law clerk to a judge or other adjudicative officer may negotiate for employment with a party or lawyer involved in a matter in which the clerk is participating personally and substantially, but only after the lawyer has notified the judge or other adjudicative officer.

(c) If a lawyer is disqualified by paragraph (a), no lawyer in a firm with which that lawyer is associated may knowingly undertake or continue representation in the matter unless:

(1) the disqualified lawyer is timely screened from any participation in the matter and is apportioned no part of the fee therefrom; and

(2) written notice is promptly given to the parties and any appropriate tribunal to enable them to ascertain compliance with the provisions of this rule.

(d) An arbitrator selected as a partisan of a party in a multimember arbitration panel is not prohibited from subsequently representing that party.

Comment

[1]   This Rule generally parallels Rule 1.11. The term "personally and substantially" signifies that a judge who was a member of a multimember court, and thereafter left judicial office to practice law, is not prohibited from representing a client in a matter pending in the court, but in which the former judge did not participate. So also the fact that a former judge exercised administrative responsibility in a court does not prevent the former judge from acting as a lawyer in a matter where the judge had previously exercised remote or incidental administrative responsibility that did not affect the merits. Compare the Comment to Rule 1.11. The term "adjudicative officer" includes such officials as judges pro tempore, referees, special masters, hearing officers and other parajudicial officers, and also lawyers who serve as part-time judges. Paragraphs C(2), D(2) and E(2) of the Application Section of the Model Code of Judicial Conduct provide that a part-time judge, judge pro tempore or retired judge recalled to active service, shall not "act as a lawyer in a proceeding in which the judge has served as a judge or in any other proceeding related thereto." Although phrased differently from this Rule, those Rules correspond in meaning.

[2]   Like former judges, lawyers who have served as arbitrators, mediators or other third-party neutrals may be asked to represent a client in a matter in which the lawyer participated personally and substantially. This Rule forbids such representation unless all of the parties to the proceedings give their informed consent, confirmed in writing. See Rule 1.0(e) and (b). Other law or codes of ethics governing third-party neutrals may impose more stringent standards of personal or imputed disqualification. See Rule 2.4.

[3]   Although lawyers who serve as third-party neutrals do not have information concerning the parties that is protected under Rule 1.6, they typically owe the parties an obligation of confidentiality under law or codes of ethics governing third-party neutrals. Thus, paragraph (c) provides that conflicts of the personally disqualified lawyer will be imputed to other lawyers in a law firm unless the conditions of this paragraph are met.

[4]   Requirements for screening procedures are stated in Rule 1.0(k). Paragraph (c)(1) does not prohibit the screened lawyer from receiving a salary or partnership share established by prior independent agreement, but that lawyer may not receive compensation directly related to the matter in which the lawyer is disqualified.

[5]   Notice, including a description of the screened lawyer's prior representation and of the screening procedures employed, generally should be given as soon as practicable after the need for screening becomes apparent.

RULE 1.13: ORGANIZATION AS CLIENT

(a) A lawyer employed or retained by an organization represents the organization acting through its duly authorized constituents.

(b) If a lawyer for an organization knows that an officer, employee or other person associated with the organization is engaged in action, intends to act or refuses to act in a matter related to the representation that is a violation of a legal obligation to the organization, or a violation of law that reasonably might be imputed to the organization, and that is likely to result in substantial injury to the organization, then the lawyer shall proceed as is reasonably necessary in the best interest of the organization. Unless the lawyer reasonably believes that it is not necessary in the best interest of the organization to do so, the lawyer shall refer the matter to higher authority in the organization, including, if warranted by the circumstances, to the highest authority that can act on behalf of the organization as determined by applicable law.

(c) Except as provided in paragraph (d), if

(1) despite the lawyer's efforts in accordance with paragraph (b) the highest authority that can act on behalf of the organization insists upon or fails to address in a timely and appropriate manner an action or a refusal to act, that is clearly a violation of law, and

(2) the lawyer reasonably believes that the violation is reasonably certain to result in substantial injury to the organization,

then the lawyer may reveal information relating to the representation whether or not Rule 1.6 permits such disclosure, but only if and to the extent the lawyer reasonably believes necessary to prevent substantial injury to the organization.

(d) Paragraph (c) shall not apply with respect to information relating to a lawyer's representation of an organization to investigate an alleged violation of law,

or to defend the organization or an officer, employee or other constituent associated with the organization against a claim arising out of an alleged violation of law.

(e) A lawyer who reasonably believes that he or she has been discharged because of the lawyer's actions taken pursuant to paragraphs (b) or (c), or who withdraws under circumstances that require or permit the lawyer to take action under either of those paragraphs, shall proceed as the lawyer reasonably believes necessary to assure that the organization's highest authority is informed of the lawyer's discharge or withdrawal.

(f) In dealing with an organization's directors, officers, employees, members, shareholders or other constituents, a lawyer shall explain the identity of the client when the lawyer knows or reasonably should know that the organization's interests are adverse to those of the constituents with whom the lawyer is dealing.

(g) A lawyer representing an organization may also represent any of its directors, officers, employees, members, shareholders or other constituents, subject to the provisions of Rule 1.7. If the organization's consent to the dual representation is required by Rule 1.7, the consent shall be given by an appropriate official of the organization other than the individual who is to be represented, or by the shareholders.

Comment

The Entity as the Client

[1]   An organizational client is a legal entity, but it cannot act except through its officers, directors, employees, shareholders and other constituents. Officers, directors, employees and shareholders are the constituents of the corporate organizational client. The duties defined in this Comment apply equally to unincorporated associations. "Other constituents" as used in this Comment means the positions equivalent to officers, directors, employees and shareholders held by persons acting for organizational clients that are not corporations.

[2]   When one of the constituents of an organizational client communicates with the organization's lawyer in that person's organizational capacity, the communication is protected by Rule 1.6. Thus, by way of example, if an organizational client requests its lawyer to investigate allegations of wrongdoing, interviews made in the course of that investigation between the lawyer and the client's employees or other constituents are covered by Rule 1.6. This does not mean, however, that constituents of an organizational client are the clients of the lawyer. The lawyer may not disclose to such constituents information relating to the representation except for disclosures explicitly or impliedly authorized by the organizational client in order to carry out the representation or as otherwise permitted by Rule 1.6.

[3]   When constituents of the organization make decisions for it, the decisions ordinarily must be accepted by the lawyer even if their utility or prudence is doubtful. Decisions concerning policy and operations, including ones entailing serious risk, are not as such in the lawyer's province. Paragraph (b) makes clear, however, that when the lawyer knows that the organization is likely to be substantially injured by action of an officer or other constituent that violates a legal obligation to the organization or is in violation of law that might be imputed to the organization, the lawyer must proceed as is reasonably necessary in the best interest of the organization. As defined in Rule 1.0(f), knowledge can be inferred from circumstances, and a lawyer cannot ignore the obvious.

[4]   In determining how to proceed under paragraph (b), the lawyer should give due consideration to the seriousness of the violation and its consequences, the responsibility in the

organization and the apparent motivation of the person involved, the policies of the organization concerning such matters, and any other relevant considerations. Ordinarily, referral to a higher authority would be necessary. In some circumstances, however, it may be appropriate for the lawyer to ask the constituent to reconsider the matter; for example, if the circumstances involve a constituent's innocent misunderstanding of law and subsequent acceptance of the lawyer's advice, the lawyer may reasonably conclude that the best interest of the organization does not require that the matter be referred to higher authority. If a constituent persists in conduct contrary to the lawyer's advice, it will be necessary for the lawyer to take steps to have the matter reviewed by a higher authority in the organization. If the matter is of sufficient seriousness and importance or urgency to the organization, referral to higher authority in the organization may be necessary even if the lawyer has not communicated with the constituent. Any measures taken should, to the extent practicable, minimize the risk of revealing information relating to the representation to persons outside the organization. Even in circumstances where a lawyer is not obligated by Rule 1.13 to proceed, a lawyer may bring to the attention of an organizational client, including its highest authority, matters that the lawyer reasonably believes to be of sufficient importance to warrant doing so in the best interest of the organization.

[5]   Paragraph (b) also makes clear that when it is reasonably necessary to enable the organization to address the matter in a timely and appropriate manner, the lawyer must refer the matter to higher authority, including, if warranted by the circumstances, the highest authority that can act on behalf of the organization under applicable law. The organization's highest authority to whom a matter may be referred ordinarily will be the board of directors or similar governing body. However, applicable law may prescribe that under certain conditions the highest authority reposes elsewhere, for example, in the independent directors of a corporation.

Relation to Other Rules

[6]   The authority and responsibility provided in this Rule are concurrent with the authority and responsibility provided in other Rules. In particular, this Rule does not limit or expand the lawyer's responsibility under Rules 1.8, 1.16, 3.3 or 4.1. Paragraph (c) of this Rule supplements Rule 1.6(b) by providing an additional basis upon which the lawyer may reveal information relating to the representation, but does not modify, restrict, or limit the provisions of Rule 1.6(b)(1)–(6). Under paragraph (c) the lawyer may reveal such information only when the organization's highest authority insists upon or fails to address threatened or ongoing action that is clearly a violation of law, and then only to the extent the lawyer reasonably believes necessary to prevent reasonably certain substantial injury to the organization. It is not necessary that the lawyer's services be used in furtherance of the violation, but it is required that the matter be related to the lawyer's representation of the organization. If the lawyer's services are being used by an organization to further a crime or fraud by the organization, Rules 1.6(b)(2) and 1.6(b)(3) may permit the lawyer to disclose confidential information. In such circumstances Rule 1.2(d) may also be applicable, in which event, withdrawal from the representation under Rule 1.16(a)(1) may be required.

[7]   Paragraph (d) makes clear that the authority of a lawyer to disclose information relating to a representation in circumstances described in paragraph (c) does not apply with respect to information relating to a lawyer's engagement by an organization to investigate an alleged violation of law or to defend the organization or an officer, employee or other person associated with the organization against a claim arising out of an alleged violation of law. This is necessary in order to enable organizational clients to enjoy the full benefits of legal counsel in conducting an investigation or defending against a claim.

[8]   A lawyer who reasonably believes that he or she has been discharged because of the lawyer's actions taken pursuant to paragraph (b) or (c), or who withdraws in circumstances that require or permit the lawyer to take action under either of these paragraphs, must proceed as

the lawyer reasonably believes necessary to assure that the organization's highest authority is informed of the lawyer's discharge or withdrawal.

Government Agency

[9] The duty defined in this Rule applies to governmental organizations. Defining precisely the identity of the client and prescribing the resulting obligations of such lawyers may be more difficult in the government context and is a matter beyond the scope of these Rules. See Scope [18]. Although in some circumstances the client may be a specific agency, it may also be a branch of government, such as the executive branch, or the government as a whole. For example, if the action or failure to act involves the head of a bureau, either the department of which the bureau is a part or the relevant branch of government may be the client for purposes of this Rule. Moreover, in a matter involving the conduct of government officials, a government lawyer may have authority under applicable law to question such conduct more extensively than that of a lawyer for a private organization in similar circumstances. Thus, when the client is a governmental organization, a different balance may be appropriate between maintaining confidentiality and assuring that the wrongful act is prevented or rectified, for public business is involved. In addition, duties of lawyers employed by the government or lawyers in military service may be defined by statutes and regulation. This Rule does not limit that authority. See Scope.

Clarifying the Lawyer's Role

[10] There are times when the organization's interest may be or become adverse to those of one or more of its constituents. In such circumstances the lawyer should advise any constituent, whose interest the lawyer finds adverse to that of the organization of the conflict or potential conflict of interest, that the lawyer cannot represent such constituent, and that such person may wish to obtain independent representation. Care must be taken to assure that the individual understands that, when there is such adversity of interest, the lawyer for the organization cannot provide legal representation for that constituent individual, and that discussions between the lawyer for the organization and the individual may not be privileged.

[11] Whether such a warning should be given by the lawyer for the organization to any constituent individual may turn on the facts of each case.

Dual Representation

[12] Paragraph (g) recognizes that a lawyer for an organization may also represent a principal officer or major shareholder.

Derivative Actions

[13] Under generally prevailing law, the shareholders or members of a corporation may bring suit to compel the directors to perform their legal obligations in the supervision of the organization. Members of unincorporated associations have essentially the same right. Such an action may be brought nominally by the organization, but usually is, in fact, a legal controversy over management of the organization.

[14] The question can arise whether counsel for the organization may defend such an action. The proposition that the organization is the lawyer's client does not alone resolve the issue. Most derivative actions are a normal incident of an organization's affairs, to be defended by the organization's lawyer like any other suit. However, if the claim involves serious charges of wrongdoing by those in control of the organization, a conflict may arise between the lawyer's duty to the organization and the lawyer's relationship with the board. In those circumstances, Rule 1.7 governs who should represent the directors and the organization.

RULE 1.14: CLIENT WITH DIMINISHED CAPACITY

(a) When a client's capacity to make adequately considered decisions in connection with a representation is diminished, whether because of minority, mental impairment or for some other reason, the lawyer shall, as far as reasonably possible, maintain a normal client-lawyer relationship with the client.

(b) When the lawyer reasonably believes that the client has diminished capacity, is at risk of substantial physical, financial or other harm unless action is taken and cannot adequately act in the client's own interest, the lawyer may take reasonably necessary protective action, including consulting with individuals or entities that have the ability to take action to protect the client and, in appropriate cases, seeking the appointment of a guardian ad litem, conservator or guardian.

(c) Information relating to the representation of a client with diminished capacity is protected by Rule 1.6. When taking protective action pursuant to paragraph (b), the lawyer is impliedly authorized under Rule 1.6(a) to reveal information about the client, but only to the extent reasonably necessary to protect the client's interests.

Comment

[1]   The normal client-lawyer relationship is based on the assumption that the client, when properly advised and assisted, is capable of making decisions about important matters. When the client is a minor or suffers from a diminished mental capacity, however, maintaining the ordinary client-lawyer relationship may not be possible in all respects. In particular, a severely incapacitated person may have no power to make legally binding decisions. Nevertheless, a client with diminished capacity often has the ability to understand, deliberate upon, and reach conclusions about matters affecting the client's own well-being. For example, children as young as five or six years of age, and certainly those of ten or twelve, are regarded as having opinions that are entitled to weight in legal proceedings concerning their custody. So also, it is recognized that some persons of advanced age can be quite capable of handling routine financial matters while needing special legal protection concerning major transactions.

[2]   The fact that a client suffers a disability does not diminish the lawyer's obligation to treat the client with attention and respect. Even if the person has a legal representative, the lawyer should as far as possible accord the represented person the status of client, particularly in maintaining communication.

[3]   The client may wish to have family members or other persons participate in discussions with the lawyer. When necessary to assist in the representation, the presence of such persons generally does not affect the applicability of the attorney-client evidentiary privilege. Nevertheless, the lawyer must keep the client's interests foremost and, except for protective action authorized under paragraph (b), must to look to the client, and not family members, to make decisions on the client's behalf.

[4]   If a legal representative has already been appointed for the client, the lawyer should ordinarily look to the representative for decisions on behalf of the client. In matters involving a minor, whether the lawyer should look to the parents as natural guardians may depend on the type of proceeding or matter in which the lawyer is representing the minor. If the lawyer represents the guardian as distinct from the ward, and is aware that the guardian is acting adversely to the ward's interest, the lawyer may have an obligation to prevent or rectify the guardian's misconduct. See Rule 1.2(d).

Taking Protective Action

[5]   If a lawyer reasonably believes that a client is at risk of substantial physical, financial or other harm unless action is taken, and that a normal client-lawyer relationship cannot be

maintained as provided in paragraph (a) because the client lacks sufficient capacity to communicate or to make adequately considered decisions in connection with the representation, then paragraph (b) permits the lawyer to take protective measures deemed necessary. Such measures could include: consulting with family members, using a reconsideration period to permit clarification or improvement of circumstances, using voluntary surrogate decisionmaking tools such as durable powers of attorney or consulting with support groups, professional services, adult-protective agencies or other individuals or entities that have the ability to protect the client. In taking any protective action, the lawyer should be guided by such factors as the wishes and values of the client to the extent known, the client's best interests and the goals of intruding into the client's decisionmaking autonomy to the least extent feasible, maximizing client capacities and respecting the client's family and social connections.

[6]   In determining the extent of the client's diminished capacity, the lawyer should consider and balance such factors as: the client's ability to articulate reasoning leading to a decision, variability of state of mind and ability to appreciate consequences of a decision; the substantive fairness of a decision; and the consistency of a decision with the known long-term commitments and values of the client. In appropriate circumstances, the lawyer may seek guidance from an appropriate diagnostician.

[7]   If a legal representative has not been appointed, the lawyer should consider whether appointment of a guardian ad litem, conservator or guardian is necessary to protect the client's interests. Thus, if a client with diminished capacity has substantial property that should be sold for the client's benefit, effective completion of the transaction may require appointment of a legal representative. In addition, rules of procedure in litigation sometimes provide that minors or persons with diminished capacity must be represented by a guardian or next friend if they do not have a general guardian. In many circumstances, however, appointment of a legal representative may be more expensive or traumatic for the client than circumstances in fact require. Evaluation of such circumstances is a matter entrusted to the professional judgment of the lawyer. In considering alternatives, however, the lawyer should be aware of any law that requires the lawyer to advocate the least restrictive action on behalf of the client.

Disclosure of the Client's Condition

[8]   Disclosure of the client's diminished capacity could adversely affect the client's interests. For example, raising the question of diminished capacity could, in some circumstances, lead to proceedings for involuntary commitment. Information relating to the representation is protected by Rule 1.6. Therefore, unless authorized to do so, the lawyer may not disclose such information. When taking protective action pursuant to paragraph (b), the lawyer is impliedly authorized to make the necessary disclosures, even when the client directs the lawyer to the contrary. Nevertheless, given the risks of disclosure, paragraph (c) limits what the lawyer may disclose in consulting with other individuals or entities or seeking the appointment of a legal representative. At the very least, the lawyer should determine whether it is likely that the person or entity consulted with will act adversely to the client's interests before discussing matters related to the client. The lawyer's position in such cases is an unavoidably difficult one.

Emergency Legal Assistance

[9]   In an emergency where the health, safety or a financial interest of a person with seriously diminished capacity is threatened with imminent and irreparable harm, a lawyer may take legal action on behalf of such a person even though the person is unable to establish a client-lawyer relationship or to make or express considered judgments about the matter, when the person or another acting in good faith on that person's behalf has consulted with the lawyer. Even in such an emergency, however, the lawyer should not act unless the lawyer reasonably believes that the person has no other lawyer, agent or other representative available. The lawyer

should take legal action on behalf of the person only to the extent reasonably necessary to maintain the status quo or otherwise avoid imminent and irreparable harm. A lawyer who undertakes to represent a person in such an exigent situation has the same duties under these Rules as the lawyer would with respect to a client.

[10] A lawyer who acts on behalf of a person with seriously diminished capacity in an emergency should keep the confidences of the person as if dealing with a client, disclosing them only to the extent necessary to accomplish the intended protective action. The lawyer should disclose to any tribunal involved and to any other counsel involved the nature of his or her relationship with the person. The lawyer should take steps to regularize the relationship or implement other protective solutions as soon as possible. Normally, a lawyer would not seek compensation for such emergency actions taken.

RULE 1.15: SAFEKEEPING PROPERTY

(a) **A lawyer shall hold property of clients or third persons that is in a lawyer's possession in connection with a representation separate from the lawyer's own property. Funds shall be kept in a separate account maintained in the state where the lawyer's office is situated, or elsewhere with the consent of the client or third person. Other property shall be identified as such and appropriately safeguarded. Complete records of such account funds and other property shall be kept by the lawyer and shall be preserved for a period of [five years] after termination of the representation.**

(b) **A lawyer may deposit the lawyer's own funds in a client trust account for the sole purpose of paying bank service charges on that account, but only in an amount necessary for that purpose.**

(c) **A lawyer shall deposit into a client trust account legal fees and expenses that have been paid in advance, to be withdrawn by the lawyer only as fees are earned or expenses incurred.**

(d) **Upon receiving funds or other property in which a client or third person has an interest, a lawyer shall promptly notify the client or third person. Except as stated in this rule or otherwise permitted by law or by agreement with the client, a lawyer shall promptly deliver to the client or third person any funds or other property that the client or third person is entitled to receive and, upon request by the client or third person, shall promptly render a full accounting regarding such property.**

(e) **When in the course of representation a lawyer is in possession of property in which two or more persons (one of whom may be the lawyer) claim interests, the property shall be kept separate by the lawyer the dispute is resolved. The lawyer shall promptly distribute all portions of the property as to which the interests are not in dispute.**

Comment

[1] A lawyer should hold property of others with the care required of a professional fiduciary. Securities should be kept in a safe deposit box, except when some other form of safekeeping is warranted by special circumstances. All property that is the property of clients or third persons, including prospective clients, must be kept separate from the lawyer's business and personal property and, if monies, in one or more trust accounts. Separate trust accounts may be warranted when administering estate monies or acting in similar fiduciary capacities. A lawyer should maintain on a current basis books and records in accordance with generally accepted accounting practice and comply with any recordkeeping rules established by law or court order. See, e.g., ABA Model Financial Recordkeeping Rule.

[2]   While normally it is impermissible to commingle the lawyer's own funds with client funds, paragraph (b) provides that it is permissible when necessary to pay bank service charges on that account. Accurate records must be kept regarding which part of the funds are the lawyer's.

[3]   Lawyers often receive funds from which the lawyer's fee will be paid. The lawyer is not required to remit to the client funds that the lawyer reasonably believes represent fees owed. However, a lawyer may not hold funds to coerce a client into accepting the lawyer's contention. The disputed portion of the funds must be kept in a trust account and the lawyer should suggest means for prompt resolution of the dispute, such as arbitration. The undisputed portion of the funds shall be promptly distributed.

[4]   Paragraph (e) also recognizes that third parties may have lawful claims against specific funds or other property in a lawyer's custody, such as a client's creditor who has a lien on funds recovered in a personal injury action. A lawyer may have a duty under applicable law to protect such third-party claims against wrongful interference by the client. In such cases, when the third-party claim is not frivolous under applicable law, the lawyer must refuse to surrender the property to the client until the claims are resolved. A lawyer should not unilaterally assume to arbitrate a dispute between the client and the third party, but, when there are substantial grounds for dispute as to the person entitled to the funds, the lawyer may file an action to have a court resolve the dispute.

[5]   The obligations of a lawyer under this Rule are independent of those arising from activity other than rendering legal services. For example, a lawyer who serves only as an escrow agent is governed by the applicable law relating to fiduciaries even though the lawyer does not render legal services in the transaction and is not governed by this Rule.

[6]   A lawyers' fund for client protection provides a means through the collective efforts of the bar to reimburse persons who have lost money or property as a result of dishonest conduct of a lawyer. Where such a fund has been established, a lawyer must participate where it is mandatory, and, even when it is voluntary, the lawyer should participate.

RULE 1.16: DECLINING OR TERMINATING REPRESENTATION

(a) Except as stated in paragraph (c), a lawyer shall not represent a client or, where representation has commenced, shall withdraw from the representation of a client if:

(1) the representation will result in violation of the rules of professional conduct or other law;

(2) the lawyer's physical or mental condition materially impairs the lawyer's ability to represent the client; or

(3) the lawyer is discharged.

(b) Except as stated in paragraph (c), a lawyer may withdraw from representing a client if:

(1) withdrawal can be accomplished without material adverse effect on the interests of the client;

(2) the client persists in a course of action involving the lawyer's services that the lawyer reasonably believes is criminal or fraudulent;

(3) the client has used the lawyer's services to perpetrate a crime or fraud;

(4) the client insists upon taking action that the lawyer considers repugnant or with which the lawyer has a fundamental disagreement;

(5) the client fails substantially to fulfill an obligation to the lawyer regarding the lawyer's services and has been given reasonable warning that the lawyer will withdraw unless the obligation is fulfilled;

(6) the representation will result in an unreasonable financial burden on the lawyer or has been rendered unreasonably difficult by the client; or

(7) other good cause for withdrawal exists.

(c) A lawyer must comply with applicable law requiring notice to or permission of a tribunal when terminating a representation. When ordered to do so by a tribunal, a lawyer shall continue representation notwithstanding good cause for terminating the representation.

(d) Upon termination of representation, a lawyer shall take steps to the extent reasonably practicable to protect a client's interests, such as giving reasonable notice to the client, allowing time for employment of other counsel, surrendering papers and property to which the client is entitled and refunding any advance payment of fee or expense that has not been earned or incurred. The lawyer may retain papers relating to the client to the extent permitted by other law.

Comment

[1] A lawyer should not accept representation in a matter unless it can be performed competently, promptly, without improper conflict of interest and to completion. Ordinarily, a representation in a matter is completed when the agreed-upon assistance has been concluded. See Rules 1.2(c) and 6.5. See also Rule 1.3, Comment [4].

Mandatory Withdrawal

[2] A lawyer ordinarily must decline or withdraw from representation if the client demands that the lawyer engage in conduct that is illegal or violates the Rules of Professional Conduct or other law. The lawyer is not obliged to decline or withdraw simply because the client suggests such a course of conduct; a client may make such a suggestion in the hope that a lawyer will not be constrained by a professional obligation.

[3] When a lawyer has been appointed to represent a client, withdrawal ordinarily requires approval of the appointing authority. See also Rule 6.2. Similarly, court approval or notice to the court is often required by applicable law before a lawyer withdraws from pending litigation. Difficulty may be encountered if withdrawal is based on the client's demand that the lawyer engage in unprofessional conduct. The court may request an explanation for the withdrawal, while the lawyer may be bound to keep confidential the facts that would constitute such an explanation. The lawyer's statement that professional considerations require termination of the representation ordinarily should be accepted as sufficient. Lawyers should be mindful of their obligations to both clients and the court under Rules 1.6 and 3.3.

Discharge

[4] A client has a right to discharge a lawyer at any time, with or without cause, subject to liability for payment for the lawyer's services. Where future dispute about the withdrawal may be anticipated, it may be advisable to prepare a written statement reciting the circumstances.

[5]   Whether a client can discharge appointed counsel may depend on applicable law. A client seeking to do so should be given a full explanation of the consequences. These consequences may include a decision by the appointing authority that appointment of successor counsel is unjustified, thus requiring self-representation by the client.

[6]   If the client has severely diminished capacity, the client may lack the legal capacity to discharge the lawyer, and in any event the discharge may be seriously adverse to the client's interests. The lawyer should make special effort to help the client consider the consequences and may take reasonably necessary protective action as provided in Rule 1.14.

Optional Withdrawal

[7]   A lawyer may withdraw from representation in some circumstances. The lawyer has the option to withdraw if it can be accomplished without material adverse effect on the client's interests. Withdrawal is also justified if the client persists in a course of action that the lawyer reasonably believes is criminal or fraudulent, for a lawyer is not required to be associated with such conduct even if the lawyer does not further it. Withdrawal is also permitted if the lawyer's services were misused in the past even if that would materially prejudice the client. The lawyer may also withdraw where the client insists on taking action that the lawyer considers repugnant or with which the lawyer has a fundamental disagreement.

[8]   A lawyer may withdraw if the client refuses to abide by the terms of an agreement relating to the representation, such as an agreement concerning fees or court costs or an agreement limiting the objectives of the representation.

Assisting the Client upon Withdrawal

[9]   Even if the lawyer has been unfairly discharged by the client, a lawyer must take all reasonable steps to mitigate the consequences to the client. The lawyer may retain papers as security for a fee only to the extent permitted by law. See Rule 1.15.

RULE 1.17: SALE OF LAW PRACTICE

A lawyer or a law firm may sell or purchase a law practice, or an area of law practice, including good will, if the following conditions are satisfied:

(a) The seller ceases to engage in the private practice of law, or in the area of practice that has been sold, [in the geographic area] [in the jurisdiction] (a jurisdiction nay elect either version) in which the practice has been conducted;

(b) The entire practice, or the entire area of practice, is sold to one or more lawyers or law firms;

(c) The seller gives written notice to each of the seller's clients regarding:

(1) the proposed sale;

(2) the client's right to retain other counsel or to take possession of the file; and

(3) the fact that the client's consent to the transfer of the client's files will be presumed if the client does not take any action or does not otherwise object within ninety (90) days of receipt of the notice.

If a client cannot be given notice, the representation of that client may be transferred to the purchaser only upon entry of an order so authorizing by a court having jurisdiction. The seller may disclose to the court in camera information relating to the representation only to the extent necessary to obtain an order authorizing the transfer of a file.

(d) The fees charged clients shall not be increased by reason of the sale.

Comment

[1]   The practice of law is a profession, not merely a business. Clients are not commodities that can be purchased and sold at will. Pursuant to this Rule, when a lawyer or an entire firm ceases to practice, or ceases to practice in an area of law, and other lawyers or firms take over the representation, the selling lawyer or firm may obtain compensation for the reasonable value of the practice as may withdrawing partners of law firms. See Rules 5.4 and 5.6.

Termination of Practice by the Seller

[2]   The requirement that all of the private practice, or all of an area of practice, be sold is satisfied if the seller in good faith makes the entire practice, or the area of practice, available for sale to the purchasers. The fact that a number of the seller's clients decide not to be represented by the purchasers but take their matters elsewhere, therefore, does not result in a violation. Return to private practice as a result of an unanticipated change in circumstances does not necessarily result in a violation. For example, a lawyer who has sold the practice to accept an appointment to judicial office does not violate the requirement that the sale be attendant to cessation of practice if the lawyer later resumes private practice upon being defeated in a contested or a retention election for the office or resigns from a judiciary position.

[3]   The requirement that the seller cease to engage in the private practice of law does not prohibit employment as a lawyer on the staff of a public agency or a legal services entity that provides legal services to the poor, or as in-house counsel to a business.

[4]   The Rule permits a sale of an entire practice attendant upon retirement from the private practice of law within the jurisdiction. Its provisions, therefore, accommodate the lawyer who sells the practice on the occasion of moving to another state. Some states are so large that a move from one locale therein to another is tantamount to leaving the jurisdiction in which the lawyer has engaged in the practice of law. To also accommodate lawyers so situated, states may permit the sale of the practice when the lawyer leaves the geographical area rather than the jurisdiction. The alternative desired should be indicated by selecting one of the two provided for in Rule 1.17(a).

[5]   This Rule also permits a lawyer or law firm to sell an area of practice. If an area of practice is sold and the lawyer remains in the active practice of law, the lawyer must cease accepting any matters in the area of practice that has been sold, either as counsel or co-counsel or by assuming joint responsibility for a matter in connection with the division of a fee with another lawyer as would otherwise be permitted by Rule 1.5(e). For example, a lawyer with a substantial number of estate planning matters and a substantial number of probate administration cases may sell the estate planning portion of the practice but remain in the practice of law by concentrating on probate administration; however, that practitioner may not thereafter accept any estate planning matters. Although a lawyer who leaves a jurisdiction or geographical area typically would sell the entire practice, this Rule permits the lawyer to limit the sale to one or more areas of the practice, thereby preserving the lawyer's right to continue practice in the areas of the practice that were not sold.

Sale of Entire Practice or Entire Area of Practice

[6]   The Rule requires that the seller's entire practice, or an entire area of practice, be sold. The prohibition against sale of less than an entire practice area protects those clients whose

matters are less lucrative and who might find it difficult to secure other counsel if a sale could be limited to substantial fee-generating matters. The purchasers are required to undertake all client matters in the practice or practice area, subject to client consent. This requirement is satisfied, however, even if a purchaser is unable to undertake a particular client matter because of a conflict of interest.

Client Confidences, Consent and Notice

[7]   Negotiations between seller and prospective purchaser prior to disclosure of information relating to a specific representation of an identifiable client no more violate the confidentiality provisions of Model Rule 1.6 than do preliminary discussions concerning the possible association of another lawyer or mergers between firms, with respect to which client consent is not required. Providing the purchaser access to client-specific information relating to the representation and to the file, however, requires client consent. The Rule provides that before such information can be disclosed by the seller to the purchaser the client must be given actual written notice of the contemplated sale, including the identity of the purchaser, and must be told that the decision to consent or make other arrangements must be made within 90 days. If nothing is heard from the client within that time, consent to the sale is presumed.

[8]   A lawyer or law firm ceasing to practice cannot be required to remain in practice because some clients cannot be given actual notice of the proposed purchase. Since these clients cannot themselves consent to the purchase or direct any other disposition of their files, the Rule requires an order from a court having jurisdiction authorizing their transfer or other disposition. The Court can be expected to determine whether reasonable efforts to locate the client have been exhausted, and whether the absent client's legitimate interests will be served by authorizing the transfer of the file so that the purchaser may continue the representation. Preservation of client confidences requires that the petition for a court order be considered in camera. (A procedure by which such an order can be obtained needs to be established in jurisdictions in which it presently does not exist).

[9]   All elements of client autonomy, including the client's absolute right to discharge a lawyer and transfer the representation to another, survive the sale of the practice or area of practice.

Fee Arrangements Between Client and Purchaser

[10]   The sale may not be financed by increases in fees charged the clients of the practice. Existing arrangements between the seller and the client as to fees and the scope of the work must be honored by the purchaser.

Other Applicable Ethical Standards

[11]   Lawyers participating in the sale of a law practice or a practice area are subject to the ethical standards applicable to involving another lawyer in the representation of a client. These include, for example, the seller's obligation to exercise competence in identifying a purchaser qualified to assume the practice and the purchaser's obligation to undertake the representation competently (see Rule 1.1); the obligation to avoid disqualifying conflicts, and to secure the client's informed consent for those conflicts that can be agreed to (see Rule 1.7 regarding conflicts and Rule 1.0(e) for the definition of informed consent); and the obligation to protect information relating to the representation (see Rules 1.6 and 1.9).

[12]   If approval of the substitution of the purchasing lawyer for the selling lawyer is required by the rules of any tribunal in which a matter is pending, such approval must be obtained before the matter can be included in the sale (see Rule 1.16).

Applicability of the Rule

[13]   This Rule applies to the sale of a law practice of a deceased, disabled or disappeared lawyer. Thus, the seller may be represented by a non-lawyer representative not subject to these

Rules. Since, however, no lawyer may participate in a sale of a law practice which does not conform to the requirements of this Rule, the representatives of the seller as well as the purchasing lawyer can be expected to see to it that they are met.

[14] Admission to or retirement from a law partnership or professional association, retirement plans and similar arrangements, and a sale of tangible assets of a law practice, do not constitute a sale or purchase governed by this Rule.

[15] This Rule does not apply to the transfers of legal representation between lawyers when such transfers are unrelated to the sale of a practice or an area of practice.

RULE 1.18: DUTIES TO PROSPECTIVE CLIENT

(a) A person who discusses with a lawyer the possibility of forming a client-lawyer relationship with respect to a matter is a prospective client.

(b) Even when no client-lawyer relationship ensues, a lawyer who has had discussions with a prospective client shall not use or reveal information learned in the consultation, except as Rule 1.9 would permit with respect to information of a former client.

(c) A lawyer subject to paragraph (b) shall not represent a client with interests materially adverse to those of a prospective client in the same or a substantially related matter if the lawyer received information from the prospective client that could be significantly harmful to that person in the matter, except as provided in paragraph (d). If a lawyer is disqualified from representation under this paragraph, no lawyer in a firm with which that lawyer is associated may knowingly undertake or continue representation in such a matter, except as provided in paragraph (d).

(d) When the lawyer has received disqualifying information as defined in paragraph (c), representation is permissible if:

(1) both the affected client and the prospective client have given informed consent, confirmed in writing, or:

(2) the lawyer who received the information took reasonable measures to avoid exposure to more disqualifying information than was reasonably necessary to determine whether to represent the prospective client; and

(i) the disqualified lawyer is timely screened from any participation in the matter and is apportioned no part of the fee therefrom; and

(ii) written notice is promptly given to the prospective client.

Comment

[1] Prospective clients, like clients, may disclose information to a lawyer, place documents or other property in the lawyer's custody, or rely on the lawyer's advice. A lawyer's discussions with a prospective client usually are limited in time and depth and leave both the prospective client and the lawyer free (and sometimes required) to proceed no further. Hence, prospective clients should receive some but not all of the protection afforded clients.

[2] Not all persons who communicate information to a lawyer are entitled to protection under this Rule. A person who communicates information unilaterally to a lawyer, without any

reasonable expectation that the lawyer is willing to discuss the possibility of forming a client-lawyer relationship, is not a "prospective client" within the meaning of paragraph (a).

[3]   It is often necessary for a prospective client to reveal information to the lawyer during an initial consultation prior to the decision about formation of a client-lawyer relationship. The lawyer often must learn such information to determine whether there is a conflict of interest with an existing client and whether the matter is one that the lawyer is willing to undertake. Paragraph (b) prohibits the lawyer from using or revealing that information, except as permitted by Rule 1.9, even if the client or lawyer decides not to proceed with the representation. The duty exists regardless of how brief the initial conference may be.

[4]   In order to avoid acquiring disqualifying information from a prospective client, a lawyer considering whether or not to undertake a new matter should limit the initial interview to only such information as reasonably appears necessary for that purpose. Where the information indicates that a conflict of interest or other reason for non-representation exists, the lawyer should so inform the prospective client or decline the representation. If the prospective client wishes to retain the lawyer, and if consent is possible under Rule 1.7, then consent from all affected present or former clients must be obtained before accepting the representation.

[5]   A lawyer may condition conversations with a prospective client on the person's informed consent that no information disclosed during the consultation will prohibit the lawyer from representing a different client in the matter. See Rule 1.0(e) for the definition of informed consent. If the agreement expressly so provides, the prospective client may also consent to the lawyer's subsequent use of information received from the prospective client.

[6]   Even in the absence of an agreement, under paragraph (c), the lawyer is not prohibited from representing a client with interests adverse to those of the prospective client in the same or a substantially related matter unless the lawyer has received from the prospective client information that could be significantly harmful if used in the matter.

[7]   Under paragraph (c), the prohibition in this Rule is imputed to other lawyers as provided in Rule 1.10, but, under paragraph (d)(1), imputation may be avoided if the lawyer obtains the informed consent, confirmed in writing, of both the prospective and affected clients. In the alternative, imputation may be avoided if the conditions of paragraph (d)(2) are met and all disqualified lawyers are timely screened and written notice is promptly given to the prospective client. See Rule 1.0(k) (requirements for screening procedures). Paragraph (d)(2)(i) does not prohibit the screened lawyer from receiving a salary or partnership share established by prior independent agreement, but that lawyer may not receive compensation directly related to the matter in which the lawyer is disqualified.

[8]   Notice, including a general description of the subject matter about which the lawyer was consulted, and of the screening procedures employed, generally should be given as soon as practicable after the need for screening becomes apparent.

[9]   For the duty of competence of a lawyer who gives assistance on the merits of a matter to a prospective client, see Rule 1.1. For a lawyer's duties when a prospective client entrusts valuables or papers to the lawyer's care, see Rule 1.15.

RULE 2.1: ADVISOR

In representing a client, a lawyer shall exercise independent professional judgment and render candid advice. In rendering advice, a lawyer may refer not only to law but to other considerations such as moral, economic, social and political factors, that may be relevant to the client's situation.

Comment

Scope of Advice

[1]   A client is entitled to straightforward advice expressing the lawyer's honest assessment. Legal advice often involves unpleasant facts and alternatives that a client may be

disinclined to confront. In presenting advice, a lawyer endeavors to sustain the client's morale and may put advice in as acceptable a form as honesty permits. However, a lawyer should not be deterred from giving candid advice by the prospect that the advice will be unpalatable to the client.

[2]   Advice couched in narrow legal terms may be of little value to a client, especially where practical considerations, such as cost or effects on other people, are predominant. Purely technical legal advice, therefore, can sometimes be inadequate. It is proper for a lawyer to refer to relevant moral and ethical considerations in giving advice. Although a lawyer is not a moral advisor as such, moral and ethical considerations impinge upon most legal questions and may decisively influence how the law will be applied.

[3]   A client may expressly or impliedly ask the lawyer for purely technical advice. When such a request is made by a client experienced in legal matters, the lawyer may accept it at face value. When such a request is made by a client inexperienced in legal matters, however, the lawyer's responsibility as advisor may include indicating that more may be involved than strictly legal considerations.

[4]   Matters that go beyond strictly legal questions may also be in the domain of another profession. Family matters can involve problems within the professional competence of psychiatry, clinical psychology or social work; business matters can involve problems within the competence of the accounting profession or of financial specialists. Where consultation with a professional in another field is itself something a competent lawyer would recommend, the lawyer should make such a recommendation. At the same time, a lawyer's advice at its best often consists of recommending a course of action in the face of conflicting recommendations of experts.

Offering Advice

[5]   In general, a lawyer is not expected to give advice until asked by the client. However, when a lawyer knows that a client proposes a course of action that is likely to result in substantial adverse legal consequences to the client, the lawyer's duty to the client under Rule 1.4 may require that the lawyer offer advice if the client's course of action is related to the representation. Similarly, when a matter is likely to involve litigation, it may be necessary under Rule 1.4 to inform the client of forms of dispute resolution that might constitute reasonable alternatives to litigation. A lawyer ordinarily has no duty to initiate investigation of a client's affairs or to give advice that the client has indicated is unwanted, but a lawyer may initiate advice to a client when doing so appears to be in the client's interest.

RULE 2.2 (Deleted)

RULE 2.3: EVALUATION FOR USE BY THIRD PERSONS

(a) A lawyer may provide an evaluation of a matter affecting a client for the use of someone other than the client if the lawyer reasonably believes that making the evaluation is compatible with other aspects of the lawyer's relationship with the client.

(b) When the lawyer knows or reasonably should know that the evaluation is likely to affect the client's interests materially and adversely, the lawyer shall not provide the evaluation unless the client gives informed consent.

(c) Except as disclosure is authorized in connection with a report of an evaluation, information relating to the evaluation is otherwise protected by Rule 1.6.

Comment

Definition

[1]   An evaluation may be performed at the client's direction or when impliedly authorized in order to carry out the representation. See Rule 1.2. Such an evaluation may be for the primary

purpose of establishing information for the benefit of third parties; for example, an opinion concerning the title of property rendered at the behest of a vendor for the information of a prospective purchaser, or at the behest of a borrower for the information of a prospective lender. In some situations, the evaluation may be required by a government agency; for example, an opinion concerning the legality of the securities registered for sale under the securities laws. In other instances, the evaluation may be required by a third person, such as a purchaser of a business.

[2] A legal evaluation should be distinguished from an investigation of a person with whom the lawyer does not have a client-lawyer relationship. For example, a lawyer retained by a purchaser to analyze a vendor's title to property does not have a client-lawyer relationship with the vendor. So also, an investigation into a person's affairs by a government lawyer, or by special counsel by a government lawyer, or by special counsel employed by the government, is not an evaluation as that term is used in this Rule. The question is whether the lawyer is retained by the person whose affairs are being examined. When the lawyer is retained by that person, the general rules concerning loyalty to client and preservation of confidences apply, which is not the case if the lawyer is retained by someone else. For this reason, it is essential to identify the person by whom the lawyer is retained. This should be made clear not only to the person under examination, but also to others to whom the results are to be made available.

Duties Owed to Third Person and Client

[3] When the evaluation is intended for the information or use of a third person, a legal duty to that person may or may not arise. That legal question is beyond the scope of this Rule. However, since such an evaluation involves a departure from the normal client-lawyer relationship, careful analysis of the situation is required. The lawyer must be satisfied as a matter of professional judgment that making the evaluation is compatible with other functions undertaken in behalf of the client. For example, if the lawyer is acting as advocate in defending the client against charges of fraud, it would normally be incompatible with that responsibility for the lawyer to perform an evaluation for others concerning the same or a related transaction. Assuming no such impediment is apparent, however, the lawyer should advise the client of the implications of the evaluation, particularly the lawyer's responsibilities to third persons and the duty to disseminate the findings.

Access to and Disclosure of Information

[4] The quality of an evaluation depends on the freedom and extent of the investigation upon which it is based. Ordinarily a lawyer should have whatever latitude of investigation seems necessary as a matter of professional judgment. Under some circumstances, however, the terms of the evaluation may be limited. For example, certain issues or sources may be categorically excluded, or the scope of search may be limited by time constraints or the noncooperation of persons having relevant information. Any such limitations that are material to the evaluation should be described in the report. If after a lawyer has commenced an evaluation, the client refuses to comply with the terms upon which it was understood the evaluation was to have been made, the lawyer's obligations are determined by law, having reference to the terms of the client's agreement and the surrounding circumstances. In no circumstances is the lawyer permitted to knowingly make a false statement of material fact or law in providing an evaluation under this Rule. See Rule 4.1.

Obtaining Client's Informed Consent

[5] Information relating to an evaluation is protected by Rule 1.6. In many situations, providing an evaluation to a third party poses no significant risk to the client; thus, the lawyer may be impliedly authorized to disclose information to carry out the representation. See Rule

1.6(a). Where, however, it is reasonably likely that providing the evaluation will affect the client's interests materially and adversely, the lawyer must first obtain the client's consent after the client has been adequately informed concerning the important possible effects on the client's interests. See Rules 1.6(a) and 1.0(e).

Financial Auditors' Requests for Information

[6] When a question concerning the legal situation of a client arises at the instance of the client's financial auditor and the question is referred to the lawyer, the lawyer's response may be made in accordance with procedures recognized in the legal profession. Such a procedure is set forth in the American Bar Association Statement of Policy Regarding Lawyers' Responses to Auditors' Requests for Information, adopted in 1975.

RULE 2.4: LAWYER SERVING AS THIRD–PARTY NEUTRAL

(a) A lawyer serves as a third-party neutral when the lawyer assists two or more persons who are not clients of the lawyer to reach a resolution of a dispute or other matter that has arisen between them. Service as a third-party neutral may include service as an arbitrator, a mediator or in such other capacity as will enable the lawyer to assist the parties to resolve the matter.

(b) A lawyer serving as a third-party neutral shall inform unrepresented parties that the lawyer is not representing them. When the lawyer knows or reasonably should know that a party does not understand the lawyer's role in the matter, the lawyer shall explain the difference between the lawyer's role as a third-party neutral and a lawyer's role as one who represents a client.

Comment

[1] Alternative dispute resolution has become a substantial part of the civil justice system. Aside from representing clients in dispute-resolution processes, lawyers often serve as third-party neutrals. A third-party neutral is a person, such as a mediator, arbitrator, conciliator or evaluator, who assists the parties, represented or unrepresented, in the resolution of a dispute or in the arrangement of a transaction. Whether a third-party neutral serves primarily as a facilitator, evaluator or decisionmaker depends on the particular process that is either selected by the parties or mandated by a court.

[2] The role of a third-party neutral is not unique to lawyers, although, in some court-connected contexts, only lawyers are allowed to serve in this role or to handle certain types of cases. In performing this role, the lawyer may be subject to court rules or other law that apply either to third-party neutrals generally or to lawyers serving as third-party neutrals. Lawyer-neutrals may also be subject to various codes of ethics, such as the Code of Ethics for Arbitration in Commercial Disputes prepared by a joint committee of the American Bar Association and the American Arbitration Association or the Model Standards of Conduct for Mediators jointly prepared by the American Bar Association, the American Arbitration Association and the Society of Professionals in Dispute Resolution.

[3] Unlike nonlawyers who serve as third-party neutrals, lawyers serving in this role may experience unique problems as a result of differences between the role of a third-party neutral and a lawyer's service as a client representative. The potential for confusion is significant when the parties are unrepresented in the process. Thus, paragraph (b) requires a lawyer-neutral to inform unrepresented parties that the lawyer is not representing them. For some parties, particularly parties who frequently use dispute-resolution processes, this information will be sufficient. For others, particularly those who are using the process for the first time, more

information will be required. Where appropriate, the lawyer should inform unrepresented parties of the important differences between the lawyer's role as third-party neutral and a lawyer's role as a client representative, including the inapplicability of the attorney-client evidentiary privilege. The extent of disclosure required under this paragraph will depend on the particular parties involved and the subject matter of the proceeding, as well as the particular features of the dispute-resolution process selected.

[4]   A lawyer who serves as a third-party neutral subsequently may be asked to serve as a lawyer representing a client in the same matter. The conflicts of interest that arise for both the individual lawyer and the lawyer's law firm are addressed in Rule 1.12.

[5]   Lawyers who represent clients in alternative dispute-resolution processes are governed by the Rules of Professional Conduct. When the dispute-resolution process takes place before a tribunal, as in binding arbitration (see Rule 1.0(m)), the lawyer's duty of candor is governed by Rule 3.3. Otherwise, the lawyer's duty of candor toward both the third-party neutral and other parties is governed by Rule 4.1.

RULE 3.1: MERITORIOUS CLAIMS AND CONTENTIONS

A lawyer shall not bring or defend a proceeding, or assert or controvert an issue therein, unless there is a basis in law and fact for doing so that is not frivolous, which includes a good faith argument for an extension, modification or reversal of existing law. A lawyer for the defendant in a criminal proceeding, or the respondent in a proceeding that could result in incarceration, may nevertheless so defend the proceeding as to require that every element of the case be established.

Comment

[1]   The advocate has a duty to use legal procedure for the fullest benefit of the client's cause, but also a duty not to abuse legal procedure. The law, both procedural and substantive, establishes the limits within which an advocate may proceed. However, the law is not always clear and never is static. Accordingly, in determining the proper scope of advocacy, account must be taken of the law's ambiguities and potential for change.

[2]   The filing of an action or defense or similar action taken for a client is not frivolous merely because the facts have not first been fully substantiated or because the lawyer expects to develop vital evidence only by discovery. What is required of lawyers, however, is that they inform themselves about the facts of their clients' cases and the applicable law and determine that they can make good faith arguments in support of their clients' positions. Such action is not frivolous even though the lawyer believes that the client's position ultimately will not prevail. The action is frivolous, however, if the lawyer is unable either to make a good faith argument on the merits of the action taken or to support the action taken by a good faith argument for an extension, modification or reversal of existing law.

[3]   The lawyer's obligations under this Rule are subordinate to federal or state constitutional law that entitles a defendant in a criminal matter to the assistance of counsel in presenting a claim or contention that otherwise would be prohibited by this Rule.

RULE 3.2: EXPEDITING LITIGATION

A lawyer shall make reasonable efforts to expedite litigation consistent with the interests of the client.

Comment

[1]   Dilatory practices bring the administration of justice into disrepute. Although there will be occasions when a lawyer may properly seek a postponement for personal reasons, it is not

proper for a lawyer to routinely fail to expedite litigation solely for the convenience of the advocates. Nor will a failure to expedite be reasonable if done for the purpose of frustrating an opposing party's attempt to obtain rightful redress or repose. It is not a justification that similar conduct is often tolerated by the bench and bar. The question is whether a competent lawyer acting in good faith would regard the course of action as having some substantial purpose other than delay. Realizing financial or other benefit from otherwise improper delay in litigation is not a legitimate interest of the client.

RULE 3.3: CANDOR TOWARD THE TRIBUNAL

(a) A lawyer shall not knowingly:

(1) make a false statement of fact or law to a tribunal or fail to correct a false statement of material fact or law previously made to the tribunal by the lawyer;

(2) fail to disclose to the tribunal legal authority in the controlling jurisdiction known to the lawyer to be directly adverse to the position of the client and not disclosed by opposing counsel; or

(3) offer evidence that the lawyer knows to be false. If a lawyer, the lawyer's client, or a witness called by the lawyer, has offered material evidence and the lawyer comes to know of its falsity, the lawyer shall take reasonable remedial measures, including, if necessary, disclosure to the tribunal. A lawyer may refuse to offer evidence, other than the testimony of a defendant in a criminal matter, that the lawyer reasonably believes is false.

(b) A lawyer who represents a client in an adjudicative proceeding and who knows that a person intends to engage, is engaging or has engaged in criminal or fraudulent conduct related to the proceeding shall take reasonable remedial measures, including, if necessary, disclosure to the tribunal.

(c) The duties stated in paragraphs (a) and (b) continue to the conclusion of the proceeding, and apply even if compliance requires disclosure of information otherwise protected by Rule 1.6.

(d) In an ex parte proceeding, a lawyer shall inform the tribunal of all material facts known to the lawyer that will enable the tribunal to make an informed decision, whether or not the facts are adverse.

Comment

[1] This Rule governs the conduct of a lawyer who is representing a client in the proceedings of a tribunal. See Rule 1.0(m) for the definition of "tribunal." It also applies when the lawyer is representing a client in an ancillary proceeding conducted pursuant to the tribunal's adjudicative authority, such as a deposition. Thus, for example, paragraph (a)(3) requires a lawyer to take reasonable remedial measures if the lawyer comes to know that a client who is testifying in a deposition has offered evidence that is false.

[2] This Rule sets forth the special duties of lawyers as officers of the court to avoid conduct that undermines the integrity of the adjudicative process. A lawyer acting as an advocate in an adjudicative proceeding has an obligation to present the client's case with persuasive force. Performance of that duty while maintaining confidences of the client, however, is qualified by the advocate's duty of candor to the tribunal. Consequently, although a lawyer in an adversary proceeding is not required to present an impartial exposition of the law or to vouch for the

evidence submitted in a cause, the lawyer must not allow the tribunal to be misled by false statements of law or fact or evidence that the lawyer knows to be false.

Representations by a Lawyer

[3] An advocate is responsible for pleadings and other documents prepared for litigation, but is usually not required to have personal knowledge of matters asserted therein, for litigation documents ordinarily present assertions by the client, or by someone on the client's behalf, and not assertions by the lawyer. Compare Rule 3.1. However, an assertion purporting to be on the lawyer's own knowledge, as in an affidavit by the lawyer or in a statement in open court, may properly be made only when the lawyer knows the assertion is true or believes it to be true on the basis of a reasonably diligent inquiry. There are circumstances where failure to make a disclosure is the equivalent of an affirmative misrepresentation. The obligation prescribed in Rule 1.2(d) not to counsel a client to commit or assist the client in committing a fraud applies in litigation. Regarding compliance with Rule 1.2(d), see the Comment to that Rule. See also the Comment to Rule 8.4(b).

Legal Argument

[4] Legal argument based on a knowingly false representation of law constitutes dishonesty toward the tribunal. A lawyer is not required to make a disinterested exposition of the law, but must recognize the existence of pertinent legal authorities. Furthermore, as stated in paragraph (a)(2), an advocate has a duty to disclose directly adverse authority in the controlling jurisdiction that has not been disclosed by the opposing party. The underlying concept is that legal argument is a discussion seeking to determine the legal premises properly applicable to the case.

Offering Evidence

[5] Paragraph (a)(3) requires that the lawyer refuse to offer evidence that the lawyer knows to be false, regardless of the client's wishes. This duty is premised on the lawyer's obligation as an officer of the court to prevent the trier of fact from being misled by false evidence. A lawyer does not violate this Rule if the lawyer offers the evidence for the purpose of establishing its falsity.

[6] If a lawyer knows that the client intends to testify falsely or wants the lawyer to introduce false evidence, the lawyer should seek to persuade the client that the evidence should not be offered. If the persuasion is ineffective and the lawyer continues to represent the client, the lawyer must refuse to offer the false evidence. If only a portion of a witness's testimony will be false, the lawyer may call the witness to testify but may not elicit or otherwise permit the witness to present the testimony that the lawyer knows is false.

[7] The duties stated in paragraphs (a) and (b) apply to all lawyers, including defense counsel in criminal cases. In some jurisdictions, however, courts have required counsel to present the accused as a witness or to give a narrative statement if the accused so desires, even if counsel knows that the testimony or statement will be false. The obligation of the advocate under the Rules of Professional Conduct is subordinate to such requirements. See also Comment [9].

[8] The prohibition against offering false evidence only applies if the lawyer knows that the evidence is false. A lawyer's reasonable belief that evidence is false does not preclude its presentation to the trier of fact. A lawyer's knowledge that evidence is false, however, can be inferred from the circumstances. See Rule 1.0(f). Thus, although a lawyer should resolve doubts about the veracity of testimony or other evidence in favor of the client, the lawyer cannot ignore an obvious falsehood.

[9]   Although paragraph (a)(3) only prohibits a lawyer from offering evidence the lawyer knows to be false, it permits the lawyer to refuse to offer testimony or other proof that the lawyer reasonably believes is false. Offering such proof may reflect adversely on the lawyer's ability to discriminate in the quality of evidence and thus impair the lawyer's effectiveness as an advocate. Because of the special protections historically provided criminal defendants, however, this Rule does not permit a lawyer to refuse to offer the testimony of such a client where the lawyer reasonably believes but does not know that the testimony will be false. Unless the lawyer knows the testimony will be false, the lawyer must honor the client's decision to testify. See also Comment [7].

Remedial Measures

[10]   Having offered material evidence in the belief that it was true, a lawyer may subsequently come to know that the evidence is false. Or, a lawyer may be surprised when the lawyer's client, or another witness called by the lawyer, offers testimony the lawyer knows to be false, either during the lawyer's direct examination or in response to cross-examination by the opposing lawyer. In such situations or if the lawyer knows of the falsity of testimony elicited from the client during a deposition, the lawyer must take reasonable remedial measures. In such situations, the advocate's proper course is to remonstrate with the client confidentially, advise the client of the lawyer's duty of candor to the tribunal and seek the client's cooperation with respect to the withdrawal or correction of the false statements or evidence. If that fails, the advocate must take further remedial action. If withdrawal from the representation is not permitted or will not undo the effect of the false evidence, the advocate must make such disclosure to the tribunal as is reasonably necessary to remedy the situation, even if doing so requires the lawyer to reveal information that otherwise would be protected by Rule 1.6. It is for the tribunal then to determine what should be done—making a statement about the matter to the trier of fact, ordering a mistrial or perhaps nothing.

[11]   The disclosure of a client's false testimony can result in grave consequences to the client, including not only a sense of betrayal but also loss of the case and perhaps a prosecution for perjury. But the alternative is that the lawyer cooperate in deceiving the court, thereby subverting the truth-finding process which the adversary system is designed to implement. See Rule 1.2(d). Furthermore, unless it is clearly understood that the lawyer will act upon the duty to disclose the existence of false evidence, the client can simply reject the lawyer's advice to reveal the false evidence and insist that the lawyer keep silent. Thus the client could in effect coerce the lawyer into being a party to fraud on the court.

Preserving Integrity of Adjudicative Process

[12]   Lawyers have a special obligation to protect a tribunal against criminal or fraudulent conduct that undermines the integrity of the adjudicative process, such as bribing, intimidating or otherwise unlawfully communicating with a witness, juror, court official or other participant in the proceeding, unlawfully destroying or concealing documents or other evidence or failing to disclose information to the tribunal when required by law to do so. Thus, paragraph (b) requires a lawyer to take reasonable remedial measures, including disclosure if necessary, whenever the lawyer knows that a person, including the lawyer's client, intends to engage, is engaging or has engaged in criminal or fraudulent conduct related to the proceeding.

Duration of Obligation

[13]   A practical time limit on the obligation to rectify false evidence or false statements of law and fact has to be established. The conclusion of the proceeding is a reasonably definite point for the termination of the obligation. A proceeding has concluded within the meaning of this Rule when a final judgment in the proceeding has been affirmed on appeal or the time for review has passed.

Ex Parte Proceedings

[14]   Ordinarily, an advocate has the limited responsibility of presenting one side of the matters that a tribunal should consider in reaching a decision; the conflicting position is

expected to be presented by the opposing party. However, in any ex parte proceeding, such as an application for a temporary restraining order, there is no balance of presentation by opposing advocates. The object of an ex parte proceeding is nevertheless to yield a substantially just result. The judge has an affirmative responsibility to accord the absent party just consideration. The lawyer for the represented party has the correlative duty to make disclosures of material facts known to the lawyer and that the lawyer reasonably believes are necessary to an informed decision.

Withdrawal

[15]   Normally, a lawyer's compliance with the duty of candor imposed by this Rule does not require that the lawyer withdraw from the representation of a client whose interests will be or have been adversely affected by the lawyer's disclosure. The lawyer may, however, be required by Rule 1.16(a) to seek permission of the tribunal to withdraw if the lawyer's compliance with this Rule's duty of candor results in such an extreme deterioration of the client-lawyer relationship that the lawyer can no longer competently represent the client. Also see Rule 1.16(b) for the circumstances in which a lawyer will be permitted to seek a tribunal's permission to withdraw. In connection with a request for permission to withdraw that is premised on a client's misconduct, a lawyer may reveal information relating to the representation only to the extent reasonably necessary to comply with this Rule or as otherwise permitted by Rule 1.6.

RULE 3.4: FAIRNESS TO OPPOSING PARTY AND COUNSEL

A lawyer shall not:

(a) unlawfully obstruct another party's access to evidence or unlawfully alter, destroy or conceal a document or other material having potential evidentiary value. A lawyer shall not counsel or assist another person to do any such act;

(b) falsify evidence, counsel or assist a witness to testify falsely, or offer an inducement to a witness that is prohibited by law;

(c) knowingly disobey an obligation under the rules of a tribunal, except for an open refusal based on an assertion that no valid obligation exists;

(d) in pretrial procedure, make a frivolous discovery request or fail to make reasonably diligent effort to comply with a legally proper discovery request by an opposing party;

(e) in trial, allude to any matter that the lawyer does not reasonably believe is relevant or that will not be supported by admissible evidence, assert personal knowledge of facts in issue except when testifying as a witness, or state a personal opinion as to the justness of a cause, the credibility of a witness, the culpability of a civil litigant or the guilt or innocence of an accused; or

(f) request a person other than a client to refrain from voluntarily giving relevant information to another party unless:

(1) the person is a relative or an employee or other agent of a client; and

(2) the lawyer reasonably believes that the person's interests will not be adversely affected by refraining from giving such information.

Comment

[1]   The procedure of the adversary system contemplates that the evidence in a case is to be marshalled competitively by the contending parties. Fair competition in the adversary system

is secured by prohibitions against destruction or concealment of evidence, improperly influencing witnesses, obstructive tactics in discovery procedure, and the like.

[2]   Documents and other items of evidence are often essential to establish a claim or defense. Subject to evidentiary privileges, the right of an opposing party, including the government, to obtain evidence through discovery or subpoena is an important procedural right. The exercise of that right can be frustrated if relevant material is altered, concealed or destroyed. Applicable law in many jurisdictions makes it an offense to destroy material for purpose of impairing its availability in a pending proceeding or one whose commencement can be foreseen. Falsifying evidence is also generally a criminal offense. Paragraph (a) applies to evidentiary material generally, including computerized information. Applicable law may permit a lawyer to take temporary possession of physical evidence of client crimes for the purpose of conducting a limited examination that will not alter or destroy material characteristics of the evidence. In such a case, applicable law may require the lawyer to turn the evidence over to the police or other prosecuting authority, depending on the circumstances.

[3]   With regard to paragraph (b), it is not improper to pay a witness's expenses or to compensate an expert witness on terms permitted by law. The common law rule in most jurisdictions is that it is improper to pay an occurrence witness any fee for testifying and that it is improper to pay an expert witness a contingent fee.

[4]   Paragraph (f) permits a lawyer to advise employees of a client to refrain from giving information to another party, for the employees may identify their interests with those of the client. See also Rule 4.2.

RULE 3.5: IMPARTIALITY AND DECORUM OF THE TRIBUNAL

A lawyer shall not:

(a) seek to influence a judge, juror, prospective juror or other official by means prohibited by law;

(b) communicate ex parte with such a person during the proceeding unless authorized to do so by law or court order;

(c) communicate with a juror or prospective juror after discharge of the jury if:

(1) the communication is prohibited by law or court order;

(2) the juror has made known to the lawyer a desire not to communicate; or

(3) the communication involves misrepresentation, coercion, duress or harassment; or

(d) engage in conduct intended to disrupt a tribunal.

Comment

[1]   Many forms of improper influence upon a tribunal are proscribed by criminal law. Others are specified in the ABA Model Code of Judicial Conduct, with which an advocate should be familiar. A lawyer is required to avoid contributing to a violation of such provisions.

[2]   During a proceeding a lawyer may not communicate ex parte with persons serving in an official capacity in the proceeding, such as judges, masters or jurors, unless authorized to do so by law or court order.

[3]   A lawyer may on occasion want to communicate with a juror or prospective juror after the jury has been discharged. The lawyer may do so unless the communication is prohibited by law or a court order but must respect the desire of the juror not to talk with the lawyer. The lawyer may not engage in improper conduct during the communication.

[4]   The advocate's function is to present evidence and argument so that the cause may be decided according to law. Refraining from abusive or obstreperous conduct is a corollary of the advocate's right to speak on behalf of litigants. A lawyer may stand firm against abuse by a judge but should avoid reciprocation; the judge's default is no justification for similar dereliction by an advocate. An advocate can present the cause, protect the record for subsequent review and preserve professional integrity by patient firmness no less effectively than by belligerence or theatrics.

[5]   The duty to refrain from disruptive conduct applies to any proceeding of a tribunal, including a deposition. See Rule 1.0(m).

RULE 3.6: TRIAL PUBLICITY

(a) A lawyer who is participating or has participated in the investigation or litigation of a matter shall not make an extrajudicial statement that the lawyer knows or reasonably should know will be disseminated by means of public communication and will have a substantial likelihood of materially prejudicing an adjudicative proceeding in the matter.

(b) Notwithstanding paragraph (a), a lawyer may state:

(1) the claim, offense or defense involved and, except when prohibited by law, the identity of the persons involved;

(2) information contained in a public record;

(3) that an investigation of a matter is in progress;

(4) the scheduling or result of any step in litigation;

(5) a request for assistance in obtaining evidence and information necessary thereto;

(6) a warning of danger concerning the behavior of a person involved, when there is reason to believe that there exists the likelihood of substantial harm to an individual or to the public interest; and

(7) in a criminal case, in addition to subparagraphs (1) through (6):

(i) the identity, residence, occupation and family status of the accused;

(ii) if the accused has not been apprehended, information necessary to aid in apprehension of that person;

(iii) the fact, time and place of arrest; and

(iv) the identity of investigating and arresting officers or agencies and the length of the investigation.

(c) Notwithstanding paragraph (a), a lawyer may make a statement that a reasonable lawyer would believe is required to protect a client from the substantial undue prejudicial effect of recent publicity not initiated by the lawyer or the lawyer's client. A statement made pursuant to this paragraph shall be limited to such information as is necessary to mitigate the recent adverse publicity.

(d) No lawyer associated in a firm or government agency with a lawyer subject to paragraph (a) shall make a statement prohibited by paragraph (a).

Comment

[1]   It is difficult to strike a balance between protecting the right to a fair trial and safeguarding the right of free expression. Preserving the right to a fair trial necessarily entails some curtailment of the information that may be disseminated about a party prior to trial, particularly where trial by jury is involved. If there were no such limits, the result would be the practical nullification of the protective effect of the rules of forensic decorum and the exclusionary rules of evidence. On the other hand, there are vital social interests served by the free dissemination of information about events having legal consequences and about legal proceedings themselves. The public has a right to know about threats to its safety and measures aimed at assuring its security. It also has a legitimate interest in the conduct of judicial proceedings, particularly in matters of general public concern. Furthermore, the subject matter of legal proceedings is often of direct significance in debate and deliberation over questions of public policy.

[2]   Special rules of confidentiality may validly govern proceedings in juvenile, domestic relations and mental disability proceedings, and perhaps other types of litigation. Rule 3.4(c) requires compliance with such rules.

[3]   The Rule sets forth a basic general prohibition against a lawyer's making statements that the lawyer knows or should know will have a substantial likelihood of materially prejudicing an adjudicative proceeding. Recognizing that the public value of informed commentary is great and the likelihood of prejudice to a proceeding by the commentary of a lawyer who is not involved in the proceeding is small, the rule applies only to lawyers who are, or who have been involved in the investigation or litigation of a case, and their associates.

[4]   Paragraph (b) identifies specific matters about which a lawyer's statements would not ordinarily be considered to present a substantial likelihood of material prejudice, and should not in any event be considered prohibited by the general prohibition of paragraph (a). Paragraph (b) is not intended to be an exhaustive listing of the subjects upon which a lawyer may make a statement, but statements on other matters may be subject to paragraph (a).

[5]   There are, on the other hand, certain subjects that are more likely than not to have a material prejudicial effect on a proceeding, particularly when they refer to a civil matter triable to a jury, a criminal matter, or any other proceeding that could result in incarceration. These subjects relate to:

   (1) the character, credibility, reputation or criminal record of a party, suspect in a criminal investigation or witness, or the identity of a witness, or the expected testimony of a party or witness;

   (2) in a criminal case or proceeding that could result in incarceration, the possibility of a plea of guilty to the offense or the existence or contents of any confession, admission, or statement given by a defendant or suspect or that person's refusal or failure to make a statement;

(3) the performance or results of any examination or test or the refusal or failure of a person to submit to an examination or test, or the identity or nature of physical evidence expected to be presented;

(4) any opinion as to the guilt or innocence of a defendant or suspect in a criminal case or proceeding that could result in incarceration;

(5) information that the lawyer knows or reasonably should know is likely to be inadmissible as evidence in a trial and that would, if disclosed, create a substantial risk of prejudicing an impartial trial; or

(6) the fact that a defendant has been charged with a crime, unless there is included therein a statement explaining that the charge is merely an accusation and that the defendant is presumed innocent until and unless proven guilty.

[6]   Another relevant factor in determining prejudice is the nature of the proceeding involved. Criminal jury trials will be most sensitive to extrajudicial speech. Civil trials may be less sensitive. Non-jury hearings and arbitration proceedings may be even less affected. The Rule will still place limitations on prejudicial comments in these cases, but the likelihood of prejudice may be different depending on the type of proceeding.

[7]   Finally, extrajudicial statements that might otherwise raise a question under this Rule may be permissible when they are made in response to statements made publicly by another party, another party's lawyer, or third persons, where a reasonable lawyer would believe a public response is required in order to avoid prejudice to the lawyer's client. When prejudicial statements have been publicly made by others, responsive statements may have the salutary effect of lessening any resulting adverse impact on the adjudicative proceeding. Such responsive statements should be limited to contain only such information as is necessary to mitigate undue prejudice created by the statements made by others.

[8]   See Rule 3.8(f) for additional duties of prosecutors in connection with extrajudicial statements about criminal proceedings.

RULE 3.7: LAWYER AS WITNESS

(a) **A lawyer shall not act as advocate at a trial in which the lawyer is likely to be a necessary witness unless:**

(1) **the testimony relates to an uncontested issue;**

(2) **the testimony relates to the nature and value of legal services rendered in the case; or**

(3) **disqualification of the lawyer would work substantial hardship on the client.**

(b) **A lawyer may act as advocate in a trial in which another lawyer in the lawyer's firm is likely to be called as a witness unless precluded from doing so by Rule 1.7 or Rule 1.9.**

Comment

[1]   Combining the roles of advocate and witness can prejudice the tribunal and the opposing party and can also involve a conflict of interest between the lawyer and client.

Advocate-Witness Rule

[2]   The tribunal has proper objection when the trier of fact may be confused or misled by a lawyer serving as both advocate and witness. The opposing party has proper objection where

the combination of roles may prejudice that party's rights in the litigation. A witness is required to testify on the basis of personal knowledge, while an advocate is expected to explain and comment on evidence given by others. It may not be clear whether a statement by an advocate-witness should be taken as proof or as an analysis of the proof.

[3]   To protect the tribunal, paragraph (a) prohibits a lawyer from simultaneously serving as advocate and necessary witness except in those circumstances specified in paragraphs (a)(1) through (a)(3). Paragraph (a)(1) recognizes that if the testimony will be uncontested, the ambiguities in the dual role are purely theoretical. Paragraph (a)(2) recognizes that where the testimony concerns the extent and value of legal services rendered in the action in which the testimony is offered, permitting the lawyers to testify avoids the need for a second trial with new counsel to resolve that issue. Moreover, in such a situation the judge has firsthand knowledge of the matter in issue; hence, there is less dependence on the adversary process to test the credibility of the testimony.

[4]   Apart from these two exceptions, paragraph (a)(3) recognizes that a balancing is required between the interests of the client and those of the tribunal and the opposing party. Whether the tribunal is likely to be misled or the opposing party is likely to suffer prejudice depends on the nature of the case, the importance and probable tenor of the lawyer's testimony, and the probability that the lawyer's testimony will conflict with that of other witnesses. Even if there is risk of such prejudice, in determining whether the lawyer should be disqualified, due regard must be given to the effect of disqualification on the lawyer's client. It is relevant that one or both parties could reasonably foresee that the lawyer would probably be a witness. The conflict of interest principles stated in Rules 1.7, 1.9 and 1.10 have no application to this aspect of the problem.

[5]   Because the tribunal is not likely to be misled when a lawyer acts as advocate in a trial in which another lawyer in the lawyer's firm will testify as a necessary witness, paragraph (b) permits the lawyer to do so except in situations involving a conflict of interest.

Conflict of Interest

[6]   In determining if it is permissible to act as advocate in a trial in which the lawyer will be a necessary witness, the lawyer must also consider that the dual role may give rise to a conflict of interest that will require compliance with Rules 1.7 or 1.9. For example, if there is likely to be substantial conflict between the testimony of the client and that of the lawyer the representation involves a conflict of interest that requires compliance with Rule 1.7. This would be true even though the lawyer might not be prohibited by paragraph (a) from simultaneously serving as advocate and witness because the lawyer's disqualification would work a substantial hardship on the client. Similarly, a lawyer who might be permitted to simultaneously serve as an advocate and a witness by paragraph (a)(3) might be precluded from doing so by Rule 1.9. The problem can arise whether the lawyer is called as a witness on behalf of the client or is called by the opposing party. Determining whether or not such a conflict exists is primarily the responsibility of the lawyer involved. If there is a conflict of interest, the lawyer must secure the client's informed consent, confirmed in writing. In some cases, the lawyer will be precluded from seeking the client's consent. See Rule 1.7. See Rule 1.0(b) for the definition of "confirmed in writing" and Rule 1.0(e) for the definition of "informed consent."

[7]   Paragraph (b) provides that a lawyer is not disqualified from serving as an advocate because a lawyer with whom the lawyer is associated in a firm is precluded from doing so by paragraph (a). If, however, the testifying lawyer would also be disqualified by Rule 1.7 or Rule 1.9 from representing the client in the matter, other lawyers in the firm will be precluded from representing the client by Rule 1.10 unless the client gives informed consent under the conditions stated in Rule 1.7.

RULE 3.8: SPECIAL RESPONSIBILITIES OF A PROSECUTOR

The prosecutor in a criminal case shall:

(a) refrain from prosecuting a charge that the prosecutor knows is not supported by probable cause;

(b) make reasonable efforts to assure that the accused has been advised of the right to, and the procedure for obtaining, counsel and has been given reasonable opportunity to obtain counsel;

(c) not seek to obtain from an unrepresented accused a waiver of important pretrial rights, such as the right to a preliminary hearing;

(d) make timely disclosure to the defense of all evidence or information known to the prosecutor that tends to negate the guilt of the accused or mitigates the offense, and, in connection with sentencing, disclose to the defense and to the tribunal all unprivileged mitigating information known to the prosecutor, except when the prosecutor is relieved of this responsibility by a protective order of the tribunal;

(e) not subpoena a lawyer in a grand jury or other criminal proceeding to present evidence about a past or present client unless the prosecutor reasonably believes:

(1) the information sought is not protected from disclosure by any applicable privilege;

(2) the evidence sought is essential to the successful completion of an ongoing investigation or prosecution; and

(3) there is no other feasible alternative to obtain the information;

(f) except for statements that are necessary to inform the public of the nature and extent of the prosecutor's action and that serve a legitimate law enforcement purpose, refrain from making extrajudicial comments that have a substantial likelihood of heightening public condemnation of the accused and exercise reasonable care to prevent investigators, law enforcement personnel, employees or other persons assisting or associated with the prosecutor in a criminal case from making an extrajudicial statement that the prosecutor would be prohibited from making under Rule 3.6 or this Rule.

Comment

[1] A prosecutor has the responsibility of a minister of justice and not simply that of an advocate. This responsibility carries with it specific obligations to see that the defendant is accorded procedural justice and that guilt is decided upon the basis of sufficient evidence. Precisely how far the prosecutor is required to go in this direction is a matter of debate and varies in different jurisdictions. Many jurisdictions have adopted the ABA Standards of Criminal Justice Relating to the Prosecution Function, which in turn are the product of prolonged and careful deliberation by lawyers experienced in both criminal prosecution and defense. Applicable law may require other measures by the prosecutor and knowing disregard of those obligations or a systematic abuse of prosecutorial discretion could constitute a violation of Rule 8.4.

[2] In some jurisdictions, a defendant may waive a preliminary hearing and thereby lose a valuable opportunity to challenge probable cause. Accordingly, prosecutors should not seek to

obtain waivers of preliminary hearings or other important pretrial rights from unrepresented accused persons. Paragraph (c) does not apply, however, to an accused appearing *pro se* with the approval of the tribunal. Nor does it forbid the lawful questioning of an uncharged suspect who has knowingly waived the rights to counsel and silence.

[3]   The exception in paragraph (d) recognizes that a prosecutor may seek an appropriate protective order from the tribunal if disclosure of information to the defense could result in substantial harm to an individual or to the public interest.

[4]   Paragraph (e) is intended to limit the issuance of lawyer subpoenas in grand jury and other criminal proceedings to those situations in which there is a genuine need to intrude into the client-lawyer relationship.

[5]   Paragraph (f) supplements Rule 3.6, which prohibits extrajudicial statements that have a substantial likelihood of prejudicing an adjudicatory proceeding. In the context of a criminal prosecution, a prosecutor's extrajudicial statement can create the additional problem of increasing public condemnation of the accused. Although the announcement of an indictment, for example, will necessarily have severe consequences for the accused, a prosecutor can, and should, avoid comments which have no legitimate law enforcement purpose and have a substantial likelihood of increasing public opprobrium of the accused. Nothing in this Comment is intended to restrict the statements which a prosecutor may make which comply with Rule 3.6(b) or 3.6(c).

[6]   Like other lawyers, prosecutors are subject to Rules 5.1 and 5.3, which relate to responsibilities regarding lawyers and nonlawyers who work for or are associated with the lawyer's office. Paragraph (f) reminds the prosecutor of the importance of these obligations in connection with the unique dangers of improper extrajudicial statements in a criminal case. In addition, paragraph (f) requires a prosecutor to exercise reasonable care to prevent persons assisting or associated with the prosecutor from making improper extrajudicial statements, even when such persons are not under the direct supervision of the prosecutor. Ordinarily, the reasonable care standard will be satisfied if the prosecutor issues the appropriate cautions to law-enforcement personnel and other relevant individuals.

RULE 3.9: ADVOCATE IN NONADJUDICATIVE PROCEEDINGS

A lawyer representing a client before a legislative body or administrative agency in a nonadjudicative proceeding shall disclose that the appearance is in a representative capacity and shall conform to the provisions of Rules 3.3(a) through (c), 3.4(a) through (c), and 3.5.

Comment

[1]   In representation before bodies such as legislatures, municipal councils, and executive and administrative agencies acting in a rule-making or policy-making capacity, lawyers present facts, formulate issues and advance argument in the matters under consideration. The decision-making body, like a court, should be able to rely on the integrity of the submissions made to it. A lawyer appearing before such a body must deal with it honestly and in conformity with applicable rules of procedure. See Rules 3.3(a) through (c), 3.4(a) through (c) and 3.5.

[2]   Lawyers have no exclusive right to appear before nonadjudicative bodies, as they do before a court. The requirements of this Rule therefore may subject lawyers to regulations inapplicable to advocates who are not lawyers. However, legislatures and administrative agencies have a right to expect lawyers to deal with them as they deal with courts.

[3]   This Rule only applies when a lawyer represents a client in connection with an official hearing or meeting of a governmental agency or a legislative body to which the lawyer or the

lawyer's client is presenting evidence or argument. It does not apply to representation of a client in a negotiation or other bilateral transaction with a governmental agency or in connection with an application for a license or other privilege or the client's compliance with generally applicable reporting requirements, such as the filing of income-tax returns. Nor does it apply to the representation of a client in connection with an investigation or examination of the client's affairs conducted by government investigators or examiners. Representation in such matters is governed by Rules 4.1 through 4.4.

RULE 4.1: TRUTHFULNESS IN STATEMENTS TO OTHERS

In the course of representing a client a lawyer shall not knowingly:

(a) make a false statement of material fact or law to a third person; or

(b) fail to disclose a material fact when disclosure is necessary to avoid assisting a criminal or fraudulent act by a client, unless disclosure is prohibited by Rule 1.6.

Comment

Misrepresentation

[1]   A lawyer is required to be truthful when dealing with others on a client's behalf, but generally has no affirmative duty to inform an opposing party of relevant facts. A misrepresentation can occur if the lawyer incorporates or affirms a statement of another person that the lawyer knows is false. Misrepresentations can also occur by partially true but misleading statements or omissions that are the equivalent of affirmative false statements. For dishonest conduct that does not amount to a false statement or for misrepresentations by a lawyer other than in the course of representing a client, see Rule 8.4.

Statements of Fact

[2]   This Rule refers to statements of fact. Whether a particular statement should be regarded as one of fact can depend on the circumstances. Under generally accepted conventions in negotiation, certain types of statements ordinarily are not taken as statements of material fact. Estimates of price or value placed on the subject of a transaction and a party's intentions as to an acceptable settlement of a claim are ordinarily in this category, and so is the existence of an undisclosed principal except where nondisclosure of the principal would constitute fraud. Lawyers should be mindful of their obligations under applicable law to avoid criminal and tortious misrepresentation.

Crime or Fraud by Client

[3]   Under Rule 1.2(d), a lawyer is prohibited from counseling or assisting a client in conduct that the lawyer knows is criminal or fraudulent. Paragraph (b) states a specific application of the principle set forth in Rule 1.2(d) and addresses the situation where a client's crime or fraud takes the form of a lie or misrepresentation. Ordinarily, a lawyer can avoid assisting a client's crime or fraud by withdrawing from the representation. Sometimes it may be necessary for the lawyer to give notice of the fact of withdrawal and to disaffirm an opinion, document, affirmation or the like. In extreme cases, substantive law may require a lawyer to disclose information relating to the representation to avoid being deemed to have assisted the client's crime or fraud. If the lawyer can avoid assisting a client's crime or fraud only by disclosing this information, then under paragraph (b) the lawyer is required to do so, unless the disclosure is prohibited by Rule 1.6.

RULE 4.2: COMMUNICATION WITH PERSON REPRESENTED BY COUNSEL

In representing a client, a lawyer shall not communicate about the subject of the representation with a person the lawyer knows to be represented by another lawyer in the matter, unless the lawyer has the consent of the other lawyer or is authorized to do so by law or a court order.

Comment

[1]   This Rule contributes to the proper functioning of the legal system by protecting a person who has chosen to be represented by a lawyer in a matter against possible overreaching by other lawyers who are participating in the matter, interference by those lawyers with the client-lawyer relationship and the uncounselled disclosure of information relating to the representation.

[2]   This Rule applies to communications with any person who is represented by counsel concerning the matter to which the communication relates.

[3]   The Rule applies even though the represented person initiates or consents to the communication. A lawyer must immediately terminate communication with a person if, after commencing communication, the lawyer learns that the person is one with whom communication is not permitted by this Rule.

[4]   This Rule does not prohibit communication with a represented person, or an employee or agent of such a person, concerning matters outside the representation. For example, the existence of a controversy between a government agency and a private party, or between two organizations, does not prohibit a lawyer for either from communicating with nonlawyer representatives of the other regarding a separate matter. Nor does this Rule preclude communication with a represented person who is seeking advice from a lawyer who is not otherwise representing a client in the matter. A lawyer may not make a communication prohibited by this Rule through the acts of another. See Rule 8.4(a). Parties to a matter may communicate directly with each other, and a lawyer is not prohibited from advising a client concerning a communication that the client is legally entitled to make. Also, a lawyer having independent justification or legal authorization for communicating with a represented person is permitted to do so.

[5]   Communications authorized by law may include communications by a lawyer on behalf of a client who is exercising a constitutional or other legal right to communicate with the government. Communications authorized by law may also include investigative activities of lawyers representing governmental entities, directly or through investigative agents, prior to the commencement of criminal or civil enforcement proceedings. When communicating with the accused in a criminal matter, a government lawyer must comply with this Rule in addition to honoring the constitutional rights of the accused. The fact that a communication does not violate a state or federal constitutional right is insufficient to establish that the communication is permissible under this Rule.

[6]   A lawyer who is uncertain whether a communication with a represented person is permissible may seek a court order. A lawyer may also seek a court order in exceptional circumstances to authorize a communication that would otherwise be prohibited by this Rule, for example, where communication with a person represented by counsel is necessary to avoid reasonably certain injury.

[7]   In the case of a represented organization, this Rule prohibits communications with a constituent of the organization who supervises, directs or regularly consults with the organiza-

tion's lawyer concerning the matter or has authority to obligate the organization with respect to the matter or whose act or omission in connection with the matter may be imputed to the organization for purposes of civil or criminal liability. Consent of the organization's lawyer is not required for communication with a former constituent. If a constituent of the organization is represented in the matter by his or her own counsel, the consent by that counsel to a communication will be sufficient for purposes of this Rule. Compare Rule 3.4(f). In communicating with a current or former constituent of an organization, a lawyer must not use methods of obtaining evidence that violate the legal rights of the organization. See Rule 4.4.

[8] The prohibition on communications with a represented person only applies in circumstances where the lawyer knows that the person is in fact represented in the matter to be discussed. This means that the lawyer has actual knowledge of the fact of the representation; but such actual knowledge may be inferred from the circumstances. See Rule 1.0(f). Thus, the lawyer cannot evade the requirement of obtaining the consent of counsel by closing eyes to the obvious.

[9] In the event the person with whom the lawyer communicates is not known to be represented by counsel in the matter, the lawyer's communications are subject to Rule 4.3.

RULE 4.3: DEALING WITH UNREPRESENTED PERSON

In dealing on behalf of a client with a person who is not represented by counsel, a lawyer shall not state or imply that the lawyer is disinterested. When the lawyer knows or reasonably should know that the unrepresented person misunderstands the lawyer's role in the matter, the lawyer shall make reasonable efforts to correct the misunderstanding. The lawyer shall not give legal advice to an unrepresented person, other than the advice to secure counsel, if the lawyer knows or reasonably should know that the interests of such a person are or have a reasonable possibility of being in conflict with the interests of the client.

Comment

[1] An unrepresented person, particularly one not experienced in dealing with legal matters, might assume that a lawyer is disinterested in loyalties or is a disinterested authority on the law even when the lawyer represents a client. In order to avoid a misunderstanding, a lawyer will typically need to identify the lawyer's client and, where necessary, explain that the client has interests opposed to those of the unrepresented person. For misunderstandings that sometimes arise when a lawyer for an organization deals with an unrepresented constituent, see Rule 1.13(f).

[2] The Rule distinguishes between situations involving unrepresented persons whose interests may be adverse to those of the lawyer's client and those in which the person's interests are not in conflict with the client's. In the former situation, the possibility that the lawyer will compromise the unrepresented person's interests is so great that the Rule prohibits the giving of any advice, apart from the advice to obtain counsel. Whether a lawyer is giving impermissible advice may depend on the experience and sophistication of the unrepresented person, as well as the setting in which the behavior and comments occur. This Rule does not prohibit a lawyer from negotiating the terms of a transaction or settling a dispute with an unrepresented person. So long as the lawyer has explained that the lawyer represents an adverse party and is not representing the person, the lawyer may inform the person of the terms on which the lawyer's client will enter into an agreement or settle a matter, prepare documents that require the person's signature and explain the lawyer's own view of the meaning of the document or the lawyer's view of the underlying legal obligations.

RULE 4.4: RESPECT FOR RIGHTS OF THIRD PERSONS

(a) In representing a client, a lawyer shall not use means that have no substantial purpose other than to embarrass, delay, or burden a third person, or use methods of obtaining evidence that violate the legal rights of such a person.

(b) A lawyer who receives a document relating to the representation of the lawyer's client and knows or reasonably should know that the document was inadvertently sent shall promptly notify the sender.

Comment

[1]   Responsibility to a client requires a lawyer to subordinate the interests of others to those of the client, but that responsibility does not imply that a lawyer may disregard the rights of third persons. It is impractical to catalogue all such rights, but they include legal restrictions on methods of obtaining evidence from third persons and unwarranted intrusions into privileged relationships, such as the client-lawyer relationship.

[2]   Paragraph (b) recognizes that lawyers sometimes receive documents that were mistakenly sent or produced by opposing parties or their lawyers. If a lawyer knows or reasonably should know that such a document was sent inadvertently, then this Rule requires the lawyer to promptly notify the sender in order to permit that person to take protective measures. Whether the lawyer is required to take additional steps, such as returning the original document, is a matter of law beyond the scope of these Rules, as is the question of whether the privileged status of a document has been waived. Similarly, this Rule does not address the legal duties of a lawyer who receives a document that the lawyer knows or reasonably should know may have been wrongfully obtained by the sending person. For purposes of this Rule, "document" includes e-mail or other electronic modes of transmission subject to being read or put into readable form.

[3]   Some lawyers may choose to return a document unread, for example, when the lawyer learns before receiving the document that it was inadvertently sent to the wrong address. Where a lawyer is not required by applicable law to do so, the decision to voluntarily return such a document is a matter of professional judgment ordinarily reserved to the lawyer. See Rules 1.2 and 1.4.

RULE 5.1: RESPONSIBILITIES OF PARTNERS, MANAGERS, AND SUPERVISORY LAWYERS

(a) A partner in a law firm, and a lawyer who individually or together with other lawyers possesses comparable managerial authority in a law firm, shall make reasonable efforts to ensure that the firm has in effect measures giving reasonable assurance that all lawyers in the firm conform to the Rules of Professional Conduct.

(b) A lawyer having direct supervisory authority over another lawyer shall make reasonable efforts to ensure that the other lawyer conforms to the Rules of Professional Conduct.

(c) A lawyer shall be responsible for another lawyer's violation of the Rules of Professional Conduct if:

(1) the lawyer orders or, with knowledge of the specific conduct, ratifies the conduct involved; or

(2) the lawyer is a partner or has comparable managerial authority in the law firm in which the other lawyer practices, or has direct supervisory authority over the other lawyer, and knows of the conduct at a time when its consequences can be avoided or mitigated but fails to take reasonable remedial action.

Comment

[1]   Paragraph (a) applies to lawyers who have managerial authority over the professional work of a firm. See Rule 1.0(c). This includes members of a partnership, the shareholders in a

law firm organized as a professional corporation, and members of other associations authorized to practice law; lawyers having comparable managerial authority in a legal services organization or a law department of an enterprise or government agency; and lawyers who have intermediate managerial responsibilities in a firm. Paragraph (b) applies to lawyers who have supervisory authority over the work of other lawyers in a firm.

[2] Paragraph (a) requires lawyers with managerial authority within a firm to make reasonable efforts to establish internal policies and procedures designed to provide reasonable assurance that all lawyers in the firm will conform to the Rules of Professional Conduct. Such policies and procedures include those designed to detect and resolve conflicts of interest, identify dates by which actions must be taken in pending matters, account for client funds and property and ensure that inexperienced lawyers are properly supervised.

[3] Other measures that may be required to fulfill the responsibility prescribed in paragraph (a) can depend on the firm's structure and the nature of its practice. In a small firm of experienced lawyers, informal supervision and periodic review of compliance with the required systems ordinarily will suffice. In a large firm, or in practice situations in which difficult ethical problems frequently arise, more elaborate measures may be necessary. Some firms, for example, have a procedure whereby junior lawyers can make confidential referral of ethical problems directly to a designated senior partner or special committee. See Rule 5.2. Firms, whether large or small, may also rely on continuing legal education in professional ethics. In any event, the ethical atmosphere of a firm can influence the conduct of all its members, and the partners may not assume that all lawyers associated with the firm will inevitably conform to the Rules.

[4] Paragraph (c) expresses a general principle of personal responsibility for acts of another. See also Rule 8.4(a).

[5] Paragraph (c)(2) defines the duty of a partner or other lawyer having comparable managerial authority in a law firm, as well as a lawyer who has direct supervisory authority over performance of specific legal work by another lawyer. Whether a lawyer has supervisory authority in particular circumstances is a question of fact. Partners and lawyers with comparable authority have at least indirect responsibility for all work being done by the firm, while a partner or manager in charge of a particular matter ordinarily also has supervisory responsibility for the work of other firm lawyers engaged in the matter. Appropriate remedial action by a partner or managing lawyer would depend on the immediacy of that lawyer's involvement and the seriousness of the misconduct. A supervisor is required to intervene to prevent avoidable consequences of misconduct if the supervisor knows that the misconduct occurred. Thus, if a supervising lawyer knows that a subordinate misrepresented a matter to an opposing party in negotiation, the supervisor as well as the subordinate has a duty to correct the resulting misapprehension.

[6] Professional misconduct by a lawyer under supervision could reveal a violation of paragraph (b) on the part of the supervisory lawyer even though it does not entail a violation of paragraph (c) because there was no direction, ratification or knowledge of the violation.

[7] Apart from this Rule and Rule 8.4(a), a lawyer does not have disciplinary liability for the conduct of a partner, associate or subordinate. Whether a lawyer may be liable civilly or criminally for another lawyer's conduct is a question of law beyond the scope of these Rules.

[8] The duties imposed by this Rule on managing and supervising lawyers do not alter the personal duty of each lawyer in a firm to abide by the Rules of Professional Conduct. See Rule 5.2(a).

RULE 5.2: RESPONSIBILITIES OF A SUBORDINATE LAWYER

(a) A lawyer is bound by the Rules of Professional Conduct notwithstanding that the lawyer acted at the direction of another person.

(b) A subordinate lawyer does not violate the Rules of Professional Conduct if that lawyer acts in accordance with a supervisory lawyer's reasonable resolution of an arguable question of professional duty.

Comment

[1]   Although a lawyer is not relieved of responsibility for a violation by the fact that the lawyer acted at the direction of a supervisor, that fact may be relevant in determining whether a lawyer had the knowledge required to render conduct a violation of the Rules. For example, if a subordinate filed a frivolous pleading at the direction of a supervisor, the subordinate would not be guilty of a professional violation unless the subordinate knew of the document's frivolous character.

[2]   When lawyers in a supervisor-subordinate relationship encounter a matter involving professional judgment as to ethical duty, the supervisor may assume responsibility for making the judgment. Otherwise a consistent course of action or position could not be taken. If the question can reasonably be answered only one way, the duty of both lawyers is clear and they are equally responsible for fulfilling it. However, if the question is reasonably arguable, someone has to decide upon the course of action. That authority ordinarily reposes in the supervisor, and a subordinate may be guided accordingly. For example, if a question arises whether the interests of two clients conflict under Rule 1.7, the supervisor's reasonable resolution of the question should protect the subordinate professionally if the resolution is subsequently challenged.

RULE 5.3: RESPONSIBILITIES REGARDING NONLAWYER ASSISTANTS

With respect to a nonlawyer employed or retained by or associated with a lawyer:

(a) a partner, and a lawyer who individually or together with other lawyers possesses comparable managerial authority in a law firm shall make reasonable efforts to ensure that the firm has in effect measures giving reasonable assurance that the person's conduct is compatible with the professional obligations of the lawyer;

(b) a lawyer having direct supervisory authority over the nonlawyer shall make reasonable efforts to ensure that the person's conduct is compatible with the professional obligations of the lawyer; and

(c) a lawyer shall be responsible for conduct of such a person that would be a violation of the Rules of Professional Conduct if engaged in by a lawyer if:

(1) the lawyer orders or, with the knowledge of the specific conduct, ratifies the conduct involved; or

(2) the lawyer is a partner or has comparable managerial authority in the law firm in which the person is employed, or has direct supervisory authority over the person, and knows of the conduct at a time when its consequences can be avoided or mitigated but fails to take reasonable remedial action.

Comment

[1]   Lawyers generally employ assistants in their practice, including secretaries, investigators, law student interns, and paraprofessionals. Such assistants, whether employees or independent contractors, act for the lawyer in rendition of the lawyer's professional services. A lawyer must give such assistants appropriate instruction and supervision concerning the ethical

aspects of their employment, particularly regarding the obligation not to disclose information relating to representation of the client, and should be responsible for their work product. The measures employed in supervising nonlawyers should take account of the fact that they do not have legal training and are not subject to professional discipline.

[2]   Paragraph (a) requires lawyers with managerial authority within a law firm to make reasonable efforts to establish internal policies and procedures designed to provide reasonable assurance that nonlawyers in the firm will act in a way compatible with the Rules of Professional Conduct. See Comment [1] to Rule 5.1. Paragraph (b) applies to lawyers who have supervisory authority over the work of a nonlawyer. Paragraph (c) specifies the circumstances in which a lawyer is responsible for conduct of a nonlawyer that would be a violation of the Rules of Professional Conduct if engaged in by a lawyer.

RULE 5.4: PROFESSIONAL INDEPENDENCE OF A LAWYER

(a) **A lawyer or law firm shall not share legal fees with a nonlawyer, except that:**

(1) **an agreement by a lawyer with the lawyer's firm, partner, or associate may provide for the payment of money, over a reasonable period of time after the lawyer's death, to the lawyer's estate or to one or more specified persons;**

(2) **a lawyer who purchases the practice of a deceased, disabled, or disappeared lawyer may, pursuant to the provisions of Rule 1.17, pay to the estate or other representative of that lawyer the agreed-upon purchase price;**

(3) **a lawyer or law firm may include nonlawyer employees in a compensation or retirement plan, even though the plan is based in whole or in part on a profit-sharing arrangement; and**

(4) **a lawyer may share court-awarded legal fees with a nonprofit organization that employed, retained or recommended employment of the lawyer in the matter.**

(b) **A lawyer shall not form a partnership with a nonlawyer if any of the activities of the partnership consist of the practice of law.**

(c) **A lawyer shall not permit a person who recommends, employs, or pays the lawyer to render legal services for another to direct or regulate the lawyer's professional judgment in rendering such legal services.**

(d) **A lawyer shall not practice with or in the form of a professional corporation or association authorized to practice law for a profit, if:**

(1) **a nonlawyer owns any interest therein, except that a fiduciary representative of the estate of a lawyer may hold the stock or interest of the lawyer for a reasonable time during administration;**

(2) **a nonlawyer is a corporate director or officer thereof or occupies the position of similar responsibility in any form of association other than a corporation ; or**

(3) **a nonlawyer has the right to direct or control the professional judgment of a lawyer.**

Comment

[1]   The provisions of this Rule express traditional limitations on sharing fees. These limitations are to protect the lawyer's professional independence of judgment. Where someone

other than the client pays the lawyer's fee or salary, or recommends employment of the lawyer, that arrangement does not modify the lawyer's obligation to the client. As stated in paragraph (c), such arrangements should not interfere with the lawyer's professional judgment.

[2]   This Rule also expresses traditional limitations on permitting a third party to direct or regulate the lawyer's professional judgment in rendering legal services to another. See also Rule 1.8(f) (lawyer may accept compensation from a third party as long as there is no interference with the lawyer's independent professional judgment and the client gives informed consent).

RULE 5.5: UNAUTHORIZED PRACTICE OF LAW; MULTIJURISDICTIONAL PRACTICE OF LAW

(a) A lawyer shall not practice law in a jurisdiction in violation of the regulation of the legal profession in that jurisdiction, or assist another in doing so.

(b) A lawyer who is not admitted to practice in this jurisdiction shall not:

(1) except as authorized by these Rules or other law, establish an office or other systematic and continuous presence in this jurisdiction for the practice of law; or

(2) hold out to the public or otherwise represent that the lawyer is admitted to practice law in this jurisdiction.

(c) A lawyer admitted in another United States jurisdiction, and not disbarred or suspended from practice in any jurisdiction, may provide legal services on a temporary basis in this jurisdiction that:

(1) are undertaken in association with a lawyer who is admitted to practice in this jurisdiction and who actively participates in the matter;

(2) are in or reasonably related to a pending or potential proceeding before a tribunal in this or another jurisdiction, if the lawyer, or a person the lawyer is assisting, is authorized by law or order to appear in such proceeding or reasonably expects to be so authorized;

(3) are in or reasonably related to a pending or potential arbitration, mediation, or other alternative dispute resolution proceeding in this or another jurisdiction, if the services arise out of or are reasonably related to the lawyer's practice in a jurisdiction in which the lawyer is admitted to practice and are not services for which the forum requires pro hac vice admission; or

(4) are not within paragraphs (c)(2) or (c)(3) and arise out of or are reasonably related to the lawyer's practice in a jurisdiction in which the lawyer is admitted to practice.

(d) A lawyer admitted in another United States jurisdiction, and not disbarred or suspended from practice in any jurisdiction, may provide legal services in this jurisdiction that:

(1) are provided to the lawyer's employer or its organizational affiliates and are not services for which the forum requires pro hac vice admission; or

(2) are services that the lawyer is authorized by federal or other law to provide in this jurisdiction.

Comment

[1]   A lawyer may practice law only in a jurisdiction in which the lawyer is authorized to practice. A lawyer may be admitted to practice law in a jurisdiction on a regular basis or may be

authorized by court rule or order or by law to practice for a limited purpose or on a restricted basis. Paragraph (a) applies to unauthorized practice of law by a lawyer, whether through the lawyer's direct action or by the lawyer assisting another person.

[2] The definition of the practice of law is established by law and varies from one jurisdiction to another. Whatever the definition, limiting the practice of law to members of the bar protects the public against rendition of legal services by unqualified persons. This Rule does not prohibit a lawyer from employing the services of paraprofessionals and delegating functions to them, so long as the lawyer supervises the delegated work and retains responsibility for their work. See Rule 5.3.

[3] A lawyer may provide professional advice and instruction to nonlawyers whose employment requires knowledge of the law; for example, claims adjusters, employees of financial or commercial institutions, social workers, accountants and persons employed in government agencies. Lawyers also may assist independent nonlawyers, such as paraprofessionals, who are authorized by the law of a jurisdiction to provide particular law-related services. In addition, a lawyer may counsel nonlawyers who wish to proceed pro se.

[4] Other than as authorized by law or this Rule, a lawyer who is not admitted to practice generally in this jurisdiction violates paragraph (b) if the lawyer establishes an office or other systematic and continuous presence in this jurisdiction for the practice of law. Presence may be systematic and continuous even if the lawyer is not physically present here. Such a lawyer must not hold out to the public or otherwise represent that the lawyer is admitted to practice law in this jurisdiction. See also Rules 7.1(a) and 7.5(b).

[5] There are occasions in which a lawyer admitted to practice in another United States jurisdiction, and not disbarred or suspended from practice in any jurisdiction, may provide legal services on a temporary basis in this jurisdiction under circumstances that do not create an unreasonable risk to the interests of their clients, the public or the courts. Paragraph (c) identifies four such circumstances. The fact that conduct is not so identified does not imply that the conduct is or is not authorized. With the exception of paragraphs (d)(1) and (d)(2), this Rule does not authorize a lawyer to establish an office or other systematic and continuous presence in this jurisdiction without being admitted to practice generally here.

[6] There is no single test to determine whether a lawyer's services are provided on a "temporary basis" in this jurisdiction, and may therefore be permissible under paragraph (c). Services may be "temporary" even though the lawyer provides services in this jurisdiction on a recurring basis, or for an extended period of time, as when the lawyer is representing a client in a single lengthy negotiation or litigation.

[7] Paragraphs (c) and (d) apply to lawyers who are admitted to practice law in any United States jurisdiction, which includes the District of Columbia and any state, territory or commonwealth of the United States. The word "admitted" in paragraph (c) contemplates that the lawyer is authorized to practice in the jurisdiction in which the lawyer is admitted and excludes a lawyer who while technically admitted is not authorized to practice, because, for example, the lawyer is on inactive status.

[8] Paragraph (c)(1) recognizes that the interests of clients and the public are protected if a lawyer admitted only in another jurisdiction associates with a lawyer licensed to practice in this jurisdiction. For this paragraph to apply, however, the lawyer admitted to practice in this jurisdiction must actively participate in and share responsibility for the representation of the client.

[9] Lawyers not admitted to practice generally in a jurisdiction may be authorized by law or order of a tribunal or an administrative agency to appear before the tribunal or agency. This

authority may be granted pursuant to formal rules governing admission pro hac vice or pursuant to informal practice of the tribunal or agency. Under paragraph (c)(2), a lawyer does not violate this Rule when the lawyer appears before a tribunal or agency pursuant to such authority. To the extent that a court rule or other law of this jurisdiction requires a lawyer who is not admitted to practice in this jurisdiction to obtain admission pro hac vice before appearing before a tribunal or administrative agency, this Rule requires the lawyer to obtain that authority.

[10] Paragraph (c)(2) also provides that a lawyer rendering services in this jurisdiction on a temporary basis does not violate this Rule when the lawyer engages in conduct in anticipation of a proceeding or hearing in a jurisdiction in which the lawyer is authorized to practice law or in which the lawyer reasonably expects to be admitted pro hac vice. Examples of such conduct include meetings with the client, interviews of potential witnesses, and the review of documents. Similarly, a lawyer admitted only in another jurisdiction may engage in conduct temporarily in this jurisdiction in connection with pending litigation in another jurisdiction in which the lawyer is or reasonably expects to be authorized to appear, including taking depositions in this jurisdiction.

[11] When a lawyer has been or reasonably expects to be admitted to appear before a court or administrative agency, paragraph (c)(2) also permits conduct by lawyers who are associated with that lawyer in the matter, but who do not expect to appear before the court or administrative agency. For example, subordinate lawyers may conduct research, review documents, and attend meetings with witnesses in support of the lawyer responsible for the litigation.

[12] Paragraph (c)(3) permits a lawyer admitted to practice law in another jurisdiction to perform services on a temporary basis in this jurisdiction if those services are in or reasonably related to a pending or potential arbitration, mediation, or other alternative dispute resolution proceeding in this or another jurisdiction, if the services arise out of or are reasonably related to the lawyer's practice in a jurisdiction in which the lawyer is admitted to practice. The lawyer, however, must obtain admission pro hac vice in the case of a court-annexed arbitration or mediation or otherwise if court rules or law so require.

[13] Paragraph (c)(4) permits a lawyer admitted in another jurisdiction to provide certain legal services on a temporary basis in this jurisdiction that arise out of or are reasonably related to the lawyer's practice in a jurisdiction in which the lawyer is admitted but are not within paragraphs (c)(2) or (c)(3). These services include both legal services and services that nonlawyers may perform but that are considered the practice of law when performed by lawyers.

[14] Paragraphs (c)(3) and (c)(4) require that the services arise out of or be reasonably related to the lawyer's practice in a jurisdiction in which the lawyer is admitted. A variety of factors evidence such a relationship. The lawyer's client may have been previously represented by the lawyer, or may be resident in or have substantial contacts with the jurisdiction in which the lawyer is admitted. The matter, although involving other jurisdictions, may have a significant connection with that jurisdiction. In other cases, significant aspects of the lawyer's work might be conducted in that jurisdiction or a significant aspect of the matter may involve the law of that jurisdiction. The necessary relationship might arise when the client's activities or the legal issues involve multiple jurisdictions, such as when the officers of a multinational corporation survey potential business sites and seek the services of their lawyer in assessing the relative merits of each. In addition, the services may draw on the lawyer's recognized expertise developed through the regular practice of law on behalf of clients in matters involving a particular body of federal, nationally-uniform, foreign, or international law.

[15] Paragraph (d) identifies two circumstances in which a lawyer who is admitted to practice in another United States jurisdiction, and is not disbarred or suspended from practice

in any jurisdiction, may establish an office or other systematic and continuous presence in this jurisdiction for the practice of law as well as provide legal services on a temporary basis. Except as provided in paragraphs (d)(1) and (d)(2), a lawyer who is admitted to practice law in another jurisdiction and who establishes an office or other systematic or continuous presence in this jurisdiction must become admitted to practice law generally in this jurisdiction.

[16]   Paragraph (d)(1) applies to a lawyer who is employed by a client to provide legal services to the client or its organizational affiliates, i.e., entities that control, are controlled by, or are under common control with the employer. This paragraph does not authorize the provision of personal legal services to the employer's officers or employees. The paragraph applies to in-house corporate lawyers, government lawyers and others who are employed to render legal services to the employer. The lawyer's ability to represent the employer outside the jurisdiction in which the lawyer is licensed generally serves the interests of the employer and does not create an unreasonable risk to the client and others because the employer is well situated to assess the lawyer's qualifications and the quality of the lawyer's work.

[17]   If an employed lawyer establishes an office or other systematic presence in this jurisdiction for the purpose of rendering legal services to the employer, the lawyer may be subject to registration or other requirements, including assessments for client protection funds and mandatory continuing legal education.

[18]   Paragraph (d)(2) recognizes that a lawyer may provide legal services in a jurisdiction in which the lawyer is not licensed when authorized to do so by federal or other law, which includes statute, court rule, executive regulation or judicial precedent.

[19]   A lawyer who practices law in this jurisdiction pursuant to paragraphs (c) or (d) or otherwise is subject to the disciplinary authority of this jurisdiction. See Rule 8.5(a).

[20]   In some circumstances, a lawyer who practices law in this jurisdiction pursuant to paragraphs (c) or (d) may have to inform the client that the lawyer is not licensed to practice law in this jurisdiction. For example, that may be required when the representation occurs primarily in this jurisdiction and requires knowledge of the law of this jurisdiction. See Rule 1.4(b).

[21]   Paragraphs (c) and (d) do not authorize communications advertising legal services to prospective clients in this jurisdiction by lawyers who are admitted to practice in other jurisdictions. Whether and how lawyers may communicate the availability of their services to prospective clients in this jurisdiction is governed by Rules 7.1 to 7.5.

RULE 5.6: RESTRICTIONS ON RIGHT TO PRACTICE

A lawyer shall not participate in offering or making:

(a) a partnership, shareholders, operating, employment, or other similar type of agreement that restricts the right of a lawyer to practice after termination of the relationship, except an agreement concerning benefits upon retirement; or

(b) an agreement in which a restriction on the lawyer's right to practice is part of the settlement of a client controversy.

Comment

[1]   An agreement restricting the right of lawyers to practice after leaving a firm not only limits their professional autonomy but also limits the freedom of clients to choose a lawyer.

Paragraph (a) prohibits such agreements except for restrictions incident to provisions concerning retirement benefits for service with the firm.

[2]   Paragraph (b) prohibits a lawyer from agreeing not to represent other persons in connection with settling a claim on behalf of a client.

[3]   This Rule does not apply to prohibit restrictions that may be included in the terms of the sale of a law practice pursuant to Rule 1.17.

RULE 5.7: RESPONSIBILITIES REGARDING LAW–RELATED SERVICES

(a) A lawyer shall be subject to the Rules of Professional Conduct with respect to the provision of law-related services, as defined in paragraph (b), if the law-related services are provided:

(1) by the lawyer in circumstances that are not distinct from the lawyer's provision of legal services to clients; or

(2) in other circumstances by an entity controlled by the lawyer individually or with others if the lawyer fails to take reasonable measures to assure that a person obtaining the law-related services knows that the services are not legal services and that the protections of the client-lawyer relationship do not exist.

(b) The term "law-related services" denotes services that might reasonably be performed in conjunction with and in substance are related to the provision of legal services, and that are not prohibited as unauthorized practice of law when provided by a nonlawyer.

Comment

[1]   When a lawyer performs law-related services or controls an organization that does so, there exists the potential for ethical problems. Principal among these is the possibility that the person for whom the law-related services are performed fails to understand that the services may not carry with them the protections normally afforded as part of the client-lawyer relationship. The recipient of the law-related services may expect, for example, that the protection of client confidences, prohibitions against representation of persons with conflicting interests, and obligations of a lawyer to maintain professional independence apply to the provision of law-related services when that may not be the case.

[2]   Rule 5.7 applies to the provision of law-related services by a lawyer even when the lawyer does not provide any legal services to the person for whom the law-related services are performed and whether the law-related services are performed through a law firm or a separate entity. The Rule identifies the circumstances in which all of the Rules of Professional Conduct apply to the provision of law-related services. Even when those circumstances do not exist, however, the conduct of a lawyer involved in the provision of law-related services is subject to those Rules that apply generally to lawyer conduct, regardless of whether the conduct involves the provision of legal services. See, e.g., Rule 8.4.

[3]   When law-related services are provided by a lawyer under circumstances that are not distinct from the lawyer's provision of legal services to clients, the lawyer in providing the law-related services must adhere to the requirements of the Rules of Professional Conduct as provided in paragraph (a)(1). Even when the law-related and legal services are provided in circumstances that are distinct from each other, for example through separate entities or different support staff within the law firm, the Rules of Professional Conduct apply to the lawyer

as provided in paragraph (a)(2) unless the lawyer takes reasonable measures to assure that the recipient of the law-related services knows that the services are not legal services and that the protections of the client-lawyer relationship do not apply.

[4]   Law-related services also may be provided through an entity that is distinct from that through which the lawyer provides legal services. If the lawyer individually or with others has control of such an entity's operations, the Rule requires the lawyer to take reasonable measures to assure that each person using the services of the entity knows that the services provided by the entity are not legal services and that the Rules of Professional Conduct that relate to the client-lawyer relationship do not apply. A lawyer's control of an entity extends to the ability to direct its operation. Whether a lawyer has such control will depend upon the circumstances of the particular case.

[5]   When a client-lawyer relationship exists with a person who is referred by a lawyer to a separate law-related service entity controlled by the lawyer, individually or with others, the lawyer must comply with Rule 1.8(a).

[6]   In taking the reasonable measures referred to in paragraph (a)(2) to assure that a person using law-related services understands the practical effect or significance of the inapplicability of the Rules of Professional Conduct, the lawyer should communicate to the person receiving the law-related services, in a manner sufficient to assure that the person understands the significance of the fact, that the relationship of the person to the business entity will not be a client-lawyer relationship. The communication should be made before entering into an agreement for provision of or providing law-related services, and preferably should be in writing.

[7]   The burden is upon the lawyer to show that the lawyer has taken reasonable measures under the circumstances to communicate the desired understanding. For instance, a sophisticated user of law-related services, such as a publicly held corporation, may require a lesser explanation than someone unaccustomed to making distinctions between legal services and law-related services, such as an individual seeking tax advice from a lawyer-accountant or investigative services in connection with a lawsuit.

[8]   Regardless of the sophistication of potential recipients of law-related services, a lawyer should take special care to keep separate the provision of law-related and legal services in order to minimize the risk that the recipient will assume that the law-related services are legal services. The risk of such confusion is especially acute when the lawyer renders both types of services with respect to the same matter. Under some circumstances the legal and law-related services may be so closely entwined that they cannot be distinguished from each other, and the requirement of disclosure and consultation imposed by paragraph (a)(2) of the Rule cannot be met. In such a case a lawyer will be responsible for assuring that both the lawyer's conduct and, to the extent required by Rule 5.3, that of nonlawyer employees in the distinct entity that the lawyer controls complies in all respects with the Rules of Professional Conduct.

[9]   A broad range of economic and other interests of clients may be served by lawyers' engaging in the delivery of law-related services. Examples of law-related services include providing title insurance, financial planning, accounting, trust services, real estate counseling, legislative lobbying, economic analysis, social work, psychological counseling, tax preparation, and patent, medical or environmental consulting.

[10]   When a lawyer is obliged to accord the recipients of such services the protections of those Rules that apply to the client-lawyer relationship, the lawyer must take special care to heed the proscriptions of the Rules addressing conflict of interest (Rules 1.7 through 1.11, especially Rules 1.7(a)(2) and 1.8(a), (b) and (f)), and to scrupulously adhere to the requirements

of Rule 1.6 relating to disclosure of confidential information. The promotion of the law-related services must also in all respects comply with Rules 7.1 through 7.3, dealing with advertising and solicitation. In that regard, lawyers should take special care to identify the obligations that may be imposed as a result of a jurisdiction's decisional law.

[11] When the full protections of all of the Rules of Professional Conduct do not apply to the provision of law-related services, principles of law external to the Rules, for example, the law of principal and agent, govern the legal duties owed to those receiving the services. Those other legal principles may establish a different degree of protection for the recipient with respect to confidentiality of information, conflicts of interest and permissible business relationships with clients. See also Rule 8.4 (Misconduct).

RULE 6.1: VOLUNTARY PRO BONO PUBLICO SERVICE

Every lawyer has a professional responsibility to provide legal services to those unable to pay. A lawyer should aspire to render at least (50) hours of pro bono publico legal services per year. In fulfilling this responsibility, the lawyer should:

(a) provide a substantial majority of the (50) hours of legal services without fee or expectation of fee to:

(1) persons of limited means or

(2) charitable, religious, civic, community, governmental and educational organizations in matters that are designed primarily to address the needs of persons of limited means; and

(b) provide any additional services through:

(1) delivery of legal services at no fee or substantially reduced fee to individuals, groups or organizations seeking to secure or protect civil rights, civil liberties or public rights, or charitable, religious, civic, community, governmental and educational organizations in matters in furtherance of their organizational purposes, where the payment of standard legal fees would significantly deplete the organization's economic resources or would be otherwise inappropriate;

(2) delivery of legal services at a substantially reduced fee to persons of limited means; or

(3) participation in activities for improving the law, the legal system or the legal profession.

In addition, a lawyer should voluntarily contribute financial support to organizations that provide legal services to persons of limited means.

Comment

[1] Every lawyer, regardless of professional prominence or professional work load, has a responsibility to provide legal services to those unable to pay, and personal involvement in the problems of the disadvantaged can be one of the most rewarding experiences in the life of a lawyer. The American Bar Association urges all lawyers to provide a minimum of 50 hours of pro bono services annually. States, however, may decide to choose a higher or lower number of hours of annual service (which may be expressed as a percentage of a lawyer's professional time)

depending upon local needs and local conditions. It is recognized that in some years a lawyer may render greater or fewer hours than the annual standard specified, but during the course of his or her legal career, each lawyer should render on average per year, the number of hours set forth in this Rule. Services can be performed in civil matters or in criminal or quasi-criminal matters for which there is no government obligation to provide funds for legal representation, such as post-conviction death penalty appeal cases.

[2] Paragraphs (a)(1) and (2) recognize the critical need for legal services that exists among persons of limited means by providing that a substantial majority of the legal services rendered annually to the disadvantaged be furnished without fee or expectation of fee. Legal services under these paragraphs consist of a full range of activities, including individual and class representation, the provision of legal advice, legislative lobbying, administrative rule making and the provision of free training or mentoring to those who represent persons of limited means. The variety of these activities should facilitate participation by government lawyers, even when restrictions exist on their engaging in the outside practice of law.

[3] Persons eligible for legal services under paragraphs (a)(1) and (2) are those who qualify for participation in programs funded by the Legal Services Corporation and those whose incomes and financial resources are slightly above the guidelines utilized by such programs but nevertheless, cannot afford counsel. Legal services can be rendered to individuals or to organizations such as homeless shelters, battered women's centers and food pantries that serve those of limited means. The term "governmental organizations" includes, but is not limited to, public protection programs and sections of governmental or public sector agencies.

[4] Because service must be provided without fee or expectation of fee, the intent of the lawyer to render free legal services is essential for the work performed to fall within the meaning of paragraphs (a)(1) and (2). Accordingly, services rendered cannot be considered pro bono if an anticipated fee is uncollected, but the award of statutory attorneys' fees in a case originally accepted as pro bono would not disqualify such services from inclusion under this section. Lawyers who do receive fees in such cases are encouraged to contribute an appropriate portion of such fees to organizations or projects that benefit persons of limited means.

[5] While it is possible for a lawyer to fulfill the annual responsibility to perform pro bono services exclusively through activities described in paragraphs (a)(1) and (2), to the extent that any hours of service remained unfulfilled, the remaining commitment can be met in a variety of ways as set forth in paragraph (b). Constitutional, statutory or regulatory restrictions may prohibit or impede government and public sector lawyers and judges from performing the pro bono services outlined in paragraphs (a)(1) and (2). Accordingly, where those restrictions apply, government and public sector lawyers and judges may fulfill their pro bono responsibility by performing services outlined in paragraph (b).

[6] Paragraph (b)(1) includes the provision of certain types of legal services to those whose incomes and financial resources place them above limited means. It also permits the pro bono lawyer to accept a substantially reduced fee for services. Examples of the types of issues that may be addressed under this paragraph include First Amendment claims, Title VII claims and environmental protection claims. Additionally, a wide range of organizations may be represented, including social service, medical research, cultural and religious groups.

[7] Paragraph (b)(2) covers instances in which lawyers agree to and receive a modest fee for furnishing legal services to persons of limited means. Participation in judicare programs and acceptance of court appointments in which the fee is substantially below a lawyer's usual rate are encouraged under this section.

[8] Paragraph (b)(3) recognizes the value of lawyers engaging in activities that improve the law, the legal system or the legal profession. Serving on bar association committees, serving

on boards of pro bono or legal services programs, taking part in Law Day activities, acting as a continuing legal education instructor, a mediator or an arbitrator and engaging in legislative lobbying to improve the law, the legal system or the profession are a few examples of the many activities that fall within this paragraph.

[9]   Because the provision of pro bono services is a professional responsibility, it is the individual ethical commitment of each lawyer. Nevertheless, there may be times when it is not feasible for a lawyer to engage in pro bono services. At such times a lawyer may discharge the pro bono responsibility by providing financial support to organizations providing free legal services to persons of limited means. Such financial support should be reasonably equivalent to the value of the hours of service that would have otherwise been provided. In addition, at times it may be more feasible to satisfy the pro bono responsibility collectively, as by a firm's aggregate pro bono activities.

[10]   Because the efforts of individual lawyers are not enough to meet the need for free legal services that exists among persons of limited means, the government and the profession have instituted additional programs to provide those services. Every lawyer should financially support such programs, in addition to either providing direct pro bono services or making financial contributions when pro bono service is not feasible.

[11]   Law firms should act reasonably to enable and encourage all lawyers in the firm to provide the pro bono legal services called for by this Rule.

[12]   The responsibility set forth in this Rule is not intended to be enforced through disciplinary process.

RULE 6.2: ACCEPTING APPOINTMENTS

A lawyer shall not seek to avoid appointment by a tribunal to represent a person except for good cause, such as:

(a) representing the client is likely to result in violation of the Rules of Professional Conduct or other law;

(b) representing the client is likely to result in an unreasonable financial burden on the lawyer; or

(c) the client or the cause is so repugnant to the lawyer as to be likely to impair the client-lawyer relationship or the lawyer's ability to represent the client.

Comment

[1]   A lawyer ordinarily is not obliged to accept a client whose character or cause the lawyer regards as repugnant. The lawyer's freedom to select clients is, however, qualified. All lawyers have a responsibility to assist in providing pro bono publico service. See Rule 6.1. An individual lawyer fulfills this responsibility by accepting a fair share of unpopular matters or indigent or unpopular clients. A lawyer may also be subject to appointment by a court to serve unpopular clients or persons unable to afford legal services.

Appointed Counsel

[2]   For good cause a lawyer may seek to decline an appointment to represent a person who cannot afford to retain counsel or whose cause is unpopular. Good cause exists if the lawyer could

not handle the matter competently, see Rule 1.1, or if undertaking the representation would result in an improper conflict of interest, for example, when the client or the cause is so repugnant to the lawyer as to be likely to impair the client-lawyer relationship or the lawyer's ability to represent the client. A lawyer may also seek to decline an appointment if acceptance would be unreasonably burdensome, for example, when it would impose a financial sacrifice so great as to be unjust.

[3] An appointed lawyer has the same obligations to the client as retained counsel, including the obligations of loyalty and confidentiality, and is subject to the same limitations on the client-lawyer relationship, such as the obligation to refrain from assisting the client in violation of the Rules.

RULE 6.3: MEMBERSHIP IN LEGAL SERVICES ORGANIZATION

A lawyer may serve as a director, officer or member of a legal services organization, apart from the law firm in which the lawyer practices, notwithstanding that the organization serves persons having interests adverse to a client of the lawyer. The lawyer shall not knowingly participate in a decision or action of the organization:

(a) if participating in the decision or action would be incompatible with the lawyer's obligations to a client under Rule 1.7; or

(b) where the decision or action could have a material adverse effect on the representation of a client of the organization whose interests are adverse to a client of the lawyer.

Comment

[1] Lawyers should be encouraged to support and participate in legal service organizations. A lawyer who is an officer or a member of such an organization does not thereby have a client-lawyer relationship with persons served by the organization. However, there is potential conflict between the interests of such persons and the interests of the lawyer's clients. If the possibility of such conflict disqualified a lawyer from serving on the board of a legal services organization, the profession's involvement in such organizations would be severely curtailed.

[2] It may be necessary in appropriate cases to reassure a client of the organization that the representation will not be affected by conflicting loyalties of a member of the board. Established, written policies in this respect can enhance the credibility of such assurances.

RULE 6.4: LAW REFORM ACTIVITIES AFFECTING CLIENT INTERESTS

A lawyer may serve as a director, officer or member of an organization involved in reform of the law or its administration notwithstanding that the reform may affect the interests of a client of the lawyer. When the lawyer knows that the interests of a client may be materially benefitted by a decision in which the lawyer participates, the lawyer shall disclose that fact but need not identify the client.

Comment

[1] Lawyers involved in organizations seeking law reform generally do not have a client-lawyer relationship with the organization. Otherwise, it might follow that a lawyer could not be involved in a bar association law reform program that might indirectly affect a client. See also Rule 1.2(b). For example, a lawyer specializing in antitrust litigation might be regarded as

disqualified from participating in drafting revisions of rules governing that subject. In determining the nature and scope of participation in such activities, a lawyer should be mindful of obligations to clients under other Rules, particularly Rule 1.7. A lawyer is professionally obligated to protect the integrity of the program by making an appropriate disclosure within the organization when the lawyer knows a private client might be materially benefitted.

RULE 6.5: NONPROFIT AND COURT–ANNEXED LIMITED LEGAL SERVICES PROGRAMS

(a) A lawyer who, under the auspices of a program sponsored by a nonprofit organization or court, provides short-term limited legal services to a client without expectation by either the lawyer or the client that the lawyer will provide continuing representation in the matter:

(1) is subject to Rules 1.7 and 1.9(a) only if the lawyer knows that the representation of the client involves a conflict of interest; and

(2) is subject to Rule 1.10 only if the lawyer knows that another lawyer associated with the lawyer in a law firm is disqualified by Rule 1.7 or 1.9(a) with respect to the matter.

(b) Except as provided in paragraph (a)(2), Rule 1.10 is inapplicable to a representation governed by this Rule.

Comment

[1]   Legal services organizations, courts and various nonprofit organizations have established programs through which lawyers provide short-term limited legal services—such as advice or the completion of legal forms—that will assist persons to address their legal problems without further representation by a lawyer. In these programs, such as legal-advice hotlines, advice-only clinics or pro se counseling programs, a client-lawyer relationship is established, but there is no expectation that the lawyer's representation of the client will continue beyond the limited consultation. Such programs are normally operated under circumstances in which it is not feasible for a lawyer to systematically screen for conflicts of interest as is generally required before undertaking a representation. See, e.g., Rules 1.7, 1.9 and 1.10.

[2]   A lawyer who provides short-term limited legal services pursuant to this Rule must secure the client's informed consent to the limited scope of the representation. See Rule 1.2(c). If a short-term limited representation would not be reasonable under the circumstances, the lawyer may offer advice to the client but must also advise the client of the need for further assistance of counsel. Except as provided in this Rule, the Rules of Professional Conduct, including Rules 1.6 and 1.9(c), are applicable to the limited representation.

[3]   Because a lawyer who is representing a client in the circumstances addressed by this Rule ordinarily is not able to check systematically for conflicts of interest, paragraph (a) requires compliance with Rules 1.7 or 1.9(a) only if the lawyer knows that the representation presents a conflict of interest for the lawyer, and with Rule 1.10 only if the lawyer knows that another lawyer in the lawyer's firm is disqualified by Rules 1.7 or 1.9(a) in the matter.

[4]   Because the limited nature of the services significantly reduces the risk of conflicts of interest with other matters being handled by the lawyer's firm, paragraph (b) provides that Rule 1.10 is inapplicable to a representation governed by this Rule except as provided by paragraph (a)(2). Paragraph (a)(2) requires the participating lawyer to comply with Rule 1.10 when the lawyer knows that the lawyer's firm is disqualified by Rules 1.7 or 1.9(a). By virtue of paragraph

(b), however, a lawyer's participation in a short-term limited legal services program will not preclude the lawyer's firm from undertaking or continuing the representation of a client with interests adverse to a client being represented under the program's auspices. Nor will the personal disqualification of a lawyer participating in the program be imputed to other lawyers participating in the program.

[5]   If, after commencing a short-term limited representation in accordance with this Rule, a lawyer undertakes to represent the client in the matter on an ongoing basis, Rules 1.7, 1.9(a) and 1.10 become applicable.

RULE 7.1: COMMUNICATIONS CONCERNING A LAWYER'S SERVICES

A lawyer shall not make a false or misleading communication about the lawyer or the lawyer's services. A communication is false or misleading if it contains a material misrepresentation of fact or law, or omits a fact necessary to make the statement considered as a whole not materially misleading.

Comment

[1]   This Rule governs all communications about a lawyer's services, including advertising permitted by Rule 7.2. Whatever means are used to make known a lawyer's services, statements about them must be truthful.

[2]   Truthful statements that are misleading are also prohibited by this Rule. A truthful statement is misleading if it omits a fact necessary to make the lawyer's communication considered as a whole not materially misleading. A truthful statement is also misleading if there is a substantial likelihood that it will lead a reasonable person to formulate a specific conclusion about the lawyer or the lawyer's services for which there is no reasonable factual foundation.

[3]   An advertisement that truthfully reports a lawyer's achievements on behalf of clients or former clients may be misleading if presented so as to lead a reasonable person to form an unjustified expectation that the same results could be obtained for other clients in similar matters without reference to the specific factual and legal circumstances of each client's case. Similarly, an unsubstantiated comparison of the lawyer's services or fees with the services or fees of other lawyers may be misleading if presented with such specificity as would lead a reasonable person to conclude that the comparison can be substantiated. The inclusion of an appropriate disclaimer or qualifying language may preclude a finding that a statement is likely to create unjustified expectations or otherwise mislead a prospective client.

[4]   See also Rule 8.4(e) for the prohibition against stating or implying an ability to influence improperly a government agency or official or to achieve results by means that violate the Rules of Professional Conduct or other law.

RULE 7.2: ADVERTISING

(a) Subject to the requirements of Rules 7.1 and 7.3, a lawyer may advertise services through written, recorded or electronic communication, including public media.

(b) A lawyer shall not give anything of value to a person for recommending the lawyer's services except that a lawyer may

(1) pay the reasonable costs of advertisements or communications permitted by this Rule;

(2) **pay the usual charges of a legal service plan or a not-for-profit or qualified lawyer referral service. A qualified lawyer referral service is a lawyer referral service that has been approved by an appropriate regulatory authority;**

(3) **pay for a law practice in accordance with Rule 1.17; and**

(4) **refer clients to another lawyer or a nonlawyer professional pursuant to an agreement not otherwise prohibited under these Rules that provides for the other person to refer clients or customers to the lawyer, if**

(i) **the reciprocal referral agreement is not exclusive, and**

(ii) **the client is informed of the existence and nature of the agreement.**

(c) **Any communication made pursuant to this rule shall include the name and office address of at least one lawyer or law firm responsible for its content.**

Comment

[1]   To assist the public in obtaining legal services, lawyers should be allowed to make known their services not only through reputation but also through organized information campaigns in the form of advertising. Advertising involves an active quest for clients, contrary to the tradition that a lawyer should not seek clientele. However, the public's need to know about legal services can be fulfilled in part through advertising. This need is particularly acute in the case of persons of moderate means who have not made extensive use of legal services. The interest in expanding public information about legal services ought to prevail over considerations of tradition. Nevertheless, advertising by lawyers entails the risk of practices that are misleading or overreaching.

[2]   This Rule permits public dissemination of information concerning a lawyer's name or firm name, address and telephone number; the kinds of services the lawyer will undertake; the basis on which the lawyer's fees are determined, including prices for specific services and payment and credit arrangements; a lawyer's foreign language ability; names of references and, with their consent, names of clients regularly represented; and other information that might invite the attention of those seeking legal assistance.

[3]   Questions of effectiveness and taste in advertising are matters of speculation and subjective judgment. Some jurisdictions have had extensive prohibitions against television advertising, against advertising going beyond specified facts about a lawyer, or against "undignified" advertising. Television is now one of the most powerful media for getting information to the public, particularly persons of low and moderate income; prohibiting television advertising, therefore, would impede the flow of information about legal services to many sectors of the public. Limiting the information that may be advertised has a similar effect and assumes that the bar can accurately forecast the kind of information that the public would regard as relevant. Similarly, electronic media, such as the Internet, can be an important source of information about legal services, and lawful communication by electronic mail is permitted by this Rule. But see Rule 7.3(a) for the prohibition against the solicitation of a prospective client through a real-time electronic exchange that is not initiated by the prospective client.

[4]   Neither this Rule nor Rule 7.3 prohibits communications authorized by law, such as notice to members of a class in class action litigation.

Paying Others to Recommend a Lawyer

[5]   Lawyers are not permitted to pay others for channeling professional work. Paragraph (b)(1), however, allows a lawyer to pay for advertising and communications permitted by this

Rule, including the costs of print directory listings, on-line directory listings, newspaper ads, television and radio airtime, domain-name registrations, sponsorship fees, banner ads, and group advertising. A lawyer may compensate employees, agents and vendors who are engaged to provide marketing or client-development services, such as publicists, public-relations personnel, business-development staff and website designers. See Rule 5.3 for the duties of lawyers and law firms with respect to the conduct of nonlawyers who prepare marketing materials for them.

[6] A lawyer may pay the usual charges of a legal service plan or a not-for-profit or qualified lawyer referral service. A legal service plan is a prepaid or group legal service plan or a similar delivery system that assists prospective clients to secure legal representation. A lawyer referral service, on the other hand, is any organization that holds itself out to the public as a lawyer referral service. Such referral services are understood by laypersons to be consumer-oriented organizations that provide unbiased referrals to lawyers with appropriate experience in the subject matter of the representation and afford other client protections, such as complaint procedures or malpractice insurance requirements. Consequently, this Rule only permits a lawyer to pay the usual charges of a not-for-profit or qualified lawyer referral service. A qualified lawyer referral service is one that is approved by an appropriate regulatory authority as affording adequate protections for prospective clients. See, e.g., the American Bar Association's Model Supreme Court Rules Governing Lawyer Referral Services and Model Lawyer Referral and Information Service Quality Assurance Act (requiring that organizations that are identified as lawyer referral services (i) permit the participation of all lawyers who are licensed and eligible to practice in the jurisdiction and who meet reasonable objective eligibility requirements as may be established by the referral service for the protection of prospective clients; (ii) require each participating lawyer to carry reasonably adequate malpractice insurance; (iii) act reasonably to assess client satisfaction and address client complaints; and (iv) do not refer prospective clients to lawyers who own, operate or are employed by the referral service.)

[7] A lawyer who accepts assignments or referrals from a legal service plan or referrals from a lawyer referral service must act reasonably to assure that the activities of the plan or service are compatible with the lawyer's professional obligations. See Rule 5.3. Legal service plans and lawyer referral services may communicate with prospective clients, but such communication must be in conformity with these Rules. Thus, advertising must not be false or misleading, as would be the case if the communications of a group advertising program or a group legal services plan would mislead prospective clients to think that it was a lawyer referral service sponsored by a state agency or bar association. Nor could the lawyer allow in-person, telephonic, or real-time contacts that would violate Rule 7.3.

[8] A lawyer also may agree to refer clients to another lawyer or a nonlawyer professional, in return for the undertaking of that person to refer clients or customers to the lawyer. Such reciprocal referral arrangements must not interfere with the lawyer's professional judgment as to making referrals or as to providing substantive legal services. See Rules 2.1 and 5.4(c). Except as provided in Rule 1.5(e), a lawyer who receives referrals from a lawyer or nonlawyer professional must not pay anything solely for the referral, but the lawyer does not violate paragraph (b) of this Rule by agreeing to refer clients to the other lawyer or nonlawyer professional, so long as the reciprocal referral agreement is not exclusive and the client is informed of the referral agreement. Conflicts of interest created by such arrangements are governed by Rule 1.7. Reciprocal referral agreements should not be of indefinite duration and should be reviewed periodically to determine whether they comply with these Rules. This Rule does not restrict referrals or divisions of revenues or net income among lawyers within firms comprised of multiple entities.

RULE 7.3: DIRECT CONTACT WITH PROSPECTIVE CLIENTS

(a) A lawyer shall not by in-person, live telephone or real-time electronic contact solicit professional employment from a prospective client when a significant motive for the lawyer's doing so is the lawyer's pecuniary gain, unless the person contacted:

(1) **is a lawyer; or**

(2) **has a family, close personal, or prior professional relationship with the lawyer.**

(b) **A lawyer shall not solicit professional employment from a prospective client by written, recorded or electronic communication or by in-person, telephone or real-time electronic contact even when not otherwise prohibited by paragraph (a), if:**

(1) **the prospective client has made known to the lawyer a desire not to be solicited by the lawyer; or**

(2) **the solicitation involves coercion, duress or harassment.**

(c) **Every written, recorded or electronic communication from a lawyer soliciting professional employment from a prospective client known to be in need of legal services in a particular matter shall include the words "Advertising Material" on the outside envelope, if any, and at the beginning and ending of any recorded or electronic communication, unless the recipient of the communication is a person specified in paragraphs (a)(1) or (a)(2).**

(d) **Notwithstanding the prohibitions in paragraph (a), a lawyer may participate with a prepaid or group legal service plan operated by an organization not owned or directed by the lawyer that uses in-person or telephone contact to solicit memberships or subscriptions for the plan from persons who are not known to need legal services in a particular matter covered by the plan.**

Comment

[1]   There is a potential for abuse inherent in direct in-person, live telephone or real-time electronic contact by a lawyer with a prospective client known to need legal services. These forms of contact between a lawyer and a prospective client subject the layperson to the private importuning of the trained advocate in a direct interpersonal encounter. The prospective client, who may already feel overwhelmed by the circumstances giving rise to the need for legal services, may find it difficult fully to evaluate all available alternatives with reasoned judgment and appropriate self-interest in the face of the lawyer's presence and insistence upon being retained immediately. The situation is fraught with the possibility of undue influence, intimidation, and over-reaching.

[2]   This potential for abuse inherent in direct in-person, live telephone or real-time electronic solicitation of prospective clients justifies its prohibition, particularly since lawyer advertising and written and recorded communication permitted under Rule 7.2 offer alternative means of conveying necessary information to those who may be in need of legal services. Advertising and written and recorded communications which may be mailed or autodialed make it possible for a prospective client to be informed about the need for legal services, and about the qualifications of available lawyers and law firms, without subjecting the prospective client to direct in-person, telephone or real-time electronic persuasion that may overwhelm the client's judgment.

[3]   The use of general advertising and written, recorded or electronic communications to transmit information from lawyer to prospective client, rather than direct in-person, live telephone or real-time electronic contact, will help to assure that the information flows cleanly as well as freely. The contents of advertisements and communications permitted under Rule 7.2 can be permanently recorded so that they cannot be disputed and may be shared with others

who know the lawyer. This potential for informal review is itself likely to help guard against statements and claims that might constitute false and misleading communications, in violation of Rule 7.1. The contents of direct in-person, live telephone or real-time electronic conversations between a lawyer and a prospective client can be disputed and may not be subject to third-party scrutiny. Consequently, they are much more likely to approach (and occasionally cross) the dividing line between accurate representations and those that are false and misleading.

[4]   There is far less likelihood that a lawyer would engage in abusive practices against an individual who is a former client, or with whom the lawyer has a close personal or family relationship, or in situations in which the lawyer is motivated by considerations other than the lawyer's pecuniary gain. Nor is there a serious potential for abuse when the person contacted is a lawyer. Consequently, the general prohibition in Rule 7.3(a) and the requirements of Rule 7.3(c) are not applicable in those situations. Also, paragraph (a) is not intended to prohibit a lawyer from participating in constitutionally protected activities of public or charitable legal-service organizations or bona fide political, social, civic, fraternal, employee or trade organizations whose purposes include providing or recommending legal services to its members or beneficiaries.

[5]   But even permitted forms of solicitation can be abused. Thus, any solicitation which contains information which is false or misleading within the meaning of Rule 7.1, which involves coercion, duress or harassment within the meaning of Rule 7.3(b)(2), or which involves contact with a prospective client who has made known to the lawyer a desire not to be solicited by the lawyer within the meaning of Rule 7.3(b)(1) is prohibited. Moreover, if after sending a letter or other communication to a client as permitted by Rule 7.2 the lawyer receives no response, any further effort to communicate with the prospective client may violate the provisions of Rule 7.3(b).

[6]   This Rule is not intended to prohibit a lawyer from contacting representatives of organizations or groups that may be interested in establishing a group or prepaid legal plan for their members, insureds, beneficiaries or other third parties for the purpose of informing such entities of the availability of and details concerning the plan or arrangement which the lawyer or lawyer's firm is willing to offer. This form of communication is not directed to a prospective client. Rather, it is usually addressed to an individual acting in a fiduciary capacity seeking a supplier of legal services for others who may, if they choose, become prospective clients of the lawyer. Under these circumstances, the activity which the lawyer undertakes in communicating with such representatives and the type of information transmitted to the individual are functionally similar to and serve the same purpose as advertising permitted under Rule 7.2.

[7]   The requirement in Rule 7.3(c) that certain communications be marked "Advertising Material" does not apply to communications sent in response to requests of potential clients or their spokespersons or sponsors. General announcements by lawyers, including changes in personnel or office location, do not constitute communications soliciting professional employment from a client known to be in need of legal services within the meaning of this Rule.

[8]   Paragraph (d) of this Rule permits a lawyer to participate with an organization which uses personal contact to solicit members for its group or prepaid legal service plan, provided that the personal contact is not undertaken by any lawyer who would be a provider of legal services through the plan. The organization must not be owned by or directed (whether as manager or otherwise) by any lawyer or law firm that participates in the plan. For example, paragraph (d) would not permit a lawyer to create an organization controlled directly or indirectly by the lawyer and use the organization for the in-person or telephone solicitation of legal employment of the lawyer through memberships in the plan or otherwise. The communication permitted by these organizations also must not be directed to a person known to need legal services in a particular matter, but is to be designed to inform potential plan members generally of another means of affordable legal services. Lawyers who participate in a legal service plan must reasonably assure that the plan sponsors are in compliance with Rules 7.1, 7.2 and 7.3(b). See 8.4(a).

RULE 7.4: COMMUNICATION OF FIELDS OF PRACTICE AND SPECIALIZATION

(a) A lawyer may communicate the fact that the lawyer does or does not practice in particular fields of law.

(b) A lawyer admitted to engage in patent practice before the United States Patent and Trademark Office may use the designation "Patent Attorney" or a substantially similar designation.

(c) A lawyer engaged in Admiralty practice may use the designation "Admiralty," "Proctor in Admiralty" or a substantially similar designation.

(d) A lawyer shall not state or imply that a lawyer is certified as a specialist in a particular field of law, unless:

(1) the lawyer has been certified as a specialist by an organization that has been approved by an appropriate state authority or that has been accredited by the American Bar Association; and

(2) the name of the certifying organization is clearly identified in the communication.

Comment

[1] Paragraph (a) of this Rule permits a lawyer to indicate areas of practice in communications about the lawyer's services. If a lawyer practices only in certain fields, or will not accept matters except in a specified field or fields, the lawyer is permitted to so indicate. A lawyer is generally permitted to state that the lawyer is a "specialist," practices a "specialty," or "specializes in" particular fields, but such communications are subject to the "false and misleading" standard applied in Rule 7.1 to communications concerning a lawyer's services.

[2] Paragraph (b) recognizes the long-established policy of the Patent and Trademark Office for the designation of lawyers practicing before the Office. Paragraph (c) recognizes that designation of Admiralty practice has a long historical tradition associated with maritime commerce and the federal courts.

[3] Paragraph (d) permits a lawyer to state that the lawyer is certified as a specialist in a field of law if such certification is granted by an organization approved by an appropriate state authority or accredited by the American Bar Association or another organization, such as a state bar association, that has been approved by the state authority to accredit organizations that certify lawyers as specialists. Certification signifies that an objective entity has recognized an advanced degree of knowledge and experience in the specialty area greater than is suggested by general licensure to practice law. Certifying organizations may be expected to apply standards of experience, knowledge and proficiency to insure that a lawyer's recognition as a specialist is meaningful and reliable. In order to insure that consumers can obtain access to useful information about an organization granting certification, the name of the certifying organization must be included in any communication regarding the certification.

RULE 7.5: FIRM NAMES AND LETTERHEADS

(a) A lawyer shall not use a firm name, letterhead or other professional designation that violates Rule 7.1. A trade name may be used by a lawyer in private practice if it does not imply a connection with a government agency or with a public or charitable legal services organization and is not otherwise in violation of Rule 7.1.

(b) A law firm with offices in more than one jurisdiction may use the same name or other professional designation in each jurisdiction, but identification of the lawyers in an office of the firm shall indicate the jurisdictional limitations on those not licensed to practice in the jurisdiction where the office is located.

(c) The name of a lawyer holding a public office shall not be used in the name of a law firm, or in communications on its behalf, during any substantial period in which the lawyer is not actively and regularly practicing with the firm.

(d) Lawyers may state or imply that they practice in a partnership or other organization only when that is the fact.

Comment

[1]   A firm may be designated by the names of all or some of its members, by the names of deceased members where there has been a continuing succession in the firm's identity or by a trade name such as the "ABC Legal Clinic." A lawyer or law firm may also be designated by a distinctive website address or comparable professional designation. Although the United States Supreme Court has held that legislation may prohibit the use of trade names in professional practice, use of such names in law practice is acceptable so long as it is not misleading. If a private firm uses a trade name that includes a geographical name such as "Springfield Legal Clinic," an express disclaimer that it is a public legal aid agency may be required to avoid a misleading implication. It may be observed that any firm name including the name of a deceased partner is, strictly speaking, a trade name. The use of such names to designate law firms has proven a useful means of identification. However, it is misleading to use the name of a lawyer not associated with the firm or a predecessor of the firm, or the name of a nonlawyer.

[2]   With regard to paragraph (d), lawyers sharing office facilities, but who are not in fact associated with each other in a law firm, may not denominate themselves as, for example, "Smith and Jones," for that title suggests that they are practicing law together in a firm.

RULE 7.6: POLITICAL CONTRIBUTIONS TO OBTAIN GOVERNMENT LEGAL EN-GAGEMENTS OR APPOINTMENTS BY JUDGES

A lawyer or law firm shall not accept a government legal engagement or an appointment by a judge if the lawyer or law firm makes a political contribution or solicits political contributions for the purpose of obtaining or being considered for that type of legal engagement or appointment.

Comment

[1]   Lawyers have a right to participate fully in the political process, which includes making and soliciting political contributions to candidates for judicial and other public office. Nevertheless, when lawyers make or solicit political contributions in order to obtain an engagement for legal work awarded by a government agency, or to obtain appointment by a judge, the public may legitimately question whether the lawyers engaged to perform the work are selected on the basis of competence and merit. In such a circumstance, the integrity of the profession is undermined.

[2]   The term "political contribution" denotes any gift, subscription, loan, advance or deposit of anything of value made directly or indirectly to a candidate, incumbent, political party or campaign committee to influence or provide financial support for election to or retention in judicial or other government office. Political contributions in initiative and referendum elections are not included. For purposes of this Rule, the term "political contribution" does not include uncompensated services.

[3]   Subject to the exceptions below, (i) the term "government legal engagement" denotes any engagement to provide legal services that a public official has the direct or indirect power to award; and (ii) the term "appointment by a judge" denotes an appointment to a position such as referee, commissioner, special master, receiver, guardian or other similar position that is made by a judge. Those terms do not, however, include (a) substantially uncompensated services; (b) engagements or appointments made on the basis of experience, expertise, professional qualifications and cost following a request for proposal or other process that is free from influence based upon political contributions; and (c) engagements or appointments made on a rotational basis from a list compiled without regard to political contributions.

[4]   The term "lawyer or law firm" includes a political action committee or other entity owned or controlled by a lawyer or law firm.

[5]   Political contributions are for the purpose of obtaining or being considered for a government legal engagement or appointment by a judge if, but for the desire to be considered for the legal engagement or appointment, the lawyer or law firm would not have made or solicited the contributions. The purpose may be determined by an examination of the circumstances in which the contributions occur. For example, one or more contributions that in the aggregate are substantial in relation to other contributions by lawyers or law firms, made for the benefit of an official in a position to influence award of a government legal engagement, and followed by an award of the legal engagement to the contributing or soliciting lawyer or the lawyer's firm would support an inference that the purpose of the contributions was to obtain the engagement, absent other factors that weigh against existence of the proscribed purpose. Those factors may include among others that the contribution or solicitation was made to further a political, social, or economic interest or because of an existing personal, family, or professional relationship with a candidate.

[6]   If a lawyer makes or solicits a political contribution under circumstances that constitute bribery or another crime, Rule 8.4(b) is implicated.

RULE 8.1: BAR ADMISSION AND DISCIPLINARY MATTERS

An applicant for admission to the bar, or a lawyer in connection with a bar admission application or in connection with a disciplinary matter, shall not:

(a) knowingly make a false statement of material fact; or

(b) fail to disclose a fact necessary to correct a misapprehension known by the person to have arisen in the matter, or knowingly fail to respond to a lawful demand for information from an admissions or disciplinary authority, except that this rule does not require disclosure of information otherwise protected by Rule 1.6.

Comment

[1]   The duty imposed by this Rule extends to persons seeking admission to the bar as well as to lawyers. Hence, if a person makes a material false statement in connection with an application for admission, it may be the basis for subsequent disciplinary action if the person is admitted, and in any event may be relevant in a subsequent admission application. The duty imposed by this Rule applies to a lawyer's own admission or discipline as well as that of others. Thus, it is a separate professional offense for a lawyer to knowingly make a misrepresentation or omission in connection with a disciplinary investigation of the lawyer's own conduct. Paragraph (b) of this Rule also requires correction of any prior misstatement in the matter that the applicant or lawyer may have made and affirmative clarification of any misunderstanding on the part of the admissions or disciplinary authority of which the person involved becomes aware.

[2]   This Rule is subject to the provisions of the fifth amendment of the United States Constitution and corresponding provisions of state constitutions. A person relying on such a provision in response to a question, however, should do so openly and not use the right of nondisclosure as a justification for failure to comply with this Rule.

[3]   A lawyer representing an applicant for admission to the bar, or representing a lawyer who is the subject of a disciplinary inquiry or proceeding, is governed by the rules applicable to the client-lawyer relationship, including Rule 1.6 and, in some cases, Rule 3.3.

RULE 8.2: JUDICIAL AND LEGAL OFFICIALS

(a) A lawyer shall not make a statement that the lawyer knows to be false or with reckless disregard as to its truth or falsity concerning the qualifications or integrity of a judge, adjudicatory officer or public legal officer, or of a candidate for election or appointment to judicial or legal office.

(b) A lawyer who is a candidate for judicial office shall comply with the applicable provisions of the Code of Judicial Conduct.

Comment

[1]   Assessments by lawyers are relied on in evaluating the professional or personal fitness of persons being considered for election or appointment to judicial office and to public legal offices, such as attorney general, prosecuting attorney and public defender. Expressing honest and candid opinions on such matters contributes to improving the administration of justice. Conversely, false statements by a lawyer can unfairly undermine public confidence in the administration of justice.

[2]   When a lawyer seeks judicial office, the lawyer should be bound by applicable limitations on political activity.

[3]   To maintain the fair and independent administration of justice, lawyers are encouraged to continue traditional efforts to defend judges and courts unjustly criticized.

RULE 8.3: REPORTING PROFESSIONAL MISCONDUCT

(a) A lawyer who knows that another lawyer has committed a violation of the Rules of Professional Conduct that raises a substantial question as to that lawyer's honesty, trustworthiness or fitness as a lawyer in other respects, shall inform the appropriate professional authority.

(b) A lawyer who knows that a judge has committed a violation of applicable rules of judicial conduct that raises a substantial question as to the judge's fitness for office shall inform the appropriate authority.

(c) This Rule does not require disclosure of information otherwise protected by Rule 1.6 or information gained by a lawyer or judge while participating in an approved lawyers assistance program.

Comment

[1]   Self-regulation of the legal profession requires that members of the profession initiate disciplinary investigation when they know of a violation of the Rules of Professional Conduct.

Lawyers have a similar obligation with respect to judicial misconduct. An apparently isolated violation may indicate a pattern of misconduct that only a disciplinary investigation can uncover. Reporting a violation is especially important where the victim is unlikely to discover the offense.

[2] A report about misconduct is not required where it would involve violation of Rule 1.6. However, a lawyer should encourage a client to consent to disclosure where prosecution would not substantially prejudice the client's interests.

[3] If a lawyer were obliged to report every violation of the Rules, the failure to report any violation would itself be a professional offense. Such a requirement existed in many jurisdictions but proved to be unenforceable. This Rule limits the reporting obligation to those offenses that a self-regulating profession must vigorously endeavor to prevent. A measure of judgment is, therefore, required in complying with the provisions of this Rule. The term "substantial" refers to the seriousness of the possible offense and not the quantum of evidence of which the lawyer is aware. A report should be made to the bar disciplinary agency unless some other agency, such as a peer review agency, is more appropriate in the circumstances. Similar considerations apply to the reporting of judicial misconduct.

[4] The duty to report professional misconduct does not apply to a lawyer retained to represent a lawyer whose professional conduct is in question. Such a situation is governed by the Rules applicable to the client-lawyer relationship.

[5] Information about a lawyer's or judge's misconduct or fitness may be received by a lawyer in the course of that lawyer's participation in an approved lawyers or judges assistance program. In that circumstance, providing for an exception to the reporting requirements of paragraphs (a) and (b) of this Rule encourages lawyers and judges to seek treatment through such a program. Conversely, without such an exception, lawyers and judges may hesitate to seek assistance from these programs, which may then result in additional harm to their professional careers and additional injury to the welfare of clients and the public. These Rules do not otherwise address the confidentiality of information received by a lawyer or judge participating in an approved lawyers assistance program; such an obligation, however, may be imposed by the rules of the program or other law.

RULE 8.4: MISCONDUCT

It is professional misconduct for a lawyer to:

(a) violate or attempt to violate the Rules of Professional Conduct, knowingly assist or induce another to do so, or do so through the acts of another;

(b) commit a criminal act that reflects adversely on the lawyer's honesty, trustworthiness or fitness as a lawyer in other respects;

(c) engage in conduct involving dishonesty, fraud, deceit or misrepresentation;

(d) engage in conduct that is prejudicial to the administration of justice;

(e) state or imply an ability to influence improperly a government agency or official or to achieve results by means that violate the Rules of Professional Conduct or other law; or

(f) knowingly assist a judge or judicial officer in conduct that is a violation of applicable rules of judicial conduct or other law.

Comment

[1] Lawyers are subject to discipline when they violate or attempt to violate the Rules of Professional Conduct, knowingly assist or induce another to do so or do so through the acts of

another, as when they request or instruct an agent to do so on the lawyer's behalf. Paragraph (a), however, does not prohibit a lawyer from advising a client concerning action the client is legally entitled to take.

[2] Many kinds of illegal conduct reflect adversely on fitness to practice law, such as offenses involving fraud and the offense of willful failure to file an income tax return. However, some kinds of offenses carry no such implication. Traditionally, the distinction was drawn in terms of offenses involving "moral turpitude." That concept can be construed to include offenses concerning some matters of personal morality, such as adultery and comparable offenses, that have no specific connection to fitness for the practice of law. Although a lawyer is personally answerable to the entire criminal law, a lawyer should be professionally answerable only for offenses that indicate lack of those characteristics relevant to law practice. Offenses involving violence, dishonesty, breach of trust, or serious interference with the administration of justice are in that category. A pattern of repeated offenses, even ones of minor significance when considered separately, can indicate indifference to legal obligation.

[3] A lawyer who, in the course of representing a client, knowingly manifests by words or conduct, bias or prejudice based upon race, sex, religion, national origin, disability, age, sexual orientation or socioeconomic status, violates paragraph (d) when such actions are prejudicial to the administration of justice. Legitimate advocacy respecting the foregoing factors does not violate paragraph (d). A trial judge's finding that peremptory challenges were exercised on a discriminatory basis does not alone establish a violation of this rule.

[4] A lawyer may refuse to comply with an obligation imposed by law upon a good faith belief that no valid obligation exists. The provisions of Rule 1.2(d) concerning a good faith challenge to the validity, scope, meaning or application of the law apply to challenges of legal regulation of the practice of law.

[5] Lawyers holding public office assume legal responsibilities going beyond those of other citizens. A lawyer's abuse of public office can suggest an inability to fulfill the professional role of lawyers. The same is true of abuse of positions of private trust such as trustee, executor, administrator, guardian, agent and officer, director or manager of a corporation or other organization.

RULE 8.5: DISCIPLINARY AUTHORITY; CHOICE OF LAW

(a) Disciplinary Authority. A lawyer admitted to practice in this jurisdiction is subject to the disciplinary authority of this jurisdiction, regardless of where the lawyer's conduct occurs. A lawyer not admitted in this jurisdiction is also subject to the disciplinary authority of this jurisdiction if the lawyer provides or offers to provide any legal services in this jurisdiction. A lawyer may be subject to the disciplinary authority of both this jurisdiction and another jurisdiction for the same conduct.

(b) Choice of Law. In any exercise of the disciplinary authority of this jurisdiction, the rules of professional conduct to be applied shall be as follows:

(1) for conduct in connection with a matter pending before a tribunal, the rules of the jurisdiction in which the tribunal sits, unless the rules of the tribunal provide otherwise; and

(2) for any other conduct, the rules of the jurisdiction in which the lawyer's conduct occurred, or, if the predominant effect of the conduct is in a different jurisdiction, the rules of that jurisdiction shall be applied to the conduct. A lawyer

shall not be subject to discipline if the lawyer's conduct conforms to the rules of a jurisdiction in which the lawyer reasonably believes the predominant effect of the lawyer's conduct will occur.

Comment

Disciplinary Authority

[1]   It is longstanding law that the conduct of a lawyer admitted to practice in this jurisdiction is subject to the disciplinary authority of this jurisdiction. Extension of the disciplinary authority of this jurisdiction to other lawyers who provide or offer to provide legal services in this jurisdiction is for the protection of the citizens of this jurisdiction. Reciprocal enforcement of a jurisdiction's disciplinary findings and sanctions will further advance the purposes of this Rule. See, Rules 6 and 22, ABA *Model Rules for Lawyer Disciplinary Enforcement.* A lawyer who is subject to the disciplinary authority of this jurisdiction under Rule 8.5(a) appoints an official to be designated by this Court to receive service of process in this jurisdiction. The fact that the lawyer is subject to the disciplinary authority of this jurisdiction may be a factor in determining whether personal jurisdiction may be asserted over the lawyer for civil matters.

Choice of Law

[2]   A lawyer may be potentially subject to more than one set of rules of professional conduct which impose different obligations. The lawyer may be licensed to practice in more than one jurisdiction with differing rules, or may be admitted to practice before a particular court with rules that differ from those of the jurisdiction or jurisdictions in which the lawyer is licensed to practice. Additionally, the lawyer's conduct may involve significant contacts with more than one jurisdiction.

[3]   Paragraph (b) seeks to resolve such potential conflicts. Its premise is that minimizing conflicts between rules, as well as uncertainty about which rules are applicable, is in the best interest of both clients and the profession (as well as the bodies having authority to regulate the profession). Accordingly, it takes the approach of (i) providing that any particular conduct of a lawyer shall be subject to only one set of rules of professional conduct, (ii) making the determination of which set of rules applies to particular conduct as straightforward as possible, consistent with recognition of appropriate regulatory interests of relevant jurisdictions, and (iii) providing protection from discipline for lawyers who act reasonably in the face of uncertainty.

[4]   Paragraph (b)(1) provides that as to a lawyer's conduct relating to a proceeding pending before a tribunal, the lawyer shall be subject only to the rules of professional conduct of that tribunal. As to all other conduct, including conduct in anticipation of a proceeding not yet pending before a tribunal, paragraph (b)(2) provides that a lawyer shall be subject to the rules of the jurisdiction in which the lawyer's conduct occurred, or, if the predominant effect of the conduct is in another jurisdiction, the rules of that jurisdiction shall be applied to the conduct. In the case of conduct in anticipation of a proceeding that is likely to be before a tribunal, the predominant effect of such conduct could be where the conduct occurred, where the tribunal sits or in another jurisdiction.

[5]   When a lawyer's conduct involves significant contacts with more than one jurisdiction, it may not be clear whether the predominant effect of the lawyer's conduct will occur in a jurisdiction other than the one in which the conduct occurred. So long as the lawyer's conduct conforms to the rules of a jurisdiction in which the lawyer reasonably believes the predominant effect will occur, the lawyer shall not be subject to discipline under this Rule.

[6]   If two admitting jurisdictions were to proceed against a lawyer for the same conduct, they should, applying this rule, identify the same governing ethics rules. They should take all

appropriate steps to see that they do apply the same rule to the same conduct, and in all events should avoid proceeding against a lawyer on the basis of two inconsistent rules.

[7] The choice of law provision applies to lawyers engaged in transnational practice, unless international law, treaties or other agreements between competent regulatory authorities in the affected jurisdictions provide otherwise.

*

APPENDIX D

ABA Model of Judicial Conduct

(1990, AS AMENDED)

[The Model Code of Judicial Conduct was adopted by the House of Delegates of the American Bar Association in August 1990. It is designed to replace the previous code, which had been adopted in 1972. It was last amended in August 2003. The Model Code of Judicial Conduct is copyrighted by the American Bar Association, and reprinted here with permission.]

PREAMBLE

[1]   Our legal system is based on the principle that an independent, fair and competent judiciary will interpret and apply the laws that govern us. The role of the judiciary is central to American concepts of justice and the rule of law. Intrinsic to all sections of this Code are the precepts that judges, individually and collectively, must respect and honor the judicial office as a public trust and strive to enhance and maintain confidence in our legal system. The judge is an arbiter of facts and law for the resolution of disputes and a highly visible symbol of government under the rule of law.

[2]   The Code of Judicial Conduct is intended to establish standards for ethical conduct of judges. It consists of broad statements called Canons, specific rules set forth in Sections under each Canon, a Terminology Section, an Application Section and Commentary. The text of the Canons and the Sections, including the Terminology and Application Sections, is authoritative. The Commentary, by explanation and example, provides guidance with respect to the purpose and meaning of the Canons and Sections. The Commentary is not intended as a statement of additional rules. When the text uses "shall" or "shall not," it is intended to impose binding obligations the violation of which can result in disciplinary action. When "should" or "should not" is used, the text is intended as hortatory and as a statement of what is or is not appropriate conduct but not as a binding rule under which a judge may be disciplined. When "may" is used, it denotes permissible discretion or, depending on the context, it refers to action that is not covered by specific proscriptions.

[3]   The Canons and Sections are rules of reason. They should be applied consistent with constitutional requirements, statutes, other court rules and decisional law and in the context of all relevant circumstances. The Code is to be construed so as not to impinge on the essential independence of judges in making judicial decisions.

[4]   The Code is designed to provide guidance to judges and candidates for judicial office and to provide a structure for regulating conduct through disciplinary agencies. It is not designed or intended as a basis for civil liability or criminal prosecution. Furthermore, the purpose of the Code would be subverted if the Code were invoked by lawyers for mere tactical advantage in a proceeding.

[5]   The text of the Canons and Sections is intended to govern conduct of judges and to be binding upon them. It is not intended, however, that every transgression will result in disciplinary action. Whether disciplinary action is appropriate, and the degree of discipline to be imposed, should be determined through a reasonable and reasoned application of the text and should depend on such factors as the seriousness of the transgression, whether there is a pattern of improper activity and the effect of the improper activity on others or on the judicial system. See ABA Standards Relating to Judicial Discipline and Disability Retirement.[1]

[6]   The Code of Judicial Conduct is not intended as an exhaustive guide for the conduct of judges. They should also be governed in their judicial and personal conduct by general ethical standards. The Code is intended, however, to state basic standards which should govern the conduct of all judges and to provide guidance to assist judges in establishing and maintaining high standards of judicial and personal conduct.

TERMINOLOGY

Terms explained below are noted with an asterisk (*) in the Sections where they appear. In addition, the Sections where terms appear are referred to after the explanation of each term below.

[1]   **"Aggregate"** in relation to contributions for a candidate under Sections 3E(1)(e) and 5C(3) and (4) denotes not only contributions in cash or in kind made directly to a candidate's committee or treasurer, but also, except in retention elections, all contributions made indirectly with the understanding that they will be used to support the election of the candidate or to oppose the election of the candidate's opponent. See Sections 3E(1)(e), 5C(3) and 5C(4).

[2]   **"Appropriate authority"** denotes the authority with responsibility for initiation of disciplinary process with respect to the violation to be reported. See Sections 3D(1) and 3D(2).

[3]   **"Candidate."** A candidate is a person seeking selection for or retention in judicial office by election or appointment. A person becomes a candidate for judicial office as soon as he or she makes a public announcement of candidacy, declares or files as a candidate with the election or appointment authority, or authorizes solicitation or acceptance of contributions or support. The term "candidate" has the same meaning when applied to a judge seeking election or appointment to nonjudicial office. See Preamble and Sections 5A, 5B, 5C and 5E.

[4]   **"Continuing part-time judge."** A continuing part-time judge is a judge who serves repeatedly on a part-time basis by election or under a continuing appointment, including a retired judge subject to recall who is permitted to practice law. See Application Section C.

---

1.   Judicial disciplinary procedures adopted in the jurisdictions should comport with the requirements of due process. The ABA Standards Relating to Judicial Discipline and Disability Retirement are cited as an example of how these due process requirements may be satisfied.

[5] **"Court personnel"** does not include the lawyers in a proceeding before a judge. See Sections 3B(7)(c) and 3B(9).

[6] **"De minimis"**† denotes an insignificant interest that could not raise reasonable question as to a judge's impartiality. See Sections 3E(1)(c) and 3E(1)(d).

[7] **"Economic interest"**[>] denotes ownership of a more than de minimis legal or equitable interest, or a relationship as officer, director, advisor or other active participant in the affairs of a party, except that:

(i) ownership of an interest in a mutual or common investment fund that holds securities is not an economic interest in such securities unless the judge participates in the management of the fund or a proceeding pending or impending before the judge could substantially affect the value of the interest;

(ii) service by a judge as an officer, director, advisor or other active participant in an educational, religious, charitable, fraternal or civic organization, or service by a judge's spouse, parent or child as an officer, director, advisor or other active participant in any organization does not create an economic interest in securities held by that organization;

(iii) a deposit in a financial institution, the proprietary interest of a policy holder in a mutual insurance company, of a depositor in a mutual savings association or of a member in a credit union, or a similar proprietary interest, is not an economic interest in the organization unless a proceeding pending or impending before the judge could substantially affect the value of the interest;

(iv) ownership of government securities is not an economic interest in the issuer unless a proceeding pending or impending before the judge could substantially affect the value of the securities. See Sections 3E(1)(c) and 3E(2).

[8] **"Fiduciary"** includes such relationships as executor, administrator, trustee, and guardian. See Sections 3E(2) and 4E.

[9] **"Impartiality"** or "impartial" denoted absence of bias or prejudice in favor of, or against particular parties or classes of parties, as well as maintaining an open mind in considering issues that may come before the judge. See Sections 2A, 3B(10), 3E(1), 5A(3)(a) and 5A(3)(d)(l).

† **Editors' note:** In contrast, Canon 3C(3)(c) of the ABA Model Code of Judicial Conduct (1972, as amended) defined "financial interest" very differently; there was no such thing as a "de minimis" legal or equitable interest. It provided:

(c) "financial interest" means ownership of a legal or equitable interest, however small, or a relationship as director, advisor, or other active participant in the affairs of a party, except that:

(i) ownership in a mutual or common investment fund that holds securities is not a "financial interest" in such securities unless the judge participates in the management of the fund;

(ii) an office in an educational, religious, charitable, fraternal, or civic organization is not a "financial interest" in securities held by the organization;

(iii) the proprietary interest of a policy holder in a mutual insurance company, of a depositor in a mutual savings association, or a similar proprietary interest, is a "financial interest" in the organization only if the outcome of the proceeding could substantially affect the value of the interest;

(iv) ownership of government securities is a "financial interest" in the issuer only if the outcome of the proceeding could substantially affect the value of the securities.

[10] **"Knowingly,"** "knowledge," "known" or "knows" denotes actual knowledge of the fact in question. A person's knowledge may be inferred from circumstances. See Sections 3D, 3E(1), and 5A(3).

[11] **"Law"** denotes court rules as well as statutes, constitutional provisions and decisional law. See Sections 2A, 3A, 3B(2), 3B(6), 4B, 4C, 4D(5), 4F, 4I, 5A(2), 5A(3), 5B(2), 5C(1), 5C(3) and 5D.

[12] **"Member of the candidate's family"** denotes a spouse, child, grandchild, parent, grandparent or other relative or person with whom the candidate maintains a close familial relationship. See Section 5A(3)(a).

[13] **"Member of the judge's family"** denotes a spouse, child, grandchild, parent, grandparent, or other relative or person with whom the judge maintains a close familial relationship. See Sections 4D(3), 4E and 4G.

[14] **"Member of the judge's family residing in the judge's household"** denotes any relative of a judge by blood or marriage, or a person treated by a judge as a member of the judge's family, who resides in the judge's household. See Sections 3E(1) and 4D(5).

[15] **"Nonpublic information"** denotes information that, by law, is not available to the public. Nonpublic information may include but is not limited to: information that is sealed by statute or court order, impounded or communicated in camera; and information offered in grand jury proceedings, presentencing reports, dependency cases or psychiatric reports. See Section 3B(11).

[16] **"Periodic part-time judge."** A periodic part-time judge is a judge who serves or expects to serve repeatedly on a part-time basis but under a separate appointment for each limited period of service or for each matter. See Application Section D.

[17] **"Political organization"** denotes a political party or other group, the principal purpose of which is to further the election or appointment of candidates to political office. See Sections 5A(1), 5B(2) and 5C(1).

[18] **"Pro tempore part-time judge."** A pro tempore part-time judge is a judge who serves or expects to serve once or only sporadically on a part-time basis under a separate appointment for each period of service or for each case heard. See Application Section E.

[19] **"Public election."** This term includes primary and general elections; it includes partisan elections, nonpartisan elections and retention elections. See Section 5C.

[20] **"Require."** The rules prescribing that a judge "require" certain conduct of others are, like all of the rules in this Code, rules of reason. The use of the term "require" in that context means a judge is to exercise reasonable direction and control over the conduct of those persons subject to the judge's direction and control. See Sections 3B(3), 3B(4), 3B(5), 3B(6), 3B(9) and 3C(2).

[21] **"Third degree of relationship."** The following persons are relatives within the third degree of relationship: great-grandparent, grandparent, parent, uncle, aunt, brother, sister, child, grandchild, great-grandchild, nephew or niece. See Section 3E(1)(d).

CANON 1

A Judge Shall Uphold the Integrity and Independence of the Judiciary

A. An independent and honorable judiciary is indispensable to justice in our society. A judge should participate in establishing, maintaining and enforcing high

standards of conduct, and shall personally observe those standards so that the integrity and independence of the judiciary will be preserved. The provisions of this Code are to be construed and applied to further that objective.

Commentary:

[1]   Deference to the judgments and rulings of courts depends upon public confidence in the integrity and independence of judges. The integrity and independence of judges depends in turn upon their acting without fear or favor. A judiciary of integrity is one in which judges are known for their probity, fairness, honesty, uprightness, and soundness of character. An independent judiciary is one free of inappropriate outside influences. Although judges should be independent, they must comply with the law, including the provisions of this Code. Public confidence in the impartiality of the judiciary is maintained by the adherence of each judge to this responsibility. Conversely, violation of this Code diminishes public confidence in the judiciary and thereby does injury to the system of government under law.

CANON 2

A Judge Shall Avoid Impropriety and the Appearance of Impropriety in all of the Judge's Activities

A.   A judge shall respect and comply with the law* and shall act at all times in a manner that promotes public confidence in the integrity and impartiality of the judiciary.

Commentary:

[1]   Public confidence in the judiciary is eroded by irresponsible or improper conduct by judges. A judge must avoid all impropriety and appearance of impropriety. A judge must expect to be the subject of constant public scrutiny. A judge must therefore accept restrictions on the judge's conduct that might be viewed as burdensome by the ordinary citizen and should do so freely and willingly. Examples of the restrictions on judicial speech imposed by Sections 3(B)(9) and (10) that are indispensable to the maintenance of the integrity, impartiality, and independence of the judiciary.

[2]   The prohibition against behaving with impropriety or the appearance of impropriety applies to both the professional and personal conduct of a judge. Because it is not practicable to list all prohibited acts, the proscription is necessarily cast in general terms that extend to conduct by judges that is harmful although not specifically mentioned in the Code. Actual improprieties under this standard include violations of law, court rules or other specific provisions of this Code. The test for appearance of impropriety is whether the conduct would create in reasonable minds a perception that the judge's ability to carry out judicial responsibilities with integrity, impartiality and competence is impaired.

[3]   See also Commentary under Section 2C.

B.   A judge shall not allow family, social, political or other relationships to influence the judge's judicial conduct or judgment. A judge shall not lend the prestige of judicial office to advance the private interests of the judge or others; nor shall a judge convey or permit others to convey the impression that they are in a special position to influence the judge. A judge shall not testify voluntarily as a character witness.

Commentary:

[1]   Maintaining the prestige of judicial office is essential to a system of government in which the judiciary functions independently of the executive and legislative branches. Respect

---

* See, Terminology.

for the judicial office facilitates the orderly conduct of legitimate judicial functions. Judges should distinguish between proper and improper use of the prestige of office in all of their activities. For example, it would be improper for a judge to allude to his or her judgeship to gain a personal advantage such as deferential treatment when stopped by a police officer for a traffic offense. Similarly, judicial letterhead must not be used for conducting a judge's personal business.

[2]   A judge must avoid lending the prestige of judicial office for the advancement of the private interests of others. For example, a judge must not use the judge's judicial position to gain advantage in a civil suit involving a member of the judge's family. In contracts for publication of a judge's writings, a judge should retain control over the advertising to avoid exploitation of the judge's office. As to the acceptance of awards, see Section 4D(5)(a) and Commentary.

[3]   Although a judge should be sensitive to possible abuse of the prestige of office, a judge may, based on the judge's personal knowledge, serve as a reference or provide a letter of recommendation. However, a judge must not initiate the communication of information to a sentencing judge or a probation or corrections officer but may provide to such persons information for the record in response to a formal request.

[4]   Judges may participate in the process of judicial selection by cooperating with appointing authorities and screening committees seeking names for consideration, and by responding to official inquiries concerning a person being considered for a judgeship. See also Canon 5 regarding use of a judge's name in political activities.

[5]   A judge must not testify voluntarily as a character witness because to do so may lend the prestige of the judicial office in support of the party for whom the judge testifies. Moreover, when a judge testifies as a witness, a lawyer who regularly appears before the judge may be placed in the awkward position of cross-examining the judge. A judge may, however, testify when properly summoned. Except in unusual circumstances where the demands of justice require, a judge should discourage a party from requiring the judge to testify as a character witness.

C.   A judge shall not hold membership in any organization that practices invidious discrimination on the basis of race, sex, religion or national origin.

Commentary:

[1]   Membership of a judge in an organization that practices invidious discrimination gives rise to perceptions that the judge's impartiality is impaired. Section 2C refers to the current practices of the organization. Whether an organization practices invidious discrimination is often a complex question to which judges should be sensitive. The answer cannot be determined from a mere examination of an organization's current membership rolls but rather depends on how the organization selects members and other relevant factors, such as that the organization is dedicated to the preservation of religious, ethnic or cultural values of legitimate common interest to its members, or that it is in fact and effect an intimate, purely private organization whose membership limitations could not be constitutionally prohibited. Absent such factors, an organization is generally said to discriminate invidiously if it arbitrarily excludes from membership on the basis of race, religion, sex or national origin persons who would otherwise be admitted to membership. *See New York State Club Ass'n. Inc. v. City of New York,* 108 S.Ct. 2225, 101 L.Ed.2d 1 (1988); *Board of Directors of Rotary International v. Rotary Club of Duarte,* 481 U.S. 537, 107 S.Ct. 1940 (1987), 95 L.Ed.2d 474; *Roberts v. United States Jaycees,* 468 U.S. 609, 104 S.Ct. 3244, 82 L.Ed.2d 462 (1984).

[2]   Although Section 2C relates only to membership in organizations that invidiously discriminate on the basis of race, sex, religion or national origin, a judge's membership in an

organization that engages in any discriminatory membership practices prohibited by the law of the jurisdiction also violates Canon 2 and Section 2A and gives the appearance of impropriety. In addition, it would be a violation of Canon 2 and Section 2A for a judge to arrange a meeting at a club that the judge knows practices invidious discrimination on the basis of race, sex, religion or national origin in its membership or other policies, or for the judge to regularly use such a club. Moreover, public manifestation by a judge of the judge's knowing approval of invidious discrimination on any basis gives the appearance of impropriety under Canon 2 and diminishes public confidence in the integrity and impartiality of the judiciary, in violation of Section 2A.

[3] When a person who is a judge on the date this Code becomes effective [in the jurisdiction in which the person is a judge][2] learns that an organization to which the judge belongs engages in invidious discrimination that would preclude membership under Section 2C or under Canon 2 and Section 2A, the judge is permitted, in lieu of resigning, to make immediate efforts to have the organization discontinue its invidiously discriminatory practices, but is required to suspend participation in any other activities of the organization. If the organization fails to discontinue its invidiously discriminatory practices as promptly as possible (and in all events within a year of the judge's first learning of the practices), the judge is required to resign immediately from the organization.

CANON 3

A Judge Shall Perform the Duties of Judicial Office Impartially and Diligently

A. JUDICIAL DUTIES IN GENERAL. The judicial duties of a judge take precedence over all the judge's other activities. The judge's judicial duties include all the duties of the judge's office prescribed by law*. In the performance of these duties, the following standards apply.

B. ADJUDICATIVE RESPONSIBILITIES.

(1) A judge shall hear and decide matters assigned to the judge except those in which disqualification is required.

(2) A judge shall be faithful to the law * and maintain professional competence in it. A judge shall not be swayed by partisan interests, public clamor or fear of criticism.

(3) A judge shall require * order and decorum in proceedings before the judge.

(4) A judge shall be patient, dignified and courteous to litigants, jurors, witnesses, lawyers and others with whom the judge deals in an official capacity, and shall require * similar conduct of lawyers, and of staff, court officials and others subject to the judge's direction and control.

Commentary:

[1] The duty to hear all proceedings fairly and with patience is not inconsistent with the duty to dispose promptly of the business of the court. Judges can be efficient and businesslike while being patient and deliberate.

2. The language within the brackets should be deleted when the jurisdiction adopts this provision.

* See, Terminology.

(5) A judge shall perform judicial duties without bias or prejudice. A judge shall not, in the performance of judicial duties, by words or conduct manifest bias or prejudice, including but not limited to bias or prejudice based upon race, sex, religion, national origin, disability, age, sexual orientation or socioeconomic status, and shall not permit staff, court officials and others subject to the judge's direction and control to do so.

Commentary:

[1]   A judge must refrain from speech, gestures or other conduct that could reasonably be perceived as sexual harassment and must require the same standard of conduct of others subject to the judge's direction and control.

[2]   A judge must perform judicial duties impartially and fairly. A judge who manifests bias on any basis in a proceeding impairs the fairness of the proceeding and brings the judiciary into disrepute. Facial expression and body language, in addition to oral communication, can give to parties or lawyers in the proceeding, jurors, the media and others an appearance of judicial bias. A judge must be alert to avoid behavior that may be perceived as prejudicial.

(6) A judge shall require* lawyers in proceedings before the judge to refrain from manifesting, by words or conduct, bias or prejudice based upon race, sex, religion, national origin, disability, age, sexual orientation or socioeconomic status, against parties, witnesses, counsel or others. This Section 3B(6) does not preclude legitimate advocacy when race, sex, religion, national origin, disability, age, sexual orientation or socioeconomic status, or other similar factors, are issues in the proceeding.

(7) A judge shall accord to every person who has a legal interest in a proceeding, or that person's lawyer, the right to be heard according to law*. A judge shall not initiate, permit, or consider ex parte communications, or consider other communications made to the judge outside the presence of the parties concerning a pending or impending proceeding except that:

(a) Where circumstances require, ex parte communications for scheduling, administrative purposes or emergencies that do not deal with substantive matters or issues on the merits are authorized; provided:

(i) the judge reasonably believes that no party will gain a procedural or tactical advantage as a result of the ex parte communication, and

(ii) the judge makes provision promptly to notify all other parties of the substance of the ex parte communication and allows an opportunity to respond.

(b) A judge may obtain the advice of a disinterested expert on the law* applicable to a proceeding before the judge if the judge gives notice to the parties of the person consulted and the substance of the advice, and affords the parties reasonable opportunity to respond.

(c) A judge may consult with court personnel * whose function is to aid the judge in carrying out the judge's adjudicative responsibilities or with other judges.

* See, Terminology.

(d) A judge may, with the consent of the parties, confer separately with the parties and their lawyers in an effort to mediate or settle matters pending before the judge.

(e) A judge may initiate or consider any ex parte communications when expressly authorized by law* to do so.

Commentary:

[1]   The proscription against communications concerning a proceeding includes communications from lawyers, law teachers, and other persons who are not participants in the proceeding, except to the limited extent permitted.

[2]   To the extent reasonably possible, all parties or their lawyers shall be included in communications with a judge.

[3]   Whenever presence of a party or notice to a party is required by Section 3B(7), it is the party's lawyer, or if the party is unrepresented the party, who is to be present or to whom notice is to be given.

[4]   An appropriate and often desirable procedure for a court to obtain the advice of a disinterested expert on legal issues is to invite the expert to file a brief *amicus curiae*.

[5]   Certain ex parte communication is approved by Section 3B(7) to facilitate scheduling and other administrative purposes and to accommodate emergencies. In general, however, a judge must discourage ex parte communication and allow it only if all the criteria stated in Section 3B(7) are clearly met. A judge must disclose to all parties all ex parte communications described in Sections 3B(7)(a) and 3B(7)(b) regarding a proceeding pending or impending before the judge.

[6]   A judge must not independently investigate facts in a case and must consider only the evidence presented.

[7]   A judge may request a party to submit proposed findings of fact and conclusions of law, so long as the other parties are apprised of the request and are given an opportunity to respond to the proposed findings and conclusions.

[8]   A judge must make reasonable efforts, including the provision of appropriate supervision, to ensure that Section 3B(7) is not violated through law clerks or other personnel on the judge's staff.

[9]   If communication between the trial judge and the appellate court with respect to a proceeding is permitted, a copy of any written communication or the substance of any oral communication should be provided to all parties.

(8) A judge shall dispose of all judicial matters promptly, efficiently and fairly.

Commentary:

[1]   In disposing of matters promptly, efficiently and fairly, a judge must demonstrate due regard for the rights of the parties to be heard and to have issues resolved without unnecessary

* See, Terminology.

cost or delay. Containing costs while preserving fundamental rights of parties also protects the interests of witnesses and the general public. A judge should monitor and supervise cases so as to reduce or eliminate dilatory practices, avoidable delays and unnecessary costs. A judge should encourage and seek to facilitate settlement, but parties should not feel coerced into surrendering the right to have their controversy resolved by the courts.

[2]   Prompt disposition of the court's business requires a judge to devote adequate time to judicial duties, to be punctual in attending court and expeditious in determining matters under submission, and to insist that court officials, litigants and their lawyers cooperate with the judge to that end.

(9) A judge shall not, while a proceeding is pending or impending in any court, make any public comment that might reasonably be expected to affect its outcome or impair its fairness or make any nonpublic comment that might substantially interfere with a fair trial or hearing. The judge shall require* similar abstention on the part of court personnel * subject to the judge's direction and control. This Section does not prohibit judges from making public statements in the course of their official duties or from explaining for public information the procedures of the court. This Section does not apply to proceedings in which the judge is a litigant in a personal capacity.

(10) A judge shall not, with respect to cases, controversies or issues that are likely to come before the court, make pledges, promises or commitments that are inconsistent with the impartial* performance of the adjudicative duties of the office.

Commentary:

[1]   Sections 3(b)(9) and (10) restrictions on judicial speech are essential to the maintenance of the integrity, impartiality, and independence of the judiciary. A pending proceeding is one that has begun but not yet reached final disposition. An impending proceeding is one that is anticipated but not yet begun. The requirement that judges abstain from public comment regarding a pending or impending proceeding continues during any appellate process and until final disposition. Sections 3B(9) and (10) do not prohibit a judge from commenting on proceedings in which the judge is a litigant in a personal capacity, but in cases such as a writ of mandamus where the judge is a litigant in an official capacity, the judge must not comment publicly. The conduct of lawyers relating to trial publicity is governed by [Rule 3.6 of the ABA Model Rules of Professional Conduct]. (Each jurisdiction should substitute an appropriate reference to its rule.)

(11) A judge shall not commend or criticize jurors for their verdict other than in a court order or opinion in a proceeding, but may express appreciation to jurors for their service to the judicial system and the community.

Commentary:

[1]   Commending or criticizing jurors for their verdict may imply a judicial expectation in future cases and may impair a juror's ability to be fair and impartial in a subsequent case.

(12) A judge shall not disclose or use, for any purpose unrelated to judicial duties, nonpublic information* acquired in a judicial capacity.

* See, Terminology.

C. ADMINISTRATIVE RESPONSIBILITIES.

(1) A judge shall diligently discharge the judge's administrative responsibilities without bias or prejudice and maintain professional competence in judicial administration, and should cooperate with other judges and court officials in the administration of court business.

(2) A judge shall require * staff, court officials and others subject to the judge's direction and control to observe the standards of fidelity and diligence that apply to the judge and to refrain from manifesting bias or prejudice in the performance of their official duties.

(3) A judge with supervisory authority for the judicial performance of other judges shall take reasonable measures to assure the prompt disposition of matters before them and the proper performance of their other judicial responsibilities.

(4) A judge shall not make unnecessary appointments. A judge shall exercise the power of appointment impartially and on the basis of merit. A judge shall avoid nepotism and favoritism. A judge shall not approve compensation of appointees beyond the fair value of services rendered.

Commentary:

[1] Appointees of a judge include assigned counsel, officials such as referees, commissioners, special masters, receivers and guardians and personnel such as clerks, secretaries and bailiffs. Consent by the parties to an appointment or an award of compensation does not relieve the judge of the obligation prescribed by Section 3C(4).

(5) A judge shall not appoint a lawyer to a position if the judge either knows that the lawyer has contributed more than [$] within the prior [ ] years to the judge's election campaign,[3] or learns of such a contribution by means of a timely motion by a party or other person properly interested in the matter, unless

(a) the position is substantially uncompensated;

(b) the lawyer has been selected in rotation from a list of qualified and available lawyers compiled without regard to their having made political contributions; or

(c) the judge or another presiding or administrative judge affirmatively finds that no other lawyer is willing, competent and able to accept the position.

D. DISCIPLINARY RESPONSIBILITIES.

(1) A judge who receives information indicating a substantial likelihood that another judge has committed a violation of this Code should take appropriate

3. This provision is meant to be applicable wherever judges are subject to public election; specific amount and time limitations, to be determined based on circumstances within the jurisdiction, should be inserted in the brackets.

action. A judge having knowledge* that another judge has committed a violation of this Code that raises a substantial question as to the other judge's fitness for office shall inform the appropriate authority *.

(2) A judge who receives information indicating a substantial likelihood that a lawyer has committed a violation of the Rules of Professional Conduct [substitute correct title if the applicable rules of lawyer conduct have a different title] should take appropriate action. A judge having knowledge * that a lawyer has committed a violation of the Rules of Professional Conduct [substitute correct title if the applicable rules of lawyer conduct have a different title] that raises a substantial question as to the lawyer's honesty, trustworthiness or fitness as a lawyer in other respects shall inform the appropriate authority *.

(3) Acts of a judge, in the discharge of disciplinary responsibilities, required or permitted by Sections 3D(1) and 3D(2) are part of a judge's judicial duties and shall be absolutely privileged, and no civil action predicated thereon may be instituted against the judge.

Commentary:

[1]   Appropriate action may include direct communication with the judge or lawyer who has committed the violation, other direct action if available, and reporting the violation to the appropriate authority or other agency or body.

E.   DISQUALIFICATION.

(1) A judge shall disqualify himself or herself in a proceeding in which the judge's impartiality* might reasonably be questioned, including but not limited to instances where:

Commentary:

[1]   Under this rule, a judge is disqualified whenever the judge's impartiality might reasonably be questioned, regardless whether any of the specific rules in Section 3E(1) apply. For example, if a judge were in the process of negotiating for employment with a law firm, the judge would be disqualified from any matters in which that law firm appeared, unless the disqualification was waived by the parties after disclosure by the judge.

[2]   A judge should disclose on the record information that the judge believes the parties or their lawyers might consider relevant to the question of disqualification, even if the judge believes there is no real basis for disqualification.

[3]   By decisional law, the rule of necessity may override the rule of disqualification. For example, a judge might be required to participate in judicial review of a judicial salary statute, or might be the only judge available in a matter requiring immediate judicial action, such as a hearing on probable cause or a temporary restraining order. In the latter case, the judge must disclose on the record the basis for possible disqualification and use reasonable efforts to transfer the matter to another judge as soon as practicable.

(a) the judge has a personal bias or prejudice concerning a party or a party's lawyer, or personal knowledge* of disputed evidentiary facts concerning the proceeding;

(b) the judge served as a lawyer in the matter in controversy, or a lawyer with whom the judge previously practiced law served during such association as a lawyer concerning the matter, or the judge has been a material witness concerning it;

Commentary:

[1]   A lawyer in a government agency does not ordinarily have an association with other lawyers employed by that agency within the meaning of Section 3E(1)(b); a judge formerly employed by a government agency, however, should disqualify himself or herself in a proceeding if the judge's impartiality might reasonably be questioned because of such association.

(c) the judge knows * that he or she, individually or as a fiduciary, or the judge's spouse, parent or child wherever residing, or any other member of the judge's family residing in the judge's household *, has an economic interest * in the subject matter in controversy or in a party to the proceeding or has any other more than de minimis * interest that could be substantially affected by the proceeding;

(d) the judge or the judge's spouse, or a person within the third degree of relationship * to either of them, or the spouse of such a person:

(i) is a party to the proceeding, or an officer, director or trustee of a party;

(ii) is acting as a lawyer in the proceeding;

(iii) is known * by the judge to have a more than de minimis * interest that could be substantially affected by the proceeding;

(iv) is to the judge's knowledge * likely to be a material witness in the proceeding.

(e) the judge knows or learns by means of a timely motion that a party or a party's lawyer has within the previous [ ] year[s] made aggregate* contributions to the judge's campaign in an amount that is greater than [[[$] for an individual or [$] for an entity]] [[is reasonable and appropriate for an individual or an entity]].[4]

(f) the judge, while a judge or a candidate * for judicial office, has made a public statement that commits, or appears to commit, the judge with respect to

---

4. This provision is meant to be applicable wherever judges are subject to public election. Jurisdictions that adopt specific dollar limits on contributions in section 5(C)(3) should adopt the same limits in section 3(E)(1)(e). Where specific dollar amounts determined by local circumstances are not used, the "reasonable and appropriate" language should be used.

* See, Terminology.

(i) an issue in the proceeding; or

(ii) the controversy in the proceeding.

Commentary:

The fact that a lawyer in a proceeding is affiliated with a law firm with which a relative of the judge is affiliated does not of itself disqualify the judge. Under appropriate circumstances, the fact that "the judge's impartiality might reasonably be questioned" under Section 3E(1), or that the relative is known by the judge to have an interest in the law firm that could be "substantially affected by the outcome of the proceeding" under Section 3E(1)(d)(iii) may require the judge's disqualification.

(2) A judge shall keep informed about the judge's personal and fiduciary* economic interests *, and make a reasonable effort to keep informed about the personal economic interests of the judge's spouse and minor children residing in the judge's household.

F. REMITTAL OF DISQUALIFICATION. A judge disqualified by the terms of Section 3E may disclose on the record the basis of the judge's disqualification and may ask the parties and their lawyers to consider, out of the presence of the judge, whether to waive disqualification. If following disclosure of any basis for disqualification other than personal bias or prejudice concerning a party, the parties and lawyers, without participation by the judge, all agree that the judge should not be disqualified, and the judge is then willing to participate, the judge may participate in the proceeding. The agreement shall be incorporated in the record of the proceeding.

Commentary:

A remittal procedure provides the parties an opportunity to proceed without delay if they wish to waive the disqualification. To assure that consideration of the question of remittal is made independently of the judge, a judge must not solicit, seek or hear comment on possible remittal or waiver of the disqualification unless the lawyers jointly propose remittal after consultation as provided in the rule. A party may act through counsel if counsel represents on the record that the party has been consulted and consents. As a practical matter, a judge may wish to have all parties and their lawyers sign the remittal agreement.

CANON 4

A Judge Shall So Conduct the Judge's Extra–Judicial Activities as to Minimize the Risk of Conflict With Judicial Obligations

A. EXTRA–JUDICIAL ACTIVITIES IN GENERAL. A judge shall conduct all of the judge's extra-judicial activities so that they do not:

(1) cast reasonable doubt on the judge's capacity to act impartially as a judge;

(2) demean the judicial office; or

(3) interfere with the proper performance of judicial duties.

Commentary:

[1] Complete separation of a judge from extra-judicial activities is neither possible nor wise; a judge should not become isolated from the community in which the judge lives.

_____

* See, Terminology.

[2] Expressions of bias or prejudice by a judge, even outside the judge's judicial activities, may cast reasonable doubt on the judge's capacity to act impartially as a judge. Expressions which may do so include jokes or other remarks demeaning individuals on the basis of their race, sex, religion, national origin, disability, age, sexual orientation or socioeconomic status. See Section 2C and accompanying Commentary.

B. AVOCATIONAL ACTIVITIES. A judge may speak, write, lecture, teach and participate in other extra-judicial activities concerning the law*, the legal system, the administration of justice and non-legal subjects, subject to the requirements of this Code.

Commentary:

[1] As a judicial officer and person specially learned in the law, a judge is in a unique position to contribute to the improvement of the law, the legal system, and the administration of justice, including revision of substantive and procedural law and improvement of criminal and juvenile justice. To the extent that time permits, a judge is encouraged to do so, either independently or through a bar association, judicial conference or other organization dedicated to the improvement of the law. Judges may participate in efforts to promote the fair administration of justice, the independence of the judiciary and the integrity of the legal profession and may express opposition to the persecution of lawyers and judges in other countries because of their professional activities.

[2] In this and other Sections of Canon 4, the phrase "subject to the requirements of this Code" is used, notably in connection with a judge's governmental, civic or charitable activities. This phrase is included to remind judges that the use of permissive language in various Sections of the Code does not relieve a judge from the other requirements of the Code that apply to the specific conduct.

C. GOVERNMENTAL, CIVIC OR CHARITABLE ACTIVITIES.

(1) A judge shall not appear at a public hearing before, or otherwise consult with, an executive or legislative body or official except on matters concerning the law*, the legal system or the administration of justice or except when acting pro se in a matter involving the judge or the judge's interests.

Commentary:

See Section 2B regarding the obligation to avoid improper influence.

(2) A judge shall not accept appointment to a governmental committee or commission or other governmental position that is concerned with issues of fact or policy on matters other than the improvement of the law*, the legal system or the administration of justice. A judge may, however, represent a country, state or locality on ceremonial occasions or in connection with historical, educational or cultural activities.

Commentary:

[1] Section 4C(2) prohibits a judge from accepting any governmental position except one relating to the law, legal system or administration of justice as authorized by Section 4C(3). The

* See, Terminology.

appropriateness of accepting extra-judicial assignments must be assessed in light of the demands on judicial resources created by crowded dockets and the need to protect the courts from involvement in extra-judicial matters that may prove to be controversial. Judges should not accept governmental appointments that are likely to interfere with the effectiveness and independence of the judiciary.

[2]   Section 4C(2) does not govern a judge's service in a nongovernmental position. See Section 4C(3) permitting service by a judge with organizations devoted to the improvement of the law, the legal system or the administration of justice and with educational, religious, charitable, fraternal or civic organizations not conducted for profit. For example, service on the board of a public educational institution, unless it were a law school, would be prohibited under Section 4C(2), but service on the board of a public law school or any private educational institution would generally be permitted under Section 4C(3).

(3) A judge may serve as an officer, director, trustee or non-legal advisor of an organization or governmental agency devoted to the improvement of the law*, the legal system or the administration of justice or of an educational, religious, charitable, fraternal or civic organization not conducted for profit, subject to the following limitations and the other requirements of this Code.

Commentary:

[1]   Section 4C(3) does not apply to a judge's service in a governmental position unconnected with the improvement of the law, the legal system or the administration of justice; see Section 4C(2).

[2]   See Commentary to Section 4B regarding use of the phrase "subject to the following limitations and the other requirements of this Code." As an example of the meaning of the phrase, a judge permitted by Section 4C(3) to serve on the board of a fraternal institution may be prohibited from such service by Sections 2C or 4A if the institution practices invidious discrimination or if service on the board otherwise casts reasonable doubt on the judge's capacity to act impartially as a judge.

[3]   Service by a judge on behalf of a civic or charitable organization may be governed by other provisions of Canon 4 in addition to Section 4C. For example, a judge is prohibited by Section 4G from serving as a legal advisor to a civic or charitable organization.

(a) A judge shall not serve as an officer, director, trustee or non-legal advisor if it is likely that the organization

(i) will be engaged in proceedings that would ordinarily come before the judge, or

(ii) will be engaged frequently in adversary proceedings in the court of which the judge is a member or in any court subject to the appellate jurisdiction of the court of which the judge is a member.

Commentary:

[1]   The changing nature of some organizations and of their relationship to the law makes it necessary for a judge regularly to reexamine the activities of each organization with which the

---

* See, Terminology.

judge is affiliated to determine if it is proper for the judge to continue the affiliation. For example, in many jurisdictions charitable hospitals are now more frequently in court than in the past. Similarly, the boards of some legal aid organizations now make policy decisions that may have political significance or imply commitment to causes that may come before the courts for adjudication.

(b) A judge as an officer, director, trustee or non-legal advisor, or as a member or otherwise:

(i) may assist such an organization in planning fund-raising and may participate in the management and investment of the organization's funds, but shall not personally participate in the solicitation of funds or other fund-raising activities, except that a judge may solicit funds from other judges over whom the judge does not exercise supervisory or appellate authority;

(ii) may make recommendations to public and private fund-granting organizations on projects and programs concerning the law*, the legal system or the administration of justice;

(iii) shall not personally participate in membership solicitation if the solicitation might reasonably be perceived as coercive or, except as permitted in Section 4C(3)(b)(i), if the membership solicitation is essentially a fund-raising mechanism;

(iv) shall not use or permit the use of the prestige of judicial office for fund-raising or membership solicitation.

Commentary:

[1] A judge may solicit membership or endorse or encourage membership efforts for an organization devoted to the improvement of the law, the legal system or the administration of justice or a nonprofit educational, religious, charitable, fraternal or civic organization as long as the solicitation cannot reasonably be perceived as coercive and is not essentially a fund-raising mechanism. Solicitation of funds for an organization and solicitation of memberships similarly involve the danger that the person solicited will feel obligated to respond favorably to the solicitor if the solicitor is in a position of influence or control. A judge must not engage in direct, individual solicitation of funds or memberships in person, in writing or by telephone except in the following cases: 1) a judge may solicit for funds or memberships other judges over whom the judge does not exercise supervisory or appellate authority, 2) a judge may solicit other persons for membership in the organizations described above if neither those persons nor persons with whom they are affiliated are likely ever to appear before the court on which the judge serves and 3) a judge who is an officer of such an organization may send a general membership solicitation mailing over the judge's signature.

[2] Use of an organization letterhead for fund-raising or membership solicitation does not violate Section 4C(3)(b) provided the letterhead lists only the judge's name and office or other position in the organization, and, if comparable designations are listed for other persons, the judge's judicial designation. In addition, a judge must also make reasonable efforts to ensure that the judge's staff, court officials and others subject to the judge's direction and control do not solicit funds on the judge's behalf for any purpose, charitable or otherwise.

* See, Terminology.

[3]   A judge must not be a speaker or guest of honor at an organization's fund-raising event, but mere attendance at such an event is permissible if otherwise consistent with this Code.

D. FINANCIAL ACTIVITIES.

(1) A judge shall not engage in financial and business dealings that:

(a) may reasonably be perceived to exploit the judge's judicial position, or

(b) involve the judge in frequent transactions or continuing business relationships with those lawyers or other persons likely to come before the court on which the judge serves.

Commentary:

[1]   The Time for Compliance provision of this Code (Application, Section F) postpones the time for compliance with certain provisions of this Section in some cases.

[2]   When a judge acquires in a judicial capacity information, such as material contained in filings with the court, that is not yet generally known, the judge must not use the information for private gain. See Section 2B; see also Section 3B(11).

[3]   A judge must avoid financial and business dealings that involve the judge in frequent transactions or continuing business relationships with persons likely to come either before the judge personally or before other judges on the judge's court. In addition, a judge should discourage members of the judge's family from engaging in dealings that would reasonably appear to exploit the judge's judicial position. This rule is necessary to avoid creating an appearance of exploitation of office or favoritism and to minimize the potential for disqualification. With respect to affiliation of relatives of judge with law firms appearing before the judge, see Commentary to Section 3E(1) relating to disqualification.

[4]   Participation by a judge in financial and business dealings is subject to the general prohibitions in Section 4A against activities that tend to reflect adversely on impartiality, demean the judicial office, or interfere with the proper performance of judicial duties. Such participation is also subject to the general prohibition in Canon 2 against activities involving impropriety or the appearance of impropriety and the prohibition in Section 2B against the misuse of the prestige of judicial office. In addition, a judge must maintain high standards of conduct in all of the judge's activities, as set forth in Canon 1. See Commentary for Section 4B regarding use of the phrase "subject to the requirements of this Code."

(2) A judge may, subject to the requirements of this Code, hold and manage investments of the judge and members of the judge's family*, including real estate, and engage in other remunerative activity.

Commentary:

[1]   This Section provides that, subject to the requirements of this Code, a judge may hold and manage investments owned solely by the judge, investments owned solely by a member or members of the judge's family, and investments owned jointly by the judge and members of the judge's family.

---

* See, Terminology.

(3) A judge shall not serve as an officer, director, manager, general partner, advisor or employee of any business entity except that a judge may, subject to the requirements of this Code, manage and participate in:

(a) a business closely held by the judge or members of the judge's family*, or

(b) a business entity primarily engaged in investment of the financial resources of the judge or members of the judge's family.

Commentary:

[1]   Subject to the requirements of this Code, a judge may participate in a business that is closely held either by the judge alone, by members of the judge's family, or by the judge and members of the judge's family.

[2]   Although participation by a judge in a closely-held family business might otherwise be permitted by Section 4D(3), a judge may be prohibited from participation by other provisions of this Code when, for example, the business entity frequently appears before the judge's court or the participation requires significant time away from judicial duties. Similarly, a judge must avoid participating in a closely-held family business if the judge's participation would involve misuse of the prestige of judicial office.

(4) A judge shall manage the judge's investments and other financial interests to minimize the number of cases in which the judge is disqualified. As soon as the judge can do so without serious financial detriment, the judge shall divest himself or herself of investments and other financial interests that might require frequent disqualification.

(5) A judge shall not accept, and shall urge members of the judge's family residing in the judge's household* not to accept, a gift, bequest, favor or loan from anyone except for:

Commentary:

[1]   Section 4D(5) does not apply to contributions to a judge's campaign for judicial office, a matter governed by Canon 5.

[2]   Because a gift, bequest, favor or loan to a member of the judge's family residing in the judge's household might be viewed as intended to influence the judge, a judge must inform those family members of the relevant ethical constraints upon the judge in this regard and discourage those family members from violating them. A judge cannot, however, reasonably be expected to know or control all of the financial or business activities of all family members residing in the judge's household.

(a) a gift incident to a public testimonial, books, tapes and other resource materials supplied by publishers on a complimentary basis for official use, or an invitation to the judge and the judge's spouse or guest to attend a bar-related function or an activity devoted to the improvement of the law*, the legal system or the administration of justice;

Commentary:

[1]   Acceptance of an invitation to a law-related function is governed by Section 4D(5)(a); acceptance of an invitation paid for by an individual lawyer or group of lawyers is governed by Section 4D(5)(h).

* See, Terminology.

[2]   A judge may accept a public testimonial or a gift incident thereto only if the donor organization is not an organization whose members comprise or frequently represent the same side in litigation, and the testimonial and gift are otherwise in compliance with other provisions of this Code. See Sections 4A(1) and 2B.

(b) a gift, award or benefit incident to the business, profession or other separate activity of a spouse or other family member of a judge residing in the judge's household, including gifts, awards and benefits for the use of both the spouse or other family member and the judge (as spouse or family member), provided the gift, award or benefit could not reasonably be perceived as intended to influence the judge in the performance of judicial duties;

(c) ordinary social hospitality;

(d) a gift from a relative or friend, for a special occasion, such as a wedding, anniversary or birthday, if the gift is fairly commensurate with the occasion and the relationship;

Commentary:

[1]   A gift to a judge, or to a member of the judge's family living in the judge's household, that is excessive in value raises questions about the judge's impartiality and the integrity of the judicial office and might require disqualification of the judge where disqualification would not otherwise be required. See, however, Section 4D(5)(e).

(e) a gift, bequest, favor or loan from a relative or close personal friend whose appearance or interest in a case would in any event require disqualification under Section 3E;

(f) a loan from a lending institution in its regular course of business on the same terms generally available to persons who are not judges;

(g) a scholarship or fellowship awarded on the same terms and based on the same criteria applied to other applicants; or

(h) any other gift, bequest, favor or loan, only if: the donor is not a party or other person who has come or is likely to come or whose interests have come or are likely to come before the judge; and, if its value exceeds $150.00, the judge reports it in the same manner as the judge reports compensation in Section 4H.

Commentary:

[1]   Section 4D(5)(h) prohibits judges from accepting gifts, favors, bequests or loans from lawyers or their firms if they have come or are likely to come before the judge; it also prohibits gifts, favors, bequests or loans from clients of lawyers or their firms when the clients' interests have come or are likely to come before the judge.

E.   FIDUCIARY ACTIVITIES.

(1) A judge shall not serve as executor, administrator or other personal

representative, trustee, guardian, attorney in fact or other fiduciary*, except for the estate, trust or person of a member of the judge's family *, and then only if such service will not interfere with the proper performance of judicial duties.

(2) A judge shall not serve as a fiduciary *if it is likely that the judge as a fiduciary will be engaged in proceedings that would ordinarily come before the judge, or if the estate, trust or ward becomes involved in adversary proceedings in the court on which the judge serves or one under its appellate jurisdiction.

(3) The same restrictions on financial activities that apply to a judge personally also apply to the judge while acting in a fiduciary* capacity.

Commentary:

[1]   The Time for Compliance provision of this Code (Application, Section F) postpones the time for compliance with certain provisions of this Section in some cases.

[2]   The restrictions imposed by this Canon may conflict with the judge's obligation as a fiduciary. For example, a judge should resign as trustee if detriment to the trust would result from divestiture of holdings the retention of which would place the judge in violation of Section 4D(4).

F. SERVICE AS ARBITRATOR OR MEDIATOR. A judge shall not act as an arbitrator or mediator or otherwise perform judicial functions in a private capacity unless expressly authorized by law *.

Commentary:

Section 4F does not prohibit a judge from participating in arbitration, mediation or settlement conferences performed as part of judicial duties.

G. PRACTICE OF LAW. A judge shall not practice law. Notwithstanding this prohibition, a judge may act pro se and may, without compensation, give legal advice to and draft or review documents for a member of the judge's family*.

Commentary:

[1]   This prohibition refers to the practice of law in a representative capacity and not in a pro se capacity. A judge may act for himself or herself in all legal matters, including matters involving litigation and matters involving appearances before or other dealings with legislative and other governmental bodies. However, in so doing, a judge must not abuse the prestige of office to advance the interests of the judge or the judge's family. See Section 2(B).

[2]   The Code allows a judge to give legal advice to and draft legal documents for members of the judge's family, so long as the judge receives no compensation. A judge must not, however, act as an advocate or negotiator for a member of the judge's family in a legal matter.

Canon 6, new in the 1972 Code, reflected concerns about conflicts of interest and appearances of impropriety arising from compensation for off-the-bench activities. Since

* See, Terminology.

1972, however, reporting requirements that are much more comprehensive with respect to what must be reported and with whom reports must be filed have been adopted by many jurisdictions. The Committee believes that although reports of compensation for extra-judicial activities should be required, reporting requirements preferably should be developed to suit the respective jurisdictions, not simply adopted as set forth in a national model code of judicial conduct. Because of the Committee's concern that deletion of this Canon might lead to the misconception that reporting compensation for extra-judicial activities is no longer important, the substance of Canon 6 is carried forward as Section 4H in this Code for adoption in those jurisdictions that do not have other reporting requirements. In jurisdictions that have separately established reporting requirements, Section 4H(2) (Public Reporting) may be deleted and the caption for Section 4H modified appropriately.

* * *

H. COMPENSATION, REIMBURSEMENT AND REPORTING.

(1) COMPENSATION AND REIMBURSEMENT. A judge may receive compensation and reimbursement of expenses for the extra-judicial activities permitted by this Code, if the source of such payments does not give the appearance of influencing the judge's performance of judicial duties or otherwise give the appearance of impropriety.

(a) Compensation shall not exceed a reasonable amount nor shall it exceed what a person who is not a judge would receive for the same activity.

(b) Expense reimbursement shall be limited to the actual cost of travel, food and lodging reasonably incurred by the judge and, where appropriate to the occasion, by the judge's spouse or guest. Any payment in excess of such an amount is compensation.

(2) PUBLIC REPORTS. A judge shall report the date, place and nature of any activity for which the judge received compensation, and the name of the payor and the amount of compensation so received. Compensation or income of a spouse attributed to the judge by operation of a community property law is not extra-judicial compensation to the judge. The judge's report shall be made at least annually and shall be filed as a public document in the office of the clerk of the court on which the judge serves or other office designated by law*.

Commentary:

[1]   See Section 4D(5) regarding reporting of gifts, bequests and loans.

[2]   The Code does not prohibit a judge from accepting honoraria or speaking fees provided that the compensation is reasonable and commensurate with the task performed. A judge should ensure, however, that no conflicts are created by the arrangement. A judge must not appear to trade on the judicial position for personal advantage. Nor should a judge spend significant time away from court duties to meet speaking or writing commitments for compensation. In addition, the source of the payment must not raise any question of undue influence or the judge's ability or willingness to be impartial.

I.   Disclosure of a judge's income, debts, investments or other assets is required only to the extent provided in this Canon and in Sections 3E and 3F, or as otherwise required by law *.

Commentary:

[1]   Section 3E requires a judge to disqualify himself or herself in any proceeding in which the judge has an economic interest. See "economic interest" as explained in the Terminology

---

* See, Terminology.

Section. Section 4D requires a judge to refrain from engaging in business and from financial activities that might interfere with the impartial performance of judicial duties; Section 4H requires a judge to report all compensation the judge received for activities outside judicial office. A judge has the rights of any other citizen, including the right to privacy of the judge's financial affairs, except to the extent that limitations established by law are required to safeguard the proper performance of the judge's duties.

CANON 5[5]

A Judge or Judicial Candidate Shall Refrain From Inappropriate Political Activity

A. ALL JUDGES AND CANDIDATES.

(1) Except as authorized in Sections 5B(2), 5C(1) and 5C(3), a judge or a candidate * for election or appointment to judicial office shall not:

(a) act as a leader or hold an office in a political organization *;

(b) publicly endorse or publicly oppose another candidate for public office;

(c) make speeches on behalf of a political organization;

(d) attend political gatherings; or

(e) solicit funds for, pay an assessment to or make a contribution to a political organization or candidate, or purchase tickets for political party dinners or other functions.

Commentary:

[1] A judge or candidate for judicial office retains the right to participate in the political process as a voter.

[2] Where false information concerning a judicial candidate is made public, a judge or another judicial candidate having knowledge of the facts is not prohibited by Section 5A(1) from making the facts public.

5. **Introductory Note to Canon 5:** There is wide variation in the methods of judicial selection used, both among jurisdictions and within the jurisdictions themselves. In a given state, judges may be selected by one method initially, retained by a different method, and selected by still another method to fill interim vacancies.

According to figures compiled in 1987 by the National Center for State Courts, 32 states and the District of Columbia use a merit selection method (in which an executive such as a governor appoints a judge from a group of nominees selected by a judicial nominating commission) to select judges in the state either initially or to fill an interim vacancy. Of those 33 jurisdictions, a merit selection method is used in 18 jurisdictions to choose judges of courts of last resort, in 13 jurisdictions to choose judges of intermediate appellate courts, in 12 jurisdictions to choose

judges of general jurisdiction courts and in 5 jurisdictions to choose judges of limited jurisdiction courts.

Methods of judicial selection other than merit selection include nonpartisan election (10 states use it for initial selection at all court levels, another 10 states use it for initial selection for at least one court level) and partisan election (8 states use it for initial selection at all court levels, another 7 states use it for initial selection for at least one level). In a small minority of the states, judicial selection methods include executive or legislative appointment (without nomination of a group of potential appointees by a judicial nominating commission) and court selection. In addition, the federal judicial system utilizes an executive appointment method. See State Court Organization 1987 (National Center for State Courts, 1988).

[3]   Section 5A(1)(a) does not prohibit a candidate for elective judicial office from retaining during candidacy a public office such as county prosecutor, which is not "an office in a political organization."

[4]   Section 5A(1)(b) does not prohibit a judge or judicial candidate from privately expressing his or her views on judicial candidates or other candidates for public office.

[5]   A candidate does not publicly endorse another candidate for public office by having that candidate's name on the same ticket.

(2) A judge shall resign from judicial office upon becoming a candidate* for a non-judicial office either in a primary or in a general election, except that the judge may continue to hold judicial office while being a candidate for election to or serving as a delegate in a state constitutional convention if the judge is otherwise permitted by law* to do so.

(3) A candidate * for a judicial office:

(a) shall maintain the dignity appropriate to judicial office and act in a manner consistent with the impartiality,* integrity and independence of the judiciary, and shall encourage members of the candidate's family * to adhere to the same standards of political conduct in support of the candidate as apply to the candidate;

Commentary:

[1]   Although a judicial candidate must encourage members of his or her family to adhere to the same standards of political conduct in support of the candidate that apply to the candidate, family members are free to participate in other political activity.

(b) shall prohibit employees and officials who serve at the pleasure of the candidate *, and shall discourage other employees and officials subject to the candidate's direction and control from doing on the candidate's behalf what the candidate is prohibited from doing under the Sections of this Canon;

(c) except to the extent permitted by Section 5C(2), shall not authorize or knowingly * permit any other person to do for the candidate * what the candidate is prohibited from doing under the Sections of this Canon;

(d) shall not:

(i) with respect to cases, controversies or issues that are likely to come before the court, make pledges, promises or commitments that are inconsistent with impartial * performance of the adjudicative duties of the office; or

(ii) knowingly * misrepresent the identity, qualifications, present position or other fact concerning the candidate or an opponent;

Commentary:

[1]   Section 5A(3)(d) prohibits a candidate for judicial office from making statements that commit the candidate regarding cases, controversies or issues likely to come before the court. As

* See, Terminology.

a corollary, a candidate should emphasize in any public statement the candidate's duty to uphold the law regardless of his or her personal views. See also Section 3B(9) and (10), the general rules on public comment by judges. Section 5A(3)(d) does not prohibit a candidate from making pledges or promises respecting improvements in court administration. Nor does this Section prohibit an incumbent judge from making private statements to other judges or court personnel in the performance of judicial duties. This Section applies to any statement made in the process of securing judicial office, such as statements to commissions charged with judicial selection and tenure and legislative bodies confirming appointment. See also Rule 8.2 of the ABA Model Rules of Professional Conduct.

(e) may respond to personal attacks or attacks on the candidate's record as long as the response does not violate Section 5A(3)(d).

B. CANDIDATES SEEKING APPOINTMENT TO JUDICIAL OR OTHER GOVERN-MENTAL OFFICE.

(1) A candidate* for appointment to judicial office or a judge seeking other governmental office shall not solicit or accept funds, personally or through a committee or otherwise, to support his or her candidacy.

(2) A candidate * for appointment to judicial office or a judge seeking other governmental office shall not engage in any political activity to secure the appointment except that:

(a) such persons may:

(i) communicate with the appointing authority, including any selection or nominating commission or other agency designated to screen candidates;

(ii) seek support or endorsement for the appointment from organizations that regularly make recommendations for reappointment or appointment to the office, and from individuals to the extent requested or required by those specified in Section 5B(2)(a); and

(iii) provide to those specified in Sections 5B(2)(a)(i) and 5B(2)(a)(ii) information as to his or her qualifications for the office;

(b) a non-judge candidate * for appointment to judicial office may, in addition, unless otherwise prohibited by law *:

(i) retain an office in a political organization *,

(ii) attend political gatherings, and

(iii) continue to pay ordinary assessments and ordinary contributions to a political organization or candidate and purchase tickets for political party dinners or other functions.

Commentary:

[1]   Section 5B(2) provides a limited exception to the restrictions imposed by Sections 5A(1) and 5D. Under Section 5B(2), candidates seeking reappointment to the same judicial office or appointment to another judicial office or other governmental office may apply for the appointment and seek appropriate support.

* See, Terminology.

[2]   Although under Section 5B(2) nonjudge candidates seeking appointment to judicial office are permitted during candidacy to retain office in a political organization, attend political gatherings and pay ordinary dues and assessments, they remain subject to other provisions of this Code during candidacy. See Sections 5B(1), 5B(2)(a), 5E and Application Section.

C.   JUDGES AND CANDIDATES SUBJECT TO PUBLIC ELECTION.

(1) A judge or a candidate* subject to public election * may, except as prohibited by law *:

(a) at any time

(i) purchase tickets for and attend political gatherings;

(ii) identify himself or herself as a member of a political party; and

(iii) contribute to a political organization *;

(b) when a candidate for election

(i) speak to gatherings on his or her own behalf;

(ii) appear in newspaper, television and other media advertisements supporting his or her candidacy;

(iii) distribute pamphlets and other promotional campaign literature supporting his or her candidacy; and

(iv) publicly endorse or publicly oppose other candidates for the same judicial office in a public election in which the judge or judicial candidate is running.

Commentary:

[1]   Section 5C(1) permits judges subject to election at any time to be involved in limited political activity. Section 5D, applicable solely to incumbent judges, would otherwise bar this activity.

(2) A candidate* shall not personally solicit or accept campaign contributions or personally solicit publicly stated support. A candidate may, however, establish committees of responsible persons to conduct campaigns for the candidate through media advertisements, brochures, mailings, candidate forums and other means not prohibited by law. Such committees may solicit and accept reasonable campaign contributions, manage the expenditure of funds for the candidate's campaign and obtain public statements of support for his or her candidacy. Such committees are not prohibited from soliciting and accepting reasonable campaign contributions and public support from lawyers. A candidate's committees may solicit contributions and public support for the candidate's campaign no

* See, Terminology.

earlier than [one year] before an election and no later than [90] days after the last election in which the candidate participates during the election year. A candidate shall not use or permit the use of campaign contributions for the private benefit of the candidate or others.

Commentary:

[1]   There is legitimate concern about a judge's impartiality when parties whose interests may come before a judge, or the lawyer who represents such parties, are known to have made contributions to the election campaigns of judicial candidates. This is among the reasons that merit selection of judges is a preferable manner in which to select the judiciary. Notwithstanding that preference, Section 5(c)(2) recognizes that in many jurisdictions judicial candidates must raise funds to support their candidacies for election to judicial office. It therefore permits a candidate, other than a candidate for appointment, to establish campaign committees to solicit and accept public support and reasonable financial contributions. In order to guard against the possibility that conflicts of interest will arise, the candidate must instruct his or her campaign committees at the start of the campaign to solicit or accept only contributions that are reasonable and appropriate under the circumstances. Though not prohibited, campaign contributions of which a judge has knowledge, made by lawyers or others who appear before the judge, may, by virtue of their size or source, raise questions about a judge's impartiality and be cause for disqualification as provided under Section3E.

[2]   Campaign committees established under Section 5C(2) should manage campaign finances responsibly, avoiding deficits that might necessitate post-election fund-raising, to the extent possible.

[3]   Section 5C(2) does not prohibit a candidate from initiating an evaluation by a judicial selection commission or bar association, or, subject to the requirements of this Code, from responding to a request for information from any organization.

(3) A candidate shall instruct his or her campaign committee(s) at the start of the campaign not to accept campaign contributions for any election that exceed, in the aggregate*, [$] from an individual or [$] from an entity. This limitation is in addition to the limitations provided in Section 5C(2).[6]

(4) In addition to complying with all applicable statutory requirements for disclosure of campaign contributions, campaign committees established by a candidate shall file with [   ][7] a report stating the name, address, occupation and employer or each person who has made campaign contributions to the committee whose value in the aggregate* exceed [$].[8] The report must be filed within [   ][9] days following the election.

---

* See, Terminology.

6. Jurisdictions wishing to adopt campaign contribution limits that are lower than generally applicable campaign finance regulations provide should adopt this provision, inserting appropriate dollar amounts where brackets appear.

7. Each jurisdiction should identify an appropriate depository for the information required under this provision, giving consideration to the public's need for convenient and timely access to the information. Electronic filing is to be preferred.

8. Jurisdictions wishing to adopt campaign contribution disclosure levels lower than those set in generally applicable campaign finance regulations should adopt this provision, inserting appropriate dollar amounts where brackets appear.

9. A time period chosen by the adopting jurisdiction should appear in the bracketed space.

(5) Except as prohibited by law *, a candidate * for judicial office in a public election * may permit the candidate's name: (a) to be listed on election materials along with the names of other candidates for elective public office, and (b) to appear in promotions of the ticket.

Commentary:

[1]   Section 5C(3) provides a limited exception to the restrictions imposed by Section 5A(1).

D.   INCUMBENT JUDGES. A judge shall not engage in any political activity except (i) as authorized under any other Section of this Code, (ii) on behalf of measures to improve the law*, the legal system or the administration of justice, or (iii) as expressly authorized by law.

Commentary:

[1]   Neither Section 5D nor any other section of the Code prohibits a judge in the exercise of administrative functions from engaging in planning and other official activities with members of the executive and legislative branches of government. With respect to a judge's activity on behalf of measures to improve the law, the legal system and the administration of justice, see Commentary to Section 4B and Section 4C(1) and its Commentary.

E.   APPLICABILITY. Canon 5 generally applies to all incumbent judges and judicial candidates *. A successful candidate, whether or not an incumbent, is subject to judicial discipline for his or her campaign conduct; an unsuccessful candidate who is a lawyer is subject to lawyer discipline for his or her campaign conduct. A lawyer who is a candidate for judicial office is subject to [Rule 8.2(b) of the ABA Model Rules of Professional Conduct]. (An adopting jurisdiction should substitute a reference to its applicable rule.)

APPLICATION OF THE CODE OF JUDICIAL CONDUCT

A.   Anyone, whether or not a lawyer, who is an officer of a judicial system[10] and who performs judicial functions, including an officer such as a magistrate, court commissioner, special master or referee, is a judge within the meaning of this Code. All judges shall comply with this Code except as provided below.

Commentary:

[1]   The four categories of judicial service in other than a full-time capacity are necessarily defined in general terms because of the widely varying forms of judicial service. For the purposes of this Section, as long as a retired judge is subject to recall the judge is considered to "perform judicial functions." The determination of which category and, accordingly, which specific Code provisions apply to an individual judicial officer, depend upon the facts of the particular judicial service.

B.   RETIRED JUDGE SUBJECT TO RECALL. A retired judge subject to recall who by law is not permitted to practice law is not required to comply:

---

10.   Applicability of this Code to administrative law judges should be determined by each adopting jurisdiction. Administrative law judges generally are affiliated with the executive branch of government rather than the judicial branch and each adopting jurisdiction should consider the unique characteristics of particular administrative law judge positions in adopting and adapting the Code for administrative law judges. See, e.g., Model Code of Judicial Conduct for Federal Administrative Law Judges, endorsed by the National Conference of Administrative Law Judges in February 1989.

(1) except while serving as a judge, with Section 4F; and

(2) at any time with Section 4E.

C. CONTINUING PART–TIME JUDGE. A continuing part-time judge*:

(1) is not required to comply

(a) except while serving as a judge, with Section 3B(9); and

(b) at any time with Sections 4C(2), 4D(3), 4E(1), 4F, 4G, 4H, 5A(1), 5B(2) and 5D.

(2) shall not practice law in the court on which the judge serves or in any court subject to the appellate jurisdiction of the court on which the judge serves, and shall not act as a lawyer in a proceeding in which the judge has served as a judge or in any other proceeding related thereto.

Commentary:

[1]   When a person who has been a continuing part-time judge is no longer a continuing part-time judge, including a retired judge no longer subject to recall, that person may act as a lawyer in a proceeding in which he or she has served as a judge or in any other proceeding related thereto only with the express consent of all parties pursuant to [Rule 1.12(a) of the ABA Model Rules of Professional Conduct]. (An adopting jurisdiction should substitute a reference to its applicable rule).

D. PERIODIC PART–TIME JUDGE. A periodic part-time judge *:

(1) is not required to comply

(a) except while serving as a judge, with Section 3B(9);

(b) at any time, with Sections 4C(2), 4C(3)(a), 4D(1)(b), 4D(3), 4D(4), 4D(5), 4E, 4F, 4G, 4H, 5A(1), 5B(2) and 5D.

(2) shall not practice law in the court on which the judge serves or in any court subject to the appellate jurisdiction of the court on which the judge serves, and shall not act as a lawyer in a proceeding in which the judge has served as a judge or in any other proceeding related thereto.

Commentary:

[1]   When a person who has been a periodic part-time judge is no longer a periodic part-time judge (no longer accepts appointments), that person may act as a lawyer in a proceeding in which he or she has served as a judge or in any other proceeding related thereto only with the express consent of all parties pursuant to [Rule 1.12(a) of the ABA Model Rules of Professional Conduct]. (An adopting jurisdiction should substitute a reference to its applicable rule).

---

* See, Terminology.

E. PRO TEMPORE PART–TIME JUDGE. A pro tempore part-time judge*:

(1) is not required to comply

  (a) except while serving as a judge, with Sections 2A, 2B, 3B(9) and 4C(1);

  (b) at any time with Sections 2C, 4C(2), 4C(3)(a), 4C(3)(b), 4D(1)(b), 4D(3), 4D(4), 4D(5), 4E, 4F, 4G, 4H, 5A(1), 5A(2), 5B(2) and 5D.

(2) A person who has been a pro tempore part-time judge * shall not act as a lawyer in a proceeding in which the judge has served as a judge or in any other proceeding related thereto except as otherwise permitted by [Rule 1.12(a) of the ABA Model Rules of Professional Conduct]. (An adopting jurisdiction should substitute a reference to its applicable rule.)

F. TIME FOR COMPLIANCE. A person to whom this Code becomes applicable shall comply immediately with all provisions of this Code except Sections 4D(2), 4D(3) and 4E and shall comply with these Sections as soon as reasonably possible and shall do so in any event within the period of one year.

Commentary:

[1]   If serving as a fiduciary when selected as judge, a new judge may, notwithstanding the prohibitions in Section 4E, continue to serve as fiduciary but only for that period of time necessary to avoid serious adverse consequences to the beneficiary of the fiduciary relationship and in no event longer than one year. Similarly, if engaged at the time of judicial selection in a business activity, a new judge may, notwithstanding the prohibitions in Section 4D(3), continue in that activity for a reasonable period but in no event longer than one year.

----

* See, Terminology.

APPENDIX E

MPRE Sample Questions

Multistate Professional Responsibility Examination[1]

N.B.: *Since 1999*, the MPRE has adopted new test specifications. Now, in addition to testing the ABA Model Rules of Professional Conduct and the ABA Model Code of Judicial Conduct, it also tests "controlling constitutional decisions and generally accepted principals established in leading federal and state cases and in procedural and evidentiary rules." This Appendix E contains 25 questions and answers that follow the MPRE testing format in effect since 1999.

Description of the Examination

The purpose of the NCBE Multistate Professional Responsibility Examination (MPRE) is to measure the examinee's knowledge and understanding of established standards related to a lawyer's professional conduct; thus, the MPRE is not a test to determine an individual's personal ethical values. Lawyers serve in many capacities: for example, as judges, as advocates, counselors, and in other roles. The law governing the conduct of lawyers in these roles is applied in disciplinary and bar admission procedures, and by courts in dealing with issues of appearance, representation, privilege, disqualification, contempt or other censure, and in lawsuits seeking to establish liability for malpractice, and other civil or criminal wrongs committed by a lawyer while acting in a professional capacity.

The law governing the conduct of lawyers is based on the disciplinary rules of professional conduct currently articulated in the American Bar Association (ABA) Model Rules of Professional Conduct and the ABA Model Code of Judicial Conduct, as well as on controlling constitutional decisions and generally accepted principles established in leading federal and state cases and in procedural and evidentiary rules.

The MPRE is developed by a six-member Drafting Committee comprised of recognized experts in the area of professional responsibility. Before a test item is selected for inclusion in the MPRE, it undergoes a multistage review process that occurs over the course of several years before the test is administered. Besides intensive reviews by the Drafting Committee and testing specialists, each test item is reviewed by other national and state experts. All test items must successfully pass all reviews before they are included in the MPRE. After an MPRE examination is administered, the statistical performance of each test item is reviewed and evaluated by content and testing experts before the items are included in the computation of examinees' scores. This final statistical review is conducted to ensure that each test item is accurate and psychometrically sound.

The MPRE consists of 50 multiple-choice test items. These test items are followed by 10 Test Center Review items that request the examinee's reactions to the testing conditions. The examination is two hours and five minutes in length.

Test items covering judicial ethics measure applications of the ABA Model Code of Judicial Conduct (CJC). Other items will deal with discipline of lawyers by state disciplinary authorities; in these items, the correct answer will be governed by the current ABA Model Rules of Professional Conduct (MRPC). The remaining items, outside the disciplinary context, are designed to measure an understanding of the generally accepted rules, principles, and common law regulating the legal profession in the United States; in these items, the correct answer will be governed by the view reflected in a majority of cases, statutes, or regulations on the subject. To the extent that questions of professional responsibility arise in the context of procedural or evidentiary issues, such as the availability of litigation sanctions or the scope of the attorney-client evidentiary privilege, the Federal Rules of Civil Procedure and the Federal Rules of Evidence will be assumed to apply, unless otherwise stated.

As a general rule, particular local statutes or rules of court will not be tested in the MPRE. However, a specific question may include the text of a local statute or rule that must be considered when answering that question. Amendments to the MRPC or the CJC will be reflected in the examination no earlier than one year after the approval of the amendments by the American Bar Association.

Each question contained in the MPRE provides a factual situation along with a specific question and four possible answer choices. Examinees should pick the best answer from the four possible answer choices. Each question may include, among others, one of the following key words or phrases:

1. <u>Subject to discipline</u> asks whether the conduct described in the question would subject the lawyer to discipline under the provisions of the ABA Model Rules of Professional Conduct. In the case of a judge, the test question also asks whether the judge would be subject to discipline under the ABA Model Code of Judicial Conduct.

2. <u>May</u> or <u>proper</u> asks whether the conduct referred to or described in the question is professionally appropriate in that it:

   a. would not subject the lawyer or judge to discipline; and

   b. is not inconsistent with the Preamble, Comments, or text of the ABA Model Rules of Professional Conduct or the ABA Code of Judicial Conduct; and

   c. is not inconsistent with generally accepted principles of the law of lawyering.

3. <u>Subject to litigation sanction</u> asks whether the conduct described in the question would subject the lawyer or the lawyer's law firm to sanction by a tribunal such as contempt, fine, fee forfeiture, disqualification, or other sanction.

4. <u>Subject to disqualification</u> asks whether the conduct described in the question would subject the lawyer or the lawyer's law firm to disqualification as counsel in a civil or criminal matter.

5. <u>Subject to civil liability</u> asks whether the conduct described in the question would subject the lawyer or the lawyer's law firm to civil liability, such as claims arising from malpractice, misrepresentation, and breach of fiduciary duty.

6. <u>Subject to criminal liability</u> asks whether the conduct described in the question would subject the lawyer to criminal liability for participation in, or aiding and abetting criminal acts, such as prosecution for insurance and tax fraud, destruction of evidence, or obstruction of justice.

When a question refers to discipline by the "bar," "state bar," or "appropriate disciplinary authority," it refers to the agency in the jurisdiction with authority to administer the standards for admission to practice and for maintenance of professional competence and integrity. Whenever a lawyer is identified as a "certified specialist," that lawyer has been so certified by the appropriate agency in the jurisdiction in which the lawyer practices. The phrases "informed consent" and "consent after consultation" are to be interpreted as having the same meaning.

Changes in MPRE in 2004

In February 2002, the American Bar Association (ABA) adopted certain changes to the Model Rules of Professional Conduct (MRPC) as a result of the recommendations of the Commission on Evaluation of the Rules of Professional Conduct (popularly known as "Ethics 2000"). In August 2002, the ABA adopted additional changes to the MRPC as a result of the recommendations of the Commission on Multijurisdictional Practice and the ABA Standing Committee on Ethics and Professional Responsibility. These 2002 changes of the MRPC will first be reflected in the content of the Multistate Professional Responsibility Examination (MPRE) beginning with the March 2004 administration. Amendments to MRPC and the CJC adopted by the ABA in August 2003 will first be reflected in the content of the MPRE beginning with the August 2004 administration.

MPRE 2004 Subject Matter Outline

The following subject matter outline indicates the 2004 examination's scope of coverage and the approximate percentage of items that are included in each major area. The outline is not intended to list every aspect of a topic mentioned. Although the test items for each MPRE are developed from these categories, each topic is not necessarily tested on each examination.

I.   Regulation of the Legal Profession (8–12%)

    A.   Inherent Powers of Courts to Regulate Lawyers

    B.   Admission to the Profession

    C.   Regulation after Admission

    D.   Maintaining Professional Standards—Peer Responsibility

    E.   Unauthorized Practice of Law

    F.   Fee Division with a Non-Lawyer

    G.   Law Firm and Other Forms of Practice

    H.   Contractual Restrictions on Practice

II. The Client-Lawyer Relationship (10–14%)

    A.   Acceptance or Rejection of Clients

    B.   Scope, Objective, and Means of the Representation

    C.   Within the Bounds of the Law

    D.   Withdrawal

    E.   Client-Lawyer Contracts

    F.   Fees

III. Privilege and Confidentiality (6–10%)

    A.   Lawyer-Client Privilege and the Work Product Doctrine

    B.   Professional Obligation of Confidentiality

    C.   Client-Authorized Disclosure

    D.   Exceptions to Confidentiality

    E.   Special Problems

IV. Independent Professional Judgment—Conflicts of Interest (12–16%)

    A.   As Affected by Lawyer's Personal Interest

    B.   Lawyer as Witness

    B. Lawyer as Custodian of Property of Client or Third Persons

    C. Disputed Claims

  IX. Communication about Legal Services (6–10%)

    A. Public Communications about Services

    B. Referrals

    C. Group Legal Services

    D. Direct Contact with Prospective Clients (Solicitation)

    E. Fields of Practice—Limitations of Practice and Specialization

  X. Lawyers and the Legal System (2–6%)

    A. Lawyer Activity in Improving the Legal System

    B. Impropriety Incident to Public Service

  XI. Judicial Ethics (6–10%)

    A. Uphold the Integrity and Independence of the Judiciary

    B. Avoid Impropriety and the Appearance of Impropriety

    C. Duties of Impartiality and Diligence

    D. Activities to Improve the Legal System

    E. Extra-Judicial Activities

    F. Political Activity of Judges

    G. Candidate for Judicial Office

Preparing for the MPRE

In addition to the Sample Examination Questions that appear in this booklet, a booklet containing additional sample questions may be obtained from the National Conference of Bar Examiners for $17.50. An order form for this study aid is on page 60.

Students who have taken and reviewed a two- or three-credit law school survey course in Professional Responsibility should be reasonably well prepared to take the MPRE. However, for those wishing to engage in additional preparation, there are numerous sources available for consultation, including the American Bar Association's Annotated Model Rules of Professional Conduct and the American Law Institute's Restatement of the Law Governing Lawyers, as well as treatises collecting and discussing the authorities.

The ABA Model Rules of Professional Conduct and the ABA Model Code of Judicial Conduct are available from the American Bar Association at 750 North Lake Shore Drive, Chicago, IL 60611 (312/988–5522 or 1–800/285–2221). The website at which these publications may be purchased is **www.abanet.org/cpr/publications.html.**

Sample Examination Questions

This section provides examples of test questions similar to those contained in the MPRE. Read and answer them to familiarize yourself with the kinds of questions contained in the examination. A sample answer sheet is provided on page 58.

Each question has four responses from which you are to select the best one. During the examination, when you have chosen the response you feel is best, find the row of ovals on your answer sheet with the same number as the question you are answering. Then find the oval in the row with the same letter as your answer. Blacken the oval completely. For example, if you choose response B for question 3, blacken oval B in the row of ovals next to the number 3 on your answer sheet. Choose only one answer for each question. Use a soft-lead pencil and make your marks heavy and black. Mark all your answers on the separate answer sheet.

The questions in the MPRE may include qualifications as part of the alternative responses. These qualifications may be essential to the correctness of the response or responses in which they appear and thus to the correct answer to the question. Consequently, you should read each question thoroughly before you select a response.

Your score on the MPRE will be based on the number of questions you answer correctly. Thus, it is to your advantage to answer every question. Do not spend too much time on any one question. Work steadily and as quickly as you can. If you cannot answer a question, leave it and go on to the next question. You may then return to all unanswered questions if you finish before time has expired.

Question 1.

Although licensed to practice law in State, Attorney Alpha does not practice law but works as an investment broker. Alpha could have elected inactive status as a member of the bar, but chose not to do so. Recently, in connection with a sale of worthless securities, Alpha made materially false representations to Victim, an investment customer. Victim sued Alpha for civil fraud, and a jury returned a verdict in Victim's favor. Alpha did not appeal.

Is Alpha <u>subject to discipline</u>?

A. Yes, because Alpha was pursuing a non-legal occupation while an active member of the bar.

B. Yes, because Alpha's conduct was fraudulent.

C. No, because Alpha was not convicted of a crime.

D. No, unless the standard of proof in State is the same in lawyer disciplinary cases and civil cases.

Question 2.

Client was an experienced oil and gas developer. Client asked Attorney for representation in a suit to establish Client's ownership of certain oil and gas royalties. Client did not have available the necessary funds to pay Attorney's reasonable hourly rate for undertaking the case. Client proposed instead to pay Attorney an amount in cash equal to 20% of the value of the proceeds received from the first year royalties Client might recover as a result of the suit. Attorney accepted the proposal and took the case.

Is Attorney <u>subject to discipline</u>?

A. Yes, because the agreement gave Attorney a proprietary interest in Client's cause of action.

B. Yes, unless the fee Attorney receives does not exceed that which Attorney would have received by charging a reasonable hourly rate.

C. No, because Client rather than Attorney proposed the fee arrangement.

D. No, because Attorney may contract with Client for a reasonable contingent fee.

<u>Question 3.</u>

Attorney represents Chemco, a producer of chemical products. Some of the waste products of Chemco's manufacturing are highly toxic and are likely to cause serious immediate physical harm if disposed of improperly. Pres, president of Chemco, recently informed Attorney that a new employee mistakenly disposed of the waste products in the ground behind the company plant, an area that is part of the source of the city's water supply. Attorney advised Pres that Chemco could be liable for negligence in lawsuits brought by any persons harmed by the waste products. As a result, Attorney advised Pres to immediately report the problem to city authorities. Fearful of adverse publicity, Pres declined to do so. Attorney further advised Pres that she believed Pres's decision was immoral. Pres continued to decline to report the matter. Attorney then informed Pres that she was withdrawing from the representation and would inform the authorities herself. Immediately after withdrawing, Attorney reported Chemco's conduct to the authorities.

Is Attorney <u>subject to discipline</u>?

A. Yes, because the information was given to Attorney in confidence and may not be revealed without the client's consent.

B. Yes, unless Chemco's conduct was criminal.

C. No, because Attorney reasonably believed that Chemco's disposal of the waste products was likely to cause serious physical harm.

D. No, because Attorney reasonably believed that Pres was pursuing an imprudent course of conduct.

<u>Question 4.</u>

Attorney, a member of the state legislature, is allowed to engage in private practice under state law. Attorney represents Plaintiff in a personal injury case. Attorney reasonably believes that the trial of the case will last at least two weeks. When the case was first scheduled for trial, Attorney requested a continuance, truthfully stating, "As the court knows, I am a member of the legislature, which will be going into special session next week. Because of my legislative duties, I must be in the state capitol for the duration of the session." The defendant objected to the continuance, but the court granted it.

Is Attorney <u>subject to discipline</u>?

A. Yes, because the defendant objected to the continuance.

B. Yes, because Attorney used her public position to influence a tribunal.

C. No, because Attorney's statements to the court were truthful.

D. No, unless the continuance will give Plaintiff an advantage in the litigation.

Question 5.

Attorney agreed to represent Able, a client, in bringing a lawsuit. Attorney and Able executed Attorney's preprinted retainer form that provides, in part:

> "The client agrees to pay promptly Attorney's fees for services. In addition, the client and Attorney agree to release each other from any and all liability arising from the representation. The client agrees that Attorney need not return the client's file prior to receiving the client's executed release. Attorney agrees to return the client's file promptly upon receipt of all fees owed and of the client's executed release."

During their initial meeting, Attorney recommended that Able consult independent counsel before signing the retainer agreement, but Able chose not to do so. Attorney reasonably believes that his fee is fair and that the quality of his work will be competent.

Is Attorney's retainer agreement with Able <u>proper</u>?

A. Yes, because Attorney furnished consideration by agreeing to release Able from liability and to return Able's files.

B. Yes, because Attorney reasonably believes that his fee is fair and that the quality of his work will be competent.

C. No, because Attorney is attempting to limit prospectively his liability for malpractice.

D. No, because Attorney uses a preprinted form for all retainers.

Question 6.

Last year, Able's house was severely damaged when a large tree in neighbor Baker's yard toppled onto Able's roof and porch. Attorney Alpha has filed suit against Baker on Able's behalf, to recover over $40,000 in damages.

Baker was represented by Attorney Beta, who has been uncooperative. When Alpha communicated Able's settlement offer to Beta, Beta said he would consider it. However, Beta did not respond further to Alpha, and Alpha suspected that Beta did not even communicate the offer to Baker. When Alpha reported this to Able, Able said, "Why can't I talk to Baker directly?" Alpha responded to Able:

> "Maybe the lawyers are getting in the way here. You two are neighbors; you could ask Baker directly if he doesn't want to put an end to this unpleasantness. As I told you, our case is strong on the law, but nothing is a dead certainty—that's why you agreed to make the settlement offer."

Is Alpha <u>subject to discipline</u>?

A. Yes, because Alpha suggested that Able communicate about the subject matter of the representation with a person known to be represented by another lawyer.

B. Yes, unless Beta had indeed failed to inform Baker of Able's settlement offer.

C. No, because Able and Baker may communicate with each other.

D. No, because by entering into settlement negotiations, Beta impliedly consented to direct communications with Baker.

<u>Question 7.</u>

Attorney represented Client in a personal injury action against the driver of the car in which Client was injured while a passenger. The personal injury action was settled, and Attorney received a check in the amount of $10,000 payable to Attorney. Attorney deposited the check in her Clients' Trust Account.

One day later, Attorney received a letter from Bank, which had heard of the settlement of the personal injury lawsuit. Bank informed Attorney that Client had failed to make his monthly mortgage payments for the last three months and demanded that Attorney immediately release $900 of the proceeds of the settlement to Bank or Bank would institute mortgage foreclosure proceedings against Client. Attorney informed Client of Bank's letter. Client responded:

> "I don't care what Bank does. The property is essentially worthless, so let Bank foreclose. If Bank wants to sue me, I'll be easy enough to find. I don't think they'll even bother. You just take your legal fees and turn the rest of the proceeds over to me."

Is Attorney <u>subject to discipline</u> if she follows Client's instructions?

A. Yes, if Client does not dispute the $900 debt to Bank.

B. Yes, because Attorney knew that Client was planning to force Bank to sue him.

C. No, unless Attorney had reason to believe that Client would not have sufficient funds to pay any subsequent judgment obtained by Bank.

D. No, because Bank has no established right to the specific proceeds of Client's personal injury judgment.

<u>Question 8.</u>

Attorney represents Client in an action by Client against Partner, Client's former partner, to recover damages for breach of contract. During the representation, Client presented Attorney with incontrovertible proof that Partner committed perjury in a prior action which was resolved in Partner's favor. Neither Attorney nor Client was involved in any way in the prior action. Attorney believes that it would be detrimental to Client's best interests to reveal the perjury because of the implication that might be drawn from the former close personal and business relationship between Client and Partner.

Would it be <u>proper</u> for Attorney to disclose the perjury to the tribunal?

A. Yes, because the information is unprivileged.

B. Yes, because Attorney has knowledge that Partner perpetrated a fraud on the tribunal.

C. No, because neither Client nor Attorney was involved in the prior action.

D. No, because Attorney believes that the disclosure would be detrimental to Client's best interests.

Question 9.

Attorney was engaged under a general retainer agreement to represent Corp, a corporation involved in the uranium industry. Under the agreement, Attorney handled all of Corp's legal work, which typically involved regulatory issues and litigation.

Corp told Attorney that a congressional committee was holding hearings concerning the extent of regulation in the copper industry. Because Corp was considering buying a copper mine during the next fiscal year, Corp wanted Attorney to testify that the industry was overregulated. Attorney subsequently testified before the relevant congressional committee. Attorney registered his appearance under his own name and did not disclose that he was appearing on behalf of a client. Afterward, Attorney billed Corp for fees and expenses related to his testimony.

Was Attorney's conduct <u>proper</u>?

A. Yes, because the duty of confidentiality prevented Attorney from disclosing the identity of his client.

B. Yes, because the attorney-client evidentiary privilege prevented disclosure of the identity of his client in this context.

C. No, because Attorney failed to disclose that he was appearing and testifying in a representative capacity.

D. No, because Attorney accepted compensation in return for his testimony.

Question 10.

Judge is one of three trustees of a trust for the educational benefit of her grandchildren. The trust owns 5,000 shares of stock in Big Oil Company. The stock has been selling for the past year at $10 per share. Big Oil is suing Oil Refining Company for breach of an oil refining agreement, and the case is assigned to Judge for trial. Judge believes that she can be fair and impartial.

<u>Should</u> Judge disqualify herself from the case?

A. Yes, because the trust has more than a de minimus financial interest in Big Oil Company.

B. Yes, unless the outcome of the lawsuit is unlikely to affect the value of the stock.

C. No, unless Judge personally owns stock in either party to the litigation.

D. No, because Judge believes she can remain impartial.

Question 11.

Attorney Alpha represented Plaintiff in a civil suit against Deft, who was represented by Attorney Beta. In the course of developing Plaintiff's case, Alpha discovered evidence that she reasonably believed showed that Deft had committed a crime. Alpha felt that Deft's crime should be reported to local prosecutorial authorities. After full disclosure, Plaintiff consented to Alpha's doing so. Without advising Beta, Alpha informed the local prosecutor of her findings, but she sought no advantage in the civil suit from her actions. Deft was subsequently indicted, tried, and acquitted of the offense.

Was Alpha's disclosure to prosecutorial authorities <u>proper</u>?

A.   Yes, because Alpha reasonably believed Deft was guilty of a crime.

B.   Yes, because Alpha was required to report unprivileged knowledge of criminal conduct.

C.   No, because Alpha did not advise Beta of her disclosure before making it.

D.   No, because Plaintiff's civil suit against Deft was still pending.

<u>Question 12.</u>

Attorney, who had represented Testator for many years, prepared Testator's will and acted as one of the two subscribing witnesses to its execution. The will gave 10% of Testator's estate to Testator's housekeeper, 10% to Testator's son and sole heir, Son, and the residue to charity.
  Upon Testator's death one year later, Executor, the executor named in the will, asked Attorney to represent him in probating the will and administering the estate. At that time Executor informed Attorney that Son had notified him that he would contest the probate of the will on the grounds that Testator lacked the required mental capacity at the time the will was executed.
  Attorney believes that Testator was fully competent at all times and will so testify, if called as a witness. The other subscribing witness to Testator's will predeceased Testator.

Is it <u>proper</u> for Attorney to represent Executor in the probate of the will?

A.   Yes, because Attorney is the sole surviving witness to the execution of the will.

B.   Yes, because Attorney's testimony will support the validity of the will.

C.   No, because Attorney will be called to testify on a contested issue of fact.

D.   No, because Attorney will be representing an interest adverse to Testator's heir at law.

<u>Question 13.</u>

Attorney Alpha is defending Bigco against a lawsuit brought in federal court by Plaintiff, a consumer injured by one of Bigco's products. Plaintiff is seeking both compensatory and punitive damages. During discovery, Plaintiff's lawyer served a set of interrogatories on Bigco, including requests for financial data of Bigco.

Pres, president of Bigco, directed Alpha to resist providing this information, although Alpha has informed him that, under the rules of discovery, Plaintiff is entitled to the information requested. Pres then demanded that Alpha assert that the information is confidential, privileged, work product, and a trade secret, but Alpha correctly informed him that it was well settled that such claims would be regarded as frivolous by the courts. Pres nonetheless directed Alpha to file objections on the bases stated, so that at least Plaintiff will have to incur the expense of compelling discovery. Alpha filed the objections as directed by Pres.

Which of the following statements would be true?

I.   Alpha is <u>subject to discipline</u>.

II. Alpha is <u>subject to litigation sanction</u>.

A. I only

B. II only

C. Both I and II

D. Neither I nor II

Question 14.

Judge needed to obtain a loan to be secured by a second mortgage on his house. Bank offered him a loan at a very favorable interest rate. The vice-president at Bank told Judge:

> "Frankly, we normally don't give such a large loan when the security is a second mortgage, and your interest rate will be 2% less than we charge our other customers. But we know that your salary is inadequate, and we are giving you special consideration."

Is it <u>proper</u> for Judge to accept the loan?

A. Yes, if Judge does not act in any case involving Bank.

B. Yes, if Bank is not likely to be involved in litigation in the court on which Judge sits.

C. No, unless the same terms are available to all judges in the state.

D. No, because the amount of the loan and interest rate were not available to persons who were not judges.

Question 15.

Law Firm has 300 lawyers in 10 states. It has placed the supervision of all routine administrative and financial matters in the hands of Admin, a nonlawyer. Admin is paid a regular monthly salary and a year-end bonus of 1% of Law Firm's net income from fees. Organizationally, Admin reports to Attorney, who is the managing partner of Law Firm. Attorney deals with all issues related to Law Firm's supervision of the practice of law.

Is it <u>proper</u> for Attorney to participate in Law Firm's use of Admin's services in this fashion?

A. Yes, unless Admin has access to client files.

B. Yes, if Admin does not control the professional judgment of the lawyers in the firm.

C. No, because Law Firm is sharing legal fees with a nonlawyer.

D. No, because Law Firm is assisting a nonlawyer in the unauthorized practice of law.

Question 16.

Attorney experienced several instances when clients failed to pay their fees in a timely manner, but it was too late in the representation to withdraw without prejudicing the clients. To avoid a recurrence of this situation, Attorney has drafted a stipulation of consent to withdraw if fees are not paid according to the fee agreement. She proposes to have all clients sign the stipulation at the outset of the representation.

Is it proper for Attorney to use the stipulation to withdraw from representation whenever a client fails to pay fees?

A. Yes, because a lawyer may withdraw when the financial burden of continuing the representation would be substantially greater than the parties anticipated at the time of the fee agreement.

B. Yes, because the clients consented to the withdrawal in the stipulation.

C. No, because a client's failure to pay fees when due may be insufficient in itself to justify withdrawal.

D. No, unless clients are provided an opportunity to seek independent legal advice before signing the stipulation.

Question 17.

Attorney was retained by Defendant to represent him in a paternity suit. Aunt, Defendant's aunt, believed the suit was unfounded and motivated by malice. Aunt sent Attorney a check for $1,000 and asked Attorney to apply it to the payment of Defendant's fee. Aunt told Attorney not to tell Defendant of the payment because "Defendant is too proud to accept gifts, but I know he really needs the money."

Is it proper for Attorney to accept Aunt's check?

A. Yes, if Aunt does not attempt to influence Attorney's conduct of the case.

B. Yes, if Attorney's charges to Defendant are reduced accordingly.

C. No, because Aunt is attempting to finance litigation to which she is not a party.

D. No, unless Attorney first informs Defendant and obtains Defendant's consent to retain the payment.

Question 18.

Attorney has a highly efficient staff of paraprofessional legal assistants, all of whom are graduates of recognized legal assistant educational programs. Recently, the statute of limitations ran against a claim of a client of Attorney's when a legal assistant negligently misplaced Client's file and suit was not filed within the time permitted by law.

Which of the following correctly states Attorney's professional responsibility?

A. Attorney is subject to civil liability and is also subject to discipline on the theory of respondent superior.

B. Attorney is subject to civil liability or is subject to discipline at Client's election.

C. Attorney is subject to civil liability but is NOT subject to discipline unless Attorney failed to supervise the legal assistant adequately.

D. Attorney is NOT <u>subject to civil liability</u> and is NOT <u>subject to discipline</u> if Attorney personally was not negligent.

Question 19.

Attorney Alpha is a general practitioner with extensive experience in personal injury litigation, including legal and medical malpractice. Baker contacted Alpha by telephone and requested that Alpha represent Baker in a legal malpractice case that Baker wanted to file against Attorney Delta, the lawyer who handled Baker's divorce. Alpha refused even to meet with Baker, saying:

> "Look, I just finished renewing my own malpractice insurance policy, and I can't believe how high the premiums have gotten. I'm not taking on any new clients with legal malpractice cases."

Baker tried to contact several other lawyers, each of whom indicated that he or she would be happy to accept the representation but was too busy to take on any new matters at this time. Six months later the statute of limitations expired without Baker filing his lawsuit.

If Baker can establish that a legal malpractice action against Delta would have succeeded, is Alpha <u>subject to civil liability</u> for refusing to accept the representation?

A. Yes, because Alpha did not have good cause to refuse the representation.

B. Yes, unless Alpha made reasonable efforts to find a competent lawyer to represent Baker.

C. No, unless Alpha holds herself out as experienced in legal malpractice cases.

D. No, because Alpha had no legal obligation to accept Baker's case.

Question 20.

Pros, a prosecutor, was assigned to try a criminal case against Deft, who was charged with robbery of a convenience store. Deft denied any involvement, contending he was home watching television with his mother on the night in question. At the trial, Wit, a customer at the convenience store, testified that he had identified Deft in a police line-up and provided other testimony connecting Deft to the crime. In addition, Pros entered into evidence a poor-quality videotape of the robbery as recorded by the store surveillance camera. The jury convicted Deft of the crime charged. Unknown to Deft's court-appointed lawyer, Wit had first identified another person in the police line-up and selected Deft only after encouragement by the detective. Pros was aware of these facts but did not notify Deft's counsel who made no pretrial discovery request to obtain this information.

Is Pros <u>subject to discipline</u>?

A. Yes, unless the jury could make its own identification of Deft from the videotape.

B. Yes, because this information tended to negate Deft's guilt.

C. No, because Deft's counsel made no pretrial discovery request to obtain this information.

D. No, unless it is likely that the jury would have acquitted Deft had it known that Wit first identified someone else.

Question 21.

Attorney and Client entered into a written retainer and hourly fee agreement that required Client to pay $5,000 in advance of any services rendered by Attorney and that required Attorney to return any portion of the $5,000 that was not earned. The agreement further provided that Attorney would render monthly statements and withdraw her fees as billed. The agreement was silent as to whether the $5,000 advance was to be deposited in Attorney's Clients' Trust Account or in a general account. Attorney deposited the entire fund in her Clients' Trust Account, which also contained the funds of other persons that had been entrusted to Attorney.

Thereafter, Attorney rendered monthly progress reports and statements for services to Client after services were rendered, showing the balance of Client's fee advance. However, Attorney did not withdraw any of the $5,000 advance until one year later when the matter was concluded to Client's complete satisfaction. At that time, Attorney had billed Client reasonable legal fees of $4,500. Attorney wrote two checks on her Clients' Trust Account: one to herself for $4,500, which she deposited in her general office account, and one for $500 to Client.

Was Attorney's conduct _proper_?

A. Yes, because Attorney deposited the funds in her Clients' Trust Account.

B. Yes, because Attorney rendered periodic and accurate billings.

C. No, because Attorney's failure to withdraw her fees as billed resulted in an impermissible commingling of her funds and Client's funds.

D. No, because Attorney required an advanced payment against her fee.

Question 22.

Attorney Alpha, a member of the bar, placed a printed flyer in the booth of each artist exhibiting works at a county fair. The face of the flyer contained the following information:

> "I, Alpha, am an attorney, with offices in 800 Bank Building, telephone (555) 555–5555. I have a J.D. degree from State Law School and an M.A. degree in fine arts from State University. My practice includes representing artists in negotiating contracts between artists and dealers and protecting artists' interests. You can find me in the van parked at the fair entrance."

All factual information on the face of the flyer was correct. There was a retainer agreement on the back of the flyer. At the entrance to the fair, Alpha parked a van with a sign that read "Alpha—Attorney at Law."

For which, if any, of the following is Alpha _subject to discipline_?

  I. Placing copies of the flyer in the booth of each artist

 II. Including a retainer agreement on the back of the flyer

III. Parking the van with the sign on it at the fair entrance

A. III only

B. I and II, but not III

C. I, II, and III

D. Neither I, nor II, nor III

Question 23.

Five years ago Attorney represented Seller in the sale of Seller's home. Attorney has not represented Seller since that time. Recently Attorney was approached by Partner, Seller's partner in a venture capital company formed two years ago. Partner and Seller have agreed to dissolve their partnership but cannot agree on the terms of the dissolution. Partner asked Attorney to sue Seller for an accounting of partnership assets.

If Attorney accepts the representation, is Attorney <u>subject to disqualification</u>?

A. Yes, because the representation is directly adverse to Seller.

B. Yes, unless at the time of the sale of Seller's home, Seller agreed that Attorney would not subsequently be precluded from representing other clients in suits against Seller.

C. No, because the partnership dissolution is unrelated to the sale of Seller's home.

D. No, unless Seller sold the home while in the partnership with Partner.

Question 24.

Judge, a judge in a criminal trial court of State, wishes to serve as guardian of her father, who has been declared incompetent. Accepting the responsibilities of the position would not interfere with the performance of Judge's official duties. Although the position in all likelihood would not involve contested litigation, it would be necessary for Judge to prepare and sign various pleadings, motions, and other papers and to appear in civil court on her father's behalf.

Would it be <u>proper</u> for Judge to undertake this guardianship?

A. Yes, unless Judge receives compensation for her services as guardian.

B. Yes, because the position involves a close family member and will not interfere with Judge's performance of her judicial duties.

C. No, because the position will require Judge to appear in court.

D. No, because the position will require Judge to prepare and sign pleadings, motions, and other papers.

Question 25.

Wife has retained Attorney to advise her in negotiating a Separation Agreement with Husband. Even though he knew Wife was represented by Attorney, Husband, who was not a lawyer, refused to obtain counsel and insisted on acting on his own behalf throughout the protracted negotiations. Attorney never met or communicated in any way with Husband during the entire course of the negotiations. After several months, Wife advised Attorney that the parties had reached agreement and presented Attorney with the terms. Attorney prepared a proposed agreement that contained all of the agreed-upon terms.

Attorney mailed the proposed agreement to Husband, with a cover letter stating the following:

"As you know, I have been retained by Wife to represent her in this matter. I enclose two copies of the Separation Agreement negotiated by you and Wife. Please read it and, if it meets with your approval, sign both copies before a notary and return them to me. I will then have Wife sign them and furnish you with a fully executed copy."

Is Attorney <u>subject to discipline</u>?

A. Yes, because Attorney did not suggest that Husband seek the advice of independent counsel before signing the agreement.

B. Yes, because Attorney directly communicated with an unrepresented person.

C. No, because Attorney acted only as a scrivener.

D. No, because Attorney's letter did not imply that Attorney was disinterested.

Answer Key

1.	B	8.	D	14.	D	20.	B
2.	D	9.	C	15.	B	21.	C
3.	C	10.	A	16.	C	22.	D
4.	C	11.	A	17.	D	23.	C
5.	C	12.	C	18.	C	24.	B
6.	C	13.	C	19.	D	25.	D
7.	D						

MPRE Sample Answer Sheet

1 Ⓐ Ⓑ Ⓒ Ⓓ   16 Ⓐ Ⓑ Ⓒ Ⓓ

2 Ⓐ Ⓑ Ⓒ Ⓓ   17 Ⓐ Ⓑ Ⓒ Ⓓ

3 Ⓐ Ⓑ Ⓒ Ⓓ   18 Ⓐ Ⓑ Ⓒ Ⓓ

4 Ⓐ Ⓑ Ⓒ Ⓓ   19 Ⓐ Ⓑ Ⓒ Ⓓ

5 Ⓐ Ⓑ Ⓒ Ⓓ   20 Ⓐ Ⓑ Ⓒ Ⓓ

6 Ⓐ Ⓑ Ⓒ Ⓓ   21 Ⓐ Ⓑ Ⓒ Ⓓ

7 Ⓐ Ⓑ Ⓒ Ⓓ   22 Ⓐ Ⓑ Ⓒ Ⓓ

8 Ⓐ Ⓑ Ⓒ Ⓓ   23 Ⓐ Ⓑ Ⓒ Ⓓ

9 Ⓐ Ⓑ Ⓒ Ⓓ   24 Ⓐ Ⓑ Ⓒ Ⓓ

10 Ⓐ Ⓑ Ⓒ Ⓓ   25 Ⓐ Ⓑ Ⓒ Ⓓ

11 Ⓐ Ⓑ Ⓒ Ⓓ

12 Ⓐ Ⓑ Ⓒ Ⓓ

13 Ⓐ Ⓑ Ⓒ Ⓓ

14 Ⓐ Ⓑ Ⓒ Ⓓ

15 Ⓐ Ⓑ Ⓒ Ⓓ

*

APPENDIX F

Text Correlation Chart

Topic in Outline	Devine, Fisch, Easton & Aronson Problems, Cases and Materials in Professional Responsibility (3d ed.)	Brown & Dauer, Planning by Lawyers	Cochran & Collett Cases and Materials on The Legal Profession (2d ed.)	Countryman, Finman & Schneyer, The Lawyer in Modern Society (2d ed.)	Crystal, Professional Responsibility (3d. ed)	Gillers, Regulation of Lawyers: Problems of Law and Ethics (6th ed.)
One: Defining Disciplinable Conduct	Ch. 1, 2A		Ch. 1	Ch. 1, 9 § B	Ch. 1	Ch. 1
Two: The Lawyer's Obligation to Support Bar Admissions and the Disciplinary System	Ch. 2A, 2B, 2C & 2E		Ch. 1	Ch. 8, §§ A"D; 9	Ch. 1	Ch. 12, 13
Three: The Lawyer's Obligation to the Client						
I Confidentiality	Ch. 4	Passim	Ch. 3	Ch. 2	Ch. 2B, 3B	Ch. 2, 3
II Conflicts	Ch. 5		Ch. 4	Ch. 2	Ch. 2C, 3C	Ch. 5, 6, 9
III Competence	Ch. 3F		Ch. 2B	Ch. 2 § A		Ch. 2, 12, 13
IV Fees	Ch. 3E	Ch. 4, § B	Ch. 6B	Ch. 2, § C	Ch. 3A	Ch. 4
V Acceptance & Termination	Ch. 3A, 3B, 3C, 3G		Ch. 2A	Ch. 2	Ch. 3A	Ch. 2A, 2D
VI Trust Funds	Ch. 3D		Ch. 6B	Ch. 2	Ch. 2A	Ch. 13D(4)
Four: The Lawyer's Obligation as a Member of a Firm	Ch. 2F	Ch. 4, §§ C, D	Ch. 6A, 7B	Ch. 5, § B	Ch. 7	Ch. 9B, 12
Five: The Lawyer's Obligation Regarding Advertising and Solicitation	Ch. 3A	Ch. 5	Ch. 7C	Ch. § A, 8, § E	Ch. 4C	Ch. 14, 16

Topic in Outline	Devine, Fisch, Easton & Aronson Problems, Cases and Materials in Professional Responsibility (3d ed.)	Brown & Dauer, Planning by Lawyers	Cochran & Collett Cases and Materials on The Legal Profession (2d ed.)	Countryman, Finman & Schneyer, The Lawyer in Modern Society (2d ed.)	Crystal, Professional Responsibility (3d. ed)	Gillers, Regulation of Lawyers: Problems of Law and Ethics (6th ed.)
Six: The Lawyer's Obligation not to Misuse the Office of Government	Ch. 5E				Ch. 2D, 3C	Ch. 8A
Seven: The Lawyer's Obligation as an Advocate	Ch. 6A		Ch. 5	Ch. 3, §B	Ch. 2, 3, 4	Ch. 7, 8, 15
Eight: The Lawyer's Obligation as Adviser	Ch. 6B	Ch. 3, 5	Ch. 2C	Ch. 3, §§ C, D	Ch. 5	Ch. 10
Nine: The Lawyer's Obligations Regarding Pro Bono Activities	Ch. 3B		Ch. 7A	Ch. 6, 7, § A	Ch. 2E, 6B	Ch. 4E, 4F, 14A
Ten: The Lawyer's Obligation as a Judge	Ch. 5F, 6D		Ch. 8	Ch. 7, § B	Ch. 6A	Ch. 11

Topic in Outline	Hazard, Koniak & Cramton, The Law and Ethics of Lawyering (3d ed.)	Kaufman & Wilkins Problems in Professional Responsibility for a Changing Profession (4th)	Martin & Fox, Traversing the Ethical Minefield (1st ed.)	Mellinkoff Lawyers and the System of Justice	Moliterno, Cases and Materials on the Law Governing Lawyers (2d ed.)	Morgan & Rotunda, Problems and Materials on Professional Responsibility (8th ed.)
One: Defining Disciplinable Conduct	Ch. 1, 2, 12	Ch. 1	Ch. 1, 2	Ch. 1	Ch. 1, 2	Ch. I
Two: The Lawyer's Obligation to Support Bar Admissions and the Disciplinary System	Ch. 9	Ch. 10, 11C	Ch. 2	Ch. 10, § 1; 13	Ch. 2	Ch. II
Three: The Lawyer's Obligation to the Client						
I Confidentiality	Ch. 4	Ch. 3, 4	Ch. 5	Ch. 14	Ch. 4	Ch. III
II Conflicts	Ch. 6F, 7, 8	Ch. 2, 5A, 5E	Ch. 6, 9H	Ch. 15	Ch. 5	Ch. III, IV
III Competence	Ch. 3	Ch. 11	Ch. 4B, 4E	Ch. 3, 16	Ch. 3D	Ch. II
IV Fees	Ch. 6C	Ch. 8A	Ch. 7	Ch. 5, §§ 1, 2	Ch. 3B	Ch. III, Problems 5, 6; VII, Problems 32, 35
V Acceptance & Termination	Ch. 6A	Ch. 7A	Ch. 8	Ch. 5, § 1	Ch. 3A, 3F	Ch. III
VI Trust Funds	Ch. 6F		Ch. 7D		Ch. 3C	Ch. III, Problem 6
Four: The Lawyer's Obligation as a Member of a Firm	Ch. 9E, 10C	Ch. 10B	Ch. 1A, 11	Ch. 5, §§ 4, 6	Ch. 8B, 8C, 8D, 8E	Ch. VII, Problems 33, 34, 37
Five: The Lawyer's Obligation Regarding Advertising and Solicitation	Ch. 10	Ch. 7C, 8	Ch. 10C	Ch. 5, § 3	Ch. 9	Ch. VII
Six: The Lawyer's Obligation not to Misuse the Office of Government	Ch. 7F, 8C	Ch. 5B, 6A	Ch. 6H	Ch. 9	Ch. 5E, 8A	Ch. IV, Problem 16; Ch. VI, Problem 29

Topic in Outline	Hazard, Koniak & Cramton, The Law and Ethics of Lawyering (3d ed.)	Kaufman & Wilkins Problems in Professional Responsibility for a Changing Profession (4th)	Martin & Fox, Traversing the Ethical Minefield (1st ed.)	Mellinkoff Lawyers and the System of Justice	Moliterno, Cases and Materials on the Law Governing Lawyers (2d ed.)	Morgan & Rotunda, Problems and Materials on Professional Responsibility (8th ed.)
Seven: The Lawyer's Obligation as an Advocate	Ch. 5	Ch. 6, 7	Ch. 9	Ch. 6, 7, 12	Ch. 6, 7	Ch. VI
Eight: The Lawyer's Obligation as Adviser	Ch. 2, 6, 7C	Ch. 5C, 5D, 6F, 7B	Ch. 4C	Ch. 8	Ch. 3E, 8D	Ch. V
Nine: The Lawyer's Obligations Regarding Pro Bono Activities	Ch. 11B	Ch. 9	Ch. 3B	Ch. 5, § 5	Ch. 7F	Ch. VII, Problem 35
Ten: The Lawyer's Obligation as a Judge	Ch. 11A	Ch. 12		Ch. 10, § 1	Ch. 10	Ch. VIII

Topic in Outline	Noonan & Painter, Professional and Personal Responsibilities of the Lawyer (2d ed.)	Hayden Ethical Lawyering (1st ed.)	Patterson & Metzloff, Legal Ethics (3d ed.)	Persig & Kirwin, Professional Responsibility (4th ed.)	Redlich Professional Responsibility (2d ed.)	Rhode & Luban Legal Ethics (4th ed.)
One: Defining Disciplinable Conduct	Ch. 11, 12(A), (B), (C)	Ch. 1	Ch. 1, 2	Ch. 1		Ch. 1, 2
Two: The Lawyer's Obligation to Support Bar Admissions and the Disciplinary System	Ch. 12		Ch. 14	Ch. 1, 2, § B, 2		Ch. 3, 14, 15A, 15B, 15C
Three: The Lawyer's Obligation to the Client						
I Confidentiality	Ch. 2	Ch. 3	Ch. 7	Ch. 3	Problems 2, 4	Ch. 5
II Conflicts	Ch. 4, 6, 12(H)	Ch. 6	Ch. 6, 10	Ch. 4	Problems 12, 13, 14	Ch. 7, 10
III Competence		Ch. 2	Ch. 5	Ch. 7, § E		Ch. 15E, 16
IV Fees	Ch. 1(D), (E), (F)	Ch. 5	Ch. 2, 4	Ch. 7, § A		Ch. 12F, 12G
V Acceptance & Termination	Ch. 1(I)	Ch. 4	Ch. 4	Ch. 7, § B	Problems 1, 3	
VI Trust Funds	Ch. 1(C)	Ch. 4(4)	Ch. 4	Ch. 7, § C		
Four: The Lawyer's Obligation as a Member of a Firm	Ch. 5, 12F, G	Ch. 2(5), 5(5)	Ch. 2	Ch. 2, § C, Ch. 7, § A, 3		Ch. 7D
Five: The Lawyer's Obligation Regarding Advertising and Solicitation	Ch. 12D	Ch. 8	Ch. 14	Ch. 8		Ch. 12, 13
Six: The Lawyer's Obligation not to Misuse the Office of Government	Ch. 3, 4(A)	Ch. 6(4)(C)	Ch. 13	Ch. 5, § B; 6, § F	Problems 15, 16, 17	Ch. 6D, 10F
Seven: The Lawyer's Obligation as an Advocate	Ch. 1, 7, 8, 9	Ch. 7	Ch. 3, 8, 9	Ch. 6	Problems 4, 5, 6, 7	Ch. 4, 6
Eight: The Lawyer's Obligation as Adviser	Ch. 1(G)	Ch. 4(3)(B), 7(6)(C)	Ch. 10, 11	Ch. 6, §§ A, B, C, E, J	Problems 8, 9, 10, 11	Ch. 7, 8, 9

Topic in Outline	Noonan & Painter, Professional and Personal Responsibilities of the Lawyer (2d ed.)	Hayden Ethical Lawyering (1st ed.)	Patterson & Metzloff, Legal Ethics (3d ed.)	Persig & Kirwin, Professional Responsibility (4th ed.)	Redlich Professional Responsibility (2d ed.)	Rhode & Luban Legal Ethics (4th ed.)
Nine: The Lawyer's Obligations Regarding Pro Bono Activities	Ch. 1(J)	Ch. 1(1)	Ch. 14	Ch. 8, § A	Problem 1	Ch. 13E, 13G, 16D
Ten: The Lawyer's Obligation as a Judge	Ch. 10(A), (B)	Ch. 9	Ch. 13			

Topic in Outline	Simon & Schwartz Lawyers and the Legal Profession (3d ed.)	Schwartz, Wydick & Perschbacher, Problems in Legal Ethics (6th ed.)	Shaffer, American Legal Ethics: Text Readings, and Discussion Topics	Sutton & Dzienkowski Professional Responsibility of Lawyers (2d ed.)	Thurman, Phillips & Cheatham, The Legal	Zitrin & Langford, Legal Ethics in the Practice of Law (2d ed.)
One: Defining Disciplinable Conduct	Ch. 33, 37	Ch. 1, 2, 13(I)(B)	Ch. 1, 2	Ch. I	Ch. I	Ch. 1, 11
Two: The Lawyer's Obligation to Support Bar Admissions and the Disciplinary System	Ch. 34, 35	Ch. 2	Ch. 10	Ch. I, VI	Ch. III, XIII	Ch. 13, §§ A, B
Three: The Lawyer's Obligation to the Client						
I Confidentiality	Ch. 1"5	Ch. 7		Ch. IIIB	Ch. XI, XII	Ch. 3
II Conflicts	Ch. 13"21	Ch. 11, 12	Ch. 3, 4	Ch. IIIB	Ch. XI, XII	Ch. 4
III Competence	Ch. 32, 36, 37, 38	Ch. 6		Ch. IIC, V	Ch. XI, XII	Ch. 2
IV Fees	Ch. 29"31	Ch. 5		Ch. IIC	Ch. XI, XII	Ch. 2, Problem 3, Ch. 12
V Acceptance & Termination	Ch. 15	Ch. 3		Ch. IIC, VD	Ch. XI, XII	Ch. 2, 5
VI Trust Funds		Ch. 5(II)		Ch. IIC	Ch. XI, XII	Ch. 13, § D
Four: The Lawyer's Obligation as a Member of a Firm	Ch. 35	Ch. 6(III), 13(I), 13(II)	Ch. 6, 7	Ch. IIA, VIF	Ch. II, § 2	Ch. 13, § C
Five: The Lawyer's Obligation Regarding Advertising and Solicitation	Ch. 39, 40, 41, 42	Ch. 4		Ch. IIB	Ch. II, § 6	Ch. 2, Problem 2, 12
Six: The Lawyer's Obligation not to Misuse the Office of Government	Ch. 18	Ch. 12(I)		Ch. IV	Ch. VIII, IX	Ch. 8
Seven: The Lawyer's Obligation as an Advocate	Ch. 6"12	Ch. 8, 9, 10	Ch. 1, 2, 11	Ch. IV	Ch. VII	Ch. 5, 6, 7
Eight: The Lawyer's Obligation as Adviser		Ch. 13(III)	Ch. 5	Ch. IIIB	Ch. V, VI	Ch. 9
Nine: The Lawyer's Obligations Regarding Pro Bono Activities	Ch. 26, 27, 28	Ch. 3(I)	Ch. 11	Ch. IIA	Ch. X	Ch. 12, Problem 30
Ten: The Lawyer's Obligation as a Judge		Ch. 14		Ch. VII	Ch. XIV	

APPENDIX G

Glossary

A

ABA Commission on Evaluation of Professional Standards (See, *Kutak Commission*).

ABA Formal Opinion If an ethics opinion written by the ABA Committee on Professional Ethics is called a *Formal Opinion*, it overrules any earlier opinions either Formal or Informal, with which it is necessarily in conflict, whether or not the earlier opinion is specifically mentioned in the later opinion. In contrast, if an opinion is called an *Informal Opinion*, it only overrules earlier Informal Opinions that necessarily conflict with it, whether or not they are specifically mentioned. An Informal Opinion cannot overrule a Formal Opinion. See ABA Formal Opinion 317 (May 23, 1967).

ABA Informal Opinion (See, *ABA Formal Opinion*).

Active Lien (See, *Lien*).

Admonition A term used in the ABA Model Standards for Lawyer Discipline and Disability Proceedings to refer to a "form of private discipline which declares the respondent's conduct to have been improper but does not limit his right to practice."

American Lawyer's Code of Conduct The title of an alternative to the ABA Model Code of Professional Responsibility or the ABA Model Rules of Professional Conduct. This alternative code was prepared under the auspices of the Roscoe Pound–American Trial Lawyers Foundation.

Attorney On a very general level, an attorney is one person (an agent) authorized to act for, or represent, another (the principal). In order for the attorney to practice law, the attorney must be a licensed member of the bar. An attorney is a lawyer.

The word "attorney" is derived from the law-French and means a person to whom one can *turn* for help.

Attorney's Lien (See, *Lien*).

B

Bar Association An association of lawyers admitted to the bar. A bar association may be limited to specialists.

Bar, Integrated (See, *Integrated Bar*).

Bar, Unified (See, *Integrated Bar*).

Belief A term used in the Model Rules to mean that the person involved actually supposed the fact in question to be true. A person's belief may be inferred from circumstances. Rule 1.0(a).

Believes (See, *Belief*).

C

Canons When used in connection with the ABA Model Code of Professional Responsibility, they refer to the titles of the nine divisions of the Model Code. They "are statements of axiomatic norms. . . . " Model Code, Preliminary Statement.

The term "Canons" may also refer to the seven divisions of the ABA Model Code of Judicial Conduct (1972), the ABA Model Code of Judicial Conduct (1990), the ABA Canons of Professional Ethics (1908), or a similar body of ethical guidance.

Charging Lien (See, *Lien*).

Comment (See, *Rules of Professional Conduct*).

Commission, Kutak (See, *Kutak Commission*).

Commission on Evaluation of Professional Standards (See, *Kutak Commission*).

Common Law Lien (See, *Lien*).

Confidence As defined in the Model Code, a confidence is information protected by the attorney-client evidentiary privilege under local law. (See, *Secret*).

Confirmed in writing A term used in the Model Rules, when used in reference to the informed consent of a person, to denote informed consent that is given in writing by the person or a writing that a lawyer promplty transmits to the person confirming an oral informed consent. If it is not feasible to obtain or transmit the writing at the time the person gives informed consent, then the lawyer must obtain or transmit it within a reasonable time thereafter. Rule 1.0(b). See also *informed consent*.

Consent (See, *Informed Consent*).

Continuing Part-time Judge A judge who serves repeatedly on a part-time basis by election or under a continuing appointment, including a retired judge subject to recall who is permitted to practice law. ABA Model Code of Judicial Conduct (1990), Terminology [4]

Counsel, Of (See, *Of Counsel*).

D

De minimis A term used in the ABA Model Code of Judicial Conduct (1990), in, Terminology [6], to signify an "insignificant interest that could not raise reasonable question as to a judge's impartiality."

Differing Interests A term used in the ABA Model Code of Professional Responsibility to include "every interest that will adversely affect either the judgment or the loyalty of a lawyer to a client, whether it be a conflicting, inconsistent, diverse, or other interest."

Discipline The sanction imposed on a lawyer after a finding or admission of misconduct is referred to as the lawyer's discipline.

Disciplinary Matter A term used in the ABA Model Standards for Lawyer Discipline and Disability Proceedings to refer to "anything involving a lawyer admitted in a jurisdiction under consideration within the discipline and disability system, e.g., complaint, reinstatement proceedings, formal charges."

Disciplinary Rules Those regulations of the ABA Model Code of Professional Responsibility that are called Disciplinary Rules are mandatory in character. They "state the minimum level of conduct below which no lawyer can fall without being subject to disciplinary action." See ABA Model Code, Preliminary Statement. See also, DR 1–102(A)(1).

See, *Rules of Professional Conduct.*

Division of Fee A division of fee is "a single billing to a client covering the fee of two or more lawyers who are not in the same firm." See Rule 1.5, Comment 7.

E

Economic Interest A term used in the ABA Model Code of Judicial Conduct

(1990), in Terminology [7], to denote ownership of a more than *de minimis* legal or equitable interest, or a relationship as officer, director, advisor, or other active participant in the affairs of a party, subject to various exceptions.

Esquire Often abbreviated, Esq., it is often used as a title signifying that the holder is a lawyer as in: John Doe, Esq.

Ethical Consideration A term used in the ABA Model Code of Professional Responsibility to refer to statements in the Model Code what are aspirational rather than mandatory. They also "constitute a body of principles upon which the lawyer can rely for guidance in many specific circumstances." See ABA Model Code, Preliminary Statement.

See, *Disciplinary Rules* and *Canons.*

F

Fiduciary A term to refer to a person having duties involving good faith, trust, special confidence, and candor towards another. A fiduciary "includes such relationships as executor, administrator, trustee, and guardian." ABA Code of Judicial Conduct (1972), Canon 3C(3)(b); ABA Model Code of Judicial Conduct (1990), Terminology [8].

A lawyer is also in a fiduciary relationship with the client.

Firm "Firm" or "law firm" is a term in the Model Rules that denotes a lawyer or lawyers in a law partnership, or professional corporation, or a sole proprietorship or other association authorized to practice law; or lawyers employed in a legal services organization or the legal department of a corporation or other organization. Rule 1.0(c).

Formal Opinion (See, *ABA Formal Opinion*).

Fraud "Fraud" or "fraudulent" is a term in the Model Rules that denotes conduct that is fraudulent under the substantive or procedural law of the applicable jurisdiction and has a purpose to deceive. Rule 1.0(d).

Fraudulent (See, *Fraud*).

G

General Retainer (See, *Retainer*).

General Counsel A term defined in the Model Code of Professional Responsibility as applying to a lawyer or law firm who is general counsel to a given client only "if he or the firm devotes a substantial amount of professional time in the representation of that client." DR 2–102(A)(4).

H

House Counsel An attorney working full time for one client is typically called the house counsel.

House of Delegates When used in connection with the American Bar Association, the House of Delegates is the body in which is vested the control and administration of the ABA. See ABA Constitution, Art. VI. It was the House of Delegates that approved the final draft of the ABA Model Code and Model Rules.

I

Informal Opinion (See, *ABA Formal Opinion*).

Informed consent A term in the Model Rules that denotes the agreement by a person to a proposed course of conduct after the lawyer has communicated adequate information and explanation about the material risks of and reasonably available alternatives to the proposed course of conduct. Rule 1.0(e).

In Propria Persona A Latin term meaning, literally, in one's own proper person. It is often abbreviated as p.p. See also, *pro se.*

Integrated Bar A term used to refer to mandatory bar membership as a prerequisite—by either legislative enactment or order of the court—to the practice of law in a given geographic area. See, e.g., *Integration of Bar Case,* 244 Wisc. 8, 11 N.W.2d 604 (1943). The term "integrated" is derived from the Latin "integer," meaning whole, untouched, one.

Interests, Differing (See, *Differing Interests*).

J

Judge, Continuing Part-time (See, *Continuing Part-time Judge*).

Judge, Lay (See, *Lay Judge*).

Judge, Part-time (See, *Part-time Judge*).

Judge, Periodic Part-time (See, *Periodic Part-time Judge*).

Judge Pro Tempore A term used in the ABA Model Code of Judicial Conduct (1972), Compliance (B), to refer to a person who is appointed to act as a judge only for a time, temporarily. (See also, *Pro tempore part-time judge,* a slightly different term that the ABA Model Code of Judicial Conduct (1990), Terminology [18], uses).

K

Knowingly "Knowingly," "known," or "knows" are terms used in the Model Rules to signify actual knowledge of the fact in question. A person's knowledge may be inferred from circumstances. Rule 1.0(f)

Known (See, *Knowingly*).

Knows (See, *Knowingly*).

Kutak Commission The popular name to refer to the ABA Commission on Evaluation of Professional Standards, the body that drafted the ABA Model Rules of Professional Conduct. The Commission was called the Kutak Commission after its first chairman, the late Robert J. Kutak.

L

Law Firm (See *Firm*).

Law Partner (See, *Partner*).

Lawyer (See, *Attorney*).

Lay Judge A judge who is not a lawyer.

Lien A lien in general is an encumbrance, a charge, imposed on specific property.

An attorney's lien is generally divided into two types: a charging lien, and a retaining lien. See, e.g., Tuite, *Something*

to Lien On, 76 A.B.A.J. 92 (Dec. 1990).

A retaining lien, or a common law lien, is "a general lien resting wholly upon possession, which is a [lawyer's] mere right to *retain,* until his whole bill is paid, all papers, deeds, vouchers, etc., in his possession upon which, or in connection with which, he has expended money or given his professional services. This 'retaining lien' is a general one for whatever may be due to him; and though a client may change his attorney at will, if the latter is without fault and willing to proceed in pending causes, none of the papers or vouchers can ordinarily be withdrawn from him except upon payment of his entire bill for professional services. This lien, like other mere possessory liens, is however, purely passive, being a base right to hold possession till payment. The articles cannot be sold or parted without the loss of the lien, nor can any active proceedings be taken at law or in equity to procure payment of the debt out of the articles so held." *In re Wilson,* 12 F. 235, 238 (S.D.N.Y.1882) (internal citations and paragraphing omitted). The retaining lien does not apply to property, such as escrow funds, that the client conveys to the lawyer unrelated to the lien. E.g., *State Bar v. Bratton,* 413 S.2d 754 (Fla.1982).

In contrast, a *charging lien* is a specific lien, which is often governed by statute. It exists on the judgment that the attorney has recovered for the client, or the money payable on the judgment or upon some fund in court. "This lien, so far as it extends, is not merely a passive lien, but entitles the attorney to take active steps to secure payment. It did not exist at common law [and] does not depend upon possession, but upon the favor of the court in protecting attorneys, as its own officers, by taking care . . . that a 'party should not run away with the fruits of the cause without satisfying the legal demands of the attorney by whose industry, and expense those fruits were obtained.' " 12 F. at 239 (internal citations omitted).

M

Malum in Se A Latin term meaning, literally, a wrong in itself. It is often used to refer to acts generally recognized as serious immoral wrongs in the nature of things, such as murder, rather than acts recognized as wrongs only because a statute so provides. Compare *malum prohibitum*.

Malum Prohibitum A Latin term meaning, literally, a wrong prohibited. It is often used to refer to acts that are not inherently immoral but wrong only because a statute so provides. Compare *malum in se*.

Model Rules of Professional Conduct (See, *Rules of Professional Conduct*).

N

Neglect DR 6–101(a)(3) provides that a lawyer shall not "[n]eglect a legal matter entrusted to him." ABA Informal Opinion 1273 (1973) explains: "Neglect involves indifference and a consistent failure to carry out the obligations which the lawyer has assumed to his clients or a conscious disregard for the responsibility owed to the client. . . . Neglect usually involves more than a single act

or omission. Neglect cannot be found if the acts or omissions complained of were inadvertent or the result of an error of judgment made in good faith." The Model Rules do not contain a prohibition of "neglect." Instead, Rule 1.1 affirmatively requires the lawyer to be competent, and Rule 1.3 affirmatively mandates "reasonable diligence and promptness in representing a client." See also, Rule 1.3, Comment 5

Nonpublic Information A term used in the Model Code of Judicial Conduct (1990), Terminology [13], to denote information not available to the public, including (but not limited to) information sealed by statute or court order; information impounded or communicated in camera; and information offered in grand jury proceedings, presentencing reports, dependency cases, or psychiatric reports.

Notice of Withdrawal A concept, used in the Model Rules, to refer to a lawyer informing third parties that the lawyer no longer represents a given client. This notice may also inform those third parties that they no longer should rely on the lawyer's participation in the case or that the lawyer is withdrawing any previously issued opinion, document, or other affirmation. A client cannot prevent a lawyer from issuing a Notice of Withdrawal, or require the lawyer to keep secret the fact of withdrawal. See Rule 1.6, Comment 15.

O

Of Counsel This term is often used in *court pleadings* to refer to a lawyer representing a party in a particular case. In briefs it is usually used to refer to the lawyer who is not the main lawyer of record but rather is assisting, or associated with, the main counsel of record.

When *law firm stationery* lists an attorney as of counsel, it typically indicates that the lawyer listed is neither a partner nor associate of the firm but has a special contractual relationship with the firm and may not be practicing law full time.

The Model Rules include a specific reference to "of counsel" in DR 2–102(A)(4), which provides that a lawyer who has a continuing relationship with a lawyer or law firm, other than as a partner or associate, may be designated "of counsel" on the firm's letterhead. The Model Rules have no specific reference, but ABA Formal Opinion 90–357 (May 10, 1990) discusses the term extensively. It concluded that it is permissible to use the title "of counsel" on the filings in a particular case even though the attorneys have only collaborated in that one case. However, when the term is used on legal stationery, professional cards, office signs and the like, it is proper to use the term only as long as the relationship between the two is close and regular (the relationship must exist for more than a single case) and the use of the title is not otherwise misleading. The Formal Opinion also concluded that not only an individual but also a law firm can be "of counsel" to another firm; that a lawyer may be "of counsel" to more than one firm, as long as the controlling criterion of a "close and regular" relationship is met; and that it is not ethically permissible to use the "of counsel" term on firm stationery and the like to designate a relationship involving only a single case (but one can use the term on court filings in a particular case), a relationship of forwarder or receiver of a legal business, a relationship involving only collaborative efforts among otherwise unrelated lawyers, and the relationship of outside consultant.

If two or more firms share the same of counsel lawyer, the law firms are treated as a single firm for purposes of attribution of disqualifications. ABA Formal Opinion 90–357.

If a lawyer who is a named partner in a law firm subsequently retires from active practice and assumed the status of "of counsel," the firm can continue to use the retired lawyer's name in the firm name. However, if a new lawyer joins a firm as "of counsel" it would be misleading for that lawyer to lend his or her name to the name of the firm when that lawyer is not undertaking the responsibilities of a partner or principle. ABA Formal Opinion 90–357.

P

Partner A term used in the Model Rules to mean a member of a partnership, a shareholder in a law firm organized as a professional corporation, or a member of an association authorized to practice law. Rule 1.0(g)

Part-time Judge A term specifically defined in the ABA Code of Judicial Conduct (1972) to refer to a judge "who serves on a continuing or periodic basis, but is permitted by law to devote time to some other profession or occupation and whose compensation for that reason is less than that of a full time judge." ABA Code of Judicial Conduct (1972), Compliance with the Code of Judicial Conduct, A. (See also, *Continuing Part-time Judge, Periodic Part-time judge,* and *Pro Tempore Part-time judge*).

Passive Lien (See, *Lien*).

Periodic Part-time Judge A term used in the Model Code of Judicial Conduct (1990), Terminology [16], to denote a judge "who serves or expects to serve repeatedly on a part-time basis but under a separate appointment for each limited period of service or for each matter."

Person A term specifically defined in the ABA Model Code of Professional Responsibility to include "a corporation, an association, a trust, a partnership, and any other organization or legal entity." See Model Code, Definitions (3).

Pro Bono Publico A Latin term meaning, literally for the public good. Often it is used to refer to lawyer giving uncompensated legal advice, or advice for which less than the usual fee is charged.

Professional Legal Corporation A corporation or an association treated as a corporation, authorized by law to practice law for profit.

Pro Hac Vice A Latin term meaning, literally, for this turn, or for this particular occasion. Often it is used to refer to a lawyer who, while not a member of the bar of a particular jurisdiction, is admitted by the court for that particular case only.

Propria Persona, In (See, *In Propria Persona*).

Pro Se A Latin term meaning, literally, for himself, or, in his own behalf. Often it is used to refer to a litigant who has no attorney and is representing himself.

See, *In Propria Persona*.

Pro Tempore, Judge (See, *Judge Pro Tempore*, and *Pro Tempore Part-time Judge*).

Pro Tempore Part-time Judge A term used in the Model Code of Judicial Conduct (1990), Terminology [18], to denote a judge "who serves or expects to serve once or only sporadically on a part-time basis under a separate appointment for each period of service or for each case heard."

Q

Qualified Legal Assistance Organization A term specifically defined in the ABA Model Code of Professional Responsibility to mean "an office or organization of one of the four types listed in DR 2–103(D)(1)–(4), inclusive that meets all of the requirements thereof." Model Code, Definitions (8).

R

Reasonable "Reasonable" or "reasonably" are terms used in the Model Rules, when used in relation to conduct by a lawyer, to denote the conduct of a reasonably prudent and competent lawyer. Rule 1.0(h)

Reasonable Belief "Reasonable belief" or "reasonably believes" are terms used in the Model Rules, when used in reference to a lawyer, denote that the lawyer believes the matter in question and that the circumstances are such that the belief is reasonable.Rule 1.0(i)

Reasonably (See, *Reasonable*).

Reasonably Believes (See, *Reasonable Belief*).

Reasonably Should Know A term used in the Model Rules, when used in reference to a lawyer, denotes that a lawyer of reasonable prudence and competence would ascertain the matter in question. Rule 1.0(j)

Reprimand A term defined in the ABA Model Standards for Lawyer Discipline and Disability Proceedings to refer to a "form of public discipline imposed after trial or formal charges, which declares the respondent's conduct to have been improper but does not limit his right to practice."

Require A term that the ABA Model Code of Judicial Conduct (1990), Terminology [20], uses to mean that the judge is to exercise reasonable direction and control over the conduct of those persons subject to the judge's direction and control. "Require" is a rule of reason.

Restatement (third) of the Law Governing Lawyers A proposed Restatement of the Law of Lawyering, prepared by the American Law Institute. The project is now in tentative draft form. There is no Restatement First, or Restatement Second.

Retainer In the practice of law, when a client hires an attorney to represent him, the client is said to have retained the attorney. This act of employment is called the retainer. The fee agreed upon is also called the retainer. (If the client employs the attorney for a specific case, that is called a *special retainer*). In contrast, if a client hires a lawyer for a specific length of time (e.g., a year) rather than for a specific project, that is called a *general retainer*. The lawyer, during the period of the general retainer, may not accept any conflicting employment. And, the attorney is to perform legal services that the client requests, and none that is not requested. Since the client is hiring the lawyer to stand ready to deliver the services requested, the lawyer is entitled to be paid for the general retainer whether or not the client actually calls upon the lawyer. See *Rhode Island Exchange Bank v. Hawkins*, 6 R.I. 198, 206 (1859). A *nonrefundable retainer* is earned when paid. It is "an agreement between lawyer and client providing for the payment of part or all of the fee in advance of the lawyer's performance. The payment is designated in the retainer agreement as nonrefundable. The dispute regarding the validity of these agreements usually arises when the client terminates the lawyer's employment without just cause before completion of the task and demands return of the unearned part of the advance fee." Nonrefundable retainers are "contractual forfeiture provisions." Brickman & Cunningham, *Nonrefundable Retainers: Impermissible Under Fiduciary, Statutory and Contract Law,* 57 Ford.L.Rev. 149, 150 n.1 & 151 (1988).

Retaining Lien (See, *Lien*).

Rules, Disciplinary (See, *Disciplinary Rules* and *Canons*).

Rules of Professional Conduct A model code developed by the ABA Commission on Evaluation of Professional Standards. The ABA House of Delegates adopted these rules on August 2, 1983. They are not positive law unless enacted into law, usually as a court rule.

The black letter *Rules* of the Rules of Professional Conduct, when cast as imperative, using the terms "shall" or "shall not," "define proper conduct for purposes of professional discipline." See ABA Model Rules, Scope 1; Rule 8.4(a).

See *Disciplinary Rules.*

The *Comment* accompanying each of these black letter Rules is intended to explain and illustrate the purpose of the Rule. "The Comments are intended as guides to interpretation, but the text of each Rule is authoritative." Model Rules, Scope 9.

S

Screened A term used in the Model Rules that denotes the isolation of a lawyer from any participation in a matter through the timely imposition of procedures within a firm that are reasonably adequate under the circumstances to protect information that the isolated lawyer is obligated to protect under these Rules or other law. Rule 1.0(k)

Secret As defined in the Model Code, a secret refers to information gained in the attorney-client relationship that is not privileged under the laws of evidence but which the client has requested be held inviolate or which would be embarrassing or is likely to be detrimental to the client if disclosed. DR 4–101(A). See *Confidence.*

Special Retainer (See *Retainer*).

Specific Lien (See, *Lien*).

Substantial A term used in the Model Rules, when used in reference to degree or extent, denotes a material matter of clear and weighty importance. Rule 1.0(*l*)

T

Third Degree of Relationship A term used in the ABA Model Code of Judicial Conduct (1990), Terminology [21], to mean great-grandparent, grandparent, parent, uncle, aunt, brother, sister, child, grandchild, great-grandchild, nephew, or niece.

Tribunal A term used in the Model Rules that denotes a court, an arbitrator in a binding arbitration proceeding or a legislative body, administrative agency or other body acting in an adjudicative capacity. A legislative body, administrative agency or other body acts in an adjudicative capacity when a neutral official, after the presentation of evidence or legal argument by a party or parties, will render a binding legal judgment directly affecting a party's interests in a particular matter. Rule 1.0(m)

U

Unified Bar (See, *Integrated Bar*).

W

Writing A "writing" or "written" are terms used in the Model Rules to denote a tangible or electronic record of a communication or representation, including handwriting, typewriting, printing, photostating, photography, audio or video recording and e-mail. A *"signed"* writing includes an electronic sound, symbol or process attached to or logically associated with a writing and executed or adopted by a person with the intent to sign the writing. Rule 1.0(n)

Z

Zeal A term, that the Model Code does not specifically define, but uses frequently. It is in the Title to Canon 7, the title to DR 7–101, and in EC 2–23, EC 7–1, EC 7–10, EC 7–19, EC 7–36, and EC 7–39. The Model Rules do not use the term in the black letter rules, though it is mentioned in Preamble, ¶ 2, and Rule 1.3, Comment 1. The drafters of the Model Rules were concerned that "zealousness" might imply or too readily suggest "over zealousness," so it is not used in any of the black letter rules.

*

APPENDIX H

Table of Cases

APPENDIX I

Index